SPECIAL OFFER FRO

FREE Expert Review College Application Essay by CAMBRIDGE EDUCATIONAL SERVICES— America's #1 Campus-Based Test-Prep Service!

Hurry! For a limited time, ARCO is offering you a professional review of your college application essay —a $30 value—and it's absolutely free! Just mail in a copy of your essay and application along with the coupon below. The experts at Cambridge Educational Services will evaluate your essay—helping you get into the school of your choice!

To take advantage of this unique offer, simply complete and mail the coupon below or a photocopy, along with one (1)copy of the essay and application you select, and your test scores, (if available).

ABOUT CAMBRIDGE EDUCATIONAL SERVICES

Cambridge Educational Services is the leading campus-based test-preparation service in the country. Currently located in 40 states, Cambridge offers test-prep courses in conjunction with continuing education departments at leading colleges, universities, and high schools. Cambridge offers preparation courses for all major tests, including the LSAT, GMAT, GRE, SAT, PSAT, MCAT, NTE, PPST, and ACT, and each course is taught by an experienced and proven instructor. And in a 1992-94 survey, 100% of Cambridge's students recommended the course to their friends! For more information about Cambridge, please check the appropriate boxes on the coupon below.

☐ **Yes! I'm interested in a free professional review from Cambridge Educational Services. I have enclosed one college application essay, a copy of the application, and my test scores (if available).**

☐ **Please send me further information about Cambridge admissions consulting services.**

☐ **Please send me information about a Cambridge test preparation course in the following City and state:______________ I plan on taking my exam:___month___year.**

Circle Exam: MCAT LSAT GMAT GRE SAT ACT TOEFL PPST NTE

Name:____________________
Address:____________________
City:____________________
State:____________________
Telephone number:____________________
Year in School (Fr., Soph., Jr., Sr.):____________________

Mail to: Cambridge Free Review Offer
Department NM—16th Floor
15 Columbus Circle
New York, New York 10023

HURRY! This is a limited offer and is open to residents of the United States and Canada only. Original coupons or photocopies only. Limit one review per person. This offer expires and all requests must be received (not postmarked) by January 15, 1996. Applications will be reviewed on a first-come, first-served basis. Not responsible for lost, or misdirected mail.

ARCO

PREPARATION FOR THE

SAT*

SCHOLASTIC ASSESSMENT TEST

Edward J. Deptula, M.A.
Glen Ridge School District
Glen Ridge, New Jersey

Gabriel P. Freedman, M.A.
The Stuyvesant Adult Center
Stuyvesant High School
New York, New York

Joan U. Levy, Ph.D.
Norman Levy, Ph.D.
NJL College Preparation
Albertson, New York

Brigitte Saunders, M.A.
Great Neck South
Senior High School
Great Neck, New York

David P. Waldherr
Cambridge Educational Services, Inc.
New York, New York

Kathy A. Zahler
Midline Editorial Services
Freeville, New York

MACMILLAN • USA

*SAT and Scholastic Assessment Test are registered trademarks that are the exclusive property of the College Entrance Examination Board. ARCO is a division of Simon & Schuster, Inc., and is not affiliated with the College Entrance Examination Board. This book has been prepared by ARCO and the authors, who bear sole responsibility for its content.

Twelfth Edition

Macmillan General Reference
A Simon & Schuster Macmillan Company
1633 Broadway
New York, NY 10019-6785

An ARCO Book

ISBN 0-02-860323-0

Manufactured in the United States of America

10 9 8 7 6 5 4 3 2 1

CONTENTS

Practice Examination 2 339

Practice Examination 3 381

Practice Examination 4 425

Practice Examination 5 465

Practice Examination 6 505

PART SIX
Final Practice Examination

Final Practice Examination 547

PART

ONE

Introduction to the SAT

CONTENTS

ABOUT THE SAT PROGRAM

The SAT Program is a program of the College Board designed to test the academic abilities of students who apply to college. The program consists of two major components designated SAT I: Reasoning Test and SAT II: Subject Tests. Together, SAT I and SAT II are known as the Scholastic Assessment Tests.

SAT I tests general verbal and mathematical reasoning skills—your ability to understand and analyze what you read, to reason clearly, and to apply fundamental mathematical principles to unfamiliar problems. SAT II tests mastery of specific subjects—such as writing, biology, or world history—which may be required by some colleges for admission or placement purposes.

SAT I: Reasoning Test

Each SAT I consists of seven sections and takes three hours to complete. The following chart shows the format, timing, and question types used on SAT I.

SAT I FORMAT

3	Verbal Reasoning Sections
	Two 30-minute sections
	One 15-minute section
3	Mathematical Reasoning Sections
	Two 30-minute sections
	One 15-minute section
1	Equating Section
	One 30-minute Verbal Reasoning section OR
	One 30-minute Mathematical Reasoning section

The equating section is experimental in nature. Your score in this section does not count; the results are used solely by the test-makers in devising future tests. However, since the order of the sections on the SAT is not fixed, and you will not be told which of the sections is the experimental one, it is important that you do your best on every part.

A TYPICAL SAT I

The chart that follows shows the sections and question types in a typical SAT I. While the ordering of the sections—as well as the timing and number of questions within each section—may vary, the overall format will follow this basic scheme.

SECTION	NUMBER OF QUESTIONS	TIME ALLOWED
Section 1: Verbal Reasoning	**30**	30 min.
Sentence Completions	9	
Analogies	6	
Critical Reading	15	
Section 2: Mathematical Reasoning	**25**	30 min.
Regular Mathematics		
Section 3: Verbal Reasoning	**13**	15 min.
Critical Reading		
Section 4: Mathematical Reasoning	**10**	15 min.
Regular Mathematics		
Section 5: Verbal Reasoning	**35**	30 min.
Sentence Completions	10	
Analogies	13	
Critical Reading	12	
Section 6: Mathematical Reasoning	**25**	30 min.
Quantitative Comparisons	15	
Student-Produced Responses	10	
Section 7: Experimental Section	**varies**	30 min.
Verbal or Mathematical Reasoning		

Verbal Reasoning Questions

The verbal sections of the SAT test vocabulary, verbal reasoning, and ability to understand reading passages. These skills are measured by means of three question types:

1. Analogies (19 questions)
2. Sentence Completions (19 questions)
3. Critical Reading (40 questions)

Analogies

Analogy questions test your ability to see a relationship between a pair of words and to recognize a similar relationship between another pair of words.

Example➤ PAINTER: STUDIO: :

(A) composer : piano
(B) teacher : faculty
(C) judge : courtroom
(D) golfer : club
(E) stage : theater

The correct answer is (**C**). A *painter* works in a *studio* as a *judge* works in a *courtroom.*

Sentence Completions

Sentence Completion questions test your ability to recognize relationships among the parts of a sentence so that you can choose the word or words that best complete each sentence.

Example➤ Conditions in the mine were ----, so the mine workers refused to return to their jobs until the dangers were ----.

(A) filthy..disbanded
(B) hazardous..eliminated
(C) deplorable..collated
(D) conducive..ameliorated
(E) illegal..enhanced

The correct answer is (**B**). The workers wanted the *hazardous* conditions *eliminated.*

Critical Reading

Critical Reading questions test your ability to read and understand passages taken from any of the following categories: humanities, social sciences, natural sciences, and fiction or nonfiction narrative.

The length of critical reading passages varies from 400 to 850 words. Passages may be followed by as few as 5 questions or as many as 13 questions. Critical reading questions may require you to

- recognize the meaning of a word as used in context
- interpret specific information presented in the passage
- analyze information in one part of the passage in terms of information presented in another part of the passage
- evaluate the author's assumptions or identify the logical structure of the passage

Some reading selections consist of a pair of passages that present different points of view on the same or related subjects. The passages may support each other, oppose each other, or in some way complement each other. Some questions relate to each passage separately, and others ask you to compare, contrast, or evaluate the two passages.

Sample Passage:

Private enterprise is no stranger to the American prison. When the United States replaced corporal punishment with confinement as the primary punishment for criminals in the early 19th century, the private sector was the most frequent employer of convict labor. Prisoners were typically either leased to private companies who set up shop in the prison or used by prison officials to produce finished goods for a manufacturer who supplied the raw materials to the prison. The former arrangement was called the contract system, while the latter came to be known as the piece-price system. In both instances, a private company paid the prison a fee for the use of prison labor, which was used to partially offset the expense of operating the prison. Blatant exploitation of inmates sometimes developed as a consequence of these systems.

Opposition to the use of prison labor from rival manufacturers and from the growing organized labor movement began to emerge in the latter part of the 19th century as more and more prisoners were put to work for the private sector. Opposition reached a peak during the Great Depression, when Congress passed a series of laws designed to prohibit the movement of prison-made goods in interstate commerce, thus ensuring that these products would not compete with those made by outside labor. Many state legislatures followed suit, forbidding the open market sale or importation of prison-made goods within their borders and effectively barring the private sector from the prison. As a consequence, prison-based manufacturing operations became state-owned and -operated businesses, selling goods in a highly restricted market.

Questions on Sample Passage:

1. Prisons stopped producing readily available goods due to all of the following *EXCEPT*

   (A) laws passed by state legislatures
   (B) laws passed by the Congress of the United States
   (C) opposition from organized labor
   (D) dissatisfaction of the prisoners
   (E) opposition from rival manufacturers

This question requires you to apply information given in the passage. The correct answer is **(D)**, because there is no mention of prisoner dissatisfaction. Choice (A) is mentioned in lines 18–20, choice (B) is mentioned in lines 15–17, and choices (C) and (E) are mentioned in lines 12–14.

2. In the arrangement known as the "contract system"

   (A) companies set up shop inside a prison and used prisoners for labor
   (B) manufacturers supplied raw materials to the prison
   (C) all of the prisoners signed a contract to produce a certain amount of goods
   (D) prisoners with suitable skills would contact the companies
   (E) exploitation inevitably ensued

This question requires you to interpret details. The correct answer is **(A)**. In lines 4–7, the contract system is defined as a system in which prisoners were "leased to private companies who set up shop in the prison."

3. According to the passage, which of the following was instrumental in the development of the private sector in prison?

   (A) Seed money from the federal government
   (B) The replacement of corporal punishment with confinement
   (C) The crudeness of the original prison system
   (D) The constant exploitation of the prisoners by manufacturers
   (E) The piece-price and contract systems

This question requires you to evaluate information. The correct answer is **(B)**, as stated in the second sentence of the passage.

4. Which of the following statements can be inferred from the passage?

   (A) There is no longer any private sector work done in prisons.
   (B) Legislatures are ready to repeal the previously passed prison laws.
   (C) Prison systems were once fully supported by the fees paid by the private sector.
   (D) The Great Depression was caused by excessive prison labor.
   (E) Piece-price was more profitable than the contract system.

This question requires you to make an inference. The correct answer is **(A)**, which follows from the last sentence of the passage.

Mathematical Reasoning Questions

The mathematical reasoning sections of the SAT test problem solving in arithmetic, elementary algebra, and geometry using three question types:

1. Standard Multiple-Choice (35 questions)
2. Quantitative Comparison (15 questions)
3. Student-Produced Responses (10 questions)

Although calculators are not required to answer any SAT math questions, students are encouraged to bring a calculator to the test and to use it wherever it is helpful.

Standard Multiple-Choice Questions

Standard Multiple-Choice questions test your knowledge of arithmetic, algebra, and geometry. You are to select the correct solution to the problem from the five choices given.

Example➤ If $(x + y)^2 = 17$, and $xy = 3$, then $x^2 + y^2 =$

(A) 11
(B) 14
(C) 17
(D) 20
(E) 23

The correct answer is **(A)**.

$$
\begin{aligned}
(x + y)^2 &= 17 \\
(x + y)(x + y) &= 17 \\
x^2 + 2xy + y^2 &= 17
\end{aligned}
$$

Since $xy = 3$

$$
\begin{aligned}
x^2 + 2(3) + y^2 &= 17 \\
x^2 + 6 + y^2 &= 17 \\
x^2 + y^2 &= 11
\end{aligned}
$$

Quantitative Comparisons

Quantitative Comparison questions test your knowledge of equalities, inequalities, and estimation. In general, quantitative comparison questions require less reading and less computation than regular mathematical questions; however, the directions may be unfamiliar to some students. Each quantitative comparison question consists of two quantities, one in Column A and one in Column B. Information concerning one or both of the quantities to be compared is centered above the two columns. You are to compare the two quantities and determine whether one quantity is greater than the other, whether the two quantities are equal, or whether the relationship cannot be determined from the information given.

Example➤ Compare the quantities in Column A and Column B. Mark your answer sheet as follows:

(A) if the quantity in Column A is greater
(B) if the quantity in Column B is greater
(C) if the two quantities are equal
(D) if the relationship cannot be determined from the information given

Column A	***Column B***
$\frac{4}{\sqrt{2}}$	$\sqrt{2}$

The correct answer is (**A**), Column A is greater than Column B. To eliminate the radical, multiply each column by $\sqrt{2}$.

$$\frac{4}{\sqrt{2}} \bullet \sqrt{2} = 4 \qquad\qquad \sqrt{2} \bullet \sqrt{2} = 2$$

Therefore, Column A is greater than Column B.

Student-Produced Responses

Student-Produced Response questions test your ability to solve mathematical problems when no choices are offered.

Example➤ On a map having a scale of $\frac{1}{4}$ inch = 20 miles, how many inches should there be between towns that are 70 miles apart?

The correct answer is either $\frac{7}{8}$ or .875, depending upon whether you choose to solve the problem using fractions or decimals.

Using Fractions

$$\frac{\frac{1}{4}}{20} = \frac{x}{70}$$

$$20x = \frac{70}{4}$$

$$x = \frac{70}{4} \bullet \frac{1}{20} = \frac{7}{8}$$

Using Decimals

$$\frac{.25}{20} = \frac{x}{70}$$

$$20x = 17.5$$

$$x = .875$$

The answer sheet for student-produced response questions consists of a grid that you fill in as shown below. One advantage of this question type is that it allows you to enter your answer as a fraction or a decimal. For this particular question you will be given credit for either of the answers shown below.

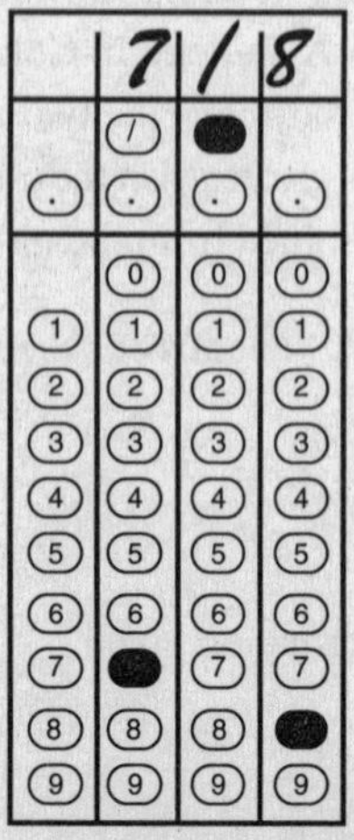

SAT II: Subject Tests

SAT II: Subject Tests consist of mastery tests in specific subject areas. Designed to help predict student performance and to facilitate course placement in college, SAT II tests take the place of the old College Board Achievement Tests. The tests fall into five general subject areas:

I. ENGLISH
- Writing Test (replaces the English Composition Test and the Test of Standard Written English)
- Literature

II. FOREIGN LANGUAGES
- Chinese with Listening
- French
- French with Listening
- German
- German with Listening
- Modern Hebrew
- Italian
- Japanese with Listening
- Latin
- Spanish
- Spanish with Listening

III. MATHEMATICS
- Level IC (with calculator)
- Level IIC (with calculator)

IV. HISTORY AND SOCIAL STUDIES
- American History and Social Studies
- World History

V. SCIENCES
- Biology
- Chemistry
- Physics

THE NEW SAT II WRITING TEST

A major feature of SAT II is the new Writing Test. This test includes both multiple-choice questions and an actual writing sample.

The multiple-choice section is 40 minutes long and includes three question types:

1. Error Recognition (30 questions)
2. Sentence Correction (20 questions)
3. Revision-in-Context 10 questions)

Error Recognition

Error Recognition questions require you to recognize errors in grammar, usage, word choice, or idiom.

Example➤ Decide which underlined part of the following sentence contains an error. If the sentence is correct, choose answer (E).

We <u>ought to</u> (A) <u>set</u> (B) our prejudices aside and <u>except</u> (C) each other as <u>equals.</u> (D) <u>No error.</u> (E)

The answer is (**C**). The verb meaning "to receive willingly" or "to agree" is *accept*, not *except*.

Sentence Correction

Sentence Correction questions require you to recognize errors in grammar or usage and to select the best rephrasing of the incorrect sentence or sentence part.

Example➤ Select the lettered answer that presents the best phrasing of the underlined part of the sentence.

Having practiced in front of a mirror, Denise's speech was delivered smoothly.

(A) Denise's speech was delivered
(B) Denise's speech should have been delivered
(C) Denise's was a speech delivered
(D) Denise delivered the speech
(E) the speech of Denise was delivered

The correct answer is (**D**). This is the only choice that eliminates the dangling modifier by placing the subject *Denise* immediately after the phrase that describes her.

Revision-in-Context

Revision-in-Context questions are based on short passages that are meant to represent the first draft of an essay. Following each passage are questions that require you to suggest improvements in structure and usage, to combine sentences into more effective prose, and to demonstrate understanding of the organization of the passage.

Sample Passage:

(1) Like the United States today, there were courts in Athens where a wrong might be righted. (2) Since any citizen might accuse another of a crime, the Athenian courts of law were very busy. (3) In fact, unless a citizen was unusually peaceful or very unimportant, they would be sure to appear in the courts at least once every few years.

(4) At a trial the accuser was allowed a certain time to speak. (5) The person accused was also allowed a certain time to speak at the trial. (6) The length of time was marked by a water clock. (7) Free men testified under oath as they do today, but the oath of a slave was counted as worthless.

Questions on Sample Passage:

1. Which of the following is the best revision of the underlined portion of sentence 1 below?

Like the United States today, there were courts in Athens where a wrong might be righted.

(A) Athens had courts
(B) there was courts in Athens
(C) the courts in Athens provided a place
(D) there were courts of law in Athens
(E) in Athens they had courts

The best revision is (**A**). It is concise, and it correctly compares the United States to Athens, rather than to courts.

2. Which of the following is the best revision of the underlined portion of sentence 3 below?

In fact, unless a citizen was unusually peaceful or very unimportant, they would be sure to appear in the courts at least once every few years.

(A) they would be sure of appearing
(B) they would certainly appear
(C) surely they would appear
(D) he would sure appear
(E) he would be sure to appear

The correct answer is **(E)**. A singular pronoun is required to refer to the singular noun *citizen.*

3. Which of the following is the best way to combine sentences 4 and 5?

(A) The accuser at the trial and the person accused by him both got time to speak.
(B) The accuser and the person accused at the trial was each allowed a certain time to speak.
(C) At the trial, the accuser and the person accused, they each were allowed time to speak.
(D) At the trial, both the accuser and the person accused were allowed a certain time to speak.
(E) The accuser could speak and the person accused could speak at a trial for a certain time.

Choice **(D)** offers the best combination of the two sentences.

The Essay section of the Writing Test allows you 20 minutes to plan and write an essay on a topic that does not require knowledge of any specific subject matter.

Each essay is scored holistically by two readers. These readers take into account the level of writing that is to be expected of someone about to enter college who is working under severe time pressure. They do not expect Nobel Prize-winning prose, but they are looking for a lot more than "Run, Spot, run"!

The topic for the essay is spelled out quite explicitly, and further information on what you should include in your essay is often provided. Here is a sample essay question.

Example➤ Consider carefully the following statement and the assignment below it. Then plan and write your essay as directed.

"Those who can, do. Those who can't, teach."

Assignment: Do you agree or disagree with this statement? Write an essay in which you support your opinion with specific examples from history, contemporary affairs, literature, or personal observation.

Notice that the assignment uses the word *or* in front of *personal observation.* That means that you can use any one or more of the sources listed for your examples. In other words, if you can't think of appropriate examples from literature, history, or current affairs, you can use examples from your own personal experiences. Obviously, you may wish to tailor your experience to fit the assignment, but that is not normally a problem. No one will hold you accountable for the absolute accuracy of your report!

Registering for the SAT

The SAT is administered on a Saturday morning in October, November, December, January, April, May, and June at established testing centers nationwide. The SAT II subject tests are offered at the same time during the November, December, January, May, and June administrations. SAT I and SAT II cannot be taken on the same day, and you must register separately for each test date.

When you apply to a college, find out whether it requires SAT I or SAT II, or both, and what its deadlines are for receiving scores. It takes five to six weeks to process your scores, so be sure to choose a test date that will allow enough time to get your scores in before the deadline.

If you plan to apply to a college for early decision, take the SAT at the end of your junior year. If you haven't yet decided which schools you will apply to, take the SAT in December or January of your senior year. Then you will be sure of having your scores reported in time wherever you apply.

It's a good idea to take SAT II tests as you finish the appropriate course. If you wait until your senior year, you may have to do an extensive review in preparation for each test.

Registration forms for the SAT may be available from your high school guidance officer. You may also obtain the form by writing to:

College Board SAT Program
P.O. Box 6200
Princeton, NJ 08541-6200

or

College Board SAT Program
P.O. Box 1025
Berkeley, CA 94701

The Registration Bulletin includes the registration form, along with information on procedures, exceptions, and special testing arrangements, times, places, and fees.

Your Score Report

About six weeks after you take the SAT, your scores will be sent to the colleges you named on your registration form, to your high school, and to you. Your score report will include your percentile ranks and interpretive information as well as SAT I and SAT II scores. You will also receive a booklet showing you how to use your scores to help with your college planning.

How to Use the Answer Grid

The Mathematical Reasoning section of SAT I includes Student-Produced Response questions. In contrast to multiple-choice questions, which require you to select the correct answer from the choices offered, student-produced response questions require you to figure out the correct answer to a problem and then record your answer in a special grid. Student-produced response questions are solved just like any other math problems, but the answer grid requires some explanation.

FEATURES OF THE ANSWER GRID

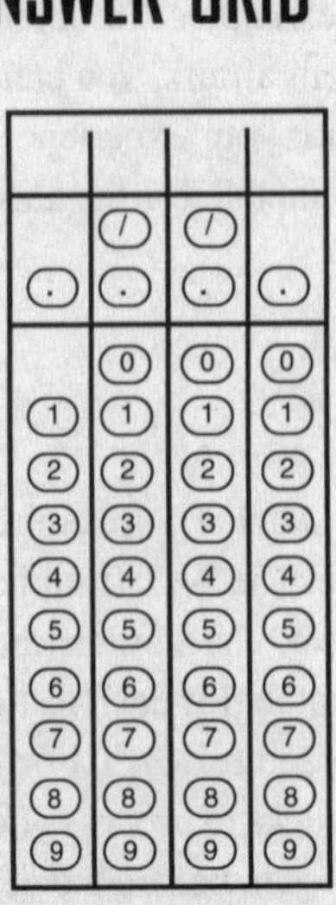

← boxes to write your numerical answer
← fraction lines—use at most one per answer
← decimal points—use at most one per answer

The empty boxes at the top of the grid are for you to write in the numerical value of your answer. The first row of ovals provides two slash marks (/), which allow you to enter numbers in fractional form. Since a fraction must have both a numerator and a denominator, it is not possible that the leftmost or rightmost positions could be a slash; therefore, no slash marks are offered in the first or last column of the grid. The second row of ovals contains four decimal points, and the following rows contain the digits 0 to 9.

RULES FOR USING THE GRID

1. Write your answer in the boxes at the top of the grid. This step is recommended but not required. You will receive credit only for answers that are recorded in the ovals. However, entering your answers in the boxes first will help you to fill in the ovals accurately.
2. Mark only one oval in any column.
3. You may start your answer in any column. Columns not needed should be left blank.

   An answer of 15 can be entered in the grid in three different ways:

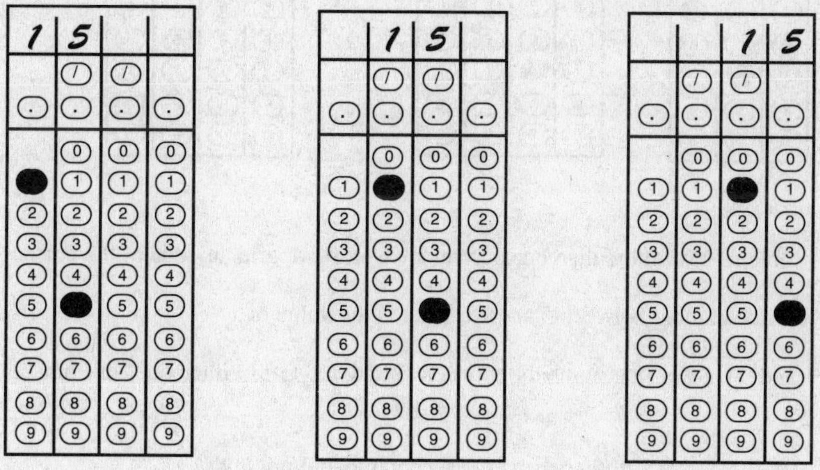

4. No grid question has a negative answer.
5. You may express your answer as a decimal or a fraction. An answer may be gridded as $\frac{3}{4}$ or as .75.
6. It is not necessary to grid a zero in front of a decimal less than 1.
7. Fractions do not have to be reduced to lowest terms unless they do not fit in the answer grid.

   You can grid an answer as $\frac{4}{16}$, but you cannot grid $\frac{12}{16}$. That is because the grid has only four columns and five columns are required to grid $\frac{12}{16}$.

8. A mixed number must be expressed as a decimal or an improper fraction.

An answer of $1\frac{3}{4}$ must be converted to 1.75 or $\frac{7}{4}$. Because the grid does not allow for a space between the integer and the fraction, if you enter your answer as $1\frac{3}{4}$, it will be read as $\frac{13}{4}$ and it will be marked as wrong.

These answers are acceptable. This answer is unacceptable.

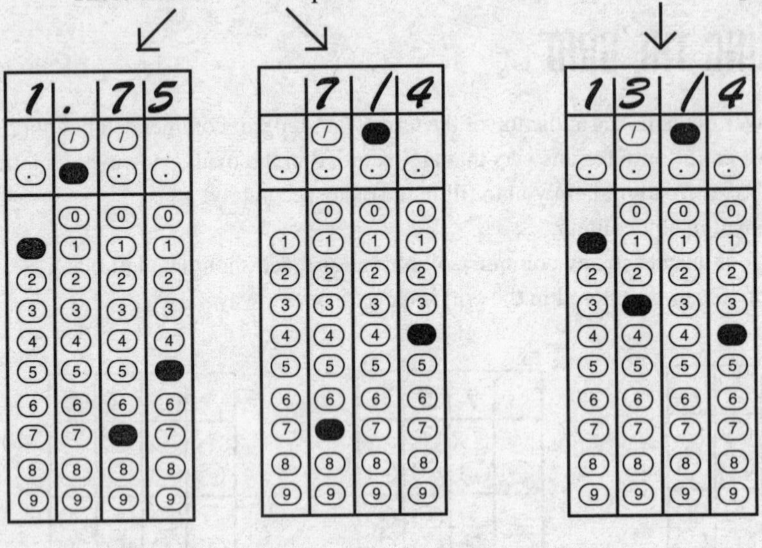

9. Some problems have more than one correct answer. If so, grid any one of the correct answers.

Example➤ If x is a prime number between 5 and 13, what is the value of x?

Solution➤ Both 7 and 11 are prime numbers between 5 and 13. Grid either one, but not both, of these answers.

Either answer is acceptable, but not both.

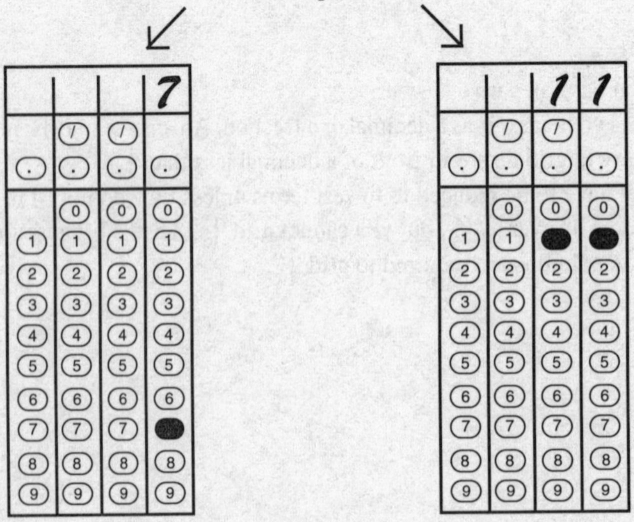

10. For decimal answers, enter the most accurate value the grid can accommodate. An answer of .1777 can be entered on the grid as follows:

Either of these answers is correct.

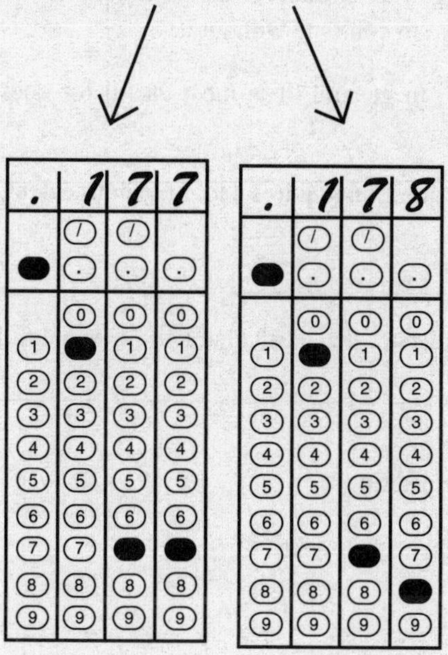

These answers are not acceptable because greater accuracy could have been achieved if additional grid columns had been used.

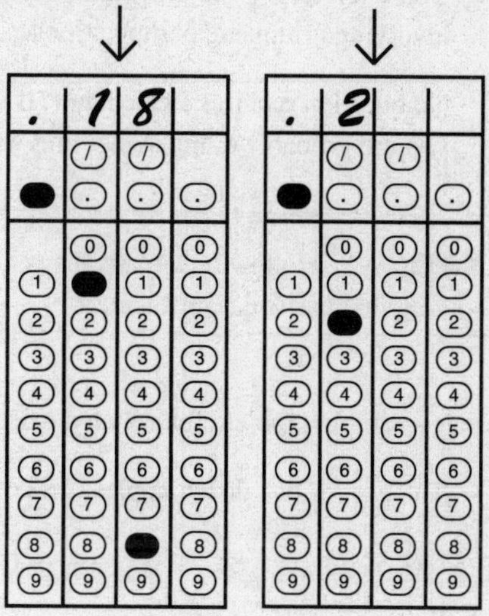

11. Answers to grid-in questions are either completely correct or completely wrong. No partial credit is given, and no points are deducted for wrong answers. For this reason, it is better to enter an answer you are not sure of than to leave a blank.

12. Check to be sure that you have gridded your answer accurately.

Calculators and the SAT

You are permitted to use a calculator for the math sections of SAT I. Although no question requires the use of a calculator, many questions can be answered more quickly or easily with the help of a calculator.

You must provide your own calculator, which can be any basic four-function, scientific or graphing calculator. You will not be allowed to share calculators with other test-takers or to use any of the following:

- calculators with paper tape or printers
- calculators with typewriter-style keypads
- calculators that "talk"
- calculators that require an external power source
- hand-held minicomputers
- laptop computers
- pocket organizers
- "clamshell" calculators

Calculator Guidelines

Make sure that the calculator you bring is one with which you are thoroughly familiar.

Check to see that your calculator is in good working order and that it has fresh batteries. If your calculator breaks down during the test, you will have to continue without it.

Don't try to use the calculator on every question. In general, it is most useful for questions involving arithmetic computations.

No question requires a calculator. If you find that a question requires a lot of tedious calculation, you are probably doing something wrong.

> **NOTE:** A [calculator icon] following a math answer explanation indicates that a calculator could be helpful in solving that particular problem.

Here is a sample problem for which a calculator would be useful:

Example➤ The cost of two dozen apples is $3.60. At this rate, what is the cost of 10 apples?

(A) $1.75
(B) $1.60
(C) $1.55
(D) $1.50
(E) $1.25

Solution➤ The correct answer is **(D)**.

Make a ratio of apples to dollars:

$$\frac{\text{apples}}{\text{dollars}} : \frac{24}{3.60} = \frac{10}{x}$$

$$24x = 36$$

$$x = \frac{36}{24} = \$1.50$$

A calculator would be useful in solving this problem. Although the calculations are fairly simple, the calculator can improve both speed and accuracy.

Here is a problem for which a calculator would *not* be useful:

Example➤ Joshua travels a distance of d miles in $t - 6$ hours. At this rate, how many miles will he travel in $t^2 - 36$ hours?

(A) $d(t + 6)$

(B) $d(t - 6)$

(C) $\frac{d}{t+6}$

(D) $\frac{d}{t-6}$

(E) $\frac{t+6}{d}$

Solution➤ The correct answer is (**A**).

$$\text{rate} = \frac{\text{distance}}{\text{time}}$$

$$\text{Joshua's rate} = \frac{d}{t-6}$$

To calculate his new distance, use $d = rt$:

$$\text{Distance} = \left(\frac{d}{t+6}\right)\left(t^2-36\right)$$

$$= \left(\frac{d}{t-6}\right)(t+6)(t-6)$$

$$= d(t+6)$$

This is an algebra question. Using a calculator would not be helpful.

Here is a problem for which a calculator would be of minimal help. Its use might mask the more appropriate method of solution.

Example➤ If $x = \left(\frac{1}{2}\right)\left(\frac{1}{3}\right)\left(\frac{3}{2}\right)\left(\frac{4}{81}\right)$, then $\sqrt{x} =$

(A) $\frac{1}{5}$

(B) $\frac{1}{9}$

(C) $\frac{1}{11}$

(D) $\frac{1}{13}$

(E) $\frac{1}{17}$

Solution➤ The correct answer is (**B**).

Without a calculator:

Reduce the fraction by canceling.

$$x = \frac{(\cancel{3})(\cancel{4})}{(\cancel{2})(\cancel{3})(\cancel{2})(81)} = \frac{1}{81} \qquad \sqrt{x} = \frac{1}{9}$$

With a calculator:

$$x = \frac{(3)(4)}{(2)(3)(2)(81)} = \frac{12}{972} = \frac{1}{81} \qquad \sqrt{x} = \frac{1}{9}$$

Fractions can be reduced. Fractions can be multiplied rapidly after canceling. Using a calculator for this problem does not simplify the arithmetic.

SAT QUESTION OVERVIEW

This section will introduce you to the types of questions that appear on the SAT. Answer all the questions to the best of your ability, check your answers, and then take the full-length *Diagnostic Examination* that follows. Your ability to answer each kind of question will increase as you become more familiar with each question's format. Remember to read *all* directions thoroughly. This is an important part of examination procedure. Use the Answer Sheet below to indicate your answers for all questions in this section.

OVERVIEW ANSWER SHEET

Verbal Reasoning

1 (A) (B) (C) (D) (E) 2 (A) (B) (C) (D) (E) 3 (A) (B) (C) (D) (E)

4 (A) (B) (C) (D) (E) 5 (A) (B) (C) (D) (E) 6 (A) (B) (C) (D) (E)

7 (A) (B) (C) (D) (E) 8 (A) (B) (C) (D) (E) 9 (A) (B) (C) (D) (E)

Mathematical Reasoning

1 (A) (B) (C) (D) (E) 2 (A) (B) (C) (D) (E) 3 (A) (B) (C) (D) (E)

4 (A) (B) (C) (D) (E) 5 (A) (B) (C) (D) (E) 6 (A) (B) (C) (D) (E)

7 (A) (B) (C) (D) (E) 8 (A) (B) (C) (D) (E) 9 (A) (B) (C) (D) (E)

10 (A) (B) (C) (D) (E) 11 (A) (B) (C) (D) (E) 12 (A) (B) (C) (D) (E)

13

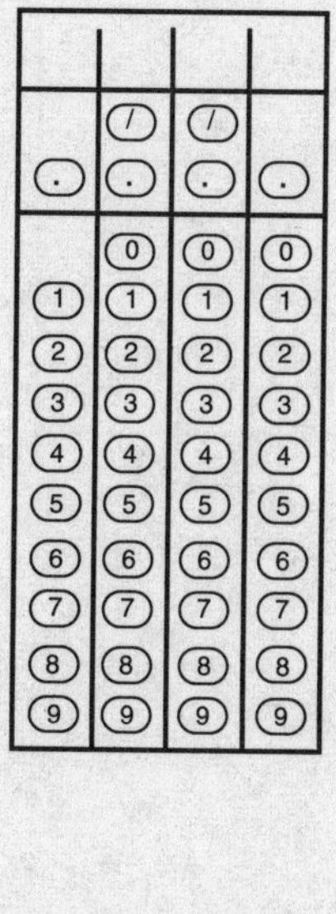

14

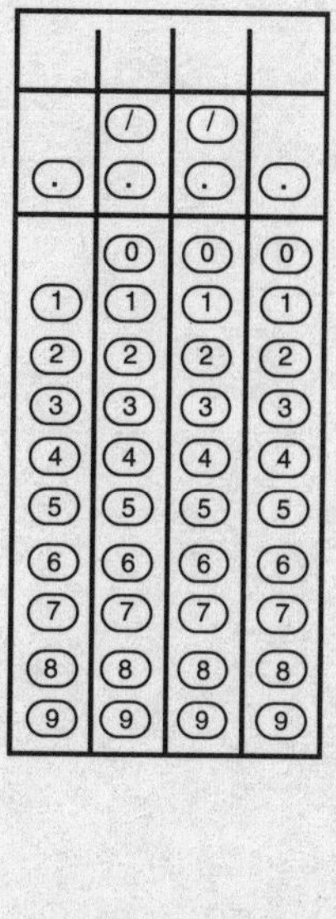

15

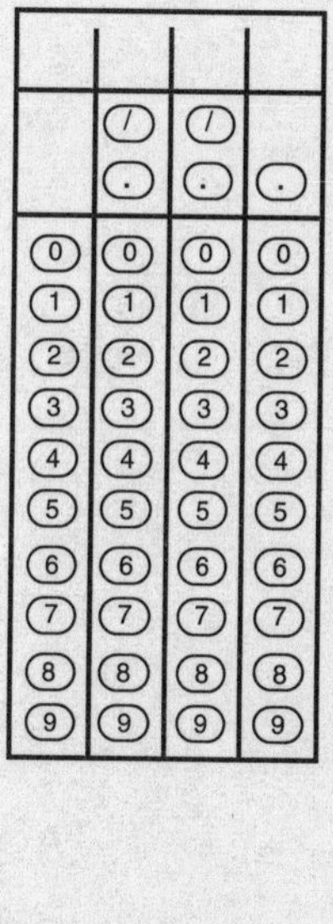

Verbal Reasoning

ANALOGIES

Directions: Each of the following items contains a pair of words in capital letters, followed by five pairs of words lettered A to E. Choose the lettered pair that *best* expresses a relationship similar to the one expressed by the capitalized pair.

1. GOAT : UNICORN : :

   (A) horse : dragon
   (B) ram : bull
   (C) sheep : dog
   (D) mountain : milk
   (E) fox : wolf

2. SPOOL : THREAD : :

   (A) bale : hay
   (B) peck : potatoes
   (C) verse : song
   (D) coil : rope
   (E) reel : line

3. RICE : WEDDING : :

   (A) food : groom
   (B) celebration : ceremony
   (C) wheat : meal
   (D) bran : cereal
   (E) confetti : parade

SENTENCE COMPLETIONS

Directions: Each of the following sentences contains one or two blank spaces to be filled in by one of the five choices listed below each sentence. Select the word or words that *best* complete the meaning of the sentence.

4. Many hours of practice are required of a successful musician, so it is often not so much---- as----which distinguishes the professional from the amateur.

   (A) genius..understanding
   (B) money..education
   (C) talent..discipline
   (D) fortitude..mediocrity
   (E) technique..pomposity

5. The sudden death of the world-renowned leader----the members of his party and----his former opponents, despite their respectful mourning.

   (A) saddened..devastated
   (B) shocked..encouraged
   (C) depressed..tempered
   (D) satisfied..aided
   (E) prostrated..depressed

6. Despite his valor on the football field, the former athlete----throughout boot camp.

(A) relaxed
(B) quivered
(C) hustled
(D) sidled
(E) embellished

CRITICAL READING

Directions: The passage below is followed by a set of questions. Read the passage and answer the accompanying questions, basing your answers on what is *stated* or *implied* in the passage.

The following passage discusses the mythical island of Atlantis.

A legendary island in the Atlantic Ocean beyond the Pillars of Hercules was first mentioned by Plato in the *Timaeus*. Atlantis was a fabulously beautiful and prosperous land, the seat of an empire nine thousand years before Solon. Its inhabitants overran part of Europe and Africa, Athens alone being able to defy them. Because of the impiety of its people, the island was destroyed by an earthquake and inundation. The legend may have existed before Plato and may have sprung from the concept of Homer's Elysium. The possibility that such an island once existed has caused much speculation, resulting in a theory that pre-Columbian civilizations in America were established by colonists from the lost island.

7. The main purpose of the passage is to discuss

(A) the legend of Atlantis
(B) Plato's description of Atlantis in the *Timaeus*
(C) the conquests made by citizens of Atlantis
(D) the possibility that America was discovered by colonists from Atlantis
(E) the destruction of Atlantis

8. According to the passage, we may safely conclude that the inhabitants of Atlantis

(A) were known personally to Homer
(B) were ruled by Plato
(C) were a religious and superstitious people
(D) used the name Columbus for America
(E) left no recorded evidence of their civilization

9. According to the legend, Atlantis was destroyed because the inhabitants

(A) failed to obtain an adequate food supply
(B) failed to conquer Greece
(C) failed to respect their gods
(D) believed in Homer's Elysium
(E) had become too prosperous

Mathematical Reasoning

STANDARD MULTIPLE-CHOICE QUESTIONS

Directions: Solve the following problems using any available space on the page for scratchwork. On your answer sheet, fill in the choice which best corresponds to the correct answer.

Notes: The figures accompanying the problems are drawn as accurately as possible unless otherwise stated in specific problems. Again, unless otherwise stated, all figures lie in the same plane. All numbers used in these problems are real numbers. Calculators are permitted for this test.

Reference Information

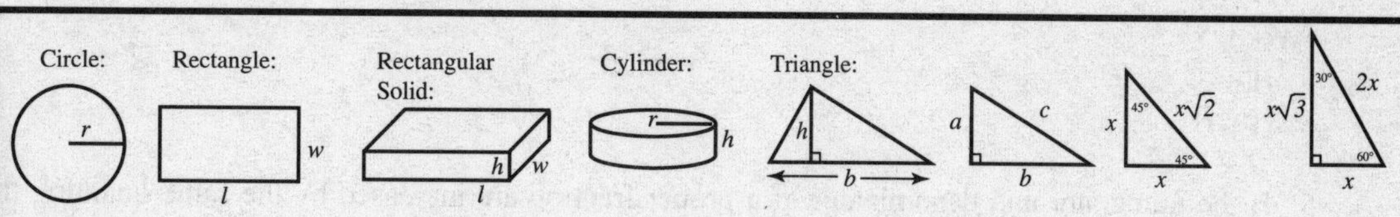

$C = 2\pi r$
$A = \pi r^2$

$A = lw$

$V = lwh$

$V = \pi r^2 h$

$A = \frac{1}{2}bh$

$a^2 + b^2 = c^2$

The number of degrees of arc in a circle is 360.
The measure in degrees of a straight angle is 180.
The sum of the measures in degrees of the angles of a triangle is 180.

1. A certain triangle has sides that are, respectively, 6 inches, 8 inches, and 10 inches long. A rectangle equal in area to that of the triangle has a width of 3 inches. The perimeter of the rectangle, expressed in inches, is

(A) 11
(B) 16
(C) 22
(D) 24
(E) 30

2. A room 27 feet by 32 feet is to be carpeted. The width of the carpet is 27 inches. The length, in yards, of the carpet needed for this floor is (1 yard = 3 feet = 36 inches)

(A) 1188
(B) 648
(C) 384
(D) 128
(E) 96

3. Given: Right ΔABC with $AB = 6$ and $AC = 7$

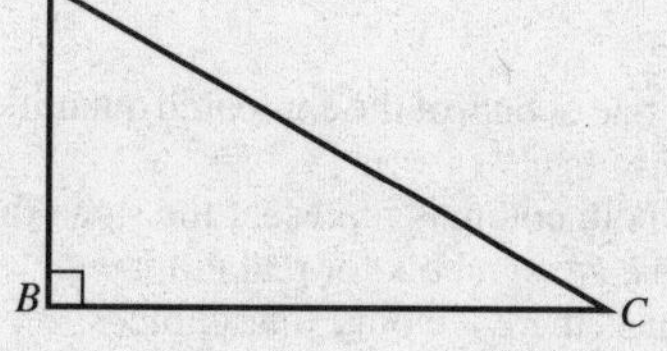

What does BC equal?

(A) 1
(B) $\sqrt{13}$
(C) 6
(D) $\sqrt{39}$
(E) $\sqrt{78}$

4. The closest approximation to the correct answer for $5-\sqrt{32.076}+1.00017^3$ is

(A) 9
(B) 7
(C) 5
(D) 3
(E) 0

5. If the numerator and denominator of a proper fraction are increased by the same quantity, the resulting fraction is

(A) always greater than the original fraction
(B) always less than the original fraction
(C) always equal to the original fraction
(D) one-half the original fraction
(E) not determinable

6. The total number of feet in x yards, y feet, and z inches is (1 yard = 3 feet = 36 inches)

(A) $3x+y+\frac{z}{12}$
(B) $12(x+y+z)$
(C) $x+y+z$
(D) $\frac{x}{36}+\frac{y}{12}+z$
(E) $x+3y+36z$

QUANTITATIVE COMPARISONS

Directions: For each of the following items, compare the quantity in Column A with the one in Column B and determine whether:

(A) the quantity is greater in Column A
(B) the quantity is greater in Column B
(C) both quantities are equal
(D) no comparison can be made with the information given

Notes:

(1) Information concerning one or both of the compared quantities will be centered between the two columns for some of the items.
(2) Symbols that appear in both columns represent the same thing in Column A as in Column B.
(3) Letters such as x, n, and k are symbols for real numbers.
(4) Do not mark choice (E), as there are only four choices.

	Column A		**Column B**
		$2 < y < x$	
7.	$\frac{120x^5y^6}{8x^3y^2}$		$\frac{120x^4y^{13/2}}{6x^0y^{1/2}}$

$a > 0$
$b > 0$
$m > 1$

8.	$(m^a)^b$	$m^a m^b$

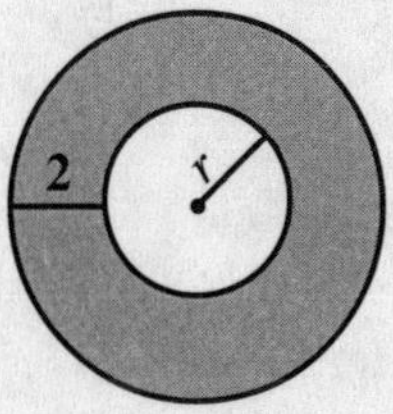

9.	Area of smaller circle	Area of shaded portion

10.	39% of 87	87% of 39

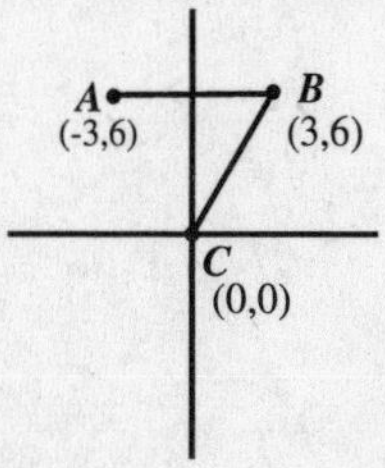

11.	Distance from A to B	Distance from B to C
12.	The sum of all the angles of an equilateral triangle	The sum of all the angles of a scalene triangle

STUDENT-PRODUCED RESPONSE QUESTIONS

Directions: Solve each of the following problems and write the arithmetic value of your answer in the open spaces at the top of the correspondingly numbered grid on your answer sheet. Then grid your answer by blackening the ovals that correspond to the decimal point, fraction line, and numbers in your answer.

Notes: If a question has more than one correct answer, grid only one of them.
To grid $4\frac{1}{4}$, use 4.25 or $\frac{17}{4}$. Do not use $4\frac{1}{4}$, as it will be read as $\frac{41}{4}$.
None of these answers requires a minus sign.
Answers may begin in any grid column.
Decimal answers should be entered with the greatest accuracy allowed by the grid.

13. The circumference of a circle is 20π. If the area of the circle is $a\pi$, what is the value of a?

14. If 35% of a number is 70, what is the number?

15. Find the mode of the following group of numbers: 8, 8, 9, 10, 11

Answer Key

VERBAL REASONING

1. A	3. E	5. B	7. A	9. C
2. E	4. C	6. B	8. E	

MATHEMATICAL REASONING

1. C	4. E	7. B	10. C	13. 100
2. D	5. A	8. D	11. B	14. 200
3. B	6. A	9. D	12. C	15. 8

Explanatory Answers

NOTE: A [calculator icon] following a math answer explanation indicates that a calculator could be helpful in solving that particular problem.

VERBAL REASONING

1. **(A)** A *goat* is a real animal and a *unicorn* an imaginary one. A *horse* is a real animal and a *dragon* an imaginary one. None of the other choices expresses this relationship.

2. **(E)** *Thread* is wrapped around a *spool*, and *line* around a *reel*. This type of direct relationship is not expressed in any of the other options.

3. **(E)** *Rice* is traditionally thrown at a *wedding* celebration, and *confetti* is usually thrown during a *parade*. A *celebration* is the observance of a *ceremony*, but this is a much more general relationship than (E).

4. **(C)** the "not so much ---- as ----" sets up a contrast between two ideas. Only choices (B) and (C) could express a contrast. However, (B) is not appropriate in the sentence. (C) provides the contrast and is appropriate in the context.

5. **(B)** The sentence implies that despite their respectful mourning, his former opponents might be *encouraged* by his absence from politics.

6. **(B)** The word *despite* introduces paradox or irony in this sentence. It is ironic that a football hero would *quiver* throughout boot camp.

7. **(A)** The entire passage concerns the legendary island of Atlantis. While each of the other choices is mentioned, none can be considered the main purpose of the passage.

8. **(E)** Since the main thrust of the passage indicates that Atlantis is a legendary island, no recorded evidence of its inhabitants could have been left. Thus, (E) is the only choice that could be derived.

9. **(C)** The passage states that the island was destroyed because of the "impiety of its people." There is no other cause mentioned.

MATHEMATICAL REASONING

1. **(C)** The area of a triangle is $A = \frac{1}{2}bh$, which in this case is $\frac{1}{2} \cdot 6 \cdot 8 = 24$. The area of a rectangle is $A = l \cdot w$. Since we know the width and area, $24 = l \cdot 3$; therefore, $l = 8$. The perimeter of the rectangle is $P = 2l + 2w$, which we find to be $2 \cdot 8 + 2 \cdot 3 = 16 + 6 = 22$.

2. **(D)** The length of one side of the room in inches is 27 ft. × 12 in. = 324 in. The width of the carpet is 27 in.; therefore, it takes 324 ÷ 27 = 12 lengths of carpet at 32 ft. per length, or 12 × 32 = 384 ft. The length needed in yards is 384 ft. ÷ 3 ft./yd. = 128 yds.

3. **(B)** By the Pythagorean Theorem, $(AB)^2 + (BC)^2 = (AC)^2$, or $(BC)^2 = (AC)^2 - (AB)^2$. Substituting the values in this equation yields $(BC)^2 = (7)^2 - (6)^2 = 49 - 36 = 13$, and $BC = \sqrt{13}$.

4. **(E)** $\sqrt{32.076}$ is slightly more than halfway between 5 and 6, say 5.6. 1.00017^3 is very slightly over $1^3 = 1$. Therefore, $5 - 5.6 + 1 = 0.4$. The closest answer given is 0.

5. **(A)** If the numerator and denominator of the fraction $\frac{n}{d}$ are increased by a quantity q, the new fraction is $\frac{n+q}{d+q}$. Compare this to the old fraction by finding a common denominator $d(d+q)$. The old fraction is $\frac{n(d+q)}{d(d+q)} = \frac{(nd+nq)}{d(d+q)}$; the new fraction is $\frac{d(n+q)}{d(d+q)} = \frac{(nd+dq)}{d(d+q)}$. Comparing the old numerator $(nd + nq)$ with the new $(nd + dq)$, the new fraction is larger, since $d > n$. The fraction of this example must be a proper fraction.

6. **(A)** x yards = $3x$ feet; y feet = y feet; z inches = $\frac{z}{12}$ feet. Therefore, x yards + y feet + z inches = $3x$ feet + y feet + $\frac{z}{12}$ feet, or $3x + y + \frac{z}{12}$ feet.

7. **(B)** If you remember to subtract the exponents in division of powers of the same base, the fraction in Column A can be reduced: $120x^5y^6/8x^3y^2 = 15x^2y^4$. In Column B, $120x^4y^{13/2}/6x^0y^{1/2} = 20x^4y^{12/2} = 20x^4y^6$. Since x and y are both greater than 2, we need not worry about powers of fractions. Therefore, Column B is obviously the larger of the two.

8. **(D)** In Column A, $(m^a)^b = m^{ab}$, with $ab > 0$, since $a,b > 0$. In Column B, $m^a m^b = m^{a+b}$, with $a + b > 0$ since $a,b > 0$. Since we know nothing else about a and b, we cannot tell if $ab > a + b$ or vice versa.

9. **(D)** The area of the larger circle is $\pi(r + 2)^2$. The area of the smaller circle is πr^2. The area of the shaded region is

   $\pi(r + 2)^2 - \pi r^2$

   $\pi(r^2 + 4r + 4) - \pi r^2$

   $\pi r^2 + 4\pi r + 4\pi - \pi r^2$

   $= 4\pi r + 4\pi = 4\pi(r + 1)$

   Since we know nothing about the radius r, we cannot tell which area is larger, $4\pi(r + 1)$ or πr^2.

10. **(C)** The trick to the problem is realizing that in both columns you will multiply 39 × 87 and move the decimal point two places to the left.

11. **(B)** The distance from *A* to *B* is

$$\sqrt{(3+3)^2+(6-6)^2}, = \sqrt{36} = 6.$$

The distance from *B* to *C* is

$$\sqrt{(0-3)^2+(0-6)^2} = \sqrt{9+36} = \sqrt{45}.$$

The square root of 45 is greater than 6. Therefore, the distance from *B* to *C* is greater than the distance from *A* to *B*.

12. **(C)** No matter what kind of triangle we speak of, the sum of all its angles is 180°.

13. $C = 2\pi r = 20\pi$

$r = 10$

$A = \pi r^2 = \pi(10)^2 = 100\pi = a\pi$

$\therefore a = 100$

14. $\frac{35x}{100} \bullet x = 70$

$\frac{35x}{100} = 70$

$x = 200$

15. The mode is the number which occurs the most frequently. The mode = 8.

PART

TWO

Full-Length Diagnostic Examination

CONTENTS

Diagnostic Examination

Answer Sheet

If a section has fewer questions than answer ovals, leave the extra ovals blank.

Section 1

1 Ⓐ Ⓑ Ⓒ Ⓓ Ⓔ	11 Ⓐ Ⓑ Ⓒ Ⓓ Ⓔ	21 Ⓐ Ⓑ Ⓒ Ⓓ Ⓔ	31 Ⓐ Ⓑ Ⓒ Ⓓ Ⓔ
2 Ⓐ Ⓑ Ⓒ Ⓓ Ⓔ	12 Ⓐ Ⓑ Ⓒ Ⓓ Ⓔ	22 Ⓐ Ⓑ Ⓒ Ⓓ Ⓔ	32 Ⓐ Ⓑ Ⓒ Ⓓ Ⓔ
3 Ⓐ Ⓑ Ⓒ Ⓓ Ⓔ	13 Ⓐ Ⓑ Ⓒ Ⓓ Ⓔ	23 Ⓐ Ⓑ Ⓒ Ⓓ Ⓔ	33 Ⓐ Ⓑ Ⓒ Ⓓ Ⓔ
4 Ⓐ Ⓑ Ⓒ Ⓓ Ⓔ	14 Ⓐ Ⓑ Ⓒ Ⓓ Ⓔ	24 Ⓐ Ⓑ Ⓒ Ⓓ Ⓔ	34 Ⓐ Ⓑ Ⓒ Ⓓ Ⓔ
5 Ⓐ Ⓑ Ⓒ Ⓓ Ⓔ	15 Ⓐ Ⓑ Ⓒ Ⓓ Ⓔ	25 Ⓐ Ⓑ Ⓒ Ⓓ Ⓔ	35 Ⓐ Ⓑ Ⓒ Ⓓ Ⓔ
6 Ⓐ Ⓑ Ⓒ Ⓓ Ⓔ	16 Ⓐ Ⓑ Ⓒ Ⓓ Ⓔ	26 Ⓐ Ⓑ Ⓒ Ⓓ Ⓔ	36 Ⓐ Ⓑ Ⓒ Ⓓ Ⓔ
7 Ⓐ Ⓑ Ⓒ Ⓓ Ⓔ	17 Ⓐ Ⓑ Ⓒ Ⓓ Ⓔ	27 Ⓐ Ⓑ Ⓒ Ⓓ Ⓔ	37 Ⓐ Ⓑ Ⓒ Ⓓ Ⓔ
8 Ⓐ Ⓑ Ⓒ Ⓓ Ⓔ	18 Ⓐ Ⓑ Ⓒ Ⓓ Ⓔ	28 Ⓐ Ⓑ Ⓒ Ⓓ Ⓔ	38 Ⓐ Ⓑ Ⓒ Ⓓ Ⓔ
9 Ⓐ Ⓑ Ⓒ Ⓓ Ⓔ	19 Ⓐ Ⓑ Ⓒ Ⓓ Ⓔ	29 Ⓐ Ⓑ Ⓒ Ⓓ Ⓔ	39 Ⓐ Ⓑ Ⓒ Ⓓ Ⓔ
10 Ⓐ Ⓑ Ⓒ Ⓓ Ⓔ	20 Ⓐ Ⓑ Ⓒ Ⓓ Ⓔ	30 Ⓐ Ⓑ Ⓒ Ⓓ Ⓔ	40 Ⓐ Ⓑ Ⓒ Ⓓ Ⓔ

Section 2

1 Ⓐ Ⓑ Ⓒ Ⓓ Ⓔ	11 Ⓐ Ⓑ Ⓒ Ⓓ Ⓔ	21 Ⓐ Ⓑ Ⓒ Ⓓ Ⓔ	31 Ⓐ Ⓑ Ⓒ Ⓓ Ⓔ
2 Ⓐ Ⓑ Ⓒ Ⓓ Ⓔ	12 Ⓐ Ⓑ Ⓒ Ⓓ Ⓔ	22 Ⓐ Ⓑ Ⓒ Ⓓ Ⓔ	32 Ⓐ Ⓑ Ⓒ Ⓓ Ⓔ
3 Ⓐ Ⓑ Ⓒ Ⓓ Ⓔ	13 Ⓐ Ⓑ Ⓒ Ⓓ Ⓔ	23 Ⓐ Ⓑ Ⓒ Ⓓ Ⓔ	33 Ⓐ Ⓑ Ⓒ Ⓓ Ⓔ
4 Ⓐ Ⓑ Ⓒ Ⓓ Ⓔ	14 Ⓐ Ⓑ Ⓒ Ⓓ Ⓔ	24 Ⓐ Ⓑ Ⓒ Ⓓ Ⓔ	34 Ⓐ Ⓑ Ⓒ Ⓓ Ⓔ
5 Ⓐ Ⓑ Ⓒ Ⓓ Ⓔ	15 Ⓐ Ⓑ Ⓒ Ⓓ Ⓔ	25 Ⓐ Ⓑ Ⓒ Ⓓ Ⓔ	35 Ⓐ Ⓑ Ⓒ Ⓓ Ⓔ
6 Ⓐ Ⓑ Ⓒ Ⓓ Ⓔ	16 Ⓐ Ⓑ Ⓒ Ⓓ Ⓔ	26 Ⓐ Ⓑ Ⓒ Ⓓ Ⓔ	36 Ⓐ Ⓑ Ⓒ Ⓓ Ⓔ
7 Ⓐ Ⓑ Ⓒ Ⓓ Ⓔ	17 Ⓐ Ⓑ Ⓒ Ⓓ Ⓔ	27 Ⓐ Ⓑ Ⓒ Ⓓ Ⓔ	37 Ⓐ Ⓑ Ⓒ Ⓓ Ⓔ
8 Ⓐ Ⓑ Ⓒ Ⓓ Ⓔ	18 Ⓐ Ⓑ Ⓒ Ⓓ Ⓔ	28 Ⓐ Ⓑ Ⓒ Ⓓ Ⓔ	38 Ⓐ Ⓑ Ⓒ Ⓓ Ⓔ
9 Ⓐ Ⓑ Ⓒ Ⓓ Ⓔ	19 Ⓐ Ⓑ Ⓒ Ⓓ Ⓔ	29 Ⓐ Ⓑ Ⓒ Ⓓ Ⓔ	39 Ⓐ Ⓑ Ⓒ Ⓓ Ⓔ
10 Ⓐ Ⓑ Ⓒ Ⓓ Ⓔ	20 Ⓐ Ⓑ Ⓒ Ⓓ Ⓔ	30 Ⓐ Ⓑ Ⓒ Ⓓ Ⓔ	40 Ⓐ Ⓑ Ⓒ Ⓓ Ⓔ

Section 3

1 Ⓐ Ⓑ Ⓒ Ⓓ Ⓔ	6 Ⓐ Ⓑ Ⓒ Ⓓ Ⓔ	11 Ⓐ Ⓑ Ⓒ Ⓓ Ⓔ	16 Ⓐ Ⓑ Ⓒ Ⓓ Ⓔ
2 Ⓐ Ⓑ Ⓒ Ⓓ Ⓔ	7 Ⓐ Ⓑ Ⓒ Ⓓ Ⓔ	12 Ⓐ Ⓑ Ⓒ Ⓓ Ⓔ	17 Ⓐ Ⓑ Ⓒ Ⓓ Ⓔ
3 Ⓐ Ⓑ Ⓒ Ⓓ Ⓔ	8 Ⓐ Ⓑ Ⓒ Ⓓ Ⓔ	13 Ⓐ Ⓑ Ⓒ Ⓓ Ⓔ	18 Ⓐ Ⓑ Ⓒ Ⓓ Ⓔ
4 Ⓐ Ⓑ Ⓒ Ⓓ Ⓔ	9 Ⓐ Ⓑ Ⓒ Ⓓ Ⓔ	14 Ⓐ Ⓑ Ⓒ Ⓓ Ⓔ	19 Ⓐ Ⓑ Ⓒ Ⓓ Ⓔ
5 Ⓐ Ⓑ Ⓒ Ⓓ Ⓔ	10 Ⓐ Ⓑ Ⓒ Ⓓ Ⓔ	15 Ⓐ Ⓑ Ⓒ Ⓓ Ⓔ	20 Ⓐ Ⓑ Ⓒ Ⓓ Ⓔ

Section 4

1 Ⓐ Ⓑ Ⓒ Ⓓ Ⓔ	6 Ⓐ Ⓑ Ⓒ Ⓓ Ⓔ	11 Ⓐ Ⓑ Ⓒ Ⓓ Ⓔ	16 Ⓐ Ⓑ Ⓒ Ⓓ Ⓔ
2 Ⓐ Ⓑ Ⓒ Ⓓ Ⓔ	7 Ⓐ Ⓑ Ⓒ Ⓓ Ⓔ	12 Ⓐ Ⓑ Ⓒ Ⓓ Ⓔ	17 Ⓐ Ⓑ Ⓒ Ⓓ Ⓔ
3 Ⓐ Ⓑ Ⓒ Ⓓ Ⓔ	8 Ⓐ Ⓑ Ⓒ Ⓓ Ⓔ	13 Ⓐ Ⓑ Ⓒ Ⓓ Ⓔ	18 Ⓐ Ⓑ Ⓒ Ⓓ Ⓔ
4 Ⓐ Ⓑ Ⓒ Ⓓ Ⓔ	9 Ⓐ Ⓑ Ⓒ Ⓓ Ⓔ	14 Ⓐ Ⓑ Ⓒ Ⓓ Ⓔ	19 Ⓐ Ⓑ Ⓒ Ⓓ Ⓔ
5 Ⓐ Ⓑ Ⓒ Ⓓ Ⓔ	10 Ⓐ Ⓑ Ⓒ Ⓓ Ⓔ	15 Ⓐ Ⓑ Ⓒ Ⓓ Ⓔ	20 Ⓐ Ⓑ Ⓒ Ⓓ Ⓔ

TEAR HERE

Section 5

1 Ⓐ Ⓑ Ⓒ Ⓓ Ⓔ 11 Ⓐ Ⓑ Ⓒ Ⓓ Ⓔ 21 Ⓐ Ⓑ Ⓒ Ⓓ Ⓔ 31 Ⓐ Ⓑ Ⓒ Ⓓ Ⓔ
2 Ⓐ Ⓑ Ⓒ Ⓓ Ⓔ 12 Ⓐ Ⓑ Ⓒ Ⓓ Ⓔ 22 Ⓐ Ⓑ Ⓒ Ⓓ Ⓔ 32 Ⓐ Ⓑ Ⓒ Ⓓ Ⓔ
3 Ⓐ Ⓑ Ⓒ Ⓓ Ⓔ 13 Ⓐ Ⓑ Ⓒ Ⓓ Ⓔ 23 Ⓐ Ⓑ Ⓒ Ⓓ Ⓔ 33 Ⓐ Ⓑ Ⓒ Ⓓ Ⓔ
4 Ⓐ Ⓑ Ⓒ Ⓓ Ⓔ 14 Ⓐ Ⓑ Ⓒ Ⓓ Ⓔ 24 Ⓐ Ⓑ Ⓒ Ⓓ Ⓔ 34 Ⓐ Ⓑ Ⓒ Ⓓ Ⓔ
5 Ⓐ Ⓑ Ⓒ Ⓓ Ⓔ 15 Ⓐ Ⓑ Ⓒ Ⓓ Ⓔ 25 Ⓐ Ⓑ Ⓒ Ⓓ Ⓔ 35 Ⓐ Ⓑ Ⓒ Ⓓ Ⓔ
6 Ⓐ Ⓑ Ⓒ Ⓓ Ⓔ 16 Ⓐ Ⓑ Ⓒ Ⓓ Ⓔ 26 Ⓐ Ⓑ Ⓒ Ⓓ Ⓔ 36 Ⓐ Ⓑ Ⓒ Ⓓ Ⓔ
7 Ⓐ Ⓑ Ⓒ Ⓓ Ⓔ 17 Ⓐ Ⓑ Ⓒ Ⓓ Ⓔ 27 Ⓐ Ⓑ Ⓒ Ⓓ Ⓔ 37 Ⓐ Ⓑ Ⓒ Ⓓ Ⓔ
8 Ⓐ Ⓑ Ⓒ Ⓓ Ⓔ 18 Ⓐ Ⓑ Ⓒ Ⓓ Ⓔ 28 Ⓐ Ⓑ Ⓒ Ⓓ Ⓔ 38 Ⓐ Ⓑ Ⓒ Ⓓ Ⓔ
9 Ⓐ Ⓑ Ⓒ Ⓓ Ⓔ 19 Ⓐ Ⓑ Ⓒ Ⓓ Ⓔ 29 Ⓐ Ⓑ Ⓒ Ⓓ Ⓔ 39 Ⓐ Ⓑ Ⓒ Ⓓ Ⓔ
10 Ⓐ Ⓑ Ⓒ Ⓓ Ⓔ 20 Ⓐ Ⓑ Ⓒ Ⓓ Ⓔ 30 Ⓐ Ⓑ Ⓒ Ⓓ Ⓔ 40 Ⓐ Ⓑ Ⓒ Ⓓ Ⓔ

Section 6

1 Ⓐ Ⓑ Ⓒ Ⓓ Ⓔ 6 Ⓐ Ⓑ Ⓒ Ⓓ Ⓔ 11 Ⓐ Ⓑ Ⓒ Ⓓ Ⓔ
2 Ⓐ Ⓑ Ⓒ Ⓓ Ⓔ 7 Ⓐ Ⓑ Ⓒ Ⓓ Ⓔ 12 Ⓐ Ⓑ Ⓒ Ⓓ Ⓔ
3 Ⓐ Ⓑ Ⓒ Ⓓ Ⓔ 8 Ⓐ Ⓑ Ⓒ Ⓓ Ⓔ 13 Ⓐ Ⓑ Ⓒ Ⓓ Ⓔ
4 Ⓐ Ⓑ Ⓒ Ⓓ Ⓔ 9 Ⓐ Ⓑ Ⓒ Ⓓ Ⓔ 14 Ⓐ Ⓑ Ⓒ Ⓓ Ⓔ
5 Ⓐ Ⓑ Ⓒ Ⓓ Ⓔ 10 Ⓐ Ⓑ Ⓒ Ⓓ Ⓔ 15 Ⓐ Ⓑ Ⓒ Ⓓ Ⓔ

Note: ONLY the answers entered on the grid are scored.
Handwritten answers at the top of the column are NOT scored.

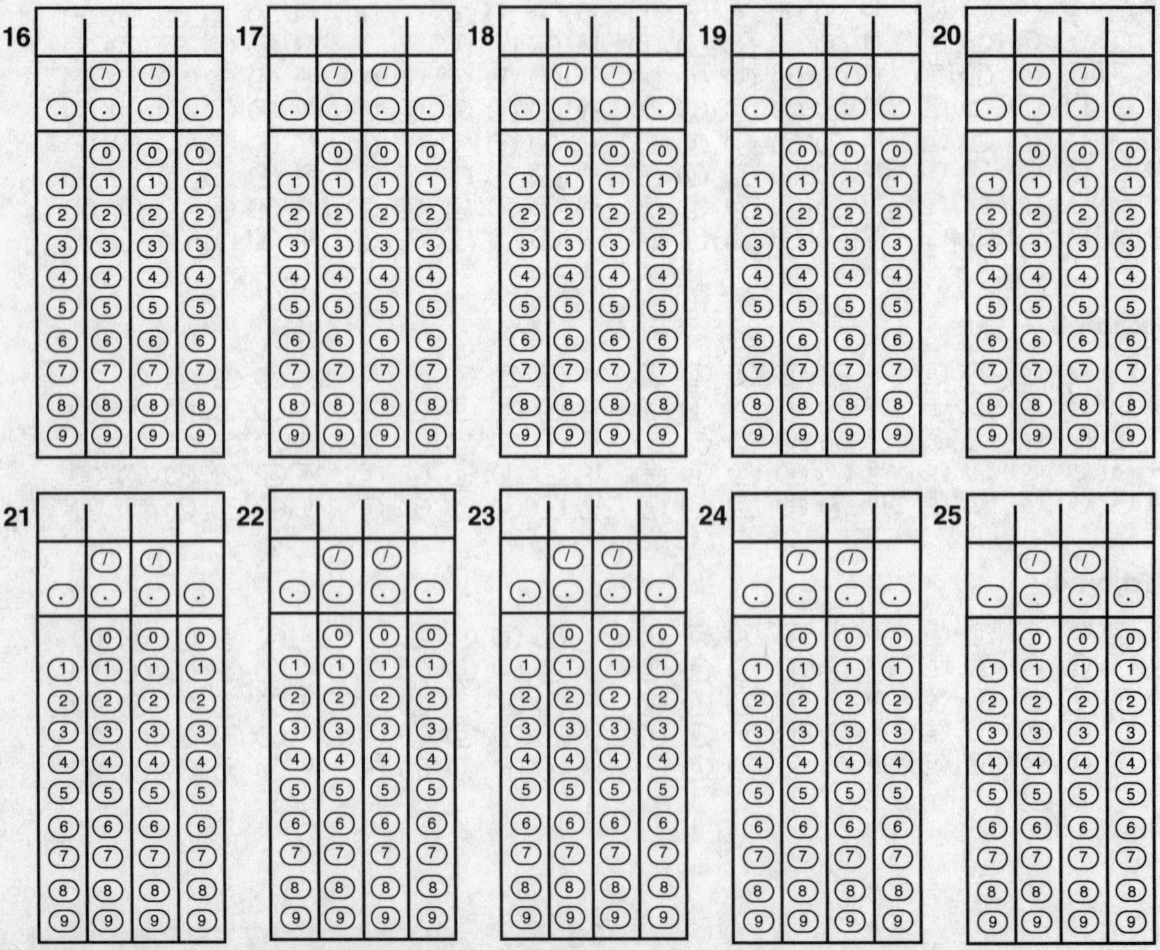

Diagnostic Examination

SECTION 1

30 Questions • Time—30 Minutes

Directions: Each of the following questions consists of an incomplete sentence followed by five words or pairs of words. Choose that word or pair of words which, when substituted for the blank space or spaces, *best* completes the meaning of the sentence and mark the letter of your choice on your answer sheet.

Example:

In view of the extenuating circumstances and the defendant's youth, the judge recommended ----.

(A) conviction (B) a defense
(C) a mistrial (D) leniency
(E) life imprisonment Ⓐ Ⓑ Ⓒ ● Ⓔ

1. Her position in the agency authorized her to award contracts and to ---- obligations for payment of expenses.

(A) rescind
(B) incur
(C) procure
(D) recur
(E) resume

2. Despite all his courtroom experience, the attorney was able to pry very little information out of the ---- witness.

(A) cooperative
(B) recalcitrant
(C) reactionary
(D) presumptive
(E) credulous

3. Although over the years ---- resources had been devoted to alleviating the problem, a satisfactory solution remained ----.

(A) natural..costly
(B) adequate..probable
(C) substantial..elusive
(D) capital..decisive
(E) conventional..abstract

4. The team attributes its ---- season to a number of ---- factors.

(A) losing..propitious
(B) long..irrelevant
(C) remarkable..derogatory
(D) embarrassing..optimistic
(E) winning..favorable

5. While fewer documents are being kept, the usefulness of those ---- is now ---- by an improved cataloging system.

(A) printed..documented
(B) discarded..concurred
(C) read..emblazoned
(D) retained..insured
(E) received..negated

GO ON TO THE NEXT PAGE

Directions: Each of the following questions consists of a capitalized pair of words followed by five pairs of words lettered A to E. The capitalized words bear some meaningful relationship to each other. Choose the lettered pair of words whose relationship is most similar to that expressed by the capitalized pair and mark its letter on your answer sheet.

Example:

DAY : SUN : :

(A) sunlight : daylight (B) ray : sun
(C) night : moon (D) heat : cold
(E) moon : star Ⓐ Ⓑ ● Ⓓ Ⓔ

6. POWERFUL : MIGHTY : :
   (A) muscular : alert
   (B) mediocre : ordinary
   (C) tense : springy
   (D) weak : small
   (E) deep : murky

7. HAIR : HORSE : :
   (A) feather : bird
   (B) wool : sheep
   (C) down : pillow
   (D) fuzz : peach
   (E) fur : animal

8. GOBBLE : TURKEY : :
   (A) shed : cobra
   (B) chop : tree
   (C) graze : elephant
   (D) twitter : bird
   (E) sleep : lion

9. SELL : PURCHASE : :
   (A) pay : charge
   (B) offer : bid
   (C) buy : earn
   (D) donate : demand
   (E) give : receive

10. NEST : BIRD : :
   (A) lair : lion
   (B) kennel : dog
   (C) ring : elephant
   (D) corral : horse
   (E) coop : chicken

11. HAMMER : HIT : :
   (A) screw : replace
   (B) wrench : leak
   (C) glue : paste
   (D) saw : cut
   (E) heat : melt

12. NOVEL : BOOK : :
   (A) act : play
   (B) article : magazine
   (C) mitten : hand
   (D) sock : foot
   (E) loafer : shoe

13. TEMERITY : CAUTION : :
   (A) trepidation : fear
   (B) effrontery : shame
   (C) cacophony : dissonance
   (D) capriciousness : whimsy
   (E) adulation : praise

Directions: Each passage below is followed by a set of questions. Read each passage; then answer the accompanying questions, basing your answers on what is stated or implied in the passage and in any introductory material provided. Mark the letter of your choice on your answer sheet.

Questions 14–21 are based on the following passage.

Abigail Smith married John Adams on October 25, 1764. As a delegate to the Continental Congress in Philadelphia, John Adams was responsible for determining the future of the colonies after independence, and it is this daunting task that Abigail addresses in this letter, sent a few months after the war with England began.

27 November, 1775

Colonel Warren returned last week to Plymouth, so that I shall not hear anything from you until he goes back again, which will not be till the last of this month. He damped my spirits greatly by telling me that the Court had prolonged your stay another month. I was pleasing myself with the thought that you would soon be upon your return. It is in vain to repine. I hope the public will reap what I sacrifice.

I wish I knew what mighty things were fabricating. If a form of government is to be established here, what one will be assumed? Will it be left to our Assemblies to choose one? And will not many men have many minds? And shall we not run into dissension among ourselves?

I am more and more convinced that man is a dangerous creature; and that power, whether vested in many or a few, is ever grasping, and, like the grave, cries, "Give, give!" The great fish swallow up the small; small; and he who is most strenuous for the rights of the people, when vested with power, is as eager after the prerogatives of government. You tell me of degrees of perfection to which human nature is capable of arriving, and I believe it, but at the same time lament that our admiration should arise from the scarcity of the instances.

The building up of a great empire, which was only hinted at by my correspondent, may now, I suppose, be realized even by the unbelievers. Yet will not ten thousand difficulties arise in the formation of it? The reins of government have been so long slackened, that I fear the people will not quietly submit to those restraints which are necessary for the peace and security of the community. If we separate from Britain, what code of laws will be established? How shall we be governed so as to retain our liberties? Can any government be free which is not administered by general stated laws? Who shall frame these laws? Who will give them force and energy? It is true, your resolutions, as a body, have hitherto had the force of laws; but will they continue to have?

When I consider these things, and the prejudice of people in favor of ancient customs and regulations, I feel anxious for the fate of our monarchy, or democracy, or whatever is to take place. I soon get lost in a labyrinth of perplexities; but, whatever occurs, may justice and righteousness be the stability of our times, and order arise out of confusion. Great difficulties may be surmounted by patience and perseverance.

I believe I have tired you with politics. As to news, we have not any at all. I shudder at the approach of winter, when I think I am to remain desolate.

I must bid you good night; 'tis late for me, who am much of an invalid. I was disappointed last week in receiving a packet by the post, and, upon unsealing it, finding only four newspapers. I think you are more cautious than you need be. All letters, I believe, have come safe to hand. I have sixteen from you, and wish I had as many more. Adieu.

Yours.

14. The word *damped* (line 4) means

(A) moistened
(B) covered
(C) freed
(D) lowered
(E) squeezed

15. When Abigail Adams says that she hopes "the public will reap what I sacrifice" (lines 7–8), she refers to

(A) giving up newspapers for the duration of the war
(B) having to live without correspondence
(C) being alone while her husband works on affairs of state
(D) living in danger thanks to the English
(E) sending food and clothing to the militia

GO ON TO THE NEXT PAGE

16. What does Adams mean when she says, "And will not many men have many minds?" (lines 12–13)?

    (A) It is hard to convince anyone that one is right.
    (B) People have conflicting opinions.
    (C) Men are always changing their minds.
    (D) Not many men have the ability to reason.
    (E) Many men will not obey the new government.

17. Adams uses the image of a great fish (line 18) to illustrate

    (A) the potential abuse of power
    (B) the natural order of things
    (C) the need for regulations
    (D) a democracy's failure to survive
    (E) monarchy's grasp on the empire

18. Why does Adams think that people will object to being governed?

    (A) They prefer the power of a monarch.
    (B) They will want to make their own laws.
    (C) They have lived too long in a lawless land.
    (D) People cannot be restrained.
    (E) Ancient customs are best.

19 When she refers to her husband's being cautious (lines 55–56), Adams means that

    (A) he should take care of himself
    (B) he need not worry about the mails
    (C) the fighting may not be over
    (D) the business of government requires discretion
    (E) he may not need to hide out in Philadelphia

20. Which line(s) makes you think that John Adams is more optimistic than his wife is?

    (A) lines 4–6
    (B) line 10
    (C) lines 12–14
    (D) lines 16–17
    (E) lines 21–23

21. Adams's main feeling about the new order of things seems to be

    (A) annoyance
    (B) delight
    (C) sorrow
    (D) astonishment
    (E) bewilderment

Questions 22–30 are based on the following passage.

Angel Decora was born Hinookmahiwi-kilinaka on the Winnebago Reservation in Nebraska in 1871. She worked as a book illustrator, particularly on books by and about Native Americans, and lectured and wrote about Indian art. The story from which this excerpt is taken, "The Sick Child," may be autobiographical.

It was about sunset when I, a little child, was sent with a handful of powdered tobacco leaves and red feathers to make an offering to the spirit who had caused the sickness of my little sister. It had been a long, hard winter, and the snow lay deep on the prairie as far as the eye could reach. The medicine-woman's directions had been that the offering must be laid upon the naked earth, and that to find it I must face toward the setting sun.

I was taught the prayer: "Spirit grandfather, I offer this to thee. I pray thee restore my little sister to health." Full of reverence and a strong faith that I could appease the anger of the spirit, I started out to plead for the life of our little one.

But now where was a spot of earth to be found in all that white monotony? They had talked of death at the house. I hoped that my little sister would live, but I was afraid of nature.

I reached a little spring. I looked down to its pebbly bottom, wondering whether I should leave my offering there, or keep on in search of a spot of earth. If I put my offering in the water, would it reach the bottom and touch the earth, or would it float away, as it had always done when I made my offering to the water spirit?

Once more I started on in my search of the bare ground.

The surface was crusted in some places, and walking was easy; in other places I would wade through a foot or more of snow. Often I paused, thinking to clear the snow away in some place and there lay my offering. But no, my faith must be in nature, and I must trust to it to lay bare the earth. It was a hard struggle for so small a child.

I went on and on; the reeds were waving their tasselled ends in the wind. I stopped and looked at them. A reed, whirling in the wind, had formed a space round its stem, making a loose socket. I stood looking into the opening. The reed must be rooted in the ground, and the hole must follow the stem to the earth. If I poured my offerings into the hole, surely they must reach the ground; so I said the prayer that I had been taught, and dropped my tobacco and red feathers into the opening that nature itself had created.

No sooner was the sacrifice accomplished than a feeling of doubt and fear thrilled me. What if my offering should never reach the earth? Would my little sister die?

Not till I turned homeward did I realize how cold I was. When at last I reached the house they took me in and warmed me, but did not question me, and I said nothing. Everyone was sad, for the little one had grown worse.

The next day the medicine-woman said my little sister was beyond hope; she could not live. Then bitter remorse was mine, for I thought I had been unfaithful, and therefore my little sister was to be called to the spirit land. I was a silent child, and did not utter my feelings; my remorse was intense. . . .

22. The word *offering* (line 3) means

(A) proposal
(B) bid
(C) advance
(D) tribute
(E) suggestion

23. By "naked earth" (lines 7–8), the medicine-woman meant

(A) the bare ground
(B) an eroded streambed
(C) a treeless plain
(D) the dirt floor of the house
(E) a patch of snow

24. The narrator's journey could be called a

(A) reverie
(B) retreat
(C) junket
(D) quest
(E) jaunt

25. "White monotony" (line 16) refers to the fact that

(A) the family lives on a reservation
(B) white people find Nebraska dull
(C) snow covers the landscape
(D) the narrator is blind
(E) nothing happens in the story

26. Lines 32–33 ("It was a hard struggle for so small a child") are

(A) an aside by an omniscient narrator
(B) the adult narrator's realization that saving her sick sister was too big a task for the child
(C) an ironic statement by an outside observer
(D) the adult narrator's excuse for placing the feathers and tobacco in a poor spot
(E) the adult narrator's explanation for the young girl's silent remorse

27. The word *thrilled* (line 45) is used to mean

(A) delighted
(B) exhilarated
(C) inflamed
(D) enraptured
(E) inspired

28. The narrator's remorse is due to her

(A) uncaring attitude toward her sister
(B) mixed feelings toward her own religion
(C) secret longing for attention
(D) perceived failure at following instructions
(E) mistrust of the medicine-woman

29. If her sister died, you would expect the narrator to feel

(A) relieved
(B) elated
(C) surprised
(D) confused
(E) guilty

GO ON TO THE NEXT PAGE

30. What feeling does the narrator have toward the child?

(A) shame
(B) bewilderment
(C) forgiveness
(D) irritation
(E) anxiety

STOP

END OF SECTION 1. IF YOU HAVE ANY TIME LEFT, GO OVER YOUR WORK IN THIS SECTION ONLY. DO NOT WORK IN ANY OTHER SECTION OF THE TEST.

SECTION 2

25 Questions • Time—30 Minutes

Directions: Solve the following problems using any available space on the page for scratchwork. On your answer sheet fill in the choice which best corresponds to the correct answer.

Notes: The figures accompanying the problems are drawn as accurately as possible unless otherwise stated in specific problems. Again, unless otherwise stated, all figures lie in the same plane. All numbers used in these problems are real numbers. Calculators are permitted for this test.

Reference Information

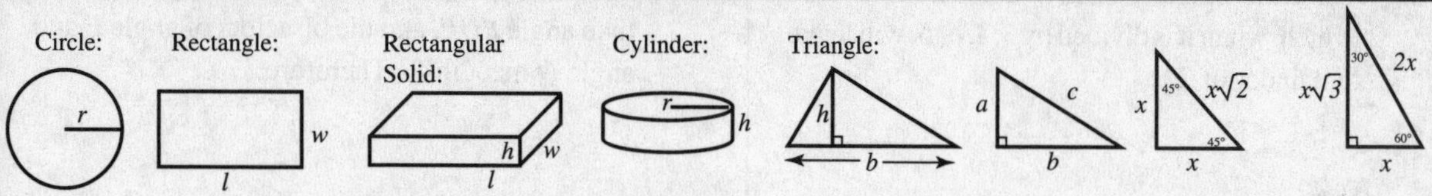

$C = 2\pi r$ $A = \pi r^2$ | $A = lw$ | $V = lwh$ | $V = \pi r^2 h$ | $A = \frac{1}{2}bh$ | $a^2 + b^2 = c^2$

The number of degrees of arc in a circle is 360.
The measure in degrees of a straight angle is 180.
The sum of the measures in degrees of the angles of a triangle is 180.

1. Which of the following fractions is more than $\frac{3}{4}$?

(A) $\frac{35}{71}$

(B) $\frac{13}{20}$

(C) $\frac{71}{101}$

(D) $\frac{19}{24}$

(E) $\frac{15}{20}$

2. If $820 + R + S - 610 = 342$, and if $R = 2S$, then $S =$

(A) 44
(B) 48
(C) 132
(D) 184
(E) 192

3. What is the cost, in dollars, to carpet a room x yards long and y yards wide, if the carpet costs five dollars per square foot?

(A) xy
(B) $5xy$
(C) $25xy$
(D) $30xy$
(E) $45xy$

4. If $7M = 3M - 20$, then $M + 7 =$

(A) 0
(B) 2
(C) 5
(D) 12
(E) 17

GO ON TO THE NEXT PAGE

5. In circle O below, AB is the diameter, angle BOD contains 15°, and angle EOA contains 85°. Find the number of degrees in angle ECA.

(A) 15
(B) 35
(C) 50
(D) 70
(E) 85

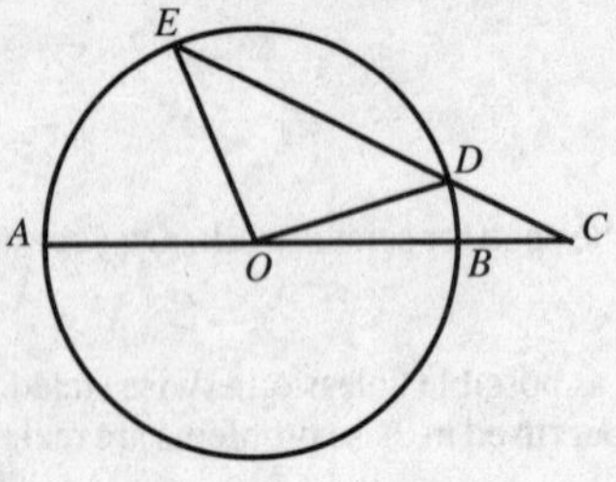

6. What is the smallest positive number, other than 2, which, when it is divided by 3, 4, or 5, will leave a remainder of 2?

(A) 22
(B) 42
(C) 62
(D) 122
(E) 182

7. A taxi charges 75 cents for the first quarter of a mile and 15 cents for each additional quarter of a mile. The charge, in cents, for a trip of d miles is

(A) $75 + 15d$
(B) $75 + 15(4d - 1)$
(C) $75 + 75d$
(D) $75 + 4(d - 1)$
(E) $75 + 75(d - 1)$

8. In a certain army post, 30% of the enlistees are from New York State, and 10% of these are from New York City. What percentage of the enlistees in the post are from New York City?

(A) .03
(B) .3
(C) 3
(D) 13
(E) 20

9. The diagonal of a rectangle is 10. What is the area of the rectangle?

(A) 24
(B) 48
(C) 50
(D) 100
(E) It cannot be determined from the information given.

10. In triangle PQR below, angle RPQ is greater than angle RQP, and the bisectors of angle P and angle Q meet in S. Therefore,

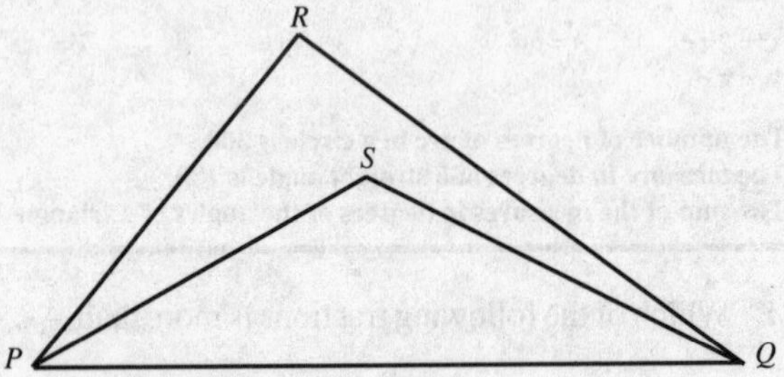

Note: Figure not drawn to scale.

(A) $SQ > SP$
(B) $SQ = SP$
(C) $SQ < SP$
(D) $SQ \geqq SP$
(E) No conclusion concerning the relative lengths of SQ and SP can be determined from the information given.

11. Which of the following is equal to 3.14×10^6?

(A) 314
(B) 3140
(C) 31,400
(D) 314,000
(E) 3,140,000

12. $\dfrac{36}{29 - \frac{4}{0.2}} =$

(A) $\dfrac{3}{4}$

(B) $\dfrac{4}{3}$

(C) 2

(D) 4

(E) 18

13. In terms of the square units in the figure below, what is the area of the semicircle?

(A) 32π
(B) 16π
(C) 8π
(D) 4π
(E) 2π

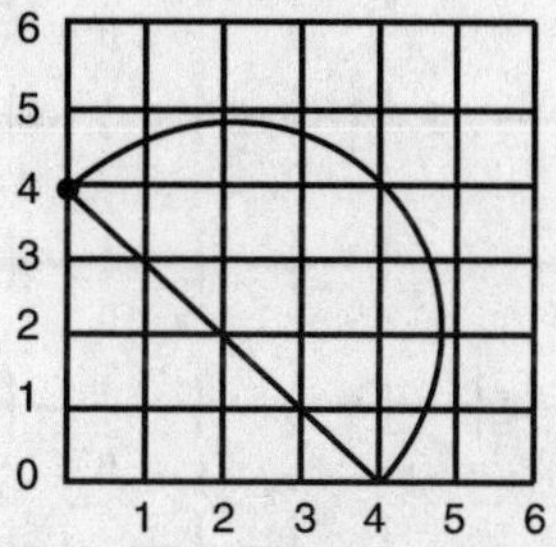

14. The sum of three consecutive odd numbers is always divisible by

I. 2
II. 3
III. 5
IV. 6

(A) I only
(B) II only
(C) I and II only
(D) I and III only
(E) II and IV only

15. In the diagram, triangle *ABC* is inscribed in a circle and *CD* is tangent to the circle. If angle *BCD* is 40°, how many degrees are there in angle *A*?

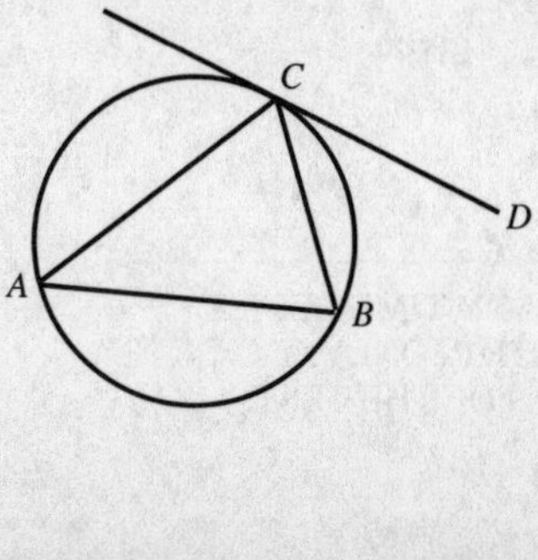

(A) 20
(B) 30
(C) 40
(D) 50
(E) 60

16. If a discount of 20% off the marked price of a jacket results in a savings of $15, what is the discounted price of the jacket?

(A) $35
(B) $60
(C) $75
(D) $150
(E) $300

17. While researching a term paper, a student read pages 7 through 49 and pages 101 through 157 of a particular source book. Altogether, how many pages from this book did this student read?

(A) 98
(B) 99
(C) 100
(D) 101
(E) 102

18. What is the sum of $\angle EBA + \angle DCF$?

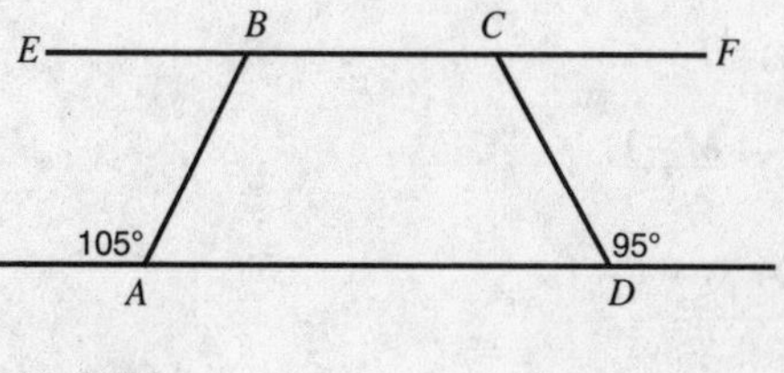

(A) 160°
(B) 180°
(C) 195°
(D) 200°
(E) It cannot be determined from the information given.

GO ON TO THE NEXT PAGE

19. A 15-gallon mixture of 20% alcohol has 5 gallons of water added to it. The strength of the mixture, as a percent, is approximately

(A) $12\frac{1}{2}$

(B) $13\frac{1}{3}$

(C) 15

(D) $16\frac{2}{3}$

(E) 20

20. In the figure below, $QXRS$ is a parallelogram and P is any point on side QS. What is the ratio of the area of triangle PXR to the area of $QXRS$?

(A) 1 : 4
(B) 1 : 3
(C) 1 : 2
(D) 2 : 3
(E) 3 : 4

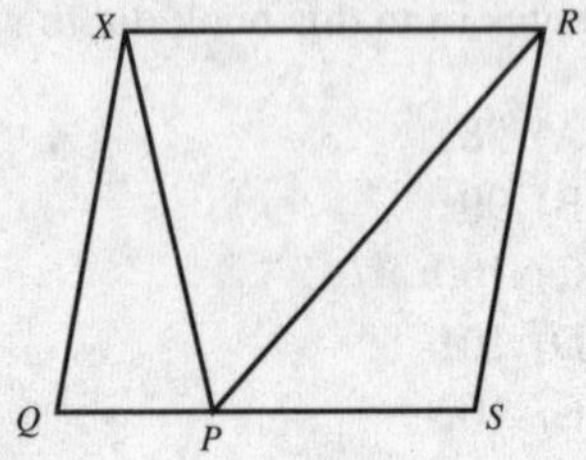

21. If $x(p + 1) = M$, then $p =$

(A) $M - 1$

(B) M

(C) $\frac{M-1}{x}$

(D) $M - x - 1$

(E) $\frac{M}{x} - 1$

22. If T tons of snow fall in 1 second, how many tons fall in M minutes?

(A) $60MT$

(B) $MT + 60$

(C) MT

(D) $\frac{60M}{T}$

(E) $\frac{MT}{60}$

23. Which of the following is the graph of $x \geq -2$ and $x \leq 3$?

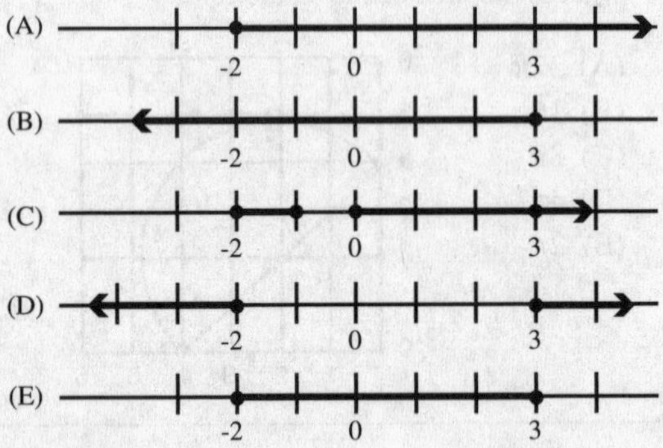

24. From 9 A.M. to 2 P.M., the temperature rose at a constant rate from –14°F to +36°F. What was the temperature at noon?

(A) –4°
(B) +6°
(C) +16°
(D) +26°
(E) +31°

25. If $\frac{P}{Q} = \frac{4}{5}$ what is the value of $2P + Q$?

(A) 14
(B) 13
(C) 3
(D) –1
(E) It cannot be determined from the information given.

STOP

END OF SECTION 2. IF YOU HAVE ANY TIME LEFT, GO OVER YOUR WORK IN THIS SECTION ONLY. DO NOT WORK IN ANY OTHER SECTION OF THE TEST.

SECTION 3

10 Questions • Time—15 Minutes

Directions: The two passages given below deal with a related topic. Following the passages are questions about the content of each passage or about the relationship between the two passages. Answer the questions based upon what is stated or implied in the passages and in any introductory material provided. Mark the letter of your choice on your answer sheet.

Questions 1–10 are based on the following passages.

Matthew Henson was born in 1866 of free black parents in Maryland. He met Commander Robert Peary in 1888 and became first his servant and then his assistant on Peary's major expeditions to the Arctic. In these two passages, Henson and Peary describe the same area in Greenland, a place known as Karnah.

Passage 1—*from Henson's Account of the 1908 Expedition*

We stopped at Kookan, the most prosperous of the Esquimo settlements, a village of five tupiks (skin tents), housing twenty-four people, and from there we sailed to the ideal community of Karnah.

Karnah is the most delightful spot on the Greenland coast. Situated on a gently southward sloping knoll are the igloos and tupiks, where I have spent many pleasant days with my Esquimo friends and learned much of the folk-lore and history. Lofty mountains, sublime in their grandeur, overtower and surround this place, and its only exposure is southward toward the sun. In winter its climate is not severe, as compared with other portions of this country, and in the perpetual daylight of summer, life here is ideal. Rivulets of clear, cold water, the beds of which are grass- and flower-covered, run down the sides of the mountain and, but for the lack of trees, the landscape is as delightful as anywhere on earth.

Passage 2—*from Peary's Account of the 1891 Expedition*

From the eastern point of Academy Bay the main shore of the gulf extends, due east, to the face of the great Heilprin Glacier, and then on beside the great ice-stream, until the crests of the cliffs disappear under the white shroud of the "Great Ice." From here on, the eastern and northern sides of the head of the gulf are an almost continuous glacier face, six great ice-streams, separated by as many precipitous nunataks, flowing down from the interior ice-cap to discharge an enormous fleet of bergs. As a result of this free discharge, the great white viscosity of the interior has settled down into a huge, and in clear weather easily discernible, semi-circular basin, similar to those of Tossukatek, Great Kariak, and Jacobshavn. In this head of the gulf, situated some in the face of the glaciers, and others a short distance beyond them, are seven or eight islands, most of which bear proof of former glaciation. Along the north-western shore of the gulf, the vertical cliffs resume their sway, back of which rise the trio of striking peaks, Mounts Daly, Adams, and Putname. The cliffs continue westward for some little distance, then gradually merge into a gentle slope, which is in turn succeeded by the face of the Hubbard Glacier. West of the glacier, cliffs of a different character (red and grey sandstone) occur, and extend to the grand and picturesque red-brown Castle Cliffs at the entrance to Bowdoin Bay. At these cliffs, the shore takes an abrupt turn to the northward, into the now familiar but previously unknown Bowdoin Bay, in which was located the headquarters of my last Expedition.

This bay has an extreme length of eleven miles, and an average width of between three and four miles. What with its southern exposure, the protection from the wind afforded by the cliffs and bluffs which enclose it, and the warmth of colouring of its shores, it presents one of the most desirable locations for a house. The scenery is also varied and attractive, offering to the eye greater contrasts, with less change of position, than any other locality occurring to me. Around the circuit of the bay are seven glaciers with exposures to all points of the compass, and varying in size from a few hundred feet to over two miles in width.

The ice-cap itself is also in evidence here, its vertical face in one place capping and forming a continuation

GO ON TO THE NEXT PAGE

of a vertical cliff which rises direct from the bay. From the western point of the bay, a line of grey sandstone cliffs—the Sculptured Cliffs of Karnah—interrupted by a single glacier in a distance of eight miles, and carved by the restless arctic elements into turrets, bastions, huge amphitheatres, and colossal statues of men and animals, extends to Cape Ackland, the Karnah of the natives. Here the cliffs end abruptly, and the shore trending north-westward to Cape Cleveland, eighteen miles distant, consists of an almost continuous succession of fan-shaped, rocky deltas formed by glacier streams. Back of the shoreline is a gradually sloping foreshore, rising to the foot of an irregular series of hills, which rise more steeply to the ice-cap lying upon their summits. In almost every depression between these hills, the face of a glacier may be seen, and it is the streams from these that have made the shore what it is, and formed the wide shoals off it, on which every year a numerous fleet of icebergs becomes stranded.

1. Henson uses the word *exposure* (line 11) to mean

   (A) denunciation
   (B) unmasking
   (C) emptiness
   (D) danger
   (E) openness

2. Henson's main impression of Karnah is one of

   (A) apprehension
   (B) dismay
   (C) indifference
   (D) pleasure
   (E) tolerance

3. Henson might prefer that Karnah

   (A) were not so far north
   (B) were warmer
   (C) were uninhabited
   (D) lay further inland
   (E) had more trees

4. Peary admires Bowdoin Bay for its

   (A) diverse vistas
   (B) incredible length
   (C) calm waters
   (D) impressive tides
   (E) great ice-streams

5. Peary compares the arctic elements to

   (A) avenging Furies
   (B) athletic challenges
   (C) stonecarvers
   (D) wild horses
   (E) ice palaces

6. Future explorers might use Peary's description to

   (A) locate their ships in Karnah's harbor
   (B) find their way around Greenland's shoreline
   (C) decide the future of native settlements
   (D) identify trees and vegetation on the island
   (E) re-enact Peary's discovery of the North Pole

7. In general, Peary's description is in

   (A) chronological order, according to his various trips
   (B) spatial order, proceeding along the coastline
   (C) chronological order, moving from past to present
   (D) spatial order, moving from west to east
   (E) spatial order, moving in a circle around the ship

8. The "lofty mountains" described by Henson (line 9) are probably Peary's

   (A) Sculptured Cliffs (line 65)
   (B) Cape Cleveland (line 71)
   (C) Heilprin Glacier (line 21)
   (D) Mount Daly (line 38)
   (E) Great Kariak (line 32)

9. Unlike Henson, Peary seems intent on

   (A) snubbing the natives
   (B) discussing flora and fauna
   (C) focusing on geology
   (D) raising political issues
   (E) extolling the delights of Karnah

10. Peary and Henson seem to agree on

(A) the severity of Greenland's weather
(B) the area's attractiveness
(C) the need for future exploration
(D) both A and B
(E) both B and C

STOP

END OF SECTION 3. IF YOU HAVE ANY TIME LEFT, GO OVER YOUR WORK IN THIS SECTION ONLY. DO NOT WORK IN ANY OTHER SECTION OF THE TEST.

SECTION 4

10 Questions • Time—15 Minutes

Directions: Solve the following problems using any available space on the page for scratchwork. On your answer sheet fill in the choice which best corresponds to the correct answer.

Notes: The figures accompanying the problems are drawn as accurately as possible unless otherwise stated in specific problems. Again, unless otherwise stated, all figures lie in the same plane. All numbers used in these problems are real numbers. Calculators are permitted for this test.

Reference Information

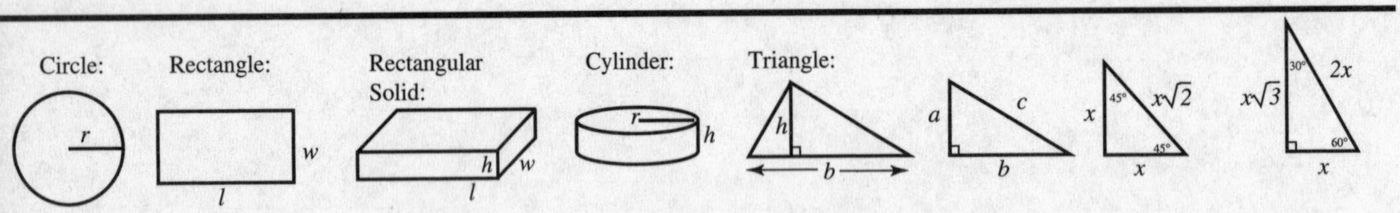

$C = 2\pi r$ $A = \pi r^2$ | $A = lw$ | $V = lwh$ | $V = \pi r^2 h$ | $A = \frac{1}{2}bh$ | $a^2 + b^2 = c^2$

The number of degrees of arc in a circle is 360.
The measure in degrees of a straight angle is 180.
The sum of the measures in degrees of the angles of a triangle is 180.

1. The coordinates of vertices X and Y of an equilateral triangle XYZ are (–4,0) and (4,0) respectively. The coordinates of Z may be

(A) $(0, 2\sqrt{3})$

(B) $(0, 4\sqrt{3})$

(C) $(4, 4\sqrt{3})$

(D) $(0, 4)$

(E) $(4\sqrt{3}, 0)$

2. There are just two ways in which 5 may be expressed as the sum of two different positive (nonzero) integers, namely, $5 = 4 + 1 = 3 + 2$. In how many ways may 9 be expressed as the sum of two different positive (nonzero) integers?

(A) 3
(B) 4
(C) 5
(D) 6
(E) 7

3. A board 7 feet 9 inches long is divided into three equal parts. What is the length of each part?

(A) 2 ft. $6\frac{1}{3}$ in.

(B) 2 ft. 7 in.

(C) 2 ft. 8 in.

(D) 2 ft. $8\frac{1}{3}$ in.

(E) 2 ft. 9 in.

4. What is the smallest possible integer $K > 1$ such that $R^2 = S^3 = K$, for some integers R and S?

(A) 4
(B) 8
(C) 27
(D) 64
(E) 81

5. The number of square units in the area of triangle *RST* is

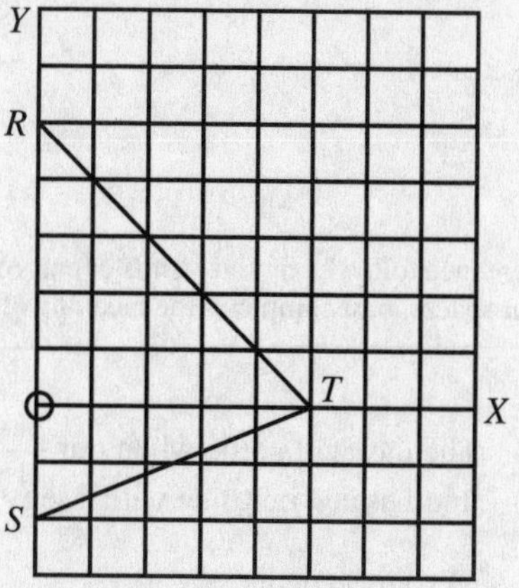

(A) 10
(B) 12.5
(C) 15.5
(D) 17.5
(E) 20

6. Which of the following has the same value as $\frac{P}{Q}$?

(A) $\frac{P-2}{Q-2}$
(B) $\frac{1+P}{1+Q}$
(C) $\frac{P^2}{Q^2}$
(D) $\frac{3P}{3Q}$
(E) $\frac{P+3}{Q+3}$

7. In the accompanying figure, *ACB* is a straight angle and *DC* is perpendicular to *CE*. If the number of degrees in angle *ACD* is represented by *x*, the number of degrees in angle *BCE* is represented by

(A) $90 - x$
(B) $x - 90$
(C) $90 + x$
(D) $180 - x$
(E) $45 + x$

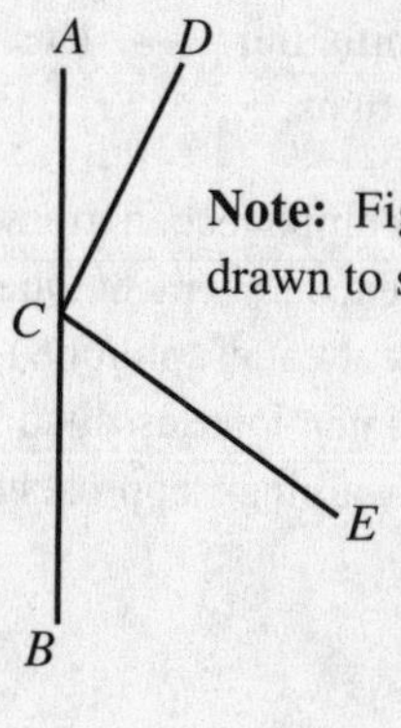

Note: Figure not drawn to scale.

Questions 8 and 9 refer to the following drawing:

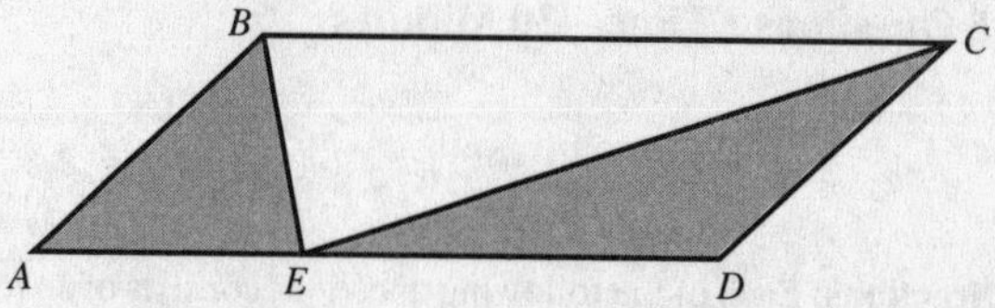

8. In parallelogram *ABCD*, what is the ratio of the shaded area to the unshaded area?

(A) 1 : 2
(B) 1 : 1
(C) 4 : 3
(D) 2 : 1
(E) It cannot be determined from the information given.

9. If the ratio of *AB* to *BC* is 4 : 9, what is the area of parallelogram *ABCD*?

(A) 36
(B) 26
(C) 18
(D) 13
(E) It cannot be determined from the information given.

10. A store owner buys eggs for *M* cents per dozen and sells them for $\frac{M}{6}$ cents apiece. At this rate, what is the profit on a dozen eggs?

(A) $\frac{M}{12}$ cents
(B) $\frac{M}{6}$ cents
(C) $\frac{M}{2}$ cents
(D) *M* cents
(E) 2*M* cents

STOP

END OF SECTION 4. IF YOU HAVE ANY TIME LEFT, GO OVER YOUR WORK IN THIS SECTION ONLY. DO NOT WORK IN ANY OTHER SECTION OF THE TEST.

SECTION 5

35 Questions • Time—30 Minutes

Directions: Each of the following questions consists of an incomplete sentence followed by five words or pairs of words. Choose that word or pair of words which, when substituted for the blank space or spaces, *best* completes the meaning of the sentence and mark the letter of your choice on your answer sheet.

Example:

In view of the extenuating circumstances and the defendant's youth, the judge recommended ----.

(A) conviction (B) a defense
(C) a mistrial (D) leniency
(E) life imprisonment Ⓐ Ⓑ Ⓒ ● Ⓔ

---

1. Human survival is a result of mutual assistance, since people are essentially ---- rather than ----.

   (A) superior..inferior
   (B) cooperative..competitive
   (C) individualistic..gregarious
   (D) physical..mental
   (E) dependent..insensate

2. For centuries, malnutrition has been ---- in the drought-stricken areas of Africa.

   (A) impalpable
   (B) evasive
   (C) endemic
   (D) divisive
   (E) redundant

3. Even as they ---- their pledges of support, they secretly planned a betrayal; their actions ---- their words.

   (A) demonstrated..echoed
   (B) confirmed..reinforced
   (C) compromised..precluded
   (D) reiterated..belied
   (E) submitted..emphasized

4. The day will come when our ---- will look back upon us and our time with a sense of superiority.

   (A) antecedents
   (B) descendants
   (C) predecessors
   (D) ancestors
   (E) contemporaries

5. Their ---- debate, billed as a(n) ---- of their opinions, was only needless repetition.

   (A) senseless..exoneration
   (B) national..travesty
   (C) incessant..distillation
   (D) primary..renunciation
   (E) final..clarification

6. With the ---- of winter storms, all drivers should take extra ---- while on the road.

   (A) demise..caution
   (B) approach..precautions
   (C) waning..care
   (D) proximity..leisure
   (E) duration..heed

7. Despite our ----, Eva ---- the stranger for directions.

   (A) compliance..harrassed
   (B) encouragement..questioned
   (C) entreaties..pinioned
   (D) intentions..assailed
   (E) warnings..approached

8. The young man was very unlikely to be hired; his appearance was disheveled, slovenly, and ----.

(A) tousled
(B) harried
(C) beleaguered
(D) mortified
(E) despondent

9. The use of trained bears in circuses was once a ---- but has now almost ----.

(A) menace..diminished
(B) precedent..extinguished
(C) sinecure..vanquished
(D) commonplace..ceased
(E) legacy..vanished

10. Although he has a reputation for aloofness, his manner on that occasion was so ---- that everyone felt perfectly at ease.

(A) reluctant
(B) gracious
(C) malign
(D) plausible
(E) spurious

11. The ---- with which the agent calmed the anxieties and soothed the tempers of the travelers ---- by the delay was a mark of frequent experience with similar crises.

(A) evasiveness..angered
(B) reverence..pleased
(C) facility..inconvenienced
(D) mannerism..destroyed
(E) acuity..accommodated

12. The lover of democracy has an ---- toward totalitarianism.

(A) antipathy
(B) empathy
(C) equanimity
(D) idolatry
(E) obstinacy

13. A ---- of employment opportunities ---- prospective employees entering the job market.

(A) surfeit..impedes
(B) paucity..discourages
(C) plethora..deters
(D) dearth..inspires
(E) deluge..enervates

GO ON TO THE NEXT PAGE

Directions: Each of the following questions consists of a capitalized pair of words followed by five pairs of words lettered A to E. The capitalized words bear some meaningful relationship to each other. Choose the lettered pair of words whose relationship is most similar to that expressed by the capitalized pair and mark its letter on your answer sheet.

Example:

DAY : SUN : :

(A) sunlight : daylight (B) ray : sun
(C) night : moon (D) heat : cold
(E) moon : star

Ⓐ Ⓑ ● Ⓓ Ⓔ

14. TRICKLE : GUSH : :
(A) flow : stream
(B) listen : hear
(C) soar : dive
(D) touch : collide
(E) drive : ride

15. WINK : EYE : :
(A) swallow : food
(B) tap : toe
(C) flirt : hand
(D) hit : nail
(E) smell : nose

16. BOWLING : PIN : :
(A) basketball : center
(B) tennis : racket
(C) baseball : glove
(D) archery : arrow
(E) golf : hole

17. LAKE : WET : :
(A) electricity : nuclear
(B) ice : cold
(C) fog : unavoidable
(D) sand : dry
(E) jewel : expensive

18. TOOTH : COMB : :
(A) book : store
(B) horse : race
(C) cog : gear
(D) hair : brush
(E) dog : hound

19. MISER : STINGINESS : :
(A) dilettante : skill
(B) demagogue : passivity
(C) tyrant : dignity
(D) altruist : selflessness
(E) miscreant : honesty

20. CHIVALROUS : GALLANT : :
(A) sanguine : cheerful
(B) doleful : happy
(C) tardy : early
(D) mercurial : slow
(E) rich : degenerate

21. LAVA : VOLCANO : :
(A) snow : mountain
(B) water : spring
(C) balloon : air
(D) eyes : makeup
(E) chimney : smoke

22. DIFFIDENT : CONFIDENCE : :
(A) magnificent : beauty
(B) voluminous : size
(C) gloomy : cheer
(D) meticulous : care
(E) athletic : strength

23. CONDUCTOR : ORCHESTRA : :
(A) violinist : bow
(B) pianist : hands
(C) author : books
(D) president : country
(E) school : principal

Directions: The reading passage below is followed by a set of questions. Read the passage and answer the accompanying questions, basing your answers on what is stated or implied in the passage. Mark the letter of your choice on your answer sheet.

Questions 24–35 are based on the following passage.

Stephen Crane (1871–1900) wrote a number of novels, short stories, and poems in his short life, as well as working as a war correspondent overseas. "The Bride Comes to Yellow Sky" (1898) is the story of a small-town sheriff who brings home a bride, changing his frontier home forever. It opens with this scene.

The great Pullman was whirling onward with such dignity of motion that a glance from the window seemed simply to prove that the plains of Texas were pouring eastward. Vast flats of green grass, dull-hued spaces of mesquit and cactus, little groups of frame houses, woods of light and tender trees, all were sweeping into the east, sweeping over the horizon, a precipice.

A newly married pair had boarded this coach at San Antonio. The man's face was reddened from many days in the wind and sun, and a direct result of his new black clothes was that his brick-colored hands were constantly performing in a most conscious fashion. From time to time he looked down respectfully at his attire. He sat with a hand on each knee, like a man waiting in a barber's shop. The glances he devoted to other passengers were furtive and shy.

The bride was not pretty, nor was she very young. She wore a dress of blue cashmere, with small reservations of velvet here and there, and with steel buttons abounding. She continually twisted her head to regard her puff sleeves, very stiff, straight, and high. They embarrassed her. It was quite apparent that she had cooked, and that she expected to cook, dutifully. The blushes caused by the careless scrutiny of some passengers as she had entered the car were strange to see upon this plain, under-class countenance, which was drawn in placid, almost emotionless lines.

They were evidently very happy. "Ever been in a parlor-car before?" he asked, smiling with delight.

"No," she answered; "I never was. It's fine, ain't it?"

"Great! And then after a while we'll go forward to the diner, and get a big lay-out. Finest meal in the world. Charge a dollar."

"Oh, do they?" cried the bride. "Charge a d o l l a r? Why, that's too much—for us—ain't it Jack?"

"Not this trip, anyhow," he answered bravely. "We're going to go the whole thing."

Later he explained to her about the trains. "You see, it's a thousand miles from one end of Texas to the other; and this train runs right across it, and never stops but for four times." He had the pride of an owner. He pointed out to her the dazzling fittings of the coach; and in truth her eyes opened wider as she contemplated the sea-green figured velvet, the shining brass, silver, and glass, the wood that gleamed as darkly brilliant as the surface of a pool of oil. At one end a bronze figure sturdily held a support for a separated chamber, and at convenient places on the ceiling were frescoes in olive and silver.

To the minds of the pair, their surroundings reflected the glory of their marriage that morning in San Antonio; this was the environment of their new estate; and the man's face in particular beamed with an elation that made him appear ridiculous to the negro porter. This individual at times surveyed them from afar with an amused and superior grin. On other occasions he bullied them with skill in ways that did not make it exactly plain to them that they were being bullied. He subtly used all the manners of the most unconquerable kind of snobbery. He oppressed them; but of this oppression they had small knowledge, and they speedily forgot that infrequently a number of travelers covered them with stares of derisive enjoyment. Historically there was supposed to be something infinitely humorous in their situation.

24. Crane highlights the newlyweds'

(A) tactlessness
(B) unsophistication
(C) wealth
(D) merriment
(E) fear

25. The bride's dress is clearly

(A) beautiful
(B) torn
(C) red
(D) comfortable
(E) unfamiliar

GO ON TO THE NEXT PAGE

26. The line "It was quite apparent that she had cooked, and that she expected to cook, dutifully" (lines 22–23) shows the bride's

(A) natural talent
(B) submissiveness
(C) commonness
(D) both A and B
(E) both B and C

27. When the bridegroom answers his bride "bravely" (line 37), the implication is that

(A) he has overcome his fear of her
(B) his usual posture is weak and sniveling
(C) gallantry is his natural mode
(D) he will conquer his anxiety about money for her sake
(E) it takes courage to speak forthrightly

28. The line "He had the pride of an owner" (line 42) is ironic because

(A) the bride has no sense of style
(B) the bridegroom could never own anything so fine
(C) Crane prefers workers to owners
(D) the owners of the train take no pride in it
(E) the bridegroom is not proud of his own belongings

29. The word *estate* (line 53) is used to mean

(A) property
(B) inheritance
(C) status
(D) statement
(E) manor

30. The figure of the porter is used to indicate

(A) a parallel between slavery and marriage
(B) where the line between worker and owner is drawn
(C) the absurdity of young love
(D) that the newlyweds are not alone in the world
(E) just how unworldly and lower-class the newlyweds are

31. The last sentence of the passage refers to

(A) the fact that newlyweds are figures of fun
(B) Crane's amusement at the behavior of the travelers
(C) people's delight at others' misfortunes
(D) the joy of the newlyweds despite their surroundings
(E) readers' sympathy with the characters

32. Crane uses the word *historically* (line 64) to mean

(A) importantly
(B) famously
(C) customarily
(D) prominently
(E) ritually

33. Crane's feeling toward the newlyweds is one of

(A) amused sympathy
(B) disgusted revulsion
(C) weary resignation
(D) scornful derision
(E) honest hatred

34. Crane probably does not name the newlyweds in this part of the story

(A) because he does not know who they are
(B) to make them seem ordinary and universal
(C) because he wants to surprise the reader
(D) to prove that they are worthless in his eyes
(E) to focus attention on the peripheral characters

35. The main goal of this passage is to

(A) introduce characters and setting
(B) illustrate a conflict between two characters
(C) resolve a crisis
(D) express an opinion
(E) instruct the reader

STOP

END OF SECTION 5. IF YOU HAVE ANY TIME LEFT, GO OVER YOUR WORK IN THIS SECTION ONLY. DO NOT WORK IN ANY OTHER SECTION OF THE TEST.

SECTION 6

25 Questions • Time—30 Minutes

Directions: Solve the following problems using any available space on the page for scratchwork. On your answer sheet fill in the choice which best corresponds to the correct answer.

Notes: The figures accompanying the problems are drawn as accurately as possible unless otherwise stated in specific problems. Again, unless otherwise stated, all figures lie in the same plane. All numbers used in these problems are real numbers. Calculators are permitted for this test.

Reference Information

Circle: Rectangle: Rectangular Solid: Cylinder: Triangle:

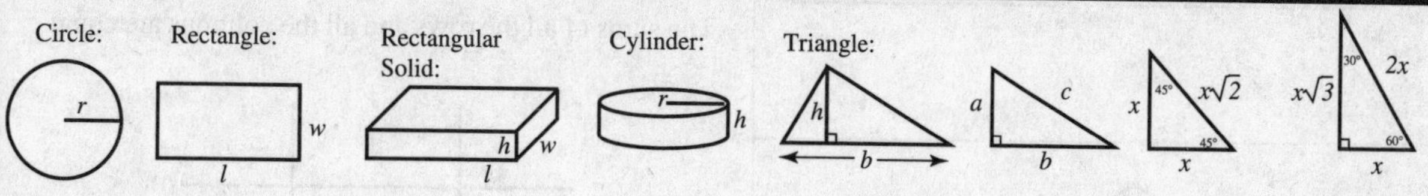

$C = 2\pi r$
$A = \pi r^2$

$A = lw$

$V = lwh$

$V = \pi r^2 h$

$A = \frac{1}{2}bh$

$a^2 + b^2 = c^2$

The number of degrees of arc in a circle is 360.
The measure in degrees of a straight angle is 180.
The sum of the measures in degrees of the angles of a triangle is 180.

PART 1: Quantitative Comparison Questions

Directions: Questions 1–15 each consist of two quantities—one in Column A, the other in Column B. Compare the two quantities and mark your answer sheet as follows:

(A) if the quantity in Column A is greater;
(B) if the quantity in Column B is greater;
(C) if the two quantities are equal;
(D) if the relationship cannot be determined from the information given.

Notes:

(1) Information concerning one or both of the compared quantities will be centered above the two columns for some items.
(2) Symbols that appear in both columns represent the same thing in Column A as in Column B.
(3) Letters such as *x*, *n*, and *k* are symbols for real numbers.

Examples

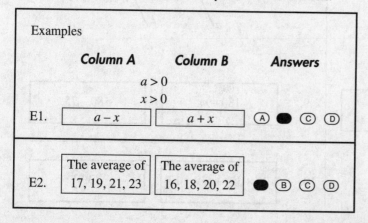

	Column A	Column B	Answers
	$a > 0$ $x > 0$		
E1.	$a - x$	$a + x$	Ⓐ ● Ⓒ Ⓓ
E2.	The average of 17, 19, 21, 23	The average of 16, 18, 20, 22	● Ⓑ Ⓒ Ⓓ

DO NOT MARK CHOICE (E) FOR THESE QUESTIONS. THERE ARE ONLY FOUR ANSWER CHOICES.

GO ON TO THE NEXT PAGE

	Column A	Column B
1.	$2x - 1$	$2x + 1$

$x < -1$

	Column A	Column B
2.	$\frac{1}{x^2}$	x

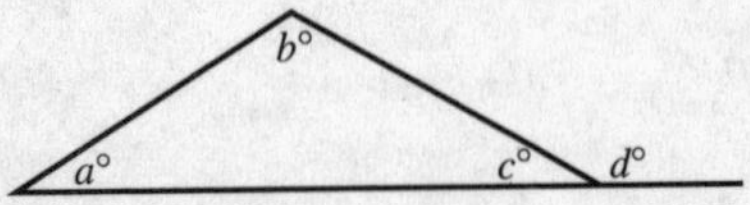

	Column A	Column B
3.	$a + b + c$	$c + d$

	Column A	Column B
4.	$\frac{1}{4}(a + b)c$	$\frac{ac + bc}{4}$

Note: Figure not drawn to scale.

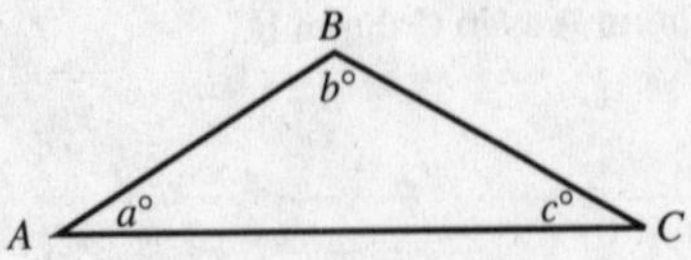

$b > c > a$

	Column A	Column B
5.	AB	AC

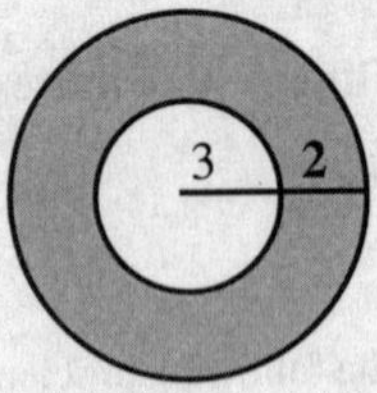

	Column A	Column B
6.	The area of the shaded region	The area of the small circle

The sums of all the rows and all the columns are equal.

w	4	y
7	x	4
v	7	z

	Column A	Column B
7.	$v + z$	$y + w$

	Column A	Column B
8.	$(n+1)^3$	$n^3 + 1$

$a \parallel b$

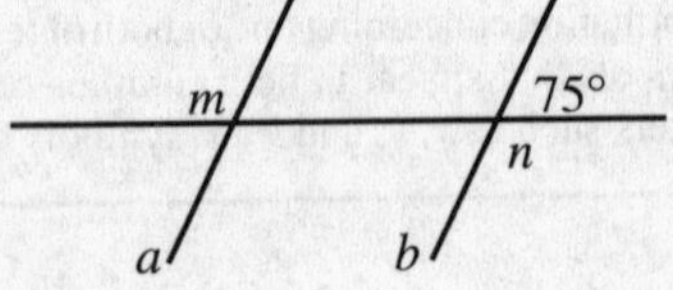

	Column A	Column B
9.	$180 - m$	$180 - 75$

	Column A	Column B
10.	$(26 \times 39) + (39 \times 13)$	$(39)^2$

	Column A	Column B
	$x = 1$ $1 > y > 0$	
11.	$\frac{1}{y}$	x

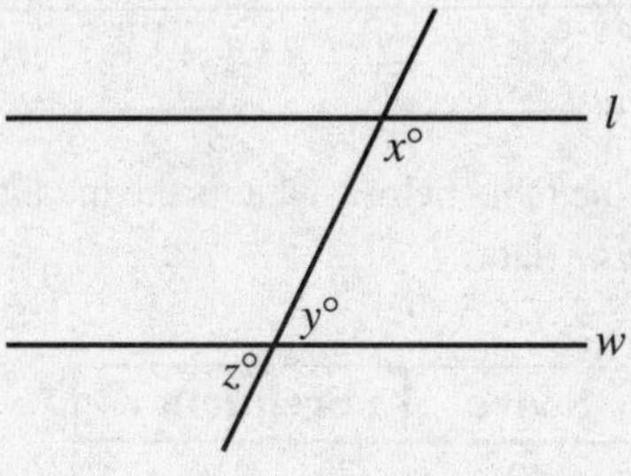

$l \parallel w$

	Column A	Column B
12.	$x + y$	$x + z$
13.	$(m^2 - 1)(2m + 2)$	$(m + 1)^2(2m - 2)$
14.	0.7% of 62	70% of 6,200
15.	The area of a square with side s	The area of an equilateral triangle with side $2s$

PART 2: Student-Produced Response Questions

Directions: Solve each of these problems. Write the answer in the corresponding grid on the answer sheet and fill in the ovals beneath each answer you write. Here are some examples.

Answer: $\frac{3}{4}$ **(= .75; show answer either way)**

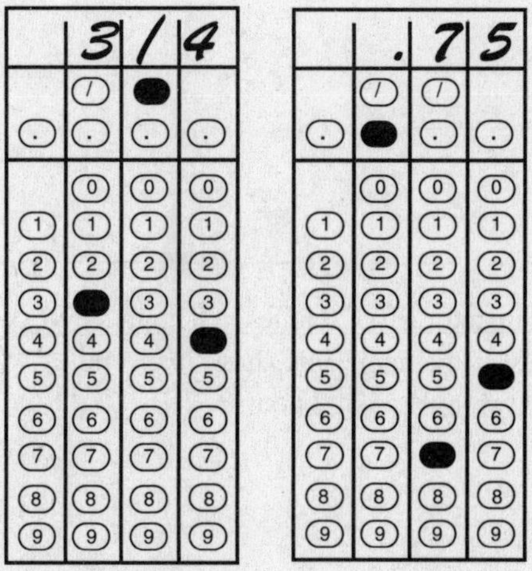

Note: A mixed number such as $3\frac{1}{2}$ must be gridded as 7/2 or as 3.5. If gridded as "31/2," it will be read as "thirty-one halves."

Answer: 325

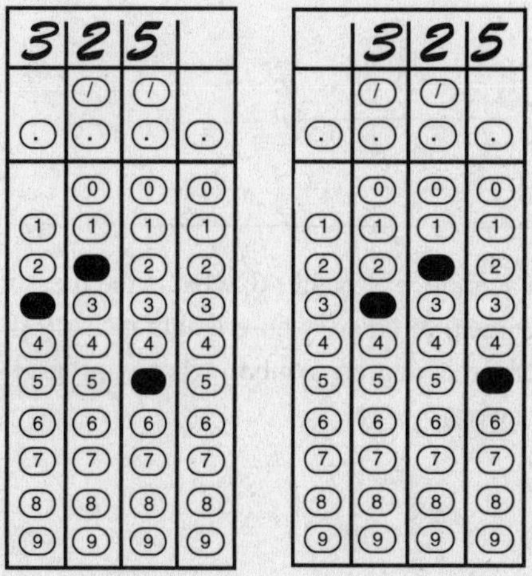

Note: Either position is correct.

16. In the figure below, $l_1 \parallel l_2$. If the measure of $\angle x = 70°$ and the measure of $\angle y = 105°$, what is the measure of $\angle r$? (Disregard the degree symbol when you grid your answer.)

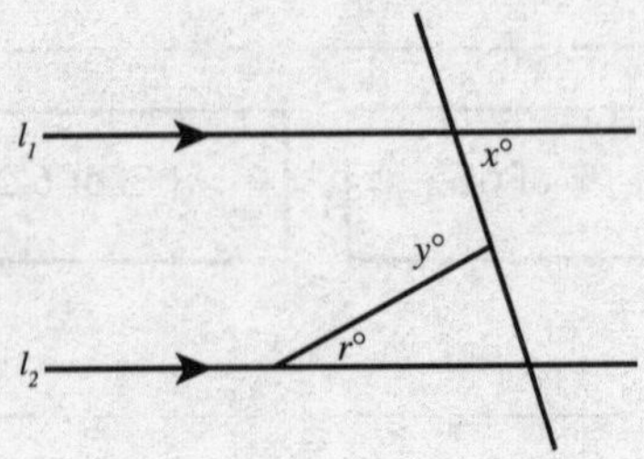

17. What is the value of $-x^2 - 2x^3$ when $x = -1$?

18. Jessica received marks of 87, 93, and 86 on three successive tests. What grade must she receive on a fourth test in order to have an average of 90?

19. In a circle with radius 6, what is the measure (in degrees) of an arc whose length is 2π? (Disregard the degree symbol when you grid your answer.)

20. If $\frac{2x}{3\sqrt{2}} = \frac{3\sqrt{2}}{x}$, what is the positive value of x?

21. Using the table below, what is the median of the following data?

Score	Frequency
20	4
30	4
50	7

22. If $A * B$ is defined as $\frac{AB - B}{-B}$, what is the value of $-2*2$?

23. A man travels 320 miles in 8 hours. If he continues at the same rate, how many miles will he travel in the next 2 hours?

24. A booklet contains 30 pages. If 9 pages in the booklet have drawings, what percent of the pages in the booklet have drawings? (Disregard the percent symbol when you grid your answer.)

25. If 3 copier machines can copy 300 sheets in 3 hours, assuming the same rate, how long (in hours) will it take 6 such copiers to copy 600 sheets?

STOP

END OF SECTION 6. IF YOU HAVE ANY TIME LEFT, GO OVER YOUR WORK IN THIS SECTION ONLY. DO NOT WORK IN ANY OTHER SECTION OF THE TEST.

Diagnostic Examination
Answer Key

Section 1: VERBAL

1. B	7. B	13. B	19. B	25. C
2. B	8. D	14. D	20. E	26. B
3. C	9. E	15. C	21. E	27. C
4. E	10. A	16. B	22. D	28. D
5. D	11. D	17. A	23. A	29. E
6. B	12. E	18. C	24. D	30. C

Section 2: MATH

1. D	6. C	11. E	16. B	21. E
2. A	7. B	12. D	17. C	22. A
3. E	8. C	13. D	18. A	23. E
4. B	9. E	14. B	19. C	24. C
5. B	10. A	15. C	20. C	25. E

Section 3: VERBAL

1. E	3. E	5. C	7. B	9. C
2. D	4. A	6. B	8. A	10. D

Section 4: MATH

1. B	3. B	5. D	7. A	9. E
2. B	4. D	6. D	8. B	10. D

Section 5: VERBAL

1. B	8. A	15. B	22. C	29. C
2. C	9. D	16. E	23. D	30. E
3. D	10. B	17. B	24. B	31. A
4. B	11. C	18. C	25. E	32. C
5. E	12. A	19. D	26. E	33. A
6. B	13. B	20. A	27. D	34. B
7. E	14. D	21. B	28. B	35. A

Section 6: MATH

Part 1

1. B	4. C	7. B	10. C	13. C
2. A	5. B	8. D	11. A	14. B
3. C	6. A	9. B	12. C	15. B

Part 2

16. 35	18. 94	20. 3	22. 3	24. 30
17. 1	19. 60	21. 30	23. 80	25. 3

Diagnostic Examination

Explanatory Answers

Note: A  following a math answer explanation indicates that a calculator could be helpful in solving that particular problem.

Section 1

1. **(B)** A position that provides authority to award contracts is also likely to allow the holder to *incur* (take on) obligations to pay bills.

2. **(B)** A witness who reveals very little information, even when questioned by an experienced attorney, is *recalcitrant* (stubborn).

3. **(C)** The word *although* signifies a shift in meaning. Even though *substantial* (large) resources had been applied, the solution was still *elusive* (hard to determine).

4. **(E)** The only logical choice is the one in which both words have the same connotation; both must be either positive or negative. Only choice (E) satisfies this condition with two positive words.

5. **(D)** The word in the first blank must be a synonym for *kept*. *Retained* and *received* both might satisfy this condition, but only *insured* makes sense in the second blank.

6. **(B)** Those who are *powerful* are also *mighty*. Those that are *mediocre* are also *ordinary*.

7. **(B)** A *horse* is a four-legged animal that is covered with an outer growth of *hair*. A *sheep* is a four-legged animal that is covered with an outer growth of *wool*.

8. **(D)** A *gobble* is a sound made by a particular kind of bird, a *turkey*. A *twitter* is a sound made by some *birds*.

9. **(E)** One *sells* something to someone, who thereby *purchases* it. One *gives* something to someone, who thereby *receives* it.

10. **(A)** A *nest* is a structure built by a *bird* as a place to live and raise young. A *lair*, or den, is a place created by a *lion* for similar purpose. All the other choices include structures that are man-made.

11. **(D)** A *hammer* is used to *hit* an object. A *saw* is used to *cut* an object.

12. **(E)** A *novel* is a type of *book*, just as a *loafer* is a type of *shoe*.

13. **(B)** *Temerity* is a lack of *caution*; *effrontery* is a lack of *shame*.

14. **(D)** Adams is referring to the delay in John Adams's return. It saddens her.

15. **(C)** Adams uses this line to express her resignation at her husband's failure to return.

16. **(B)** Adams is concerned about dissension in the ranks; many men may have too many opinions, leading to conflict.

17. **(A)** A great fish swallowing a small fish may be natural (B), but it disturbs Adams to think of the powerful destroying the weak.

18. **(C)** "The reins of government have been so long slackened" (lines 29–30) that Adams fears people will not accept being governed.

19. **(B)** Adams was disappointed not to receive mail; she tells her husband that she has safely received his letters to date.

20. **(E)** In these lines, Adams tells of her desire to believe her husband's assertion that human nature is capable of achieving degrees of perfection—but she has doubts.

21. **(E)** In her questioning, Adams finds herself in a "labyrinth of perplexities" (lines 44–45).

22. **(D)** The word is used several times to refer to the feathers and leaves with which the narrator will appease the spirit. It is thus a *tribute* rather than any of the other synonyms.

23. **(A)** This interpretation question is quite literal. Go with your first answer on questions of this kind. The narrator's entire dilemma surrounds the difficulty of finding bare ground in a snowy landscape.

24. **(D)** It is a quest, because she is looking for a patch of bare ground where she can perform a religious rite.

25. **(C)** This is the essential problem of the story: How can bare ground be found in this snowy landscape?

26. **(B)** Looking back on the events, the adult narrator feels sorry for the small child she was. She now sees that the task was too great for someone so small—that a child could not hope or be expected to save her sister's life.

27. **(C)** Try the various synonyms in context, and you will see that only *inflamed* makes any sense.

28. **(D)** The child is afraid that the offering did not reach the ground, and therefore, her sister will not be saved. If it did not reach the ground, perhaps it is because she did not have faith in nature to show her a bare patch of ground and did not follow the medicine-woman's instructions.

29. **(E)** If you understand question 28, you probably answered this question correctly. The small child blames herself for her lack of faith, which she sees as causing her sister's turn for the worse.

30. **(C)** This evaluation question is a restatement of interpretation question 26. Throughout the passage, the reader is made aware of the child's struggle and her essential decency. The author wants us to like the child and forgive her as she herself has done.

Section 2

1. **(D)** $\frac{3}{4} = .75$

$\frac{35}{71}$ is slightly less than $\frac{35}{70} = .5$

$\frac{13}{20} = \frac{13 \times 5}{20 \times 5} = \frac{65}{100} = .65$

$\frac{71}{101}$ is very close to $\frac{7}{10}$ or .7

$\frac{15}{20} = \frac{15 \times 5}{20 \times 5} = \frac{75}{100} = .75$

$\frac{19}{24} = 24\overline{)19.00}$ = .79 which is more than $\frac{3}{4}$

$$\begin{array}{r} 168 \\ \hline 220 \\ 216 \\ \hline \end{array}$$

2. **(A)**

$$\begin{aligned} 820 + R + S - 610 &= 342 \\ R + S + 210 &= 342 \\ R + S &= 132 \\ \text{If } R = 2S, \text{ Then } 2S + S &= 132 \\ 3S &= 132 \\ S &= 44 \end{aligned}$$

3. **(E)**

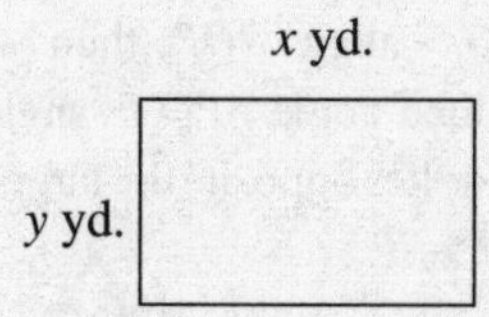

Area = xy sq. yd. = 9 xy sq. ft.
$9\,xy \bullet 5 = 45\,xy$

4. **(B)**

$$\begin{aligned} 7M &= 3M - 20 \\ 4M &= -20 \\ M &= -5 \\ M + 7 &= -5 + 7 = 2 \end{aligned}$$

5. **(B)** Arc $EA = 85°$ and arc $BD = 15°$. Since a central angle is measured by its arc, then

$$\text{angle } ECA = \frac{1}{2}(AE - BD) = \frac{1}{2}(85 - 15) = \frac{1}{2} \bullet 70 = 35°$$

6. **(C)** The smallest positive number divisible by 3, 4, or 5 is $3 \bullet 4 \bullet 5 = 60$. Hence, the desired number is $60 + 2 = 62$.

7. **(B)** Since there are $4d$ quarter miles in d miles the charge $= 75 + 15(4d - 1)$.

8. **(C)** Assume that there are 100 enlistees on the post; then 30 are from New York State and $\frac{1}{10} \times 30 = 3$ are from New York City. $\frac{3}{100} = 3\%$.

9. **(E)** If you know only the hypotenuse of a right triangle, you cannot determine its legs. Hence, the area of the rectangle cannot be determined from the data given.

10. **(A)** If angle $RPQ >$ angle RQP, then $\frac{1}{2}$ angle $P > \frac{1}{2}$ angle Q; then angle $SPQ >$ angle SQP. Since the larger side lies opposite the larger angle, it follows that $SQ > SP$.

11. **(E)** $3.14 \times 10^6 = 3.14 \times 1{,}000{,}000 = 3{,}140{,}000$

12. **(D)** $\dfrac{36}{29 - \dfrac{4}{0.2}} = \dfrac{36}{29 - 20} = \dfrac{36}{9} = 4$

13. **(D)** Diameter $= 4\sqrt{2}$, since it is the hypotenuse of a right isosceles triangle of leg 4.

Then the radius $= 2\sqrt{2}$

Area of semicircle $= \frac{1}{2} \times \pi\left(2\sqrt{2}\right)^2 = \frac{1}{2} \times \pi 8 = 4\pi$

14. **(B)** Consecutive odd numbers may be represented as

$$\begin{array}{l} 2n + 1 \\ 2n + 3 \\ 2n + 5 \\ \hline \text{Sum} = 6n + 9 \end{array}$$

Always divisible by 3. Thus, only II.

15. **(C)** Angle BCD is formed by tangent and chord and is equal to one-half of arc BC. Angle A is an inscribed angle and is also equal to one-half of arc BC. Hence, angle A = angle $BCD = 40°$.

16. **(B)** Let x = amount of marked price. Then

$$\frac{1}{5}x = 15$$
$$x = 75$$
$$75 - 15 = \$60$$

17. **(C)** This problem cannot be solved by simply doing subtraction. To give an example: if you read pages 1 and 2 of a book, how many pages have you read? The answer is obviously 2; we can conclude then that we do not obtain the answer by subtracting 1 from 2. Instead we subtract 1 from 2 and add 1.

$$49 - 7 + 1 = 43$$
$$157 - 101 + 1 = 57$$
$$43 + 57 = 100$$

18. **(A)** When we are asked for the sum of two items, we often *cannot* state the values of the individual items. This is the case in this problem. We can say that $\angle BAD$ is 75° and $\angle CDA$ is 85°. We also know that $ABCD$ is a quadrilateral and must contain 360°. Therefore, $\angle ABC + \angle BCD = 200°$

$$\angle EBA + \angle ABC = 180°$$
$$\angle BCD + \angle DCF = 180°$$
$$\angle EBA + \angle ABC + \angle BCD + \angle DCF = 360°$$
$$\angle EBA + 200° + \angle DCF = 360°$$
$$\angle EBA + \angle DCF = 160°$$

(1)

(1) [E] ✓
(2) (D) ✓
(3) ~~B~~ ✗
(4 A) ✓
(5) — CNC
6 ~~A~~ ✗
(7) C ✗
8 A NC
9 C ✓
10 E ✗ (D)

19. **(C)** The new solution is $\frac{3}{20}$ pure alcohol or 15%.

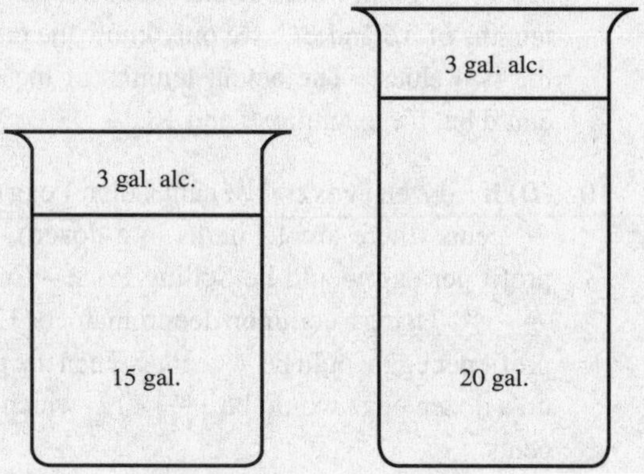

STARTING SOL. **RESULTING SOL.**

20. **(C)** Area of $QXRS = XR \times$ altitude from P to XR. Area of $\Delta PXR = \frac{1}{2} XR \times$ altitude from P to XR. Hence, ratio of area of Δ to $QXRS = 1 : 2$.

21. **(E)** $x(p + 1) = M$

Divide both sides by x.

$$p + 1 = \frac{M}{x} \text{ or } p = \frac{M}{x} - 1$$

22. **(A)** $\frac{T}{1} = \frac{x}{60M}$

$$x = 60MT$$

23. **(E)** It can be helpful to graph each of the inequalities and then put the two graphs together to find the overlapping area.

24. **(C)** Rise in temperature $= 36 - (-14) = 36 + 14 = 50°$. $\frac{50}{5} = 10°$ (hourly rise). Hence, at noon, temperature $= -14 + 3(10) = -14 + 30 = +16°$.

25. **(E)** If $\frac{P}{Q} = \frac{4}{5}$, then $5P = 4Q$. However, there is no way of determining from this the value of $2P + Q$.

Section 3

1. **(E)** The town's only exposure is southward toward the sun; it is open only on the south side.

2. **(D)** Henson calls Karnah "pleasant," "delightful," even "ideal."

3. **(E)** The lack of trees (lines 16–17) is the only thing that keeps Karnah from having a landscape "as delightful as anywhere on earth."

4. **(A)** "The scenery is also varied and attractive, offering to the eye greater contrasts. . . ." (lines 54–57), writes Peary. This diversity is one of the attractions of the bay.

5. **(C)** Lines 67–68 describe the "restless arctic elements" carving the cliffs into "turrets, bastions, huge amphitheatres, and colossal statues. . . ."

6. **(B)** Peary does not talk about vegetation (D), nor is this passage about the North Pole (E). The passage follows the coast of Greenland with enough specific detail that a reader could use it as a map.

7. **(B)** The description of the geology and scenery of Greenland seems to be from the vantage point of a ship traveling along the coastline. Everything that is mentioned is along the shore.

8. **(A)** Henson's "lofty mountains" surround Karnah; the only mention of landmarks around Karnah in Peary's description is to the "Sculptured Cliffs of Karnah."

9. **(C)** Peary's descriptions are much more technical than Henson's; his purpose is not to write a simple travelogue, but to detail an expedition for future explorers.

10. **(D)** Both writers mention the severity of most of the arctic, Henson in comparing it to Karnah's more moderate climate (line 12), and Peary in his description of the restless arctic elements. Both, too, remark on the unusual attractiveness of Karnah and the bay.

Section 4

1. **(B)** Since Z is equidistant from X and Y, it must lie on the y-axis. Then $\Delta\ OZY$ is a 30°-60°-90° triangle with $YZ = 8$. Hence $OZ = \frac{8}{2}\sqrt{3} = 4\sqrt{3}$.

Coordinates of Z are $(0, 4\sqrt{3})$.

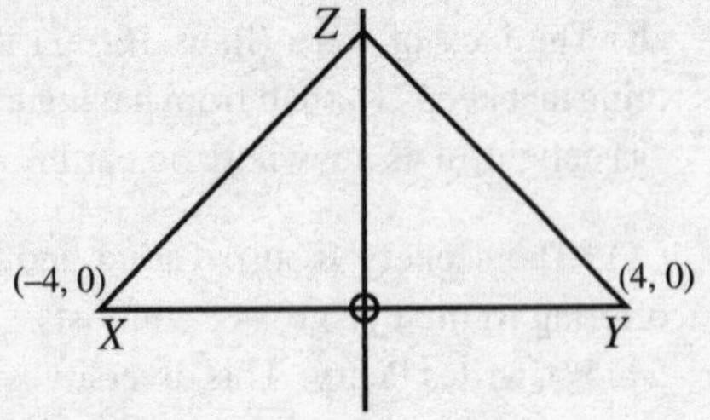

2. **(B)** $9 = 8 + 1 = 7 + 2 = 6 + 3 = 5 + 4$.
Thus, 4 ways.

3. **(B)** $\dfrac{7 \text{ ft. } 9 \text{ in.}}{3} = \dfrac{6 \text{ ft. } 21 \text{ in.}}{3} = 2 \text{ ft. } 7 \text{ in.}$

4. **(D)** Since K is an integer and R and S are integers, K must be a perfect square and perfect cube. The smallest such number listed is $64 = 8^2 = 4^3$.

5. **(D)** The Δ RST has a base of 7 and an altitude of 5. Hence the area $= \frac{1}{2} \cdot 7 \cdot 5 = 17\frac{1}{2}$

6. **(D)** $\dfrac{3P}{3Q}$ is obviously reducible to $\dfrac{P}{Q}$.

The others cannot be reduced.

7. **(A)** Since ACB is a straight angle and angle DCE is a right angle, then angle ACD and angle BCE are complementary. Hence $BCE = 90 - x$.

8. **(B)** When a triangle is inscribed in a parallelogram or a rectangle, the area inside the inscribed triangle will always be the same as the area outside the inscribed triangle. All three triangles have the same altitude. Since AE plus ED equals BC, the two shaded triangles combined have the same base as the unshaded triangle. If the base and the altitude are the same, then the area is the same.

9. **(E)** The most important point here is that we do not know the altitude of the parallelogram; the area of a parallelogram is altitude times base. A secondary point would be that we do not know the lengths of AB and BC; we only know the ratio of the two sides. The actual lengths of the sides could be, for example, 8 and 18.

10. **(D)** If a dozen eggs cost M cents, then 1 egg costs $\frac{M}{12}$ cents (there are 12 items in a dozen). The profit per egg would be Selling Price – Cost or $\frac{M}{6} - \frac{M}{12}$. Using a common denominator of 12, the profit per egg would be $\frac{M}{12}$ cents. Then the profit on a dozen eggs would be $\left(\frac{M}{12}\right) \times 12$, which is M cents.

Section 5

1. **(B)** "Mutual assistance" implies that people are *cooperative*. Since "rather than" indicates a shift in meaning, the word in the second blank must have an opposing connotation; only *competitive* satisfies this condition.

2. **(C)** A condition that has existed for a long time in a particular place is said to be *endemic* to that location.

3. **(D)** The first blank could logically be filled by any of the choices. However, the secret betrayal implies that the actions *belied* (showed to be untrue) the words of the *reiterated* (repeated) pledges of support.

4. **(B)** Of the choices, the only one that could "look back upon us and our time" is our *descendants.*

5. **(E)** Choices (B), (D), and (E) are possibilities for the first blank. However, the second words in choices (B) and (D) make no logical sense. A *final* debate is likely to offer *clarification* of opinions.

6. **(B)** This is the only logical answer. "With the *duration*" is poor diction.

7. **(E)** The sentence establishes an opposition between "our" wishes and Eva's action. Only (E) satisfies this requirement.

8. **(A)** A key word in this sentence is *appearance.* The words following all tell how a person physically looks. Choices (B), (C), (D), and (E) describe feelings or behaviors. The only word describing physical appearance is *tousled* (A), which means "unkempt."

9. **(D)** The word *but* is your clue that the two words must have opposite connotations. The only choice that satisfies this condition is (D): the use of trained bears was once a *commonplace* (ordinary occurrence) but has now almost *ceased* (stopped).

10. **(B)** The word *although* signals that the second part of the sentence will describe the opposite of *aloofness* (coldness of manner). Therefore, the correct answer is *gracious* (courteous and kind).

11. **(C)** The first blank needs a positive word to describe the way the agent calmed the travelers; the second blank needs a negative word to describe the delayed travelers. Only choice (C) meets both conditions.

12. **(A)** The lover of democracy has an *aversion* or *antipathy* toward totalitarianism.

13. **(B)** This answer needs either two negative or two positive words. The other four choices have a combination of positive and negative words. Since choice (B) has two negative words describing the situation, it is the only correct response.

14. **(D)** To *trickle* is to flow slowly; to *gush*, to flow profusely. Similarly, to *touch* is to come into gentle contact and to *collide* is to come into violent contact.

15. **(B)** We intentionally use the *eye* to *wink* and the *toe* to *tap* but we couldn't be said to intentionally use the *nose* to *smell.*

16. **(E)** In *bowling* you aim at the *pin* as in *golf* you aim at the *hole.*

17. **(B)** A *lake* will necessarily be experienced as *wet*, and *ice* necessarily as *cold.*

18. **(C)** A *tooth* is part of a *comb*; a *cog* is part of a *gear.*

19. **(D)** A *miser* is characterized by *stinginess.* An *altruist* (a person concerned with the welfare of others) is characterized by *selflessness.*

20. **(A)** One who is *chivalrous* is *gallant* and one who is *sanguine* is *cheerful.* Answers (B), (C), and (D) are antonyms.

21. **(B)** *Lava* flows out of a *volcano* and *water* flows out of a *spring.* Although answer choice (E) has some appeal, it reverses the order.

22. **(C)** To be *diffident* (timid) is to be lacking in *confidence.* Similarly, to be *gloomy* is to be lacking in *cheer.*

23. **(D)** A *conductor* leads an *orchestra* and a *president* leads a *country.*

24. **(B)** Their preoccupation with their stiff, new clothing, their awe at the train's typical conveniences, and their blushes at the glances of travelers—all of these combine to paint the picture of an innocent, unworldly pair.

25. **(E)** The bride constantly "twisted her head to regard her puff sleeves" (lines 20–21) and is embarrassed by them. Her dress is probably brand new, and she is certainly unused to such finery.

26. **(E)** With this single line, Crane paints a life of hard work and resignation.

27. **(D)** The bridegroom is putting on a brave face for the sake of his bride, who is even more unsophisticated than he.

28. **(B)** The bridegroom's pride is part of his delight in his "new estate" of marriage. He can show off for his bride, but there is no doubt that such elegance is rare for him.

29. **(C)** The charmingly decorated train is thought by the newlyweds to be indicative of their new status in life. Because they feel exalted by their new marriage, they imagine that they deserve such luxury.

30. **(E)** The porter is a lower-class working man, and is probably looked down upon by travelers, but he welcomes this opportunity to sneer at those lower on the ladder than himself.

31. **(A)** Travelers look at the newlyweds with "derisive enjoyment" (line 64). It is clear that they are just married, and there is something amusing about this.

32. **(C)** Customarily, people in the position of the newlyweds are amusing to others. None of the other synonyms makes sense in this context.

33. **(A)** Crane is not derisive (D); he leaves that to the other travelers and the porter. On the contrary, his attitude seems to be a slightly detached air of sympathy at the newlyweds' embarrassment and innocence.

34. **(B)** Their names are unimportant; what is vital is their provincialism and ordinariness. The reader can thus identify a type without feeling overly empathetic.

35. **(A)** This is, in fact, the beginning of the story, and, as with most short stories, its object is to introduce characters and setting. No opinion is expressed (D); the passage is simply descriptive.

Section 6

Part 1

1. **(B)** Since $2x$ is the same in both columns, adding 1 to $2x$ will surely be larger than subtracting 1 from it. The answer is (B).

2. **(A)** In Column A, x^2 will be a positive number, therefore $\frac{1}{x^2}$ will also be positive. In Column B, x will always be negative, so (A) is greater.

3. **(C)** $a + b + c$ is the sum of the angles of a triangle and therefore equals 180°. $c + d$ is the sum of supplementary angles and, therefore, also equals 180°.

4. **(C)** Using the distributive property in Column A, $(a + b)\ c = ac + bc$. Therefore $\frac{1}{4}(ac + bc) = \frac{ac+bc}{4}$. Column A and Column B are equal.

5. **(B)** Angle b is the largest in the triangle, so the side opposite b, side AC, is the largest side of the triangle. Therefore AC is larger than AB. Answer (B) is correct.

6. **(A)** The area of the small circle is $\pi\,(3)^2 = 9\pi$. The area of the shaded region is the area of the large circle minus that of the small circle. The area of the large circle is $\pi\,(5)^2 = 25\pi$. The area of the shaded region is $25\pi - 9\pi = 16\pi$. The area of the shaded region is larger than that of the smaller circle. Hence, answer (A) is correct.

7. **(B)** We are told that the sums of all the rows and columns are the same. We could set up an equation:

$$\begin{array}{rcl} v + z + 7 & = & w + y + 4 \\ -4 & & -4 \\ \hline v + z + 3 & = & w + y \end{array}$$

Therefore, $w + y$ must be greater than $v + z$.

8. **(D)** It is impossible to determine which is larger. Taking two examples: $n = -\frac{1}{2}$; $(n + 1)^3 = (\frac{1}{2})^3 = \frac{1}{8}$ and $n^3 + 1 = (-\frac{1}{2})^3 + 1 = -\frac{1}{8} + 1 = \frac{7}{8}$. In this example, Column B is greater than Column A. However, $n = \frac{1}{2}$, $(n + 1)^3 = (1\frac{1}{2})^3 = 3\frac{3}{8}$ and $n^3 + 1 = \left(\frac{1}{2}\right)^3 + 1 = 1\frac{1}{8}$. In this example, Column A is greater than Column B.

9. **(B)** m and n are alternate interior angles, so $m = n$. n and 75° are supplementary angles, so $n = 180° – 75° = 105° = m$ and $180° – m = 75°$. Therefore, $180° – 75° > 180° – m$, and (B) is the correct choice.

10. **(C)** Using the distributive property, $(26 \times 39) + (39 \times 13) = 39(26 + 13) = 39 \times 39 = (39)^2$. Therefore, Column A and Column B are equal.

11. **(A)** Since y is a positive fraction less than 1, $\frac{1}{y}$ is a positive fraction greater than 1. Therefore, $\frac{1}{y} > x$. Answer (A) is the correct choice.

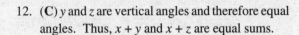

12. **(C)** y and z are vertical angles and therefore equal angles. Thus, $x + y$ and $x + z$ are equal sums.

13. **(C)** Factoring Column A, $(m^2 - 1)(2m + 2) = (m - 1)(m + 1) \cdot 2(m + 1)$. Rearrange the factor so that $(m + 1)^2 \cdot 2(m - 1) = (m + 1)^2(2m - 2)$, which is equal to Column B.

14. **(B)** In Column A, 0.7% of 62 is $(0.007) \times (62) = 0.434$. In Column B, 70% of 6200 is 4340. Column B is larger.

15. **(B)** The area of a square with side s is s^2. The height of the triangle, using the Pythagorean Theorem, is $\sqrt{(2s)^2 + s^2} = \sqrt{3s^2} = s\sqrt{3}$. The area of the triangle is $\frac{1}{2}(2s)\left(s\sqrt{3}\right) = s^2\sqrt{3}$. Thus, the area of the triangle (Column B) is larger.

Part 2

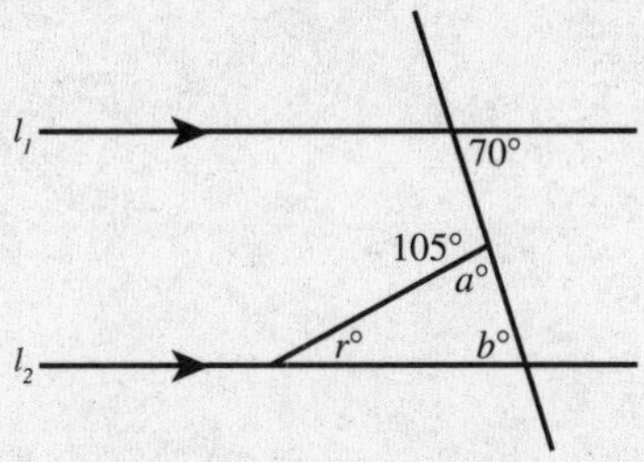

16. The measure of $\angle b = 70°$. It is an alternate interior angle with angle x.

The measure of $\angle a = 75°$. It is the supplement of angle y.

$\angle r + \angle a + \angle b = 180°$. They form a triangle.

$\angle r + 75° + 70° = 180°$

$\angle r = 35°$

17. $-x^2 - 2x^3$

Substitute the value -1 for x

$$-(-1)^2 - 2(-1)^3 =$$
$$-(-1) - 2(-1) =$$
$$-1 + 2 = 1$$

18. $$\text{Average} = \frac{\text{Sum of the test scores}}{\text{Quantity of tests}}$$

$$90 = \frac{87 + 93 + 86 + x}{4}$$

By cross-multiplication:

$4(90) = 87 + 93 + 86 + x$

$360 = 266 + x$

$x = 94$

19. Circumference $= 2\pi r = 2\pi(6) = 12\pi$. 2π is $\frac{2\pi}{12\pi} = \frac{1}{6}$ of the circumference. In turn, the central angle is $\frac{1}{6}(360°) = 60°$,

or

$$\frac{\text{arc length}}{\text{circumference}} = \frac{x°}{360°}$$

$$\frac{2\pi}{12\pi} = \frac{x}{360}$$

$$\frac{1}{6} = \frac{x}{360}$$

$$6x = 360$$

$$x = 60$$

20. $$\frac{2x}{3\sqrt{2}} = \frac{3\sqrt{2}}{x}$$

By cross-multiplication

$$2x(x) = (3\sqrt{2})(3\sqrt{2})$$

$$2x^2 = 9(2) = 18$$

$$x^2 = 9$$

$$x = \pm 3$$

The positive value of x is 3.

21. The median is the "middle" data element when the data is arranged in numerical order. 20, 20, 20, 20, 30, 30, 30, 30, 50, 50, 50, 50, 50, 50, 50
↑
The "middle" data element is 30.

22. $A * B = \dfrac{AB - B}{-B}$

$$-2 * 2 = \frac{(-2)(2) - 2}{-2} = \frac{-4 - 2}{-2} = \frac{-6}{-2} = 3$$

23. distance = rate × time → rate = $\dfrac{\text{distance}}{\text{time}}$

$$\frac{320 \text{ miles}}{8 \text{ hrs}} = 40 \text{ mph}$$

40 mph × 2 hrs = 80 miles

24. $\dfrac{\text{part}}{\text{whole}} \times 100 = \dfrac{9}{30} \times 100 = 30\%$

25. The number of sheets is directly proportional to the number of machines and also directly proportional to the amount of time.
Mathematically this can be expressed as:

$$\frac{\text{sheets}}{(\text{number of machines})(\text{time})} = \frac{\text{sheets}}{(\text{number of machines})(\text{time})}$$

$$\frac{300}{3(3)} = \frac{600}{6(t)}$$

$$\frac{300}{9} = \frac{600}{6t}$$

Reduce the fractions and then cross-multiply:

$$\frac{100}{3} = \frac{100}{t}$$

$$100t = 300$$

$$t = 3$$

Evaluating the Diagnostic Examination

To determine your Verbal Reasoning Score:

1. Using the Analysis Worksheet, enter the number of correct answers for each verbal reasoning section on the appropriate line in Column A of the Verbal Reasoning grid.
2. Enter the number of incorrect answers for each verbal reasoning section on the appropriate line in Column B of the Verbal Reasoning grid.
3. Total Columns A and B and enter these totals in boxes A and B, respectively.
4. Perform the indicated calculation to find your Raw Score; (value in box A) minus (one-quarter of the value in box B) = Raw Score.
5. Consult the Conversion Chart to find your approximate Scaled Score.

To determine your Mathematical Reasoning Score:

1. Enter the number of correct answers for each mathematical reasoning section on the appropriate line in Column C of the Mathematical Reasoning grid.
2. Enter the number of incorrect answers for each mathematical reasoning section on the appropriate line in Column D, E, or F of the Mathematical Reasoning grid.
3. Total Columns C, D, and E, and enter these totals in boxes C, D, and E, respectively.
4. Perform the indicated calculation to find your Raw Score: (value in box C) minus (one-quarter of the value in box D) minus (one-third of the value in box E) = Raw Score.
5. Consult the Conversion Chart to find your approximate Scaled Score.

Note: Box F is not used in this calculation.

Analysis Worksheet

VERBAL REASONING

Section	Number of Questions	Column A Number of Correct Answers	Column B Number of Incorrect Answers
1	30		
3	10		
5	35		
	Total	A	B

A − ¼ B = Raw Score → Use Conversion Chart → Scaled Score

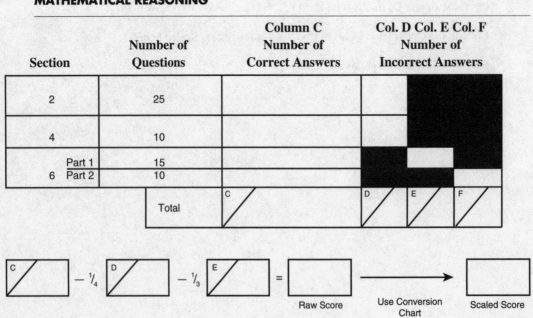

MATHEMATICAL REASONING

Section		Number of Questions	Column C Number of Correct Answers	Col. D Number of Incorrect Answers	Col. E	Col. F
2		25				
4		10				
6	Part 1	15				
	Part 2	10				
		Total	C	D	E	F

C − ¼ D − ⅓ E = Raw Score → Use Conversion Chart → Scaled Score

Conversion Scales for Diagnostic Examination

VERBAL REASONING:

Raw Score	Scaled Score	Raw Score	Scaled Score
75	800	40	550
70	800	35	520
65	760	30	480
60	710	25	440
55	670	20	410
50	620	15	370
45	590	10	340
		5	290
		0	230

MATHEMATICAL REASONING:

Raw Score	Scaled Score	Raw Score	Scaled Score
60	800	25	510
55	760	20	480
50	690	15	440
45	650	10	410
40	610	5	340
35	580	0	200
30	550		

Although you now have some idea of what your scores would like had they been scaled according to unofficial ETS standards, you will probably want to know how to interpret your Raw Scores in more familiar terms. If so, use the following Self-Evaluation Charts to see what your Raw Scores actually mean.

SELF-EVALUATION CHARTS

VERBAL REASONING: RAW SCORE

Excellent	60 – 75
Good	50 – 60
Average	30 – 50
Fair	20 – 30
Poor	0 – 20

MATHEMATICAL REASONING: RAW SCORE

Excellent	50 – 60
Good	40 – 50
Average	20 – 40
Fair	10 – 20
Poor	0 – 10

PART THREE

Review of SAT Subject Areas

CONTENTS

MATHEMATICS REVIEW

This section offers a comprehensive review of the mathematics you will need for the SAT. It contains 15 sections, each concentrating on a particular area of mathematics. Model examples with worked-through solutions are provided for specific topics within each subject area. These examples illustrate common student errors and should be carefully studied. At the end of each section are practice exercises with explanatory solutions. Work out each problem before looking at its solution. If you miss an answer, review the problem to learn where you made your mistake. This will help you to understand the mathematical concepts involved in the problem. Note that there are no concepts presented beyond beginning geometry. Familiarity with the types of problems contained here will help you attain a higher score on the examination.

About Answering SAT Math Questions

The SAT is mainly a multiple-choice test. For each multiple-choice question, credit is given for a correct answer, a lesser credit is deducted for each incorrect answer, and credit is neither given nor deducted for an omitted answer. There is no penalty for an incorrect answer to a student-produced response question. The guessing penalty imposed for the multiple-choice questions makes it a disadvantage to guess wildly. If a question lists five possible answers, you have four chances of guessing incorrectly for every one chance of guessing correctly. That means you have four times as many chances of losing credit as you have of gaining credit. If, however, you can narrow your choices among the given answers to two or three, your chances of gaining credit increase substantially, and it would be worth your while to guess.

You should also remember that the test you will take is prepared by persons highly skilled in test construction. The questions on the SAT test your ability to make careful and logical decisions. The choices listed as possible answers for each question are there for a reason. In many cases, the wrong choices offered are the answers that result from common student errors. Do *not* assume your answer is correct just because it appears among the choices. The key to success is careful reading and accurate computation.

I. Operations With Integers and Decimals

In preparing for the mathematics section of the SAT, it is especially important to overcome any fear of mathematics. The level of this examination extends no further than simple geometry and much of the material involves only basic arithmetic.

The four basic arithmetic operations are addition, subtraction, multiplication, and division. The results of these operations are called sum, difference, product, and quotient, respectively. Because these words are often used in problems, you should be thoroughly familiar with them.

When adding integers and/or decimals, remember to keep your columns straight and to write all digits in their proper columns, according to place value.

Example➤ Add 43.75, .631, and 5

Solution➤

$$\begin{array}{r} 43.75 \\ .631 \\ 5. \\ \hline 49.381 \end{array}$$

When subtracting integers and/or decimals, it is likewise important to put numbers in their proper columns. Be particularly careful in subtracting a longer decimal from a shorter one.

Example➤ Subtract .2567 from 3.8

Solution➤

$$\begin{array}{r} 3.8000 \\ .2567 \\ \hline 3.5433 \end{array}$$

In order to perform this subtraction, zeros must be added to the top number to extend it to equal length with the bottom number. The zeros in this case are only place fillers and in no way change the value of the number.

When multiplying integers, pay particular attention to zeros.

Example➤ Find the product of 403 and 30.

Solution➤

$$\begin{array}{r} 403 \\ 30 \\ \hline 12{,}090 \end{array}$$

When multiplying decimals, remember that the number of decimal places in the product must be equal to the sum of the number of decimal places in the numbers being mutiplied.

Example➤ Find the product of 4.03 and .3

Solution➤

$$\begin{array}{r} 4.03 \\ .3 \\ \hline 1.209 \end{array}$$

When dividing, it is also important to watch for zeros.

Example➤ Divide 4935 by 7

Solution➤

$$7\overline{)4935}\quad \text{quotient } 705$$

Since 7 divides evenly into 49, there is no remainder to carry to the next digit. However, 7 will not divide into 3, so you must put a 0 into the quotient. Carrying the 3, you can then divide 7 into 35 evenly.

When dividing by a decimal, always change the decimal to an integer by moving the decimal point to the end of the divisor. To do this, multiply the divisor by a power of 10. (Multiplying by 10 moves a decimal point one place to the right. Multiplying by 100 moves it two places to the right, and so forth.) Then multiply the number in the division sign by the same power of 10. Since division can always be written as a fraction in which the divisor is the denominator and the number being divided is the numerator, when you remove a decimal point from the divisor, you are really multiplying both parts of the fraction by the same number, which changes its form, but not its value.

Example➤ Divide 4.935 by .07

Solution➤ $.07\overline{)4.935}$ (Multiply by 100 to move the decimal point two places to the right.)

$$\begin{array}{r} 70.5 \\ 7\overline{)493.5} \end{array}$$

PRACTICE EXERCISES I

Work out each problem in the space provided.

Add:

1. 6 + 37 + 42,083 + 125
2. .007 + 32.4 + 1.234 + 7.3
3. .37 + .037 + .0037 + 37

Subtract:

4. 3701 – 371
5. 1000 – 112
6. 40.37 – 6.983

Multiply:

7. 3147 by 206
8. 2.137 by .11
9. .45 by .06

Divide:

10. 12,894 by 42
11. 34.68 by 3.4
12. .175 by 25

SOLUTIONS TO PRACTICE EXERCISES I

1.
```
      6
     37
  42083
    125
  -----
  42251
```

2.
```
   .007
  32.4
   1.234
   7.3
  ------
  40.941
```

3.
```
    .37
    .037
    .0037
  37.
  -------
  37.4107
```

4.
```
  3701
 - 371
 -----
  3330
```

5.
```
  1000
 - 112
 -----
   888
```

6.
```
  40.370
 - 6.983
 -------
  33.387
```

7.
```
    3147
   ×206
  ------
   18882
  62940
  ------
  648282
```

8.
```
  2.137
   ×.11
  -----
   2137
  2137
  ------
  .23507
```

9.
```
    .45
   ×.06
  -----
  .0270
```

10.
```
       307
  42)12894
     126
     ---
       294
       294
       ---
```

11.
```
       10.2
  3.4)34.68
      34
      --
        68
        68
        --
```

12.
```
     .007
  25).175
      175
      ---
```

II. Operations With Fractions

In adding or subtracting fractions, you must remember that the numbers must have the same (common) denominator.

Example➤ Add $\frac{1}{3}+\frac{2}{5}+\frac{3}{4}$

Solution➤ The least number into which 3, 5, and 4 all divide evenly is 60. Therefore, use 60 as the common denominator. To add the fractions, divide each denominator into 60 and multiply the result by the given numerator.

$$\frac{20+24+45}{60}=\frac{89}{60}\text{, or }1\frac{29}{60}$$

To add or subtract two fractions quickly, remember that a sum can be found by adding the two cross-products and putting this answer over the denominator product.

$$\frac{a}{b}\times\frac{c}{d}=\frac{ad+bc}{bd}$$

A similar shortcut applies to subtraction.

$$\frac{a}{b}-\frac{c}{d}=\frac{ad-bc}{bd}$$

Example➤ $\frac{3}{4}-\frac{5}{7}=\frac{21-20}{28}=\frac{1}{28}$

All fractions should be left in their lowest terms. That is, there should be no factor common to both numerator and denominator. Often in multiple-choice questions you may find that the answer you have correctly computed is not among the choices but an equivalent fraction is. Be careful!

In reducing fractions involving large numbers, it is helpful to be able to tell whether a factor is common to both numerator and denominator before a lengthy trial division. Certain tests for divisibility help with this.

To test if a number is divisible by:	Check to see:
2	if it is even
3	if the sum of the digits is divisible by 3
4	if the last two digits are divisible by 4
5	if it ends in 5 or 0
6	if it is even *and* the sum of the digits is divisible by 3
8	if the last three digits are divisible by 8
9	if the sum of the digits is divisible by 9
10	if it ends in 0

Example➤ $\frac{3525}{4341}$

Solution➤ This fraction is reducible by 3, since the sum of the digits of the numerator is 15 and those of the denominator add up to 12, both divisible by 3.

$$\frac{3525}{4341} = \frac{1175}{1447}$$

The resulting fraction meets no further divisibility tests and therefore has no common factor listed above. Larger divisors would be unlikely on an SAT test.

To add or subtract mixed numbers, it is again important to remember common denominators. In subtraction, you must borrow in terms of the common denominator.

Addition:

$$\begin{array}{r} 43\frac{2}{5} \\ +\ 8\frac{1}{3} \\ \hline \end{array} \qquad \begin{array}{r} 43\frac{6}{15} \\ +\ 8\frac{5}{15} \\ \hline 51\frac{11}{15} \end{array}$$

Subtraction:

$$\begin{array}{r} 43\frac{2}{5} \\ -\ 6\frac{2}{3} \\ \hline \end{array} \qquad \begin{array}{r} 43\frac{6}{15} \\ -\ 6\frac{10}{15} \\ \hline \end{array} \qquad \begin{array}{r} 42\frac{21}{15} \\ -\ 6\frac{10}{15} \\ \hline 36\frac{11}{15} \end{array}$$

To multiply fractions, always try to cancel where possible before actually multiplying. In multiplying mixed numbers, always change them to improper fractions first.

Multiply: $$\frac{2}{\cancel{5}} \cdot \frac{\overset{2}{\cancel{10}}}{\cancel{11}} \cdot \frac{\overset{9}{\cancel{99}}}{\underset{55}{\cancel{110}}} = \frac{18}{55}$$

Multiply: $$4\frac{1}{2} \cdot 1\frac{2}{3} \cdot 5\frac{1}{5}$$

$$\frac{\overset{3}{\cancel{9}}}{\cancel{2}} \cdot \frac{\cancel{5}}{\cancel{3}} \cdot \frac{\overset{13}{\cancel{26}}}{\cancel{5}} = 39$$

To divide fractions or mixed numbers, remember to invert the divisor (the number after the division sign) and multiply.

Divide: $$4\frac{1}{2} \div \frac{3}{4} = \frac{\overset{3}{\cancel{9}}}{\cancel{2}} \cdot \frac{\overset{2}{\cancel{4}}}{\cancel{3}} = 6$$

Divide: $62\frac{1}{2} \div 5 = \frac{\overset{25}{\cancel{125}}}{2} \cdot \frac{1}{\cancel{5}} = 12\frac{1}{2}$

To simplify complex fractions (fractions within fractions), multiply every term by the lowest number needed to clear all fractions in the given numerator and denominator.

Example➤ $$\frac{\frac{1}{2}+\frac{1}{3}}{\frac{1}{4}+\frac{1}{6}}$$

Solution➤ The lowest number which can be used to clear all fractions is 12. Multiplying each term by 12 yields:

$$\frac{6+4}{3+2} = \frac{10}{5} = 2$$

Example➤ $$\frac{\frac{3}{4}+\frac{2}{3}}{1-\frac{1}{2}}$$

Solution➤ Again, multiply by 12.

$$\frac{9+8}{12-6} = \frac{17}{6} = 2\frac{5}{6}$$

PRACTICE EXERCISES II

Work out each problem in the space provided.

Add:

1. $12\frac{5}{6} + 2\frac{3}{8} + 21\frac{1}{4}$

2. $\frac{1}{2}+\frac{1}{3}+\frac{1}{4}+\frac{1}{5}+\frac{1}{6}$

Subtract:

3. $5\frac{3}{4}$ from $10\frac{1}{2}$

4. $17\frac{2}{3}$ from 50

5. $25\frac{3}{5}$ from $30\frac{9}{10}$

Multiply:

6. $5\frac{1}{4} \bullet 1\frac{5}{7}$

7. $\frac{3}{4} \bullet \frac{3}{4} \bullet \frac{3}{4}$

8. $12\frac{1}{2} \bullet 16$

Divide:

9. $\frac{1}{5} \div 5$

10. $5 \div \frac{1}{5}$

11. $3\frac{2}{3} \div 1\frac{5}{6}$

Simplify:

12. $\dfrac{\frac{5}{6} - \frac{1}{3}}{2 + \frac{1}{5}}$

13. $\dfrac{3 + \frac{1}{4}}{5 - \frac{1}{2}}$

SOLUTIONS TO PRACTICE EXERCISES II

1.
$$12\frac{5}{6}=\frac{20}{24}$$
$$2\frac{3}{8}=\frac{9}{24}$$
$$21\frac{1}{4}=\frac{6}{24}$$
$$35\quad\frac{35}{24}$$
$$36\frac{11}{24}$$

2.
$$\frac{1}{2}=\frac{30}{60}$$
$$\frac{1}{3}=\frac{20}{60}$$
$$\frac{1}{4}=\frac{15}{60}$$
$$\frac{1}{5}=\frac{12}{60}$$
$$\frac{1}{6}=\frac{10}{60}$$
$$\frac{87}{60}=1\frac{27}{60}=1\frac{9}{20}$$

3.
$$10\frac{1}{2}=9\frac{3}{2}=9\frac{6}{4}$$
$$-5\frac{3}{4}$$
$$4\frac{3}{4}$$

4.
$$\overset{49}{\cancel{50}}\frac{3}{3}$$
$$17\frac{2}{3}$$
$$32\frac{1}{3}$$

5.
$$30\frac{9}{10}$$
$$25\frac{3}{5}=\frac{6}{10}$$
$$5\frac{3}{10}$$

6.
$$\frac{\overset{3}{\cancel{21}}}{\cancel{4}}\bullet\frac{\overset{3}{\cancel{12}}}{\cancel{7}}=9$$

7.
$$\frac{3}{4}\bullet\frac{3}{4}\bullet\frac{3}{4}=\frac{27}{64}$$

8.
$$\frac{25}{\cancel{2}}\bullet\overset{8}{\cancel{16}}=200$$

9.
$$\frac{1}{5}\bullet\frac{1}{5}=\frac{1}{25}$$

10.
$$5\bullet5=25$$

11.
$$\frac{\cancel{11}}{\cancel{3}}\bullet\frac{\overset{2}{\cancel{6}}}{\cancel{11}}=2$$

12.
$$\frac{25-10}{60+6}=\frac{15}{66}=\frac{5}{22}$$

Each term was multiplied by 30.

13.
$$\frac{12+1}{20-2}=\frac{13}{18}$$

Each term was multiplied by 4.

III. Verbal Problems Involving Fractions

In dealing with fractional problems, you are usually dealing with a part of a whole.

Example➤ If a class consists of 12 boys and 18 girls, what part of the class is boys?

Solution➤ 12 out of 30 students, or $\frac{12}{30} = \frac{2}{5}$

Be careful to read all the questions carefully. Often a problem may refer to a part of a previously mentioned part.

Example➤ $\frac{1}{4}$ of this year's seniors have averages above 90. $\frac{1}{2}$ of the remainder have averages between 80 and 90. What part of the senior class have averages below 80?

Solution➤ $\frac{1}{4}$ have averages above 90.

$\frac{1}{2}$ of $\frac{3}{4}$ or $\frac{3}{8}$ have averages between 80 and 90.

$\frac{1}{4} + \frac{3}{8}$ or $\frac{5}{8}$ have averages above 80.

Therefore, $\frac{3}{8}$ of the class have averages below 80.

When a problem can easily be translated into an algebraic equation, remember that algebra is a very useful tool.

Example➤ 14 is $\frac{2}{3}$ of what number?

Solution➤ $14 = \frac{2}{3}x$

Multiply each side by $\frac{3}{2}$

$21 = x$

If a problem is given with letters in place of numbers, the same reasoning must be used as if numbers were given. If you are not sure how to proceed, replace the letters with numbers to determine the steps that must be taken.

Example➤ If John has p hours of homework and has worked for r hours, what part of his homework is yet to be done?

Solution➤ If John had 5 hours of homework and had worked for 3 hours, you would first find he had 5–3 hours, or 2 hours, yet to do. This represents $\frac{2}{5}$ of his work. Using letters, his remaining work is represented by $\frac{p-r}{p}$.

PRACTICE EXERCISES III

Work out each problem. Circle the letter that appears before your answer.

1. A team played 30 games of which it won 24. What part of the games played did it lose?

   (A) $\frac{4}{5}$ (B) $\frac{1}{4}$ (C) $\frac{1}{5}$ (D) $\frac{3}{4}$ (E) $\frac{2}{3}$

2. If a man's weekly salary is $\$X$ and he saves $\$Y$, what part of his weekly salary does he spend?

   (A) $\frac{X}{Y}$ (B) $\frac{X-Y}{X}$ (C) $\frac{X-Y}{Y}$ (D) $\frac{Y-X}{X}$ (E) $\frac{Y-X}{Y}$

3. What part of an hour elapses between 11:50 A.M. and 12:14 P.M.?

   (A) $\frac{2}{5}$ (B) $\frac{7}{30}$ (C) $\frac{17}{30}$ (D) $\frac{1}{6}$ (E) $\frac{1}{4}$

4. One-half of the employees of Acme Co. earn salaries above \$18,000 annually. One-third of the remainder earn salaries between \$15,000 and \$18,000. What part of the staff earns below \$15,000?

   (A) $\frac{1}{6}$ (B) $\frac{2}{3}$ (C) $\frac{1}{2}$ (D) $\frac{1}{10}$ (E) $\frac{1}{3}$

5. David received his allowance on Sunday. He spends $\frac{1}{4}$ of his allowance on Monday and $\frac{2}{3}$ of the remainder on Tuesday. What part of his allowance is left for the rest of the week?

   (A) $\frac{1}{3}$ (B) $\frac{1}{12}$ (C) $\frac{1}{4}$ (D) $\frac{1}{2}$ (E) $\frac{4}{7}$

6. 12 is $\frac{3}{4}$ of what number?

   (A) 16 (B) 9 (C) 36 (D) 20 (E) 15

7. A piece of fabric is cut into three sections so that the first is three times as long as the second and the second section is three times as long as the third. What part of the entire piece is the smallest section?

   (A) $\frac{1}{12}$ (B) $\frac{1}{9}$ (C) $\frac{1}{3}$ (D) $\frac{1}{7}$ (E) $\frac{1}{13}$

8. What part of a gallon is one quart?

   (A) $\frac{1}{2}$ (B) $\frac{1}{4}$ (C) $\frac{2}{3}$ (D) $\frac{1}{3}$ (E) $\frac{1}{5}$

9. A factory employs M men and W women. What part of its employees are women?

   (A) $\frac{W}{M}$ (B) $\frac{M+W}{W}$ (C) $\frac{W}{M-W}$ (D) $\frac{W}{M+W}$ (E) W

10. A motion was passed by a vote of 5 : 3. What part of the votes cast were in favor of the motion?

    (A) $\frac{5}{8}$ (B) $\frac{5}{3}$ (C) $\frac{3}{5}$ (D) $\frac{2}{5}$ (E) $\frac{3}{8}$

11. If the ratio of $x : y$ is $9 : 7$, what is the value of $x + y$?

(A) 2 (B) 14 (C) 16 (D) 63 (E) It cannot be determined from the information given.

12. In a certain class the ratio of men to women is 3 : 5. If the class has 24 people in it, how many are women?

(A) 9 (B) 12 (C) 15 (D) 18 (E) 21

13. If the ratio of men to women in a class is 3 : 5 and the class contains 24 people, how many additional men would have to enroll to make the ratio of men to women 1 : 1?

(A) 3 (B) 6 (C) 9 (D) 12 (E) 15

14. If x is $\frac{2}{3}$ of y and y is $\frac{3}{4}$ of z, what is the ratio of $z : x$?

(A) 1 : 2 (B) 1 : 1 (C) 2 : 1 (D) 3 : 2 (E) 4 : 3

15. What fraction of 8 tons is 1,000 lbs?

(A) $\frac{1}{32}$ (B) $\frac{1}{16}$ (C) $\frac{1}{8}$ (D) $\frac{8}{1}$ (E) $\frac{16}{1}$

SOLUTIONS TO PRACTICE EXERCISES III

1. **(C)** The team lost 6 games out of 30. $\frac{6}{30} = \frac{1}{5}$.

2. **(B)** The man spends $X–Y$ out of X. $\frac{X-Y}{X}$

3. **(A)** 10 minutes elapse by noon, and another 14 after noon, making a total of 24 minutes. There are 60 minutes in an hour. $\frac{24}{60} = \frac{2}{5}$

4. **(E)** One-half earn over $18,000. One-third of the other $\frac{1}{2}$, or $\frac{1}{6}$, earn between $15,000 and $18,000. This accounts for $\frac{1}{2} + \frac{1}{6}$, or $\frac{3}{6} + \frac{1}{6} = \frac{4}{6} = \frac{2}{3}$ of the staff, leaving $\frac{1}{3}$ to earn below $15,000.

5. **(C)** David spends $\frac{1}{4}$ on Monday and $\frac{2}{3}$ of the other $\frac{3}{4}$, or $\frac{1}{2}$, on Tuesday, leaving only $\frac{1}{4}$ for the rest of the week.

6. **(A)** $12 = \frac{3}{4}x$. Multiply each side by $\frac{4}{3}$.
$16 = x$

7. **(E)** Let the third or shortest section $= x$. Then the second section $= 3x$, and the first section $= 9x$. The entire piece of fabric is then $13x$, and the shortest piece represents $\frac{x}{13x}$ or $\frac{1}{13}$ of the entire piece.

8. **(B)** There are four quarts in one gallon.

9. **(D)** The factory employs $M + W$ people, out of which W are women.

10. **(A)** For every 5 votes in favor, 3 were cast against. 5 out of every 8 votes cast were in favor of the motion.

11. **(E)** Remember, a ratio is a fraction. If x is 18 and y is 14, the ratio $x : y$ is $9 : 7$, but $x + y$ is 32. The point of this problem is that x and y can take on *many* possible values, just as long as the ratio $9 : 7$ is preserved. Given the multiplicity of possible values, it is not possible here to establish *one* definite value for the sum of x and y.

12. **(C)** The ratio of women to the total number of people is $5 : 8$. We can set up a proportion. If $\frac{5}{8} = \frac{x}{24}$, then $x = 15$.

13. **(B)** From the previous problem we know that the class contains 15 women and 9 men. In order to have the same number of men and women, 6 additional men would have to enroll.

14. **(C)** There are several ways to attack this problem. If x is $\frac{2}{3}$ of y then y is $\frac{3}{2}$ of x. If y is $\frac{3}{4}$ of z then z is $\frac{4}{3}$ of y. Therefore, y is $\frac{3}{2}x$ and z is $2x$. The ratio of $z : x$ is $2 : 1$. You could also plug in a real number and solve. If x is 2, figure out what y and z would be. y would be 3 and z would be 4, so the ratio of z to x is $2 : 1$.

15. **(B)** A ton contains 2,000 pounds. So the fraction would be $\frac{1{,}000}{16{,}000}$, which is $\frac{1}{16}$.

IV. Variation

Two quantities are said to vary directly if they change in the same direction. As one increases, the other increases.

For example, the amount owed to the milkman varies directly with the number of quarts of milk purchased. The amount of sugar needed in a recipe varies directly with the amount of butter used. The number of inches between two cities on a map varies directly with the number of miles between the cities.

Whenever two quantities vary directly, a problem can be solved by using a proportion. However, be very careful to compare the same units, in the same order in both fractions.

Example➤ If a two-ounce package of peanuts costs 20¢, what is the cost of a pound of peanuts?

Solution➤ Here you are comparing cents with ounces, so $\frac{20}{2} = \frac{x}{16}$

In solving a proportion, it is easiest to cross-multiply, remembering that the product of the means (the second and third terms of a proportion) is equal to the product of the extremes (the first and last terms of a proportion).

$2x = 320$

$x = 160$

Remember that the original units were cents, so the cost is $1.60.

When two fractions are equal, as in a proportion, it is sometimes easier to see what change has taken place in the given numerator or denominator and then to apply the same change to the missing term. In keeping fractions equal, the change will always involve multiplying or dividing by a constant. In the previous example, the denominator was changed from 2 to 16. This involved multiplication by 8; therefore, the numerator (20) must also be multiplied by 8, giving 160 as an answer without any written work necessary. Since time is a very important factor in this type of examination, shoutcuts such as this could be critical.

Example➤ If a truck can carry *m* pounds of coal, how many trucks are needed to carry *p* pounds of coal?

Solution➤ You are comparing trucks with pounds. This again is a direct variation, because the number of trucks increases as the number of pounds increases.

$$\frac{1}{m} = \frac{x}{p}$$

$$mx = p$$

$$x = \frac{p}{m}$$

Two quantities are said to vary inversely if they change in opposite directions. As one increases, the other decreases.

For example, the number of workers hired to paint a house varies inversely with the number of days the job will take. A doctor's stock of flu vaccine varies inversely with the number of patients injected. The number of days a given supply of cat food lasts varies inversely with the number of cats being fed.

Whenever two quantities vary inversely, the problem is not solved by a proportion. Instead of dividing the first quantity by the second and setting the quotients equal, as in direct variation, multiply the first quantity by the second and set the products equal.

Example➤ If a case of cat food can feed 5 cats for 4 days, how long would it feed 8 cats?

Solution➤ Since this is a case of inverse variation (the more cats, the fewer days), multiply the number of cats by the number of days in each instance and set them equal.

$5 \cdot 4 = 8 \cdot x$

$20 = 8x$

$2\frac{1}{2} = x$

PRACTICE EXERCISES IV

Work out each problem. Circle the letter that appears before your answer.

1. If 60 feet of uniform wire weighs 80 pounds, what is the weight of 2 yards of the same wire?

   (A) $2\frac{2}{3}$ (B) 6 (C) 2400 (D) 120 (E) 8

2. A gear 50 inches in diameter turns a smaller gear 30 inches in diameter. If the larger gear makes 15 revolutions, how many revolutions does the smaller gear make in that time?

   (A) 9 (B) 12 (C) 20 (D) 25 (E) 30

3. If x men can do a job in h days, how long would y men take to do the same job?

   (A) $\frac{x}{h}$ (B) $\frac{xh}{y}$ (C) $\frac{hy}{x}$ (D) $\frac{xy}{h}$ (E) $\frac{x}{y}$

4. If a furnace uses 40 gallons of oil in a week, how many gallons, to the nearest gallon, does it use in 10 days?

   (A) 57 (B) 4 (C) 28 (D) 400 (E) 58

5. A recipe requires 13 ounces of sugar and 18 ounces of flour. If only 10 ounces of sugar are used, how much flour, to the nearest ounce, should be used?

   (A) 13 (B) 23 (C) 24 (D) 14 (E) 15

6. If a car can drive 25 miles on two gallons of gasoline, how many gallons will be needed for a trip of 150 miles?

   (A) 12 (B) 3 (C) 6 (D) 7 (E) 10

7. A school has enough bread to feed 30 children for 4 days. If 10 more children are added, how many days will the bread last?

   (A) $5\frac{1}{3}$ (B) $1\frac{1}{3}$ (C) $2\frac{2}{3}$ (D) 12 (E) 3

8. At c cents per pound, what is the cost of a ounces of salami?

   (A) $\frac{c}{a}$ (B) $\frac{a}{c}$ (C) ac (D) $\frac{ac}{16}$ (E) $\frac{16c}{a}$

9. If 3 miles are equivalent to 4.83 kilometers, then 11.27 kilometers are equivalent to how many miles?

(A) $7\frac{1}{3}$ (B) $2\frac{1}{3}$ (C) 7 (D) 5 (E) $6\frac{1}{2}$

10. If p pencils cost d dollars, how many pencils can be bought for c cents?

(A) $\frac{100pc}{d}$ (B) $\frac{pc}{100d}$ (C) $\frac{pd}{c}$ (D) $\frac{pc}{d}$ (E) $\frac{cd}{p}$

SOLUTIONS TO PRACTICE EXERCISES IV

1. **(E)** You are comparing *feet* with pounds. The more feet the more pounds. This is DIRECT. Remember to change yards to feet:

$$\frac{60}{80} = \frac{6}{x}$$
$$60x = 480$$
$$x = 8$$

2. **(D)** The larger a gear, the fewer times it revolves in a given period of time. This is INVERSE.

$$50 \bullet 15 = 30 \bullet x$$
$$750 = 30x$$
$$25 = x$$

3. **(B)** The more men, the fewer days. This is INVERSE.

$$x \bullet h = y \bullet ?$$
$$\frac{xh}{y} = ?$$

4. **(A)** The more days, the more oil. This is DIRECT. Remember to change the week to 7 days.

$$\frac{40}{7} = \frac{x}{10}$$
$$7x = 400$$
$$x = 57\frac{1}{7}$$

5. **(D)** The more sugar, the more flour. This is DIRECT.

$$\frac{13}{18} = \frac{10}{x}$$
$$13x = 180$$
$$x = 13\frac{11}{13}$$

6. **(A)** The more miles, the more gasoline. This is DIRECT.

$$\frac{25}{2} = \frac{150}{x}$$
$$25x = 300$$
$$x = 12$$

7. **(E)** The more children, the fewer days. This is INVERSE.

$$30 \bullet 4 = 40 \bullet x$$
$$120 = 40x$$
$$3 = x$$

8. **(D)** The more salami, the more it will cost. This is DIRECT. Remember to change the pound to 16 ounces.

$$\frac{c}{16} = \frac{x}{a}$$
$$x = \frac{ac}{16}$$

9. **(C)** The more miles, the more kilometers. This is DIRECT.

$$\frac{3}{4.83} = \frac{x}{11.27}$$
$$4.83x = 33.81$$
$$x = 7$$

10. **(B)** The more pencils, the more cost. This is DIRECT. Remember to change dollars to cents.

$$\frac{p}{100d} = \frac{x}{c}$$
$$x = \frac{pc}{100d}$$

V. Percent

"Percent" means "out of 100." If you understand this concept, it becomes very easy to change a percent to an equivalent decimal or fraction.

$$5\% = \frac{5}{100} = .05$$

$$2.6\% = \frac{2.6}{100} = .026$$

$$c\% = \frac{c}{100} = \frac{1}{100} \bullet c = .01c$$

$$\frac{1}{2}\% = \frac{\frac{1}{2}}{100} = \frac{1}{100} \bullet \frac{1}{2} = \frac{1}{100} \bullet .5 = .005$$

To change a % to a decimal, remove the % sign and divide by 100. This has the effect of moving the decimal point two places to the LEFT.

Example➤ $37\% = .37$

To change a decimal to a %, add the % sign and multiply by 100. This has the effect of moving the decimal point two places to the RIGHT.

Example➤ $.043 = 4.3\%$

To change a % to a fraction, remove the % sign and divide by 100. This has the effect of putting the % over 100 and reducing the resulting fraction.

Example➤ $75\% = \frac{75}{100} = \frac{3}{4}$

To change a fraction to a %, add the % sign and multiply by 100.

Example➤ $\frac{1}{8} = \frac{1}{8} \bullet 100\% = \frac{100}{8}\% = 12\frac{1}{2}\%$

Certain fractional equivalents of common percents occur frequently enough that they should be memorized. Learning the values in the following table will make your work with percent problems much easier.

PERCENT–FRACTION EQUIVALENT TABLE

$50\% = \frac{1}{2}$	$33\frac{1}{3}\% = \frac{1}{3}$	$12\frac{1}{2}\% = \frac{1}{8}$
$25\% = \frac{1}{4}$	$66\frac{2}{3}\% = \frac{2}{3}$	$37\frac{1}{2}\% = \frac{3}{8}$
$75\% = \frac{3}{4}$	$20\% = \frac{1}{5}$	$62\frac{1}{2}\% = \frac{5}{8}$
$10\% = \frac{1}{10}$	$40\% = \frac{2}{5}$	$87\frac{1}{2}\% = \frac{7}{8}$
$30\% = \frac{3}{10}$	$60\% = \frac{3}{5}$	$16\frac{2}{3}\% = \frac{1}{6}$
$70\% = \frac{7}{10}$	$80\% = \frac{4}{5}$	$83\frac{1}{3}\% = \frac{5}{6}$
$90\% = \frac{9}{10}$		

Most percentage problems can be solved by using the following proportion:

$$\frac{\%}{100} = \frac{\text{part}}{\text{whole}}$$

Although this method works, it often yields unnecessarily large numbers that are difficult to compute. Following are examples of the three basic types of percent problems and different methods for solving them.

A. To find a % of a number.

Example➤ Find 27% of 92.

PROPORTION METHOD

$$\frac{27}{100} = \frac{x}{92}$$

$$100x = 2484$$

$$x = 24.84$$

SHORT METHOD

Change the % to its decimal or fraction equivalent and multiply. Use fractions only when they are among the familiar ones given in the previous chart.

$$\begin{array}{r} 92 \\ .27 \\ \hline 644 \\ 184 \\ \hline 24.84 \end{array}$$

Example➤ Find $12\frac{1}{2}\%$ of 96.

PROPORTION METHOD

$$\frac{12\frac{1}{2}}{100} = \frac{x}{96}$$

$$100x = 1200$$

$$x = 12$$

DECIMAL METHOD

$$\begin{array}{r} 96 \\ .125 \\ \hline 480 \\ 192 \\ 96 \\ \hline 12.000 \end{array}$$

FRACTION METHOD

$$\frac{1}{8} \bullet 96 = 12$$

Which method is easiest? It really pays to memorize those fractional equivalents.

B. To find a number when a % of it is given.

Example➤ 7 is 5% of what number?

PROPORTION METHOD

$$\frac{5}{100} = \frac{7}{x}$$

$$5x = 700$$

$$x = 140$$

SHORTER METHOD

Translate the problem into an algebraic equation. In doing this, the % must be written as a fraction or decimal.

$$7 = .05x$$

$$700 = 5x$$

$$140 = x$$

Example➤ 20 is $33\frac{1}{3}\%$ of what number?

PROPORTION METHOD

$$\frac{33\frac{1}{3}}{100} = \frac{20}{x}$$

$$33\frac{1}{3}x = 2000$$

$$\frac{100}{3}x = 2000$$

$$100x = 6000$$

$$x = 60$$

SHORTER METHOD

$$20 = \frac{1}{3}x$$

$$60 = x$$

Just think of the time you save and the number of extra problems you will get to solve if you know that $33\frac{1}{3}\% = \frac{1}{3}$.

C. To find what % one number is of another.

Example➤ 90 is what % of 1500?

PROPORTION METHOD

$$\frac{x}{100} = \frac{90}{1500}$$
$$1500x = 9000$$
$$15x = 90$$
$$x = 6$$

SHORTER METHOD

Put the part over the whole. Reduce the fraction and multiply by 100.

$$\frac{90}{1500} = \frac{9}{150} = \frac{3}{50} \bullet 100 = 6$$

Example➤ 7 is what % of 35?

PROPORTION METHOD

$$\frac{x}{100} = \frac{7}{35}$$
$$35x = 700$$
$$x = 20$$

SHORTER METHOD

$$\frac{7}{35} = \frac{1}{5} = 20\%$$

Example➤ 18 is what % of 108?

PROPORTION METHOD

$$\frac{x}{100} = \frac{18}{108}$$
$$108x = 1800$$

Time-consuming long division is necessary to get:

$$x = 16\frac{2}{3}$$

SHORTER METHOD

$$\frac{18}{108} = \frac{9}{54} = \frac{1}{6} = 16\frac{2}{3}\%$$

Once again, if you know the fraction equivalents of common percents, computation can be done in a few seconds.

D. When the percentage involved is over 100, the same methods apply.

Example➤ Find 125% of 64.

PROPORTION METHOD

$$\frac{125}{100} = \frac{x}{64}$$
$$100x = 8.000$$
$$x = 80$$

DECIMAL METHOD

$$\begin{array}{r} 64 \\ 1.25 \\ \hline 320 \\ 128 \\ 64 \\ \hline 80.00 \end{array}$$

FRACTION METHOD

$$1\frac{1}{4} \bullet 64$$
$$\frac{5}{\not{4}} \bullet \overset{16}{\not{64}} = 80$$

Example➤ 36 is 150% of what number?

PROPORTION METHOD

$$\frac{150}{100} = \frac{36}{x}$$
$$150x = 3600$$
$$15x = 360$$
$$x = 24$$

DECIMAL METHOD

$$36 = 1.50x$$
$$360 = 15x$$
$$24 = x$$

FRACTION METHOD

$$36 = 1\frac{1}{2}x$$
$$36 = \frac{3}{2}x$$
$$72 = 3x$$
$$24 = x$$

Example➤ 60 is what % of 50?

PROPORTION METHOD

$$\frac{x}{100} = \frac{60}{50}$$
$$50x = 6000$$
$$5x = 600$$
$$x = 120$$

FRACTION METHOD

$$\frac{60}{50} = \frac{6}{5} = 1\frac{1}{5} = 120\%$$

PRACTICE EXERCISES V (PART 1)

Work out each problem. Circle the letter that appears before your answer.

1. Write .2% as a decimal.

   (A) .2 (B) .02 (C) .002 (D) 2 (E) 20

2. Write 3.4% as a fraction.

   (A) $\frac{34}{1000}$ (B) $\frac{34}{10}$ (C) $\frac{34}{100}$ (D) $\frac{340}{100}$ (E) $\frac{34}{10,000}$

3. Write $\frac{3}{4}$% as a decimal.

   (A) .75 (B) .075 (C) .0075 (D) .00075 (E) 7.5

4. Find 60% of 70.

   (A) 420 (B) 4.2 (C) $116\frac{2}{3}$ (D) 4200 (E) 42

5. What is 175% of 16?

   (A) $9\frac{1}{7}$ (B) 28 (C) 24 (D) 12 (E) 22

6. What percent of 40 is 16?

   (A) 20 (B) $2\frac{1}{2}$ (C) $33\frac{1}{3}$ (D) 250 (E) 40

7. What percent of 16 is 40?

(A) 20 (B) $2\frac{1}{2}$ (C) 200 (D) 250 (E) 40

8. $4 is 20% of what?

(A) $5 (B) $20 (C) $200 (D) $5 (E) $10

9. 12 is 150% of what number?

(A) 18 (B) 15 (C) 6 (D) 9 (E) 8

10. How many sixteenths are there in $87\frac{1}{2}\%$?

(A) 7 (B) 14 (C) 3.5 (D) 13 (E) 15

SOLUTIONS TO PRACTICE EXERCISES V (PART I)

1. **(C)** .2% = .002 The decimal point moves to the LEFT two places.

2. **(A)** $3.4\% = \frac{3.4}{100} = \frac{34}{1000}$

3. **(C)** $\frac{3}{4}\% = .75\% = .0075$

4. **(E)** $60\% = \frac{3}{5} \quad \frac{3}{5} \bullet 70 = 42$

5. **(B)** $175\% = 1\frac{3}{4} \quad \frac{7}{4} \bullet 16 = 28$

6. **(E)** $\frac{16}{40} = \frac{2}{5} = 40\%$

7. **(D)** $\frac{40}{16} = \frac{5}{2} = 2\frac{1}{2} = 250\%$

8. **(B)** $20\% = \frac{1}{5}$, so $4 = \frac{1}{5}x \quad 20 = x$

9. **(E)** $150\% = 1\frac{1}{2} \quad \frac{3}{2}x = 12 \quad 3x = 24 \quad x = 8$

10. **(B)** $87\frac{1}{2}\% = \frac{7}{8} = \frac{14}{16}$

VERBAL PROBLEMS INVOLVING PERCENT

Certain types of business situations are excellent applications of percent.

A. Percent of Increase or Decrease

The percent of increase or decrease is found by putting the amount of increase or decrease over the original amount and changing this fraction to a percent, as explained in a previous section.

Example➤ Over a five-year period, the enrollment at South High dropped from 1,000 students to 800. Find the percent of decrease.

Solution➤ $\frac{200}{1000} = \frac{20}{100} = 20\%$

Example➤ A company normally employs 100 people. During a slow spell, it fired 20% of its employees. By what % must it now increase its staff to return to full capacity?

Solution➤ $20\% = \frac{1}{5} \quad \frac{1}{5} \bullet 100 = 20$

The company now has $100 - 20 = 80$ employees. If it then increases by 20, the percent of increase is $\frac{20}{80} = \frac{1}{4}$, or 25%.

B. Discount

A discount is usually expressed as a percent of the marked price that will be deducted from the marked price to determine the sale price.

Example➤ Bill's Hardware offers a 20% discount on all appliances during a sale week. If they take advantage of the sale, how much must the Russells pay for a washing machine marked at $280?

LONG METHOD

$20\% = \frac{1}{5}$

$\frac{1}{5} \bullet 280 = \$56$ discount

$\$280 - \$56 = \$224$ sale price

The danger inherent in this method is that $56 is sure to be among the multiple-choice answers.

SHORTCUT METHOD

If there is a 20% discount, the Russells will pay 80% of the marked price.

$80\% = \frac{4}{5}$

$\frac{4}{5} \bullet 280 = \$224$ sale price.

Example➤ A store offers a television set marked at $340 less discounts of 10% and 5%. Another store offers the same set with a single discount of 15%. How much does the buyer save by buying at the better price?

Solution➤ In the first store, the initial discount means the buyer pays 90% or $\frac{9}{10}$ of 340, which is $306. The additional 5% discount means the buyer pays 95% of $306, or $290.70. Note that the second discount must be figured on the first sale price. Taking 5% of $306 is a smaller amount than taking the additional 5% off $340. The second store will therefore have a lower sale price. In the second store, the buyer will pay 85% of $340, or $289, making the price $1.70 less than in the first store.

C. Commission

Many salesmen earn money on a commission basis. In order to encourage sales, they are paid a percentage of the value of goods sold. This amount is called a commission.

Example➤ A salesperson at Brown's Department Store is paid \$80 per week in salary plus a 4% commission on all his sales. How much will that salesperson earn in a week in which he sells \$4,032 worth of merchandise?

Solution➤ Find 4% of \$4,032 and add this amount to \$80.

$$\begin{array}{r} 4032 \\ \underline{.04} \\ \$161.28 + \$80 = \$241.28 \end{array}$$

Example➤ Bill Olson delivers newspapers for a dealer and keeps 8% of all money collected. One month he was able to keep \$16. How much did he forward to the newspaper?

Solution➤ First, determine how much he collected by finding the number that 16 is 8% of.

$$16 = .08x$$
$$1600 = 8x$$
$$200 = x$$

If Bill collected \$200 and kept \$16, he gave the dealer \$200 – \$16, or \$184.

D. Taxes

Taxes are a percent of money spent or money earned.

Example➤ Noname County collects a 7% sales tax on automobiles. If the price of a car is \$8,532 before taxes, what will this car cost once sales tax is added in?

Solution➤ Find 7% of \$8,532 to determine tax and then add it to \$8,532. This can be done in one step by finding 107% of \$8,532.

$$\begin{array}{r} 8532 \\ \underline{1.07} \\ 59724 \\ \underline{85320} \\ \$9129.24 \end{array}$$

Example➤ If the tax rate in Anytown is \$3.10 per \$100, what is the annual real estate tax on a house assessed at \$47,200?

Solution➤ Annual tax = Tax rate × Assessed value

= (\$3.10/\$100)(\$47,200)

= (.031) (47,200)

= \$1463.20

PRACTICE EXERCISES V (PART 2)

Work out each problem. Circle the letter that appears before your answer.

1. A suit marked at \$80 is sold for \$68. What is the rate of discount?

   (A) 15% (B) 12% (C) $17\frac{11}{17}\%$ (D) 20% (E) 24%

2. What was the original price of a radio that sold for \$70 during a 20%-off sale?

   (A) \$84 (B) \$56 (C) \$87.50 (D) \$92 (E) \$90

3. How many dollars does a salesperson earn on a sale of s dollars at a commission of r%?

   (A) rs (B) $\frac{r}{s}$ (C) $100rs$ (D) $\frac{r}{100s}$ (E) $\frac{rs}{100}$

4. At a selling price of \$273, a refrigerator yields a 30% profit on the cost. What selling price will yield a 10% profit on the cost?

   (A) \$210 (B) \$231 (C) \$221 (D) \$235 (E) \$240

5. What single discount is equivalent to two successive discounts of 10% and 15%?

   (A) 25% (B) 24% (C) 24.5% (D) 23.5% (E) 22%

6. The net price of a certain article is \$306 after successive discounts of 15% and 10% off the marked price. What is the marked price?

   (A) \$234.09 (B) \$400 (C) \$382.50 (D) \$408 (E) None of these

7. If a merchant makes a profit of 20% based on the selling price of an article, what percent does the merchant make on the cost?

   (A) 20 (B) 40 (C) 25 (D) 80 (E) None of these

8. A certain radio costs a merchant \$72. At what price must the merchant sell this radio in order to make a profit of 20% of the selling price?

   (A) \$86.40 (B) \$92 (C) \$90 (D) \$144 (E) \$148

9. A baseball team has won 40 games out of 60 played. It has 32 more games to play. How many of these must the team win to make its record 75% for the season?

   (A) 26 (B) 29 (C) 28 (D) 30 (E) 32

10. If prices are reduced 25% and sales increase 20%, what is the net effect on gross receipts?

    (A) They increase by 5%.

    (B) They decrease by 5%.

    (C) They remain the same.

    (D) They increase by 10%.

    (E) They decrease by 10%.

11. A salesperson earns 5% on all sales between \$200 and \$600, and 8% on all sales over \$600. What is her commission in a week in which her sales total \$800?

(A) \$20 (B) \$46 (C) \$88 (D) \$36 (E) \$78

12. If the enrollment at State U. was 3,000 in 1965 and 12,000 in 1990, what was the percent of increase in enrollment?

(A) 125% (B) 25% (C) 300% (D)400% (E) 3%

13. If 6 students, representing $16\frac{2}{3}\%$ of the class, failed algebra, how many students passed the course?

(A) 48 (B) 36 (C) 42 (D) 30 (E) 32

14. If 95% of the residents of Coral Estates live in private homes and 40% of these live in air-conditioned homes, what percent of the residents of Coral Estates live in air-conditioned homes?

(A) 3% (B) 30% (C) 3.8% (D) 40% (E) 38%

15. A salesperson receives a salary of \$100 a week and a commission of 5% on all sales. What must be the amount of sales for a week in which the salesperson's total weekly income is \$360?

(A) \$6,200 (B) \$5,200 (C) \$2,600 (D) \$720 (E) \$560

SOLUTIONS TO PRACTICE EXERCISES V (PART 2)

1. **(A)** The amount of discount is \$12. Rate of discount is figured on the original price.

$$\frac{12}{80}=\frac{3}{20} \quad \frac{3}{20}\bullet 100=15\%$$

2. **(C)** \$70 represents 80% of the original price.

$$70=.80x$$
$$700=8x$$
$$\$87.50=x$$

3. **(E)** $r\%=\frac{r}{100}$

The commission is $\frac{r}{100}\bullet s=\frac{rs}{100}$

4. **(B)** \$273 represents 130% of the cost.

$$1.30x=273$$
$$13x=2730$$
$$x=\$210=\text{cost}$$

The new price will add 10% of cost, or \$21, for profit.
New price = \$231

5. **(D)** Work with a simple figure, such as 100.
First sale price is 90% of \$100, or \$90.
Final sale price is 85% of \$90, or \$76.50
Total discount is \$100 – \$76.50 = \$23.50
% of discount = $\frac{23.50}{100}$ or 23.5%

6. **(B)** If marked price = m, first sale price = $.85m$ and net price = $.90(.85m) = .765m$

$$.765m = 306$$
$$m = 400$$

In this case, it would be easy to work from the answer choices.
15% of \$400 is \$60, making a first sale price of \$340.
10% of this price is \$34, making the net price \$306.
Answers (A), (C), and (D) would not give a final answer in whole dollars.

7. **(C)** Use an easy amount of \$100 for the selling price. If the profit is 20% of the selling price, or \$20, the cost is \$80. Profit based on cost is $\frac{20}{80} = \frac{1}{4} = 25\%$.

8. **(C)** If the profit is to be 20% of the selling price, the cost must be 80% of the selling price.

$$72 = .80x$$
$$720 = 8x$$
$$90 = x$$

9. **(B)** The team must win 75%, or $\frac{3}{4}$, of the games played during the entire season. With 60 games played and 32 more to play, the team must win $\frac{3}{4}$ of 92 games in all. $\frac{3}{4} \bullet 92 = 69$. Since 40 games have already been won, the team must win 29 additional games.

10. **(E)** Let original price = p, and original sales = s. Therefore, original gross receipts = ps. Let new price = $.75p$, and new sales = $1.20s$. Therefore, new gross receipts = $.90ps$. Gross receipts are only 90% of what they were.

11. **(D)** 5% of sales between \$200 and \$600 is .05(400) = \$20. 8% of sales over \$600 is .08(200) = \$16. Total commission = \$20 + \$16 = \$36.

12. **(C)** Increase is 9,000. Percent of increase is figured on original. $\frac{9000}{3000} = 3 = 300\%$

13. **(D)** $16\frac{2}{3}\% = \frac{1}{6}$

$$6 = \frac{1}{6}x$$
$$36 = x$$

36 students in class. 6 failed. 30 passed.

14. **(E)** $40\% = \frac{2}{5}$

$\frac{2}{5}$ of $95\% = 38\%$

15. **(B)** Let s = sales

$$\$100 + .05s = \$360$$
$$.05s = 260$$
$$5s = 26{,}000$$
$$s = \$5{,}200$$

VI. Averages

The concept of average is familiar to most students. To find the average of n numbers, simply add the numbers and divide by n.

Example➤ Find the average of 32, 50, and 47.

Solution➤

$$\begin{array}{r} 32 \\ 50 \\ \underline{47} \\ 3\overline{)129} \\ 43 \end{array}$$

A more frequently encountered type of average problem will give the average and ask you to find a missing term.

Example➤ The average of three numbers is 43. If two of the numbers are 32 and 50, find the third number.

Solution➤ Using the definition of average, write the equation

$$\frac{32+50+x}{3} = 43$$

$$32+50+x = 129$$

$$82+x = 129$$

$$x = 47$$

Another concept to be understood is the weighted average.

Example➤ Andrea has four grades of 90 and two grades of 80 during the spring semester of calculus. What is her average in the course for this semester?

Solution➤

$$\begin{array}{r} 90 \\ 90 \\ 90 \\ 90 \\ 80 \\ \underline{80} \\ 6\overline{)520} \\ 86\frac{2}{3} \end{array} \qquad \text{or} \qquad \begin{array}{r} 90 \bullet 4 = 360 \\ 80 \bullet 2 = \underline{160} \\ 6\overline{)520} \\ 86\frac{2}{3} \end{array}$$

Be sure to understand that you cannot simply average 90 and 80, since there are more grades of 90 than 80.

The final concept of average that should be mastered is that of average rate. The average rate for a trip is the total distance covered, divided by the total time used.

Example➤ In driving from New York to Boston, Mr. Portney drove for 3 hours at 40 miles per hour and 1 hour at 48 miles per hour. What was his average rate for this portion of the trip?

Solution➤

$$\text{Average rate} = \frac{\text{Total distance}}{\text{Total time}}$$

$$\text{Average rate} = \frac{3(40)+1(48)}{3+1}$$

$$\text{Average rate} = \frac{168}{4} = 42 \text{ miles per hour}$$

Since more of the trip was driven at 40 mph than at 48 mph, the average should be closer to 40 than to 48, which it is. This will help you to check your answer, or to pick out the correct choice in a multiple-choice question.

It is very important to realize that the average of a group of positive numbers is always a fraction of the sum of the numbers based on the number of elements. Put in simpler terms: If there are five numbers in a set, then the average must be 20% or $\frac{1}{5}$ of the sum of the numbers. If there are three numbers in a set, the average of the three numbers must be $\frac{1}{3}$, or $33\frac{1}{3}\%$, of the sum.

Example➤ The average of 147, y, 193, and 287 is what percent of the sum of the four positive integers?

(A) 15
(B) 20
(C) 25
(D) 30
(E) It cannot be determined from the above information.

Solution➤ The correct answer is (C) 25%. It will not matter what number y is; the average of these four numbers will always be 25% of their sum.

PRACTICE EXERCISES VI

Work out each problem. Circle the letter that appears before your answer.

1. Dan had an average of 72 on his first four math tests. After taking the next test, his average dropped to 70. Which of the following is his most recent test grade?

   (A) 60 (B) 62 (C) 64 (D) 66 (E) 68

2. What is the average of $\sqrt{.64}$, .85, and $\frac{9}{10}$?

   (A) $\frac{21}{25}$ (B) 3.25 (C) 2.55 (D) 85% (E) $\frac{4}{5}$

3. The average of two numbers is XY. If the first number is Y, what is the other number?

   (A) $2XY - Y$ (B) $XY - 2Y$ (C) $2XY - X$ (D) X (E) $XY - Y$

4. 30 students had an average of X, while 20 students had an average of 80. What is the average for the entire group?

(A) $\frac{X+80}{50}$ (B) $\frac{X+80}{2}$ (C) $\frac{50}{X+80}$ (D) $\frac{3}{5}X+32$ (E) $\frac{30X+80}{50}$

5. What is the average of the first 15 positive integers?

(A) 7 (B) 7.5 (C) 8 (D) 8.5 (E) 9

6. A man travels a distance of 20 miles at 60 miles per hour and then returns over the same route at 40 miles per hour. What is his average rate for the round trip in miles per hour?

(A) 50 (B) 48 (C) 47 (D) 46 (E) 45

7. A number p equals $\frac{3}{2}$ the average of 10, 12, and q. What is q in terms of p?

(A) $\frac{2}{3}p-22$ (B) $\frac{4}{3}p-22$ (C) $2p-22$ (D) $\frac{1}{2}p+11$ (E) $\frac{9}{2}p-22$

8. Susan has an average of 86 in three examinations. What grade must she receive on her next test to raise her average to 88?

(A) 94 (B) 90 (C) 92 (D) 100 (E) 96

9. The heights of the five starters on Redwood High's basketball team are 5'11", 6'3", 6', 6'6", and 6'2". The average height of these players is

(A) 6'1" (B) 6'2" (C) 6'3" (D) 6'4" (E) 6'5"

10. What is the average of all numbers from 1 to 100 that end in 2?

(A) 46 (B) 47 (C) 48 (D) 50 (E) None of these

SOLUTIONS TO PRACTICE EXERCISES VI

1. **(B)** $\frac{4(72)+x}{5}=70$

$$288+x=350$$
$$x=62$$

2. **(D)** In order to average these three numbers, they should all be expressed as decimals.

$$\sqrt{.64}=.8$$
$$.85=.85$$
$$\frac{9}{10}=.9$$

$$\text{Average}=\frac{.8+.85+.9}{3}=\frac{2.55}{3}=.85$$

This is equal to 85%.

3. **(A)** $\frac{Y+x}{2}=XY$
$Y+x=2XY$
$x=2XY-Y$

4. **(D)** $\frac{30(X)+20(80)}{50}=\text{Average}$

$\frac{30X+1600}{50}=\frac{3X+160}{5}=\frac{3}{5}X+32$

5. **(C)** Positive integers begin with 1.

$$\frac{1+2+3+4+5+6+7+8+9+10+11+12+13+14+15}{15}$$

Since these numbers are evenly spaced, the average will be the middle number, 8.

6. **(B)** Average rate = $\frac{\text{Total distance}}{\text{Total time}}$

Total distance = 20 + 20 = 40
Since time = $\frac{\text{distance}}{\text{rate}}$, time for first part of trip is $\frac{20}{60}$, or $\frac{1}{3}$ hour, while time for the second part of trip is $\frac{20}{40}$, or $\frac{1}{2}$ hour.
Total time = $\frac{1}{3}+\frac{1}{2}$, or $\frac{5}{6}$ hour.
Average rate $\frac{40}{\frac{5}{6}}=40 \bullet \frac{6}{5}=48$ mph

7. **(C)** $p=\frac{3}{2}\left(\frac{10+12+q}{3}\right)$
$p=\frac{10+12+q}{2}$
$2p=22+q$

$2p-22=q$

8. **(A)** $\frac{3(86)+x}{4}=88$
$258+x=352$
$x=94$

9. **(B)** 5'11"
6'3"
6'
6'6"
6'2"
29'22" = 5)30'10"
6'2"

10. **(B)** $\frac{2+12+22+32+42+52+62+72+82+92}{10}$

Since these numbers are equally spaced, the average is the middle number. However, since there is an even number of addends, the average will be halfway between the middle two. Halfway between 42 and 52 is 47.

VII. Signed Numbers and Equations

COMPUTATION

Basic to successful work in algebra is the ability to compute accurately with signed numbers.

Addition: To add signed numbers with the same sign, add the magnitudes of the numbers and keep the same sign. To add signed numbers with different signs, subtract the magnitudes of the numbers and use the sign of the number with the greater magnitude.

Subtraction: Change the sign of the number being subtracted and follow the rules for addition.

Multiplication: If there are an odd number of negative signs, the product is negative. An even number of negative signs gives a positive product.

Division: If the signs are the same, the quotient is positive. If the signs are different, the quotient is negative.

PRACTICE EXERCISES VII (PART 1)

Work out each problem. Circle the letter that appears before your answer.

1. When +3 is added to –5, the sum is

   (A) –8 (B) +8 (C) –2 (D) +2 (E) –15

2. When –4 and –5 are added, the sum is

   (A) –9 (B) +9 (C) –1 (D) +1 (E) +20

3. Subtract $\begin{array}{r} +3 \\ \underline{-6} \end{array}$

   (A) –3 (B) +3 (C) +18 (D) –9 (E) +9

4. When –5 is subtracted from +10 the result is

   (A) +5 (B) +15 (C) –5 (D) –15 (E) –50

5. (–6)(–3) equals

   (A) –18 (B) +18 (C) +2 (D) –9 (E) +9

6. The product of $(-6)(+\frac{1}{2})(-10)$ is

   (A) $-15\frac{1}{2}$ (B) $+15\frac{1}{2}$ (C) –30 (D) +30 (E) +120

7. When the product of (–4) and (+3) is divided by (–2), the quotient is

   (A) $\frac{1}{2}$ (B) $3\frac{1}{2}$ (C) 6 (D) $-\frac{1}{2}$ (E) –6

SOLUTIONS TO PRACTICE EXERCISES VII (PART I)

1. **(C)** In adding numbers with opposite signs, subtract their magnitudes $(5 - 3 = 2)$ and use the sign of the number with the greater magnitude (negative).

2. **(A)** In adding numbers with the same sign, add their magnitudes $(4 + 5 = 9)$ and keep the same sign.

3. **(E)** Change the sign of the bottom number and follow the rules for addition.

$$\begin{array}{r} +\ 3 \\ +\ \ominus\ 6 \\ \hline +\ 9 \end{array}$$

4. **(B)** Change the sign of the bottom number and follow the rules for addition.

$$\begin{array}{r} +\ 10 \\ +\ \ominus\ 5 \\ \hline +\ 15 \end{array}$$

5. **(B)** The product of two negative numbers is a positive number.

6. **(D)** The product of an even number of negative numbers is positive.

$$\overset{3}{\cancel{(6)}}\left(\frac{1}{\cancel{2}}\right)(10) = 30$$

7. **(C)** $(-4)(+3) = -12$ Dividing a negative number by a negative number gives a positive quotient.

$$\frac{-12}{-2} = +6$$

LINEAR EQUATIONS

The next step in gaining confidence in algebra is mastering linear equations. Whether an equation involves numbers or only letters, the basic steps are the same.

1. If there are fractions or decimals, remove them by multiplication.
2. Collect all terms containing the unknown for which you are solving on the same side of the equation. Remember that whenever a term crosses the equal sign from one side of the equation to the other, it must pay a toll. That is, it must change its sign.
3. Determine the coefficient of the unknown by combining similar terms or factoring when terms cannot be combined.
4. Divide both sides of the equation by this coefficient.

Example➤ Solve for x: $5x - 3 = 3x + 5$

Solution➤

$$2x = 8$$
$$x = 4$$

Example➤ Solve for x: $ax - b = cx + d$

Solution➤

$$ax - cx = b + d$$
$$x(a - c) = b + d$$
$$x = \frac{b+d}{a-c}$$

Example➤ Solve for x: $\frac{3}{4}x + 2 = \frac{2}{3}x + 3$

Solution➤ Multiply by 12: $9x + 24 = 8x + 36$

$$x = 12$$

Example➤ Solve for x: $.7x + .04 = 2.49$

Solution➤ Multiply by 100: $70x + 4 = 249$

$$70x = 245$$
$$x = 3.5$$

In solving equations with two unknowns, it is necessary to work with two equations simultaneously. The object is to eliminate one of the two unknowns, and solve the resulting single unknown equation.

Example➤ Solve for x: $2x - 4y = 12$

$$3x + 5y = 14$$

Solution➤ Multiply the first equation by 5:

$$10x - 20y = 10$$

Multiply the second equation by 4:

$$12x + 20y = 56$$

Since the y terms now have the same numerical coefficients, but with opposite signs, you can eliminate them by adding the two equations. If they had the same signs, you would eliminate them by subtracting the equations.

Add the equations:
$$\begin{aligned} 10x - 20y &= 10 \\ 12x + 20y &= 56 \\ \hline 22x \quad &= 66 \\ x &= 3 \end{aligned}$$

Since you were only asked to solve for x, stop here. If you were asked to solve for both x and y, you would now substitute 3 for x in either equation and solve the resulting equation for y.

$$\begin{aligned} 3(3) + 5y &= 14 \\ 9 + 5y &= 14 \\ 5y &= 5 \\ y &= 1 \end{aligned}$$

Example➤ Solve for x: $ax + by = c$
$dx + ey = f$

Solution➤ Multiply the first equation by e:
$$aex + bey = ce$$

Multiply the second equation by b:
$$bdx + bey = bf$$

Since the y terms now have the same coefficient, with the same sign, eliminate these terms by subtracting the two equations.

$$\begin{aligned} aex + bey &= ce \\ -(bdx + bey &= bf) \\ \hline aex - bdx &= ce - bf \end{aligned}$$

Factor to determine the coefficient of x.
$$x(ae - bd) = ce - bf$$

Divide by the coefficient of x.
$$x = \frac{ce - bf}{ae - bd}$$

PRACTICE EXERCISES VII (PART 2)

Work out each problem. Circle the letter that appears before your answer.

1. If $5x + 6 = 10$, then x equals

   (A) $\frac{16}{5}$ (B) $\frac{5}{16}$ (C) $-\frac{5}{4}$ (D) $\frac{4}{5}$ (E) $\frac{5}{4}$

2. Solve for x: $ax = bx + c, a \neq b$

   (A) $\frac{b+c}{a}$ (B) $\frac{c}{a-b}$ (C) $\frac{c}{b-a}$ (D) $\frac{a-b}{c}$ (E) $\frac{c}{a+b}$

3. Solve for k: $\frac{k}{3} + \frac{k}{4} = 1$

   (A) $\frac{11}{8}$ (B) $\frac{8}{11}$ (C) $\frac{7}{12}$ (D) $\frac{12}{7}$ (E) $\frac{1}{7}$

4. If $x + y = 8p$ and $x - y = 6q$, then x is

   (A) $7pq$ (B) $4p + 3q$ (C) pq (D) $4p - 3q$ (E) $8p + 6q$

5. If $7x = 3x + 12$, then $2x + 5 =$

   (A) 10 (B) 11 (C) 12 (D) 13 (E) 14

6. In the equation $y = x^2 + rx - 3$, for what value of r will $y = 11$ when $x = 2$?

   (A) 6 (B) 5 (C) 4 (D) $3\frac{1}{2}$ (E) 0

7. If $1 + \frac{1}{t} = \frac{t+1}{t}$, what does t equal?

   (A) +1 only (B) +1 or –1 only (C) +1 or +2 only
   (D) No values (E) All values except 0

8. If $.23m = .069$, then $m =$

   (A) .003 (B) .03 (C) .3 (D) 3 (E) 30

9. If $35rt + 8 = 42rt$, then $rt =$

   (A) $\frac{8}{7}$ (B) $\frac{8}{87}$ (C) $\frac{7}{8}$ (D) $\frac{87}{8}$ (E) $-\frac{8}{7}$

10. For what values of n is $n + 5$ equal to $n - 5$?

    (A) No value (B) 0 (C) All negative values
    (D) All positive values (E) All values

SOLUTIONS TO PRACTICE EXERCISES VII (PART 2)

1. **(D)** $5x = 4 \quad x = \frac{4}{5}$

2. **(B)** $ax - bx = c \quad x(a - b) = c \quad x = \frac{c}{a - b}$

3. **(D)** Multiply by 12: $4k + 3k = 12$

$$7k = 12$$
$$k = \frac{12}{7}$$

4. **(B)** Add equations to eliminate *y*:

$$\begin{aligned} x + y &= 8p \\ x - y &= 6q \\ \hline 2x \quad &= 8p + 6q \end{aligned}$$

Divide by 2: $x = 4p + 3q$

5. **(B)** Solve for *x*: $4x = 12$

$$x = 3$$
$$2x + 5 = 2(3) + 5 = 11$$

6. **(B)** Substitute given values: $11 = 4 + 2r - 3$

$$10 = 2r$$
$$r = 5$$

7. **(E)** Multiply by *t*: $t + 1 = t + 1$
This is an identity and is therefore true for all values. However, since *t* was a denominator in the given equation, *t* may not equal 0, because you can never divide by 0.

8. **(C)** Multiply by 100 to make coefficient an integer.
$23x = 6.9$
$x = .3$

9. **(A)** Even though this equation has two unknowns, you are asked to solve for *rt*, which may be treated as a single unknown.
$8 = 7rt$
$\frac{8}{7} = rt$

10. **(A)** There is no number such that when 5 is added, you get the same result as when 5 is subtracted. Do not confuse choices (A) and (B). Choice (B) would mean that the number 0 satisfies the equation, which it does not.

EXPONENTS

Exponents are simply a form of mathematical shorthand. In the examples below, x is called the base and the numerical superscript is called the exponent.

$x^3 = x$ times x times x
$x^2 = x$ times x
$x^1 = x$
$x^0 = 1$

Manipulating exponents:

1. When multiplying exponents with the same base, add the exponents.
2. When dividing exponents with the same base, subtract the exponents.
3. When an exponent is raised to another exponent, multiply the exponents.

Example➤

1. x^2 times $x^3 = x^{2+3} = x^5$

   x^5 times $x^4 = x^{5+4} = x^9$

2. $\dfrac{x^6}{x^2} = x^{6-2} = x^4$

   $\dfrac{x^{10}}{x^3} = x^{10-3} = x^7$

3. $(x^2)^3 = x^{(2)(3)} = x^6$

   $(x^3y^5)^2 = x^{(3)(2)}y^{(5)(2)} = x^6y^{10}$

Common pitfalls:

1. When the exponent is an even number, there are two values for the variable, one positive and one negative.

Example➤ $x^2 = 25$. x could be positive 5 or negative 5.

2. Unless it is stated explicitly or implicitly, you must consider zero as a possible value for the variable.

Example➤ Is x^4 always greater than x^2? No, if x is zero, then x^4 and x^2 are equal.

3. Fractions between zero and one present a small problem: The larger the exponent for a given fraction, the smaller the actual value of the fraction.

Example➤ Which is greater, $(\frac{37}{73})$ or $(\frac{37}{73})^2$? The correct answer is $(\frac{37}{73})$. $(\frac{37}{73})$ is almost $\frac{1}{2}$, while $(\frac{37}{73})^2$ is about $\frac{1}{4}$.

PRACTICE EXERCISES VII (PART 3)

Work out the problem. Circle the letter that appears before your answer.

1. If x and y are not equal to 0, then $x^{12}y^6$ must be

I. Positive II. Negative III. An integer IV. A mixed fraction

(A) I only (B) II only (C) III only (D) IV only (E) I and III

2. $(x^2y^3)^4 =$

(A) x^6y^7 (B) x^8y^{12} (C) $x^{12}y^8$ (D) x^2y (E) x^6y^9

3. $\dfrac{x^{16}y^6}{x^4y^2} =$

(A) $x^{20}y^8$ (B) x^4y^3 (C) x^5y^6 (D) $x^{12}y^3$ (E) $x^{12}y^4$

4. If $x^4 = 16$ and $y^2 = 36$, then the *maximum* possible value for $x - y$ is

(A) –20 (B) 20 (C) –4 (D) 6 (E) 8

5. $p^8 \times q^4 \times p^4 \times q^8 =$

(A) $p^{12}q^{12}$ (B) p^4q^4 (C) $p^{32}q^{32}$ (D) $p^{64}q^{64}$ (E) $p^{16}q^{16}$

SOLUTIONS TO PRACTICE EXERCISES VII (PART 3)

1. **(A)** If x and y are not 0, then the even exponents would force x^{12} and y^6 to be positive.
2. **(B)** To raise a power to a power, multiply the exponents. $x^{(2)(4)}y^{(3)(4)} = x^8y^{12}$
3. **(E)** All fractions are implied division. When dividing terms with a common base and different exponents, subtract the exponents. 16 – 4 = 12 and 6 – 2 = 4.
4. **(E)** x could be positive 2 or negative 2. y could be positive 6 or negative 6. The four possible values for $x - y$ are as follows:

$$2 - 6 = -4$$
$$2 - (-6) = 8$$
$$-2 - 6 = -8$$
$$-2 - (-6) = 4$$

The maximum value would be 8.

5. **(A)** The multiplication signs do not change the fact that this is the multiplication of terms with a common base and different exponents. Solve this kind of problem by adding the exponents. $p^{8+4} \times q^{4+8} = p^{12}q^{12}$

QUADRATIC EQUATIONS

In solving quadratic equations, remember that there will always be two roots, even though these roots may be equal. A complete quadratic equation is of the form $ax^2 + bx + c = 0$ and, in the SAT, can always be solved by factoring.

Example➤ $x^2 + 7x + 12 = 0$

Solution➤ $(x \quad)(x \quad) = 0$

The last term of the equation is positive; therefore, both factors must have the same sign, since the last two terms multiply to a positive product. The middle term is also positive; therefore, both factors must be positive, since they also add to a positive sum.

$(x + 4)(x + 3) = 0$

If the product of two factors is 0, each factor may be set equal to 0, yielding the values for x of -4 or -3

Example➤ $x^2 + 7x - 18 = 0$

Solution➤ $(x \quad)(x \quad) = 0$

Now you are looking for two numbers with a product of –18; therefore, they must have opposite signs. To yield +7 as a middle coefficient, the numbers must be +9 and –2.

$(x + 9)(x - 2) = 0$

This equation gives the roots –9 and +2.

Incomplete quadratic equations are those in which b or c is equal to 0.

Example➤ $x^2 - 16 = 0$

Solution➤ $x^2 = 16$

$x = \pm 4$ Remember, there must be 2 roots.

Example➤ $4x^2 - 9 = 0$

Solution➤

$$4x^2 = 9$$
$$x^2 = \frac{9}{4}$$
$$x = \pm\frac{3}{2}$$

Example➤ $x^2 + 4x = 0$

Solution➤ Never divide through an equation by the unknown, as this would yield an equation of lower degree having fewer roots than the original equation. Always factor this type of equation.

$x(x + 4) = 0$

The roots are 0 and –4.

Example➤ $4x^2 - 9x = 0$

Solution➤ $x(4x - 9) = 0$

The roots are 0 and $\frac{9}{4}$.

In solving equations containing radicals, always get the radical alone on one side of the equation; then square both sides to remove the radical and solve. Remember that all solutions to radical equations must be checked, as squaring both sides may sometimes result in extraneous roots.

Example➤ $\sqrt{x+5} = 7$

Solution➤

$$x + 5 = 49$$
$$x = 44$$

Checking, we have $\sqrt{49} = 7$, which is true.

Example➤ $\sqrt{x} = -6$

Solution➤ $x = 36$

Checking, we have $\sqrt{36} = -6$, which is not true, as the radical sign means the positive, or principal, square root only. $\sqrt{36} = 6$, not -6, and therefore this equation has no solution.

Example➤ $\sqrt{x^2 + 6} - 3 = 6$

Solution➤

$$\sqrt{x^2 + 6} - 3 = x$$
$$\sqrt{x^2 + 6} = x + 3$$
$$x^2 + 6 = x^2 + 6x + 9$$
$$6 = 6x + 9$$
$$-3 = 6x$$
$$-\frac{1}{2} = x$$

Checking, we have

$$\sqrt{6\frac{1}{4}} - 3 = -\frac{1}{2}$$
$$\sqrt{\frac{25}{4}} - 3 = -\frac{1}{2}$$
$$\frac{5}{2} - 3 = -\frac{1}{2}$$
$$2\frac{1}{2} - 3 = -\frac{1}{2}$$
$$-\frac{1}{2} = -\frac{1}{2}$$

This is a true statement. Therefore, $-\frac{1}{2}$ is a true root.

PRACTICE EXERCISES VII (PART 4)

Work out the problem. Circle the letter that appears before your answer.

1. Solve for x: $x^2 - 2x - 15 = 0$

   (A) $+5$ or -3 (B) -5 or $+3$ (C) -5 or -3 (D) $+5$ or $+3$ (E) None of these

2. Solve for x: $x^2 + 12 = 8x$

   (A) $+6$ or -2 (B) -6 or $+2$ (C) -6 or -2 (D) $+6$ or $+2$ (E) None of these

3. Solve for x: $4x^2 = 12$

   (A) $\sqrt{3}$ (B) 3 or -3 (C) $\sqrt{3}$ or $-\sqrt{3}$ (D) $\sqrt{3}$ or $\sqrt{-3}$ (E) 9 or -9

4. Solve for x: $3x^2 = 4x$

   (A) $\frac{4}{3}$ (B) $\frac{4}{3}$ or 0 (C) $-\frac{4}{3}$ or 0 (D) $\frac{4}{3}$ or $-\frac{4}{3}$ (E) None of these

5. Solve for x: $x^2 + 7 - 2 = x - 1$

   (A) No values (B) $\frac{1}{3}$ (C) $-\frac{1}{3}$ (D) -3 (E) 3

SOLUTIONS TO PRACTICE EXERCISES VII (PART 4)

1. **(A)** $(x-5)(x+3) = 0$

   $x = 5$ or -3

2. **(D)** $x^2 - 8x + 12 = 0$

   $(x-6)(x-2) = 0$

   $x = 6$ or 2

3. **(C)** $x^2 = 3$

   $x = \pm\sqrt{3}$

4. **(B)** $3x^2 - 4x = 0$

   $x(3x-4) = 0$

   $x = 0$ or $\frac{4}{3}$

5. **(E)** $\sqrt{x^2 + 7} = x + 1$

   $x^2 + 7 = x^2 + 2x + 1$

   $6 = 2x$

   $x = 3$

   Checking: $\sqrt{16} - 2 = 3 - 1$

   $4 - 2 = 3 - 1$

   $2 = 2$

VIII. Literal Expressions

Many students who can compute easily with numbers become confused when they work with letters. The computational processes are exactly the same. Just think of how you would do the problem with numbers and do exactly the same thing with letters.

Example➤ Find the number of inches in 2 feet 5 inches.

Solution➤ Since there are 12 inches in a foot, multiply 2 feet by 12 to change it to 24 inches and then add 5 more inches, giving an answer of 29 inches.

Example➤ Find the number of inches in f feet and i inches.

Solution➤ Doing exactly as you did above, multiply f by 12, giving $12f$ inches, and add i more inches, giving an answer of $12f + i$ inches.

Example➤ A telephone call from New York to Chicago costs 85 cents for the first three minutes and 21 cents for each additional minute. Find the cost of an eight minute call at this rate.

Solution➤ The first three minutes cost 85 cents. There are five additional minutes above the first three. These five are billed at 21 cents each, for a cost of \$1.05. The total cost is \$1.90.

Example➤ A telephone call costs c cents for the first three minutes and d cents for each additional minute. Find the cost of a call which lasts m minutes if $m > 3$.

Solution➤ The first three minutes cost c cents. The number of *additional* minutes is $(m - 3)$. These are billed at d cents each, for a cost of $d(m - 3)$ or $dm - 3d$. Thus the total cost is $c + dm - 3d$. Remember that the first three minutes have been paid for in the basic charge; therefore, you must subtract 3 from the total number of minutes to find the *additional* minutes.

PRACTICE EXERCISES VIII

Work out each problem. Circle the letter that appears before your answer.

1. David had d dollars. After a shopping trip, he returned with c cents. How many cents did he spend?

   (A) $d - c$ (B) $c - d$ (C) $100d - c$ (D) $100c - d$ (E) $d - 100c$

2. How many ounces are there in p pounds and q ounces?

   (A) $\frac{p}{16} + q$ (B) pq (C) $p + 16q$ (D) $p + q$ (E) $16p + q$

3. How many passengers can be seated on a plane with r rows, if each row consists of d double seats and t triple seats?

   (A) rdt (B) $rd + rt$ (C) $2dr + 3tr$ (D) $3dr + 2tr$ (E) $rd + t$

4. How many dimes are there in $4x - 1$ cents?

   (A) $40x - 10$ (B) $\frac{2}{5}x - \frac{1}{10}$ (C) $40x - 1$ (D) $4x - 1$ (E) $20x - 5$

5. If u represents the tens' digit of a certain number and t represents the units' digit, then the number with the digits reversed can be represented by

(A) $10t + u$ (B) $10u + t$ (C) tu (D) ut (E) $t + u$

6. Joe spent k cents of his allowance and has r cents left. What was his allowance in dollars?

(A) $k + r$ (B) $k - r$ (C) $100(k + r)$ (D) $\frac{k+r}{100}$ (E) $100kr$

7. If p pounds of potatoes cost \$$K$, find the cost (in cents) of one pound of potatoes.

(A) $\frac{K}{p}$ (B) $\frac{K}{100p}$ (C) $\frac{p}{K}$ (D) $\frac{100K}{p}$ (E) $\frac{100p}{K}$

8. Mr. Rabner rents a car for d days. He pays m dollars per day for each of the first 7 days, and half that rate for each additional day. Find the total charge if $d > 7$.

(A) $m + 2m(d - 7)$ (B) $m + \frac{m}{2}(d - 7)$ (C) $7m + \frac{m}{2}(d - 7)$

(D) $7m + \frac{md}{2}$ (E) $7m + 2md$

9. A salesperson earns 900 dollars per month plus a 10% commission on all sales over 1,000 dollars. One month she sells R dollars' worth of merchandise $(R > 1{,}000)$. How many dollars does she earn that month?

(A) $800 + .1R$ (B) $800 - .1R$ (C) $900 + .1R$ (D) $900 - .1R$ (E) $810 + .1R$

10. Elliot's allowance was just raised to k dollars per week. He gets a raise of c dollars per week every 2 years. How much will his allowance be per week y years from now?

(A) $k + cy$ (B) $k + 2cy$ (C) $k + \frac{1}{2}cy$ (D) $k + 2c$ (E) $ky + 2c$

SOLUTIONS TO PRACTICE EXERCISES VIII

1. **(C)** Since the answer is to be in cents, change d dollars to cents by multiplying it by 100 and subtract from that the c cents he spent.

2. **(E)** There are 16 ounces in a pound. Therefore, you must multiply p pounds by 16 to change it to ounces and then add q more ounces.

3. **(C)** Each double seat holds 2 people, so d double seats hold $2d$ people. Each triple seat holds 3 people, so t triple seats hold $3t$ people. Therefore, each row holds $2d + 3t$ people. There are r rows, so multiply the number of people in each row by r.

4. **(B)** To change cents to dimes, divide by 10.

$$\frac{4x-1}{10} = \frac{4}{10}x - \frac{1}{10} = \frac{2}{5}x - \frac{1}{10}$$

5. **(A)** The original number would be $10u + t$. The number with the digits reversed would be $10t + u$.

6. **(D)** Joe's allowance was $k + r$ cents. To change this to dollars, divide by 100.

7. **(D)** This can be solved by using a proportion. Remember to change \$*K* to 100*K* cents.

$$\frac{p}{100k} = \frac{1}{x}$$
$$px = 100k$$
$$x = \frac{100k}{p}$$

8. **(C)** He pays *m* dollars for each of 7 days, for a total of 7*m* dollars. Then he pays $\frac{1}{2}m$ dollars for $(d-7)$ days, for a cost of $\frac{m}{2}(d-7)$.
The total charge is $7m + \frac{m}{2}(d-7)$.

9. **(A)** She gets a commission of 10% of (*R* – 1000), or .1(*R* –1000), which is .1*R* – 100. Adding this to 900 yields 800 + .1*R*.

10. **(C)** Since he gets a raise only every 2 years, in *y* years, he will get $\frac{1}{2}y$ raises. Each raise is *c* dollars, so with $\frac{1}{2}y$ raises his present allowance will be increased by $c(\frac{1}{2}y)$.

IX. Roots and Radicals

Rules for addition and subtraction of radicals are much the same as for addition and subtraction of letters. Radicals must be exactly the same if they are to be added or subtracted, and they merely serve as a label that does not change.

Example➤ $4\sqrt{2} + 3\sqrt{2} = 7\sqrt{2}$

Example➤ $\sqrt{2} + 2\sqrt{3}$ cannot be added.

Example➤ $\sqrt{2} + \sqrt{3}$ cannot be added.

Sometimes, when radicals are not the same, simplification of one or more radicals will make them the same. Remember that radicals are simplified by removing any perfect square factors.

Example➤ $\sqrt{27} + \sqrt{75}$

Solution➤ $\sqrt{9 \cdot 3} + \sqrt{25 \cdot 3}$

$3\sqrt{3} + 5\sqrt{3} = 8\sqrt{3}$

In multiplication and division, radicals are again treated the same way as letters. They are factors and must be handled as such.

Example➤ $\sqrt{2} \cdot \sqrt{3} = \sqrt{6}$

Example➤ $2\sqrt{5} \cdot 3\sqrt{7} = 6\sqrt{35}$

Example➤ $(2\sqrt{3})^2 = 2\sqrt{3} \cdot 2\sqrt{3} = 4 \cdot 3 = 12$

Example➤ $\dfrac{\sqrt{75}}{\sqrt{3}} = \sqrt{25} = 5$

Example➤ $\dfrac{10\sqrt{3}}{5\sqrt{3}} = 2$

In simplifying radicals that contain a sum or difference under the radical sign, add or subtract first then take the square root.

Example➤ $\sqrt{\dfrac{x^2}{9} + \dfrac{x^2}{16}}$

Solution➤ $\sqrt{\dfrac{16x^2 + 9x^2}{144}} = \sqrt{\dfrac{25x^2}{144}} = \dfrac{5x}{12}$

If you take the square root of each term before combining, you would have $\frac{x}{3} + \frac{x}{4}$, or $\frac{7x}{12}$, which is clearly not the same answer. Remember that $\sqrt{25}$ is 5. However, if you write that $\sqrt{25}$ as $\sqrt{16+9}$, you cannot say it is 4 + 3 or 7. *Always* combine the quantities within a radical sign into a single term before taking the square root.

To find the number of digits in the square root of a number, remember that the first step in the procedure for finding a square root is to pair off the numbers in the radical sign on either side of the decimal point. Every pair of numbers under the radical gives one number in the answer.

Example➤ $\sqrt{\overset{\frown}{32}\ \overset{\frown}{14}\ \overset{\frown}{89}}$ will have 3 digits.

If you are given several choices for $\sqrt{321489}$, look first for a three-digit number. If there is only one among the answers, that is the one you should select. If there is more than one, you will have to reason further. If a number ends in 9, such as in the example, its square root would have to end in a digit that would end in 9 when multiplied by itself. This might be either 3 or 7. Only one of these would probably be among the choices, as very few SAT problems call for much computation. This is an aptitude test, which tests your ability to reason.

Example➤ The square root of 61504 is exactly

(A) 245

(B) 246

(C) 247

(D) 248

(E) 249

Solution➤ The only answer among the choices which will end in 4 when squared is (D).

PRACTICE EXERCISES IX

Work out each problem. Circle the letter that appears before your answer.

1. What is the sum of $\sqrt{12} + \sqrt{27}$?

   (A) $\sqrt{29}$ (B) $3\sqrt{5}$ (C) $13\sqrt{3}$ (D) $5\sqrt{3}$ (E) $7\sqrt{3}$

2. What is the difference between $\sqrt{150}$ and $\sqrt{54}$?

   (A) $2\sqrt{6}$ (B) $16\sqrt{6}$ (C) $\sqrt{96}$ (D) $6\sqrt{2}$ (E) $8\sqrt{6}$

3. What is the product of $\sqrt{18x}$ and $\sqrt{2x}$?

   (A) $6x^2$ (B) $6x$ (C) $36x$ (D) $36x^2$ (E) $6\sqrt{x}$

4. If $\frac{1}{x} = \sqrt{.25}$, what does x equal?

   (A) 2 (B) .5 (C) .2 (D) 20 (E) 5

5. If $n = 3.14$, find n^3 to the nearest hundredth.

   (A) 3.10 (B) 30.96 (C) 309.59 (D) 3095.91 (E) 30959.14

6. The square root of 24336 is exactly

(A) 152 (B) 153 (C) 155 (D) 156 (E) 158

7. The square root of 306.25 is exactly

(A) .175 (B) 1.75 (C) 17.5 (D) 175 (E) 1750

8. Divide $6\sqrt{45}$ by $3\sqrt{5}$.

(A) 9 (B) 4 (C) 54 (D) 15 (E) 6

9. $\sqrt{\frac{y^2}{25}+\frac{y^2}{16}} =$

(A) $\frac{2y}{9}$ (B) $\frac{9y}{20}$ (C) $\frac{y}{9}$ (D) $\frac{y\sqrt{41}}{20}$ (E) $\frac{41y}{20}$

10. $\sqrt{a^2+b^2}$ is equal to

(A) $a+b$ (B) $a-b$ (C) $(a+b)(a-b)$ (D) $\sqrt{a^2}+\sqrt{b^2}$ (E) None of these

SOLUTIONS TO PRACTICE EXERCISES IX

1. **(D)** $\sqrt{12}=\sqrt{4}\sqrt{3}=2\sqrt{3}$

$\sqrt{27}=\sqrt{9}\sqrt{3}=3\sqrt{3}$

$2\sqrt{3}+3\sqrt{3}=5\sqrt{3}$

2. **(A)** $\sqrt{150} = \sqrt{25}\ \sqrt{6} = 5\sqrt{6}$

$\sqrt{54} = \sqrt{9}\ \sqrt{6} = 3\sqrt{6}$

$5\sqrt{6}-3\sqrt{6} = 2\sqrt{6}$

3. **(B)** $\sqrt{18x} \bullet \sqrt{2x} = \sqrt{36x^2} = 6x$

4. **(A)** $\sqrt{.25} = .5$

$\frac{1}{x} = .5$

$1 = 5x$

$10 = 5x$

$2 = x$

5. **(B)** $(3)^3$ would be 27, so the answer should be a little larger than 27.

6. **(D)** The only answer that will end in 6 when squared is (D).

7. **(C)** The square root of this number must have two digits before the decimal point.

8. **(E)** $\frac{6\sqrt{45}}{3\sqrt{5}} = 2\sqrt{9} = 2 \cdot 3 = 6$

9. **(D)** $\sqrt{\frac{y^2}{25} + \frac{y^2}{16}} = \sqrt{\frac{16y^2 + 25y^2}{400}}$

$= \sqrt{\frac{41y^2}{400}} = \frac{y\sqrt{41}}{20}$

10. **(E)** Never take the square root of a sum separately. There is no way to simplify $\sqrt{a^2 + b^2}$.

X. Factoring and Algebraic Fractions

To reduce algebraic fractions, you must divide the numerator and denominator by the same factor, just as you do in arithmetic. You can never cancel terms, as this would be adding or subtracting the same number from the numerator and denominator, which changes the value of the fraction. When you reduce $\frac{6}{8}$ to $\frac{3}{4}$, you are really saying that $\frac{6}{8} = \frac{2 \cdot 3}{2 \cdot 4}$ and then dividing numerator and denominator by 2. You do not say $\frac{6}{8} = \frac{3+3}{3+5}$ and then say $\frac{6}{8} = \frac{3}{5}$. This is faulty reasoning in algebra as well. If you have $\frac{6t}{8t}$, you can divide numerator and denominator by $2t$, giving $\frac{3}{4}$ as an answer. However, if you have $\frac{6+t}{8+t}$, you can do no more, as there is no factor that divides into the *entire* numerator as well as the *entire* denominator. Cancelling terms is one of the most frequent student errors. Don't get caught! Be careful!

Example➤ Reduce $\frac{3x^2 + 6x}{4x^3 + 8x^2}$ to its lowest terms.

Solution➤ Factor the numerator and denominator to get $\frac{3x(x+2)}{4x^2(x+2)}$. The factors common to both numerator and denominator are x and $(x + 2)$. Divide these out to arrive at the correct answer of $\frac{3}{4x}$.

To add or subtract fractions, work with a common denominator and the same shortcuts used in arithmetic.

Example➤ Find the sum of $\frac{1}{a}$ and $\frac{1}{b}$.

Solution➤ Remember to add the two cross products and put the sum over the denominator product. $\frac{b+a}{ab}$.

Example➤ Add: $\frac{2n}{3} + \frac{3n}{2}$

Solution➤ $\frac{4n+9n}{6} = \frac{13n}{6}$

To multiply or divide fractions, cancel a factor common to any numerator and any denominator. Always remember to invert the fraction following the division sign. Where exponents are involved, they are added in multiplication and subtracted in division.

Example➤ Find the product of $\frac{a^3}{b^2}$ and $\frac{b^3}{a^2}$.

Solution➤ Divide a^2 into the first numerator and second denominator, giving $\frac{a}{b^2} \cdot \frac{b^3}{1}$. Then divide b^2 into the first denominator and second numerator, giving $\frac{a}{1} \cdot \frac{b}{1}$. Finally, multiply the resulting fractions, giving an answer of ab.

Example➤ Divide $\frac{6x^2y}{5}$ by $2x^3$.

Solution➤ $\frac{6x^2y}{5} \cdot \frac{1}{2x^3}$. Divide the first numerator and second denominator by $2x^2$, giving $\frac{3y}{5} \cdot \frac{1}{x}$. Multiply the resulting fractions to get $\frac{3y}{5x}$.

Complex algebraic fractions are simplified by the same methods used in arithmetic. Multiply *each term* of the complex fraction by the lowest quantity that will eliminate the fraction within the fraction.

Example➤ $\dfrac{\frac{1}{a} + \frac{1}{b}}{ab}$

Solution➤ Multiply *each term* by ab, giving $\frac{b+a}{a^2b^2}$. Since no reduction beyond this is possible, $\frac{b+a}{a^2b^2}$ is the final answer.

Certain types of problems may involve factoring the difference of two squares. If an expression consists of two terms that are perfect squares separated by a minus sign, the expression can always be factored into two binomials, with one containing the sum of the square roots and the other the difference of the square roots. This can be expressed by the identity $a^2 - b^2 = (a+b)(a-b)$.

Example➤ If $x^2 - y^2 = 100$ and $x + y = 2$, find $x - y$.

Solution➤ Since $x^2 - y^2$ can be written as $(x+y)(x-y)$, these two factors must multiply to 100. If one is 2, the other must be 50.

Example➤ If $a + b = \frac{1}{2}$ and $a - b = \frac{1}{4}$, find $a^2 - b^2$.

Solution➤ $a^2 - b^2$ is the product of $(a+b)$ and $(a-b)$. Therefore, $a^2 - b^2$ must be equal to $\frac{1}{8}$.

PRACTICE EXERCISES X

Work out the problem. Circle the letter that appears before your answer.

1. Find the sum of $\frac{n}{6} + \frac{2n}{5}$.

   (A) $\frac{13n}{30}$ (B) $17n$ (C) $\frac{3n}{30}$ (D) $\frac{17n}{30}$ (E) $\frac{3n}{11}$

2. Combine into a single fraction: $1 - \frac{x}{y}$

   (A) $\frac{1-x}{y}$ (B) $\frac{y-x}{y}$ (C) $\frac{x-y}{y}$ (D) $\frac{1-x}{1-y}$ (E) $\frac{y-x}{xy}$

3. Divide $\frac{x-y}{x+y}$ by $\frac{y-x}{y+x}$

   (A) 1 (B) –1 (C) $\frac{(x-y)^2}{(x+y)^2}$ (D) $-\frac{(x-y)^2}{(x+y)^2}$ (E) 0

4. Simplify: $\dfrac{1+\frac{1}{x}}{\frac{y}{x}}$

   (A) $\frac{x+1}{y}$ (B) $\frac{x+1}{x}$ (C) $\frac{x+1}{xy}$ (D) $\frac{x^2+1}{xy}$ (E) $\frac{y+1}{y}$

5. Find an expression equivalent to $\left(\frac{2x^2}{y}\right)^3$.

   (A) $\frac{8x^5}{3y}$ (B) $\frac{6x^6}{y^3}$ (C) $\frac{6x^5}{y^3}$ (D) $\frac{8x^5}{y^3}$ (E) $\frac{8x^6}{y^3}$

6. Simplify: $\dfrac{\frac{1}{x}+\frac{1}{y}}{3}$

   (A) $\frac{3x+3y}{xy}$ (B) $\frac{3xy}{x+y}$ (C) $\frac{xy}{3}$ (D) $\frac{x+y}{3xy}$ (E) $\frac{x+y}{3}$

7. $\frac{1}{a} + \frac{1}{b} = 7$ and $\frac{1}{a} - \frac{1}{b} = 3$. Find $\frac{1}{a^2} - \frac{1}{b^2}$.

   (A) 10 (B) 7 (C) 3 (D) 21 (E) 4

8. If $(a-b)^2 = 64$ and $ab = 3$, find $a^2 + b^2$.

   (A) 61 (B) 67 (C) 70 (D) 58 (E) 69

9. If $c + d = 12$ and $c^2 - d^2 = 48$, then $c - d =$

(A) 4 (B) 36 (C) 60 (D) 5 (E) 3

10. The trinomial $x^2 + x - 20$ is exactly divisible by

(A) $x - 5$ (B) $x + 4$ (C) $x - 10$ (D) $x - 4$ (E) $x - 2$

SOLUTIONS TO PRACTICE EXERCISES X

1. **(D)** $\frac{n}{6} + \frac{2n}{5} = \frac{5n + 12n}{30} = \frac{17n}{30}$

2. **(B)** $\frac{1}{1} - \frac{x}{y} = \frac{y - x}{y}$

3. **(B)** $\frac{x - y}{x + y} \bullet \frac{y + x}{y - x}$

Since addition is commutative, you can cancel $x + y$ with $y + x$, as they are the same quantity. However, subtraction is not commutative, so you cannot cancel $x - y$ with $y - x$, as they are *not* the same quantity. Change the form of $y - x$ by factoring out a –1. Thus, $y - x = (-1)(x - y)$. In this form, you can cancel $x - y$, leaving an answer of $\frac{1}{-1}$, or –1.

4. **(A)** Multiply every term of the fraction by *x*, giving $\frac{x+1}{y}$.

5. **(E)** $\frac{2x^2}{y} \bullet \frac{2x^2}{y} \bullet \frac{2x^2}{y} = \frac{8x^6}{y^3}$

6. **(D)** Multiply every term of the fraction by *xy*, giving $\frac{y+x}{3xy}$.

7. **(D)** $\frac{1}{a^2} - \frac{1}{b^2}$ is equivalent to $\left(\frac{1}{a} + \frac{1}{b}\right)\left(\frac{1}{a} - \frac{1}{b}\right)$.
Therefore, multiply 7 by 3 for an answer of 21.

8. **(C)** $(a - b)^2$ is $(a - b)(a - b)$, or $a^2 - 2ab + b^2$, which is equal to 64.

$a^2 - 2ab + b^2 = 64$

$a^2 + b^2 = 64 + 2ab$

Since $ab = 3$, $2ab = 6$, and $a^2 + b^2 = 64 + 6$, or 70.

9. **(A)** $c^2 - d^2 = (c + d)(c - d)$

$48 = 12(c - d)$

$4 = (c - d)$

10. **(D)** The factors of $x^2 + x - 20$ are $(x + 5)$ and $(x - 4)$.

XI. Problem-Solving in Algebra

In solving verbal problems, the most important technique is to read accurately. Be sure you understand exactly what you are asked to find. Once this is done, represent what you are looking for algebraically. Write an equation that translates the words of the problem to the symbols of mathematics. Then solve that equation by the techniques reviewed previously.

This section reviews the types of algebra problems most frequently encountered on the SAT. Thoroughly familiarizing yourself with the problems that follow will help you to translate and solve all kinds of verbal problems.

Coin Problems

In solving coin problems, it is best to change the value of all monies involved to cents before writing an equation. Thus, the number of nickels must be multiplied by 5 to give their value in cents; dimes must be multiplied by 10; quarters by 25; half dollars by 50; and dollars by 100.

Example➤ Richard has \$3.50 consisting of nickels and dimes. If he has 5 more dimes than nickels, how many dimes does he have?

Solution➤

Let x = the number of nickels

$x + 5$ = the number of dimes

$5x$ = the value of the nickels in cents

$10x + 50$ = the value of the dimes in cents

350 = the value of the money he has in cents

$5x + 10x + 50 = 350$

$15x = 300$

$x = 20$

He has 20 nickels and 25 dimes.

In a problem such as this, you can be sure that 20 would be among the multiple-choice answers. You must be sure to read carefully what you are asked to find and then continue until you have found the quantity sought.

Consecutive Integer Problems

Consecutive integers are one apart and can be represented by $x, x + 1, x + 2$, etc. Consecutive even or odd integers are two apart and can be represented by $x, x + 2, x + 4$, etc.

Example➤ Three consecutive odd integers have a sum of 33. Find the average of these integers.

Solution➤ Represent the integers as x, $x + 2$ and $x + 4$. Write an equation indicating the sum is 33.

$3x + 6 = 33$

$3x = 27$

$x = 9$

The integers are 9, 11, and 13. In the case of evenly spaced numbers such as these, the average is the middle number, 11. Since the sum of the three numbers was given originally, all you really had to do was to divide this sum by 3 to find the average, without ever knowing what the numbers were.

Age Problems

Problems of this type usually involve a comparison of ages at the present time, several years from now, or several years ago. A person's age x years from now is found by adding x to his present age. A person's age x years ago is found by subtracting x from his present age.

Example➤ Michelle was 12 years old y years ago. Represent her age b years from now.

Solution➤ Her present age is $12 + y$. In b years, her age will be $12 + y + b$.

Interest Problems

The annual amount of interest paid on an investment is found by multiplying the amount of principal invested by the rate (percent) of interest paid.

Principal • Rate = Interest income

Example➤ A student invests $4,000, part at 6% and part at 7%. The income from these investments in one year is $250. Find the amount invested at 7%.

Solution➤ Represent each investment.

Let x = the amount invested at 7%. Always try to let x represent what you are looking for.

$4000 - x$ = the amount invested at 6%

$.07x$ = the income from the 7% investment

$.06(4000 - x)$ = the income from the 6% investment

$$\begin{aligned} .07x + .06(4000 - x) &= 250 \\ 7x + 6(4000 - x) &= 25000 \\ 7x + 24000 - 6x &= 25000 \\ x &= 1000 \end{aligned}$$

The student invested $1,000 at 7%.

Fraction Problems

A fraction is a ratio between two numbers. If the value of a fraction is $\frac{2}{3}$, it does not mean the numerator must be 2 and the denominator 3. The numerator and denominator could be 4 and 6, respectively, or 1 and 1.5, or 30 and 45, or any of infinitely many other combinations. All you know is that the ratio of numerator to denominator will be 2 : 3. Therefore, the numerator may be represented by $2x$, the denominator by $3x$, and the fraction by $\frac{2x}{3x}$.

Example➤ The value of a fraction is $\frac{3}{4}$. If 3 is subtracted from the numerator and added to the denominator, the value of the fraction is $\frac{2}{5}$. Find the original fraction.

Solution➤ Let the original fraction be represented by $\frac{3x}{4x}$. If 3 is subtracted from the numerator and added to the denominator, the new fraction becomes $\frac{3x-3}{4x+3}$.

The value of the new fraction is $\frac{2}{5}$.

$$\frac{3x - 3}{4x + 3} = \frac{2}{5}$$

Cross multiply to eliminate fractions.

$$15x - 15 = 8x + 6$$
$$7x = 21$$
$$x = 3$$

Therefore, the original fraction is

$$\frac{3x}{4x} = \frac{9}{12}$$

Mixture Problems

There are two kinds of mixture problems with which you should be familiar. The first is sometimes referred to as dry mixture, in which dry ingredients of different values are mixed. Also solved by the same method are problems such as those dealing with tickets at different prices. In solving this type of problem, it is best to organize the data in a chart of three rows and three columns, labeled as illustrated in the following example.

Example➤ A dealer wishes to mix 20 pounds of nuts selling for 45 cents per pound with some more expensive nuts selling for 60 cents per pound to make a mixture that will sell for 50 cents per pound. How many pounds of the more expensive nuts should be used?

Solution➤

	No. of lbs. •	Price/lb. =	Total Value
Original	20	.45	.45(20)
Added	x	.60	.60(x)
Mixture	20 + x	.50	.50(20 + x)

The value of the original nuts plus the value of the added nuts must equal the value of the mixture. Almost all mixture problems require an equation that comes from adding the final column:

$.45(20) + .60(x) = .50(20 + x)$

Multiply by 100 to remove the decimals.

$$45(20) + 60(x) = 50(20 + x)$$
$$900 + 60(x) = 1000 + 50x$$
$$10x = 100$$
$$x = 10$$

The dealer should use 10 lbs. of 60-cent nuts.

The second type of mixture problem concerns chemical mixtures. These problems deal with percents rather than prices and with amounts instead of values.

Example➤ How much water must be added to 20 gallons of a solution that is 30% alcohol to dilute it to a solution that is only 25% alcohol?

Solution➤

	No. of gals. •	% alcohol =	Amt. alcohol
Original	20	.30	.30(20)
Added	x	0	0
Mixture	20 + x	.25	.25(20 + x)

Note that the percent of alcohol in water is 0. Had you added pure alcohol to strengthen the solution, the percent would have to be 100. The equation again comes from the last column. The amount of alcohol added (none in this case) plus the amount you had to start with must equal the amount of alcohol in the new solution.

$$.30(20) = .25(20 + x)$$
$$30(20) = 25(20 + x)$$
$$600 = 500 + 25x$$
$$100 = 25x$$
$$x = 4$$

Motion Problems

The fundamental relationship in all motion problems is that of Rate • Time = Distance. The problems at the level of this examination usually derive their equations from relationships concerning distance. Most problems fall into one of three types:

1. *Motion in opposite directions.* When two objects start at the same time and move in opposite directions, or when two objects start at points at a given distance apart and move toward each other until they meet, the total distance traveled equals the sum of the distances traveled by each object.

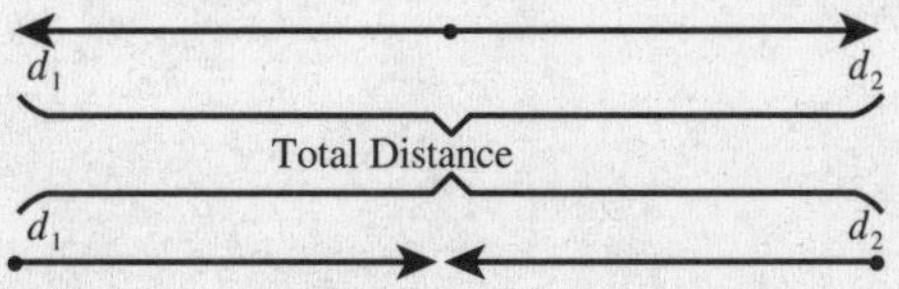

In either of the above cases, $d_1 + d_2$ = Total distance.

2. *Motion in the same direction.* This type of problem is sometimes called the "catch-up" problem. Two objects leave the same place at different times and different rates, but one "catches up" to the other. In such a case, the two distances must be equal.

3. *Round Trip.* In this type of problem, the rate going is usually different from the rate returning. The times are also different. But if you go somewhere and then return to the starting point, the distances must be the same.

To solve any motion problem, it is helpful to organize the data in a box with columns for rate, time, and distance. Use a separate line for each moving object. Remember that if the rate is given in *miles per hour*, the time must be in *hours* and the distance in *miles*.

Example➤ Two cars leave a restaurant at 1 P.M., with one car traveling east at 60 miles per hour and the other west at 40 miles per hour along a straight highway. At what time will they be 350 miles apart?

Solution➤

	Rate •	Time =	Distance
Eastbound	60	x	$60x$
Westbound	40	x	$40x$

Notice that the time is unknown, since it is necessary to find the number of hours traveled. However, since the cars start at the same time and stop when they are 350 miles apart, their times are the same.

$$60x + 40x = 350$$

$$100x = 350$$

$$x = 3\frac{1}{2}$$

In $3\frac{1}{2}$ hours, it will be 4:30 P.M.

Example➤ Gloria leaves home for school, riding her bicycle at a rate of 12 mph. Twenty minutes after she leaves, her mother sees Gloria's English paper on her bed and leaves to bring it to her. If her mother drives at 36 mph, how far must she drive before she reaches Gloria?

Solution➤

	Rate	•	Time	=	Distance
Gloria	12		x		$12x$
Mother	36		$x - \frac{1}{3}$		$36\left(x - \frac{1}{3}\right)$

Notice that 20 minutes has been changed to $\frac{1}{3}$ of an hour. In this problem the times are not equal, but the distances are.

$$12x = 36\left(x - \frac{1}{3}\right)$$

$$12x = 36x - 12$$

$$12 = 24x$$

$$x = \frac{1}{2}$$

If Gloria rode for $\frac{1}{2}$ hour at 12 mph, the distance covered was 6 miles.

Example➤ Judy leaves home at 11 A.M. and rides to Mary's house to return Mary's bicycle. She travels at 12 miles per hour and arrives at 11:30 A.M. She turns right around and walks home. How fast does she walk if she returns home at 1 P.M.?

Solution➤

	Rate	•	Time	=	Distance
Going	12		$\frac{1}{2}$		6
Return	x		$1\frac{1}{2}$		$\frac{3}{2}x$

The distances are equal.

$$6 = \frac{3}{2}x$$

$$12 = 3x$$

$$x = 4$$

She walked at 4 mph.

Work Problems

In most work problems, a complete job is broken into several parts, each representing a fractional part of the entire job. For each fractional part, which represents the portion completed by one person, one machine, one pipe, etc., the numerator should represent the time actually spent working, while the denominator should represent the total time needed to do the entire job alone. The sum of all the individual fractions should be 1.

Example➤ John can wax his car in 3 hours. Jim can do the same job in 5 hours. How long will it take them if they work together?

Solution➤ If multiple-choice answers are given, you should realize that the correct answer must be smaller than the shortest time given, for no matter how slow a helper may be, he will do some of the work. Therefore, the job will be completed in less time than it would take for one person working alone.

John Jim

$$\frac{\text{Time spent}}{\text{Total time needed to do job alone}}: \quad \frac{x}{3} + \frac{x}{5} = 1$$

Multiply by 15 to eliminate fractions.

$5x + 3x = 15$

$8x = 15$

$x = 1\frac{7}{8}$ hours

PRACTICE EXERCISES XI

Work out the problem. Circle the letter that appears before your answer.

1. Sue and Nancy wish to buy a snack. They combine their money and find they have \$4.00, consisting of quarters, dimes, and nickels. If they have 35 coins and the number of quarters is half the number of nickels, how many quarters do they have?

   (A) 5 (B) 10 (C) 20 (D) 3 (E) 6

2. Three times the first of three consecutive odd integers is 3 more than twice the third. Find the third integer.

   (A) 9 (B) 11 (C) 13 (D) 15 (E) 7

3. Robert is 15 years older than his brother Stan. However, y years ago Robert was twice as old as Stan. If Stan is now b years old and $b > y$, find the value of $b - y$.

   (A) 13 (B) 14 (C) 15 (D) 16 (E) 17

4. How many ounces of pure acid must be added to 20 ounces of a solution that is 5% acid to strengthen it to a solution that is 24% acid?

   (A) $2\frac{1}{2}$ (B) 5 (C) 6 (D) $7\frac{1}{2}$ (E) 10

5. A dealer mixes a pounds of nuts worth b cents per pound with c pounds of nuts worth d cents per pound. At what price should he sell a pound of the mixture if he wishes to make a profit of 10 cents per pound?

(A) $\frac{ab+cd}{a+c}+10$ (B) $\frac{ab+cd}{a+c}+.10$ (C) $\frac{b+d}{a+c}+10$

(D) $\frac{b+d}{a+c}+.10$ (E) $\frac{b+d+10}{a+c}$

6. Barbara invests $2,400 in the National Bank at 5%. How much additional money must she invest at 8% so that the total annual income will be equal to 6% of her entire investment?

(A) $2,400 (B) $3,600 (C) $1,000 (D) $3,000 (E) $1,200

7. Frank left Austin to drive to Boxville at 6:15 P.M. and arrived at 11:45 P.M. If he averaged 30 miles per hour and stopped one hour for dinner, how far is Boxville from Austin?

(A) 120 (B) 135 (C) 180 (D) 165 (E) 150

8. A plane traveling 600 miles per hour is 30 miles from Kennedy Airport at 4:58 P.M. At what time will it arrive at the airport?

(A) 5:00 P.M. (B) 5:01 P.M. (C) 5:02 P.M. (D) 5:20 P.M. (E) 5:03 P.M.

9. Mr. Bridges can wash his car in 15 minutes, while his son Dave takes twice as long to do the same job. If they work together, how many minutes will the job take them?

(A) 5 (B) $7\frac{1}{2}$ (C) 10 (D) $22\frac{1}{2}$ (E) 30

10. The value of a fraction is $\frac{2}{5}$. If the numerator is decreased by 2 and the denominator increased by 1, the resulting fraction is equivalent to $\frac{1}{4}$. Find the numerator of the original fraction.

(A) 3 (B) 4 (C) 6 (D) 10 (E) 15

SOLUTIONS TO PRACTICE EXERCISES XI

1. **(B)** Let x = number of quarters

$2x$ = number of nickels

$35 - 3x$ = number of dimes

Write all money values in cents.

$$25(x) + 5(2x) + 10(35 - 3x) = 400$$
$$25x + 10x + 350 - 30x = 400$$
$$5x = 50$$
$$x = 10$$

2. **(D)** Let x = first integer

$x + 2$ = second integer

$x + 4$ = third integer

$$3(x) = 3 + 2(x + 4)$$
$$3x = 3 + 2x + 8$$
$$x = 11$$

The third integer is 15.

3. **(C)** $b =$ Stan's age now
$b + 15 =$ Robert's age now
$b - y =$ Stan's age y years ago
$b + 15 - y =$ Robert's age y years ago
$b + 15 - y = 2(b - y)$
$b + 15 - y = 2b - 2y$
$15 = b - y$

4. **(B)**

	No. of oz. •	% acid =	Amt. acid
Original	20	.05	1
Added	x	1.00	x
Mixture	$20 + x$	.24	$.24(20 + x)$

$1 + x = .24(20 + x)$.
Multiply by 100 to eliminate decimal.
$100 + 100x = 480 + 24x$
$76x = 380$
$x = 5$

5. **(A)** The a pounds of nuts are worth a total of ab cents. The c pounds of nuts are worth a total of cd cents. The value of the mixture is $ab + cd$ cents. Since there are $a + c$ pounds, each pound is worth $\frac{ab+cd}{a+c}$ cents.

Since the dealer wants to add 10 cents to each pound for profit, and the value of each pound is in cents, add 10 to the value of each pound.

6. **(E)** If Barbara invests x additional dollars at 8%, her total investment will amount to $2400 + x$ dollars.
$.05(2400) + .08(x) = .06(2400 + x)$
$5(2400) + 8(x) = 6(2400 - x)$
$12000 + 8x = 14400 + 6x$
$2x = 2400$
$x = 1200$

7. **(B)** Total time elapsed is $5\frac{1}{2}$ hours. However, one hour was used for dinner. Therefore, Frank drove at 30 mph for $4\frac{1}{2}$ hours, covering 135 miles.

8. **(B)** Time $= \frac{\text{Distance}}{\text{Rate}} = \frac{30}{600} = \frac{1}{20}$ hour, or 3 minutes.

9. **(C)** Dave takes 30 minutes to wash the car alone.
$\frac{x}{15} + \frac{x}{30} = 1$
$2x + x = 30$
$3x = 30$
$x = 10$

10. **(C)** Let $2x$ = original numerator
$5x$ = original denominator

$$\frac{2x-2}{5x+1}=\frac{1}{4}$$

Cross-multiply:

$$8x-8=5x+1$$
$$3x=9$$
$$x=3$$

Original numerator is 2(3), or 6.

XII. Geometry

Numerical relationships from geometry should be reviewed thoroughly. A list of the most important formulas with illustrations follows.

Areas

1. Rectangle = bh

   Area = $6 \cdot 3 = 18$

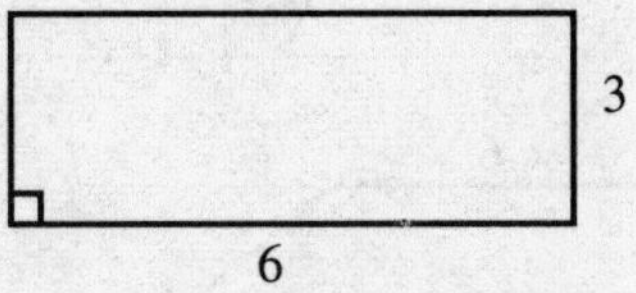

2. Parallelogram = bh

   Area = $8 \cdot 4 = 32$

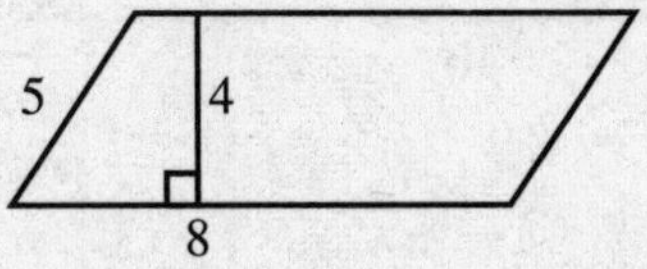

3. Rhombus $= \frac{1}{2} d_1 d_2$

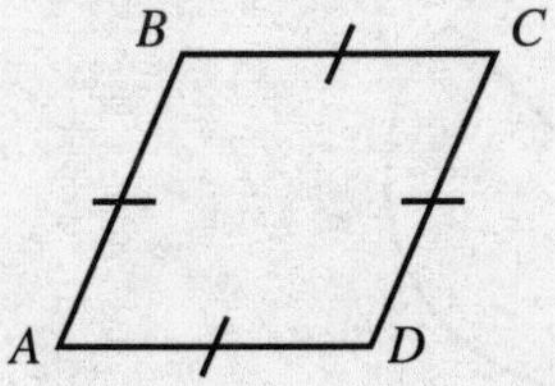

   If $AC = 10$ and $BD = 8$, then area is $\frac{1}{2}(10)(8) = 40$

4. Square $= s^2$ or $\frac{1}{2} d^2$

   Area $= 6^2 = 36$

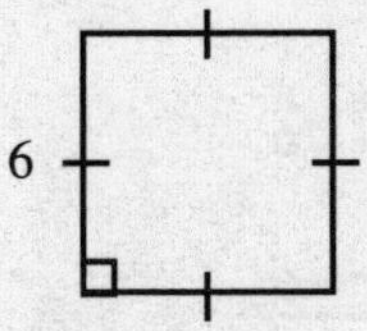

   Area $= \frac{1}{2}(10)(10) = 50$

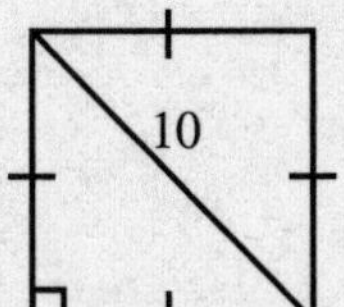

5. Triangle $= \frac{1}{2} bh$

   Area $= \frac{1}{2}(12)(4) = 24$

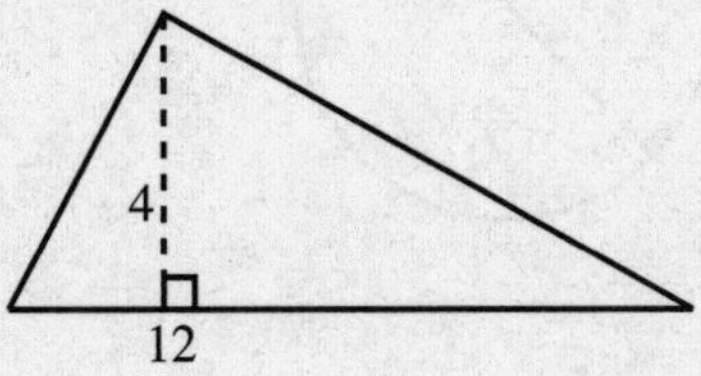

6. Equilateral triangle $= \frac{s^2}{4}\sqrt{3}$

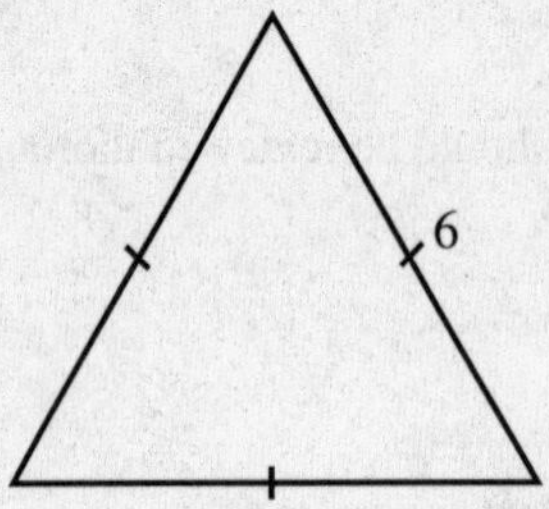

Area $= \frac{36}{4}\sqrt{3} = 9\sqrt{3}$

7. Trapezoid $= \frac{1}{2}h(b_1 + b_2)$

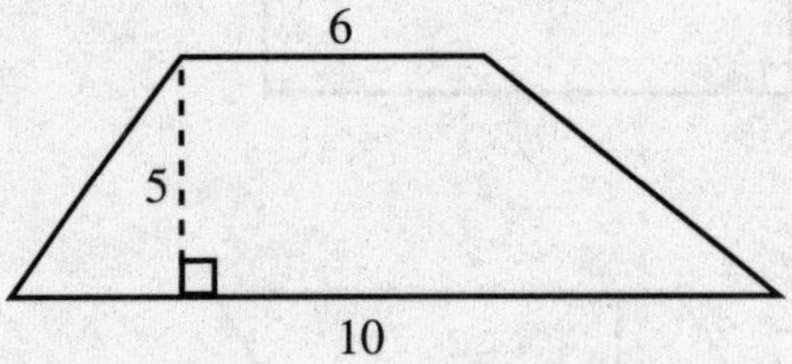

Area $= \frac{1}{2}(5)(16) = 40$

8. Circle $= \pi r^2$

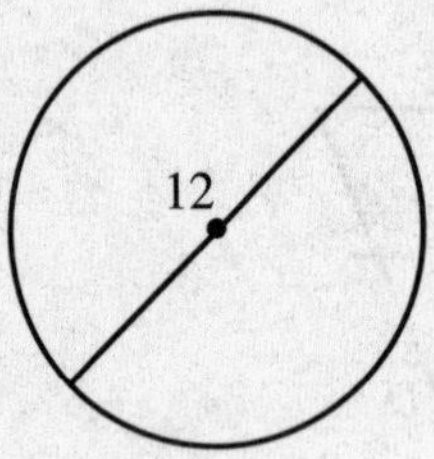

Area $= \pi(6)^2 = 36\pi$

Perimeters

1. Any polygon = sum of all sides

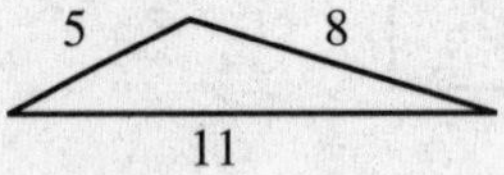

P = 5 + 8 + 11 = 24

2. Circle $= \pi d$
(called circumference)

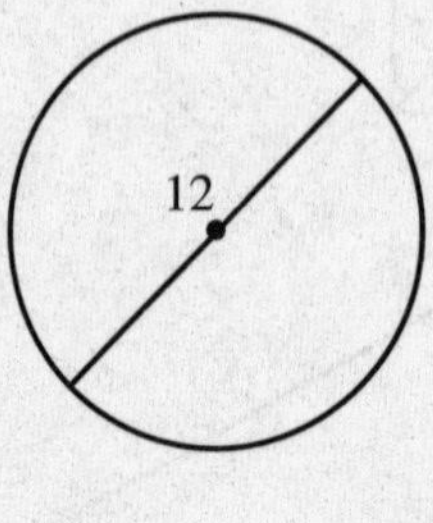

Circle $= \pi(12) = 12\pi$

3. The distance covered by a wheel in one revolution is equal to the circumference of the wheel.

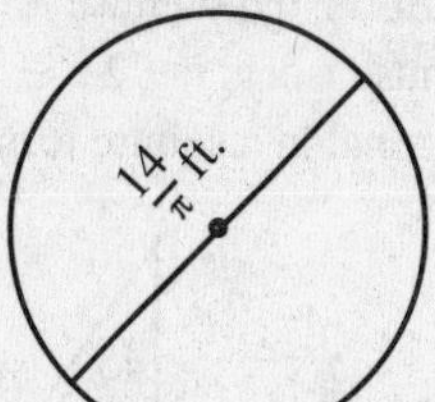

In one revolution, this wheel covers $\pi \cdot \frac{14}{\pi}$, or 14 feet.

Right Triangles

1. Pythagorean Theorem
   $(\text{leg})^2 + (\text{leg})^2 = (\text{hypotenuse})^2$

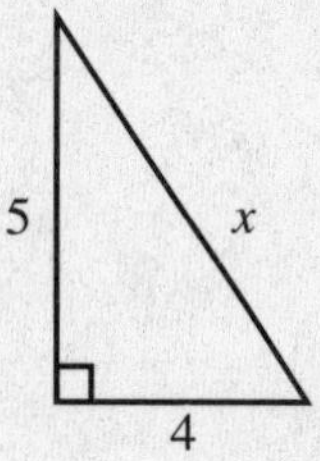

$$4^2 + 5^2 = x^2$$
$$16 + 25 = x^2$$
$$41 = x^2$$
$$\sqrt{41} = x$$

2. Pythagorean triples: These are sets of numbers that satisfy the Pythagorean Theorem. When a given set of numbers such as 3, 4, 5 forms a Pythagorean triple $(3^2 + 4^2 = 5^2)$, any multiples of this set such as 6, 8, 10 or 15, 20, 25 also form a Pythagorean triple. The most common Pythagorean triples, which should be memorized, are:

   3, 4, 5
   5, 12, 13
   8, 15, 17
   7, 24, 25

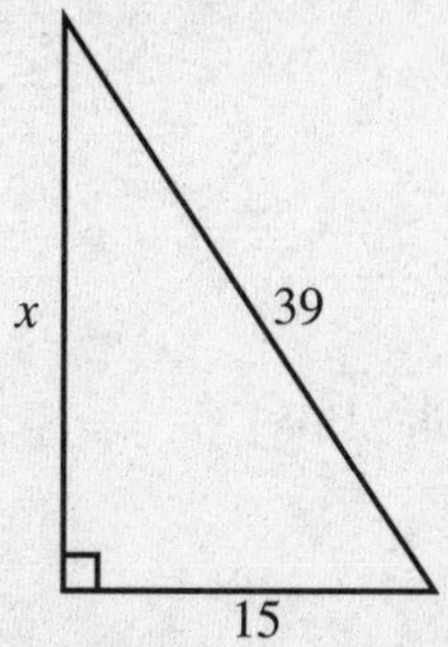

Squaring these numbers in order to apply the Pythagorean Theorem would take too much time. Instead, recognize the hypotenuse as 3(13). Suspect a 5, 12, 13 triangle. Since the given leg is 3(5), the missing leg must be 3(12), or 36, with no computation and a great saving of time.

3. The 30°-60°-90° triangle
   a) The leg opposite the 30° angle is $\frac{1}{2}$ hypotenuse.
   b) The leg opposite the 60° angle is $\frac{1}{2}$ hypotenuse • $\sqrt{3}$.
   c) An altitude in an equilateral triangle forms a 30°-60°-90° triangle and is therefore equal to $\frac{1}{2}$ hypotenuse • $\sqrt{3}$.

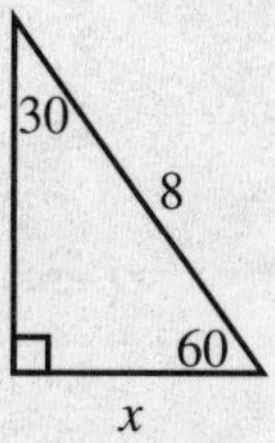

$x = 4$

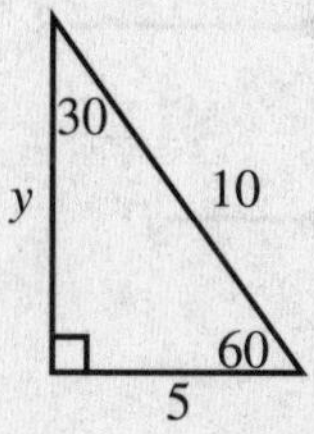

$y = 5\sqrt{3}$

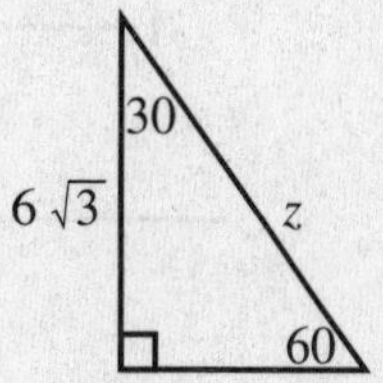

$z = 12$

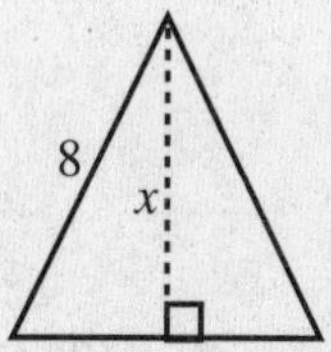

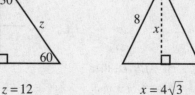

$x = 4\sqrt{3}$

4. The 45°-45°-90° triangle (isosceles right triangle)
   a) Each leg is $\frac{1}{2}$ hypotenuse • $\sqrt{2}$.
   b) Hypotenuse is leg • $\sqrt{2}$.
   c) The diagonal in a square forms a 45°-45°-90° triangle and is therefore equal to a side • $\sqrt{2}$.

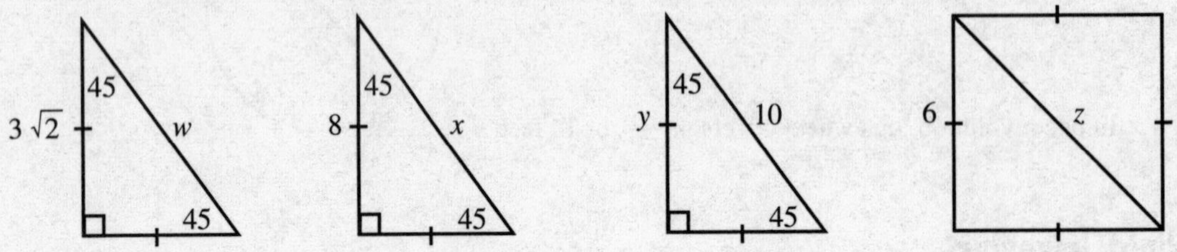

$w = 6$ $\quad x = 8\sqrt{2}$ $\quad y = 5\sqrt{2}$ $\quad z = 6\sqrt{2}$

Coordinate Geometry

1. Distance between two points

   $\sqrt{(x_2 - x_1)^2 + (y_2 - y_1)^2}$

   The distance from (–2, 3) to (4, –1) is

   $\sqrt{[4-(-2)]^2 + [-1-(3)]^2}$

   $\sqrt{(6)^2 + (-4)^2} = \sqrt{36+16} = \sqrt{52}$

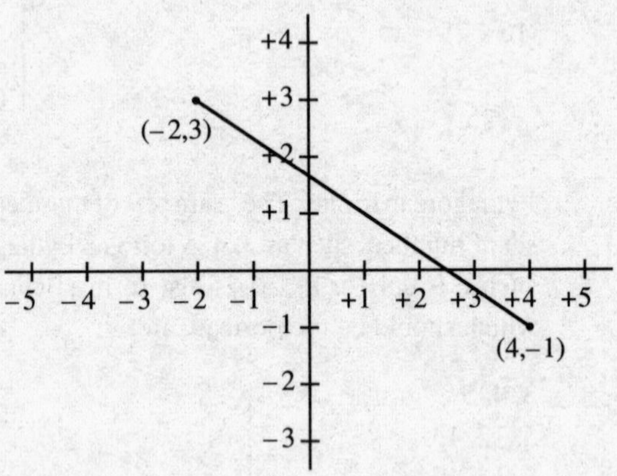

2. The midpoint of a line segment

   $\left(\frac{x_1 + x_2}{2}, \frac{y_1 + y_2}{2}\right)$

   The midpoint of the segment joining (–2, 3) to (4, –1) is

   $\left(\frac{-2+4}{2}, \frac{3+(-1)}{2}\right) = \left(\frac{2}{2}, \frac{2}{2}\right) = 1,1$

Parallel Lines

1. If two parallel lines are cut by a transversal, the alternate interior angles are congruent.

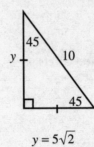

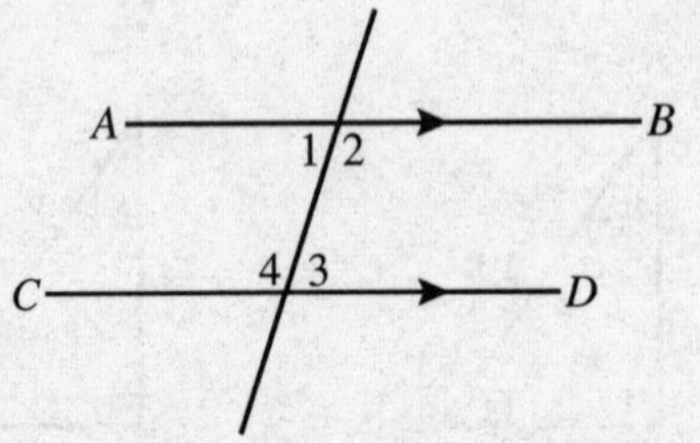

If $AB \parallel CD$, then
$\angle 1 \cong \angle 3$ and
$\angle 2 \cong \angle 4$.

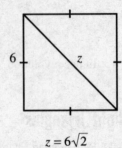

2. If two parallel lines are cut by a transversal, the corresponding angles are congruent.

If $AB \| CD$, then

$\angle 1 \cong \angle 5$,
$\angle 2 \cong \angle 6$,
$\angle 3 \cong \angle 7$, and
$\angle 4 \cong \angle 8$.

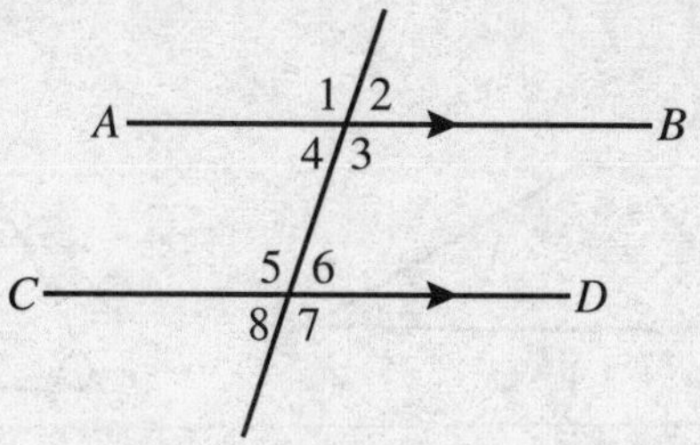

3. If two parallel lines are cut by a transversal, interior angles on the same side of the transversal are supplementary.

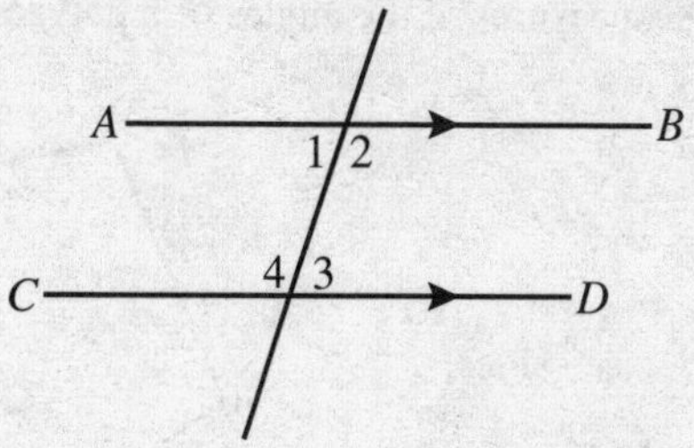

If $AB \| CD$, then
$\angle 1$ is supplementary to $\angle 4$ and
$\angle 2$ is supplementary to $\angle 3$.

Triangles

1. If two sides of a triangle are congruent, the angles opposite these sides are congruent.

If $AB \cong AC$, then
$\angle B \cong \angle C$.

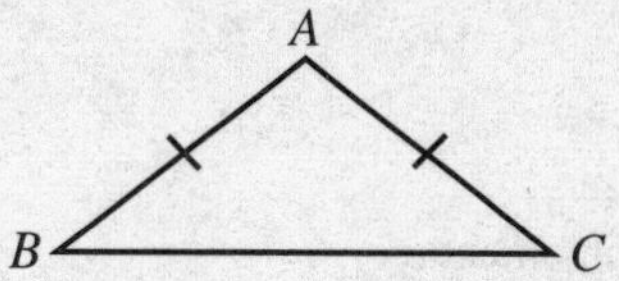

2. If two angles of a triangle are congruent, the sides opposite these angles are congruent.

If $\angle B \cong \angle C$, then
$AB \cong AC$.

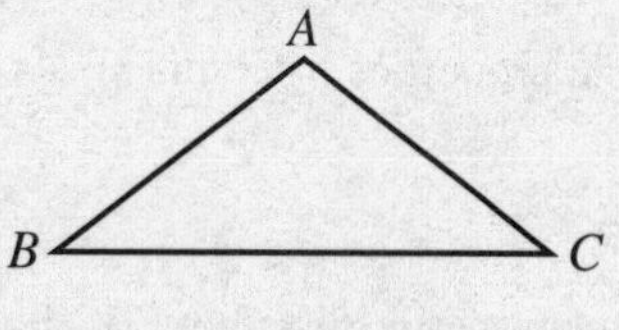

3. The sum of the measures of the angles of a triangle is 180°.

4. The measure of an exterior angle of a triangle is equal to the sum of the measures of the two remote interior angles.

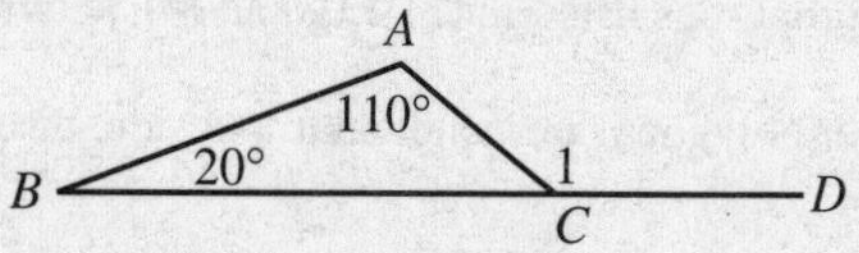

$\angle 1 = 130°$

5. If two angles of one triangle are congruent to two angles of a second triangle, the third angles are congruent.

$\measuredangle D \cong \measuredangle A$

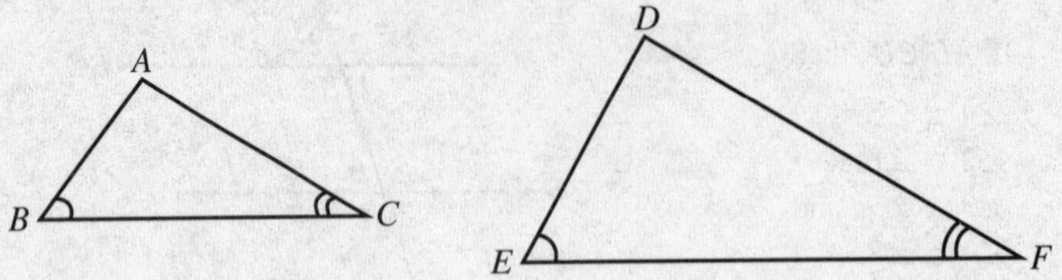

Polygons

1. The sum of the measures of the angles of a polygon of n sides is $(n - 2)180°$.

Since *ABCDE* has 5 sides,
$\angle A + \angle B + \angle C + \angle D + \angle E = (5 - 2)180 = 3(180) = 540°$.

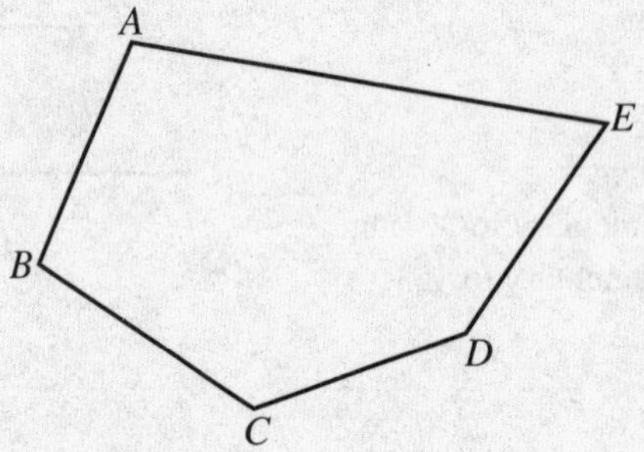

2. In a parallelogram:
   a) Opposite sides are parallel.
   b) Opposite sides are congruent.
   c) Opposite angles are congruent.
   d) Consecutive angles are supplementary.
   e) Diagonals bisect each other.
   f) Each diagonal bisects the parallelogram into two congruent triangles.

3. In a rectangle, in addition to the properties listed in (2), above:
   a) All angles are right angles.
   b) Diagonals are congruent.

4. In a rhombus, in addition to the properties listed in (2), above:
   a) All sides are congruent.
   b) Diagonals are perpendicular.
   c) Diagonals bisect the angles.

5. A square has *all* of the properties listed in (2), (3), and (4), above.

6. The apothem of a regular polygon is perpendicular to a side, bisects that side, and also bisects a central angle.

OX is an *apothem*.
It bisects *AB*, is perpendicular to *AB*, and bisects $\angle AOB$.

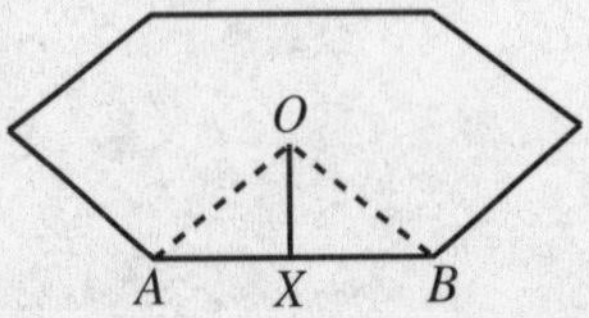

7. The area of a regular polygon is equal to one-half the product of its apothem and perimeter.

$A = \frac{1}{2}(3)(30) = 45$

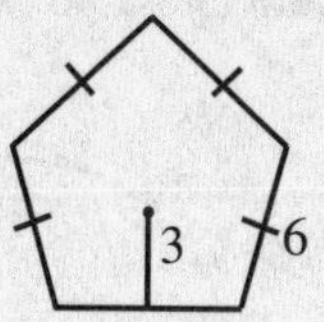

Circles

1. A central angle is equal in degrees to its intercepted arc.

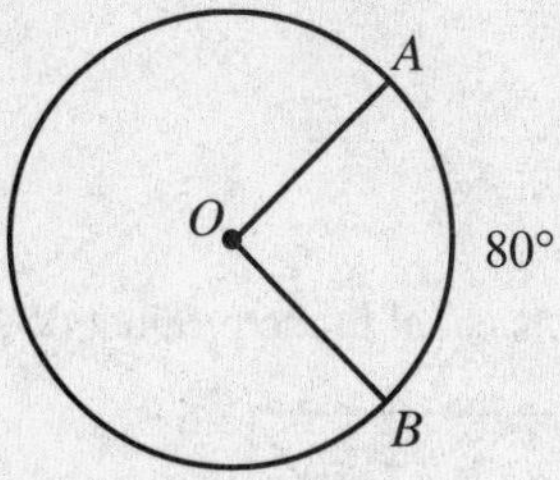

If $\widehat{AB} = 80°$, then $\angle AOB = 80°$.

2. An inscribed angle is equal in degrees to one-half its intercepted arc.

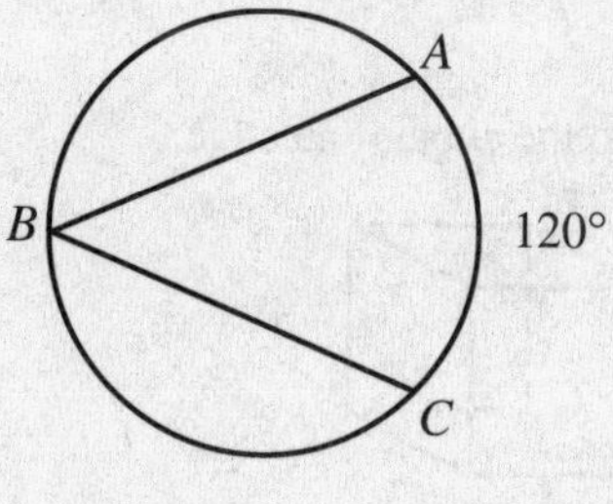

If $\widehat{AC} = 120°$, then $\angle ABC = 60°$.

3. An angle formed by two chords intersecting in a circle is equal in degrees to one-half the sum of its intercepted arcs.

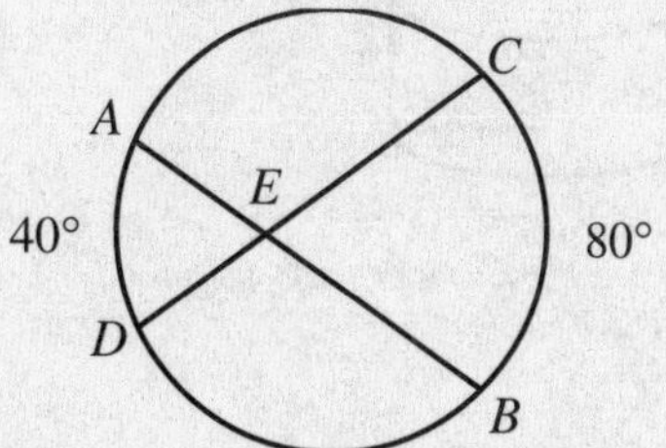

If $\widehat{AD} = 40°$ and $\widehat{CB} = 80°$, then $\angle CEB = 60°$.

4. An angle formed outside a circle by two secants, a secant and a tangent, or two tangents is equal in degrees to one-half the difference of its intercepted arcs.

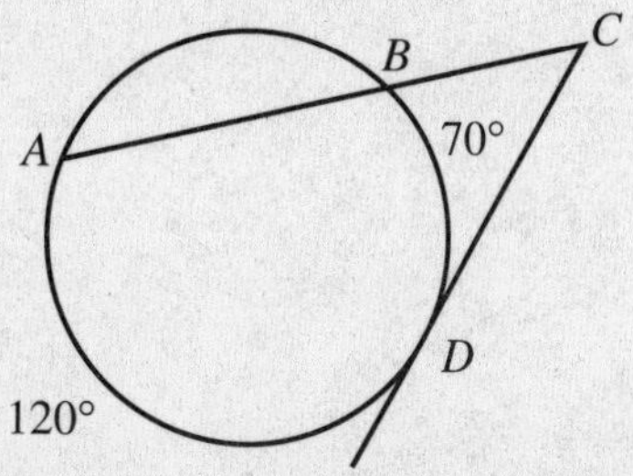

If $\widehat{AD} = 120°$ and $\widehat{BD} = 70°$, then $\angle ACD = 25°$.

5. Two tangent segments drawn to a circle from the same external point are congruent.

If AC and CE are tangent to circle O at B and D, then $CB \cong CD$.

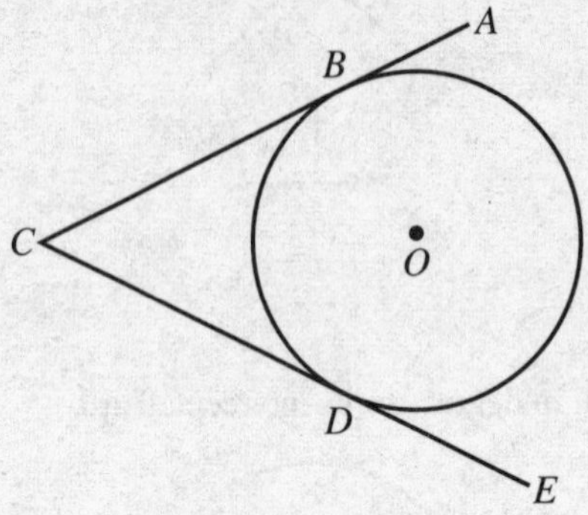

Volumes

1. The volume of a rectangular solid is equal to the product of its length, width, and height.

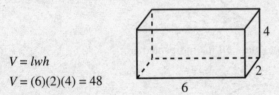

$V = lwh$

$V = (6)(2)(4) = 48$

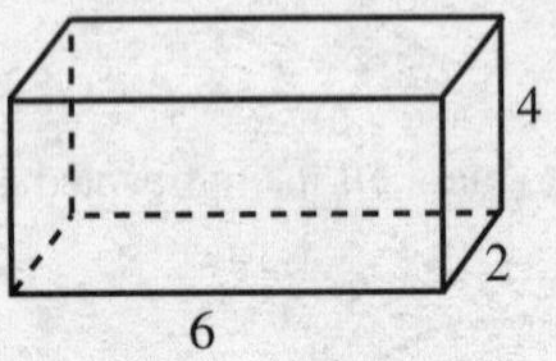

2. The volume of a cube is equal to the cube of an edge.

$V = e^3$

$V = (5)^3 = 125$

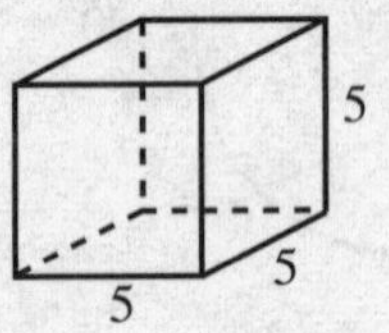

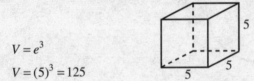

3. The volume of a cylinder is equal to π times the square of the radius of the base times the height.

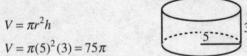

$V = \pi r^2 h$

$V = \pi(5)^2(3) = 75\pi$

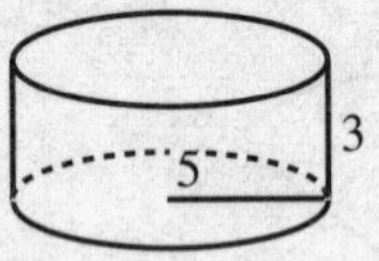

Similar Polygons

1. Corresponding angles of similar polygons are congruent.

2. Corresponding sides of similar polygons are in proportion.

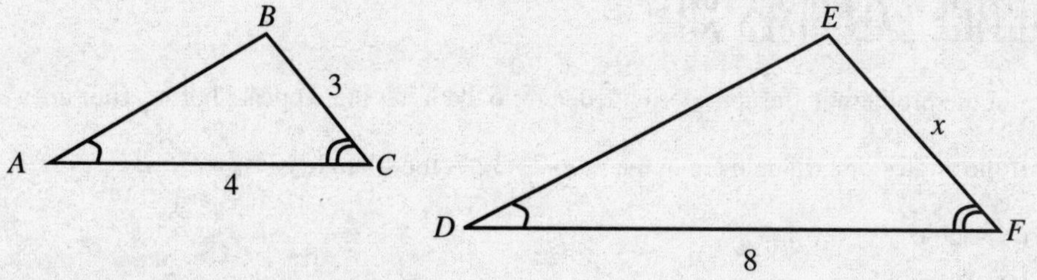

If triangle *ABC* is similar to triangle *DEF*, and the sides are given as marked, then *EF* must be equal to 6, as the ratio between corresponding sides is 4 : 8 or 1 : 2.

3. When figures are similar, all corresponding linear ratios are equal. The ratio of one side to its corresponding side is the same as perimeter to perimeter, apothem to apothem, altitude to altitude, etc.

4. When figures are similar, the ratio of their areas is equal to the square of the ratio between two corresponding linear quantities.

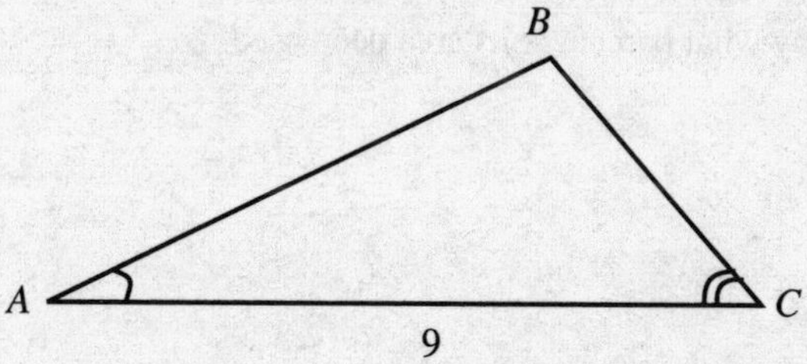

If triangle *ABC* is similar to triangle *DEF*, the area of triangle *ABC* will be 9 times as great as that of triangle *DEF*. The ratio of sides is 9 : 3, or 3 : 1. The ratio of areas will be the square of 3 : 1, or 9 : 1.

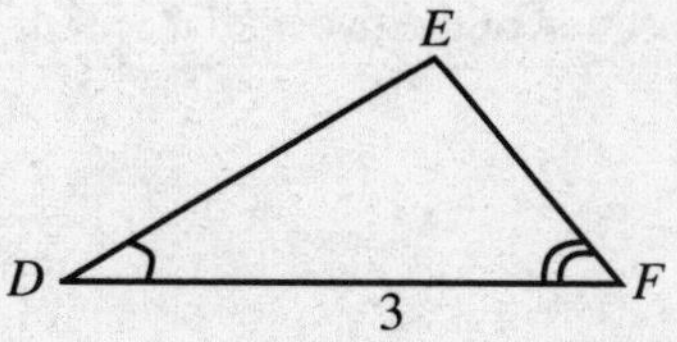

5. When figures are similar, the ratio of their volumes is equal to the cube of the ratio between two corresponding linear quantities.

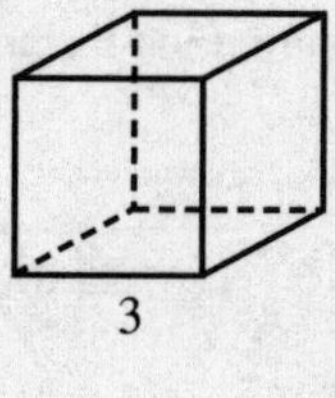

The volume of the larger cube is 8 times as large as the volume of the smaller cube. If the ratio of sides is 3 : 6, or 1 : 2, the ratio of volumes is the cube of this, or 1 : 8.

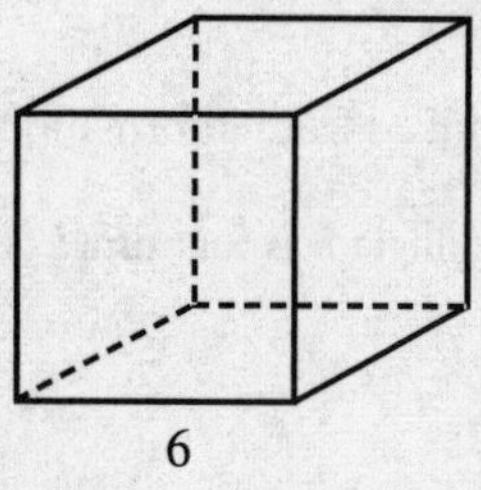

PRACTICE EXERCISES XII

Work out the problem in the space provided. Circle the letter that appears before your answer.

1. If the angles of a triangle are in the ratio 2 : 3 : 7, the triangle is

(A) acute
(B) isosceles
(C) obtuse
(D) right
(E) equilateral

2. If the area of a square of side x is 5, what is the area of a square of side $3x$?

(A) 15
(B) 45
(C) 95
(D) 75
(E) 225

3. If the radius of a circle is decreased by 10%, by what percent is its area decreased?

(A) 10
(B) 19
(C) 21
(D) 79
(E) 81

4. A spotlight is 5 feet from one wall of a room and 10 feet from the wall at right angles to it. How many feet is it from the intersection of the two walls?

(A) 15
(B) $5\sqrt{2}$
(C) $5\sqrt{5}$
(D) $10\sqrt{2}$
(E) $10\sqrt{5}$

5. A dam has the dimensions indicated in the figure. Find the area of this isosceles trapezoid.

(A) 1300
(B) 1560
(C) 1400
(D) 1440
(E) It cannot be determined from information given.

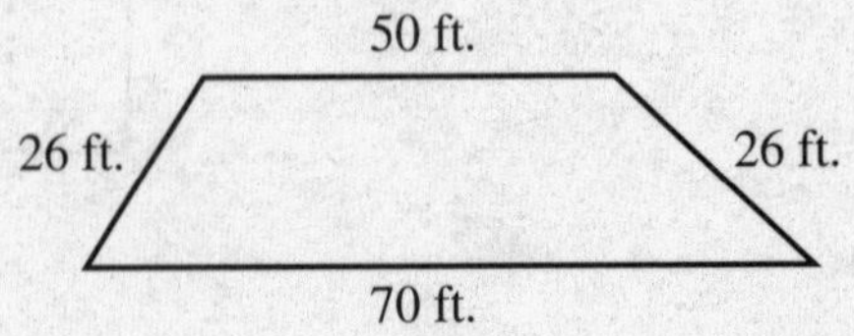

6. In parallelogram $PQRS$, angle P is four times angle Q. What is the measure in degrees of angle P?

(A) 36
(B) 72
(C) 125
(D) 144
(E) 150

7. If $PQ \cong QS$, $QR \cong RS$ and angle $PRS = 100°$, what is the measure, in degrees, of angle QPS?

(A) 10
(B) 15
(C) 20
(D) 25
(E) 30

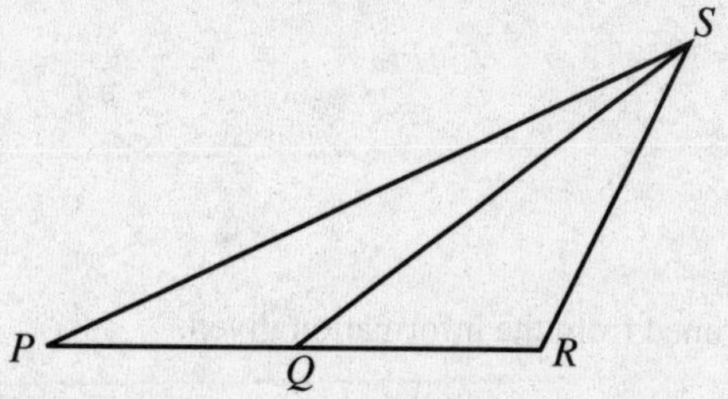

8. A line segment is drawn from the point (3, 5) to the point (9, 13). What are the coordinates of the midpoint of this line segment?

(A) (3, 4)
(B) (12, 18)
(C) (6, 8)
(D) (9, 6)
(E) (6, 9)

9. A rectangular box with a square base contains 6 cubic feet. If the height of the box is 18 inches, how many feet are there in each side of the base?

(A) 1

(B) 2

(C) $\sqrt{3}$

(D) $\frac{\sqrt{3}}{3}$

(E) 4

10. The surface area of a cube is 150 square feet. How many cubic feet are there in the volume of the cube?

(A) 30
(B) 50
(C) 100
(D) 125
(E) 150

11. Peter lives 12 miles west of school and Bill lives north of the school. Peter finds that the direct distance from his house to Bill's is 6 miles shorter than the distance by way of school. How many miles north of the school does Bill live?

(A) 6

(B) 9

(C) 10

(D) $6\sqrt{2}$

(E) None of these

12. A square is inscribed in a circle of area 18π. Find a side of the square.

(A) 3
(B) 6
(C) $3\sqrt{2}$
(D) $6\sqrt{2}$
(E) It cannot be determined from the information given.

13. A carpet is y yards long and f feet wide. How many dollars will it cost if the carpet sells for x cents per square foot?

(A) xyf
(B) $3xyf$
(C) $\frac{xyf}{3}$
(D) $\frac{.03yf}{x}$
(E) $.03xyf$

14. If a triangle of base 6 has the same area as a circle of radius 6, what is the altitude of the triangle?

(A) 6π
(B) 8π
(C) 10π
(D) 12π
(E) 14π

15. The vertex angle of an isosceles triangle is p degrees. How many degrees are there in one of the base angles?

(A) $180 - p$
(B) $90 - p$
(C) $180 - 2p$
(D) $180 - \frac{p}{2}$
(E) $90 - \frac{p}{2}$

16. In a circle with center O, arc $RS = 132$ degrees. How many degrees are there in angle RSO?

(A) 66
(B) 20
(C) 22
(D) 24
(E) 48

17. The ice compartment of a refrigerator is 8 inches long, 4 inches wide, and 5 inches high. How many ice cubes will it hold if each cube is 2 inches on an edge?

(A) 8
(B) 10
(C) 12
(D) 16
(E) 20

18. In the figure, PSQ is a straight line and RS is perpendicular to ST. If angle $RSQ = 48°$, how many degrees are there in angle PST?

(A) 48
(B) 132
(C) 90
(D) 136
(E) 138

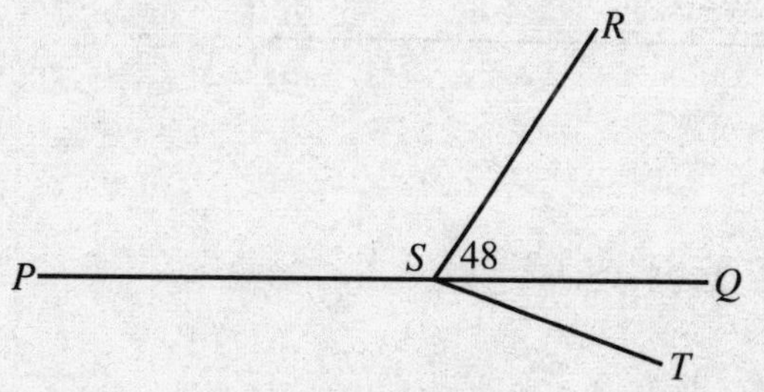

19. A cylindrical pail has a radius of 7 inches and a height of 9 inches. If there are 231 cubic inches to a gallon, approximately how many gallons will this pail hold?

(A) 6

(B) $\frac{12}{7}$

(C) 7.5

(D) 8.2

(E) 9

20. In triangle PQR, QS and SR are angle bisectors and angle $P = 80°$. How many degrees are there in angle QSR?

(A) 115
(B) 120
(C) 125
(D) 130
(E) 135

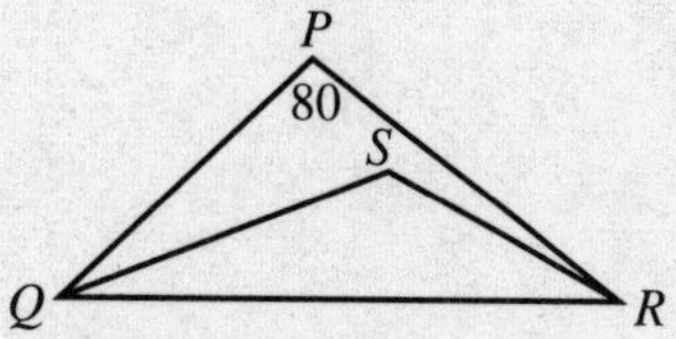

SOLUTIONS TO PRACTICE EXERCISES XII

1. **(C)** Represent the angles as $2x$, $3x$, and $7x$.

$$2x + 3x + 7x = 180$$
$$12x = 180$$
$$x = 15$$

The angles are 30°, 45°, and 105°. Since one angle is between 90° and 180°, the triangle is called an obtuse triangle.

2. **(B)** If the sides have a ratio 1 : 3, the areas have a ratio 1 : 9. Therefore, the area of the large square is 9(5), or 45.

3. **(B)** If the radii of the two circles have a ratio of 10 : 9, the areas have a ratio of 100 : 81. Therefore, the decrease is 19 out of 100, or 19%.

4. **(C)**

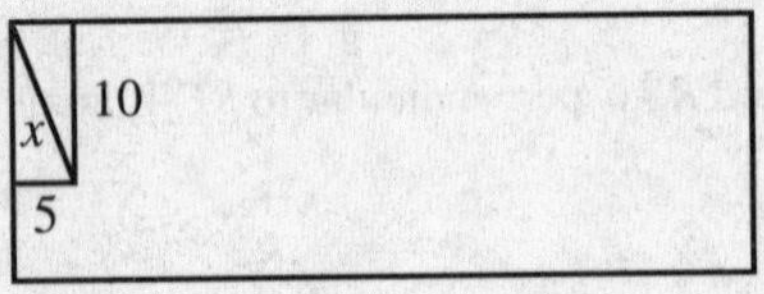

$$5^2 + 10^2 = x^2$$
$$25 + 100 = x^2$$
$$x^2 = 125$$
$$x = \sqrt{125} = \sqrt{25}\sqrt{5} = 5\sqrt{5}$$

5. **(D)**

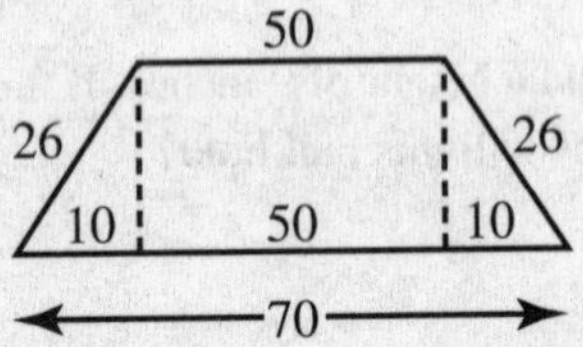

When altitudes are drawn from both ends of the upper base in an isosceles trapezoid, the figure is divided into a rectangle and two congruent right triangles. The center section of the lower base is equal to the upper base, and the remainder of the lower base is divided equally between both ends. The altitude can then be found using the Pythagorean Theorem. In this case, we have a 5, 12, 13 triangle with all measures doubled, so the altitude is 24.

The area is $\frac{1}{2}(24)(120)$, or 1440.

6. **(D)** The consecutive angles of a parallelogram are supplementary,

so $x + 4x = 180$
$$5x = 180$$
$$x = 36$$

Angle P is 4(36), or 144°.

7. **(C)**

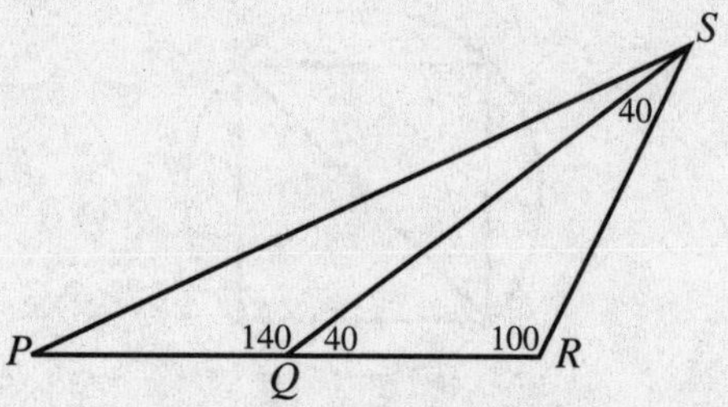

Since $QR \cong RS$, angle $RQS \cong$ angle RSQ. There are 80° left in the triangle, so each of these angles is 40°. Angle SQP is supplementary to angle SQR, making it 140°. Since $QP \cong QS$, angle $QPS \cong$ angle QSP. There are 40° left in the triangle, so each of these angles is 20°.

8. **(E)** Add the x values and divide by 2. Add the y values and divide by 2.

9. **(B)** Change 18 inches to 1.5 feet. Letting each side of the base be x, the volume is $1.5x^2$.

$$\begin{aligned} 1.5x^2 &= 6 \\ 15x^2 &= 60 \\ x^2 &= 4 \\ x &= 2 \end{aligned}$$

10. **(D)** The surface area of a cube is made up of 6 equal squares. If each edge of the cube is x, then,

$$\begin{aligned} 6x^2 &= 150 \\ x^2 &= 25 \\ x &= 5 \end{aligned}$$

Volume = (edge)$^3 = 5^3 = 125$

11. **(B)**

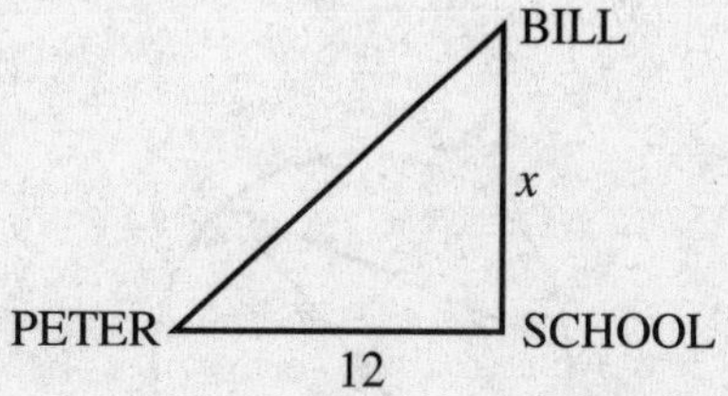

The direct distance from Peter's house to Bill's can be represented by means of the Pythagorean Theorem as $\sqrt{144 + x^2}$. Then

$$\begin{aligned} \sqrt{144 + x^2} &= (12 + x) - 6 \\ \sqrt{144 + x^2} &= x + 6 \end{aligned}$$

Square both sides.

$$\begin{aligned} 144 + x^2 &= x^2 + 12x + 36 \\ 144 &= 12x + 36 \\ 108 &= 12x \\ 9 &= x \end{aligned}$$

12. **(B)**

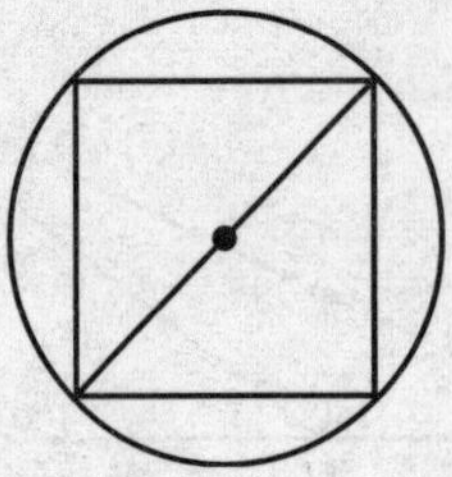

The diagonal of the square will be a diameter of the circle.

$$\pi r^2 = 18\pi$$
$$r^2 = 18$$
$$r = \sqrt{18} = \sqrt{9}\sqrt{2} = 3\sqrt{2}$$

The diameter is $6\sqrt{2}$ and, since the triangles are 45°-45°-90°, a side of the square is 6.

13. **(E)** To find the area in square feet, change *y* yards to 3*y* feet. The area is then (3*y*)(*f*), or 3*yf* square feet. If each square foot costs *x* cents, change this to dollars by dividing *x* by 100. Thus, each square foot costs $\frac{x}{100}$ dollars.

The cost of 3*yf* square feet will be $(3yf)\left(\frac{x}{100}\right)$, or $\frac{3xyf}{100}$.

Since $\frac{3}{100} = .03$, the correct answer is (E).

14. **(D)** The area of the circle is $(6)^2$, or 36π.

In the triangle $\frac{1}{2}(6)(h) = 36\pi$
$$3h = 36\pi$$
$$h = 12\pi$$

15. **(E)** There are $(180 - p)$ degrees left, which must be divided between 2 congruent angles. Each angle will contain $\frac{(180-p)}{2}$, or $90 - \frac{p}{2}$ degrees.

16. **(D)**

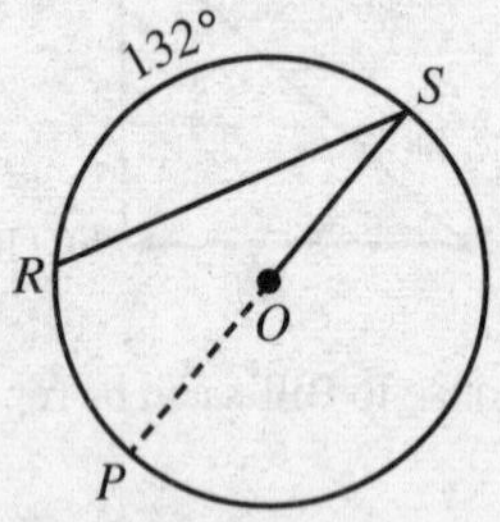

By extending *SO* until it hits the circle at *P*, arc *PRS* is a semicircle. Therefore, arc *PR* = 48°, and inscribed angle *RSO* = 24°.

17. **(D)**

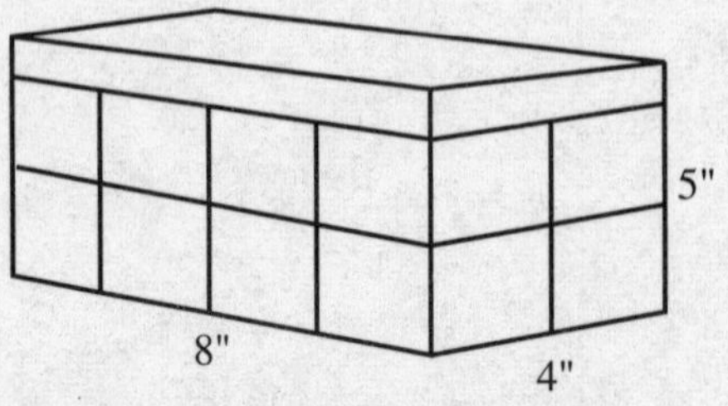

The compartment will hold 2 layers, each of which contains 2 rows of 4 cubes each. This leaves a height of 1 inch on top empty. Therefore, the compartment can hold 16 cubes.

18. **(E)**

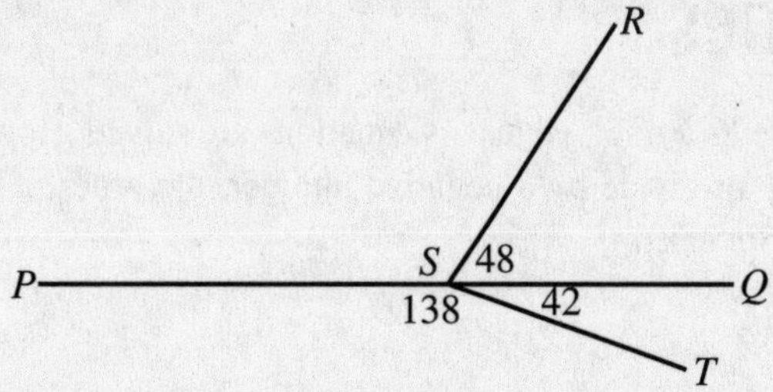

Since $\angle RST$ is a right angle, 42° are left for $\angle QST$. Since PSQ is a straight angle of 180°, $\angle PST$ contains 138°.

19. **(A)** The volume of the pail is found using the formula $V = \pi r^2 h$. Since the answers are not in terms of π, it is best to use $\frac{22}{7}$ as a value for π because the 7 will cancel with r^2: $V = \frac{22}{\cancel{7}} \cdot \cancel{49}^{7} \cdot 9$. Rather than multiply this out, which will take unnecessary time, divide by 231 and cancel wherever possible.

$$\frac{\overset{2}{\cancel{22}} \cdot \cancel{7} \cdot \overset{3}{\cancel{9}}}{\cancel{231}\ \cancel{33}\ \cancel{3}} = 6$$

20. **(D)** If $\angle P = 80°$, there are 100° left between angles PQR and PRQ. If they are both bisected, there will be 50° between angles SQR and SRQ, leaving 130° in triangle SRQ for angle QSR.

XIII. Inequalities

Algebraic inequality statements are solved just as equations are solved. However, you must remember that whenever you multiply or divide by a negative number, the order of the inequality, that is, the inequality symbol, must be reversed.

Example➤ Solve for x: $3 - 5x > 18$

Solution➤ Add –3 to both sides:
$-5x > 15$
Divide by –5, remembering to reverse the inequality:
$x < -3$

Example➤ $5x - 4 > 6x - 6$

Solution➤ Collect all x terms on the left and numerical terms on the right. As with equations, remember that if a term crosses the inequality symbol, the term changes sign.
$-x > -2$
Divide (or multiply) by –1:
$x < 2$

In working with geometric inequalities, certain postulates and theorems should be reviewed. The list follows:

1. If unequal quantities are added to unequal quantities of the same order, the result is unequal quantities in the same order.

2. If equal quantities are added to, or subtracted from, unequal quantities, the results are unequal in the same order.

3. If unequal quantities are subtracted from equal quantities, the results are unequal in the opposite order.

4. Doubles, or halves, or unequals are unequal in the same order.

5. If the first of three quantities is greater than the second, and the second is greater than the third, then the first is greater than the third.

6. The sum of two sides of a triangle must be greater than the third side.

7. If two sides of a triangle are unequal, the angles opposite these sides are unequal, with the larger angle opposite the larger side.

8. If two angles of a triangle are unequal, the sides opposite these angles are unequal, with the larger side opposite the larger angle.

9. An exterior angle of a triangle is greater than either remote interior angle.

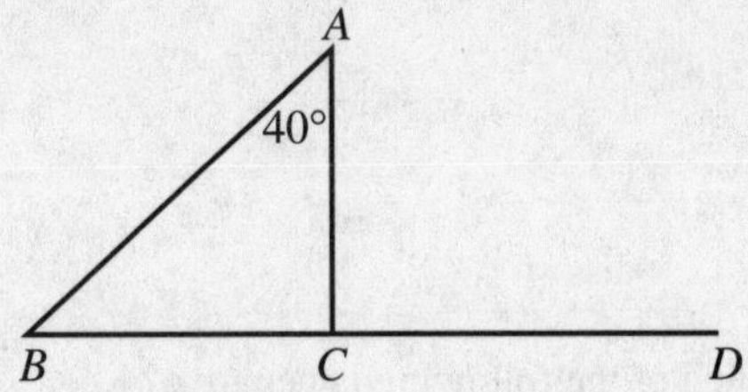

Example➤ If BCD is a straight line and $\angle A = 40°$, then angle ACD contains

(A) 40°
(B) 140°
(C) less than 40°
(D) more than 40°
(E) 100°

Solution➤ The correct answer is (D), since an exterior angle of a triangle is always greater than either of the remote interior angles.

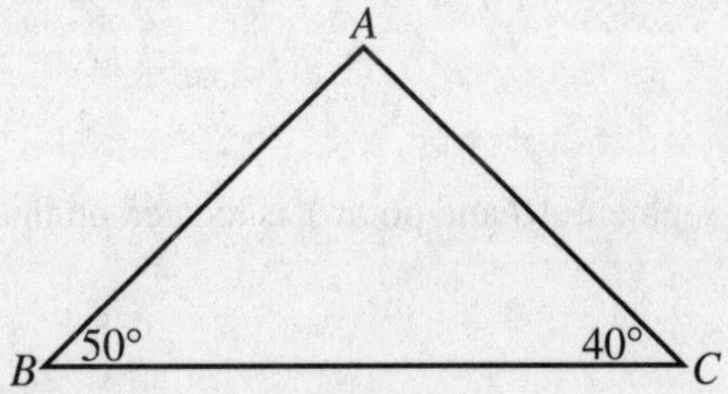

Example➤ Which of the following statements is true regarding the above triangle?

(A) $AB > AC$
(B) $AC > BC$
(C) $AB > BC$
(D) $AC > AB$
(E) $BC > AB + AC$

Solution➤ The correct answer is (D), since a comparison between two sides of a triangle depends upon the angles opposite these sides. The larger side is always opposite the larger angle. Since angle A contains 90°, the largest side of this triangle is BC, followed by AC and then AB.

PRACTICE EXERCISES XIII

Work out the problems in the space provided. Circle the letter that appears before your answer.

1. If $x < y$, $2x = A$, and $2y = B$, then

(A) $A = B$
(B) $A < B$
(C) $A > B$
(D) $A < x$
(E) $B < y$

2. If $a > b$ and $c > d$, then

(A) $a = c$
(B) $a < d$
(C) $a + d = b + c$
(D) $a + c < b + d$
(E) $a + c > b + d$

3. If $ab > 0$ and $a < 0$, which of the following is negative?

(A) b
(B) $-b$
(C) $-a$
(D) $(a - b)^2$
(E) $-(a + b)$

4. If $4 - x > 5$, then

(A) $x > 1$
(B) $x > -1$
(C) $x < 1$
(D) $x < -1$
(E) $x = -1$

5. Point X is located on line segment AB and point Y is located on line segment CD. If $AB = CD$ and $AX > CY$, then

(A) $XB > YD$
(B) $XB < YD$
(C) $AX > XB$
(D) $AX < XB$
(E) $AX > AB$

6. In triangle ABC, $AB = BC$. D is any point on side AB. Which of the following statements is always true?

(A) $AD < DC$
(B) $AD = DC$
(C) $AD > DC$
(D) $AD \leq DC$
(E) $AD \geq DC$

7. In the diagram at the right,

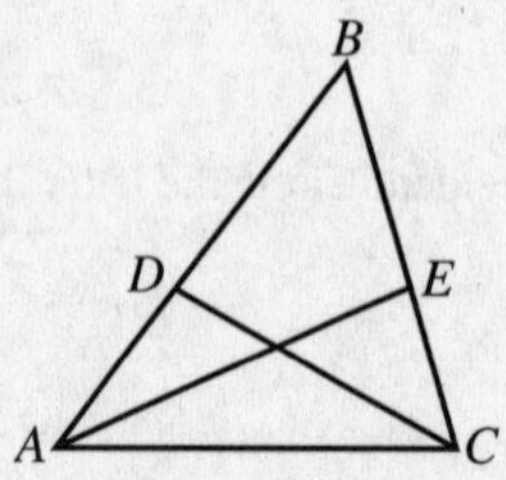

$BD = BE$ and $DA > EC$. Then

(A) $AE > DC$
(B) $\angle BCA < \angle BAC$
(C) $\angle DCA < \angle EAC$
(D) $AB < BC$
(E) $AD < BD$

8. In the diagram below, which of the following is always true?

I. $a > b$
II. $c > a$
III. $d > a$

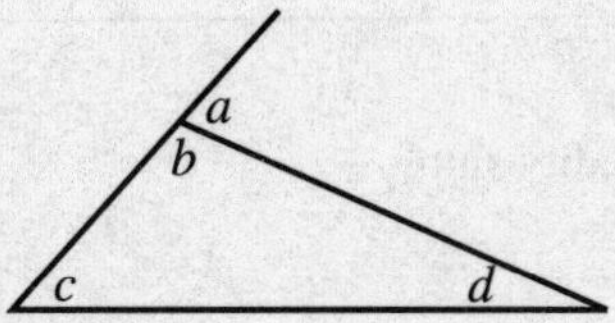

(A) I only
(B) II and III only
(C) I, II, and III
(D) II only
(E) None of these

9. If point X is on line segment AB, all of the following may be true *except*

(A) $AX = XB$
(B) $AX > XB$
(C) $AX < XB$
(D) $AB > XB$
(E) $AX + XB < AB$

10. If $x > 0$, $y > 0$, and $x - y < 0$, then

(A) $x > y$
(B) $x < y$
(C) $x + y < 0$
(D) $y - x < 0$
(E) $x = -y$

SOLUTIONS TO PRACTICE EXERCISES XIII

1. **(B)** Doubles of unequals are unequal in the same order.

2. **(E)** If unequal quantities are added to unequal quantities of the same order, the results are unequal in the same order.

3. **(A)** If the product of two numbers is > 0 (positive), then either both numbers are positive or both are negative. Since $a < 0$ (negative), b must also be negative.

4. **(D)** $4 - x > 5$
   $-x > 1$. Divide by -1 and change the inequality sign.
   $x < -1$

5. **(B)**

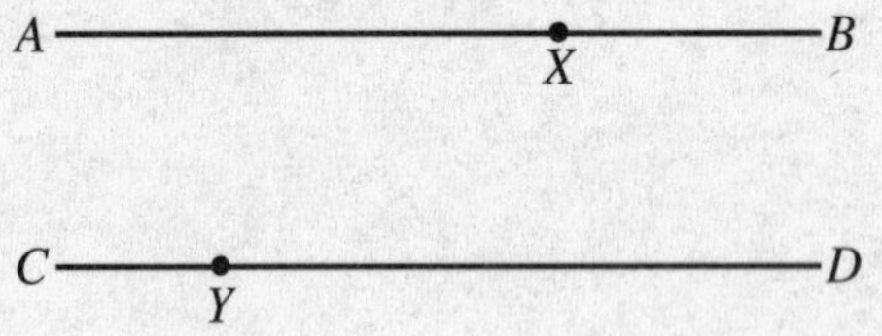

If unequal quantities are subtracted from equal quantities, the results are unequal in the same order.

6. **(A)**

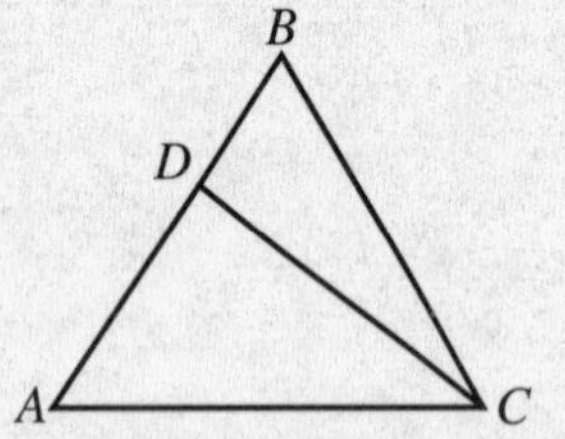

Since $AB = BC$, $\angle BAC = \angle BCA$. Since $\angle BCA > \angle DCA$, it follows that $\angle BAC$ is also greater than $\angle DCA$. Then $DC > DA$. If two angles of a triangle are unequal, the sides opposite these angles are unequal, with the larger side opposite the larger angle.

7. **(B)** $BA > BC$. If equal quantities are added to unequal quantities, the sums are unequal in the same order. It follows, in triangle ABC, that the angle opposite BA will be greater than the angle opposite BC.

8. **(E)** An exterior angle of a triangle must be greater than either remote interior angle. There is no fixed relationship between an exterior angle and its adjacent interior angle.

9. **(E)** Point X could be so located to make each of the other choices true, but the whole segment AB will always be equal to the sum of its parts AX and XB.

10. **(B)** If x and y are both positive, but $x - y$ is negative, then y must be a larger number than x.

XIV. Quantitative Comparisons

Questions of this type give you two quantities, one listed in Column A and one in Column B. For some items, information concerning one or both of the compared quantities will be centered above the quantities to be compared. You are to decide which quantity, if any, is the greater of the two. If A is greater choose answer (A). If B is greater, choose answer (B). If they are equal, choose answer (C). If there isn't enough information to tell, choose answer (D). In contrast to the other multiple-choice questions on the examination, which have five possible choices for answers, these questions have only four possible choices.

Unnecessary involvement with tedious computation can really slow you down here. Always remember that if you are doing lengthy written work to find an answer, there must be an easier way. None of these problems should involve multiplication or division with large numbers.

Example➤

Column A	*Column B*
$\frac{(8)(45)(17)}{(462)(8)}$	$\frac{(17)(9)(42)}{(231)(16)}$

Solution➤ The denominators of both fractions are equal, since 462 is 231 times 2, making both denominators (231)(2)(8). The numerator of B is larger than A, as they both have a factor of 17, but (9)(42) is greater than (8)(45). Therefore, B is the greater fraction—a conclusion reached with no major computation at all.

Another important concept to remember is that the product of any number of factors will be zero if and only if one of the factors is 0.

Example➤

$$x > 0, y > 0, z = 0$$

Column A	*Column B*
$3z(2x + 5y)$	$3x(2z + 5y)$

Solution➤ If $z = 0$, then $3z = 0$ and the product of the factors in Column A is 0. In Column B, the product will be $(3x)(5y)$, which is positive. Therefore, B is greater.

Example➤

$$x < 0, y > 0, z = 0$$

Column A	*Column B*
$3z(2x + 5y)$	$3x(2z + 5y)$

Solution➤ Again, the product of the factors in Column A will be 0, since $3z = 0$. In Column B, $3x$ will be negative, $5y$ will be positive, so their product will be a negative number. This time, A is greater.

When making comparisons in this type of question, be sure to consider all possibilities.

Example➤

Column A		Column B
	$x^2 = 81$ $y^2 = 64$	
x		y

Solution➤ Remember that a quadratic equation has two roots. If $x^2 = 81$, x may be 9 or –9. If $y^2 = 64$, y may be 8 or –8. If x is 9 while y is 8, x will be greater. But if x is –9 while y is –8, y will be greater. Therefore, the correct answer is (D), there is not enough information.

Example➤

Column A	Column B
x^3	x^2

Solution➤ If x is greater than 1, A is greater. If x is a fraction between 0 and 1, or any negative number, B is greater. If x is 0 or 1, both A and B are equal. Therefore, the correct answer is (D).

Example➤

Column A		Column B
	$1 < x < 3$ $1 < y < 99$	
x		y

Solution➤ If x and y are both 2, A and B are equal. If x is $2\frac{1}{2}$ and y is 2, A is greater. If x is 2 and y is 17, B is greater. Again, the correct answer is (D).

In each of the above examples, it is important to consider all possible values of the variable before jumping to a conclusion.

Triangle relationships in geometry also lend themselves to this type of question.

Examples➤

Column A — Column B

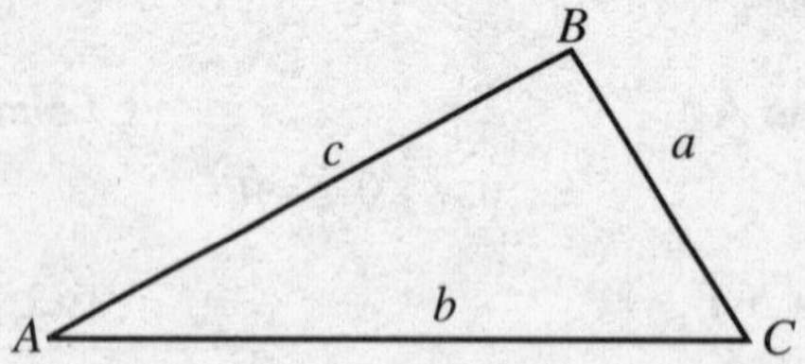

$c > a$

	Column A	Column B
1.	$\angle A$	$\angle C$
2.	$\angle A$	$\angle B$
3.	$a + b$	c

Solutions➤

1. If two sides of a triangle are unequal, the angles opposite are unequal, with the greater angle opposite the greater side. Therefore, the correct answer is (B).
2. Since we do not know whether a or b is greater, we cannot tell which angle is greater. The correct answer is (D).
3. The sum of any two sides of a triangle must always be greater than the third. Therefore, the correct answer is (A).

PRACTICE EXERCISES XIV

Compare the two quantities in Column A and Column B and determine whether:

(A) the quantity is greater in Column A
(B) the quantity is greater in Column B
(C) both quantities are equal
(D) no comparison can be made with the information given

Write your answer next to the question number.

Notes: (1) Information concerning one or both of the compared quantities will be centered between the two columns when given.
(2) Symbols that appear in both columns represent the same thing in Column A as in Column B.
(3) Letters such as *x*, *n*, and *k* are symbols for real numbers.
(4) Figures are not necessarily drawn to scale.

	Column A	Column B
1.	$\frac{2}{3} \times 2$	30%
2.	$\frac{4}{17}$	$\frac{2}{15}$
3.	$3\frac{1}{2}$ expressed as a percent	3.5%
4.	$\sqrt{25.1}$	5.1
5.	Cost per egg if 2 dozen cost $1.90	9¢
6.	$(2+.2)(2-.2)\left(\frac{1}{5}\right)$	(.2)(1.8)(2.2)
7.	$\sqrt{\frac{1}{4}+\frac{1}{9}}$	$\frac{1}{2}+\frac{1}{3}$

$m = 3, n = -2$

	Column A	Column B
8.	$(m+n)^2$	$(m-n)^2$

The distance from *A* to *B* is 3 miles.
The distance from *B* to *C* is 4 miles.

	Column A	Column B
9.	5 miles	The distance from *A* to *C*
10.	x^5	x^2

The area of a circle is 16π.

	Column A	Column B
11.	Diameter of the circle	16

The average of 5 numbers is 20.

	Column A	Column B
12.	The sum of the five numbers	110
13.	$\frac{1}{.5}$	$\frac{1}{.05}$

	Column A	Column B
14.	$.1\pi$	$\sqrt{.9}$
15.	Area of a square having perimeter 32	Area of circle having radius 5

$x = 8 = y^2 - 1$

	Column A	Column B
16.	x	y

$a^2 = 49$

	Column A	Column B
17.	a	7

$a > b > 0$

	Column A	Column B
18.	$\frac{1}{a}$	$\frac{1}{b}$

$(2)(2)(a) = (3)(3)(3)$

	Column A	Column B
19.	a	2

$-4 < x < -2$

	Column A	Column B
20.	$\frac{1}{x^4}$	$\frac{1}{x^5}$
21.	(16)(351)(10)	(15)(351)(11)

$a^2 > 0$

	Column A	Column B
22.	a	0

	Column A	Column B
23.	A single discount of 10%	Two successive discounts of 5% and 5%
24.	50%	$\frac{1}{.02}$
25.	Time elapsed from 11:50 P.M. to 12:02 A.M.	$\frac{1}{3}$ hour

The diagram below applies to problems 26–29.

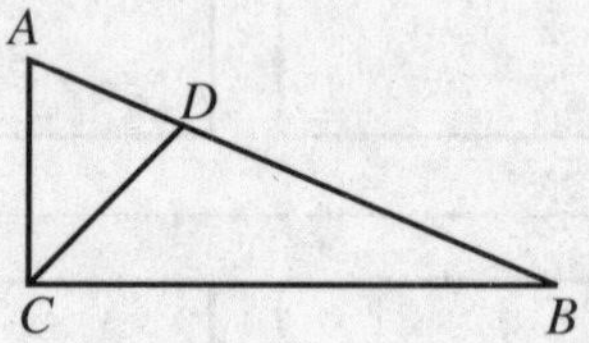

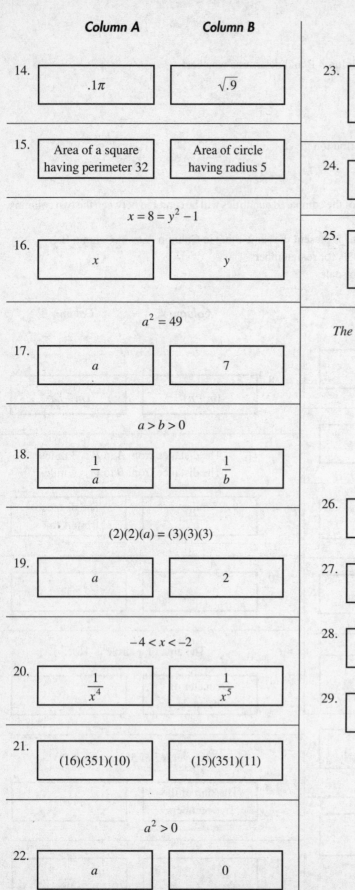

$AC \cong CD \cong AD$ $\quad AC \perp CB$

	Column A	Column B
26.	CD	DB
27.	$\angle A$	$\angle B$
28.	CD	CB
29.	AD	DB

Column A	Column B

Questions 30–31 refer to the figure below.

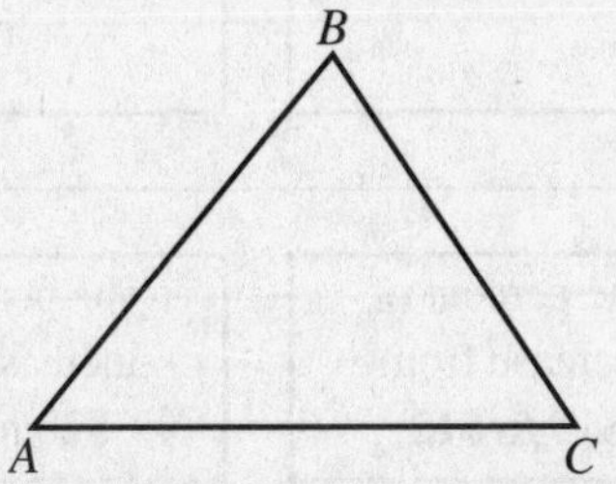

$AB \cong BC$	Angle $B <$ Angle A

	Column A	Column B
30.	$\angle B$	$\angle C$
31.	AB	AC

Questions 32–34 refer to the figure below.

$EC \perp AD$

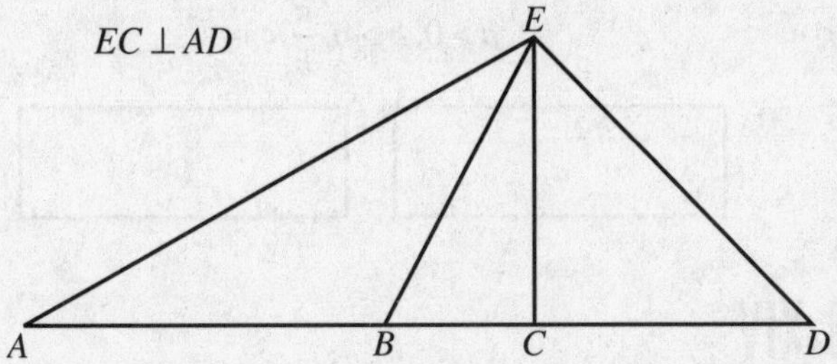

	Column A	Column B
32.	EC	ED
33.	$\angle EBA$	$\angle ECD$
34.	$\angle A$	$\angle ECB$

Column A	Column B

Questions 35–37 refer to the figure below.

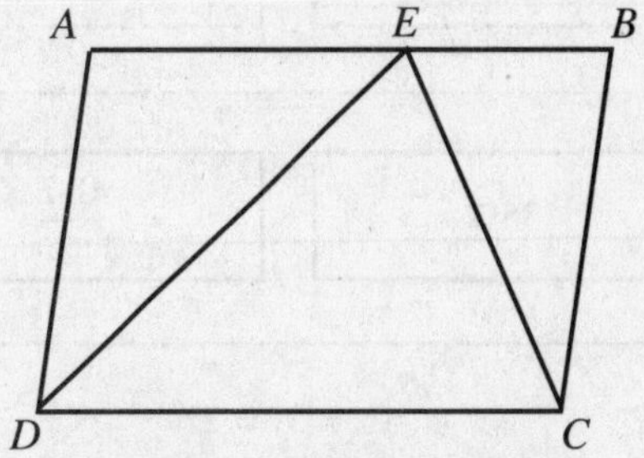

ABCD is a parallelogram.
E is any point on *AB*.

	Column A	Column B
35.	Twice the area of triangle *DEC*	Area of parallelogram *ABCD*
36.	$\angle A$	$\angle B$
37.	AD	DC

Questions 38–40 apply to the figure below.

Radius of outer circle = 10
Radius of inner circle = 5

	Column A	Column B
38.	Twice area of inner circle	Area of shaded portion
39.	Area of inner circle	75
40.	Circumference of inner circle	50% of circumference of outer circle

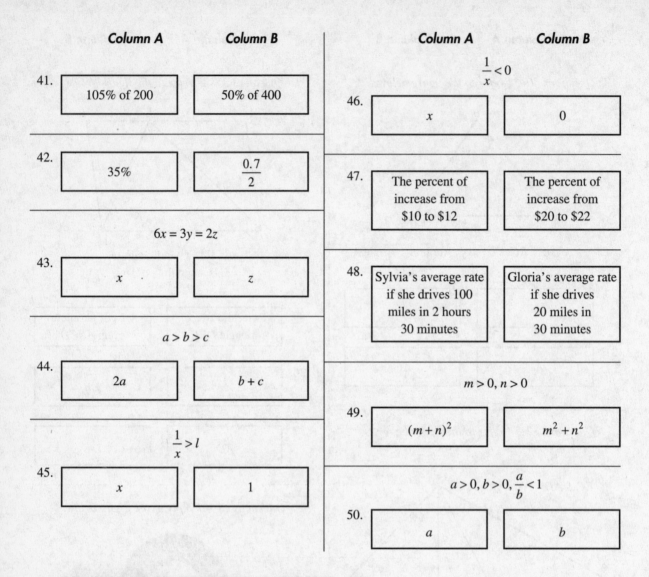

	Column A	Column B
41.	105% of 200	50% of 400

	Column A	Column B
42.	35%	$\frac{0.7}{2}$

$6x = 3y = 2z$

	Column A	Column B
43.	x	z

$a > b > c$

	Column A	Column B
44.	$2a$	$b + c$

$\frac{1}{x} > 1$

	Column A	Column B
45.	x	1

$\frac{1}{x} < 0$

	Column A	Column B
46.	x	0

	Column A	Column B
47.	The percent of increase from \$10 to \$12	The percent of increase from \$20 to \$22

	Column A	Column B
48.	Sylvia's average rate if she drives 100 miles in 2 hours 30 minutes	Gloria's average rate if she drives 20 miles in 30 minutes

$m > 0, n > 0$

	Column A	Column B
49.	$(m+n)^2$	$m^2 + n^2$

$a > 0, b > 0, \frac{a}{b} < 1$

	Column A	Column B
50.	a	b

SOLUTIONS TO PRACTICE EXERCISES XIV

1. **(A)** $\frac{2}{3} \div 2 = \frac{2}{3} \bullet \frac{1}{2} = \frac{1}{3} = 33\frac{1}{3}\%$

2. **(A)** To compare $\frac{a}{b}$ with $\frac{c}{d}$, compare ad with bc.
   If $ad < bc$, then the first fraction is smaller. If $ad = bc$, the fractions are equal. If $ad > bc$, then the first fraction is larger. 4 times 15 is greater than 17 times 2. Therefore, the first fraction is greater.

3. **(A)** $3\frac{1}{2} = 3.5 = 350\%$

4. **(B)** $(5.1)^2 = 26.01$
   $(\sqrt{25.1})^2 = 25.1$

5. **(B)** There are 24 eggs in 2 dozen.'

$$24\overline{)1.90} = .079$$

```
     .079
 24)1.90
    1 68
    ----
     220
```

Each egg costs almost 8 cents.

6. **(C)** $2 + .2 = 2.2$
$2 - .2 = 1.8$
$\frac{1}{5} = .2$

Factors on both sides are the same.

7. **(B)** $\sqrt{\frac{1}{4} + \frac{1}{9}} = \sqrt{\frac{13}{36}} = \frac{\sqrt{13}}{6}$

$\frac{1}{2} + \frac{1}{3} = \frac{5}{6}$

8. **(B)** $(m+n)^2 = (1)^2 = 1$
$(m-n)^2 = (5)^2 = 25$

9. **(D)** There is no indication as to the direction from B to C.

10. **(D)** If $x > 1$, A is bigger. If $x = 1$, A and B are equal. If $x < 0$, B is bigger.

11. **(B)**
$$\text{Area of a circle} = \pi r^2$$
$$16\pi = \pi r^2$$
$$16 = r^2$$
$$r = 4$$
$$\text{diameter} = 8$$

12. **(B)** If the average is 20, then the 5 numbers were added and the sum divided by 5 to give 20. The sum of these numbers must be 100.

13. **(B)** $\frac{1}{.5} = \frac{10}{5} = 2$

$\frac{1}{.05} = \frac{100}{5} = 20$

14. **(B)** $.1(3.14) = .314$

$\sqrt{.90}$ (.9)

15. **(B)** Each side of the square is 8. Area of the square is 64. Area of the circle is 25π. $25(3.14)$ is greater than 64.

16. **(A)** $8 = y^2 - 1$
$9 = y^2$
$y = 3$ or -3

Since $x = 8$, x is greater for either value of y.

17. **(D)** a may be either 7 or –7.

18. **(B)** When fractions have equal numerators, the fraction having the smaller denominator has the greater value.

19. **(A)** $4a = 27$ $\quad a = 6\frac{3}{4}$

20. **(A)** Since x is negative, any even power of x is positive, while any odd power of x is negative.

21. **(B)** (16)(10) is less than (15)(11).

22. **(D)** If a^2 is positive, a can be either negative or positive.

23. **(A)** Consider a marked price of \$100. A single discount of 10% gives \$10 off. An initial discount of 5% gives \$5 off, making the new price \$95. The second 5% discount is 5% of \$95 or \$4.75, making the total discount only \$5 + \$4.75 or \$9.75.

24. **(B)** $50\% = \frac{1}{2}$

$$\frac{1}{.02} = \frac{100}{2} = 50$$

25. **(B)** From 11:50 P.M. to 12:02 A.M. is 12 minutes. One third of an hour is 20 minutes.

26. **(C)**

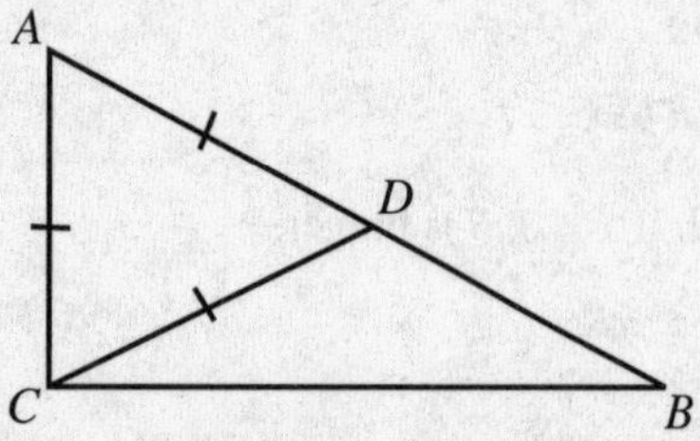

Triangle *ACD* is equilateral, making each angle 60°. Angle *DCB* is then 30°, and angle *CDB* is 120°, leaving 30° for angle *B*. Therefore, triangle *DCB* is isosceles.

27. **(A)** Angle *A* is 60° and angle *B* is 30°.

28. **(B)** In triangle *CDB*, *CD* is opposite a 30° angle, while *CB* is opposite 120°.

29. **(C)** Both of these segments are equal to *CD*.

30. **(B)** Since $\angle A$ and $\angle C$ must be equal, because the sides opposite are congruent, $\angle B$ is also less than $\angle C$.

31. **(A)** Since $\angle B$ is less than $\angle C$, *AC* will be less than *AB*.

32. **(B)** The shortest distance from a point to a line is the perpendicular.

33. **(A)** Angle *EBA* is an exterior angle of triangle *EBC* and is therefore greater than angle *ECB*. Since angle *ECD* is also a right angle, angle *EBA* will be greater than angle *ECD*.

34. **(B)** Triangle *ECA* has a right angle. Since there will be 90° left to divide between the two remaining angles, angle *A* must be less than 90°.

35. **(C)** The altitude of triangle *EDC* is equal to the altitude of the parallelogram. Both the triangle and the parallelogram have the same base. Since the area of a triangle is $\frac{1}{2}bh$ and the area of a parallelogram is bh, these quantities are equal.

36. **(D)** There is no way to tell which is greater.

37. **(D)** There is no way to tell which is greater.

38. **(B)** Area of outer circle = $\pi r^2 = 100\pi$
Area of inner circle = 25π
Shaded portion is outer circle minus inner circle, or 75π.

39. **(A)** Area of inner circle = $\pi r^2 = 25\pi$.
25(3.14) is more than 75.

40. **(C)** Circumference = πd
Circumference of outer circle = $\pi(20)$
Circumference of inner circle = $\pi(10)$
$50\% = \frac{1}{2}$
$\frac{1}{2}$ of outer circumference = 10π

41. **(A)** 105% of 200 is more than 200.
50% or $\frac{1}{2}$ of 400 is 200.

42. **(C)** 35% = .35
$$\frac{0.7}{2} = .35$$

43. **(D)** If $6x = 2z$, then $3x = z$, or $x = \frac{1}{3}z$. If either x or z is zero, both quantities are equal; if both are positive, z is larger. If both are negative, x is larger.

44. **(A)**
$$\begin{array}{l} a > b \\ a > c \\ \hline 2a > b + c \end{array}$$

45. **(B)** If $\frac{1}{x} > 1$, multiply each side by x to get $1 > x$. There should be no concern about reversing the inequality, as x must be positive if $\frac{1}{x} > 1$.

46. **(B)** If $\frac{1}{x}$ is to be negative, x must be negative, since a positive number divided by a negative number gives a negative quotient. 0 is larger than any negative number.

47. **(A)** Percent of increase = $\frac{\text{Amount of increase}}{\text{Original}} \bullet 100$. The percent of increase in A is $\frac{2}{10} \bullet 100$. The percent of increase in B is $\frac{2}{20}$, or $\frac{1}{10} \bullet 100$.

48. **(C)** Average rate = $\frac{\text{Total distance}}{\text{Total time}}$
Sylvia's average rate = $\frac{100}{2.5} = 40$
Gloria's average rate = $\frac{20}{.5} = 40$

49. **(A)** $(m+n)^2 = m^2 + 2mn + n^2$. Since m and n are both positive, $2mn$ is positive.

50. **(B)** If $\frac{a}{b} < 1$, the denominator must be greater than the numerator.

XV. Function or Operation Problems

Functions are another way that mathematicians save time. A real function problem might look like this: $f(x)=3x^2$. The function of x is obtained by squaring x and then multiplying the result by 3. If you wanted to know $f(4)$, you would square 4 and multiply that product by 3; the answer would be 48. On the SAT the $f(x)$ symbol is not normally used. Instead the test-makers use arbitrary symbols. You still have to approach these symbols as you would a function: Talk to yourself about what the function does. In math you usually change words into mathematical notation, but with functions you change mathematical notation into words.

$!x = 2x + 4$

What does the "!" do in this problem? It takes x and doubles it and then adds four.

What is the value of !6?

$!6 = 2(6) + 4 = 16$

PRACTICE EXERCISES XV

1. &x is such that $\&x = \frac{x^2}{2}$. What is the value of &4?

(A) 8
(B) 16
(C) 32
(D) 40
(E) 64

2. \$$x$ is such that \$$x$ is equal to the nearest low integer to x. What is the value of \$6.99 times \$ –2.01?

(A) 18
(B) 12
(C) –12
(D) –18
(E) –21

3. The operation # is defined in the following way for any two numbers:
$p \# q = (p - q)$ times $(q - p)$.
If $p \# q = -1$ then which of the following are true:

I. p could equal 5 and q could equal 4
II. p could equal 4 and q could equal 5
III. p could equal 1 and q could equal –1
IV. p could equal –1 and q could equal 1

(A) I and II only
(B) I and III only
(C) II and IV only
(D) III and IV only
(E) I, II, III, IV

4. Every letter in the alphabet has a number value which is equal to its place in the alphabet; the letter A has a value of 1 and C a value of 3. The number value of a word is obtained by adding up the value of the letters in the word and then multiplying that sum by the length of the word. The word "DFGH" would have a number value of

(A) 22
(B) 44
(C) 66
(D) 100
(E) 108

5. Let $\wedge x \wedge$ be defined such that $\wedge x \wedge = x + \frac{1}{x}$. The value of $\wedge 6 \wedge + \wedge 4 \wedge + \wedge 2 \wedge$ is

(A) 12

(B) $12\frac{7}{12}$

(C) $12\frac{11}{12}$

(D) $13\frac{1}{12}$

(E) $13\frac{5}{12}$

SOLUTIONS TO PRACTICE EXERCISES XV

1. **(C)** $4^3 = 64$ and 64 divided by 2 is 32.

2. **(D)** The key phrase in the problem is "the nearest low integer." The nearest low integer to 6.99 is 6 (not 7, this problem does not say to round the numbers) and the nearest low integer to –2.01 is –3(not –2 as –2 is higher than –2.01).

3. **(A)** The best way to solve this is to plug the values into the equation:

$(5-4)\#(4-5) = -1$
$(4-5)\#(5-4) = -1$
$(1--1)\#(-1-1) = -4$
$(-1-1)\#(1--1) = -4$

Statements I and II give the stated value, –1.

4. **(D)** D = 4, F = 6, G = 7, and H = 8 so the sum of the letters would be 25. 25 multiplied by 4 (the length of the word) is 100.

5. **(C)** The work of this problem is adding up the reciprocals of the numbers.

6 + 4 + 2 is clearly 12. $\frac{1}{6} + \frac{1}{4} + \frac{1}{2} = \frac{2}{12} + \frac{3}{12} + \frac{6}{12} = \frac{11}{12}$

VERBAL REVIEW

This section will help you strengthen your vocabulary and prepare you to score high in every SAT verbal skill. To increase your vocabulary, there's an introduction to word building, a list of common word parts, and a 500-word SAT vocabulary list. To boost your verbal reasoning scores, there are helpful hints for answering Verbal Analogy, Sentence Completion, and Critical Reading questions, along with practice tests and explanatory answers for each SAT verbal skill area.

The Building Blocks of Words

One of the most efficient ways to increase your vocabulary is to study the basic parts from which most English words are built. Once you know some of these basic building blocks, you will find it easier to remember words you have learned and to figure out unfamiliar words you come across in your school work or on the SAT.

Let's look at some examples of word parts at work. The word *biography* is made up of two important parts. *Graphy* comes from a Greek word meaning "writing." Many English words use this root. *Graphology*, for instance, is the study of handwriting; *graphite* is the carbon material used in "lead" pencils; and the *telegraph* is a device for writing at a distance. The *bio* part, also from Greek, means "life." It, too, is at the root of many English words, such as *biology* (the study of life) and *biochemistry* (the chemistry of life). Putting *bio* and *graphy* together creates a word that means "writing about a person's life." You can make another word by adding another part, this time from the Latin word *auto*, meaning "self." An *autobiography* is a person's written account of his or her own life.

The study of how words are formed is called *etymology*, from the Greek words *etymon*, meaning "word source," and *logos*, meaning "knowledge." Any good dictionary will give you the etymology of words. Whenever you look up an unfamiliar word, make it a habit to look at how the word was formed. Does the word have a root that helps to explain its meaning? Is it related to other words you already know?

The following list of common word parts is divided into three categories:

Prefixes—word parts that attach to the beginning of a word to alter its meaning or create a new word;
Suffixes—word parts that attach to the end of a word to change its meaning, give it grammatical function, or form a new word;
Roots—the fundamental elements of words that are the basis for their meaning. Groups of words deriving from the same root are called word families.

By studying the word parts that follow, and by observing their basic, secondary, concrete, and abstract meanings, you will be able to figure out the fundamental meaning of most words. The essence of the study of word parts is to find out not just what a word means, but, rather, *why* it means what it means. Each word part below is defined and an example is given of a word in which it appears. Don't try to memorize the whole list at once. Study one small section at a time, and once you've learned one of the building blocks, remember to look for it in your reading. See if you can think of other words in which the word part appears. Use the dictionary to check your guesses. To help you apply what you've learned, there are several etymology exercises following the list of word parts.

List of Common Word Parts

PREFIXES

Prefix	Meaning	Example
a-	in, on, of, to	*abed*—in bed
a-, ab-, abs-	from, away	*abrade*—wear off *absent*—away, not present
a-, an-	lacking, not	*asymptomatic*—showing no symptoms *anaerobic*—able to live without air
ad-, ac-, af-, ag-, al-, an-, ap-, ar-, as-, at-	to, toward	*accost*—approach and speak to *adjunct*—something added to *aggregate*—bring together
ambi-, amphi-	around, both	*ambidextrous*—using both hands equally *amphibious*—living both in water and on land
ana-	up, again, anew, throughout	*analyze*—loosen up, break up into parts *anagram*—word spelled by mixing up letters of another word
ante-	before	*antediluvian*—before the Flood
anti-	against	*antiwar*—against war
arch-	first, chief	*archetype*—first model
auto-	self	*automobile*—self-moving vehicle
bene-, ben-	good, well	*benefactor*—one who does good deeds
bi-	two	*bilateral*—two-sided
circum-	around	*circumnavigate*—sail around

Prefix	Meaning	Example
com-, co-, col-, con-, cor-	with, together	*concentrate*—bring closer together *cooperate*—work with *collapse*—fall together
contra-, contro-, counter-	against	*contradict*—speak against *counterclockwise*—against the clock
de-	away from, down, opposite of	*detract*—draw away from
demi-	half	*demitasse*—half cup
di-	twice, double	*dichromatic*—having two colors
dia-	across, through	*diameter*—measurement across
dis-, di-	not, away from	*dislike*—to not like *digress*—turn away from the subject
dys-	bad, poor	*dyslexia*—poor reading
equi-	equal	*equivalent*—of equal value
ex-, e-, ef-	from, out	*expatriate*—one who lives outside his or her native country *emit*—send out
extra-	outside, beyond	*extraterrestrial*—from beyond the earth
fore-	in front of, previous	*forecast*—tell ahead of time *foreleg*—front leg
geo-	earth	*geography*—science of the earth's surface
homo-	same, like	*homophonic*—sounding the same
hyper-	too much, over	*hyperactive*—overly active
hypo-	too little, under	*hypothermia*—state of having too little body heat

Prefix	**Meaning**	**Example**
in-, il-, ig-, im-, ir-	not	*innocent*—not guilty *ignorant*—not knowing *illogical*—not logical *irresponsible*—not responsible
in-, il-, im-, ir-,	on, into, in	*impose*—place on *invade*—go into
inter-	between, among	*interplanetary*—between planets
intra-, intro-,	within, inside	*intrastate*—within a state
mal-, male-	bad, wrong, poor	*maladjust*—adjust poorly *malevolent*—ill-wishing
mis-	badly, wrongly	*misunderstand*—understand wrongly
mis-, miso-	hatred	*misogyny*—hatred of women
mono-	single, one	*monorail*—train that runs on a single rail
neo-	new	*neolithic*—of the New Stone Age
non-	not	*nonentity*—a nobody
ob-	over, against, toward	*obstruct*—stand against
omni-	all	*omnipresent*—present in all places
pan-	all	*panorama*—a complete view
peri-	around, near	*periscope*—device for seeing all around
poly-	many	*polygonal*—many-sided
post-	after	*postmortem*—after death
pre-	before, earlier than	*prejudice*—judgment in advance
pro-	in favor of, forward, in front of	*proceed*—go forward *prowar*—in favor of war
re-	back, again	*rethink*—think again *reimburse*—pay back

Prefix	Meaning	Example
retro-	backward	*retrospective*—looking backward
se-	apart, away	*seclude*—keep away
semi-	half	*semiconscious*—half conscious
sub-, suc-, suf-, sug-, sus-	under, beneath	*subscribe*—write underneath *suspend*—hang down *suffer*—undergo
super-	above, greater	*superfluous*—overflowing, beyond what is needed
syn-, sym-, syl-, sys-	with, at the same time	*synthesis*—a putting together *sympathy*—a feeling with
tele-	far	*television*—machine for seeing far
trans-	across	*transport*—carry across a distance
un-	not	*uninformed*—not informed
vice-	acting for, next in rank to	*viceroy*—one acting for the king

SUFFIXES

Suffix	Meaning	Example
-able, -ble	able, capable	*acceptable*—able to be accepted
-acious, -cious	characterized by, having the quality of	*fallacious*—having the quality of a fallacy
-age	sum, total	*mileage*—total number of miles
-al	of, like, suitable for	*theatrical*—suitable for theater
-ance, -ancy	act or state of	*disturbance*—act of disturbing
-ant, -ent	one who	*defendant*—one who defends him- or herself

Suffix	Meaning	Example
-ary, -ar	having the nature of, concerning	*military*—relating to soldiers *polar*—concerning the pole
-cy	act, state, or position of	*presidency*—position of president *ascendency*—state of being raised up
-dom	state, rank, that which belongs to	*wisdom*—state of being wise
-ence	act, state, or quality of	*dependence*—state of depending
-er, -or	one who, that which	*doer*—one who does *conductor*—that which conducts
-escent	becoming	*obsolescent*—becoming obsolete
-fy	to make	*pacify*—make peaceful
-hood	state, condition	*adulthood*—state of being adult
-ic, -ac	of, like	*demonic*—of or like a demon
-il, -ile	having to do with, like, suitable for	*civil*—having to do with citizens *tactile*—having to do with touch
-ion	act or condition of	*operation*—act of operating
-ious	having, characterized by	*anxious*—characterized by anxiety
-ish	like, somewhat	*foolish*—like a fool
-ism	belief or practice of	*racism*—belief in racial superiority
-ist	one who does, makes, or is concerned with	*scientist*—one concerned with science
-ity, -ty, -y	character or state of being	*amity*—friendship *jealousy*—state of being jealous
-ive	of, relating to, tending to	*destructive*—tending to destroy

Suffix	Meaning	Example
-logue, -loquy	speech or writing	*monologue*—speech by one person *colloquy*—conversation
-logy	speech, study of	*geology*—study of the earth
-ment	act or state of	*abandonment*—act of abandoning
-mony	a resulting thing, condition, or state	*patrimony*—property inherited from one's father
-ness	act or quality	*kindness*—quality of being kind
-ory	having the quality of; a place or thing for	*compensatory*—having the quality of a compensation *lavatory*—place for washing
-ous, -ose	full of, having	*glamorous*—full of glamor
-ship	skill, state of being	*horsemanship*—skill in riding *ownership*—state of being an owner
-some	full of, like	*frolicsome*—playful
-tude	state or quality of	*rectitude*—state of being morally upright
-ward	in the direction of	*homeward*—in the direction of home
-y	full of, like, somewhat	*wily*—full of wiles

ROOTS

Root	Meaning	Example
acr	bitter	*acrid, acrimony*
act, ag	do, act, drive	*action, react, agitate*
acu	sharp, keen	*acute, acumen*
agog	leader	*pedagogue, demagogic*
agr	field	*agronomy, agriculture*
ali	other	*alias, alienate, inalienable*

Root	Meaning	Example
alt	high	*altitude, contralto*
alter, altr	other, change	*alternative, altercation, altruism*
am, amic	love, friend	*amorous, amiable*
anim	mind, life, spirit	*animism, animate, animosity*
annu, enni	year	*annual, superannuated, biennial*
anthrop	man	*anthropoid, misanthropy*
apt, ept	fit	*apt, adapt, ineptitude*
aqu	water	*aquatic, aquamarine*
arbit	judge	*arbiter, arbitrary*
arch	chief	*anarchy, matriarch*
arm	arm, weapon	*army, armature, disarm*
art	skill, a fitting together	*artisan, artifact, articulate*
aster, astr	star	*asteroid, disaster, astral*
aud, audit, aur	hear	*auditorium, audition, auricle*
aur	gold	*aureate, aureomycin*
aut	self	*autism, autograph*
bell	war	*antebellum, belligerent*
ben, bene	well, good	*benevolent, benefit*
bibli	book	*bibliography, bibliophile*
bio	life	*biosphere, amphibious*
brev	short	*brevity, abbreviation*
cad, cas, cid	fall	*cadence, casualty, occasion, accident*
cand	white, shining	*candid, candle, incandescent*
cant, chant	sing, charm	*cantor, recant, enchant*
cap, capt, cept, cip	take, seize, hold	*capable, captive, accept, incipient*

Root	Meaning	Example
capit	head	*capital, decapitate, recapitulate*
carn	flesh	*carnal, incarnate*
cede, ceed, cess	go, yield	*secede, exceed, process, intercession*
cent	hundred	*percentage, centimeter*
cern, cert	perceive, make certain, decide	*concern, certificate, certain*
chrom	color	*monochrome, chromatic*
chron	time	*chronometer, anachronism*
cide, cis	cut, kill	*genocide, incision*
cit	summon, impel	*cite, excite, incitement*
civ	citizen	*uncivil, civilization*
clam, claim	shout	*clamorous, proclaim, claimant*
clar	clear	*clarity, clarion, declare*
clin	slope, lean	*inclination, recline*
clud, clus, clos	close, shut	*seclude, recluse, closet*
cogn	know	*recognize, incognito*
col, cul	till	*colony, cultivate, agriculture*
corp	body	*incorporate, corpse*
cosm	order, world	*cosmetic, cosmos, cosmopolitan*
crac, crat	power, rule	*democrat, theocracy*
cre, cresc, cret	grow	*increase, crescent, accretion*
cred	trust, believe	*credit, incredible*
crux, cruc	cross	*crux, crucial, crucifix*
crypt	hidden	*cryptic, cryptography*
culp	blame	*culprit, culpability*
cur, curr, curs	run, course	*occur, current, incursion*

Root	Meaning	Example
cura	care	*curator, accurate*
cycl	wheel, circle	*bicycle, cyclone*
dec	ten	*decade, decimal*
dem	people	*demographic, demagogue*
dent	tooth	*dental, indentation*
derm	skin	*dermatitis, pachyderm*
di, dia	day	*diary, quotidian*
dic, dict	say, speak	*indicative, edict, dictation*
dign	worthy	*dignified, dignitary*
doc, doct	teach, prove	*indoctrinate, docile, doctor*
domin	rule	*predominate, domineer, dominion*
dorm	sleep	*dormitory, dormant*
du	two	*duo, duplicity, dual*
duc, duct	lead	*educate, abduct, ductile*
dur	hard, lasting	*endure, obdurate, duration*
dyn	force, power	*dynamo, dynamite*
ego	I	*egomania, egotist*
equ	equal	*equation, equitable*
erg, urg	work, power	*energetic, metallurgy, demiurge*
err	wander	*error, aberrant*
ev	time, age	*coeval, longevity*
fac, fact, fect, fic	do, make	*facility, factual, perfect, artifice*
fer	bear, carry	*prefer, refer, conifer, fertility*
ferv	boil	*fervid, effervesce*
fid	belief, faith	*infidelity, confidant, perfidious*

Root	Meaning	Example
fin	end, limit	*finite, confine*
firm	strong	*reaffirm, infirmity*
flect, flex	bend	*reflex, inflection*
flor	flower	*florescent, floral*
flu, fluct, flux	flow	*fluid, fluctuation, influx*
form	shape	*formative, reform, formation*
fort	strong	*effort, fortitude*
frag, fract	break	*fragility, infraction*
fug	flee	*refuge, fugitive*
fus	pour, join	*infuse, transfusion*
gam	marry	*exogamy, polygamous*
ge, geo	earth	*geology, geode, perigee*
gen	birth, kind, race	*engender, general, generation*
gest	carry, bear	*gestation, ingest, digest*
gon	angle	*hexagonal, trigonometry*
grad, gress	step, go	*regress, gradation*
gram	writing	*grammar, cryptogram*
graph	writing	*telegraph, graphics*
grat	pleasing, agreeable	*congratulate, gratuitous*
grav	weight, heavy	*gravamen, gravity*
greg	flock, crowd	*gregarious, segregate*
habit, hibit	have, hold	*habitation, inhibit, habitual*
heli	sun	*helium, heliocentric, aphelion*
hem	blood	*hemoglobin, hemorrhage*
her, hes	stick, cling	*adherent, cohesive*
hydr	water	*dehydration, hydrofoil*
iatr	heal, cure	*pediatrics, psychiatry*

Root	Meaning	Example
iso	same, equal	*isotope, isometric*
it	journey, go	*itinerary, exit*
ject	throw	*reject, subjective, projection*
jud	judge	*judicial, adjudicate*
jug, junct	join	*conjugal, juncture, conjunction*
jur	swear	*perjure, jurisprudence*
labor	work	*laborious, belabor*
leg	law	*legal, illegitimate*
leg, lig, lect	choose, gather, read	*illegible, eligible, select, lecture*
lev	light, rise	*levity, alleviate*
liber	free	*liberal, libertine*
liter	letter	*literate, alliterative*
lith	rock, stone	*eolithic, lithograph*
loc	place	*locale, locus, allocate*
log	word, study	*logic, biology, dialogue*
loqu, locut	talk, speech	*colloquial, loquacious, interlocutor*
luc, lum	light	*translucent, pellucid, illumine, luminous*
lud, lus	play	*allusion, ludicrous, interlude*
magn	large, great	*magnificent, magnitude*
mal	bad, ill	*malodorous, malinger*
man, manu	hand	*manifest, manicure, manuscript*
mar	sea	*maritime, submarine*
mater, matr	mother	*matrilocal, maternal*
medi	middle	*intermediary, medieval*
mega	large, million	*megaphone, megacycle*

Root	Meaning	Example
ment	mind	*demented, mental*
merg, mers	plunge, dip	*emerge, submersion*
meter, metr, mens	measure	*chronometer, metronome, geometry, commensurate*
micr	small	*microfilm, micron*
min	little	*minimum, minute*
mit, miss	send	*remit, admission, missive*
mon, monit	warn	*admonish, monument, monitor*
mor	custom	*mores, immoral*
mor, mort	death	*mortify, mortician*
morph	shape	*amorphous, anthropomorphic*
mov, mob, mot	move	*removal, automobile, motility*
multi	many	*multiply, multinational*
mut	change	*mutable, transmute*
nasc, nat	born	*native, natural, nascent, innate*
nav	ship, sail	*navy, navigable*
necr	dead, die	*necropolis, necrosis*
neg	deny	*renege, negative*
neo	new	*neologism, neoclassical*
nomen, nomin	name	*nomenclature, cognomen, nominate*
nomy	law, rule	*astronomy, antinomy*
nov	new	*novice, innovation*
ocul	eye	*binocular, oculist*
omni	all	*omniscient, omnibus*
onym	name	*pseudonym, eponymous*
oper	work	*operate, cooperation, inoperable*
ora	speak, pray	*oracle, oratory*

Root	Meaning	Example
orn	decorate	*adorn, ornate*
orth	straight, correct	*orthodox, orthopedic*
pan	all	*panacea, pantheon*
pater, patr	father	*patriot, paternity*
path, pat, pass	feel, suffer	*telepathy, patient, compassion, passion*
ped	child	*pedagogue, pediatrics*
ped, pod	foot	*pedestrian, impede, tripod*
pel, puls	drive, push	*impel, propulsion*
pend, pens	hang	*pendulous, suspense*
pet, peat	seek	*petition, impetus, repeat*
phil	love	*philosopher, Anglophile*
phob	fear	*phobic, agoraphobia*
phon	sound	*phonograph, symphony*
phor	bearing	*semaphore, metaphor*
phot	light	*photograph, photoelectric*
pon, pos	place, put	*component, repose, postpone*
port	carry	*report, portable, deportation*
pot	power	*potency, potential*
press	press	*pressure, impression*
prim	first	*primal, primordial*
proto, prot	first	*proton, protagonist*
psych	mind	*psychic, metempsychosis*
pyr	fire	*pyrite, pyrophobia*
quer, quir, quis, ques	ask, seek	*query, inquiry, inquisitive, quest*
reg, rig, rect	straight, rule	*regulate, dirigible, corrective*
rid, ris	laugh	*deride, risible, ridiculous*
rog	ask	*rogation, interrogate*

Root	Meaning	Example
rupt	break	*erupt, interruption, rupture*
sanct	holy	*sacrosanct, sanctify, sanction*
sci, scio	know	*nescient, conscious, omniscience*
scop	watch, view	*horoscope, telescopic*
scrib, script	write	*scribble, proscribe, description*
sed, sid, sess	sit, seat	*sedate, residence, session*
seg, sect	cut	*segment, section, intersect*
sent, sens	feel, think	*nonsense, sensitive, sentient, dissent*
sequ, secut	follow	*sequel, consequence, consecutive*
sign	sign, mark	*signature, designate, assign*
sol	alone	*solitary, solo, desolate*
solv, solu, solut	loosen	*dissolve, soluble, absolution*
somn	sleep	*insomnia, somnolent*
son	sound	*sonorous, unison*
soph	wise, wisdom	*philosophy, sophisticated*
spec, spic, spect	look	*specimen, conspicuous, spectacle*
spir	breathe	*spirit, conspire, respiration*
stab, stat	stand	*unstable, status, station, establish*
stead	place	*instead, steadfast*
string, strict	bind	*astringent, stricture, restrict*
stru, struct	build	*construe, structure, destructive*
sum, sumpt	take	*presume, consumer, assumption*
tang, ting, tact, tig	touch	*tangent, contingency, contact, tactile, contiguous*

Root	Meaning	Example
tax, tac	arrange, arrangement	*taxonomy, tactic*
techn	skill, art	*technique, technician*
tele	far	*teletype, telekinesis*
tempor	time	*temporize, extemporaneous*
ten, tain, tent	hold	*tenant, tenacity, retention, contain*
tend, tens, tent	stretch	*contend, extensive, intent*
tenu	thin	*tenuous, attenuate*
term	end	*terminal, terminate*
terr, ter	land, earth	*inter, terrain*
test	witness	*attest, testify*
the	god	*polytheism, theologist*
therm	heat	*thermos, isotherm*
tom	cut	*atomic, appendectomy*
tort, tors	twist	*tortuous, torsion, contort*
tract	pull, draw	*traction, attract, protract*
trib	assign, pay	*attribute, tribute, retribution*
trud, trus	thrust	*obtrude, intrusive*
turb	agitate	*perturb, turbulent, disturb*
umbr	shade	*umbrella, penumbra, umbrage*
uni	one	*unify, disunity, union*
urb	city	*urbane, suburb*
vac	empty	*vacuous, evacuation*
vad, vas	go	*invade, evasive*
val, vail	strength, worth	*valid, avail, prevalent*
ven, vent	come	*advent, convene, prevention*
ver	true	*aver, veracity, verity*
verb	word	*verbose, adverb, verbatim*

Root	Meaning	Example
vert, vers	turn	*revert, perversion*
vest	dress	*vestment*
vid, vis	see	*video, evidence, vision, revise*
vinc, vict	conquer	*evince, convict, victim*
viv, vit	life	*vivid, revive, vital*
voc, vok	call	*vociferous, provocative, revoke*
vol	wish	*involuntary, volition*
voly, volut	roll, turn	*involve, convoluted, revolution*
vulg	common	*divulge, vulgarity*
zo	animal	*zoologist, paleozoic*

Exercises

In each of the following exercises, the words in the left-hand column are built on roots given in the etymology chart. Match each word with its definition from the right-hand column. Refer to the chart if necessary. Can you identify the roots of each word? If there is any word you can't figure out, look it up in a dictionary.

EXERCISE 1

1. mutable	A. able to be touched
2. culpable	B. laughable
3. interminable	C. empty of meaning or interest
4. amiable	D. of the first age
5. vacuous	E. holding firmly
6. vital	F. necessary to life
7. primeval	G. unending
8. tenacious	H. stable, not able to be loosened or broken up
9. tangible	I. changeable
10. inoperable	J. friendly
11. risible	K. blameworthy
12. indissoluble	L. not working, out of order

EXERCISE 2

1. infinity	A. list of things to be done
2. duplicity	B. sum paid yearly
3. levity	C. a throwing out or from
4. brevity	D. shortness
5. ejection	E. endlessness
6. edict	F. body of teachings
7. infraction	G. killing of a race
8. genocide	H. lightness of spirit
9. agenda	I. a breaking
10. annuity	J. double-dealing
11. microcosm	K. official decree; literally, a speaking out
12. doctrine	L. world in miniature

EXERCISE 3

1. recede	A. state as the truth
2. abdicate	B. throw light on
3. homogenize	C. forswear, give up a power
4. illuminate	D. put into words
5. supervise	E. make freer
6. verbalize	F. go away
7. liberalize	G. bury
8. legislate	H. oversee
9. intervene	I. make laws
10. inter	J. draw out
11. aver	K. make the same throughout
12. protract	L. come between

EXERCISE 4

1. abduction	A. arrival, a coming to
2. fortitude	B. a pressing together
3. consequence	C. a flowing together
4. confluence	D. something added to
5. compression	E. a coming back to life
6. locus	F. place
7. status	G. truthfulness
8. disunity	H. that which follows as a result
9. veracity	I. strength
10. revival	J. lack of oneness
11. advent	K. a leading away, kidnapping
12. adjunct	L. standing, position

EXERCISE 5

1. nascent	A. being born
2. centennial	B. before the war
3. prospective	C. believing easily
4. circumspect	D. going against
5. multinational	E. in name only
6. clamorous	F. hard, unyielding
7. antebellum	G. looking, forward
8. contrary	H. careful, looking in all directions
9. impassioned	I. hundred year anniversary
10. credulous	J. have interests in many countries
11. obdurate	K. full of strong feeling
12. nominal	L. shouting

Answer Key

Exercise 1

1. I	4. J	7. D	9. A	11. B
2. K	5. C	8. E	10. L	12. H
3. G	6. F			

Exercise 2

1. E	4. D	7. I	9. A	11. L
2. J	5. C	8. G	10. B	12. F
3. H	6. K			

Exercise 3

1. F	4. B	7. E	9. L	11. A
2. C	5. H	8. I	10. G	12. J
3. K	6. D			

Exercise 4

1. K	4. C	7. L	9. G	11. A
2. I	5. B	8. J	10. E	12. D
3. H	6. F			

Exercise 5

1. A	4. H	7. B	9. K	11. F
2. I	5. J	8. D	10. C	12. E
3. G	6. L			

SAT Word List

Vocabulary questions appear in the Critical Reading section of the SAT, where you are asked to define a word as it is used in the context of the reading. However, a good vocabulary is also required to answer verbal analogy and sentence completion questions, so vocabulary building remains an essential part of SAT preparation.

The word list that follows contains over 500 words that have appeared on recent SATs. Many of these words may be familiar to you, although you may not be certain precisely what they mean or how they are used. Each word is identified by part of speech and briefly defined. For information about the roots of these words or for more extensive definitions, check your dictionary.

As part of your SAT study plan, try to learn as many of these words as you can. Below are two techniques to help you expand your vocabulary in preparation for the SAT. Try them both to see which one works best for you.

MAKING LISTS

Read through the SAT word list and choose 15 or 20 words whose meanings you don't know. Write these words on a sheet of paper, one word to a line. Then go back and fill in the definition of each word as it appears in the word list. Now you have a smaller list that you can carry with you and review whenever you have some spare time. When you have mastered this list, prepare another in the same way.

MAKING FLASHCARDS

As you read through the SAT word list, prepare an index card for each word you do not know. Write the word on one side of the card and the definition on the other side. Prepare 15 or 20 cards at a time. Then study the words and definitions and test yourself. Arrange the cards so that the words are face up. On a separate sheet of paper, write the meaning of the word shown on the top card. Turn this card over and write the meaning of the second word, and so on through the deck. Check yourself by comparing your answers with the definitions on the backs of your flashcards. You can also reverse the cards and, looking at the definitions, write the correct words. Then, too, you can ask a friend to hold the cards up for you as you call out the correct meaning of each word.

Following the word list is a vocabulary drill to test your mastery of these words.

Word List

aberration *(noun)* Deviation from what is correct or right.
abeyance *(noun)* Suspension of an activity; postponement.
abstemious *(adj)* Sparing in use of food or drink; moderate.
abstruse *(adj)* Concealed; difficult to comprehend; obscure.
accolade *(noun)* Embrace; award; commendation.
acerbic *(adj)* Bitter; harsh; caustic.
acrimonious *(adj)* Sarcastic; caustic; angry; mordant.
acuity *(noun)* Sharpness; acuteness; keenness.
acute *(adj)* 1. Perceptive. 2. Excruciating.
adept *(adj)* Proficient; masterful; expert.
adherent *(noun)* Believer; supporter; devotee.
adjunct *(noun)* 1. Attachment; appendage. 2. Subordinate or auxiliary capacity.
admonish *(verb)* Caution; reprove mildly; reprimand.
adroit *(adj)* Dexterous; proficient; skillful.
adulation *(noun)* Excessive flattery; adoration; idolization.
adulterate *(verb)* Make impure or inferior by adding improper ingredients; contaminate; pollute.
advocate *(verb)* 1. Argue for a cause; defend. 2. Support; uphold.
aesthete *(noun)* Person who cultivates beauty or art; connoisseur.
aggrandize *(verb)* Make more powerful; amplify; increase.
alacrity *(noun)* Eagerness; zeal; speed.
altruistic *(adj)* Concerned about the general welfare of others; charitable; generous.
ambivalence *(noun)* Uncertainty; doubt; indecisiveness.
ambulatory *(adj)* Able to walk; not stationary.
ameliorate *(verb)* Make better; improve.
amiable *(adj)* Cordial; of pleasant disposition; friendly.
amorphous *(adj)* Without structure; shapeless; nebulous.
animate *(verb)* Energize; enliven.
anomaly *(noun)* Abnormality; deviation from the general rule; irregularity.
antediluvian *(adj)* Ancient; antiquated; obsolete.
antipathy *(noun)* Feeling of opposition or repugnance; aversion; dislike.
apathy *(noun)* Lack of concern, emotion or interest; indifference.
aperture *(noun)* Gap; opening; orifice.
apocryphal *(adj)* False; unauthenticated; disputed.
apotheosis *(noun)* 1. Essence; epitome. 2. Canonization.
appease *(verb)* Satisfy; make peace; placate.
approbatory *(adj)* Expressing approval.
arable *(adj)* Suitable for cultivation or plowing.
arrogant *(adj)* Feeling superior to other people; egotistical.
ascetic *(adj)* Strict; austere.
assuage *(verb)* Ease; make less burdensome; mitigate.
atrophy *(verb)* Waste away from lack of use; degenerate.
audacity *(noun)* Boldness or adventurousness; gall.
authoritarian *(noun)* 1. Person who acts like a dictator; tyrant. 2. Disciplinarian.
avarice *(noun)* Extreme desire for wealth; greed; acquisitiveness.
aviary *(noun)* Large enclosure confining birds.
avouch *(verb)* Guarantee; take responsibility for; affirm.
avow *(verb)* Affirm; assert; declare; acknowledge.

baleful *(adj)* Sorrowful; sinister; evil.
balm *(noun)* Soothing ointment for pain or healing; salve.
banal *(adj)* Trite; insipid; ordinary.
bane *(noun)* Deadly affliction; curse; plague.
barbarity *(noun)* Cruel action; inhuman act; harsh conduct.
barren *(adj)* 1. Infertile; impotent. 2. Arid; unproductive.
befuddle *(verb)* Stupefy or confuse; misconstrue.
belated *(adj)* Tardy; overdue.
beleaguer *(verb)* Besiege; surround.
belittle *(verb)* Humiliate; tease; diminish in importance.
bemoan *(verb)* 1. Experience pain or distress. 2. Express pity for; mourn.
bemused *(adj)* Preoccupied by thought; bewildered; perplexed.
bilk *(verb)* Defraud; deceive; hoodwink.
blandishment *(noun)* Cajolery; enticement.
bliss *(noun)* Gaiety; happiness; enjoyment.
blithe *(adj)* Happy; pleased; delighted.
boisterous *(adj)* Noisy; loud; violent; rowdy.
boorish *(adj)* Ill-mannered; rude; gauche.
brevity *(noun)* Briefness; succinctness; terseness.
broach *(verb)* Introduce; bring up; mention.
browbeat *(verb)* Intimidate; harass; dominate.
bungle *(verb)* Botch; mismanage; spoil.
buttress *(noun)* Truss; foundation; support.

cacophonous *(adj)* Discordant; dissident; harsh.
callow *(adj)* Inexperienced; immature; naive.
candid *(adj)* Frank; blunt; open.
carouse *(verb)* Drink to excess; live it up.
cease *(verb)* Stop; end; halt.
celerity *(noun)* Swift motion; speed; alacrity.
censorious *(adj)* Critical; attacking; denouncing.
charlatan *(noun)* Fraud; person claiming knowledge he/she does not have; humbug; fake; hustler.
chary *(adj)* Careful; cautious.
chasten *(verb)* Castigate; punish; reprove.
cherubic *(adj)* Sweet; kind; innocent.
chimerical *(adj)* Fanciful; whimsical; playful.
chronic *(adj)* Compulsive; typical; habitual; inveterate.
churlish *(adj)* Selfish; rancorous; surly.
circuitous *(adj)* Indirect; roundabout; rambling.
clamor *(noun)* Loud noise or complaint; commotion; din.
clandestine *(adj)* Furtive; surreptitious; secret.
clemency *(noun)* Lenience; mercy; compassion.
cloister *(noun)* Convent; monastery; religious place.
coagulate *(verb)* Congeal; curdle; clot.
coalesce *(verb)* Combine; incorporate; merge.
coddle *(verb)* Pamper; overindulge; baby; spoil.
coercion *(noun)* Intimidation; duress; force; compulsion.
cognate *(adj)* Related by blood; having the same origin.

commensurate *(adj)* Equal in measure; of the same duration or size.
compile *(verb)* Collect data; accumulate; amass.
concomitant *(adj)* Concurrent; attendant; occurring with something else.
concordance *(noun)* Agreement; treaty; accord.
confluence *(noun)* Nexus; union; meeting; conflux.
confound *(verb)* Perplex; baffle; confuse.
conglomerate *(noun)* Corporation; partnership; firm.
conjugal *(adj)* Matrimonial; nuptial; marital.
constrict *(verb)* Squeeze; pinch; obstruct; block.
contentious *(adj)* Argumentative; pugnacious; quarrelsome.
contrite *(adj)* Penitent; apologetic; remorseful.
conundrum *(noun)* Mystery; puzzle.
convoke *(verb)* Convene; assemble.
copious *(adj)* Plentiful; ample; profuse.
corpulence *(noun)* Stoutness; obesity.
coterie *(noun)* Small group of people who share interests and meet frequently.
crass *(adj)* Vulgar, grossly ignorant; indelicate.
credulous *(adj)* Gullible; unsuspecting; naive.
cryptic *(adj)* Enigmatic; obscure; secret; puzzling.
ctenoid *(adj)* Comblike; having narrow segments.
cuboid *(adj)* Having the shape of a cube.
cucullate *(adj)* Hood-shaped.
curmudgeon *(noun)* Cantankerous person.

daub *(verb)* Blur; smear; spread.
dawdle *(verb)* Procrastinate; loiter; idle; dally.
dearth *(noun)* Paucity; shortage; deficiency.
debased *(adj)* Lowered in status or character; degenerate.
decipher *(verb)* Solve or figure out a puzzle; translate; untangle.
declivity *(noun)* Downward slope.
decorum *(noun)* Appropriate conduct; polite or proper behavior, protocol.
delectable *(adj)* Delicious; delightful; savory.
deleterious *(adj)* Destructive; poisonous; unhealthy.
delineate *(verb)* Describe; outline; depict.
delusion *(noun)* Untrue belief; hallucination; fallacy; misconception.
demagogue *(noun)* Incendiary; agitator; opportunist.
denounce *(verb)* Reprove; accuse; condemn.
depravity *(noun)* Perverted disposition; wickedness; vileness; corruption.
deprecatory *(adj)* Disapproving; belittling.
desecrate *(verb)* Contaminate; profane; defile.
desist *(verb)* Discontinue or stop; cease; renounce.
desolate *(adj)* Alone; without hope or comfort; forsaken.
despoil *(verb)* Ravage; rob; loot.
despot *(noun)* Dictator; tyrant; totalitarian.
diatribe *(noun)* Extreme, bitter, and abusive speech; vituperation; tirade.
didactic *(adj)* Pedantic; academic; for teaching.
diffidence *(noun)* Self-doubt; timidity; shyness.
dilatory *(adj)* Lackadaisical; lazy; remiss.
diligent *(adj)* Assiduous; studious; hard-working.

diminution *(noun)* Decrease; reduction.
disaffected *(adj)* Disillusioned; dissatisfied; discontented.
disapprobation *(noun)* Dislike; reservation; denunciation.
disband *(verb)* Disperse; dissipate; scatter; dispel.
discontent *(adj)* Unhappy; displeased; miserable.
discursive *(adj)* Circuitous; digressive; rambling.
dishearten *(verb)* Dismay; daunt; depress.
disinterment *(noun)* Exhumation; removal of a body from a grave.
disoblige *(verb)* Slight or offend.
disparage *(verb)* Deprecate; belittle or abuse.
dispassionate *(adj)* Imperturbable; unemotional; calm; composed.
disputatious *(adj)* Quarrelsome; contentious; argumentative.
dissemble *(verb)* Disguise; conceal; mask; camouflage.
dissension *(noun)* Conflict; disagreement; strife.
dissonant *(adj)* Cacophonous; inharmonious; discordant; strident.
dissuade *(verb)* Obstruct; hinder; deter.
distend *(verb)* Bloat, bulge; swell; stretch.
dither *(noun)* Commotion; turmoil.
divination *(noun)* Prediction; prophecy; forecast.
dolt *(noun)* Cretin; fool; dimwit; idiot.
dotard *(noun)* Senile person.
dubious *(adj)* Irresolute; uncertain; moot.
duplicity *(noun)* Cunning; fraud; trickery; deception.

edify *(verb)* Instruct; enlighten; educate.
efface *(verb)* Cancel; delete; obliterate.
effervescent *(adj)* Lively; volatile.
effigy *(noun)* Mannequin; likeness; image.
effrontery *(noun)* Impudence; nerve; gall.
egregious *(adj)* Flagrant; glaring; outrageous.
elegiac *(adj)* Mournful; sorrowful; sad.
elucidate *(verb)* Interpret; define; clarify; explain.
emanate *(verb)* Radiate; flow from; emit.
emasculate *(verb)* Deprive of strength.
embroil *(verb)* Implicate; enmesh; involve.
emcee *(noun)* Master of ceremonies.
empathize *(verb)* Identify with; understand.
emulate *(verb)* Model; pattern.
enervate (*verb*) Exhaust or weaken; debilitate.
engender *(verb)* Generate; produce; cause.
enigmatic *(adj)* Cryptic; baffling; mysterious.
enmesh *(verb)* Tangle or involve.
ennui *(noun)* Dullness; boredom; monotony.
enthrall *(verb)* Mesmerize; captivate; thrill.
entrench *(verb)* Fortify; reinforce; secure.
ephemeral *(adj)* Transitory; fleeting; passing; temporary.
epicure *(noun)* Person devoted to luxurious living; person with refined tastes.
epithet *(noun)* Word used to describe or characterize a person or thing.
equilibrium *(noun)* Balance; stability; poise.

equivocate *(verb)* Prevaricate; dodge; evade; hedge.
erudition *(noun)* Learning; knowledge; enlightenment.
escapade *(noun)* Adventurous conduct; unusual behavior.
esoteric *(adj)* Confidential; personal; private; privileged.
espouse *(verb)* Embrace; defend; support.
ethereal *(adj)* Incorporeal; intangible; airy.
eulogy *(noun)* Commendation; speech giving great tribute.
euphonic *(adj)* Pertaining or agreeable to the ear.
evanescent *(adj)* Ephemeral; fading; brief.
exigent *(adj)* Pressing; insistent; urgent.
exonerate *(verb)* Acquit; vindicate; free from responsibility.
exorcise *(verb)* Cast out evil spirits; expel demons.
expatriate *(verb)* Send into exile; renounce one's own country.
expedite *(verb)* Speed up matters; accelerate; quicken.
expunge *(verb)* Obliterate; remove; erase; exterminate.
expurgate *(verb)* Remove erroneous or objectionable material; delete; edit.
extemporaneous *(adj)* Spontaneous; impromptu.
extol *(verb)* Praise; laud; hail; glorify.
extradite *(verb)* Transfer a person to another jurisdiction for possible prosecution for an alleged offense.
extricate *(verb)* Remove; loosen; untie.

fallible *(adj)* Faulty; imperfect.
fallow *(adj)* Idle; dormant.
fastidious *(adj)* Meticulous; exacting.
fathom *(verb)* Measure; discover; perceive.
fatuous *(adj)* Ludicrous; inane; idiotic; silly.
fecund *(adj)* Prolific; productive; fruitful.
felicity *(noun)* Great happiness; bliss.
fetid *(adj)* Possessing an offensive smell; malodorous; foul; gamey.
fetter *(verb)* Restrain; restrict; curb.
fickle *(adj)* Capricious; erratic; spasmodic.
fledgling *(noun)* Young or inexperienced person; young bird.
flippant *(adj)* Nonchalant; frivolous, superficial; light.
florid *(adj)* Ornate; flushed with rosy color, ruddy.
flout *(verb)* Ridicule; scoff; mock; scorn.
foible *(noun)* Frailty; imperfection; weakness.
forswear *(verb)* Repudiate; forsake; eschew.
fulsome *(adj)* Loathsome; excessive.
fume *(noun)* Gas; vapor; harmful or irritating smoke.
furtive *(adj)* Clandestine; secretive; surreptitious; covert.

gambol *(verb)* Play; frolic; romp.
garble *(verb)* Confuse; scramble; distort.
garish *(adj)* Gaudy; ostentatious; excessive.
garner *(verb)* Collect; receive; attain; acquire.
giddy *(adj)* Scatterbrained; silly; frivolous.
goad *(verb)* Incite; pressure; irk; arouse; awaken.
grandiloquence *(noun)* Pompous or bombastic speech; lofty, welling language.

grisly *(adj)* Frightening; ghastly; gory; hideous.
grovel *(verb)* Act in a servile way; cringe; kneel.
guile *(noun)* Wiliness; deceit; cunning.
guzzle *(verb)* Gulp; swill; consume to excess.

hackneyed *(adj)* Trite; common; overdone; banal.
haggle *(verb)* Dicker; barter; make a deal.
hallow *(verb)* Make holy; consecrate; sanctify.
hamper *(verb)* Hinder; frustrate; impede.
harbor *(verb)* Preserve; conceal; secure; shelter.
hardy *(adj)* Stalwart; robust; sturdy.
haughty *(adj)* Arrogant; disdainful; blatantly proud; contemptuous.
hearten *(verb)* Encourage; give strength.
hedge *(verb)* Enclose; surround; fence.
hedonism *(noun)* Intemperance; self-indulgence; excess.
herald *(verb)* Announce; broadcast; report.
heretic *(noun)* Nihilist; infidel; radical; dissenter.
hiatus *(noun)* Interruption; pause; gap.
hilarity *(noun)* Boisterous merriment; enjoyment.
histrionic *(adj)* Pertaining to actors; melodramatic.
hoary *(adj)* Frosted; grey; grizzled.
hyperbole *(noun)* Exaggeration; fanciful statement; enhancement.

iconoclasm *(noun)* Attack on religious values or symbols.
ignoramus *(noun)* Moron; fool; dimwit.
immutable *(adj)* Incorruptible; enduring; unchanging.
impecunious *(adj)* Poor; destitute; penniless.
imperturbable *(adj)* Even-tempered; level-headed; calm.
impervious *(adj)* Airtight; sealed; impenetrable.
impetuous *(adj)* Hasty; rash; impulsive.
impregnable *(adj)* Invincible; invulnerable; unable to capture or enter.
impromptu *(adj)* Makeshift; spontaneous.
improvident *(adj)* Reckless; rash.
impugn *(verb)* Denounce; censor; attack.
inauspicious *(adj)* Unfavorable.
inaudible *(adj)* Faint; soft; hard to hear.
incipient *(adj)* Embryonic; developing; in the beginning stages.
incisive *(adj)* Perceptive; astute.
inclusive *(adj)* All-encompassing; broad in scope; comprehensive.
incoherent *(adj)* Illogical; inconsistent.
incongruous *(adj)* Inconsistent; unsuitable; contradictory.
incorrigible *(adj)* Unruly; delinquent; incapable of reform.
indecorous *(adj)* Inappropriate; indelicate; unseemly.
indefatigable *(adj)* Diligent; persistent inexhaustible.
indenture *(noun)* Contract binding a person to work for another.
indolence *(noun)* Lethargy; idleness; sloth.
inebriation *(noun)* Drunkenness; intoxication.
ingenuous *(adj)* Genuine; open; candid; frank.
inimical *(adj)* Antagonistic; hurtful; harmful; adverse.

innocuous *(adj)* Dull; harmless; innocent.
inscrutable *(adj)* Mysterious; perplexing.
insipid *(adj)* Dull; banal; tasteless.
insolvent *(adj)* Bankrupt; unable to pay debts.
intercede *(verb)* Intervene; negotiate.
intonate *(verb)* Speak or utter with a particular tone.
intractable *(adj)* Unruly; disobedient.
intrinsic *(adj)* Inherent; natural; innate.
inveigh *(verb)* Abuse; criticize; rebuke.
inveterate *(adj)* Habitual; chronic.
irascible *(adj)* Testy; touchy; irritable.
issue *(verb)* Discharge; emerge; emanate.

jettison *(verb)* Eliminate; discharge.
jollity *(noun)* Gaiety; merriment.
judicious *(adj)* Logical; reasonable; clever.
juncture *(noun)* Joint; seam; intersection; joining.
juxtapose *(verb)* Place side by side.

knotty *(adj)* Snarled; tangled.

labyrinth *(noun)* Maze; network; puzzle.
lachrymose *(adj)* Weepy; tearful.
laconic *(adj)* Concise; terse; curt.
lamentation *(noun)* Complaint; moan.
lampoon *(verb)* Mock; ridicule.
languish *(verb)* Decline; diminish; weaken.
largess *(noun)* Charity; philanthropy; gift.
lassitude *(noun)* Fatigue; weariness; debility.
laudable *(adj)* Commendable; admirable; exemplary.
laxity *(noun)* Carelessness; indifference.
lethargy *(noun)* Idleness; listlessness; passivity.
levity *(noun)* Lightness; frivolity.
linger *(verb)* Loiter; remain; hesitate.
lithe *(adj)* Flexible; agile; mobile; bendable.
loutish *(adj)* Clumsy; idiotic; buffoonlike.
ludicrous *(adj)* Outlandish; silly; ridiculous.
lurid *(adj)* Shockingly vivid; horrifying; sensational.

maladroit *(adj)* Clumsy; unskilled.
malapropism *(noun)* Inappropriate or ludicrous use of a word.
malevolent *(adj)* Venomous; spiteful; malignant.
malinger *(verb)* Feign illness to escape work; shirk.
marred *(adj)* Having blemishes; damaged; defaced.
maudlin *(adj)* Overemotional; mushy.
meander *(verb)* Twist; bend; zigzag.
mendicant *(noun)* Almsman; beggar; leech; parasite.
meticulous *(adj)* Precise; scrupulous; particular.
mettle *(noun)* Stamina; bravery; courage.
mince *(verb)* Chop; mitigate.

mire *(noun)* Mud; slime; muck.
moribund *(adj)* Failing; waning; ailing.
motley *(adj)* Multicolored; spotted; mixed.
multifarious *(adj)* Diverse; many-sided; multiple.
mundane *(adj)* Boring; ordinary; typical; tedious.
munificent *(adj)* Generous; extravagant; philanthropic.

nascent *(adj)* Beginning; embryonic; incipient.
nefarious *(adj)* Evil; vile; sinister; wicked.
neologism *(noun)* Newly coined phrase or expression.
noxious *(adj)* Nocuous; harmful; malignant.

obdurate *(adj)* Stubborn; intractable.
obsequious *(adj)* Servile; groveling.
obviate *(verb)* Make unnecessary.
odious *(adj)* Detestable; loathsome; revolting; sickening.
officious *(adj)* Meddlesome.
opaque *(adj)* Impenetrable by light; dull; dark; obscure.
optimum *(noun)* Peak or prime; ideal.
opulent *(adj)* Affluent; well-to-do; plentiful.
ostentatious *(adj)* Conspicuous; showy.
ostracize *(verb)* Exclude; isolate; bar; shun.

palpable *(adj)* Noticeable; obvious; apparent.
paltry *(adj)* Minor; petty; insignificant.
panegyric *(noun)* Elaborate praise, public compliment.
paragon *(noun)* Model or standard of excellence.
pariah *(noun)* Outcast; misfit; refugee.
parochial *(adj)* Religious; restricted.
parsimony *(noun)* Miserliness; unusually excessive frugality.
partisan *(noun)* Fan or supporter; enthusiast supporting a particular cause or issue.
pastiche *(noun)* Hodgepodge; literary or musical piece imitating other works.
paucity *(noun)* Scarcity; shortage; dearth.
peccadillo *(noun)* Small sin or fault.
pedantic *(adj)* Stuffy or dogmatic; meticulous; academic.
peevish *(adj)* Irritable; grouchy; ill-tempered.
pejorative *(adj)* Degrading; derogatory; negative.
percipient *(adj)* Able to perceive or see things as they actually are.
perfidy *(noun)* Deliberate breach of faith or trust; treachery.
peripheral *(adj)* Marginal; outer; surrounding.
perspicacious *(adj)* Astute; keen; perceptive.
philistine *(noun)* Barbarian; person lacking artistic judgment.
pique *(verb)* Irritate; miff; offend.
pithy *(adj)* 1. Substantial; profound. 2. Brief; concise.
placid *(adj)* Sincere; tranquil; composed; sedate.
plaintive *(adj)* Sad; mournful; pathetic.
platitude *(noun)* 1. Triteness. 2. Cliché; trivial remark.
plaudit *(noun)* Enthusiastic expression.
pliable *(adj)* Limber; malleable; flexible.
poignant *(adj)* Intense; powerful; biting; piercing.

polemical *(adj)* Controversial; argumentative; debatable.
polyphony *(noun)* Music with two or more melodies blended together.
porous *(adj)* Permeable; absorbent; having holes.
posthumous *(adj)* Arising or continuing after someone's death.
potable *(adj)* Drinkable.
prattle *(verb)* Gab; babble.
precocious *(adj)* Showing premature development.
precursor *(noun)* Forerunner.
prescient *(adj)* Showing foresight; predicting events before they occur.
primeval *(adj)* Belonging to a primitive age.
primordial *(adj)* Belonging to a primitive age; first in time.
proclivity *(noun)* Tendency; inclination; propensity.
procrastinate *(verb)* Postpone; stall; defer.
prodigious *(adj)* Exceptional; impressive; of huge quantity; immense.
proficient *(adj)* Skillful; masterful; expert.
progeny *(noun)* Heir; descendant; offspring.
prolific *(adj)* Fruitful; abundant; fertile.
prosaic *(adj)* Common; routine; ordinary.
protean *(adj)* Taking many forms; changeable; variable.
protract *(verb)* Elongate; lengthen; prolong.
prudent *(adj)* Careful; cautious; judicious.
puerile *(adj)* Juvenile; immature; childish.
pugilism *(noun)* Boxing.
pugnacity *(noun)* Eagerness to fight; belligerence.
pulchritude *(noun)* Beauty; physical appeal.
pulverize *(verb)* Grind; crush; smash.

quagmire *(noun)* Marsh; quicksand; swamp.
quandary *(noun)* Dilemma; mire; entanglement.
querulous *(adj)* Difficult; testy; disagreeable.
quibble *(verb)* Argue or bicker.
quixotic *(adj)* Romantic; whimsical; unrealistic.

rabid *(adj)* Berserk; diseased; sick.
ramble *(verb)* Meander; roam.
rancorous *(adj)* Antagonistic; hostile; spiteful.
rarefy *(verb)* Make thin; purify; make less dense.
raucous *(adj)* Harsh; annoying; piercing; shrill.
raze *(verb)* Demolish; level; topple.
reactionary *(adj)* Opposing progress; characterized by reaction.
recalcitrant *(adj)* Headstrong; disobedient; stubborn.
recant *(verb)* Rescind; retract; take back.
reconciliation *(noun)* Settlement or resolution.
redundant *(adj)* Excessive; repetitious; unnecessary.
refractory *(adj)* Unmanageable; obstinate; not responsive to treatment.
refurbish *(verb)* Overhaul; remodel.
regimen *(noun)* Administration; government; system.
remedial *(adj)* Restorative; corrective; healing.
remuneration *(noun)* Compensation; wages.

rend *(verb)* Rip; tear; splinter.
reprobate *(noun)* Degenerate; person without morals.
repudiate *(verb)* Recant; disclaim; reject; disavow.
rescind *(verb)* Cancel; repeal; veto.
resilient *(adj)* Elastic; stretchy; rebounding.
resonant *(adj)* Reverberant; ringing.
resplendent *(adj)* Dazzling; glorious; intense.
restive *(adj)* Nervous; restless; uneasy.
retrospection *(noun)* Contemplation of past things.
reverent *(adj)* Devout; solemn; worshipful.
ribald *(adj)* Lewd; obscene; irreverent.
rudiment *(noun)* Beginning; foundation or source.
ruffian *(noun)* Brutal person; cruel and sadistic person.
ruminate *(verb)* Contemplate; think about.

saccharine *(adj)* Sugary; syrupy.
savant *(noun)* Intellectual; scholar; philosopher.
scanty *(adj)* Meager; scarce.
scoff *(verb)* Mock; ridicule.
sequester *(verb)* Separate; isolate; segregate.
soporific *(adj)* Hypnotic; lethargic; causing sleep.
spurious *(adj)* Bogus; false.
spurn *(verb)* Defy; reject.
squalor *(noun)* 1. Severe poverty. 2. Filthiness.
stratagem *(noun)* Plot; tactic; deception.
strident *(adj)* Discordant; harsh; piercing.
strife *(noun)* Conflict; turmoil; struggle.
stultify *(verb)* Inhibit; make ineffective; cripple.
supercilious *(adj)* Egotistic; proud; arrogant.
surfeit *(noun)* Overabundance; excess; surplus.
surly *(adj)* Choleric; rude; sullen.
surreptitious *(adj)* Covert; furtive; acquired by stealthy means.
svelte *(adj)* Graceful; slim.
sybarite *(noun)* Someone devoted to luxury; pleasure-seeker.
sycophant *(noun)* Flatterer.

taciturn *(adj)* Reserved; shy; uncommunicative.
tantamount *(adj)* Indistinguishable; equivalent.
taper *(verb)* Diminish; thin; narrow.
tawdry *(adj)* Gaudy; showy; loud.
temerity *(noun)* Rashness; audacity; recklessness.
tensile *(adj)* Pertaining to tension; stretchable; ductile.
tenuous *(adj)* Attenuated; flimsy; thin.
tirade *(noun)* Diatribe; angry speech.
torpor *(noun)* Lethargy; apathy; dormancy.
trepidation *(noun)* Anxiety; alarm; apprehension.
truant *(adj)* Indolent; absent; idle.
turgid *(adj)* Swollen; bombastic; distended.
turpitude *(noun)* Depravity; baseness; shamefulness.

undulate *(verb)* Move in a wavy manner.
unfathomable *(adj)* Baffling; puzzling; incomprehensible.
unkempt *(adj)* Uncombed; messy; untidy.
unscathed *(adj)* Unhurt; uninjured.
unwieldy *(adj)* Clumsy; awkward; unmanageable.
upbraid *(verb)* Rebuke; scold; criticize.
upshot *(noun)* Final result; conclusion; end.

vacillate *(verb)* Hedge; waver; fluctuate.
variegated *(adj)* Multicolored; polychromatic; varied.
vehement *(adj)* Fierce; emphatic; intense.
venerate *(verb)* Admire; show respect.
veracity *(noun)* Truth; sincerity; honesty; candor.
verbose *(adj)* Wordy; talkative; profuse.
verdant *(adj)* Lush; thick with vegetation; leafy.
viable *(adj)* Living; alive; feasible.
vigilance *(noun)* Attentiveness; prudence; care.
vilify *(verb)* Defame; denigrate.
virulent *(adj)* Fatal; lethal; toxic.
vitriolic *(adj)* Scathing; caustic.
vociferous *(adj)* Clamorous; outspoken; noisy; vocal.
voluble *(adj)* Verbose; wordy; garrulous.
voluminous *(adj)* Huge; immense; bulky.
voracious *(adj)* 1. Enthusiastic; overly eager. 2. Starving.
vouchsafe *(verb)* Confer; grant; permit.

wan *(adj)* Anemic; colorless; pale.
waver *(verb)* Totter; fluctuate.
whet *(verb)* Stimulate; sharpen; intensify.
wistful *(adj)* Yearning; pensive; sad.
woe *(noun)* Anguish; grief; affliction.
writhe *(verb)* Squirm; twist.

zealot *(noun)* Fanatic; radical; enthusiast.
zenith *(noun)* Apex; summit; peak.

Verbal Drill

Directions: For each of the following questions, select the one word that has most nearly the same meaning as the italicized word in the context of the sentence. An answer key appears at the end of the test.

1. The young girl listened to her grandfather's endless and repetitious stories with *laudable* patience.

   (A) exorbitant
   (B) meticulous
   (C) unwavering
   (D) exemplary
   (E) intractable

2. When the right job comes along, act with *celerity* to take advantage of the opportunity.

   (A) alacrity
   (B) resourcefulness
   (C) pragmatism
   (D) compunction
   (E) diligence

3. His *diffidence* caused him to miss many opportunities.

   (A) ignorance
   (B) timidity
   (C) indifference
   (D) indolence
   (E) arrogance

4. The business survived on a *tenuous* relationship with one customer.

   (A) tentative
   (B) insubstantial
   (C) lucrative
   (D) salient
   (E) amatory

5. He asked for compensation *commensurate* to his work.

   (A) approximate
   (B) previous
   (C) equal
   (D) appropriate
   (E) incongruous

6. Visitors to impoverished countries are often shocked at the number of *mendicants* in the streets.

   (A) beggars
   (B) criminals
   (C) vendors
   (D) drunkards
   (E) soldiers

7. It will take more than good intentions to *ameliorate* the conditions in the schools.

   (A) understand
   (B) counteract
   (C) eliminate
   (D) camouflage
   (E) improve

8. *Ephemeral* pleasures may leave long-lasting memories.

   (A) enervated
   (B) irresolute
   (C) frivolous
   (D) adventurous
   (E) transitory

9. The critic *belittled* her talent by suggesting that her beauty, rather than her acting ability, was responsible for her success.

   (A) illuminated
   (B) disparaged
   (C) declared
   (D) diminished
   (E) inveighed

10. The father *upbraided* his children for their extravagance.

   (A) scolded
   (B) scorned
   (C) advocated
   (D) bolstered
   (E) flouted

11. Imagination and curiosity are the antidotes for *ennui.*

(A) inactivity
(B) indolence
(C) boredom
(D) jollity
(E) woe

12. His friends *dissuaded* him from that unwise course of action.

(A) protected
(B) ostracized
(C) deterred
(D) sequestered
(E) enmeshed

13. They *rescinded* their offer of aid when they became disillusioned with the project.

(A) renegotiated
(B) withdrew
(C) reinstated
(D) rethought
(E) validated

14. The novel told a *lurid* tale of murder and lust.

(A) sensational
(B) nonsensical
(C) esoteric
(D) unrealistic
(E) dubious

15. She made many enemies because of her *acerbic* wit.

(A) boorish
(B) caustic
(C) inane
(D) ingratiating
(E) magnanimous

16. The ancient town was a *labyrinth* of narrow, winding streets.

(A) confusion
(B) model
(C) maze
(D) collection
(E) path

17. I will *ruminate* on your proposal and let you know my decision next week.

(A) ameliorate
(B) linger
(C) report
(D) procrastinate
(E) contemplate

18. One *contentious* student can disrupt an entire class.

(A) rambunctious
(B) vociferous
(C) quarrelsome
(D) humorous
(E) garrulous

19. The hot, humid weather can *enervate* even hearty souls.

(A) intimidate
(B) invigorate
(C) weaken
(D) incite
(E) impugn

20. Insisting on a luxury car you cannot afford is *fatuous.*

(A) inane
(B) avarice
(C) nefarious
(D) impetuous
(E) pretentious

21. They had to *jettison* the cargo to lighten the plane.

(A) relocate
(B) divide
(C) eject
(D) disregard
(E) consume

22. His ideas were *quixotic* and thoroughly useless.

(A) erroneous
(B) dubious
(C) incomprehensible
(D) unrealistic
(E) incoherent

23. He was *candid* about his financial difficulties.

(A) incredulous
(B) apprehensive
(C) enigmatic
(D) blunt
(E) ambiguous

24. Because of the drug's *soporific* effect, you should not drive after taking it.

(A) noxious
(B) sedative
(C) inimical
(D) poignant
(E) incongruous

25. He is always *chary* with a new acquaintance.

(A) eager
(B) amiable
(C) impudent
(D) baleful
(E) cautious

26. An *intractable* person is slow to adapt to a new way of life.

(A) timid
(B) bemused
(C) ascetic
(D) stubborn
(E) antediluvian

27. She responded with *alacrity* to every customer request.

(A) indignation
(B) aggression
(C) laxity
(D) diffidence
(E) zeal

28. Knowing how sensitive she was about money, he did not *broach* the subject of who should pay for the ticket.

(A) introduce
(B) avoid
(C) postpone
(D) prolong
(E) bemoan

29. United States law *emanates* from English common law.

(A) fluctuates
(B) merges
(C) mitigates
(D) originates
(E) amasses

30. He was expelled from the club because of his *nefarious* activities.

(A) unsolicited
(B) questionable
(C) sinister
(D) unauthorized
(E) pejorative

31. They met *surreptitiously* in the night to exchange information.

(A) clandestinely
(B) egregiously
(C) punctiliously
(D) exigently
(E) indecorously

32. Only a personal apology will *appease* his rage at having been slighted.

(A) control
(B) entrench
(C) placate
(D) obviate
(E) modify

33. Health benefits are part of the *remuneration* that goes with the position.

(A) paucity
(B) surfeit
(C) pay
(D) advantages
(E) package

34. The band of terrorists threatened to *despoil* the town unless it surrendered.

(A) infiltrate
(B) ravage
(C) scoff
(D) browbeat
(E) stultify

35. She was surprised to find that the *callow* youth had grown into a sophisticated man.

(A) awkward
(B) immature
(C) banal
(D) gauche
(E) coddled

36. *Impetuous* actions often lead to trouble.

(A) contentious
(B) malicious
(C) irrational
(D) dilatory
(E) impulsive

37. A *recalcitrant* child is a difficult pupil.

(A) indefatigable
(B) churlish
(C) unfocused
(D) impudent
(E) obdurate

38. *Brevity* is the essence of journalistic writing.

(A) continuity
(B) opacity
(C) succinctness
(D) incisiveness
(E) hedonism

39. Supporting her *impecunious* aunt was a drain on her resources.

(A) extravagant
(B) thrifty
(C) munificent
(D) eccentric
(E) destitute

40. The silly costumes and party hats epitomized the *levity* of the occasion.

(A) inebriation
(B) frivolity
(C) emotion
(D) banality
(E) mettle

41. The jury's deliberation was *protracted* because of their confusion over a point of law.

(A) lengthened
(B) befuddled
(C) decided
(D) illuminated
(E) distended

42. She had a *proclivity* for getting into trouble.

(A) compulsion
(B) propensity
(C) guile
(D) antipathy
(E) vulnerability

43. Only a few scrubby trees clung to the rocky soil of that *barren* landscape.

(A) verdant
(B) undesirable
(C) odious
(D) arid
(E) insolvent

44. The *dearth* of rain can create a desert in a few years.

(A) contamination
(B) deficiency
(C) hiatus
(D) equilibrium
(E) abundance

45. The rock sample was a *conglomerate* of quartz pebbles.

(A) mixture
(B) collusion
(C) emulation
(D) paragon
(E) apotheosis

46. Squeezing through the *aperture* between the rocks, she found herself in a cool, dark cave.

(A) chasm
(B) confluence
(C) path
(D) orifice
(E) anomaly

47. Sometimes a *circuitous* route is the best way to reach your destination.

(A) scenic
(B) alternative
(C) roundabout
(D) audacious
(E) desolate

48. To *expedite* delivery of the letter, he sent it by overnight mail.

(A) accelerate
(B) assure
(C) efface
(D) extradite
(E) secure

49. The *adroit* juggler held the attention of the crowd.

(A) inept
(B) stunning
(C) magnificent
(D) confident
(E) skillful

50. The confession of one prisoner *exonerated* the other suspects.

(A) infuriated
(B) acquitted
(C) condemned
(D) implicated
(E) denounced

Answer Key

1. D	11. C	21. C	31. A	41. A
2. A	12. C	22. D	32. C	42. B
3. B	13. B	23. D	33. C	43. D
4. B	14. A	24. B	34. B	44. B
5. C	15. B	25. E	35. B	45. A
6. A	16. C	26. D	36. E	46. D
7. E	17. E	27. E	37. E	47. C
8. E	18. C	28. A	38. C	48. A
9. B	19. C	29. D	39. E	49. E
10. A	20. A	30. C	40. B	50. B

Verbal Analogies

Verbal Analogies test your ability to see a relationship between two words and to recognize a similar relationship between two other words. Analogy questions measure both vocabulary and verbal reasoning ability.

On the SAT, analogies are presented in the form of a mathematical proportion, in which : stands for *is to* and : : stands for *as*. Thus, the analogy
MAN : BOY : : WOMAN : GIRL is read as
MAN *is to* BOY *as* WOMAN *is to* GIRL.

HOW TO ANSWER ANALOGY QUESTIONS

The first step in approaching an analogy question is to define the capitalized words. The vocabulary of analogy questions is usually not very difficult, but occasionally an unfamiliar word will appear. If you cannot define both words of the initial capitalized pair, you cannot identify their relationship and you are probably better off skipping the question.

Most often, however, you will know the meanings of both words. In that case, the next step is to determine how the words are related to each other. Suppose you are confronted with an analogy question like this:

Example➤ BRIM : HAT : :

(A) hand : glove
(B) spoke : umbrella
(C) skirt : hem
(D) snood : hood
(E) lace : shoe

What is the relationship between BRIM and HAT? A *brim* is a part of a *hat*, so the relationship is that of part to whole. The next step is to examine the answer choices to find another pair of words which bear the same relation to each other. Consider each answer choice in turn.

(A) A *hand* is not a part of a *glove*, so eliminate (A).

(B) A *spoke* is part of an *umbrella*, so (B) is a likely choice. But don't mark your answer yet. You must always look at all five choices before making your final decision.

(C) A *hem* is part of a *skirt*, but BEWARE. The relationship in (C) is whole (the skirt) to part (the hem), which is the reverse of the initial relationship. Your answer must maintain the same relationship in the same sequence as the original pair. Eliminate (C).

(D) If you know that a *snood* is a hair net, you can see that *snood, hood*, and *hat* are all headgear. However, a snood is not a part of a hood, so (D) is incorrect. If you do not know the meaning of one word among the choices, do not fall into the trap of choosing that answer just because it's unfamiliar. Consider all the choices carefully before you mark an unknown answer as correct.

(E) A *lace* is a part of a *shoe*, so (E) appears to be a perfectly good answer.

Having found two likely answers, (B) and (E), you must go back to the original pair and determine its other distinguishing characteristics. A brim is a part of a hat, but it is not a necessary part. Not all hats have brims. A lace is a part of a shoe, but it is not a necessary part. Some shoes have buckles and some are slip-ons. A spoke, however, is a necessary part of an umbrella. Furthermore, a brim is part of a hat, which is wearing apparel. A lace is part of a shoe, which is also wearing apparel. But an umbrella is not something to wear. Thus there are two counts on which to eliminate (B) and to choose (E) as the *best* answer.

Usually the problem with analogies is refining the relationship to find the best answer. Sometimes, however, the difficulty will be in finding even one correct answer. If this happens, you may have to redefine the relationship. Consider an analogy which begins LETTER : WORD. Your first thought is probably that a letter is part of a word, and so you look for an answer choice that shows a part-to-whole relationship. However, suppose the question looks like this:

Example➤ LETTER : WORD : :

(A) procession : parade
(B) dot : dash
(C) whisper : orate
(D) song : note
(E) spell : recite

Not one of these choices offers a part-to-whole relationship. Returning to the original pair, you must then consider other relationships between *letter* and *word*. If *letter* is not "letter of the alphabet," but, rather, "written communication," then a *word* is part of a *letter* and the relationship becomes that of the whole to its part. Now the answer is immediately clear. A *song* is the whole of which a *note* is a part, making choice (D) correct.

To summarize the steps in solving an analogy question:

1. Define the capitalized terms.
2. Describe the relationship of these terms.
3. Eliminate incorrect answers.
4. If necessary, redefine the initial relationship.
5. Choose the *best* answer.

Examples of some common analogy relationships:

Part to whole	BRANCH : TREE
Whole to part	OCEAN : WATER
Cause and effect	GERM : DISEASE
Effect and cause	HONORS : STUDY
Degree	HUT : MANSION
Sequence	ELEMENTARY : SECONDARY
Function	OVEN : BAKE
Characteristic	WISE : OWL
Antonym	BAD : GOOD
Synonym	SPRING : JUMP

The Analogy Test that follows offers practice with the kind of analogy questions you will find on the SAT. An answer key and explanations follow the test.

Analogy Practice Test

Directions: Each of the following questions consists of a capitalized pair of words followed by five pairs of words lettered A to E. The capitalized words bear some meaningful relationship to each other. Choose the lettered pair of words whose relationship is most similar to that expressed by the capitalized pair and mark its letter on your answer sheet.

Example:

DAY : SUN : :

(A) sunlight : daylight (B) ray : sun
(C) night : moon (D) heat : cold
(E) moon : star

Ⓐ Ⓑ ● Ⓓ Ⓔ

1. HAIR : BALD : :

(A) wig : curly
(B) egg : cooked
(C) rain : arid
(D) skin : scarred
(E) medicine : healthy

2. DINGHY : BOAT : :

(A) novel : book
(B) canoe : paddle
(C) oar : water
(D) deck : stern
(E) land : sea

3. APPLE : TREE : :

(A) silver : ore
(B) bronze : copper
(C) plank : wood
(D) glass : sand
(E) pearl : oyster

4. CARNIVORE : MEAT : :

(A) carnivore : vegetables
(B) herbivore : plants
(C) vegetarian : vitamins
(D) botanist : herbs
(E) pollinator : plants

5. MAUVE : COLOR : :

(A) basil : spice
(B) salt : sugar
(C) light : dark
(D) tan : brown
(E) blue : rainbow

6. MUFFLE : SILENCE : :

(A) cover : report
(B) sound : alarm
(C) cry : hear
(D) stymie : defeat
(E) glimpse : look

7. DEARTH : PAUCITY : :

(A) individual : person
(B) scarcity : shortage
(C) shortage : plethora
(D) prairie : forest
(E) commodity : expectation

8. WATERMARK : PAPER : :

(A) landmark : monument
(B) birthmark : person
(C) tide : character
(D) line : signal
(E) signature : author

9. BRIGHT : BRILLIANT : :

(A) orange : red
(B) tall : high
(C) warm : light
(D) white : cold
(E) happy : ecstatic

10. DISCIPLINE : ORDER : :

(A) military : rank
(B) authority : follower
(C) parent : child
(D) teacher : student
(E) training : preparation

11. NEWS REPORT : DESCRIPTIVE : :

(A) weather report : unpredictable
(B) editorial : one-sided
(C) feature story : newsworthy
(D) commercial : prescriptive
(E) joke : funny

12. AGREEMENT : CONSENSUS : :

(A) discord : harmony
(B) pleasure : hatred
(C) tranquility : peace
(D) argument : solution
(E) action : conclusion

13. WATER : HYDRAULIC : :

(A) energy : atomic
(B) power : electric
(C) gasoline : inflammable
(D) pressure : compressible
(E) air : pneumatic

14. STABLE : HORSE : :

(A) pond : duck
(B) sty : pig
(C) fold : ram
(D) coop : hen
(E) zoo : lioness

15. ROLE : ACTOR : :

(A) aria : soprano
(B) private : soldier
(C) melody : singer
(D) position : ballplayer
(E) character : part

16. PROW : SHIP : :

(A) snout : hog
(B) nose : airplane
(C) bird : beak
(D) wheel : car
(E) point : shaft

17. MAXIMUM : MINIMUM : :

(A) pessimistic : chauvinistic
(B) minimum : optimum
(C) best : good
(D) most : least
(E) waning : less

18. SENSATION : ANESTHETIC : :

(A) breath : lung
(B) drug : reaction
(C) satisfaction : disappointment
(D) poison : antidote
(E) observation : sight

19. DISEMBARK : SHIP : :

(A) board : train
(B) dismount : horse
(C) intern : jail
(D) discharge : navy
(E) dismantle : clock

20. PROTEIN : MEAT : :

(A) calories : cream
(B) energy : sugar
(C) cyclamates : diet
(D) starch : potatoes
(E) fat : cholesterol

21. NECK : NAPE : :

(A) foot : heel
(B) head : forehead
(C) arm : wrist
(D) stomach : back
(E) eye : lid

22. GRIPPING : PLIERS : :

(A) appealing : picture
(B) breaking : hammer
(C) elevating : jack
(D) killing : knife
(E) fastening : screwdriver

23. RADIUS : CIRCLE : :

(A) rubber : tire
(B) bisector : angle
(C) equator : earth
(D) cord : circumference
(E) spoke : wheel

24. MISDEMEANOR : FELONY : :

(A) police : prison
(B) thief : burglar
(C) murder : manslaughter
(D) mishap : catastrophe
(E) crime : degree

25. HYGROMETER : HUMIDITY : :

(A) clock : second
(B) gauge : air
(C) odometer : speed
(D) barometer : weather
(E) thermometer : temperature

26. ASTUTE : STUPID : :

(A) pedantic : idiotic
(B) agile : clumsy
(C) lonely : wary
(D) dull : ignorant
(E) intelligent : smart

27. WHALE : FISH : :

(A) collie : dog
(B) fly : insect
(C) bat : bird
(D) alligator : crocodile
(E) mako : shark

28. GOLD : PROSPECTOR : :

(A) medicine : doctor
(B) prayer : preacher
(C) wood : carpenter
(D) clue : detective
(E) iron : machinist

29. COUPLET : POEM : :

(A) letter : page
(B) sentence : paragraph
(C) address : house
(D) epic : poetry
(E) biography : novel

30. ENTREPRENEUR : PROFIT : :

(A) interloper : trade
(B) business : monopoly
(C) miner : ore
(D) nemesis : peace
(E) captain : boat

31. RUDDER : SHIP : :

(A) wheel : car
(B) motor : truck
(C) oar : boat
(D) string : kite
(E) wing : plane

32. STALLION : ROOSTER : :

(A) buck : doe
(B) filly : colt
(C) horse : chicken
(D) foal : calf
(E) mare : hen

33. READ : BOOK : :

(A) taste : salt
(B) attend : movie
(C) smell : odor
(D) listen : record
(E) touch : paper

34. PARROT : SPARROW : :

(A) dog : poodle
(B) elephant : ant
(C) goldfish : guppy
(D) lion : cat
(E) eagle : butterfly

35. BONE : LIGAMENT : :

(A) fracture : cast
(B) muscle : tendon
(C) fat : cell
(D) knuckle : finger
(E) knee : joint

36. SPICY : INSIPID : :

(A) peppery : salty
(B) hot : creamy
(C) keen : dull
(D) pickled : sweet
(E) bland : chewy

37. SCYTHE : DEATH : :

(A) fall : winter
(B) knife : murder
(C) sickle : grain
(D) harvest : crops
(E) arrow : love

38. YEAST : LEAVEN : :

(A) soda : bubble
(B) iodine : antiseptic
(C) aspirin : medicine
(D) flour : dough
(E) penicillin : plant

39. POLYGLOT : LANGUAGE : :

(A) teacher : students
(B) tourist : countries
(C) linguist : words
(D) polygamist : children
(E) factotum : trades

40. EXPURGATE : PASSAGES : :

(A) defoliate : leaves
(B) cancel : checks
(C) incorporate : ideas
(D) invade : privacy
(E) till : fields

41. PHARMACIST : DRUGS : :

(A) psychiatrist : ideas
(B) mentor : drills
(C) mechanic : troubles
(D) chef : foods
(E) nurse : diseases

42. CONQUER : SUBJUGATE : :

(A) esteem : respect
(B) slander : vilify
(C) discern : observe
(D) ponder : deliberate
(E) free : enslave

43. ENGRAVING : CHISEL : :

(A) printing : paper
(B) photography : camera
(C) lithography : stone
(D) printing : ink
(E) etching : acid

44. DECIBEL : SOUND : :

(A) calorie : weight
(B) volt : electricity
(C) temperature : weather
(D) color : light
(E) area : distance

45. HOMONYM : SOUND : :

(A) antonym : confusion
(B) synonym : meaning
(C) acronym : ideas
(D) pseudonym : fake
(E) synopsis : summary

46. WHET : KNIFE : :

(A) file : spur
(B) chop : ax
(C) hone : razor
(D) stab : sword
(E) fence : rapier

47. VALUELESS : INVALUABLE : :

(A) miserly : philanthropic
(B) frugal : wealthy
(C) thrifty : cheap
(D) costly : cut-rate
(E) incomprehensible : unreadable

48. TRIANGLE : PRISM : :

(A) sphere : earth
(B) square : rhomboid
(C) rectangle : building
(D) circle : cylinder
(E) polygon : diamond

ALL ABOUT THE PSAT/NMSQT

The Preliminary SAT/National Merit Scholarship Qualifying Test (PSAT/NMSQT) is designed to help you plan for college. It gives you a first chance to test your skills against those of other college-bound high school students. It also allows you to compete for scholarships offered by the National Merit Scholarship Corporation.

Registering for the PSAT/NMSQT

Most students take the PSAT/NMSQT test on a Tuesday or Saturday in October of their junior year in high school. Taking the exam as a junior qualifies students for the Merit Program scholarship competition corresponding to the year they would normally enter college—two years later.

To register to take the PSAT/NMSQT at your school, talk to your guidance counselor. You may find out more about registration by writing to:

PSAT/NMSQT
P.O. Box 6720
Princeton, NJ 08541-6720

Special Features of the Answer Sheet

The PSAT/NMSQT answer sheet contains a few special features. It has a section that asks you to select a possible college major and career. Do not worry if you have not made a decision yet—you may choose something quite general from the list. When you receive your scores, you will also receive a list of suggestions and recommendations related to that major and career choice.

Make sure to complete the sections on Scholarship Programs if you are interested in participating. One section covers general eligibility, and two others ask about your qualifications to enter the National Achievement Scholarship Program for Outstanding Negro Students or the National Hispanic Scholar Recognition Program.

Types of Questions

The PSAT/NMSQT measures your verbal and math reasoning skills. The question types that it contains are the same as those on the SAT: analogies, sentence completions, critical reading, multiple-choice math, quantitative comparison, and student-produced-response math questions. As on the SAT, answers to student-produced response questions must be entered in special grids on the answer sheet. (For more about these grids, see page 12.) You may use a calculator to answer any math question. To learn more about the question types and the subjects they cover, see Parts 1, 3, and 4 of this book.

Your Score Report

Approximately six weeks after you take the test, your school will give you your score report and test book. You can review your test to see what areas need improvement. This will help you prepare for the SAT. The PSAT/NMSQT scores are not sent to colleges unless you specially request that they be forwarded. They are, however, sent to the National Merit Scholarship Corporation (NMSC). In April, approximately 50,000 high-scoring students will be invited to name two colleges or universities to which they would like to be referred by the NMSC. Of these, approximately 15,000 of the highest scorers are selected as semifinalists; the rest receive commendations. Scholarships are awarded to about 6,500 finalists by the NMSC and by colleges and private corporations, based on scores, academic record, geographic location, and other factors.

PSAT/NMSQT Practice Examination

Answer Sheet

Section 1—Verbal 30 minutes
1 Ⓐ Ⓑ Ⓒ Ⓓ Ⓔ
2 Ⓐ Ⓑ Ⓒ Ⓓ Ⓔ
3 Ⓐ Ⓑ Ⓒ Ⓓ Ⓔ
4 Ⓐ Ⓑ Ⓒ Ⓓ Ⓔ
5 Ⓐ Ⓑ Ⓒ Ⓓ Ⓔ
6 Ⓐ Ⓑ Ⓒ Ⓓ Ⓔ
7 Ⓐ Ⓑ Ⓒ Ⓓ Ⓔ
8 Ⓐ Ⓑ Ⓒ Ⓓ Ⓔ
9 Ⓐ Ⓑ Ⓒ Ⓓ Ⓔ
10 Ⓐ Ⓑ Ⓒ Ⓓ Ⓔ
11 Ⓐ Ⓑ Ⓒ Ⓓ Ⓔ
12 Ⓐ Ⓑ Ⓒ Ⓓ Ⓔ
13 Ⓐ Ⓑ Ⓒ Ⓓ Ⓔ
14 Ⓐ Ⓑ Ⓒ Ⓓ Ⓔ
15 Ⓐ Ⓑ Ⓒ Ⓓ Ⓔ
16 Ⓐ Ⓑ Ⓒ Ⓓ Ⓔ
17 Ⓐ Ⓑ Ⓒ Ⓓ Ⓔ
18 Ⓐ Ⓑ Ⓒ Ⓓ Ⓔ
19 Ⓐ Ⓑ Ⓒ Ⓓ Ⓔ
20 Ⓐ Ⓑ Ⓒ Ⓓ Ⓔ
21 Ⓐ Ⓑ Ⓒ Ⓓ Ⓔ
22 Ⓐ Ⓑ Ⓒ Ⓓ Ⓔ
23 Ⓐ Ⓑ Ⓒ Ⓓ Ⓔ
24 Ⓐ Ⓑ Ⓒ Ⓓ Ⓔ
25 Ⓐ Ⓑ Ⓒ Ⓓ Ⓔ
26 Ⓐ Ⓑ Ⓒ Ⓓ Ⓔ
27 Ⓐ Ⓑ Ⓒ Ⓓ Ⓔ
28 Ⓐ Ⓑ Ⓒ Ⓓ Ⓔ
29 Ⓐ Ⓑ Ⓒ Ⓓ Ⓔ
30 Ⓐ Ⓑ Ⓒ Ⓓ Ⓔ

Section 2—Math 30 minutes
1 Ⓐ Ⓑ Ⓒ Ⓓ Ⓔ
2 Ⓐ Ⓑ Ⓒ Ⓓ Ⓔ
3 Ⓐ Ⓑ Ⓒ Ⓓ Ⓔ
4 Ⓐ Ⓑ Ⓒ Ⓓ Ⓔ
5 Ⓐ Ⓑ Ⓒ Ⓓ Ⓔ
6 Ⓐ Ⓑ Ⓒ Ⓓ Ⓔ
7 Ⓐ Ⓑ Ⓒ Ⓓ Ⓔ
8 Ⓐ Ⓑ Ⓒ Ⓓ Ⓔ
9 Ⓐ Ⓑ Ⓒ Ⓓ Ⓔ
10 Ⓐ Ⓑ Ⓒ Ⓓ Ⓔ
11 Ⓐ Ⓑ Ⓒ Ⓓ Ⓔ
12 Ⓐ Ⓑ Ⓒ Ⓓ Ⓔ
13 Ⓐ Ⓑ Ⓒ Ⓓ Ⓔ
14 Ⓐ Ⓑ Ⓒ Ⓓ Ⓔ
15 Ⓐ Ⓑ Ⓒ Ⓓ Ⓔ
16 Ⓐ Ⓑ Ⓒ Ⓓ Ⓔ
17 Ⓐ Ⓑ Ⓒ Ⓓ Ⓔ
18 Ⓐ Ⓑ Ⓒ Ⓓ Ⓔ
19 Ⓐ Ⓑ Ⓒ Ⓓ Ⓔ
20 Ⓐ Ⓑ Ⓒ Ⓓ Ⓔ
21 Ⓐ Ⓑ Ⓒ Ⓓ Ⓔ
22 Ⓐ Ⓑ Ⓒ Ⓓ Ⓔ
23 Ⓐ Ⓑ Ⓒ Ⓓ Ⓔ
24 Ⓐ Ⓑ Ⓒ Ⓓ Ⓔ
25 Ⓐ Ⓑ Ⓒ Ⓓ Ⓔ

Section 3—Verbal 30 minutes
31 Ⓐ Ⓑ Ⓒ Ⓓ Ⓔ
32 Ⓐ Ⓑ Ⓒ Ⓓ Ⓔ
33 Ⓐ Ⓑ Ⓒ Ⓓ Ⓔ
34 Ⓐ Ⓑ Ⓒ Ⓓ Ⓔ
35 Ⓐ Ⓑ Ⓒ Ⓓ Ⓔ
36 Ⓐ Ⓑ Ⓒ Ⓓ Ⓔ
37 Ⓐ Ⓑ Ⓒ Ⓓ Ⓔ
38 Ⓐ Ⓑ Ⓒ Ⓓ Ⓔ
39 Ⓐ Ⓑ Ⓒ Ⓓ Ⓔ
40 Ⓐ Ⓑ Ⓒ Ⓓ Ⓔ
41 Ⓐ Ⓑ Ⓒ Ⓓ Ⓔ
42 Ⓐ Ⓑ Ⓒ Ⓓ Ⓔ
43 Ⓐ Ⓑ Ⓒ Ⓓ Ⓔ
44 Ⓐ Ⓑ Ⓒ Ⓓ Ⓔ
45 Ⓐ Ⓑ Ⓒ Ⓓ Ⓔ
46 Ⓐ Ⓑ Ⓒ Ⓓ Ⓔ
47 Ⓐ Ⓑ Ⓒ Ⓓ Ⓔ
48 Ⓐ Ⓑ Ⓒ Ⓓ Ⓔ
49 Ⓐ Ⓑ Ⓒ Ⓓ Ⓔ
50 Ⓐ Ⓑ Ⓒ Ⓓ Ⓔ
51 Ⓐ Ⓑ Ⓒ Ⓓ Ⓔ
52 Ⓐ Ⓑ Ⓒ Ⓓ Ⓔ
53 Ⓐ Ⓑ Ⓒ Ⓓ Ⓔ
54 Ⓐ Ⓑ Ⓒ Ⓓ Ⓔ
55 Ⓐ Ⓑ Ⓒ Ⓓ Ⓔ
56 Ⓐ Ⓑ Ⓒ Ⓓ Ⓔ
57 Ⓐ Ⓑ Ⓒ Ⓓ Ⓔ
58 Ⓐ Ⓑ Ⓒ Ⓓ Ⓔ
59 Ⓐ Ⓑ Ⓒ Ⓓ Ⓔ
60 Ⓐ Ⓑ Ⓒ Ⓓ Ⓔ

Section 4—Math
30 minutes

26 Ⓐ Ⓑ Ⓒ Ⓓ Ⓔ
27 Ⓐ Ⓑ Ⓒ Ⓓ Ⓔ
28 Ⓐ Ⓑ Ⓒ Ⓓ Ⓔ
29 Ⓐ Ⓑ Ⓒ Ⓓ Ⓔ
30 Ⓐ Ⓑ Ⓒ Ⓓ Ⓔ
31 Ⓐ Ⓑ Ⓒ Ⓓ Ⓔ
32 Ⓐ Ⓑ Ⓒ Ⓓ Ⓔ
33 Ⓐ Ⓑ Ⓒ Ⓓ Ⓔ
34 Ⓐ Ⓑ Ⓒ Ⓓ Ⓔ
35 Ⓐ Ⓑ Ⓒ Ⓓ Ⓔ
36 Ⓐ Ⓑ Ⓒ Ⓓ Ⓔ
37 Ⓐ Ⓑ Ⓒ Ⓓ Ⓔ
38 Ⓐ Ⓑ Ⓒ Ⓓ Ⓔ
39 Ⓐ Ⓑ Ⓒ Ⓓ Ⓔ
40 Ⓐ Ⓑ Ⓒ Ⓓ Ⓔ

41 42 43 44 45

46 47 48 49 50

PSAT/NMSQT Practice Examination

SECTION 1

30 Questions (1–30) • Time: 30 Minutes

Directions: Each of the following questions consists of an incomplete sentence followed by five words or pairs of words. Choose that word or pair of words which, when substituted for the blank space or spaces, *best* completes the meaning of the sentence and mark the letter of your choice on your answer sheet.

Example:

In view of the extenuating circumstances and the defendant's youth, the judge recommended ----.

(A) conviction
(B) a defense
(C) a mistrial
(D) leniency
(E) life imprisonment

Ⓐ Ⓑ Ⓒ ● Ⓔ

1. The speaker fascinated us with his knowledge, but his ---- toward the end onto other topics confused us.

   (A) digression
   (B) removal
   (C) preoccupation
   (D) tipoff
   (E) apprehension

2. My accountant suggested that I should organize my ---- more carefully.

   (A) regulations
   (B) annals
   (C) profits
   (D) remainders
   (E) receipts

3. He swept into the room like a ----, blowing papers and journals off the desk.

   (A) tyrant
   (B) zephyr
   (C) cyclone
   (D) viper
   (E) satyr

4. If you make a ---- movement, you might ---- the bear.

   (A) vast..disturb
   (B) sudden..startle
   (C) graceful..perturb
   (D) slow..aggrieve
   (E) rash..promote

5. Because the motorist had been unable to control his car, the police officer questioned his ----.

   (A) sobriety
   (B) fecundity
   (C) passivity
   (D) frailty
   (E) virility

6. After the recital we all ---- to the salon for tea and cakes.

   (A) retired
   (B) restored
   (C) retorted
   (D) reviewed
   (E) remanded

7. He soon ---- that she was making fun of him; with that ---- came a feeling of intense shame.

   (A) forgot..withdrawal
   (B) apprised..wisdom
   (C) realized..contentment
   (D) recognized..awareness
   (E) believed..contrivance

GO ON TO THE NEXT PAGE

8. Her easy win in the cross-country ski race gained her much ---- from skiers in her northern community.

(A) condemnation
(B) consternation
(C) tribulation
(D) demarcation
(E) approbation

9. The house looked ---- situated on the crumbling cliff.

(A) prudently
(B) precariously
(C) predominantly
(D) vicariously
(E) aimlessly

10. Should we allow Paul to ---- his brother's time at the computer?

(A) usurp
(B) renege
(C) depict
(D) marshal
(E) entail

11. The treaty was ---- almost as soon as the signatures were ----.

(A) broken..revamped
(B) abrogated..affixed
(C) signed..appended
(D) funded..initialed
(E) prepared..fulfilled

12. The stark trees were ---- against the gray sky.

(A) silhouetted
(B) shackled
(C) established
(D) conflicted
(E) oscillated

13. It makes no difference what we ----; her opinion is ----.

(A) understand..reflective
(B) assert..unwavering
(C) opine..shifting
(D) modify..subversive
(E) delineate..volatile

14. In love he was lucky; however, in business, he was somewhat ----.

(A) foreshortened
(B) singular
(C) favored
(D) hapless
(E) attuned

15. After the divorce she returned to the way she had lived before her ----.

(A) nuptials
(B) annulment
(C) epoch
(D) progeny
(E) vocation

16. First ---- to the right, and then ---- in a straight line.

(A) turn..meander
(B) continue..veer
(C) veer..proceed
(D) pivot..waver
(E) digress..drift

17. His ---- annoyed us; never had we met a more ---- man.

(A) jealousy..piquant
(B) obtuseness..astute
(C) patience..temperate
(D) obstinacy..stubborn
(E) petulance..zealous

Directions: Each reading passage below is followed by a set of questions. Read the passage and answer the accompanying questions, basing your answers on what is stated or implied in the passage. Mark the letter of your choice on your answer sheet.

Questions 18–22 are based on the following passage.

In 1891 in China, a collection of descriptive essays on other countries was compiled by a native of Kiangsu named Wang Hsi-ch'i. This excerpt is from an essay entitled "Europe to a Chinese Observer."

Europe's people are all tall and white. Only those who live in the northeast where it is very cold are short, and dwarfish. They have big noses and deep eyes. But their eyes are not of the same color, with brown, green, and black being most frequent. They have heavy beards that go up to their temples, or are wound around their jaws. Some of their beards are straight like those of the Chinese. Some are crooked and twisted like curly hairs. Some shave them all off. Some leave them all on. Some cut their beards but leave their mustaches. Some cut off their mustaches and leave their beards. They do what they wish. Whether old or young, all have beards. They let their hair grow to two or three inches. But if it gets longer they cut it. The women leave on all of their hair. The women dress their hair somewhat like Chinese women, but gather it together in a net. The color of their whiskers and hair is different. They have yellow, red, mottled, or black, all kinds. The men wear flat-topped, tubelike, narrow-brimmed hats of different heights ranging from four inches to over one foot. They are made of felt or silk. When they meet people, they lift their hats as a sign of respect. Their clothes are narrow and their sleeves are tight. The length only goes down to their bellies. Their trousers are bound tightly around their waists. But their outer garments are loose and long, and reach as far down as their knees. They wear collars in front and back. Their inner garments are of cotton, but their outer garments are of wool. They often wear boots which are made of leather.

Women's clothes are also tight and their sleeves stick to their bodies. They wear skirts which are long and brush the ground. This is how they generally dress. For their ceremonial hats, ceremonial clothes, their military helmets and garments, they have different practices.

For their eating and drinking utensils they use gold, silver, and ceramics. When they eat they use knife and fork, and they do not use chopsticks. They eat mainly bread. Potatoes are staple. They mostly roast or broil fowl and game. They usually season it with preserves or olive oil. They drink spirits and soda water, as well as coffee in which they mix sugar. Its fragrance enlivens teeth and jaws, and makes the spirit fresh and clear.

18. When Wang Hsi-ch'i says that European people's "eyes are not of the same color" (line 4), he means that

(A) they often have two eyes that do not match in color
(B) their eyes are different from Chinese people's eyes
(C) different Europeans have different-colored eyes
(D) their eyes are a different color from their hair
(E) northern Europeans have eyes that are a different color from those of southern Europeans

19. The word *dress* (line 15) is used to mean

(A) clothe
(B) attire
(C) style
(D) bandage
(E) decorate

20. How does paragraph 3 differ from paragraphs 1 and 2?

(A) It does not refer to personal appearance.
(B) It compares European ways to Chinese ways.
(C) It does not discuss European customs.
(D) Both A and B
(E) Both B and C

21. This passage was intended primarily as

(A) entertainment and amusement
(B) digression and exchange
(C) persuasion and argument
(D) narration and diversion
(E) description and instruction

GO ON TO THE NEXT PAGE

22. How does Wang Hsi-ch'i feel about European customs?

    (A) They are not to be trusted.
    (B) They are unusual but interesting.
    (C) They are bizarre and hilarious.
    (D) They are pathetic.
    (E) They are preferable to Chinese customs.

Charles Darwin (1809-1882) was best known for his own observational studies, which led to his theory of natural selection, but he was quite capable of using other people's observations to support his theories, as shown in this excerpt from The Descent of Man.

Birds sometimes exhibit benevolent feelings; they will feed the deserted young ones even of distinct species, but this perhaps ought to be considered as a mistaken instinct. They will feed, as shown in an earlier part of this work, adult birds of their own species which have become blind. Mr. Buxton gives a curious account of a parrot which took care of a frost-bitten and crippled bird of a distinct species, cleansed her feathers and defended her from the attacks of the other parrots which roamed freely about his garden. It is a still more curious fact that these birds apparently evince some sympathy for the pleasures of their fellows. When a pair of cockatoos made a nest in an acacia tree "it was ridiculous to see the extravagant interest taken in the matter by the others of the same species." These parrots also evinced unbounded curiosity and clearly had "the idea of property and possession." They have good memories, for in the Zoological Gardens they have plainly recognized their former masters after an interval of some months.

Birds possess acute powers of observation. Every mated bird, of course, recognizes its fellow. Audubon states that a certain number of mating thrushes *(Mimus polyglottus)* remain all the year round in Louisiana, while others migrate to the Eastern States; these latter on their return are instantly recognized and always attacked by their southern brethren. Birds under confinement distinguish different persons, as is proved by the strong and permanent antipathy or affection which they show without any apparent cause toward certain individuals. I have heard of numerous instances with jays, partridges, canaries, and especially bullfinches. Mr. Hussey has described in how extraordinary a manner a tamed partridge recognized everybody; and its likes and dislikes were very strong. This bird seemed "fond of gay colors, and no new gown or cap could be put on without catching his attention." Mr. Hewitt has described the habits of some ducks (recently descended from wild birds) which at the approach of a strange dog or cat would rush headlong into the water and exhaust themselves in their attempts to escape; but they knew Mr. Hewitt's own dogs and cats so well that they would lie down and bask in the sun close to them. They always moved away from a strange man, and so they would from the lady who attended them if she made any great change in her dress. Audubon relates that he reared and tamed a wild turkey which always ran away from any strange dog; this bird escaped into the woods, and some days afterward Audubon saw, as he thought, a wild turkey and made his dog chase it; but to his astonishment the bird did not run away, and the dog when he came up did not attack the bird, for they mutually recognized each other as old friends.

Mr. Jenner Weir is convinced that birds pay particular attention to the colors of other birds, sometimes out of jealousy and sometimes as a sign of kinship. Thus he turned a reed-bunting *(Emberiza schoeniculus)*, which had acquired its black headdress, into his aviary, and the newcomer was not noticed by any bird except by a bullfinch, which is likewise black-headed. This bullfinch was a very quiet bird, and had never before quarreled with any of its comrades, including another reed-bunting, which had not as yet become black-headed; but the reed-bunting with a black head was so unmercifully treated that it had to be removed.

23. Why does Darwin cite Mr. Buxton?

    (A) To support his theory about birds' powers of observation
    (B) To support his statement about birds' benevolence
    (C) To contrast with his own observations of birds
    (D) Both A and B
    (E) Both B and C

24. The word *distinct* (line 8) is used to mean

    (A) special
    (B) apparent
    (C) intelligible
    (D) definite
    (E) different

25. The word *antipathy* (line 29) means

(A) dislike
(B) remedy
(C) disappointment
(D) amusement
(E) argument

26. Why does Darwin mention jays, partridges, canaries, and bullfinches?

(A) To explain why some birds cannot be trained
(B) To educate his reader on types of local birds
(C) To contrast with a later discussion of shore birds
(D) To support his discussion of birds' memories
(E) To show the variety of birds in England

27. The word *reared* (line 46) is used to mean

(A) backed
(B) raised
(C) leaped
(D) ended
(E) constructed

28. What does Darwin mean by "a sign of kinship" (line 56)?

(A) Mark of common parentage
(B) Premonition of future union
(C) Symbol of compatibility
(D) Evidence of family relationship
(E) Indication of mutual interest

29. A good title for paragraph 3 might be

(A) "Different-Colored Birds"
(B) "Bullfinches and Their Colors"
(C) "An Example of Color Recognition in Birds"
(D) "Captive Birds"
(E) "Birds in Peace and War"

30. The main purpose of this passage is to

(A) contrast birds with humans
(B) compare three species of birds
(C) review current studies of birds
(D) compare wild birds to confined birds
(E) discuss some traits of birds

STOP

END OF SECTION 1. IF YOU HAVE ANY TIME LEFT, GO OVER YOUR WORK IN THIS SECTION ONLY. DO NOT WORK IN ANY OTHER SECTION OF THE TEST.

SECTION 2

25 Questions (26–50) • Time: 30 Minutes

Directions: Solve the following problems using any available space on the page for scratchwork. On your answer sheet fill in the choice which best corresponds to the correct answer.

Notes: The figures accompanying the problems are drawn as accurately as possible, unless otherwise stated in specific problems. Again, unless otherwise stated, all figures lie in the same plane. All numbers used in these problems are real numbers. Calculators are permitted for this test.

Reference Information

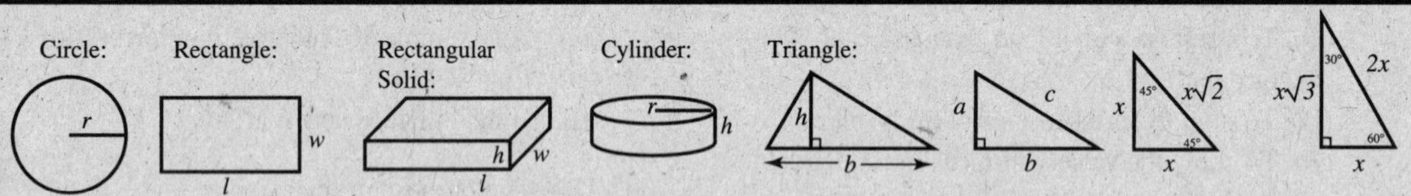

$C=2\pi r$ $A=\pi r^2$ $A=lw$ $V=lwh$ $V=\pi r^2 h$ $A=\frac{1}{2}bh$ $a^2+b^2=c^2$

The number of degrees of arc in a circle is 360.
The measure in degrees of a straight angle is 180.
The sum of the measures in degrees of the angles of a triangle is 180.

1. $0.1 \times 0.01 \times 0.001 =$

(A) .01
(B) .03
(C) .003
(D) .0001
(E) .000001

2. The average height of the four-member gymnastics squad is 5 feet. Three of the girls are 4 feet 10 inches tall. How tall is the fourth member?

(A) 5 feet
(B) 5 feet 2 inches
(C) 5 feet 4 inches
(D) 5 feet 6 inches
(E) It cannot be determined from the information given.

3. $\frac{1}{5}$ times its reciprocal is

(A) $\frac{2}{5}$
(B) $\frac{1}{25}$
(C) 1
(D) 5
(E) 25

4. How many sixteenths are in $5\frac{1}{4}$?

(A) 17
(B) 20
(C) 80
(D) 81
(E) 84

5. Whenever a particular organism reproduces, it doubles in number each hour. If you start with one organism at 3:00, how many will you have by 6:00?

(A) 4
(B) 6
(C) 8
(D) 24
(E) 120

6. If $x = \frac{1}{4}y$, what is the value of $\frac{x}{4}$?

(A) 16
(B) $\frac{y}{16}$
(C) $\frac{y}{4}$
(D) y
(E) $4y$

7. If the sides of a square are tripled, what always happens to its perimeter?

(A) It remains the same.
(B) It is cubed.
(C) It increases by 100%.
(D) It is tripled.
(E) It increases by 900%.

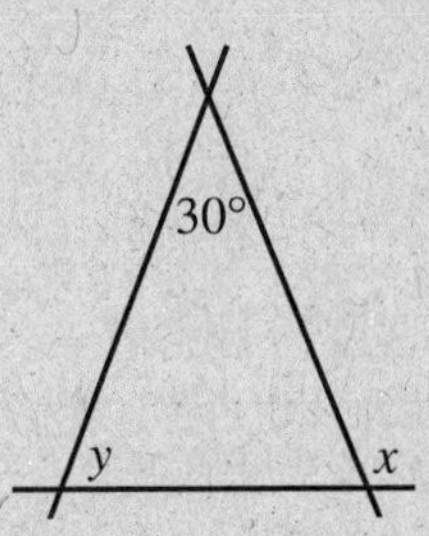

8. In the figure above, what is the value of x?

(A) 30
(B) 60
(C) 90
(D) $2y$
(E) It cannot be determined from the information given.

9. Leo is 67. His son Robert is 29. In how many years will Robert be exactly half his father's age?

(A) 2
(B) 5
(C) 7
(D) 9
(E) 12

10. When the numbers $\frac{1}{4}$, $\frac{3}{10}$, 0.23, and $\frac{4}{15}$ are arranged in ascending order of size, the result is

(A) 0.23, $\frac{3}{10}$, $\frac{1}{4}$, $\frac{4}{15}$
(B) $\frac{1}{4}$, 0.23, $\frac{3}{10}$, $\frac{4}{15}$
(C) 0.23, $\frac{1}{4}$, $\frac{3}{10}$, $\frac{4}{15}$
(D) $\frac{4}{15}$, $\frac{3}{10}$, $\frac{1}{4}$, 0.23
(E) 0.23, $\frac{1}{4}$, $\frac{4}{15}$, $\frac{3}{10}$

11. If $a + b = 12$ and $\frac{b}{a} = 3$, then

(A) $a = 9$
(B) $b = \frac{a}{3}$
(C) $12 = 3b$
(D) $b - a = 9$
(E) $ab = 27$

12. The side of a square forms the radius of a circle with a circumference of 10. What is the perimeter of the square?

(A) $\frac{5}{\pi}$
(B) $\frac{10}{\pi}$
(C) $\frac{20}{\pi}$
(D) 4π
(E) 100π

GO ON TO THE NEXT PAGE

13. Station KBAZ is on the air 24 hours a day. Yesterday it sold ads and took in money at this rate: 20% from drive-time ads at \$20/minute, 50% from daytime ads at \$10/minute, and 30% from nighttime ads at \$5/minute. If the station made \$500 yesterday, how much air time was dedicated to ads?

(A) 30 minutes
(B) 1 hour
(C) 2 hours
(D) 3 hours
(E) 3 hours, 30 minutes

14. In the figure below, the area of the circle is equivalent to

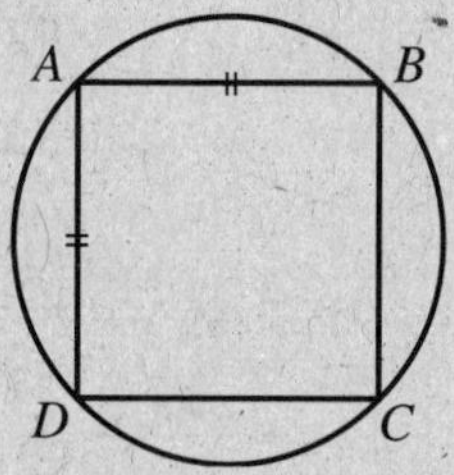

(A) $\frac{AB}{\pi}$
(B) AB
(C) πAB
(D) $\pi\left(\frac{AC}{2}\right)^2$
(E) πAC^2

15. A motorist drives 90 miles at an average speed of 52 miles per hour and returns at an average speed of 60 miles per hour. What is her average speed in miles per hour for the entire trip?

(A) 55
(B) 56
(C) 56.5
(D) 58
(E) It cannot be determined from the information given.

16. If $17x - 32 = 308$, what is $\frac{x}{4}$?

(A) 5
(B) 10
(C) 20
(D) 50
(E) 85

17. In the figure below, ΔUQR and ΔRST are equal in area. If $QR = 2$, what is the area of triangle RUT?

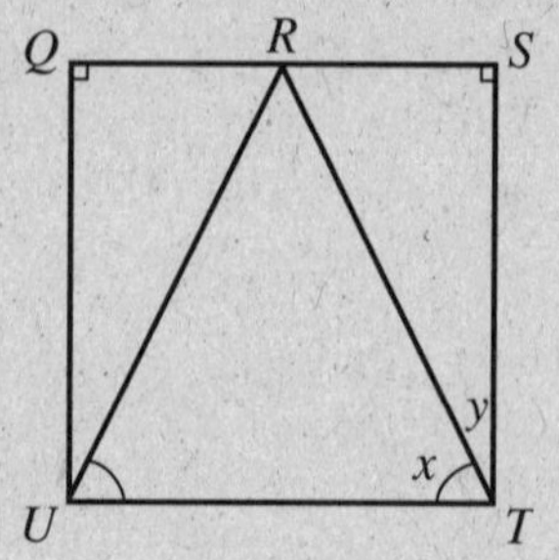

(A) 2
(B) 4
(C) 8
(D) 12
(E) 16

18. If the radius of a circle is increased by 10%, the area of the circle is increased by

(A) 10%
(B) 21%
(C) 100%
(D) 110%
(E) 121%

19. If 2! means 2×3 and 3! means 3×4, what does $7! + 8!$ mean?

(A) 56
(B) 128
(C) 392
(D) 448
(E) 4,032

20. If one faucet fills the sink in 3 minutes and the other fills it in 2 minutes, how long will it take both faucets to fill the sink if both are turned on together?

(A) .5 minutes
(B) 1 minute
(C) 1.2 minutes
(D) 1.5 minutes
(E) 1.8 minutes

21. A pica is equal to about $\frac{1}{6}$ inch. Bodoni bold typeface gives you 3.4 characters per pica. If you are working on a page that is $8\frac{1}{2}$ inches across, and you wish to leave a 1-inch margin on all sides, about how many Bodoni bold characters can you expect to fit per line?

(A) 11
(B) 22
(C) 51
(D) 91
(E) 132

22. If the outer diameter of a pipe is 4 inches and the inner diameter is 3.75 inches, the thickness of the pipe in inches is

(A) .125
(B) .25
(C) .5
(D) .625
(E) 1

23. The points (2,0) and (4,y) are $\sqrt{8}$ units apart. What does y equal?

(A) –2
(B) 0
(C) 1
(D) 2
(E) 3

24. $(x-2)(x-(-2))=$

(A) x^2+4
(B) x^2-4
(C) x^2+2x-4
(D) $2x+4$
(E) $2x^2$

25. Between the hours of 2:15 and 2:27, how many degrees does the minute hand on a clock move?

(A) 12
(B) 27
(C) 30
(D) 45
(E) 72

STOP

END OF SECTION 2. IF YOU HAVE ANY TIME LEFT, GO OVER YOUR WORK IN THIS SECTION ONLY. DO NOT WORK IN ANY OTHER SECTION OF THE TEST.

SECTION 3

30 Questions (31–60) • Time: 30 Minutes

Directions: Each of the following questions consists of a capitalized pair of words followed by five pairs of words lettered A to E. The capitalized words bear some meaningful relationship to each other. Choose the lettered pair of words whose relationship is most similar to that expressed by the capitalized pair and mark its letter on your answer sheet.

Example:

DAY : SUN ::

(A) sunlight : daylight (B) heat : cold
(C) ray : sun (D) moon : star
(E) night : moon Ⓐ Ⓑ Ⓒ Ⓓ ●

31. COLLAR : NECK ::

(A) hat : head
(B) mitten : hand
(C) lapel : jacket
(D) cuff : wrist
(E) sock : ankle

32. MASTER : CHESS ::

(A) prodigy : game
(B) genius : contest
(C) acme : skill
(D) slave : fashion
(E) virtuoso : music

33. SNOW : BLIZZARD ::

(A) rain : fog
(B) hail : tornado
(C) wind : typhoon
(D) water : rainbow
(E) sleet : winter

34. SONG : LYRICIST ::

(A) tune : musician
(B) play : dramatist
(C) poet : author
(D) show : cast
(E) book : publisher

35. GEOMETRY : MATHEMATICS ::

(A) painting : calculation
(B) astronomy : accounting
(C) hygiene : health care
(D) art : arithmetic
(E) botany : science

36. DOLLAR : DIME ::

(A) decade : year
(B) century : time
(C) nickel : quarter
(D) metal : paper
(E) value : cost

37. GRAMMAR : LANGUAGE ::

(A) training : puppy
(B) hanger : clothing
(C) story : building
(D) English : French
(E) scale : music

38. WHEEL : WAGON ::

(A) runner : sled
(B) circle : square
(C) fin : fish
(D) engine : automobile
(E) skate : blade

39. DEFEND : PROSECUTE ::

(A) protect : serve
(B) allay : berate
(C) fortify : assail
(D) liberate : free
(E) deliberate : judge

40. SAPPHIRE : BLUE ::

(A) ruby : red
(B) tree : green
(C) silver : tarnished
(D) gem : polished
(E) jewelry : ornate

41. CASTOFFS : CLOTHING ::

(A) closet : coat
(B) castaway : ship
(C) rummage : sale
(D) trash : garbage
(E) scrap : metal

42. FOX : KIT ::

(A) pup : seal
(B) manx : cat
(C) male : female
(D) lion : cub
(E) wolf : pack

43. SHARECROPPER : PLANTATION ::

(A) renter : apartment
(B) farmer : crop
(C) worker : job
(D) assembly line : factory
(E) potato : root

Directions: The reading passage below is followed by a set of questions. Read the passage and answer the accompanying questions, basing your answers on what is stated or implied in the passage. Mark the letter of your choice on your answer sheet.

Questions 44-48 are based on the following passage.

Kate Chopin wrote a number of short stories about the Louisiana Creoles, but she is famous for her novel of a woman trapped in a stifling marriage. The Awakening *is a strange, moody book, basing much of its appeal on a strong sense of character and setting. In this excerpt from the beginning of the novel, we meet the main characters.*

Mr. Pontellier finally lit a cigar and began to smoke, letting the paper drag idly from his hand. He fixed his gaze upon a white sunshade that was advancing at snail's pace from the beach. He could see it plainly between the gaunt trunks of the water-oaks and across the stretch of yellow camomile. The gulf looked far away, melting hazily into the blue of the horizon. The sunshade continued to approach slowly. Beneath its pink-lined shelter were his wife, Mrs. Pontellier, and young Robert Lebrun. When they reached the cottage, the two seated themselves with some appearance of fatigue upon the upper step of the porch, facing each other, each leaning against a supporting post.

"What folly! to bathe at such an hour in such heat!" exclaimed Mr. Pontellier. He himself had taken a plunge at daylight. That was why the morning seemed long to him.

"You are burnt beyond recognition," he added, looking at his wife as one looks at a valuable piece of personal property which has suffered some damage. She held up her hands, strong, shapely hands, and surveyed them critically, drawing up her lawn sleeves above the wrists. Looking at them reminded her of her rings, which she had given to her husband before leaving for the beach. She silently reached out to him, and he, understanding, took the rings from his vest pocket and dropped them into her open palm. She slipped them upon her fingers; then clasping her knees, she looked across at Robert and began to laugh. He sent back an answering smile.

"What is it?" asked Pontellier, looking lazily and amused from one to the other. It was some utter nonsense; some adventure out there in the water, and they both tried to relate it at once. It did not seem half so amusing when told. They realized this, and so did Mr. Pontellier. He yawned and stretched himself. Then he got up, saying he had half a mind to go over to Klein's hotel and play a game of billiards.

"Come go along, Lebrun," he proposed to Robert. But Robert admitted quite frankly that he preferred to stay where he was and talk to Mrs. Pontellier.

"Well, send him about his business when he bores you, Edna," instructed her husband as he prepared to leave.

"Here, take the umbrella," she exclaimed, holding it out to him. He accepted the sunshade, and lifting it over his head descended the steps and walked away.

GO ON TO THE NEXT PAGE

44. The word *folly* (line 14) is used to mean

(A) temerity
(B) gaiety
(C) clumsiness
(D) tactlessness
(E) foolishness

45. The narrator refers to "a valuable piece of personal property" (lines 19–20) to

(A) show how very much her husband values Mrs. Pontellier
(B) imply that Mr. Pontellier considers his wife to be his possession
(C) remind the reader of Mr. Pontellier's great wealth
(D) show how much the author values Mrs. Pontellier
(E) contrast Mrs. Pontellier with her beach property

46. The incident with Mrs. Pontellier's rings symbolizes

(A) her bondage
(B) her love for Lebrun
(C) her traditional values
(D) her desire to grow
(E) her bravery

47. The word *relate* (line 34) is used to mean

(A) unite
(B) recount
(C) integrate
(D) involve
(E) compare

48. How does the narrator feel about Mr. Pontellier?

(A) He is mischievous.
(B) He is dull.
(C) He is rude.
(D) He is vain.
(E) He is fiendish.

Directions: The two passages given below deal with a related topic. Following the passages are questions about the content of each passage or about the relationship between the two passages. Answer the questions based upon what is stated or implied in the passages and in any introductory material provided. Mark the letter of your choice on your answer sheet.

Questions 49-60 are based on the following passages.

As many in pre-Revolutionary Virginia cried for conciliation with Britain, Patrick Henry advocated preparing for war in a speech to the delegates to the Continental Congress. A year later, a group of writers who signed themselves Hutchinson, Cooper, Cato, & c. *submitted a stinging article to the* Pennsylvania Evening Post.

Passage 1—Patrick Henry to the Virginia Delegation, March 23, 1775

No man thinks more highly than I do of the patriotism, as well as abilities, of the very worthy gentlemen who have just addressed the House. But different men often see the same subject in different lights; and, therefore, I hope it will not be thought disrespectful to those gentlemen, if, entertaining as I do opinions of a character very opposite to theirs, I shall speak forth my sentiments freely and without reserve. This is no time for ceremony. The question before the House is one of awful moment to this country. For my own part, I consider it as nothing less than a question of freedom or slavery. . . .

Mr. President, it is natural to man to indulge in the illusions of hope. We are apt to shut our eyes against a painful truth, and listen to the song of that siren till she transforms us into beasts. Is this the part of wise men, engaged in a great and arduous struggle for liberty? Are we disposed to be of the number of those who, having eyes, see not, and, having ears, hear not, the things which so nearly concern their temporal salvation? For my part, whatever anguish of spirit it may cost, I am willing to know the whole truth; to know the worst, and to provide for it.

I have but one lamp by which my feet are guided, and that is the lamp of experience. I know of no way of judging the future but by the past. And judging by the past, I wish to know what there has been in the conduct of the British ministry for the last ten years to justify those hopes with which gentlemen have been pleased to solace themselves and the House.

Passage 2—In the Pennsylvania Evening Post, *June 1, 1776*

Notwithstanding the savage treatment we have met with from the King of Britain, and the impossibility of the colonies ever being happy under his government again, according to the usual operation of natural and moral causes, yet we still find some people wishing to be dependent once more upon the crown of Britain. I have too good an opinion of the human understanding, to suppose that there is a man in America who believes that we ever shall be happy again in our old connection with that crown. I, therefore, beg leave to oblige the advocates for dependence to speak for themselves in the following order:—

1. I shall lose my office. 2. I shall lose the honor of being related to men in office. 3. I shall lose the rent of my houses for a year or two. 4. We shall have no more rum, sugar, tea nor coffee, in this country, except at a most exorbitant price. 5. We shall have no more gauze or fine muslins imported among us. 6. The New England men will turn Goths and Vandals, and overrun all the Southern Colonies. N.B.—It is the fashion with the people who make this objection to independence, to despise the courage and discipline of the New England troops, and to complain that they are unwilling to fight out of their own colonies. 7. The church will have no king for a head. 8. The Presbyterians will have a share of power in this country. N.B.—These people have been remarked, ever since the commencement of our disputes with Great Britain, to prefer a Quaker or an Episcopalian, to one of their own body, where he was equally hearty in the cause of liberty. 9. I shall lose my chance of a large tract of land in a new purchase. 10. I shall want the support of the first officers of government, to protect me in my insolence, injustice, and villany. 11. The common people will have too much power in their hands. N.B.—The common people are composed of tradesmen and farmers, and include nine-tenths of the people of America.

Finally.—Sooner than submit to the chance of these probable evils, we will have our towns burnt, our country desolated, and our fathers, brothers, and children butchered by English, Scotch, and Irishmen. . . . And, after all, such of us as survive these calamities, will submit to such terms of slavery as King George and his Parliament may impose upon us.

GO ON TO THE NEXT PAGE

49. Henry uses the phrase "in different lights" (line 4) to mean

(A) in a frivolous manner
(B) in a hopeful way
(C) based on varied preconceptions
(D) according to level of intelligence
(E) as if in bright sunlight

50. The phrase "awful moment" (line 10) is used by Henry to mean

(A) terrible time
(B) unpleasant point
(C) dreadful value
(D) great importance
(E) sudden amazement

51. Why does Henry refer to the myth about the siren?

(A) To remind us that sweet sounds may lull us falsely
(B) To advise us to prepare for war as the Greeks once did
(C) To compare our democracy with that of the Greeks
(D) To persuade us to heed the song as it is sung
(E) To stress the need for alarm

52. The word *solace* (line 30) means

(A) distress
(B) reassure
(C) sedate
(D) overturn
(E) applaud

53. In Passage 2, the phrase "beg leave" (line 40) means

(A) demand egress
(B) desire respite
(C) plead abandonment
(D) ask permission
(E) solicit allowance

54. The numbered list in Passage 2 contains

(A) articles of confederation
(B) arguments in favor of independence from Britain
(C) moral causes
(D) the author's opinions about independence
(E) supposed excuses for remaining dependent on Britain

55. In Passage 2, the notes labeled "N.B." (for *nota bene,* or "mark well") are apparently

(A) ironic asides by the author
(B) the author's notes to himself
(C) references to previous writings
(D) remarks by a second author
(E) additions by the editor/translator

56. "Goths and Vandals" (line 49) are used as examples of

(A) haphazard events
(B) tribal rites
(C) games
(D) barbaric peoples
(E) famous cowards

57. The word *want* (line 62) is used in Passage 2 to mean

(A) covet
(B) need
(C) lack
(D) crave
(E) prefer

58. How does the author of Passage 2 feel about commoners?

(A) They must be tolerated.
(B) They have too much power.
(C) They are in the majority.
(D) Both A and B
(E) Both B and C

59. Passage 1 differs from Passage 2 in its

(A) politics
(B) tone
(C) attitude toward the British
(D) both A and B
(E) both B and C

60. With which of the following would both authors agree?

(A) The question is one of freedom or slavery.
(B) Men indulge in illusions of hope.
(C) The British have done nothing to inspire hope.
(D) All of the above
(E) None of the above

STOP

END OF SECTION 3. IF YOU HAVE ANY TIME LEFT, GO OVER YOUR WORK IN THIS SECTION ONLY. DO NOT WORK IN ANY OTHER SECTION OF THE TEST.

SECTION 4

25 Questions (26–50) • Time: 30 Minutes

Directions: Solve the following problems using any available space on the page for scratchwork. On your answer sheet fill in the choice which best corresponds to the correct answer.

Notes: The figures accompanying the problems are drawn as accurately as possible unless otherwise stated in specific problems. Again, unless otherwise stated, all figures lie in the same plane. All numbers used in these problems are real numbers. Calculators are permitted for this test.

Reference Information

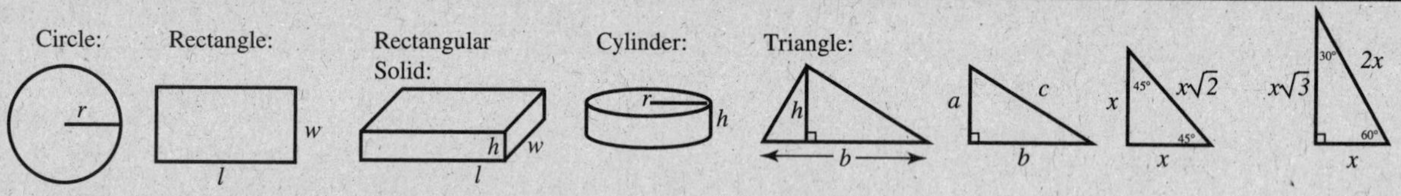

$C = 2\pi r$
$A = \pi r^2$

$A = lw$

$V = lwh$

$V = \pi r^2 h$

$A = \frac{1}{2}bh$

$a^2 + b^2 = c^2$

The number of degrees of arc in a circle is 360.
The measure in degrees of a straight angle is 180.
The sum of the measures in degrees of the angles of a triangle is 180.

PART 1: Quantitative Comparison Questions

Directions: Questions 26–40 each consist of two quantities—one in Column A, the other in Column B. Compare the two quantities and mark your answer sheet as follows:

(A) if the quantity in Column A is greater;
(B) if the quantity in Column B is greater;
(C) if the two quantities are equal;
(D) if the relationship cannot be determined from the information given.

Notes:

(1) Information concerning one or both of the compared quantities will be centered above the two columns for some items.
(2) Symbols that appear in both columns represent the same thing in Column A as in Column B.
(3) Letters such as x, n, and k are symbols for real numbers.

Examples

	Column A	*Column B*	*Answers*
		$a > 0$ $x > 0$	
E1.	$a - x$	$a + x$	Ⓐ ● Ⓒ Ⓓ
E2.	The average of 17, 19, 21, 23	The average of 16, 18, 20, 22	● Ⓑ Ⓒ Ⓓ

DO NOT MARK CHOICE (E) FOR THESE QUESTIONS. THERE ARE ONLY FOUR ANSWER CHOICES.

	Column A	Column B
26.	Area of a circle with a radius of z	Area of a square with sides measuring z

$$\frac{a}{2} = -b$$

	Column A	Column B
27.	ab	$\frac{a}{b}$

	Column A	Column B
28.	The number of odd numbers greater than 3 and less than or equal to 13.	4

$$x^2 = 144$$
$$2y - 18 = 32$$

	Column A	Column B
29.	$2x$	y

$$m < n$$

	Column A	Column B
30.	$\frac{m}{n}$	$\frac{n}{m}$

	Column A	Column B
31.	$\frac{1}{3}(c+d)$	$\frac{c}{3}+\frac{d}{3}$

two dice packed exactly into a box

	Column A	Column B
32.	the volume of the box	the volumes of the dice added together

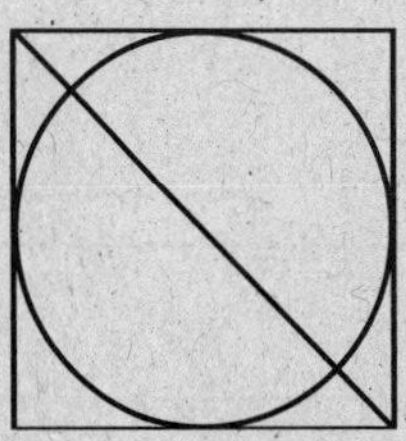

	Column A	Column B
33.	the perimeter of the triangle	the circumference of the circle

	Column A	Column B
34.	5% of 7	7% of 5

a and b are positive integers

	Column A	Column B
35.	$(a + b) - a$	$(b + a) - b$

	Column A	Column B
36.	$(x + 2)(x - 2)$	$x^2 - 4$

	Column A	Column B
37.	The average of the even numbers greater than 2 and less than 12	The average of the odd numbers greater than 3 and less than 13

	Column A	Column B
38.	$\left(\frac{1}{3}+\frac{1}{5}\right)^2$	$\left(\frac{1}{3}\right)^2+\left(\frac{1}{5}\right)^2$

GO ON TO THE NEXT PAGE

Questions 39–40 refer to the figure below.

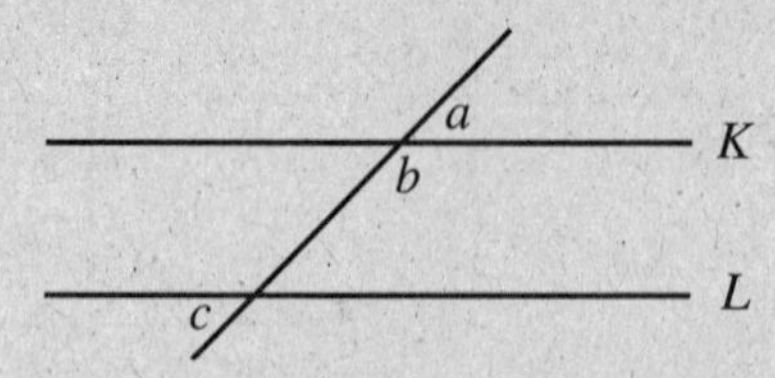

$K \parallel L$

$a = 60°$

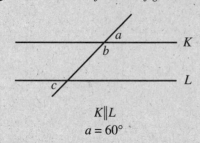

	Column A	Column B
39.	120	$a + c$
40.	360	$a + b + c$

PART 2: Student-Produced Response Questions

Directions: Solve each of these problems. Write the answer in the corresponding grid on the answer sheet and fill in the ovals beneath each answer you write. Here are some examples.

Answer: $\frac{3}{4}$ **(= .75; show answer either way)**

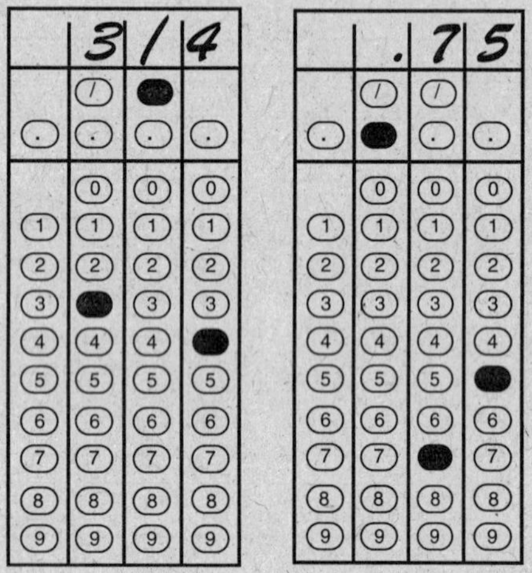

Note: A mixed number such as $3\frac{1}{2}$ must be gridded as 7/2 or as 3.5. If gridded as "31/2," it will be read as "thirty-one halves."

Answer: 325

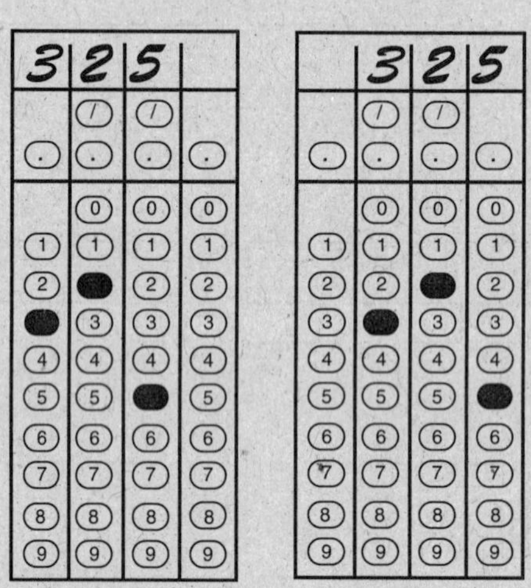

Note: Either position is correct

41. If $4x - 9 = 27$, what is x^3?

42. One-half of the contents of a container evaporates in one week, and three-fourths of the remainder evaporates in the following week. At the end of two weeks, what fractional part of the original contents remains? Express your answer in lowest terms.

43. The distance from the center of a circle to the midpoint of a chord is 3. If the length of the chord is 8, what is the length of the radius of the circle?

44. Three friends decide to split the cost of a pizza, with each chipping in \$3.25. If two more friends join them, and each pays an equal share, how much less will each of the three friends have to pay?

45. Five members of the baseball team weigh 130, 115, 120, 140, and 145 pounds. If the average weight of the nine-person team is 130 pounds, what is the average weight in pounds of the remaining four players?

46. In the figure below, what is the measure in degrees of angle n?

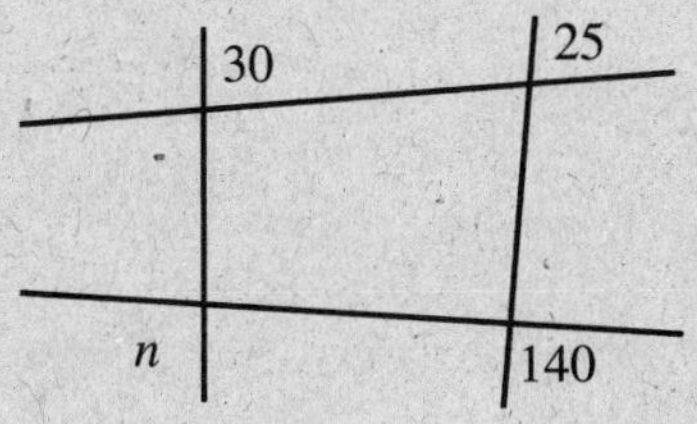

47. If $a + b = -4$ and $b^2 = 49$, what positive whole number can a be?

48. Danielle ate $\frac{1}{4}$ of a bag of popcorn and gave $\frac{1}{6}$ of the remainder to Phil. How much of the original container was left? Express your answer in lowest terms.

49. $\dfrac{.2 \times .3 \times .4}{12} =$

50. .004 is the ratio of .4 to what number?

STOP

END OF SECTION 4. IF YOU HAVE ANY TIME LEFT, GO OVER YOUR WORK IN THIS SECTION ONLY. DO NOT WORK IN ANY OTHER SECTION OF THE TEST.

Answer Key

SECTION 1: VERBAL

1. A	6. A	11. B	16. C	21. E	26. D
2. E	7. D	12. A	17. D	22. B	27. B
3. C	8. E	13. B	18. C	23. B	28. D
4. B	9. B	14. D	19. C	24. E	29. C
5. A	10. A	15. A	20. A	25. A	30. E

SECTION 2: MATH

1. E	6. B	11. E	16. A	21. E
2. D	7. D	12. C	17. C	22. A
3. C	8. E	13. B	18. B	23. D
4. E	9. D	14. D	19. B	24. B
5. C	10. E	15. B	20. C	25. E

SECTION 3: VERBAL

31. D	36. A	41. E	46. A	51. A	56. D
32. E	37. E	42. D	47. B	52. B	57. C
33. A	38. A	43. A	48. B	53. D	58. C
34. B	39. C	44. E	49. C	54. E	59. B
35. E	40. A	45. B	50. D	55. A	60. D

SECTION 4: MATH

Part 1

26. A	31. C	36. C
27. B	32. C	37. B
28. A	33. A	38. A
29. B	34. C	39. C
30. D	35. D	40. A

Part 2

41. 729	46. 45
42. $\frac{1}{8}$	47. 3
43. 5	48. $\frac{5}{8}$
44. 1.30	49. .002
45. 130	50. 100

Explanatory Answers

SECTION 1

1. **(A)** The word *confused* is your clue. The speaker has made a *digression,* or departure from the topic.

2. **(E)** What might concern an accountant? *Profits* (C) are one possibility, but they could not be *organized,* as the sentence indicates. *Receipts,* on the other hand, might be.

3. **(C)** The words *swept* and *blowing* indicate a windlike movement. A *zephyr* (B) is a kind of wind, but it is very gentle. Only *cyclone,* of the choices given, names a big, blustery wind.

4. **(B)** Both words must fit the context here. In choice (A), only the second word fits; the first makes no sense. In choices (C) and (D), if the first is true, the second is not; and choice (E) makes no sense at all.

5. **(A)** A motorist who cannot control a car may be intoxicated; in other words, lacking in *sobriety.*

6. **(A)** *Retired* has many meanings, and the one that means "retreated" or "withdrew" is the one used here.

7. **(D)** A parallelism is set up in this sentence; the second word will be an extension of the first. Once you recognize that, you will see that only choice (D) works.

8. **(E)** She would not be *condemned* (A) or "criticized" for her win; nor would other skiers be *consternated* (B) or "alarmed." *Tribulation* (C) means "hardship," and *demarcation* (D) means "limitation." Only *approbation,* meaning "congratulations" or "praise," has the proper meaning.

9. **(B)** If the house is on a crumbling cliff, it does not look *prudently* or "carefully" situated (A). It looks *precariously* or "shakily" positioned.

10. **(A)** The words *allow* and *time* are your clues here. If Paul *usurped,* or "took over," his brother's computer time, that might be a questionable offense.

11. **(B)** Both words must fit in order for your choice to be correct. In choice (A), the first word fits, but signatures cannot be *revamped.* Choice (C) is absurd—the treaty would be signed at exactly the same time as the signatures were appended. Choice (D) makes no sense, because a treaty would not be *funded,* and choice (E) makes no sense, because signatures cannot be *fulfilled.* The answer is choice (B)—the treaty was *abrogated,* or "broken," almost as soon as the signatures were *affixed,* or "added."

12. **(A)** The sentence has to do with appearance. The trees were *silhouetted*—only their outlines were apparent.

13. **(B)** Try filling in the second word first. That means choices (B), (C), and (D) are possibilities. Now add the first word, and you will see that only choice (B) is logical.

14. **(D)** *However* is the clue that lets you know that the second clause will be somehow antithetical to the first. Since the first clause has him being *lucky,* you must look for a word that means the opposite. *Hapless* is that word.

15. **(A)** She would not return to the way she had lived before her *annulment,* since that would imply that she would return to married life. Presumably, the divorce returns her to the way she lived before marriage, so *nuptials,* meaning "wedding," is the correct choice.

16. **(C)** You can *turn, continue, veer,* or *pivot* to the right, but you cannot *meander, veer, drift,* or *waver* "in a straight line." Only choice (C) makes sense.

17. **(D)** The second clause will support the first one in this kind of sentence construction. Any of the first words except *patience* might work in context, but only *obstinacy,* or "stubbornness," has a parallel in the second word of the pair.

18. **(C)** Return to the cited line, and you will see that the only eyes referred to are those of the Europeans, which come in brown, green, and black.

19. **(C)** Any of these might be a synonym for *dress,* but only *style* fits the context of fixing hair.

20. **(A)** Paragraph 3 *does* compare European ways to Chinese ways and discuss European customs. However, it deals with eating habits rather than with personal appearance.

21. **(E)** Looking at the passage as a whole, you can see that it primarily describes the people and customs of Europe, all with an instructive tone.

22. **(B)** The author rarely inserts himself into the passage, and he certainly says nothing negative, as choices (A), (C), and (D) would suggest. Nor does he ever imply that European customs are better than Chinese customs. He focuses on the strangeness of what he observes, stressing what his reader might find most interesting.

23. **(B)** Mr. Buxton is cited in paragraph 1. His account of a parrot who took care of a crippled bird is clearly included to support the discussion of benevolent behavior in birds.

24. **(E)** *Distinct* has several meanings, but in this case, the bird is of a *different* species from the parrot.

25. **(A)** The birds show "antipathy or affection," two opposite reactions.

26. **(D)** The list of birds appears in paragraph 2 as supporting evidence for Darwin's discussion of birds' powers of observation and recall.

27. **(B)** Returning to the cited phrase, you will see that only *raised* fits the context.

28. **(D)** Test the choices in context, and you will find that, while (A) and (C) are close, (D) is the best choice.

29. **(C)** Choice (A) is too broad, and choice (B) is too narrow. Choices (D) and (E) are off the mark. Only choice (C) is an accurate summary of the author's intent.

30. **(E)** You might be fooled into choosing choice (C), but Darwin really only cites studies to support his own observations, and there is no indication whether they are "current studies," unscientific observations by friends, or writings from long ago. Only choice (E) is accurate.

SECTION 2

1. **(E)** You can solve simply by counting decimal places to the right of the decimal and recognizing that the answer will have six (1 + 2 + 3).

(This sign will appear whenever it is easy or preferable to use a calculator to solve the problem.)

2. **(D)** Convert first to inches. The average height is 60 inches. Three girls are 58 inches tall. The fourth is x.

$(58 + 58 + 58 + x) \div 4 = 60$
$(174 + x) = 240$
$x = 66$ inches, or 5 feet 6 inches 

3. **(C)** *Any* number times its reciprocal is 1.

4. **(E)** Think: $5\frac{1}{4} = \frac{x}{16}$

$\frac{21}{4} = \frac{84}{16}$

5. **(C)** This lends itself to a draw-a-picture strategy.

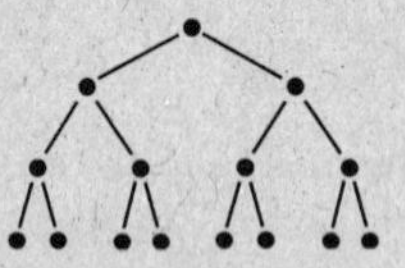

The answer is 8.

6. **(B)** You know that $x = \frac{y}{4}$. Therefore, stated in terms of y, $\frac{x}{4} = \frac{y}{4} \div 4$, or $\frac{y}{4} \times \frac{1}{4}$, or $\frac{y}{16}$.

7. **(D)** If you have any doubts, simply plug in a few numbers to test your ideas. If the side of a square = 2, the perimeter = 4 × 2, or 8. If the side is tripled to 6, the perimeter = 4 × 6, or 24. The perimeter is tripled.

8. **(E)** You can determine only these few facts, and they are not enough to find for *x*.

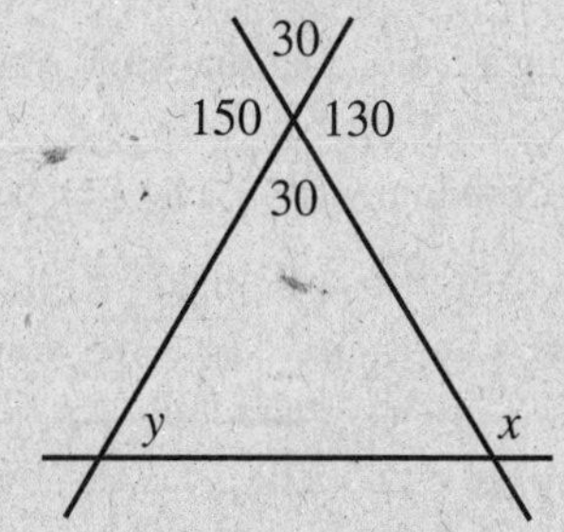

9. **(D)** The easiest way to solve is to determine the age Leo was when Robert was born: $67 - 29 = 38$. Then you know that when Robert reaches age 38, he will be half his father's age. That will occur in *x* years, where $29 + x = 38$ years. In 9 years, Robert will be 38, and his father will be $67 + 9 = 76$ years old—twice Robert's age.

10. **(E)** You can convert all the numbers to fractions with the same denominator and compare them:

$$\frac{75}{300}, \frac{90}{300}, \frac{69}{300}, \frac{80}{300}.$$

Alternatively, you can use a calculator to do the division and compare the numbers in decimal form.

11. **(E)** You know that $\frac{b}{a} = 3$, so you can refer to *b* as 3*a*. Plugging that into the first number sentence, you get

$a + 3a = 12$, so $4a = 12$, so $a = 3$
Since $b = 3a$, $b = 9$.
Therefore, $ab = 27$.

12. **(C)** First, draw the picture.

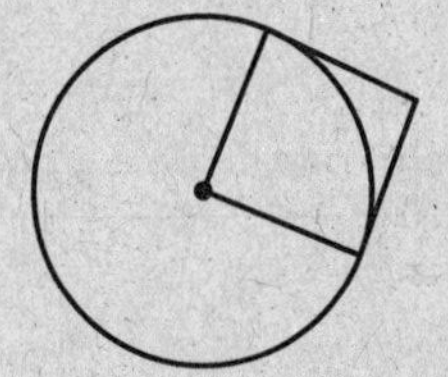

The reference information tells you that the circumference, 10, equals $2\pi r$.
Therefore, $\pi r = 5$.

Since $r = \frac{5}{\pi}$, the perimeter of the square $= 4 \times \frac{5}{\pi}$, or $\frac{20}{\pi}$.

13. **(B)** The station got $500 in all. Of this, 20%, or $100, was from drive-time ads at $20/minute—5 minutes of ads. 50%, or $250, was from daytime ads at $10/minute—25 minutes of ads. Finally, 30%, or $150, was from nighttime ads at $5/minute—30 minutes of ads. Add the numbers of minutes: $5 + 25 + 30 = 60$ minutes, or 1 hour.

14. **(D)** You should not need to do any calculating here. You know that the area of any circle is equal to πr^2. The radius of the circle pictured is equal to $\frac{AC}{2}$.

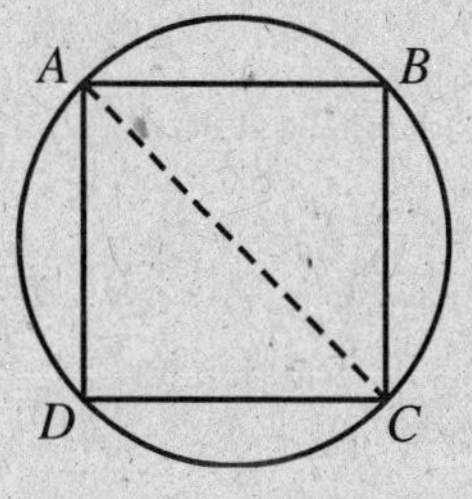

Therefore, the circle's area is $\pi\left(\frac{AC}{2}\right)^2$.

15. **(B)** Again, this problem needs very little calculation. The motorist drove the same distance there and back; only her average speed changed. You can add the averages for the two legs of the journey and divide by 2:

$52 + 60 = 112$
$112 \div 2 = 56$

16. **(A)** Solve for *x*:

$17x - 32 = 308$
$17x = 340$
$x = 20$

Knowing the value of *x*, you can see that $\frac{x}{4} = 5$.

17. **(C)** The area of any triangle is $\frac{1}{2}$ base × height. Since ΔUQR and ΔRST are equal in area and have equal heights, they must also have equal bases. In other words $QR = RS$, and each equals 2. That means that $QS = 4$, so each side of the square = 4.

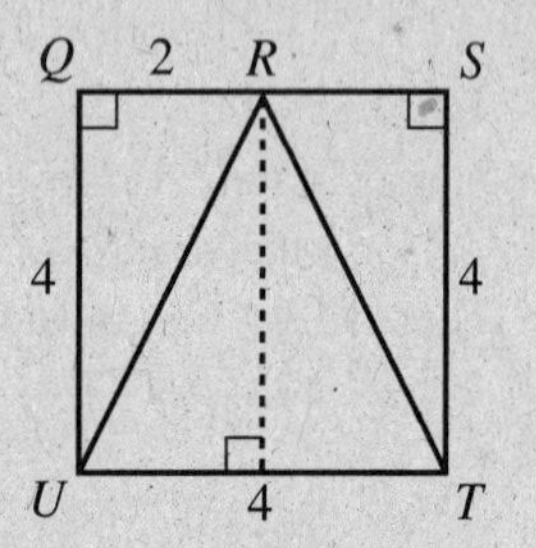

Now, to find the area of ΔRUT,

$\frac{1}{2}UT \times ST = \frac{1}{2}(4 \times 4) = 8.$

18. **(B)** This is trickier than it looks. Express the increase in the radius as $r + .1r$. Then the area, which before was πr^2, now is $\pi(r + .1r)^2$, or $\pi(1.1r)^2$. $(1.1)^2 = 1.21$, so the new area is 21% greater than the old.

19. **(B)** The sign ! appears to mean "multiply the number by the next greater whole number." Therefore, $7! = 7 \times 8$, and $8! = 8 \times 9$. Solving for $7! + 8!$, you add $56 + 72$ for a sum of 128.

20. **(C)** In one minute, the faucets working together will fill $\frac{1}{3} + \frac{1}{2}$ of the sink. In two minutes, they will fill $\frac{2}{3} + \frac{2}{2}$—overflowing the sink. Returning to the first set of numbers, you can see that the faucets will fill $\frac{2}{6} + \frac{3}{6}$, or $\frac{5}{6}$ of the sink in one minute. If $\frac{5}{6}x = 1$, then $x = \frac{6}{5}$, $1\frac{1}{5}$, or 1.2 minutes.

21. **(E)** The page is $8\frac{1}{2}$ inches across, but you are leaving a 1-inch margin, which subtracts 2 inches from each line. That leaves you with $6\frac{1}{2}$ inches. There are about 6 picas to the inch, so that makes 6.5×6, or 39 picas per line. Bodoni bold gives you 3.4 characters per pica, so multiplying the number of picas, 39, by the number of characters per pica, 3.4, gives you your answer: 132.6. Since a fraction of a character is useless, round to 132.

22. **(A)** Draw the picture:

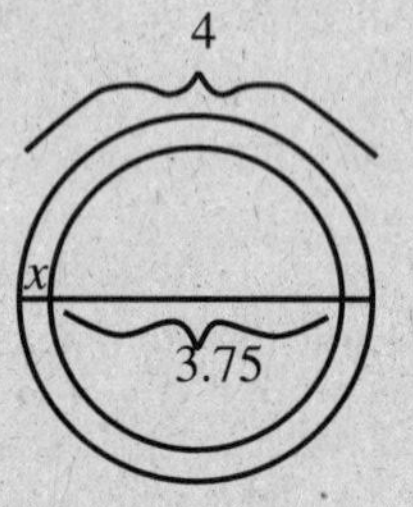

You can see that the difference in diameters is $4 - 3.75 = 2x$, so $x = .125$

23. **(D)** Again, draw the picture to help you solve.

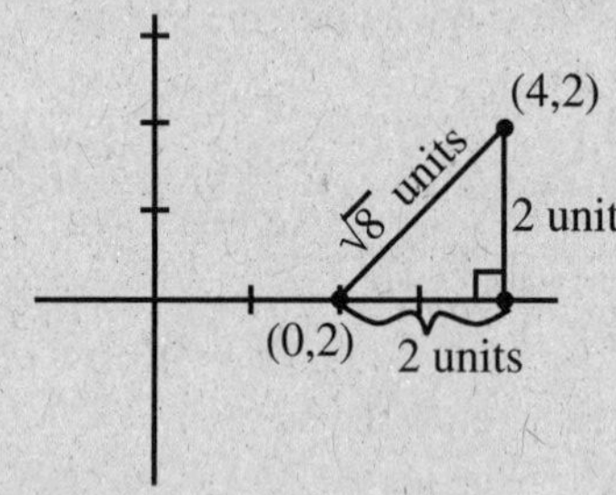

In the right triangle, $2^2 + y^2 = 8$, so $y = 2$.

24. **(B)** $(x - 2)(x - (-2)) =$

$(x - 2)(x + 2) =$
$x^2 - 2x + 2x - 4 =$
$x^2 - 4.$

25. **(E)** Converting the minutes on a clockface—60—to the degrees in a circle—360—means that each minute is equivalent to 6 degrees. The difference between 2:15 and 2:27, then—12 minutes—equals 12×6, or 72 degrees.

SECTION 3

31. **(D)** A *collar* fastens around the *neck* just as a *cuff* fastens around a *wrist.*

32. **(E)** A very great chess player is a *master,* and a very great musician is a *virtuoso.*

33. **(A)** A *blizzard* is a storm characterized by heavy, blowing snow, and a *typhoon* is a storm characterized by strong *wind.*

34. **(B)** The writer of a *song* is called a *lyricist,* and the writer of a *play* is called a *dramatist.* A musician may write a tune (A), but the more accurate word is *composer.* In addition, both lyricists and dramatists deal in words.

35. **(E)** As *geometry* is a branch of *mathematics,* so *botany* is a branch of *science.*

36. **(A)** Think of relative values here. A *dollar* equals 10 *dimes,* and a *decade* equals 10 *years.*

37. **(E)** *Grammar* is the structure on which *language* is built. In a similar way, *scales* are used to structure *music.*

38. **(A)** The *wheel* helps propel the *wagon* in the same way that the *runner* helps propel the *sled.* A fin might help propel a fish (C), but it works more like a rudder than like a wheel. An engine might help propel an automobile (D), but it does not do it in the same way that a wheel does.

39. **(C)** These words are used in their antithetical meanings. Of the answer choices, the only one that is a pair of opposites is (C), *fortify* and *assail.*

40. **(A)** A *sapphire* is a *blue* gem, and a *ruby* is a *red* gem. A tree may be green (B), but it is not a gem.

41. **(E)** We call discarded *clothing* "*castoffs*," and we call discarded *metal* "*scrap.*"

42. **(D)** A *kit* is a baby *fox,* and a *cub* is a baby *lion.*

43. **(A)** A *sharecropper* has a relationship to a *plantation* much as a *renter* does to an *apartment*—neither has ownership; both lease the space.

44. **(E)** Mr. Pontellier regards much of his wife's actions as *folly,* by which he means "foolishness" rather than the more negative connotations.

45. **(B)** If you read the introduction, you know that this is the story of a woman "trapped in a stifling marriage." Even if you didn't know this, you could infer from Mr. Pontellier's amused and patronizing attitude toward his wife that (B) is the correct answer.

46. **(A)** Mrs. Pontellier has removed her rings, including, presumably, her wedding ring, and has left them in the care of her husband while she set off for a morning of freedom. The scene in question makes it seem as though Mrs. Pontellier is putting out her arms to be handcuffed once more.

47. **(B)** Of all of these synonyms, only *recount,* meaning "retell," has the meaning that fits the context.

48. **(B)** We see Mr. Pontellier moving ponderously about, mystified by the laughter of others, and confined to a routine. There is no support for any of the other choices, but the author plainly feels he is dull.

49. **(C)** This phrase is still commonly used to mean "according to their various preconceived ideas and viewpoints."

50. **(D)** This is *awful* as meaning "full of awe" and *moment* as the root of *momentous.* Henry means that this is a time of great importance.

51. **(A)** Rereading the entire sentence in which the reference is found will help you recognize that this myth is referred to as a parallel for those men who cling to false hope.

52. **(B)** Men have had false hopes, and these hopes have *reassured* them. They may also have *sedated* them to some degree (C), but (B) is closer to the connotation intended.

53. **(D)** The author is asking permission to obtain some information from those who advocate dependence.

54. **(E)** If you understand the passage at all, you will see that the list is one of excuses those who advocate dependence use to explain why America should remain connected to Britain.

55. **(A)** Return to the passage and look for those N.B. references. *N.B.* stands for *nota bene,* meaning "mark well" or "pay attention to this important item." The author has used this device to comment directly on the items in his list.

56. **(D)** The clues in the sentence are *men* and *overrun.* The author suggests that people fear that New Englanders will take over the South, much as the barbarian Goths and Vandals took over Europe long ago.

57. **(C)** One fear cited is that the independent Americans will *want,* or "lack," protection.

58. **(C)** This is delineated in one of the N.B. asides. The author does not believe (B); he believes that those in favor of dependence believe it.

59. **(B)** The passages share the same political bent and attitude toward the British, but whereas Passage 1 is heartfelt and solemn, Passage 2 is tongue-in-cheek and ironic.

60. **(D)** Both authors refer to slavery—in line 12 in Passage 1, and in line 73 in Passage 2. Both remark on the fact that some people have deluded themselves with vain hopes about the British, despite the fact that the British have done nothing to inspire such hope. Since (A), (B), and (C) are correct, the answer is (D).

SECTION 4

Part 1

26. **(A)** Draw a picture to help you solve this problem. Just looking at the picture will convince you that the area of the circle will be greater than that of the square.

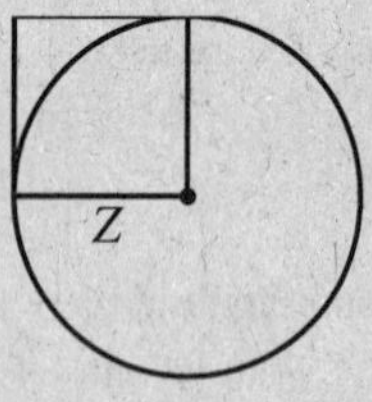

27. **(B)** Try plugging in some numbers. Suppose a is a positive number such as 4.

$\frac{4}{2} = -(-2)$

In that case, ab, 4(–2), equals –8.

$\frac{a}{b}$, $\frac{4}{-2}$, equals –2.

Now suppose a is a negative number such as –4.

$\frac{-4}{2} = -2$

In that case, ab, –4(2), equals –8 again.

$\frac{a}{b}$, $\frac{-4}{2}$, equals –2.

28. **(A)** There are five odd numbers greater than 3 and less than or equal to 13: 5, 7, 9, 11, and 13.

29. **(B)** If $x^2 = 144$, $x = 12$, and $2x = 24$.

If $2y - 18 = 32$, $2y = 50$, and $y = 25$.

30. **(D)** There is not enough information to solve this. If m and n are positive whole numbers, then $\frac{n}{m}$ is greater, but if n is positive and m negative, then $\frac{m}{n}$ is greater.

31. **(C)** One glance should tell you that these numbers are equivalent, but if you wish, try some numbers in place of c and d. If $c = 1$ and $d = 2$, $\frac{1}{3}(c+d) = 1$.

$\frac{c}{3} + \frac{d}{3} = \frac{1}{3} + \frac{2}{3} = 1$.

32. **(C)** You may wish to draw a picture to check this.

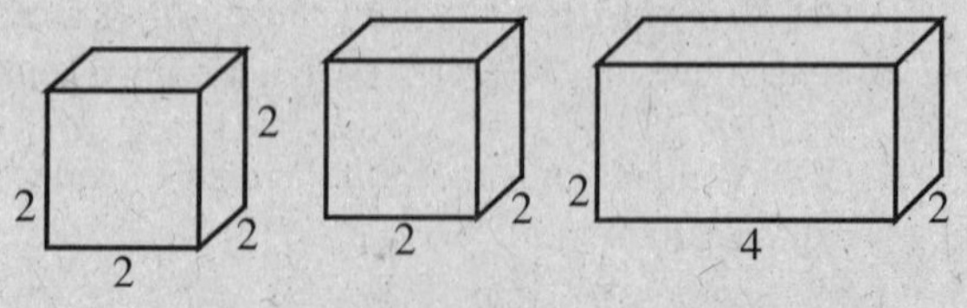

The volume of the large box = $2 \times 4 \times 2 = 16$.
The volume of each of the dice = $2 \times 2 \times 2 = 8$.
$8 + 8 = 16$

33. **(A)** Draw a picture, ascribe values, and solve.

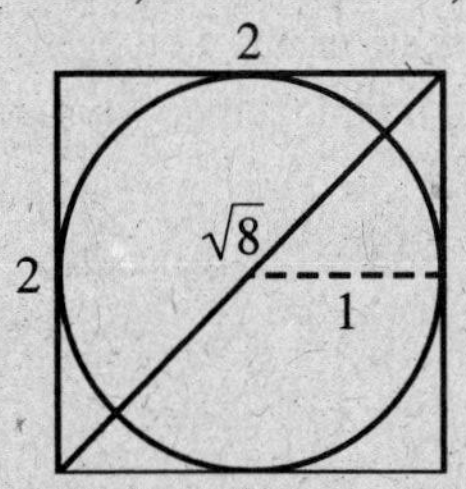

The perimeter of the triangle = $2 + 2 + \sqrt{8}$.
The circumference of the circle = $2\pi r$, and since $r = 1$, you can restate that as 2π.
$\pi \approx 3.14$, so $2\pi \approx 6.28$.
$\sqrt{8}$ lies between 2.8 and 2.9, so $2 + 2 + \sqrt{8} \approx 6.8$ or 6.9.

34. **(C)** If you do not recognize the equivalence immediately, use your calculator to solve.

5% of 7 = .35
7% of 5 = .35

35. **(D)** Unless you know which is greater, *a* or *b*, you cannot answer this question.

36. **(C)** $(x + 2)(x - 2) = x^2 + 2x - 2x - 4$, or $x^2 - 4$.

37. **(B)** The even numbers greater than 2 and less than 12 are 4, 6, 8, and 10. Their average is 5. The odd numbers greater than 3 and less than 13 are 5, 7, 9, and 11. Their average is 8.

38. **(A)** $\left(\frac{1}{3}+\frac{1}{5}\right)$ can be restated as $\left(\frac{5}{15}+\frac{3}{15}\right)$ or $\frac{8}{15}$.
That number squared is $\frac{64}{225}$. $\frac{1}{3^2}=\frac{1}{9}$, and $\frac{1}{5^2}=\frac{1}{25}$. $\left(\frac{1}{9}+\frac{1}{25}\right)$ can be restated as $\left(\frac{25}{225}+\frac{9}{225}\right)$, or $\frac{34}{225}$.

39. **(C)** If *K* is parallel to *L*, then $a = c$. Since $a + b = 180$, and you know that $a = 60$, you know that $b = 120$.

40. **(A)** You should be able to solve this even had you not done the calculations above. $a + b + c$ equals 240.

41. **(729)** $4x - 9 = 27$, so $4x = 36$. $9^3 = 729$

42. **(1/8)** At the end of week 2, you have the following:

$$1-\left[\frac{1}{2}+\left(\frac{1}{2}\times\frac{3}{4}\right)\right]=$$

$$1-\left(\frac{4}{8}+\frac{3}{8}\right)=$$

$$\frac{1}{8}$$

43. **(5)** If the chord is 8, half of it is 4, which sets you up with a nice 3-4-5 right triangle, as here:

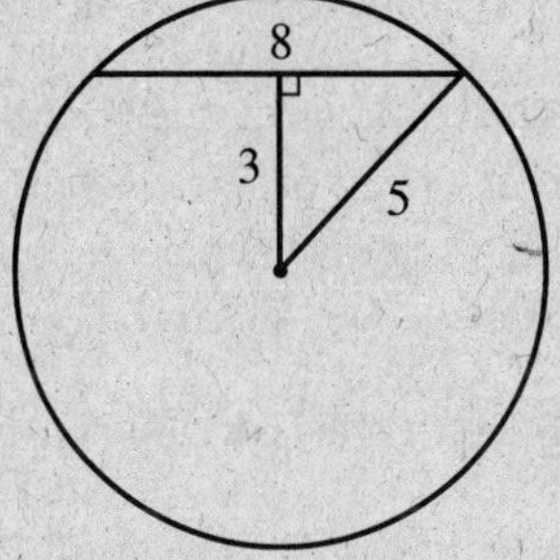

44. **(1.30)** The pizza costs 3 × \$3.25, or \$9.75. If that is now divided by 5, each person pays \$9.75 ÷ 5, or \$1.95. That is \$1.30 less for each of the original friends. (Although you will not record a dollar sign, do not forget the final 0.)

45. **(130)** This is less difficult than it may at first seem. Average the five players you know:

(130 + 115 + 120 + 140 + 145) ÷ 5 = 130
In order to maintain the 130 average, the average weight of the remaining players must be 130 as well.

46. **(45)** You can solve this if you recall that the sum of the measures of the angles of a quadrilateral will equal 360. Redraw the picture, writing in all the measures you know or can calculate:

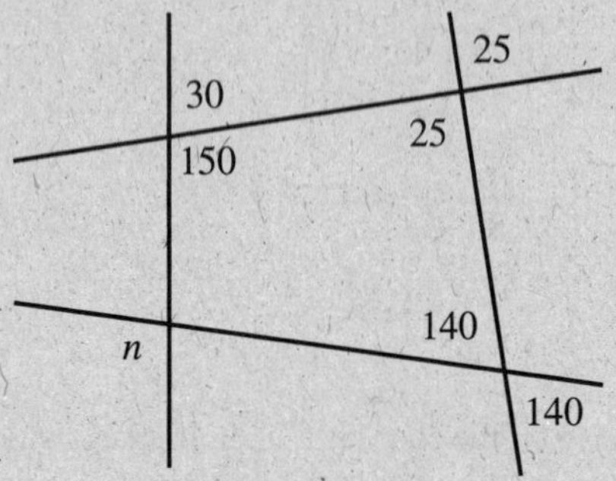

$360 - (150 + 25 + 140) = 45$

47. **(3)** The key to this is the phrase "positive whole number." If a is positive, b must be negative, and the only negative number whose square is 49 is -7. If $a + (-7) = -4$, $a = 3$.

48. **(5/8)** Express the consumed popcorn this way:

$$1-\left[\frac{1}{4}+\left(\frac{3}{4}\times\frac{1}{6}\right)\right]=$$

$$1-\left(\frac{1}{4}+\frac{3}{24}\right)=$$

$$1-\left(\frac{2}{8}+\frac{1}{8}\right)=$$

$$\frac{5}{8}$$

49. **(.002)** This is the kind of question where it pays to use your calculator and eliminate the chance of a careless misplacement of a decimal point.

$.2 \times .3 \times .4 = .024$

$.024 \div 12 = .002$

50. **(100)** Think: $\frac{.4}{x} = .004$

$x = 100$

49. YOKE : OX : :

(A) saddle : stallion
(B) tether : cow
(C) herd : sheep
(D) brand : steer
(E) harness : horse

50. SYMPHONY : CODA : :

(A) drama : prologue
(B) letter : introduction
(C) music : note
(D) opera : aria
(E) novel : epilogue

Answer Key

1. C	11. D	21. A	31. A	41. D
2. A	12. C	22. C	32. E	42. B
3. E	13. E	23. E	33. D	43. E
4. B	14. B	24. D	34. C	44. B
5. A	15. D	25. E	35. B	45. B
6. D	16. B	26. B	36. C	46. C
7. B	17. D	27. C	37. E	47. A
8. B	18. D	28. D	38. B	48. D
9. E	19. B	29. B	39. E	49. E
10. E	20. D	30. C	40. A	50. E

Explanatory Answers

1. **(C)** To be *bald* is to lack *hair*. To be *arid* is to lack *rain*.

2. **(A)** A *dinghy* is a type of *boat*, and a *novel* is a type of *book*.

3. **(E)** An *apple* is produced by a *tree*, and a *pearl* is produced by an *oyster*.

4. **(B)** A *carnivore* eats only *meat*, and an *herbivore* eats only *plants*.

5. **(A)** *Mauve* is a *color*, and *basil* is a *spice*.

6. **(D)** To *muffle* something is almost to *silence* it. To *stymie* something is almost to *defeat* it.

7. **(B)** *Paucity* is a synonym for *dearth*, as is *shortage* for *scarcity*.

8. **(B)** *Paper* is sometimes identified by a *watermark*, and a *person* by a *birthmark*.

9. **(E)** A person who is extremely *bright* is *brilliant*. A person who is extremely *happy* is *ecstatic*.

10. **(E)** *Discipline* brings about *order* rather than disorder. *Training* brings about *preparation* rather than lack of preparation.

11. **(D)** A *news report* is *descriptive* of an event, but a *commercial* is *prescriptive*, recommending rather than describing.

12. **(C)** In a case of *consensus* among individuals, there is necessarily an *agreement*. Where there is *tranquility* among individuals, there is also *peace*.

13. **(E)** *Hydraulic* describes something that is operated by means of *water*; *pneumatic* describes something that is operated by means of *air*.

14. **(B)** A *horse* is usually kept and fed in a *stable*; a *pig* is usually kept and fed in a *sty*.

15. **(D)** The *actor* plays a *role*, as a *ballplayer* plays a *position*.

16. **(B)** The *prow* is the forward part of the *ship*, as the *nose* is the forward part of the *airplane*.

17. **(D)** *Maximum* and *minimum* mark extremes in quantity, as do *most* and *least*.

18. **(D)** One can counteract a *sensation* with an *anesthetic* and a *poison* with an *antidote*.

19. **(B)** One leaves a *ship* by *disembarking* and a *horse* by *dismounting*.

20. (**D**) *Meat* is a food that supplies us with *protein*; *potatoes* are a food that supplies us with *starch*.

21. (**A**) The *nape* is the back of the *neck*, and the *heel* is the back of the *foot*.

22. (**C**) *Pliers* are designed for *gripping*, as is a *jack* for *elevating*.

23. (**E**) The *radius* is a line extending from the center of the *circle* to the edge, as the *spoke* is a bar extending from the center of the *wheel* to the edge.

24. (**D**) A *misdemeanor* is not as serious as a *felony*. A *mishap* is not as serious as a *catastrophe*.

25. (**E**) A *hygrometer* is used to measure *humidity*, as a *thermometer* measures *temperature*.

26. (**B**) As *astute* is in emphatic opposition to *stupid*, so is *agile* in opposition to *clumsy*. Both terms go beyond simple denials of the opposing terms.

27. (**C**) A *whale* is a mammal that is mistakenly thought to be a *fish*, and a *bat* is a mammal that is mistakenly thought to be a *bird*.

28. (**D**) A *prospector* seeks *gold*, and a *detective* seeks a *clue*.

29. (**B**) A *couplet* makes up part of a *poem*, and a *sentence* makes up part of a *paragraph*.

30. (**C**) The goal of an *entrepreneur* is to obtain *profit*, just as the goal of a *miner* is to obtain *ore*.

31. (**A**) A *rudder* is used in directing a *ship*. A *wheel* is used in directing a *car*.

32. (**E**) A *stallion* and a *rooster* are two different animals of the same sex, as are a *mare* and a *hen*.

33. (**D**) We assimilate a *book* through *reading*, and a *record* through *listening*.

34. (**C**) A *parrot* and a *sparrow* are two different sorts of birds. A *goldfish* and a *guppy* are two different sorts of fish.

35. (**B**) *Muscles* are connected to bones by *tendons*, just as *bones* are connected to bones by *ligaments*.

36. (**C**) *Spicy* is the opposite of *insipid* as *keen* is the opposite of *dull*.

37. (**E**) A *scythe* is used as a symbol of *death*, and an *arrow* is used as a symbol of *love*.

38. (**B**) *Yeast* is used as a *leaven* and *iodine* as an *antiseptic*. These functions are more specific than *aspirin's* function as a *medicine*.

39. (**E**) A *polyglot* is adept at many *languages* as a *factotum* is adept at many skilled jobs, or *trades*.

40. (**A**) *Passages* can be eliminated by *expurgation* and *leaves* by *defoliation*.

41. (**D**) The basic materials of a *pharmacist* are *drugs*; the basic materials of a *chef* are *foods*.

42. (**B**) To *conquer* someone is to *subjugate* that person. To *slander* someone is to *vilify* him or her. In both cases, the subject is hostile toward the object.

43. (**E**) A *chisel* can be used to cut out an *engraving*. *Acid* can be used to cut through a surface to create an *etching*.

44. (**B**) *Sound* is measured in *decibels*, and *electricity* in *volts*.

45. (**B**) *Sound* determines whether two words are *homonyms*. *Meaning* determines whether two words are *synonyms*.

46. (**C**) One *whets* a *knife* to sharpen it. One *hones* a *razor* to sharpen it.

47. (**A**) At one extreme something can be *valueless*, and at another extreme something can be *invaluable*. At one extreme an individual can be *miserly*, and, at another extreme, *philanthropic*.

48. (**D**) A *triangle* has three sides, and a *prism* is a three-sided solid figure. A *circle* is circular, and a *cylinder* is a solid figure that is circular.

49. (**E**) An *ox* is controlled by means of a *yoke*. A *horse* is controlled by means of a *harness*.

50. (**E**) A *symphony* can end with a *coda*, as can a *novel* with an *epilogue*.

Sentence Completions

In sentence completion questions, you are given a sentence containing one or more blanks. A number of words or pairs of words are suggested to fill the blank spaces. You must select the word or pair of words that will *best* complete the meaning of the sentence as a whole.

Sentence completion questions test not only your knowledge of basic vocabulary but also your ability to understand what you read. In a typical sentence completion question, if *any* of the answer choices is inserted into the blank spaces, the resulting sentence will be technically correct, but it may not make sense. Usually, more than one choice makes sense, but only one completely carries out the full meaning of the sentence. There is one *best* answer.

HOW TO ANSWER SENTENCE COMPLETION QUESTIONS

1. Read the sentence. Try to figure out what it means.
2. Consider the blank or blanks with relation to the meaning of the sentence. Is a negative connotation called for or a positive one? If there are two blanks, should the pair be comparative, contrasting, or complementary? Are you looking for a term that best defines a phrase in the sentence?
3. Eliminate those answer choices that do not meet the criteria you established in step two.
4. Read the sentence to yourself, trying out each of the remaining choices, one by one. Which choice is the most exact, appropriate, or likely considering the information given in the sentence? Which of the choices does the *best* job of completing the sentence?
5. First answer the questions you find easy. If you have trouble with a question, leave it and go back to it later. If a fresh look does not help you to come up with a sure answer, make an educated guess.

Before you go on to the practice test, study the following examples:

1. Those who feel that war is stupid and unnecessary think that to die on the battlefield is ----.

(A) courageous
(B) pretentious
(C) useless
(D) illegal
(E) heroic

The correct answer is (C). The key to this answer is the attitude expressed—that war is stupid and unnecessary. Those who are antagonistic toward war would consider a battlefield death to be *useless*. While it is true that giving one's life on the field of battle is *courageous* (A), that is not the answer in the context of this sentence. Choice (B), *pretentious*, meaning "affectedly grand or ostentatious," does not go along with the idea that war is stupid. Choice (D) does not make sense in relation to a battlefield death. Choice (E), like choice (A), would not be consistent with the attitude of those who think war is stupid and unnecessary.

2. An unruly person may well become ---- if he is treated with ---- by those around him.

(A) angry..kindness
(B) calm..respect
(C) peaceful..abuse
(D) interested..medicine
(E) dangerous..love

The correct answer is (B). This sentence is about how a person's behavior is affected by the way he is treated. "Unruly" is a word with a negative connotation, but this unruly person may become ----. The implication is that the person will change for the better, so the first blank should be filled by a word with a positive connotation. The sentence further implies a cause-and-effect relationship. Positive treatment logically results in a positive change in behavior, so the second blank should also be filled by a word with a positive connotation. Choices (A), (C), and (E) all contain words that have a negative connotation. Of the remaining choices, (B) makes more sense than (D).

Sentence Completion Practice Test

Directions: Each of the following questions consists of an incomplete sentence followed by five words or pairs of words. Choose that word or pair of words which, when substituted for the blank space or spaces, *best* completes the meaning of the sentence and mark the letter of your choice on your answer sheet.

Example:

In view of the extenuating circumstances and the defendant's youth, the judge recommended ----.

(A) conviction
(B) a defense
(C) a mistrial
(D) leniency
(E) life imprisonment

Ⓐ Ⓑ Ⓒ ● Ⓔ

1. The ---- workroom had not been used in years.

(A) derelict
(B) bustling
(C) bereft
(D) bereaved
(E) stricken

2. Tempers ran hot among the old-timers, who ---- the young mayor and his ---- city council.

(A) despised..attractive
(B) admired..elite
(C) resented..reforming
(D) forgave..activist
(E) feared..apathetic

3. With the discovery of ---- alternative fuel source, oil prices dropped significantly.

(A) a potential
(B) a feasible
(C) a possible
(D) a variant
(E) an inexpensive

4. The product of a ---- religious home, he often found ---- in prayer.

(A) zealously..distraction
(B) devoutly..solace
(C) vigorously..comfort
(D) fanatically..misgivings
(E) pious..answers

5. Our ---- objections finally got us thrown out of the stadium.

(A) hurled
(B) modest
(C) wary
(D) vocal
(E) pliant

6. We should have ---- trouble ahead when the road ---- into a gravel path.

(A) interrogated..shrank
(B) anticipated..dwindled
(C) expected..grew
(D) enjoyed..transformed
(E) seen..collapsed

7. The ---- of the house, fresh lobster, was all gone, so we ---- ourselves with crab.

(A) suggestion..resolved
(B) embarrassment..consoled
(C) recommendation..contented
(D) specialty..pelted
(E) regret..relieved

8. ---- mob began to form, full of angry men ---- incoherent threats.

(A) An excited..whispering
(B) A listless..shouting
(C) An ugly..gesturing
(D) A lynch..muttering
(E) A huge..waving

9. In the ---- downpour, the women managed to ---- us and disappear.

(A) ensuing..evade
(B) incessant..pervade
(C) uncouth..escape
(D) torrential..provoke
(E) insipid..avoid

10. As a staunch ---- of our right to leisure time, Ken had few ----.

(A) proponent..friends
(B) advocate..defenders
(C) disciple..rivals
(D) defender..equals
(E) opponent..duties

11. A single wall still stood in mute ---- to Nature's force.

(A) evidence
(B) tribute
(C) remainder
(D) memory
(E) testimony

12. With the current wave of crime, tourists are ---- to make sure their passports are secure.

(A) required
(B) invited
(C) permitted
(D) forbidden
(E) urged

13. Over the ---- of the sirens, you could still hear the hoarse ---- of his voice.

(A) babble..roar
(B) drone..power
(C) gibbering..cries
(D) wail..sound
(E) groaning..whisper

14. Working ---- under the pressure of time, Edmond didn't notice his ---- mistake.

(A) leisurely..stupid
(B) frantically..inevitable
(C) rapidly..careless
(D) sporadically..simple
(E) continually..redundant

15. Held up only by a ---- steel cable, the chairlift was ---- to carry only two people.

(A) slender..instructed
(B) single..intended
(C) sturdy..obliged
(D) massive..designed
(E) narrow..appointed

16. After completing her usual morning chores, Linda found herself ---- tired.

(A) surprisingly
(B) erratically
(C) buoyantly
(D) forcibly
(E) unceasingly

17. With a ---- roar, the Concorde took off from New York on its ---- flight to Europe.

(A) deafening..subterranean
(B) thunderous..transoceanic
(C) sickening..transcontinental
(D) frightening..perennial
(E) supersonic..eventual

18. The cheerful, lively sound of dance music ---- almost everyone.

(A) accosted
(B) drained
(C) flaunted
(D) revived
(E) expired

19. With ---- grin, Mark quickly ---- his way through the crowd toward us.

(A) an infectious..demolished
(B) a sappy..devoured
(C) an irrepressible..maneuvered
(D) a surly..crawled
(E) a hapless..lost

20. Though a ---- of four campaigns, he had never seen action on the front lines.

(A) veteran
(B) victim
(C) volunteer
(D) reveler
(E) recruit

21. The ---- of the early morning light ---- the room, making it larger and cozier at once.

(A) brilliance..shattered
(B) softness..transformed
(C) harshness..transfigured
(D) warmth..disfigured
(E) glare..annihilated

22. As ---- of the original team, Mickey had free ---- for all their games.

(A) a survivor..advice
(B) a scholar..passage
(C) an institution..admission
(D) an organizer..submission
(E) a member..entrance

23. From his ---- manner, we could all tell that he was of ---- birth.

(A) boorish..noble
(B) aristocratic..humble
(C) regal..royal
(D) refined..common
(E) courteous..illegitimate

24. The presence of armed guards ---- us from doing anything disruptive.

(A) defeated
(B) excited
(C) irritated
(D) prevented
(E) encouraged

25. A careful ---- of the house revealed no clues.

(A) dissemination
(B) incineration
(C) autopsy
(D) dereliction
(E) examination

26. For his diligent work in astronomy, Professor Wilson was ---- at the banquet as ---- of the Year.

(A) taunted..Teacher
(B) praised..Lobotomist
(C) lauded..Scientist
(D) honored..Astrologer
(E) welcomed..Administrator

27. Because of his ---- sense of his own importance, Larry often tried to ---- our activities.

(A) exaggerated..monopolize
(B) inflated..autonomize
(C) insecure..violate
(D) modest..dominate
(E) egotistic..diffuse

28. After such ---- meal, we were all quick to ---- Arlene for her delicious cooking.

(A) a fearful..congratulate
(B) an enormous..console
(C) a delightful..avoid
(D) a heavy..thank
(E) a wonderful..applaud

29. If you hear the ---- of a gun, don't worry; it's only my car backfiring.

(A) burst
(B) report
(C) retort
(D) flash
(E) volume

30. He demanded ---- obedience from us, and was always telling us we must be ---- subjects.

(A) total..foolish
(B) partial..cringing
(C) formal..rigorous
(D) complete..compliant
(E) marginal..loyal

31. The ---- of the *Titanic* could have been avoided if more safety ---- had been taken.

(A) tragedy..precautions
(B) embargo..preservers
(C) disaster..reservations
(D) crew..measures
(E) fiasco..inspectors

32. We are ---- going to have to face the reality that the resources of Earth are ----.

(A) finally..worthless
(B) gradually..limitless
(C) eventually..finite
(D) quickly..unavailable
(E) seldom..vanished

33. A native wit, Angela never ---- for her words.

(A) groaned
(B) breathed
(C) asked
(D) groped
(E) worried

34. With ---- a thought for his own safety, Gene ---- dashed back across the courtyard.

(A) even..quickly
(B) scarcely..nimbly
(C) barely..cautiously
(D) seldom..swiftly
(E) hardly..randomly

35. As she ---- retirement, Laura became more thoughtful and withdrawn.

(A) circled
(B) sighted
(C) withdrew
(D) neared
(E) derived

36. Though many thought him a tedious old man, he had a ---- spirit that delighted his friends.

(A) perverse
(B) juvenile
(C) meek
(D) leaden
(E) youthful

37. ----, the factories had not closed, and those who needed work most were given a chance to survive during the economic disaster.

(A) Unintentionally
(B) Mercifully
(C) Blithely
(D) Importunately
(E) Tragically

38. There was a ---- all about the estate, and the ---- concerned the guards.

(A) pall..shroud
(B) focus..scrutiny
(C) hush..quiet
(D) coolness..temper
(E) talent..genius

39. The stubborn families feuded for generations, and ---- feelings are still fixed in their ----.

(A) begrudging..acceptance
(B) bitter..generosity
(C) inimical..antagonism
(D) suspicious..relief
(E) chary..helplessness

40. As the archaeologist expected, living conditions in the ancient culture were ---- worse than those of today.

(A) awfully
(B) surprisingly
(C) significantly
(D) begrudgingly
(E) boldly

41. Our reunion was completely ---- ; who'd have guessed we would have booked the same flight?

(A) illogical
(B) fortuitous
(C) expected
(D) abandoned
(E) usurped

42. There is one ---- thing about them: They have nothing in common and never will have.

(A) immutable
(B) atypical
(C) indiscriminate
(D) indigenous
(E) alliterative

43. Always one for a long, pleasant talk, Nancy went on ---- for hours.

(A) volubly
(B) tiresomely
(C) incessantly
(D) relentlessly
(E) articulately

44. He should be ---- to complain, since his salary is ---- with his productivity.

(A) right..proportionate
(B) brought..balanced
(C) foolish..gratuitous
(D) loath..commensurate
(E) entitled..alleviated

45. Paul's ---- at work is a natural product of his ---- nature.

(A) wastefulness..unpleasant
(B) thoughtfulness..rarefied
(C) diligence..sedulous
(D) candor..familial
(E) stubbornness..intrepid

46. Blustery winds knocked off hats and rattled windows, and the adventurous children were ----.

(A) frightened
(B) terrified
(C) improved
(D) anxious
(E) delighted

47. The ---- youngster thought old people should be polite to *him*!

(A) impertinent
(B) classless
(C) cultured
(D) submissive
(E) alternate

48. Wild beasts roamed the deserted country, which had not been ---- for hundreds of years.

(A) temperate
(B) active
(C) winnowed
(D) lived in
(E) civilized

49. At night, the inn turned into a theater, not one of actors and actresses, but one of the ---- of real people.

(A) sciences
(B) psychologies
(C) dramas
(D) jokes
(E) novels

50. "He who laughs last laughs ----."

(A) least
(B) fast
(C) best
(D) never
(E) softest

Answer Key

1. A	11. E	21. B	31. A	41. B
2. C	12. E	22. E	32. C	42. A
3. E	13. D	23. C	33. D	43. A
4. B	14. C	24. D	34. B	44. D
5. D	15. B	25. E	35. D	45. C
6. B	16. A	26. C	36. E	46. E
7. C	17. B	27. A	37. B	47. A
8. D	18. D	28. E	38. C	48. E
9. A	19. C	29. B	39. C	49. C
10. D	20. A	30. D	40. C	50. C

Explanatory Answers

1. **(A)** *Derelict* in this sense means "empty," or "abandoned." Only people are *bereaved* or *bereft*.

2. **(C)** This sentence implies discord between the old-timers and the young mayor. Old-timers are likely to *resent* those officials who are trying to change, or *reform*, things.

3. **(E)** There may be many possible alternative fuel sources, but unless they are *inexpensive*, they won't affect the price of oil.

4. **(B)** To say a *pious religious home* is redundant. Only (B) completes the thought and intent of the sentence.

5. **(D)** The objections mentioned must have been *vocal* to get them thrown out.

6. **(B)** Most people do not *enjoy* trouble, and you can't *interrogate* it, but you may logically conclude that they foresaw, or *anticipated*, trouble. A road doesn't *grow* into a path; nor does it *collapse* into one.

7. **(C)** No restaurant would advertise an *embarrassment* of the house, but you may logically conclude that lobster was their *recommendation*.

8. **(D)** In this item, the final two words are the key. It is impossible to *gesture* or *wave* incoherent threats. An excited mob wouldn't *whisper* and a listless mob wouldn't *shout*.

9. **(A)** In this question, only (A) logically completes the thought of the sentence.

10. **(D)** This sentence assumes that most people support having leisure time, ruling out (A) and (B). A *staunch disciple* is bad usage. That an opponent of leisure would have few *duties* is illogical.

11. **(E)** A *single wall* implies that, formerly, there were other walls. That only one wall still stood is *testimony*, not a *tribute*, to Nature's power. *Evidence to* is poor diction.

12. **(E)** Checking your passport can only be a suggestion, not an order. As losing your passport can pose serious problems to a tourist, *urged* is a better choice than *invited*.

13. **(D)** Sirens may *drone* or *wail*, but they don't *babble*, *gibber*, or *groan*. *Hoarse sound* is a better choice than *hoarse power*.

14. **(C)** *The pressure of time* indicates a need to work quickly. Assuming that mistakes are not *inevitable* or *redundant*, answer (C) is the only logical choice.

15. **(B)** This sentence is concerned with the design of the lift. As it says "held up only by," you may assume that the cable is not large, which eliminates (C) and (D). Of the three remaining options, only *intended* (B) completes the sentence logically.

16. **(A)** Assuming that routine activity is not exhausting, it would be *surprising* to find yourself exhausted by it one day.

17. **(B)** A *transoceanic* flight is one that goes over an ocean, in this case, the Atlantic.

18. **(D)** This sentence assumes that cheerful, lively music has a positive effect on people.

19. **(C)** As there is no such thing as a *surly*, or sullen, grin, choice (C) is the only answer that supplies the appropriate words for Mark's expression as well as for the manner in which he made his way through the crowd.

20. **(A)** One may be a *veteran* without ever having seen action, but a *victim* has to have seen it.

21. **(B)** For the light to make the room cozier, it must be *soft*, not *harsh*. This implies that the light enhanced the room, rather than disfigured it.

22. **(E)** A person may be an *institution*, but not an institution of a team. It is more likely that a *member* of the original team rather than a *scholar* would have a free pass.

23. **(C)** This is the only answer in which the first and second words are consistent.

24. **(D)** Armed guards are intended to *prevent* any kind of disruption. Answer (D) is the only logical and grammatical choice.

25. **(E)** The sentence implies that the house was being searched, and since you don't perform an *autopsy* on a house, (E) is the best choice.

26. **(C)** An astronomer would not be honored as an *astrologer*, much less as an *administrator*.

27. **(A)** Someone with a high opinion of his own importance tends to try to run others' activities. Choice (A) best reflects this attitude.

28. **(E)** One doesn't generally *avoid* or *console* someone for a tasty meal. Thus, (E) is the only logical answer.

29. **(B)** The sound of an explosion, whether from a gun or a car, is called a *report*.

30. **(D)** You may assume that no one demands *partial* or *marginal* obedience. *Compliant* is the best adjective for *subjects*.

31. **(A)** The loss of the *Titanic* is best described as a *tragedy* or a *disaster*. *Precautions*, not *reservations*, is the second word that is required, making (A) the correct response.

32. **(C)** As the Earth's resources are not *limitless*, *worthless*, or *unavailable*, only (C) logically completes this sentence.

33. **(D)** A person may *grope* for words; to say that he or she *worries* for them is bad usage.

34. **(B)** If Gene dashed across the courtyard, he must have run *swiftly* or *nimbly*. He couldn't have taken time to think of himself.

35. **(D)** Retirement has no physical presence, so it can't be either *circled* or *sighted*. One approaches, or *nears*, retirement.

36. **(E)** A *meek* spirit may comfort or console people, but it won't delight them. A *juvenile* spirit is immature and thus is also inappropriate. A *youthful* spirit, however, may be mature as well as vigorous.

37. **(B)** According to the sense of this sentence, it was *merciful*, not *unintentional, blithe, importunate,* or *tragic*, that the factories remained open.

38. **(C)** It follows that a *hush* or a *quiet* about an estate would concern the guards, not a *pall, focus, coolness,* or *talent.*

39. **(C)** This sentence describes enmity and a persistence of ill will. Answer (C) best completes the thought of this sentence.

40. **(C)** The archaeologist would expect conditions to be *significantly* worse, not *surprisingly, awfully, begrudgingly,* or *boldly* worse.

41. **(B)** The sentence implies that the reunion occurred by chance, so it was *fortuitous.*

42. **(A)** *Immutable* means "unchanging." Since the second part of the sentence concerns finality and since the other choices are not appropriate, (A) is the answer.

43. **(A)** According to the sentence, Nancy is "one for a long, pleasant talk." *Voluble* means "garrulous," but does not necessarily imply unpleasantness, while *tiresome, incessant,* and *relentless* all imply offense. *Articulate* is simply speaking clearly.

44. **(D)** He should be *loath* (or reluctant) to complain if his salary is *commensurate* with (or equal to) his productivity.

45. **(C)** "Natural product" in this sentence means "logical extension or outgrowth of" and joins like characteristics. *Diligence* and *sedulousness* are synonyms.

46. **(E)** Adventurous children will be *delighted* by blustery winds and rattling windows.

47. **(A)** This sentence describes a rebellious attitude. *Impertinence* means "insolence."

48. **(E)** This sentence concerns a wilderness and an absence of people, or *civilization. Lived in* has a meaning similar to *civilized*, but it implies a home or a town and not a countryside.

49. **(C)** The concept of theater is satisfied by *dramas,* not *sciences, psychologies, jokes,* or *novels.*

50. **(C)** The last (i.e., "end-of-line") position in certain activities connotes a positive result or a favored position. Some examples are: having the *last* word; being assigned the *last* (closing) spot in a show; being up *last* in baseball; or having a *last* (final) rebuttal in a debate. Laughing last, then, could not imply laughing *least, fast, never,* or *softest,* because these are not positive terms. The person who laughs last laughs *best*, because being last by definition precludes any possibility of someone else laughing back.

Critical Reading

Critical reading questions test your ability to read, understand, analyze, and evaluate material presented in a single reading passage or in two related passages. These questions account for approximately half of all the verbal reasoning questions on the SAT.

Reading passages on the SAT vary in length from 400 words to 850 words, and they can treat virtually any subject, including humanities, natural sciences, and social sciences, as well as fiction and nonfiction narratives. Despite the range of subject matter, this is a test of your reading ability—not your knowledge of a particular subject—and so everything you need to answer the questions will be contained in the passage.

HOW TO ANSWER CRITICAL READING QUESTIONS

1. Start with a passage that is familiar or interesting to you. Since all questions count the same, you are better off tackling what is easy for you first. Then you can turn to a passage that is likely to take you longer to read and understand.
2. Before reading the passage, glance quickly at the questions that follow it. Just look at the questions, not the answer choices. Knowing what kinds of questions you'll be asked helps you to focus your attention as you read the passage.
3. Read the passage carefully, noting the author's attitude and tone as well as the purpose of the passage.
4. Watch for transitions. Transitional words and phrases illustrate the relationship of one topic to another and highlight the underlying logic of the passage.

   For example, here are some common transitional words and their purposes.

Purpose	*Examples*
Contrast	although, and yet, at the same time, but, however, in contrast, nevertheless, on the other hand, yet
Comparison	in like manner, likewise, similarly
Purpose	for this purpose, to this end, with this object
Result	accordingly, consequently, hence, therefore, thereupon, thus, wherefore
Summary	as I have said, as has been noted, for example, for instance, in brief, in fact, in short, in other words, on the whole, to be sure, to sum up

5. If the author has quoted material from another source, be sure that you understand the purpose of the quote. Does the author agree or disagree?
6. Read each question carefully and determine exactly what is being asked. Watch out for words such as *always, never, all, only, every,* and *none.* These little words can have a big effect on your answer.
7. Read all five answer choices. The task is to choose the *best* answer. One answer choice may seem correct, but another may prove to be more exact and therefore better.
8. Avoid inserting your own judgments into your answers. Answer each question on the basis of what is stated or implied in the passage, not on what you think should be there.
9. Don't spend too much time on any one question. Laboring over one difficult question may cause you to miss the opportunity to answer three easier questions.

Critical Reading Practice Test

Directions: Each reading passage below is followed by a series of questions that require you to analyze, interpret, or evaluate the written work. Answer these questions on the basis of what each passage states or implies. Circle the letter that appears before your answer.

In the eleventh century, the Muslim empire was taken over by Turks of the Seljuk tribes. The main Seljuk sultan had as his advisor a Persian called Nizam al-Mulk. Nizam al-Mulk took it upon himself to reform the government, writing many of his ideas in a treatise called The Book of Government. *This passage is from a chapter entitled "Advice to Governors."*

When ambassadors come from foreign countries, nobody is aware of their movements until they actually arrive at the city gates; nobody gives any information [that they are coming] and nobody makes any preparation for them; and they will surely attribute this to our negligence and indifference. So officers at the frontiers must be told that whenever anyone approaches their stations, they should at once dispatch a rider and find out who it is who is coming, how many men there are with him, mounted and unmounted, how much baggage and equipment he has, and what is his business. A trustworthy person must be appointed to accompany them and conduct them to the nearest big city; there he will hand them over to another agent who will likewise go with them to the next city (and district), and so on until they reach the court. Whenever they arrive at a place where there is cultivation, it must be a standing order that officers, tax-collectors and assignees should give them hospitality and entertain them well so that they depart satisfied. When they return, the same procedure is to be followed. Whatever treatment is given to an ambassador, whether good or bad, it is as if it were done to the very king who sent him; and kings have always shewn the greatest respect to one another and treated envoys well, for by this their own dignity has been enhanced. And if at any time there has been disagreement or enmity between kings, and if ambassadors have still come and gone as occasion requires, and discharged their missions according to their instructions, never have they been molested or treated with less than usual courtesy. Such a thing would be disgraceful, as God (to Him be power and glory) says [in the Quran 24.53], "The messenger has only to convey the message plainly."

It should also be realized that when kings send ambassadors to one another their purpose is not merely the message or the letter which they communicate openly, but secretly they have a hundred other points and objects in view. In fact they want to know about the state of roads, mountain passes, rivers and grazing grounds, to see whether an army can pass or not; where fodder is available and where not; who are the officers in every place; what is the size of that king's army and how well it is armed and equipped; what is the standard of his table and company; what is the organization and etiquette of his court and audience hall; does he play polo and hunt; where are his qualities and manners, his designs and intentions, his appearance and bearing; is he cruel or just, old or young; is his country flourishing or decaying; are the peasants rich or poor; is he avaricious or generous; is he alert or negligent in affairs. . . .

1. What alarms the author about the way ambassadors are currently treated upon their arrival?

(A) An ambassador might assume that the natives are discourteous and negligent in regard to foreigners.
(B) Ambassadors may use the opportunity to spy on the natives.
(C) Ambassadors are often molested at the border.
(D) No one checks to see if ambassadors are smuggling arms.
(E) Ambassadors can easily become lost because no one guides them.

2. The word *stations* (line 8) is used to mean

(A) levels
(B) ranks
(C) depots
(D) posts
(E) postures

3. Why does Nizam al-Mulk want to hand ambassadors from one agent to the next?

(A) To watch their every move
(B) To make sure their needs are met
(C) To remove them from the country quickly
(D) To keep them from seeing the king
(E) To stop their complaints

4. The word *envoys* (line 24) means

(A) methods
(B) heralds
(C) substitutes
(D) accounts
(E) representatives

5. Which of these phrases best summarizes the main idea of paragraph 1?

(A) Favor everyone with equal care.
(B) Never molest an ambassador.
(C) Kings must respect each other.
(D) Politeness pays.
(E) Be sure to treat envoys well.

6. Unlike paragraph 1, paragraph 2 deals with

(A) ambassadors
(B) kings
(C) messages
(D) intelligence
(E) procedures

7. By "objects in view" (line 38) Nizam al-Mulk means

(A) goals in mind
(B) disagreements with opinions
(C) commodities to investigate
(D) complaints in mind
(E) artwork to see

8. The word *fodder* (line 41) means

(A) light
(B) animal food
(C) armaments
(D) trees
(E) tobacco

9. The phrase "standard of his table" (line 43–44) refers to the king's

(A) flag
(B) requirements
(C) hospitality
(D) performance
(E) language

10. The word *avaricious* (line 50) means

(A) savage
(B) stingy
(C) violent
(D) fickle
(E) charitable

Uvedale Price, a British writer of the 1790s, became obsessed with the idea of the picturesque, its nature and definition. He wrote a series of essays on this topic, often in answer to work by essayists Humphrey Repton and Richard Payne Knight.

I am therefore persuaded that the . . . qualities of roughness and of sudden variation joined to that of irregularity are the most efficient causes of the picturesque.

This, I think, will appear very clearly if we take a view of those objects, both natural and artificial, that are allowed to be picturesque, and compare them with those which are as generally allowed to be beautiful.

A temple or palace of Grecian architecture in its perfect, entire state, and with its surface and color smooth and even, either in painting or reality is beautiful; in ruin it is picturesque. Observe the process by which time, the great author of such changes, converts a beautiful object into a picturesque one. First, by means of weather stains, partial incrustations, mosses, etc., it at the same time takes off from the uniformity of the surface and of the color; that is, gives a degree of roughness and variety of tint. Next, the various accidents of weather loosen the stones themselves; they tumble in irregular masses upon what was perhaps smooth turf or pavement, or nicely trimmed walks and shrubberies, now mixed and overgrown with wild plants and creepers, that crawl over and shoot among the fallen ruins. Sedums, wallflowers, and other vegetables that bear drought find nourishment in the decayed cement from which the stones have been detached; birds convey their food into the chinks, and yew, elder, and other berried plants project from the sides, while the ivy mantles over other parts and crowns the top. The even, regular lines of the doors and windows are broken, and through their ivy-fringed openings is displayed in a more broken and picturesque manner that striking image in Virgil:

["The home within appears, and the long
corridors are laid open; the chambers of
Priam and ancient kings are shown."]

Gothic architecture is generally considered as more picturesque, though less beautiful, than Grecian; and upon the same principle that a ruin is more so than a new edifice. The first thing that strikes the eye in approaching any building is the general outline and the effect of the openings: in Grecian buildings the general lines of the roof are straight, and even when varied and adorned by a dome or a pediment, the whole has a character of symmetry and regularity. But symmetry, which in works of art, particularly, accords with the beautiful, is in the same degree adverse to the picturesque; and among the various causes of the superior picturesqueness of ruins compared with entire buildings, the destruction of symmetry is by no means the least powerful.

11. The phrase "joined to that of" (line 2) means

(A) fastened to
(B) combined with
(C) adhered to
(D) enlisted by
(E) with or without

12. The word *efficient* (line 3) is used to mean

(A) capable
(B) businesslike
(C) valuable
(D) qualified
(E) effective

13. The phrase "allowed to be" (line 7) means

(A) enabled
(B) bestowed
(C) considered
(D) yielded
(E) tolerated

14. In paragraph 2, Price

(A) makes an ironic statement about beauty
(B) gives examples of picturesque items
(C) denies that the beautiful can be picturesque
(D) introduces his method of comparison
(E) contrasts natural objects with picturesque ones

15. Price compares time to

(A) an author
(B) an artist
(C) an architect
(D) ancient Greece
(E) a temple

16. The word *mantles* (line 29) means

(A) shrouds
(B) disfigures
(C) comforts
(D) erodes
(E) blinds

17. Price quotes Virgil to

(A) allow the reader to know him better
(B) contrast with his notion of beauty
(C) expand upon his idea of the picturesque
(D) end his discussion of architecture
(E) cite someone for whom beauty was all

18. The word *pediment* (line 44) means

(A) obstacle
(B) imperfection
(C) obstruction
(D) decorative gable
(E) foundation

19. In general, Price thinks that beautiful things are

(A) trivial and imperfect
(B) decorative and ornate
(C) massive and awe-inspiring
(D) harmonious and uniform
(E) intricate and complex

20. Which of these might Price find picturesque?

(A) A brand-new skyscraper
(B) A child with a balloon
(C) A crumbling stone wall
(D) The Washington Monument
(E) A storm at sea

"The Goodman Who Saved Another from Drowning" is a French tale from the Middle Ages. In today's litigious times, the lesson it teaches remains relevant.

It happened one day that a fisherman putting out to sea in a boat was just about to cast a net, when right in front of him he saw a man on the point of drowning. Being a stout-hearted and at the same time an agile man, he jumped up and, seizing a boathook, thrust it towards the man's face. It caught him right in the eye and pierced it. The fisherman hauled the man into the boat and made for the shore without casting any of his nets. He had the man carried to his house and given the best possible attention and treatment, until he had got over his ordeal.

For a long time, that man thought about the loss of his eye, considering it a great misfortune. "That wretched fellow put my eye out, but I didn't do *him* any harm. I'll go and lodge a complaint against him—why, I'll make things really hot for him!" Accordingly he went and complained to the magistrate, who fixed a day for the hearing. They both waited till the day came round, and then went to the court. The one who had lost an eye spoke first, as was appropriate. "Gentlemen," he said, "I'm bringing a complaint against this worthy, who, only the other day, savagely struck me with a boathook and knocked my eye out. Now I'm handicapped. Give me justice, that's all I ask. I've nothing more to say."

The other promptly spoke up and said, "Gentlemen, I cannot deny that I knocked his eye out, but if what I did was wrong, I'd like to explain how it all happened. This man was in mortal danger in the sea, in fact he was on the point of drowning. I went to his aid. I won't deny I struck him with my boathook, but I did it for his own good: I saved his life on that occasion. I don't know what more I can say. For God's sake, give me justice!"

The court was quite at a loss when it came to deciding the rights of the case, but a fool who was present at the time said to them, "Why this hesitation? Let the first speaker be thrown back into the sea on the spot where the other man hit him in the face, and if he can get out again, the defendant shall compensate him for the loss of his eye. That I think, is a fair judgment." Then they all cried out as one man, "You're absolutely right! That's exactly what we'll do!" Judgment was then pronounced to that effect. When the man heard that he was to be thrown into the sea, just where he had endured all that cold water before, he wouldn't have gone back there for all the world. He released the goodman from any liability, and his earlier attitude came in for much criticism.

In the light of this incident, you can take it from me that it's a waste of time to help a scoundrel. Release a guilty thief from the gallows, and he will never like you for it. A wicked man will never be grateful to anyone who does him a good turn: he'll forget all about it; it will mean nothing to him. On the contrary, he would be only too glad to make trouble for his benefactor if he ever saw him at a disadvantage.

21. The word *cast* (line 2) is used to mean

(A) tint
(B) perform
(C) hurl
(D) mold
(E) copy

22. Paragraph 1 makes it clear that the fisherman is

(A) essentially well-meaning
(B) clumsy and foolish
(C) fat but nimble
(D) hard-working and honest
(E) basically unlucky

23. The word *fixed* (line 16) is used to mean

(A) corrected
(B) secured
(C) set
(D) mended
(E) attached

24. The word *worthy* (line 20) is used to mean

(A) caliber
(B) significance
(C) morality
(D) gentleman
(E) prize

25. Paragraph 3 concerns

(A) the narrator's beliefs
(B) the court's wishes
(C) the one-eyed man's complaint
(D) the fisherman's plea
(E) the magistrate's judgment

26. The fool's suggested solution to the case was

(A) pitiless and spiteful
(B) absurd but lawful
(C) harsh but fair
(D) just and merciful
(E) sensible but unjust

27. The phrase "as one man" (line 39) means

(A) manfully
(B) as someone once said
(C) one by one
(D) together
(E) as he believed

28. "In the light of this incident" (line 47) means

(A) Thanks to that event
(B) Because of this tale
(C) Without further ado
(D) As darkness falls
(E) As you can see from this story

29. The narrator clearly believes that the one-eyed man

(A) showed good sense
(B) had bad luck
(C) deserved better
(D) was a scoundrel
(E) did the right thing

30. The moral of this story might be

(A) "Do unto others as you would have them do unto you."
(B) "A wicked man is never satisfied."
(C) "You can only be good so long."
(D) "There is no such thing as justice."
(E) "The one-eyed man is king."

Bernal Díaz del Castillo was a member of the band of Spanish soldiers that conquered Mexico, Guatemala, and Honduras for Spain. His commander was the conquistador Hernando Cortés. At the age of eighty-four, Don Bernal, then magistrate of Santiago, Guatemala, sat down to record his memories of the conquest. This excerpt describes some of the wonders of Mexico City, which the soldiers invaded on November 8, 1519.

It seems to me that the great *cu* must have been as big around as six of the very large mansions they have in this country. It tapered from the bottom up to a small tower at the top, and in the center of the top there were five open indentations, like crenels in a battlement. As there are many *cúes* painted on the horse trappings of the *conquistadores*—I have one—anyone who has seen them can tell what they looked like on the outside; but that isonly a small part of the story.

It was said that when they built the great *cu,* the residents of the city placed gold, silver, pearls, and precious stones in the foundations as an offering, bathed with the blood of many sacrificed prisoners of war. They had also placed there every kind of seed that the land produces, so that the idols would give them victories and wealth and abundant crops. After we captured that great city and allocated building sites, we decided to build a church dedicated to St. James, our patron and guide, on the site of the *cu.* When we opened the foundations to reinforce them, we found a great deal of gold, silver, *chalchiuis,* pearls, and other stones. A settler in Mexico who was assigned another part of the same site found the same things. The officials of His Majesty's Treasury demanded them for His Majesty, and there was a lawsuit about it. I do not remember any of the details, except that they questioned Cuauhtémoc, who was alive then, and other Mexican chiefs, and they said that according to their ancient books and paintings, it was true that the old residents of Mexico had thrown the jewels and all the rest of it into the foundations; and so the treasure was left to the church of St. James.

A short distance from the great *cu* there was a small tower that also was a house for idols, a true hell, for the entrance was the horrible open mouth of one of their lords of the underworld, with great fangs to devour souls. Here too there were images of devils and the bodies of serpents near the entrance, and close by a place of sacrifice, black with smoke and crusted with blood. . . .

Beyond the court there was another *cu* where the great Mexican lords were buried. Here too there were many idols and everything was covered with blood and smoke. Close by there was another *cu* filled with skulls and bones very neatly arranged, the skulls together and the bones in separate piles. It would have been impossible to count them, there were so many. . . .

I have dwelt a long time on this great *cu* of Tatelulco and its courts, but it was the most important temple in all Mexico, although there were many other splendid ones; for every four or five city districts they had a temple with all its idols. They were so numerous that I have no idea how many there were altogether.

The great oratory in Cholula was higher than the one in Mexico, for it had 120 steps. The idol of Cholula was held to be very good, and people made pilgrimages to it from all parts of New Spain to obtain pardons; that was the reason for such a splendid *cu.* It was made entirely differently from the one in Mexico, although the large courts were the same, and the double wall surrounding them.

The *cu* in Texcoco was also very high, with 117 steps, and with fine broad courts, but differently shaped from the others. It is an amusing thing that every province had its idols, and the people of one province or city did not make use of the others; so they had an infinite number of idols, and sacrificed to all of them.

When our captain and all of us got tired from walking around and looking at such a variety of idols and the sacrifices to them, we returned to our quarters, still accompanied by the chiefs Montezuma sent with us. I will leave off here and tell what else we did.

31. A *cu* is apparently a

(A) captain
(B) priest
(C) prison
(D) temple
(E) castle

32. The word *crenels* in line 5 probably means

(A) soldiers
(B) notches
(C) crowns
(D) wars
(E) swords

33. Díaz's insertion of the phrase "I have one" (line 7) indicates that he

(A) is a painter
(B) owns a mansion
(C) collects Mexican art
(D) brought horses from Mexico home to Spain
(E) was a conquistador

34. Unlike paragraph 1, paragraph 2 deals with

(A) the outside of the *cu*
(B) the interior of the *cu*
(C) the size of the *cu*
(D) the height of the *cu*
(E) the *cúes* in other Mexican cities

35. The word *patron* (line 18) means

(A) supporter
(B) friend
(C) shopper
(D) customer
(E) client

36. The word *stones* (line 21) is used to mean

(A) gems
(B) boulders
(C) foundations
(D) memorials
(E) seeds

37. How does Díaz feel about the religion of the Mexicans?

(A) Tolerant
(B) Wistful
(C) Horrified
(D) Suspicious
(E) Indifferent

38. The word *oratory* (line 53) is used to mean

(A) speaking ability
(B) lecture
(C) rhetoric
(D) prayer
(E) church

39. Unlike the preceding paragraphs, paragraphs 6 and 7 concern

(A) places in Mexico
(B) the conquest of the Mexicans
(C) sacrifices
(D) burial grounds
(E) other *cúes*

40. Díaz's purpose is primarily to

(A) invent
(B) argue
(C) preach
(D) describe
(E) persuade

Answer Key

1. A	9. C	17. C	25. D	33. E
2. D	10. B	18. D	26. C	34. B
3. B	11. B	19. D	27. D	35. A
4. E	12. E	20. C	28. E	36. A
5. E	13. C	21. C	29. D	37. C
6. D	14. D	22. A	30. B	38. E
7. A	15. A	23. C	31. D	39. E
8. B	16. A	24. D	32. B	40. D

Explanatory Answers

1. **(A)** The answer to this is found in paragraph 1, lines 5-6. The author never mentions spying, molestation, or lost ambassadors; he is just worried that the messengers will think his countrymen negligent and indifferent.

2. **(D)** This multiple-meaning word has only one synonym given that fits the context of the sentence. If you plug the choices into the line cited, you will easily make the correct choice.

3. **(B)** The author's concerns have to do with behaving in a dignified and appropriate manner. He apparently wants to make sure the ambassadors are led to their destination courteously and swiftly.

4. **(E)** *Envoy* and *ambassador* are used interchangeably by the author to refer to representatives of foreign lands.

5. **(E)** This is an accurate summing up of paragraph 1. (A) is irrelevant, as is (C). (B) is not hinted at here, and (D) is never directly stated.

6. **(D)** In the connotation of information gleaned by visiting a foreign land, *intelligence* is precisely the subject of paragraph 2. Even if you do not know the word, you should be able to eliminate the other choices as irrelevant or incorrect.

7. **(A)** Plug the choices into the context of the sentence to determine the correct response. Only (A) makes sense.

8. **(B)** If this is a familiar word, you will have no problem. If not, substitute the choices into the sentence to find the one that makes the most sense.

9. **(C)** The phrase uses *standard* to mean "measure"; the ambassador is interested in gauging the measure of the king's table and company—the extent of his hospitality and the quality of his companions.

10. **(B)** The passage sets up a list of opposites. If you recognize this, it should be easy enough to find the word among the choices that is the opposite of *generous;* that is, *stingy.*

11. **(B)** This is an archaic construction, but if you try the choices in context, you will find that only (B) makes sense as a replacement.

12. **(E)** The first sentence might be paraphrased: "I think that roughness, variation, and irregularity make things picturesque." Only (E) is a meaningful replacement for *efficient.*

13. **(C)** Again, this is an archaic construction and may be unfamiliar to you. The author is writing about "objects . . . that are *allowed to be* picturesque. . . ." Any of the choices can be a synonym for *allowed,* but only (C) works as a substitute in this sentence.

14. **(D)** Paragraph 2 does nothing but introduce the method Price will use to compare and contrast the beautiful with the picturesque.

15. **(A)** Careful reading will show you that Price literally refers to time as "the great author of . . . changes" (line 13)

16. **(A)** It is unusual to see this word used as a verb, but rereading lines 28–29 shows that Price refers to ivy that "*mantles* over other parts [of the ruin] and crowns the top." The ivy is covering up, or *shrouding* the ruin.

17. **(C)** The quote has no purpose other than to add to Price's discussion of the picturesque. He shows with the quote that the ruin he describes reveals an ancient world.

18. **(D)** You know from the citation that a *pediment* must be something that "adorns"; it must be (D), since a foundation (E) cannot be said to adorn. (A), (B), and (C) are synonyms for *impediment.*

19. **(D)** In Price's view, beautiful things share the traits of harmony, symmetry, and uniformity.

20. **(C)** If you have understood Price's main idea, you will know that he believes a picturesque object must be rough and partly in ruins.

21. **(C)** It is used in relation to nets, so the only appropriate synonym for *cast* is *hurl* (C).

22. **(A)** The fisherman may be (D), but that is never made clear. He is certainly not (B), and he is stout-hearted, not stout (C). There is no support for (E). The only answer possible is (A), and, in fact, the narrator makes it clear that the fisherman has done everything possible to help the drowning man.

23. **(C)** *Fixed* has many meanings, and each choice is a possible synonym. However, in the context of "[fixing] a day for the hearing," only (C) makes sense.

24. **(D)** This archaic term means "man of worth," or gentleman. Testing the choices in context should lead you to this conclusion.

25. **(D)** All of paragraph 3 is given over to the fisherman's tale of what happened.

26. **(C)** The fool's suggestion to throw the one-eyed man back into the sea may have been harsh, but it offered a certain rough justice.

27. **(D)** Try the choices in context, and you will find that *together* is the only meaningful substitute.

28. **(E)** Choice (B) is incorrect—the narrator did not draw this conclusion *because* of the incident, but rather uses the incident to illustrate a moral.

29. **(D)** The scoundrel mentioned in line 48 is a reference to the man helped in the story—the one-eyed man.

30. **(B)** This is a reasonable paraphrase of the final paragraph. When you see the word *moral,* you know that you need to draw conclusions about the theme of what you have read. It may help to look back at the end of the story to see whether the author has done that for you, as in this case.

31. **(D)** A *cu* is as big as six mansions (lines 1–2), which certainly eliminates (A) and (B). Further reading shows that the *cu* holds offerings to idols, which makes (D) the likeliest answer.

32. **(B)** The sentence parallels *crenels* to *indentations,* leading you to suppose that they are notches in the top of the tower.

33. **(E)** First think: What does the author have? He has a *cu* painted on his horse trappings, as do many conquistadors. You can conclude that he was a conquistador. None of the other answers is supported by the passage.

34. **(B)** Paragraph 1 covers the exterior; paragraph 2 takes the reader inside the *cu.* Size and height are discussed in paragraph 1. *Cúes* in other cities are discussed later in the passage.

35. **(A)** Saint James is the conquistadors' patron saint, which is to say the saint who supports and guides them.

36. **(A)** The list that precedes the word *stones* tells you that the stones are precious.

37. **(C)** He is not tolerant (A); the sacrifices horrify him, and he refers to the house for idols as "a true hell." Although he finds the architecture awe-inspiring, he does not admire the religion.

38. (**E**) *Oratory* is used here to mean the same thing as *cu* or temple. Since it is referred to as having 120 steps, the answer is clearly not (A), (B), (C), or (D).

39. (**E**) The other paragraphs deal with the great *cu,* but in paragraphs 6 and 7, the author describes the *cu* at Cholula and the *cu* at Texcoco.

40. (**D**) The passage as a whole is descriptive; it tells what the *cúes* looked like in great detail.

Double Passages

Each SAT verbal reasoning test contains a pair of passages on similar or related subjects. The two passages may support each other or oppose each other, or one may supplement the opinions stated in the other.

Double passages are intended to assess higher-level thinking skills. Among the questions asked are these:

Vocabulary-in-Context. In this type of question you must choose the best meaning for a word or phrase as it is used in the passage. Several meanings may seem correct, but only one is *best* in the context of the passage.

Interpreting Meanings. These questions are related to vocabulary questions but are usually broader in scope. You are asked to interpret a phrase selected from the passage. To answer this kind of question, you must look before and after the actual quote to determine the larger context in which it is given before selecting the best answer choice.

Predicting Results. You may be asked to predict results based on the point of view of Author 1 or Author 2. For this type of question, you must evaluate the material presented and formulate a conclusion based on what you have read.

Spotting Assumptions. These questions ask you to spot the assumptions made about the data used in building the author's hypothesis. These assumptions may or may not be justified. The key issue is that they are not proven to be true. You can sometimes spot an assumption by the use of "weak" phrases such as "this may be," or "it is likely that," or "this could indicate."

Selecting Arguments. In this type of question you are asked to select the best argument for or against the hypothesis. To do this, you should concentrate on the assumptions made about the data, as well as on the central point of the author's passage. The assumption is the weakest part of the hypothesis; therefore, an argument attacking or supporting the assumption will have the most telling effect on the hypothesis.

Sample Double Passages Analyzed and Explained

Directions: Each pair of passages below deals with a related topic. Following the passages are questions about the content of each passage or about the relationship between the two passages. Answer the questions based upon what is stated or implied in the passages and in any introductory material provided.

Narrative Double Passage

Among the great historic loves are those of composer Robert Schumann for his wife, Clara, and of Napoleon Bonaparte for his wife, Josephine. Their love is public knowledge due to the hundreds of love letters they left behind. These excerpts are from a letter from Schumann to his then fiancée and from a letter from Napoleon on the battlefield to his wife at home.

Passage 1—Robert Schumann to Clara Wieck (1838)

I have a hundred things to write to you, great and small, if only I could do it neatly, but my writing grows more and more indistinct, a sign, I fear, of heart weakness. There are terrible hours when your image forsakes me, when I wonder anxiously whether I have ordered my life as wisely as I might, whether I had any right to bind you to me, my angel, or can really make you as happy as I should wish. These doubts all arise, I am inclined to think, from your father's attitude towards me. It is so easy to accept other people's estimate of oneself. Your father's behaviour makes me ask myself if I am really so bad—of such humble standing—as to invite such treatment from anyone. Accustomed to easy victory over difficulties, to the smiles of fortune, and to affection, I have been spoiled by having things made too easy for me, and now I have to face refusal, insult and calumny. I have read of many such things in novels, but I thought too highly of myself to imagine I could ever be the hero of a family tragedy of the Kotzebue sort myself. If I had ever done your father an injury, he might well hate me; but I cannot see why he should despise me and, as you say, hate me without any reason. But my turn will come, and I will then show him how I love you and himself; for I will tell you, as a secret, that I really love and respect your father for his many great and fine qualities, as no one but yourself can do. I have a natural inborn devotion and reverence for him, as for all strong characters, and it makes his antipathy for me doubly painful. Well, he may some time declare peace, and say to us, "Take each other, then."

You cannot think how your letter has raised and strengthened me.... You are splendid, and I have much more reason to be proud of you than of me. I have made up my mind, though, to read all your wishes in your face. Then you will think,even though you don't say it, that your Robert is a really good sort, that he is entirely yours, and loves you more than words can say. You shall indeed have cause to think so in the happy future. I still see you as you looked in your little cap that last evening. I still hear you call me *du*. Clara, I heard nothing of what you said but that *du.* Don't you remember?

Passage 2—Napoleon Bonaparte to Josephine Bonaparte (1796)

I have not spent a day without loving you; I have not spent a night without embracing you; I have not so much as drunk a single cup of tea without cursing the pride and ambition which force me to remain separated from the moving spirit of my life. In the midst of my duties, whether I am at the head of my army or inspecting the camps, my beloved Josephine stands alone in my heart, occupies my mind, fills my thoughts. If I am moving away from you with the speed of the Rhône torrent, it is only that I may see you again more quickly. If I rise to work in the middle of the night, it is because this may hasten by a matter of days the arrival of my sweet love. Yet in your letter of the 23rd. and 26th. Ventôse, you call me *vous. Vous* yourself! Ah! wretch, how could you have written this letter? How cold it is! And then there are those four days between the 23rd. and the 26th.; what were you doing that you failed to write to your husband? . . . Ah, my love, that *vous,* those four days make me long for my former indifference. Woe to the person responsible! May he, as punishment and penalty, experience what my convictions and the evidence (which is in your friend's favour) would make me experience! Hell has no torments great enough! Nor do the Furies have serpents enough! *Vous! Vous!* Ah! How will things stand in two weeks? . . . My spirit is heavy; my heart is fettered and I am terrified by my fantasies. . . . You love me less; but you will get over the loss. One day you will love me no longer; at least tell me; then I shall know how I have come to deserve this misfortune. . . .

1. In Passage 1, the word *calumny* (line 17) means

   (A) remorse
   (B) chance
   (C) victory
   (D) kindness
   (E) slander

This is a vocabulary-in-context question. In general, it is easiest to locate the citation and then test each choice in place of the italicized word. In this case, Schumann is listing the difficulties he now faces from Clara's father. Among these is the italicized word *calumny.* You can easily eliminate choices (C) and (D)—they have positive connotations that do not fit this context. Choice (B) makes no sense here. Choice (A) is possible, but the rest of Schumann's list refers to negatives that issue from Clara's father to Schumann—insult and refusal. The word that best fits within this list is choice (E), *slander.*

2. To what does Napoleon refer in Passage 2 when he writes of "the moving spirit of my life" (lines 45–46)?

   (A) France
   (B) Ambition
   (C) The army
   (D) His wife
   (E) The Rhône

This is an interpretation question. You are asked to determine why the author makes a particular statement or chooses particular words or phrases. To do this, you must understand the author's intent. Locate the citation in context. Reread the text surrounding the phrase. In this case, the entire sentence deals with Napoleon's love for Josephine. He curses his pride and ambition, so choice (B) is not correct. There is no evidence to support choice (E). He is with his army (C), not separate from it, and he is still in France (A). The only possible answer is choice (D).

3. How do the authors feel about being separated from their lovers?

   (A) Separation raises doubts and fears.
   (B) Separation is due to parental disapproval.
   (C) Separations never last long.
   (D) Separations improve a relationship.
   (E) Separations between lovers are inevitable.

This evaluation question asks you to consider and compare both passages. While choice (B) might be true of Passage 1, it is not true of Passage 2. There is little direct evidence of choice (C); in fact, both authors consider any separation too long. Both Schumann and Napoleon express doubts and fears (A)—Schumann expresses his in the first paragraph of his letter, and Napoleon saves his for the end. Neither Schumann nor Napoleon expresses the sentiments in choices (D) and (E).

4. Why do the writers refer to the words *du* and *vous?*

   (A) To remind their readers of their rank
   (B) To refer to their lovers' intimacy or lack thereof
   (C) To ask their lovers to be faithful
   (D) To demonstrate their knowledge of languages
   (E) To address their unborn children

A synthesis/analysis question requires you to analyze the author's structural choices and composition. In this case, you must look at both passages, locate the citations, and use your understanding of the authors' intent to determine why they included this material. Schumann, in his last paragraph, remembers fondly the time when Clara called him by the informal second-person German pronoun, *du.* Napoleon, on the other hand, is unnerved by Josephine's use of the formal second-person French pronoun, *vous.* In the first case, Clara's words imply intimacy; in the second case, Josephine's words imply distance and coldness, as her husband notes with dismay. None of the other choices are supported by a careful reading of the passages. The answer is choice (B).

Expository Double Passage—Social Science

Fanny Wright was a reformer, author, and orator, unusual occupations for a woman in the early nineteenth century. Young Robert Emmet was condemned to death for treason after organizing a rebellion against the English in Ireland. He, too, had achieved fame as an orator, with speeches decrying tyranny.

Passage 1—Fanny Wright to a Fourth-of-July Audience at New Harmony, Indiana (1828)

In continental Europe, of late years, the words patriotism and patriot have been used in a more enlarged sense than it is usual here to attribute to them, or than is attached to them in Great Britain. Since the political struggles of France, Italy, Spain, and Greece, the word patriotism has been employed, throughout continental Europe, to express a love of the public good; a preference for the interests of the many to those of the few; a desire for the emancipation of the human race from the thrall of despotism, religious and civil: in short, patriotism there is used rather to express the interest felt in the human race in general than that felt for any country, or inhabitants of a country, in particular. And patriot, in like manner, is employed to signify a lover of human liberty and human improvement rather than a mere lover of the country in which he lives, or the tribe to which he belongs. Used in this sense, patriotism is a virtue, and a patriot is a virtuous man. With such an interpretation, a patriot is a useful member of society, capable of enlarging all minds and bettering all hearts with which he comes in contact; a useful member of the human family, capable of establishing fundamental principles and of merging his own interests, those of his associates, and those of his nation in the interests of the human race. Laurels and statues are vain things, and mischievous as they are childish; but could we imagine them of use, on *such* a patriot alone could they be with any reason bestowed. . . .

Passage 2—Robert Emmet to the Court That Condemned Him to Death (1803)

I am charged with being an emissary of France. An emissary of France! and for what end? It is alleged that I wish to sell the independence of my country; and for what end? Was this the object of my ambition? . . . No; I am no emissary; and my ambition was to hold a place among the deliverers of my country, not in power nor in profit, but in the glory of the achievement. Sell my country's independence to France! and for what? Was it a change of masters? No, but for ambition. Oh, my country! was it personal ambition that could influence me? Had it been the soul of my actions, could I not, by my education and fortune, by the rank and consideration of my family, have placed myself amongst the proudest of your oppressors? My country was my idol! To it I sacrificed every selfish, every endearing sentiment; and for it I now offer up myself, O God! No, my lords; I acted as an Irishman, determined on delivering my country from the yoke of a foreign and unrelenting tyranny, and the more galling yoke of a domestic faction, which is its joint partner and perpetrator in the patricide, from the ignominy existing with an exterior of splendor and a conscious depravity. It was the wish of my heart to extricate my country from this double riveted despotism—I wished to place her independence beyond the reach of any power on earth. I wished to exalt her to that proud station in the world. Connection with France was, indeed, intended, but only as far as mutual interest would sanction or require. Were the French to assume any authority inconsistent with the purest independence, it would be the signal for their destruction. . . .

Let no man dare, when I am dead, to charge me with dishonor; let no man attaint my memory by believing that I could have engaged in any cause but that of my country's liberty and independence; or that I could have become the pliant minion of power in the oppression and misery of my country. The proclamation of the provisional government speaks for our views; no inference can be tortured from it to countenance barbarity or debasement at home, or subjection, humiliation, or treachery from abroad. I would not have submitted to a foreign oppressor, for the same reason that I would resist the foreign and domestic oppressor. In the dignity of freedom, I would have fought upon the threshold of my country, and its enemy should enter only by passing over my lifeless corpse. And am I, who lived but for my country, and who have subjected myself to the dangers of the jealous and watchful oppressor, and the bondage of the grave, only to give my countrymen their rights, and my country its independence—am I to be loaded with calumny, and not suffered to resent it? No; God forbid!

1. In Passage 1, the word *thrall* (line 10) is used to mean

   (A) freedom
   (B) bondage
   (C) tremor
   (D) excitement
   (E) stimulation

This is a vocabulary-in-context question. Replace the word cited with the five choices and choose the word that best fits the context. In this case, only one of the words has the same meaning as the italicized word. At times, all five choices will be synonyms, but only one will fit the shade of meaning in the citation. Here, Wright speaks of emancipating the human race "from the *thrall* of despotism." If you know that *emancipating* means "freeing" and that *despotism* is "dictatorship," you will know to look for a word that implies the opposite of *freeing*—in this case, choice (B), *bondage.* Even if you do not recognize the words *emancipating* or *despotism,* reading the entire sentence will help you understand the meaning of the italicized word.

2. How could you restate Wright's last sentence?

   (A) Laurels and statues are silly, but if they had any meaning at all, a patriot like the one I describe might deserve them.
   (B) Tributes make men vain, but such a man could wear them wisely.
   (C) We decorate men in vain, but a useful man could be called a patriot.
   (D) A patriot such as the one I have mentioned will have no need for statues and laurels.
   (E) In vain do we search for appropriate laurels and statues with which to reward such a patriot.

This kind of interpretation question asks you to paraphrase a phrase or sentence. Often the language cited is archaic or difficult because of its use of figures of speech. If you merely read the choices above, (A), (B), (D), and (E) might make some kind of sense to you, in light of the passage you read. In order to choose correctly, you must return to the sentence in question and compare it piece by piece to the choices. Here, "Laurels and statues are vain things. . ." might be paraphrased "Laurels and statues are silly." "Could we imagine them of use" might be paraphrased "if they had any meaning at all," and so on. The choice that is closest to the original meaning is choice (A).

3. In what way does Emmet fail to fit Wright's definition of a patriot?

   (A) He prefers the despotism of France to that of England.
   (B) He wants to free his people.
   (C) He idolizes his own country over all.
   (D) He declares the court's sentence to be unjust.
   (E) He sees no dishonor in his actions.

This evaluation question requires you to use Passage 1 to evaluate Passage 2—in this case, to apply a definition from one passage to something in the other passage. In a science selection, you might be asked to apply one writer's hypothesis to another writer's results or to compare two theories. Here, first you must look at Wright's definition of a patriot. She believes that a patriot is a lover of human liberty in general rather than a lover of country in particular. Next, you must look at the choices in light of what you recall about Passage 2. Choice (A) has nothing to do with Wright's definition, and in terms of Emmet's speech, it is simply wrong. He does not prefer one type of tyranny; he hates all tyranny. Choice (B) is certainly true of Emmet, but it does not contradict Wright's definition, and you are looking for some aspect of Emmet's speech that does. The answer is choice (C)—Wright does not believe in blind chauvinism, but Emmet continually repeats the point that everything he has done, he has done for his country alone. In fact, Emmet supported the French Revolution and probably would have been admired by Fanny Wright, but you must base your answer solely on the material given in the passages. Neither (D) nor (E) discusses actions or attitudes that are part of Wright's definition of patriotism.

4. Emmet's speech moves from

(A) a plea for mercy to acceptance
(B) interpretation to description
(C) polite refusal to calm denial
(D) impassioned denial to angry challenge
(E) expressions of remorse to expressions of fear

This kind of synthesis/analysis question asks you to look at the flow of a passage and analyze the author's intent in light of the structure of the work. Skim the passage and look for a point where the tone or intent of the passage changes. Usually this will happen between paragraphs, so the paragraphing of the passage is a definite clue. Paragraph 1 of Passage 2 begins with a statement of the charge against Emmet and his denial of that charge. The tone is impassioned rather than polite (C). He never asks for mercy (A) or expresses remorse (E). Nor could this paragraph be termed "interpretation" (B). To test whether choice (D) is correct, go on to paragraph 2. Here, Emmet begins with the words "Let no man dare," angrily challenging those who might call him a dishonorable man. Choice (D) is the only possible answer.

PART

FOUR

Test Busters

CONTENTS

TEST BUSTERS

In the Mathematics and Verbal Reviews you studied the content areas that you must know for the SAT. In this section, you will learn strategies that will help you apply what you know to the exam. To help you remember these strategies, each one is signaled by the Test Busters symbol. The day before the test, do a final review of this section by rereading each Test Buster.

Let's begin with strategies that you can use throughout the entire exam.

TEST-WISE TEST BUSTERS

Try to think of the SAT as an obstacle course. Your score on the course is determined by the number of obstacles you handle successfully within the time limit (with an adjustment for those obstacles you attempt but fail to surmount).

Pacing

An important element of the obstacle course is a time limit. You have only 15 or 30 minutes to complete the course, so you must learn to pace yourself.

It is possible to determine the average time you spend per question to finish all questions in the time allowed. For example, in a verbal section with 35 questions, you can attempt all the obstacles if you spend 50 seconds on each one. But spending the same amount of time on each obstacle won't work.

For Any Given Kind of Question, the Obstacles Get Progressively More Difficult.

For example, in a typical verbal section, the first analogy may be easy, the eighth more difficult, and the thirteenth very difficult. The same pattern will be repeated for sentence completions and for the math questions. Critical reading is the only exception to this rule. The questions about a critical reading selection are *not* necessarily arranged in any particular order of difficulty.

Difficult obstacles require more time than easy ones. Therefore:

Work as Quickly as Possible Through the Easier Problems in a Group.

This is essential if you hope to complete the course in the allotted time. Of course, you can't afford to be careless.

Work as Quickly as You Can Without Making Foolish Errors.

Remember that a fraction of a point is taken off your score for each question that you answer incorrectly. If you work too quickly, you may make silly mistakes.

What is the best speed at which to work? The answer to this question varies from person to person. You must find the best rate for yourself. As you do the practice tests in this book, check your results to see whether you are pacing yourself correctly. If you find that you are not answering every question in a section but are very accurate, then take a chance and speed up. If you find that you are answering most of the questions but are missing too many, then slow down.

One pitfall you must avoid is the trap of spending too much time on any one question.

When You Realize That You Are Not Making Progress on a Question, Go on to the Next Item.

Suppose, for example, that you are working on an analogy item. You have narrowed your options to two choices (and eliminated the other three), and you can't recall the exact meaning of a key word. Once you realize you are in this position, you should select one of the two choices as a guess (more on guessing shortly) and move on to the next question.

Sometimes you may not realize that you are just spinning your wheels. You may think you are making progress and that if you spend "just a little more time" you will find a solution. No one wants to abandon a question while there is still hope, so you need an absolute rule:

If You're Stuck on a Question and You Have Other Questions Within a Section, Stop Working on That Question Before You Spend Twice the Average Time Per Question on It.

For a section with 35 questions, the average time per question would be 50 seconds. Do not spend 100 seconds on any one question if you still have other questions to attack. If you fail to follow this rule, you may succeed in answering that difficult question. But that difficult question is worth only one point—the same value as other (perhaps easier) questions you will find later in the section.

There are some other strategies you can use to make the most effective use of your time:

Do Not Read the Directions.

This advice may seem somewhat surprising. After all, you are usually told to read directions carefully so that you understand what is required. But by the time you take your SAT, you will have practiced solving many SAT model questions. You will already know what is required. For example, you will be able to recognize a sentence completion (fill-in-the-blank) item and will know what to do with it without reading the directions that precede the group of items. So don't waste any of your valuable time reading directions you are already familiar with.

Finally, make sure you are able to keep track of the passing time.

Bring a Watch With You to the Exam.

Your watch doesn't have to be a fancy stopwatch. A simple wristwatch with a minute hand works well. As time for a section begins, just set the minute hand on the half hour (or the hour). Time will be up when the hand reaches the hour (or the half hour). You can see at a glance from the position of the minute hand in relation to the six (or the 12) approximately how much time remains. For a digital watch, at the beginning of each section do a quick calculation to determine when that section will end. (Add 15 or 30 minutes to the current time.) Jot this number down next to the stop notice at the end of the section. Don't use a watch alarm (your watch may be taken by a proctor).

Don't Become Preoccupied With Keeping Track of Time.

The time limit is an important element of the obstacle course, but don't become obsessed with keeping track of exactly how much time remains.

Guessing

For all multiple-choice questions, a fraction of a point is deducted from your score for each wrong answer (questions you do not answer at all don't affect your score either way). This feature of the scoring formula is often called "the guessing penalty." In reality, however, it is not intended to be a "penalty" or punishment. Instead, it is just a statistical adjustment that makes sure that scores are not artificially inflated by random guessing.

Do Not Guess Randomly.

If time is called before you even get a chance to read a question or if you read a question and have literally no idea how to answer it, don't answer that question. Leave the corresponding space on the answer sheet blank.

If You Can Make an Educated Guess, You Must Answer the Question.

Notice the wording of this strategy. It states that you *must* guess if you can eliminate one or more of the answer choices.

Do Not Pick Easy Answers to Difficult Questions.

As you learned above, questions on the SAT (except for critical reading questions) are arranged in increasing order of difficulty. A question that appears in the last third of a group is likely to be a difficult one, and difficult problems require difficult solutions. If you think that the last question in a group is easy, then your approach to the question is probably incorrect. Suppose the following example were to appear as the last problem in a math section of the SAT.

Example➤ A bicyclist rode to school at an average rate of 10 miles per hour and returned home along the same route at an average rate of 20 miles per hour. If her entire traveling time was 1 hour, what was the total number of miles in the round trip?

(A) 10

(B) $13\frac{1}{3}$

(C) 15

(D) $15\frac{2}{3}$

(E) 20

Solution➤ Because this is the last problem, it must be a difficult one. Some students will try to solve it by simply averaging 10 and 20: $(10+20)/2=15$. They select choice (C) and are happy to have found such an easy solution. But the fact that the solution is easy should tell those students that they have made an error! If this question could be answered so simply, then it wouldn't be found in the final third of the questions.

Use Common Sense to Eliminate Impossible Choices.

Common sense will help you eliminate one or more choices and make an educated guess. Let's return to the math problem above. We have already decided that choice (C) must be wrong. What about (A)? If the cyclist rode for an hour at the rate of 10 miles per hour, then she would have covered exactly 10 miles. But we know that she rode part of that hour at 10 miles per hour. So she covered more than

10 miles, and (A) must be wrong. Apply the same reasoning to (E). If she rode for an hour at the rate of 20 miles per hour, then she would have covered exactly 20 miles. But we know that she rode part of that hour at only 10 miles per hour. So she covered less than 20 miles, and (E) must be wrong. We have now eliminated three of the five choices and must (if we can't solve the problem) make an educated guess. If you guessed (B), you were correct.

Each Question Is Usually Worth Ten Points on the Scaled Score.

While SAT scores are reported on a scale that runs from 200 to 800, the final digit is always zero, as illustrated by the following excerpt from a scoring table:

Raw Score	Verbal Score	Math Score
55	670	760
54	660	745
53	640	730
52	640	715
51	630	700

As you can see, most often a single question changes the score by ten points. (There are some "lumps" in the scaled scores. For example, raw scores of 52 and 53 both generate verbal scores of 640.)

Finally, you should know that you are not expected to answer every single question.

You Can Get a Very Good Score Without Answering Every Question.

The "average" student gets a raw score of about 35 (out of a possible 80) on the verbal sections and a raw score of about 27 (out of a possible 60) on the math sections.

Answer Sheets

After you have decided upon your answer to a question, you must enter your response on the machine-graded answer sheet. Use the next strategy as a time-saver when answering questions.

Mark Your Answers in Groups.

Moving back and forth between the answer sheet and the test booklet takes time. Don't do it more often than you need to. The most efficient system is to work a small group of problems (like a page of five math problems or a set of ten analogies), noting your responses by circling the letter of each choice in the test booklet. Then mark all of those responses on the answer sheet. One trip to the answer sheet is more efficient than five or ten trips to the answer sheet. (This system will also help you avoid the most annoying error of all: putting a right answer in the wrong space. When you enter your responses on the answer sheet, you will be concentrating on that task alone.)

MATH TEST BUSTERS

The SAT uses three different types of math questions:

Standard multiple-choice questions
Quantitative comparison questions
Student-produced response questions

Math Test Busters address techniques for answering both standard multiple-choice and quantitative comparison questions. A combination of test-busting techniques and mathematics knowledge is necessary for success on the student-produced response math questions.

STANDARD MULTIPLE-CHOICE QUESTIONS

The Higher the Question Number Within the Same Question Group, the More Difficult the Problem.

Look at, but do not attempt to solve, the following three problems.

Examples➤

1. If $x - 2 = 5$, then $x =$

(A) –10

(B) –3

(C) $\frac{5}{2}$

(D) 3

(E) 7

12. For how many integers x is $-7 < 2x < -5$?

(A) None
(B) One
(C) Two
(D) Three
(E) Indefinite Number

25. In a set of five books, no two of which have the same number of pages, the longest book has 150 pages and the shortest book has 130 pages. If x pages is the average (arithmetic mean) of the number of pages in the five-book set, which of the following best indicates all possible values of x and only possible values of x?

(A) $130 < x < 150$
(B) $131 < x < 149$
(C) $133 < x < 145$
(D) $134 < x < 145$
(E) $135 < x < 145$

Notice that the first question has the number "1," the second question the number "12," and the last question the number "25." This indicates that the second question is much more difficult than the first and that the third is much more difficult than the second. And you can easily see that this is true. (Don't worry about how to solve these problems just yet. We'll get to that issue shortly.)

Easy Questions Have Easy Answers.

This is of course true by definition: the definition of an easy question is that it is easy to answer. With an easy question, there are no "hidden tricks." So what seems to be an obviously correct answer is probably the correct answer. Let's consider the first example on page 251:

Example➤ 1. If $x - 2 = 5$, then $x =$

(A) -10
(B) -3
(C) $\frac{5}{2}$
(D) 3
(E) 7

Solution➤ The correct answer is (E). Just solve for x.

$x - 2 = 5$

Add 2 to both sides of the equation:

$x - 2 + 2 = 5 + 2$
$x = 7$

If easy questions have easy answers, then it stands to reason that hard questions have difficult answers. Again, this is true by definition. But this point is the basis for an important strategy.

Don't Pick Easy Answers to Hard Questions.

Return to the third example on page 251:

Example➤ 25. In a set of five books, no two of which have the same number of pages, the longest book has 150 pages and the shortest book has 130 pages. If x pages is the average (arithmetic mean) of the number of pages in the five-book set, which of the following best indicates all possible values of x and only possible values of x?

(A) $130 < x < 150$
(B) $131 < x < 149$
(C) $133 < x < 145$
(D) $134 < x < 145$
(E) $135 < x < 145$

Solution➤ Since this is question "25," it is difficult. And it is a difficult question because the process you have to use to get the right answer is difficult.

Look first at answer choice (A). It cannot possibly answer this difficult question. (A) reasons that "The shortest book is 130 pages long and the longest is 150 pages long; therefore, the average is between 130 and 150." That's very simple and incorrect.

Apply the same analysis to choice (B). If it were possible to answer this question just by thinking, "Since no two books have the same number of pages, the average must be one page more than the shortest book and one page less than the longest book," then this would be an easy question.

The correct answer is (E), and the solution shows why this is a difficult question. To find the minimum possible value for x, assume that the other three books contain 131, 132, and 133 pages. (Remember, the question states that no two books contain the same number of pages.) The average would be:

$$\frac{130+131+132+133+150}{5} = \frac{676}{5} = 135.2$$

So x must be more than 135. Now assume that the other three books contain 149, 148, and 147 pages. The average length of all five books would be:

$$\frac{150+149+148+147+130}{5} = \frac{724}{5} = 144.8$$

So x must be less than 145. Therefore, x is greater than 135 but less than 145.

When Guessing at Difficult Questions, Eliminate Easy Answers.

Having just learned about the "sucker" play (picking an easy answer to a difficult question), you can actually turn this point into a guessing strategy. Even if you can't solve a math problem (like the one above), you may still be entitled to make a guess. If one or more of the choices appear to be "sucker bait," then eliminate them and choose one of the others.

Example➤ 25. In a certain laboratory experiment, a beaker containing liquid is heated over a flame so that 10 percent of the liquid (by volume) evaporates. If at the conclusion of the experiment one cup of liquid remains in the beaker, how many cups of liquid were originally in the beaker?

(A) $1\frac{1}{8}$

(B) $1\frac{1}{9}$

(C) $1\frac{1}{10}$

(D) $1\frac{1}{11}$

(E) $1\frac{1}{12}$

Solution➤ This is a difficult question (as signaled by the question number), so it has a difficult answer. Choice (C) is "sucker bait." You get choice (C) if you think "10 percent is $\frac{1}{10}$, so the original volume was 1 cup plus $\frac{1}{10}$ of a cup." But the solution can't be that easy. You can safely eliminate (C) and are already in a position to make an educated guess. (You have only four answers to choose from.)

The correct answer to the problem above is (B). Let V be the volume of liquid in the beaker at the beginning of the experiment. After losing 10 percent of V, the beaker still contains 1 cup:

$$V - (10 \text{ percent of } V) = 1$$
$$V - 0.1V = 1$$
$$0.9V = 1$$
$$V = 1 \div \frac{9}{10}$$
$$V = 1 \times \frac{10}{9}$$
$$V = 1\frac{1}{9}$$

Finally, questions of moderate difficulty have solutions that are moderately challenging—not too easy but not too hard.

For Questions of Moderate Difficulty, Trust Your Judgment.

Now let's consider the second problem on page 251:

Example➤ 12. For how many integers x is $-7 < 2x < -5$?

(A) None
(B) One
(C) Two
(D) Three
(E) Indefinite number

Solution➤ This is a question of moderate difficulty because it is question number 12. The problem is solved in this way: There is only one integer between –7 and –5, and that integer is –6. And there is only one value of x (an integer) such that $2x$ is equal to –6, and that, of course, is –3. So the correct answer to this question of moderate difficulty is (B). Although this question is more difficult than the first example, it contains no hidden tricks—so trust your judgment.

Each standard multiple-choice math problem includes five answer choices. One of them is correct: the other four are wrong. This means that the right answer is printed on the page. All you have to do is find it. Of course, that's not always easy. In this respect, the SAT is like one of those puzzles you find in children's magazines: How many farm animals can you find hidden in this picture?

Fortunately, there are some tried-and-true methods to help you locate the right answer.

If Answer Choices Are Presented Using a Three-Statement Format, Use the Process of Elimination.

Example➤ If x-y is positive, which of the following statements about x and y could be true?

I. $0 > x > y$
II. $x > 0 > y$
III. $y > x > 0$

(A) I only
(B) II only
(C) III only
(D) I and II only
(E) II and III only

Solution➤ The answer choices above are all various combinations of the three statements. Start with statement I. If x and y are negative numbers such that x is greater than y, then y has a greater absolute value than x. Since both are negative, however, x-y will be positive. For example, $-3 > -4$ and $-3-(-4) = -3+4 = 1$, and $1 > 0$. Therefore, statement I will appear in the correct answer choice. Since (B), (C), and (E) do not contain statement I, you should eliminate them. The correct answer must be either (A) or (D). Next take statement II. If x is positive and y negative, then $x - y$ is an expression in which a negative number is subtracted from a positive number. Since subtracting a negative number is equivalent to adding a positive number, $x - y$ must be positive. Because statement II must appear in the correct answer, you should eliminate (A). By the process of elimination, you have learned that (D) is the correct choice—even without looking at statement III.

The technique above is not the only way that you can use the answer choices to your advantage. When you look at a group of answer choices, you know that one of them must be right.

Test Answer Choices Until You Find One That Works.

Example➤ If a rectangle has sides of $2x$ and $3x$ and an area of 24, what is the value of x?

(A) 2
(B) 3
(C) 4
(D) 5
(E) 6

Solution➤ Since this is the SAT, you know that the value of x is 2, 3, 4, 5, or 6. Take the first possibility. If $x = 2$, then the rectangle has sides with lengths of $2(2) = 4$ and $3(2) = 6$ and an area of $4 \times 6 = 24$. The question states that the rectangle in question does have an area of 24, so the value of x is 2 and (A) is the correct answer.

Was this a lucky try? After all, the answer choices might have been arranged differently:

(A) 6
(B) 5
(C) 4
(D) 3
(E) 2

Now it seems as though you would need to do five calculations to get the right answer. This impression, however, is wrong. You shouldn't start with choice (A). You should start with choice (C). Why? Notice that the answers are arranged in order (either smallest to largest or largest to smallest). If you test (C) and it doesn't work, determine which answer you should test next. Take the choices given in the original problem.

(A) 2
(B) 3
(C) 4
(D) 5
(E) 6

Assume that $x = 4$. Then the sides have lengths of $2(4) = 8$ and $3(4) = 12$, and the rectangle has an area of $8 \times 12 = 96$. Since 96 is more than 24, the area given in the problem, this proves that 4 is too large a number. You should then try the next smaller number, in this case 3. If $x = 3$, then the sides have lengths of $2(3) = 6$ and $3(3) = 9$, and the rectangle has an area of $6 \times 9 = 54$. This eliminates (B). You need a number that's even smaller than 3, and there is only one possibility left: 2. Should you plug 2 into the question? No. Since 2 is the only possibility left, by the process of elimination you have determined that (A) is the correct choice.

Let's return to a problem studied earlier:

Example➤ In a certain laboratory experiment, a beaker containing liquid is heated over a flame until 10 percent of the liquid (by volume) evaporates. If at the conclusion of the experiment one cup of liquid remains in the beaker, how many cups of liquid were originally in the beaker?

(A) $1\frac{1}{7}$ (B) $1\frac{1}{8}$ (C) $1\frac{1}{9}$ (D) $1\frac{1}{10}$ (E) $1\frac{1}{11}$

Solution➤ Earlier, this problem was solved using a variable, but you can actually solve the problem without doing any algebra at all. Just test answer choices until you find one that works. Start with choice (C). Assume that the beaker contains $1\frac{1}{9}$ or $\frac{10}{9}$ cups of the liquid at the beginning of the experiment. $\frac{1}{10}$ of $\frac{10}{9}$ is equal to $\frac{1}{9}$. And $\frac{10}{9}$ minus $\frac{1}{9}$ is equal to 1. Therefore, (C) must be the right answer.

This technique of testing answer choices is not some parlor trick that is fun to know but has no real value. You must *believe* in this technique and look for opportunities to use it. Here are five examples of *difficult* questions. These questions are difficult because it is difficult to answer them using conventional strategies such as algebra. But with this TEST BUSTER, they become easy items.

Example➤ A farmer raises chickens and cows. If his animals have a total of 120 heads and a total of 300 feet, how many chickens does the farmer have?

(A) 50
(B) 60
(C) 70
(D) 80
(E) 90

Solution➤ Test answer choices—starting with (C). If the farmer has 70 chickens, he has 50 cows. The chickens have a total of $70 \times 2 = 140$ feet and the cows a total of $50 \times 4 = 200$ feet. Combined, the animals have a total of $140 + 200 = 340$ feet. But the problem says that they have only 300 feet. How can you adjust the numbers to get fewer feet? By assuming more chickens and fewer cows. (The cows have more feet than the chickens.) So test (D). If the farmer has 80 chickens, he has 40 cows. Eighty chickens have $2 \times 80 = 160$ feet, and 40 cows have $4 \times 40 = 160$, for a total of 320 feet. But 320 is also too many feet. Now you know, by the process of elimination, that the correct answer is (E). (With 90 chickens and 30 cows, you have $2 \times 90 = 180$ chicken feet and $4 \times 30 = 120$ cow feet, for a total of 300 feet—just what the problem calls for.)

Example➤ A vendor sold $\frac{1}{2}$ of his hot dogs in the first three innings of a baseball game, and he sold another five hot dogs in the fourth inning. If he still has $\frac{3}{8}$ of the number of hot dogs he started with, how many hot dogs did he start with?

(A) 60
(B) 50
(C) 40
(D) 30
(E) 20

Solution➤ Test choices, starting with (C). Assume that the vendor originally had 40 hot dogs. In the first three innings he sells half of them, or 20 hot dogs: $40 - 20 = 20$. In the fourth inning he sells another five: $20 - 15 = 15$. Is $\frac{15}{40}$ equal to $\frac{3}{8}$? Yes! So the vendor must have started with 40 hot dogs, and (C) must be the correct answer.

Example➤ Two identical cylindrical tanks are to be filled with water at the same uniform rate. It takes four hours to fill each tank. If water begins to fill one tank at 1:00 P.M. and the other at 2:00 P.M., at what time will the water level in the first tank be exactly three times the water level in the second?

(A) 1:30 P.M.
(B) 2:30 P.M.
(C) 4:00 P.M.
(D) 4:30 P.M.
(E) 5:00 P.M.

Solution➤ Test choices, starting with (C). At 4:00 P.M., water has been running into the first tank for 3 hours, so the first tank is $\frac{3}{4}$ full, and the water level in the tank is equal to $\frac{3}{4}$ the height of the cylinder. And at 4:00 P.M., the water has been running into the second tank for 2 hours, so the second tank is $\frac{1}{2}$ full, and the water level in the tank is equal to $\frac{1}{2}$ the height of the cylinder. Is $\frac{3}{4}$ three times $\frac{1}{2}$? No. So (C) is a wrong answer. But which choice should you test next? Before you read on, stop to think about this question.

In another hour, the first tank will be completely full and the second getting fuller. So the water levels will be getting closer together. Therefore, the critical time (at which the height of the water level in the first tank was three times the height of the water level in the second tank) must have occurred earlier than 4:00. So next try 2:30. At 2:30, water has been flowing into the tank for $1\frac{1}{2}$ hours, and the height of the water level is $\frac{1\frac{1}{2}}{4} = \frac{\frac{3}{2}}{4} = \frac{3}{8}$ of the height of the cylinder. And at 2:30, water has been flowing into the second tank for $\frac{1}{2}$ hour, and the height of the water level in the second tank is $\frac{\frac{1}{2}}{4} = \frac{1}{8}$. Three-eighths is exactly three times $\frac{1}{8}$, so the correct answer must be (B).

Example➤ If the sum of $\frac{2}{3}$ of an even integer and $\frac{1}{2}$ of the next consecutive even integer is equal to 36, what is the odd integer between these two even integers?

(A) 15
(B) 23
(C) 25
(D) 29
(E) 31

Solution➤ Just test answer choices, starting with (C). If the odd integer is 25, then the even integers are 24 and 26. Two-thirds of 24 is 16, and $\frac{1}{2}$ of 26 is 13: $16 + 13 = 29$, not 36. Since 29 is less than 36, this indicates that 25 is too small. Try the next larger choice. If the odd integer is 29, then the even integers are 28 and 30. Take $\frac{1}{3}$ of 28: $\frac{28}{3} = 9\frac{1}{3}$. That's not an integer, so the sum described by the question stem cannot be the integer 36. This proves that the correct answer is (E). (If 31 is the odd integer, then the even integers are 30 and 32. $\frac{2}{3}$ of $30 = 20$, and $\frac{1}{2}$ of $32 = 16$, and $20 + 16 = 36$).

Example➤ For a certain woodworking project, a carpenter must make five successive cuts from a single board such that each cut reduces the length of the board by $\frac{1}{3}$ of its previous length. If the length of the board following the fifth cut is 1 meter, then the length of the board (in meters) following the third cut was

(A) $\frac{2}{3}$ (B) $1\frac{1}{2}$ (C) 2 (D) $2\frac{1}{4}$ (E) 3

Start by testing choice (C). If the length of the board following the third cut was 2, then following the fourth cut the length would be:

$$2-\left(\frac{1}{3}\text{ of }2\right)=2-\left(\frac{2}{3}\right)=1\frac{1}{3}$$

$$1\frac{1}{3}-\left(\frac{1}{3}\text{ of }1\frac{1}{3}\right)=\frac{12}{9}-\frac{4}{9}=\frac{8}{9}$$

Eight-ninths, however, is less than 1, so the board must have been longer than 2 meters after the third cut. And you should next try (D):

$$2\frac{1}{4}-\left(\frac{1}{3}\text{ of }2\frac{1}{4}\right)=\frac{9}{4}-\frac{3}{4}=\frac{6}{4}=\frac{3}{2}$$

$$\frac{3}{2}-\left(\frac{1}{3}\text{ of }\frac{3}{2}\right)=\frac{3}{2}-\frac{1}{2}=1$$

After the fifth cut, the board is only 1 meter long, so (D) must be the correct answer.

The technique of testing answer choices allows you to work with numbers (arithmetic rather than variables (algebra). There is a closely related technique:

Instead of Working with Letters, Use Numbers.

Example➤ $S1$ and $S2$ are two lists of five consecutive positive integers. If $S1$ and $S2$ have exactly one element in common, then what is the difference between the sums of the two lists?

(A) 4
(B) 5
(C) 8
(D) 10
(E) 20

Solution➤ You can attack this question by thinking about all lists, $S1$ and $S2$, that have five consecutive integers with one integer in common. To do this, you use a variable such as x to represent the first integer in the list with the smaller numbers. The second number in that list is $x + 1$, the third is $x + 2$, the fourth is $x + 3$, and the fifth is $x + 4$. Since the two lists have only one number in common, the smallest number of the larger list must be the same number as the largest number of the smaller list, $x + 4$. So the second integer of the larger list is $x + 5$, the third is $x + 6$, the fourth is $x + 7$, and the fifth is $x + 8$. Now add the elements of each list:

$$S1 = x + (x + 1) + (x + 2) + (x + 3) + (x + 4) = 5x + 10$$

$$S2 = (x + 4) + (x + 5) + (x + 6) + (x + 7) + (x + 8) = 5x + 30$$

So the difference is $(5x + 30) - (5x + 10) = 20$

You can make things a lot easier for yourself if you just make up some numbers. Since *S*1 and *S*2 can be any lists, assume that *S*1 is the list, 1, 2, 3, 4, and 5. Then *S*2 is the list 5, 6, 7, 8, and 9. The sum of numbers in *S*1 is 15, and the sum of the numbers in *S*2 is 35. The difference between the two sums is 35 – 15 = 20. And arithmetic is always much easier than algebra!

Arithmetic is also easier than geometry.

Example➤ If the length of a rectangle is increased by 10 percent and the width of the rectangle is decreased by 10 percent, what is the percent change in the area of the figure?

(A) An increase of 20 percent
(B) An increase of 1 percent
(C) No net change
(D) A decrease of 1 percent
(E) A decrease of 20 percent

Solution➤ One way to attack this problem is to use w and l to represent the width and length of the rectangle. The rectangle originally has an area of $w \times l = wl$. Its new width is $w - 0.1w = 0.9w$ and its new length is $l + 0.1l = 1.1l$. And its new area is $0.9w \times 1.1l = 0.99wl$. The difference between the original area and the new area is $wl - 0.99wl = 0.01wl$. A percent decline of 0.01 = 1%. You can reach the same conclusions, however, just by picking some numbers for w and l. Assume that the original rectangle has a width of 4 and a length of 5. The original area is $4 \times 5 = 20$. The new width will be:

4 – (10% of 4) = 3.6

And the new length will be:

5 + (10% of 5) = 5.5

The new area is $3.6 \times 5.5 = 19.8$. The net change in area is $20 - 19.8 = 0.2$. So the percent change is:

$$\frac{0.2}{20} = 1\% \text{ decrease}$$

Since this is such an important strategy, here are five more problems for practice. Solve each problem by using numbers. (Try the problems yourself *before* you read the explanation.)

Example➤ If x and y are positive integers such that x divided by 6 leaves a remainder of 4 and y divided by 6 leaves a remainder of 3, what is the remainder when xy is divided by 6?

(A) 0
(B) 1
(C) 2
(D) 3
(E) 4

Solution➤ What do you know about x and y? Only that they are positive integers and that when they are divided by 6 you get a remainder of 4 or 3. Can you think of such numbers? Try 10 and 9. (When you divide 10 by 6, you get a remainder of 4, and when you divide 9 by 6, you get a remainder of 3.) $10 \times 9 = 90$, and 90 divided by 6 is equal to 15 with no remainder. Therefore, the correct answer is (A).

Example➤ If $x-4$ is 2 greater than y, then $x+5$ is how much greater than y?

(A) 1
(B) 3
(C) 7
(D) 9
(E) 11

Solution➤ Pick a value for x. You can even let x be equal to 4. Then, $4-4=0$ and 0 is 2 greater than y. So y is equal to -2. If $x=4$, then $x+5=4+5=9$, and so $x+5$ is 11 more than y. Therefore, the right answer is (E).

Example➤ If x is 125 percent of y, then y is what percent of x?

(A) $66\frac{2}{3}$
(B) 75
(C) 80
(D) 92
(E) 110

Solution➤ Pick values for x and y. If x is 125 and y is 100, then x is 125% of y. What percent of y is x?

$$\frac{100}{125}=\frac{4}{5}=80\%$$

So the correct answer is (C).

Example➤ In a certain school, the number of sophomores is 50 percent of the rest of the student body. Sophomores account for what percent of the entire student body?

(A) 20
(B) 25
(C) $33\frac{1}{3}$
(D) 40
(E) 50

Solution➤ How many sophomores are there in this school? Pick a number, say 100. Since the number of sophomores is equal to 50 percent of the rest of the student body, there must be another 200 students in the school. (100 is 50 percent of 200). The total student population is $100+200=300$. So sophomores account for $\frac{100}{300}=33\frac{1}{3}\%$ of all students. And the correct answer is (C).

Example➤ If x is 10 percent greater than y, and m is 20 percent greater than n, then xm is what percent greater than yn?

(A) 10
(B) 20
(C) 24
(D) 28
(E) 32

Solution➤ Let y be 10 and x be 11 (11 is 10 percent greater than 10). And let m be 12 and n be 10 (12 is 20 percent greater than 10). $xm = (11)(12) = 132$, and $yn = (10)(10) = 100$. And 132 is 32 percent more than 100. The correct answer is (E).

You can use a similar technique when the answer choices contain variables:

If Answer Choices Are Algebraic Formulas, Make Up Numbers and Test the Choices.

Example➤ The unit cost of pens is the same regardless of how many pens are purchased. If the cost of p pens is d dollars, what is the cost, in dollars of x pens?

(A) xd

(B) xpd

(C) $\frac{xd}{p}$

(D) $\frac{xp}{d}$

(E) $\frac{pd}{x}$

Solution➤ Turn this problem into a real, everyday situation. Assume that four pens cost $2. In other words, a pen costs 50 cents. And assume that you need to buy only one pen. You could spend only $0.50. So assuming that $p = 4$, $d = 2$, and $x = 1$, the right answer should give you the number 0.5. Plug numbers into the choices:

(A) $xd = (1)(2) = 2$ A wrong answer.

(B) $xpd = (1)(4)(2) = 8$ Another wrong answer.

(C) $\frac{xd}{p} = (1)(2) / 4 = 0.5$ The right answer.

(D) $\frac{xp}{d} = (1)(4) / 2 = 2$ A wrong answer.

(E) $\frac{pd}{x} = (4)(2) / 1 = 8$ Another wrong answer.

Example➤ If p is an odd integer, which of the following is an even integer?

(A) $p+2$
(B) p^2
(C) p^2+2
(D) $(p+2)^2$
(E) p^2+p

Solution➤ Just pick any odd integer and substitute that integer for p in the choices. 1 is an odd integer and easy to work with:

(A) $p+2=1+2=3$ An odd number.
(B) $p^2=1^2=1$ Another odd number.
(C) $p^2+2=1^2+2=3$ Another odd number.
(D) $(p+2)^2=(1+2)^2=3^2=9$ Again, an odd number.
(E) $p^2+p=1^2+1=1+1=2$ An even number.

Therefore, the correct answer must be (E).

Again, this is an important strategy, so you should practice using it.

Example➤ If the sum of three consecutive even integers is N, then in terms of N, what is the sum of the next three consecutive odd integers that follow the greatest of the three even integers?

(A) $N+3$
(B) $N+6$
(C) $N+12$
(D) $N+15$
(E) $N+21$

Solution➤ Select a series of three consecutive even integers, say 2, 4, and 6. Their sum is $2+4+6=12$. The next largest odd integer after 6 is 7. So the odd integers are 7, 9, and 11. Their sum is $7+9+11=27$. So the correct answer choice must produce the number 27.

(A) $N+3=12+3=15$ A wrong answer.
(B) $N+6=12+6=18$ Another wrong answer.
(C) $N+12=12+12=24$ And another wrong answer.
(D) $N+15=12+15=27$ The right answer.
(E) $N+21=12+21=33$ Another wrong one.

Example➤ If $\frac{1}{(1+\frac{1}{y})}=x$, then which of the following is equal to $2x$?

(A) $\frac{2}{(2+\frac{2}{y})}$

(B) $\frac{2}{(2+\frac{1}{2}y)}$

(C) $\frac{1}{(\frac{1}{2}+\frac{1}{2}y)}$

(D) $\frac{1}{(\frac{1}{2}+2y)}$

(E) $\frac{1}{(2+2y)}$

Solution➤ Pick a value of y, say, $y = 1$:

$$\frac{1}{(1+\frac{1}{y})} = \frac{1}{(1+\frac{1}{1})} = \frac{1}{(1+1)} = \frac{1}{2}$$

So if $y = 1$, $x = \frac{1}{2}$. $2x$, therefore, is equal to 1. Substitute 1 for y in each of the answer choices. The correct choice will give you the value 1:

(A) $\frac{2}{(2+\frac{2}{y})} = \frac{2}{(2+\frac{2}{1})} = \frac{1}{2}$ Wrong.

(B) $\frac{2}{(2+\frac{1}{2y})} = \frac{2}{(2+\frac{1}{2}(1))} = \frac{4}{5}$ Wrong.

(C) $\frac{1}{(\frac{1}{2}+\frac{1}{2y})} = \frac{1}{(\frac{1}{2}+\frac{1}{2}(1))} = 1$ Correct.

(D) $\frac{1}{(\frac{1}{2}+2y)} = \frac{1}{(\frac{1}{2}+2(1))} = \frac{2}{5}$ Wrong.

(E) $\frac{1}{(2+2y)} = \frac{1}{(2+2(1))} = \frac{1}{4}$ Wrong.

Example➤ If $x < -1$, then which of the following must be true?

(A) $x^3 > x^2 > x$

(B) $x^2 > x^3 > x$

(C) $x^2 > x > x^3$

(D) $x > x^3 > x^2$

(E) $x > x^2 > x^3$

Solution➤ Just pick a value for x, say, -2:

(A) $x^3 > x^2 > x$

$(-2)^3 > (-2)^2 > -2$

$-8 > 4 > -2$ False.

(B) $x^2 > x^3 > x$

$(-2)^2 > (-2)^3 > -2$

$4 > -8 > -2$ False.

(C) $x^2 > x > x^3$

$(-2)^2 > -2 > (-2)^3$

$4 > -2 > -8$ True.

(D) $x > x^3 > x^2$

$-2 > (-2)^3 > (-2)^2$

$-2 > -8 > 4$ False.

(E) $x > x^2 > x^3$

$-2 > (-2)^2 > (-2)^3$

$-2 > 4 > -8$ False.

Therefore, the correct answer is (C).

Example➤ Today, Ted is twice as old as Fran was five years ago. If Ted is now x years old, how old is Fran today?

(A) $\frac{x}{2}-5$

(B) $\frac{x}{2}+5$

(C) $x+5$

(D) $2x-5$

(E) $2(x-5)$

Solution➤ Pick a value for x, say, $x = 20$. If Ted is now 20 years old, then five years ago, Fran was 10 years old. And today, five years later, Fran is 15 years old. So when you plug in 20 for x, the correct choice will produce the number 15.

(A) $\frac{x}{2}-5=\frac{20}{2}-5=5$ Wrong.

(B) $\frac{x}{2}+5=\frac{20}{2}+5=15$ Correct.

(C) $x+5=20+5=25$ Wrong.

(D) $2x-5=2(20)-5=35$ Wrong.

(E) $2(x-5)=2(20-5)=30$ Wrong.

Example➤ On a certain toll road, the toll is 60 cents for the first half mile and 10 cents for each additional half mile. If x is an integer, what is the toll for a trip x miles in length?

(A) $60 + 10x$

(B) $60+10\left(\frac{x}{2}\right)$

(C) $60 + 10(2x)$

(D) $60+10\left(x-\frac{1}{2}\right)$

(E) $60 + 10(2x - 1)$

Solution➤ How long is the trip? Try 1 mile. For a trip exactly 1 mile long, the toll will be 60 cents for the first half mile and 10 cents for the second half mile, for a total of 70 cents. When you substitute 1 for x into the answer choices, the correct choice will yield the value 70:

(A) $60 + 10x = 60 + 10(1) = 70$ Correct.

(B) $60+10\left(\frac{x}{2}\right)=60+10\left(\frac{1}{2}\right)=65$ Wrong.

(C) $60 + 10(2x) = 60 + 10(2(1)) = 80$ Wrong.

(D) $60+10\left(x-\frac{1}{2}\right)=60+10\left(1-\frac{1}{2}\right)=65$ Wrong.

(E) $60 + 10(2x - 1) = 60 + 10(2(1) - 1) = 70$ Correct.

But how can there be two correct answers? Only one choice can be correct. Just by coincidence, two choices produce the same results when you use 1. To find the correct choice, test another number. Suppose a trip is 2 miles long. The toll would be 60 cents for the first half mile and 30 cents for the next three half miles. So when $x = 2$, the correct answer yields 90.

(A) $60 + 10x = 60 + 10(2) = 80$ Wrong.

(E) $60 + 10(2x - 1) = 60 + 10(2(2) - 1) = 90$ Correct.

For word problems involving geometry figures, we have special test busters. Most geometry problems on the SAT require you to apply your knowledge of geometry principles to new situations.

The Area of an Unusual Shape Is the Difference Between the Areas of Two Ordinary Figures.

Example➤

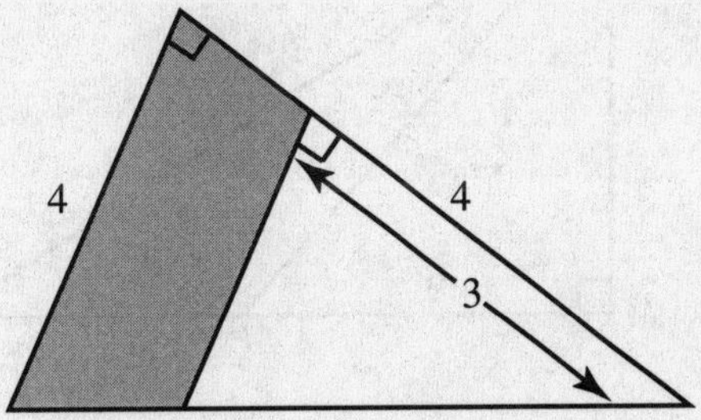

In the figure above, what is the area of the shaded region?

(A) $2\frac{1}{2}$

(B) 4

(C) $3\frac{1}{2}$

(D) 6

(E) 8

Solution➤ When you isolate the shaded portion of the figure, it looks like this:

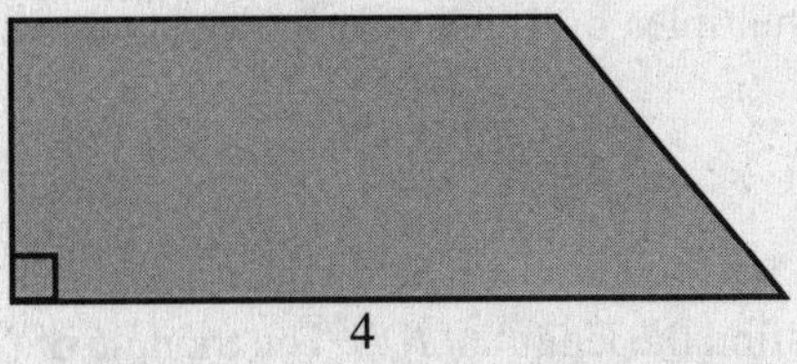

This figure is a trapezoid, and there is a special formula for finding the area of a trapezoid. You can, however, solve the problem even without the special formula. The shaded portion of the figure is the difference between the area of the large triangle and the area of the small triangle. And you surely know how to find the area of a triangle. Since the larger triangle has one right angle and two equal sides, it is an isosceles right triangle. Since the side of the smaller triangle is parallel to the side of the larger triangle, the smaller triangle is also an isosceles right triangle with sides of 3 and 3. Now find the area of each triangle.

$$\text{Area of Smaller} = \frac{1}{2}(3)(3) = \frac{9}{2}$$

$$\text{Area of Larger} = \frac{1}{2}(4)(4) = 8$$

So the shaded portion of the figure has an area of:

$$8 - \frac{9}{2} = 3\frac{1}{2}$$

In a Complex Figure, Different Shapes Can Share a Common Aspect.

Example➤

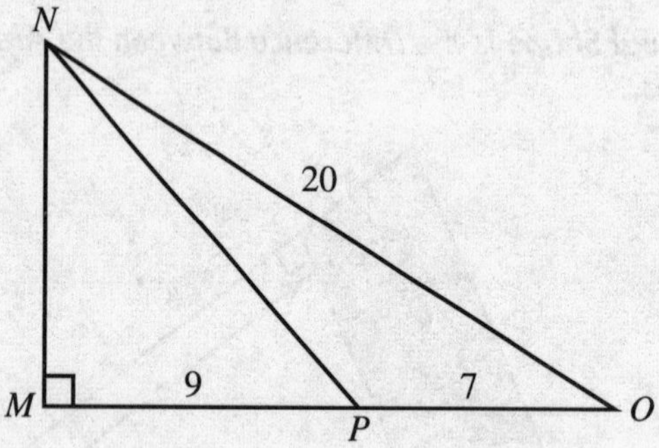

In the figure above, what is the length of *NP*?

(A) 3
(B) 8
(C) 9
(D) 12
(E) 15

Solution➤ The figure above consists of two right triangles, *NMO* and *NMP*. *NM* is a side of both triangles. If you can find the length of *NM*, you can also find the length of *NP*. Use the Pythagorean Theorem to find *NM*:

$$NM^2 + MO^2 = NO^2$$
$$NM^2 + 16^2 = (20)^2$$

Notice that 16 and 20 are multiples of 4 and 5, respectively, so this is a 3, 4, 5 right triangle. Therefore:

$NM = 12$

Now you are in a position to find the length of *NP*. The triangle of *NMP* has sides of 9 and 12, so it too is a 3, 4, 5 right triangle, and *NP* must be 15.

Use Your Eye to Estimate Quantities.

Figures in this section are always drawn to scale unless they are accompanied by a warning that reads "**Note:** Figure NOT drawn to scale." Therefore, you can sometimes solve a problem just by looking at the picture.

Example➤

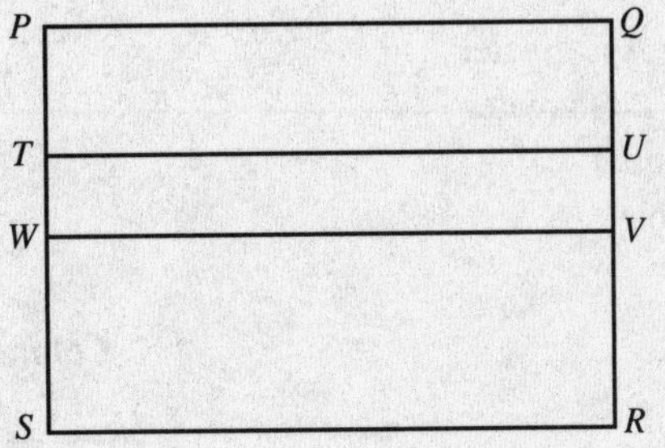

In the rectangle *PQRS* shown, *TU* and *WV* are parallel to *SR*. If *PS* = 6, *UV* = 1, and *PR* (not shown) = 10, what is the area of rectangle *TUVW?*

(A) 8
(B) 12
(C) 16
(D) 24
(E) 32

Solution➤ To solve the problem, you will need to find the length of *TU*. You can do this by using the Pythagorean Theorem. The triangle *PSR* has sides of 6 and 10, so *SR* = 8. Since *TU* = *SR*, *TU* = 8, so the area of the small rectangle is equal to $1 \times 8 = 8$. As an alternative, you could simply estimate the length of *TU*. *TU* appears to be longer than *PS* (6), and *TU* must be shorter than *PR* (10). Therefore, *TU* appears to be approximately 8. And the area must be approximately $1 \times 8 = 8$. Is that sufficiently accurate to get the right answer? Look at the choices. (A) is 8, and it is the only choice that is even close to 8.

QUANTITATIVE COMPARISONS

Quantitative comparisons are a special kind of math problem found on the SAT, so it is important that you become familiar with their peculiar format. The object of quantitative comparisons is to compare two quantities (one appearing in Column A and the other in Column B).

Memorize the Following Directions.

(A) if the quantity in Column A is greater
(B) if the quantity in Column B is greater
(C) if the two quantities are equal
(D) if no comparison is possible

Examples➤

	Column A	Column B
1.	$\frac{1}{4}+\frac{3}{8}$	$\frac{1}{5}+\frac{3}{10}$
2.	5%	$\frac{1}{10}$
3.	$x(x+y)+y(x+y)$	$(x+y)^2$
4.	x^2	x^3

Solutions➤ 1. The correct answer to the first comparison is (A). Just do the arithmetic:

$$\frac{1}{4}+\frac{3}{8}=\frac{2}{8}+\frac{3}{8}=\frac{5}{8}$$

$$\frac{1}{5}+\frac{3}{10}=\frac{2}{10}+\frac{3}{10}=\frac{5}{10}=\frac{1}{2}$$

Since $\frac{5}{8}$ is greater than $\frac{1}{2}$, Column A is greater.

2. The correct answer to the second comparison is (B). Since $\frac{1}{10}$ is equal to 10 percent, Column B is greater.

3. The correct answer to the third comparison is (C). Do the algebra:

$$x(x+y)+y(x+y)=x^2+xy+xy+y^2=x^2+2xy+y^2$$
$$(x+y)^2=(x+y)(x+y)=x^2+xy+xy+y^2=x^2+2xy+y^2$$

The two expressions are identical, so the two columns must be equal (no matter what values x and y have).

4. The correct answer to the last comparison is (D). Sometimes Column B is greater, for example when $x = 2$. At other times Column A is greater, for example, when $x = -2$. And the two columns can even be equal, for example, when $x = 0$.

An important key to doing well on this part of the test is:

Do Only as Much Work as You Need to Do to Arrive at a Comparison.

All you have to do is determine which column is greater (or whether the columns are equal, or whether the comparison cannot be made). You don't have to determine how much bigger one column is than the other.

Example➤

Column A	*Column B*
$31 \times 32 \times 33 \times 34 \times 35$	$32 \times 33 \times 34 \times 35 \times 36$

Solution➤ To make this comparison, you don't have to do the multiplication. Column A is the product of the consecutive integers 31 through 35, and Column B is the product of the consecutive integers 32 through 36. Since the numbers in Column B are larger, Column B is the greater quantity.

Example➤

The formula for the volume of a right circular cylinder is $V = \pi r^2 h$

Column A	*Column B*
The volume of a right circular cylinder with $r = 3$ and $h = 6$	The volume of a right circular cylinder with $r = 6$ and $h = 3$

Solution➤ Your first reaction to this comparison might be to use the formula to find the volume of each cylinder.

Volume $A = \pi(3^2)(6) = (3.14)(3)(3)(6)$
Volume $B = \pi(6^2)(3) = (3.14)(6)(6)(3)$

If you do the multiplication, you'll be wasting time. Why multiply by 3.14? Since you are doing the same operation to both formulas, it won't make any difference as to which is larger. So the problem becomes which is greater: $(3^2)(6)$ or $(6^2)(3)$. You should be able to see that the second is larger. If you can't then you will have to multiply: $(3^2)(6) = (9)(6) = 54$ and $(6^2)(3) = (36)(3)$. Don't finish the multiplication, however, because you should see that (36) (3) is more than 54. And that's all you need to know.

There are several strategies you can use to help reach the point at which you can make a comparison.

If the Math Is Not Difficult, Do It.

Example➤

Column A	*Column B*
(0.6) (0.6)	$\frac{36}{100}$

Solution➤ The math required here is very simple. Do it, and deposit that question in your account:

$(0.6)(0.6) = 0.36$

$\frac{36}{100} = 0.36$

So the correct response is (C).

Example➤

Column A		*Column B*
	The toll on a certain highway is 80 cents for the first mile and 20 cents for each additional mile.	
The toll for a 7-mile drive on the highway.		\$2.00

Solution➤ Again, the calculation is a simple one, so do it: 80 cents for the first mile plus 20 cents for 6 additional miles = \$2.00. So the correct response is (C).

If the Comparison Includes an Equation Centered Between the Columns, Solve for Unknowns.

Example➤

Column A		*Column B*
	$x + y = 6$ $x = -2$	
y		4

Solution➤ To answer the question, you must use the centered information to find the value of y. Substitute -2 for x in the first equation:

$$(-2) + y = 6$$
$$y = 8$$

Therefore, Column A is greater than Column B.

Example➤

Column A		*Column B*
	$x + y = 6$ $x - 2y = 3$	
x		y

Solution➤ Treat the centered information as a system of simultaneous equations and solve for y and x:

$$x + y = 6$$
$$x = 6 - y$$

Substitute this value for x into the second equation:

$$(6 - y) - 2y = 3$$
$$6 - 3y = 3$$
$$-3y = -3$$
$$y = 1$$

And find the value of x:

$$x + y = 6$$
$$x + 1 = 6$$
$$x = 5$$

Since $x = 5$ and $y = 1$, Column A is larger, and the correct answer is (A).

Example➤

Column A		Column B
	If twice x is added to half of x, the sum is 50.	
x		25

Solution➤ Solve for x:

$$2x + \frac{x}{2} = 50$$

$$\frac{5x}{2} = 50$$

$$5x = 100$$

$$x = 20$$

Therefore, Column B is larger, and the correct answer is (B).

Many times, comparisons are presented in such a way that the comparison is not immediately evident. It is obscured by the form of the elements.

Example➤

Column A		Column B
	$x \neq 0$	
$\frac{(x^2 + 6x)}{2}$		$3x$

Given the complexity of the expression in Column A, it's difficult to make a judgment about which column is greater.

Simplify Across the Comparison.

In algebra, you learned that it is possible to do certain manipulations to inequalities. You can add to and subtract from both sides of an inequality without changing the direction of the inequality, and you can multiply or divide both sides of an inequality without changing its direction. (Remember, however, that when you multiply or divide by a negative number, you do change the direction of the inequality.)

When you approach a quantitative comparison, you don't know whether you are looking at an equality or an inequality (nor in which direction the inequality runs). But you can add to or subtract from both sides without upsetting the balance. And you can multiply or divide without upsetting the balance—so long as you use positive quantities. This is a very powerful strategy for attacking quantitative comparisons. Let's go back to the example above.

Example➤

Column A		Column B
	$x \neq 0$	
$\frac{(x^2 + 6x)}{2}$		$3x$

Solution➤ Begin by multiplying both columns by 2. The outcome is:

Column A		Column B
	$x \neq 0$	
$x^2 + 6x$		$6x$

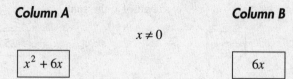

Now subtract 6x from both sides. The outcome is:

Column A		Column B
	$x \neq 0$	
x^2		0

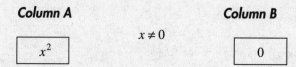

Now you are in a position to make the comparison. Since x is not equal to zero, x^2 must be a positive quantity. Therefore, Column A is larger.

Example➤

Column A	Column B
6^{12}	$6^{13} - 6^{12}$

Solution➤ This is a very difficult problem. With the TEST BUSTER, however, it becomes almost easy. Add 6^{12} to both columns. The result is:

Column A	Column B
$2(6^{12})$	6^{13}

Now you may be able to make the comparison. Column A is 2 times 6^{12}, but Column B is 6 times 6^{12}. (6^{13} is equal to 6^{12} times 6.) If you don't yet see the comparison, you can continue by dividing both columns by 6^{12}. The result is:

Column A	Column B
2	6

At this point it is obvious that Column B is greater.

Example➤

Column A	Column B
$9\sqrt{3}$	$3\sqrt{3}$

Solution➤ Start by multiplying both columns by $\sqrt{3}$. The result is:

Column A	Column B
9(3)	3(3)

Now you can see that Column A is greater and the correct answer is (A).

Example➤

Column A	*Column B*
12% of 3610	3610% of 12

Solution➤ The comparison here can be made by doing the arithmetic:

Column A	*Column B*
0.12×3610	36.10×12

But that's too much work. Multiply each column by 100 to get rid of the decimal fraction. The result is:

Column A	*Column B*
12×3610	3610×12

Now you can easily see that the two columns are equal and that the correct answer is (C).

This Test Buster is extremely important. Here are some examples for you to practice on. Try to simplify each comparison by doing the same thing to both columns. Try to solve the problem on your own *before* you read the solution.

Example➤

Column A	*Column B*
$\frac{1}{5}+\frac{1}{7}+\frac{1}{12}$	$\frac{1}{12}+\frac{1}{6}+\frac{1}{7}$

Solution➤ You could, of course, add these fractions by finding a lowest common denominator. But there is an easier route. Notice that $\frac{1}{12}$ appears in both columns. Subtract it from both columns. And $\frac{1}{7}$ appears in both columns, so subtract that from both sides. You are left with the fractions that follow:

Column A	*Column B*
$\frac{1}{5}$	$\frac{1}{6}$

Obviously Column A is larger, so the correct answer must be (A).

Example➤

Column A	*Column B*
$\frac{x}{0.25}$	$4x$

Solution➤ Multiply both columns by 0.25. The result is:

Column A	*Column B*
x	x

Now it is easy to see that the two columns are equal and the correct answer must be (C).

Example➤

Column A		Column B
	Peter is x years old and Mary is y years older than Peter.	
$x - y$		$y - x$

Solution➤ Add x to both columns and add y to both columns. The result is:

Column A	Column B
$2x$	$2y$

If the solution is not yet clear to you, you can divide both columns by 2:

Column A	Column B
x	y

Do you have any information about x and y? No. So it is impossible to determine which of the two columns is greater, and the correct answer is (D).

Example➤

Column A		Column B
	x is a positive integer, and $0 < a < 1$	
x		$\frac{x}{a}$

Solution➤ Since a is a positive number, you can multiply both columns by a:

Column A	Column B
$x(a)$	x

And you can divide both columns by x:

Column A	Column B
a	1

Since the note above the two columns stipulates that a is less than 1, Column B must be greater.

Example➤

Column A		Column B
	$x > y$	
x^2y		xy^2

Solution➤ Should you divide both columns by x and y? NO! Although you know that x is greater than y, you don't know whether x and y are positive or negative. You cannot multiply or divide by a quantity unless you are certain the quantity is positive. If you forget this, here is what happens. (Divide by both x and y.)

Column A		Column B
	$x > y$	
x		y

And you select choice (A). But the correct answer to this comparison is (D). For example, let $x = 1$ and $y = 0$. On that assumption, both columns have the value 0 and are equal. Or let $x = 1$ and $Y = -1$. On that assumption, Column A is –1 and Column B is 1. This proves that the correct choice is (D).

Do Not Multiply or Divide Across the Comparison Unless You Are Certain the Quantity You Are Using Is Positive.

In the solution to the preceding problem, you tested the comparison by using a negative number.

Remember that an unknown can have any value:

Unless Otherwise Restricted, an Unknown Can Be Negative, Zero, or Positive.

Example➤

Column A		Column B
	$3x = 4y$	
x		y

Solution➤ The correct answer to this question is not (A). It is true that if x and y are positive, then x is greater than y. But x and y might be negative: $3(-4) = 4(-3)$. If x and y are negative, then y is greater than x. And x and y might be zero and therefore equal. Thus (D) is the correct answer.

Remember also that fractions behave peculiarly.

A Proper Fraction Raised to a Power Is Smaller Than the Fraction Itself.

Example➤

Column A	Column B
$\frac{27}{41}$	$\left(\frac{27}{41}\right)^{15}$

Solution➤ Obviously, it would be foolish to try to do the arithmetic in Column B. The key to this comparison is to see that each successive multiplication results in a smaller product. Therefore, Column A is larger than Column B, and the correct answer is (A).

Since fractions are funny things, be sure to keep them in mind when working with unknowns.

Unless Otherwise Restricted, an Unknown Can Be a Fraction.

Example➤

Column A		Column B
	$x > 0$ and $x \neq 1$	
x^2		x

Solution➤ The correct answer to this comparison is (D). If x is a number larger than 1, then x^2 is larger than x. But if x is a number between 0 and 1 (a fraction), then x^2 is smaller than x:

$$\left(\frac{1}{2}\right)^2 = \frac{1}{4} \text{ and } \frac{1}{4} < \frac{1}{2}$$

When you attack a comparison involving unknowns, try to determine systematically what possible values there are for them.

When Testing the Value of an Unknown, Check With Negative Numbers, Zero, Fractions, 1, and Other Positive Numbers.

Example➤

Column A	Column B
$x^3 > x^2$	
x	1

Solution➤ The correct answer to this is (A). Can x be a negative number? No, for then x^3 would be negative and x^2 would be positive. But the centered information tells us that x^3 is greater than x^2. Can x be 0? No, for then x^3 and x^2 would both be 0 and equal (x^3 would not be more than x^2). Can x be a fraction? No, for then x^3 would be less than x^2. (Remember, when you raise a fraction to a power, it keeps getting smaller.) Can x be 1? No, for then x^3 and x^2 would be equal. Therefore, x must be a positive number larger than 1, and Column A is greater.

Frequently, the geometry figures in this section are accompanied by a warning "**Note:** Figure not drawn to scale."

If a Figure Is Accompanied by a Warning That It Is Not Drawn to Scale, Do Not Make a Comparison by Estimating or Measuring.

Example➤

Column A **Column B**

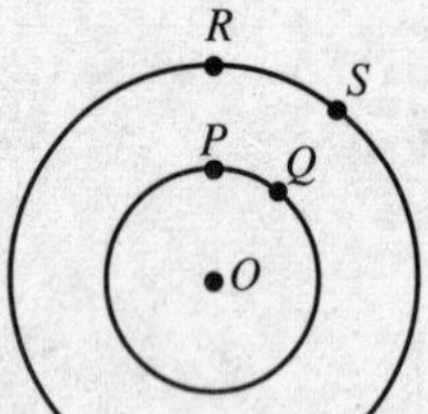

Minor arcs PQ and RS have equal length
and each circle has center O.
Note: Figure not drawn to scale.

Column A	Column B
Degree measure of angle POQ	Degree measure of angle ROS

Solution➤ The correct answer to this comparison is not (C). In the figure, angle *POQ* seems to be equal to angle *ROS*, but we are warned that the figure is not drawn to scale. The correct answer is (A), as shown by the following figure, which is drawn to scale.

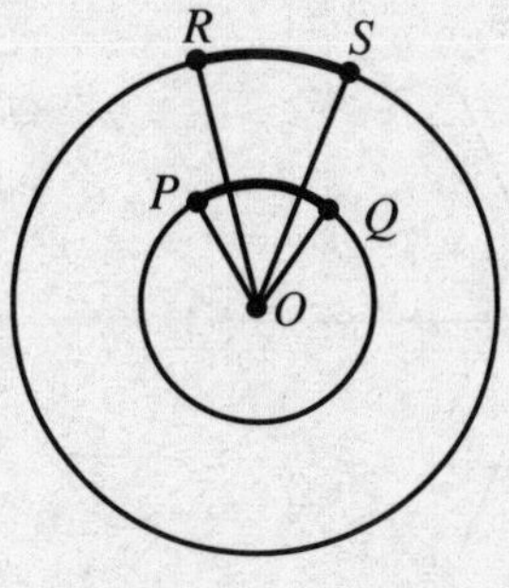

Example➤

Column A	Column B

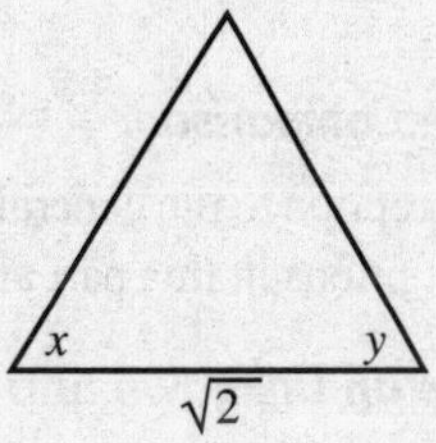

Note: Figure not drawn to scale.

Column A	Column B
x^0	y^0

Solution➤ The correct answer to this comparison is not (C). Although x and y appear to be equal, the note warns that the figure is not drawn to scale. And the fact that one side of the triangle has length of $\sqrt{2}$ does not prove that the triangle is an isosceles triangle. The correct answer is (D).

Example➤

Column A	Column B

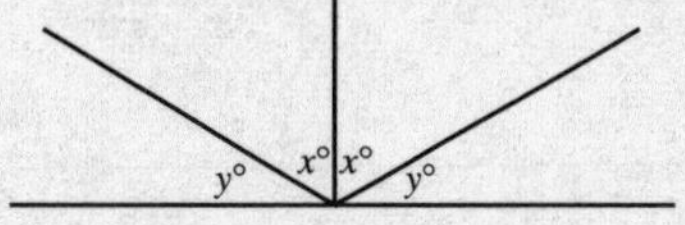

Note: Figure not drawn to scale.

Column A	Column B
x	y

Solution➤ The correct answer to this question is not (A). Although x appears to be larger than y in the figure, the note indicates that the figure is not drawn to scale. The correct answer to this comparison is (D), as shown by the following figures:

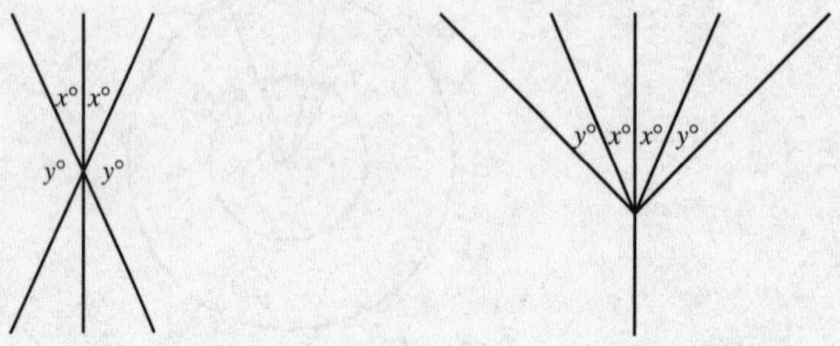

Finally, there are a couple of points to keep in mind about guessing on this part of the test:

Never Guess (E) to a Quantitative Comparison.

Quantitative comparisons are the exception to the general rule that each multiple-choice question on the SAT has five answer choices. The options in this part are only (A), (B), (C), and (D).

If a Comparison Does Not Involve an Unknown or a Figure, Guess (A), (B), or (C) — Not (D).

Why would a comparison ever be classified as (D)? This would happen only if it were not possible to determine which column is greater. And this situation can occur only when the comparison involves an unknown of some kind, for example, a variable or an unknown aspect of a figure. If the comparison involves only numbers, do not guess (D).

Example➤

Column A	*Column B*
Sum of all integers from –20 to 50, inclusive	Sum of all integers from 21 to 50, inclusive

Solution➤ When you first see the comparison, you may want to start adding. (It is only arithmetic.) But you won't have time to do such a lengthy calculation. Suppose, therefore, that you have to guess. Don't guess (D)! You know that it is possible to make the comparison—you just don't have time to do it. [The correct answer is (C). The sum of the integers from –20 to 20 is 0., e.g., $-20 + 20 = 0$, $-19 + 19 = 0$, and so on. So Column A is really just the sum of all integers from 21 to 50.]

VERBAL REASONING TEST BUSTERS

CRITICAL READING

The phrase "critical reading" really doesn't prepare you for what to expect on this part of the SAT. In the first place, the passages used by the SAT are drawn from many categories:

Reading Selections Can Be Taken From Novels, Biographies, Essays, Medicine, Botany, Zoology, Chemistry, Physics, Astronomy, Art, Literature, Music, Philosophy, Folklore, History, Economics, Sociology, Government, or Any Other Source.

Your reaction is probably "I've studied some of those areas, but how can I answer a question on a topic I haven't studied?" The answer to this question is that the SAT questions don't presuppose that you have studied any particular area:

The Passage Contains Everything You Need to Answer the Questions.

Some questions test your ability to *interpret* words or phrases based on the author's intent. These questions are usually worded in these ways:

> In line 26, why does the author say . . . ?
> What does the author mean by . . . ?

Some questions require you to *evaluate* the author's key assumptions, point of view, or main idea. These questions might take one of these forms:

> How does the author feel about . . . ?
> Which evidence does the author provide to support the idea that . . . ?
> Which of these three phrases best summarizes the author's intent?

A final type of question asks you to *synthesize* the whole package and *analyze* the author's structural choices and the composition of the package. For example:

> Why does the author mention . . . ?
> How does part 1 of the passage differ from/support part 2?

Learning to recognize the different kinds of questions will make it easier for you to plan your strategy and recognize the right (and wrong) answers.

Since every critical reading exercise is designed along these lines, there are some procedures you can follow regardless of the content of the selection.

SAT Reading Passages are Not Likely to Be Familiar to You.

The SAT intentionally uses obscure materials to make sure that no examinee has an unfair advantage because he or she is familiar with the material.

The people who write the SAT are not particularly interested in whether you have a certain piece of knowledge. Instead, they are interested in how well you read. They have a certain idea about what constitutes good reading. According to their theory, a good reader does several different things:

- A good reader can decipher unfamiliar words from the context in which they are found.
- A good reader can interpret words and phrases based on an understanding of the author's intent.

- A good reader can discern an author's assumptions, point of view, and main idea.
- A good reader can analyze the logical structure and composition of a piece of writing.

Every critical reading question is designed to test one of these reading skills.

Some questions test whether you understand *vocabulary in context*. These questions may have one of the following forms.

The word --- in line 16 means . . . ?
In line 48, what is the best definition of --- ?

First Do the Selections That Are Familiar to You. Save Until Last the Selection That Seems Most Difficult.

Even though a selection may treat a topic that seems familiar to you, the selection will probably still seem difficult for several reasons. First, though the general topic is familiar, the specific treatment given the topic by the author may be unusual. Second, the selection will seem to begin in the middle of nowhere. Third, the selection has been carefully edited to contain many ideas in a few words. A good technique for getting over these difficulties is "previewing" (after deciding on the "easiest" passage to do first).

Begin Your Attack on a Critical Reading Exercise by Reading the Question Stems.

The "stem" of the question is the part that introduces the answer choices; in other words, the stem is everything but the choices. Why should you read the stem before you read the selection? For two reasons. First, some stems will actually tell you what the selection is about. Second, some stems will tell you what specific points to look for as you read the selection.

Here are four question stems. Later you will see the passage on which the questions are based. For now, just read the question stems to see what you can learn from them. You are previewing the question stems before you read the passage.

1. In line 7, the word *mortal* is used to mean . . . .
2. What does the author mean when he says that "particularly the Europeans" are fearful of the black snake's appearance (lines 10–12).
3. To support his statement that copperhead snakes are very dangerous to humans, the author cites . . . .
4. Why does the author mention handling rattlesnakes?

Stem 3 doesn't really provide any information. It is a stock question that could be used with any selection. The other stems, however, refer to a greater or lesser degree to specific content in the passage you will see on pages 281–282.

Stem 1 introduces a vocabulary word that has several meanings. You are given a specific line reference in which to locate the word.

Stems 2 and 4 let you know that the author is discussing snakes. They suggest that you stay alert as you read lines 10–12 and as you read the section where the author discusses handling rattlesnakes.

After you have previewed the question stems, you should next read the introduction and the opening sentence.

Before Reading the Passage, Read the Introduction and the Opening Sentence.

The introduction will often suggest the main idea of the passage, and the opening sentence may confirm that. Here is the introduction and opening sentence from the selection you will see on pages 281–282:

J. Hector St. John Crèvecoeur wrote a long series of letters to a friend in England, describing his life as a frontier farmer in the colony of Pennsylvania. These letters were collected and printed in 1782 as Letters from an American Farmer. *They remain a fascinating record of the natural history, politics, and customs of the colonial era.*

You insist on my saying something about our snakes; and relating what I know concerning them, were it not for two singularities, the one of which I saw, the other I received from an eyewitness, I should have but very little to observe.

The introduction tells you who the author is, when he wrote, and what he generally wrote about. The opening sentence tells you that he plans to "[say] something about our snakes."

When you have finished your preview, read the selection. Don't try to go through it too quickly. Critical reading is not a speed-reading contest.

Do Not Merely Skim the Passage, and Do Not Try to "Speed Read."

This part of the SAT tests reading *comprehension,* not reading *speed.* Even if you read slowly, you should be able to complete the longest selections in three to four minutes.

Of course, since this is a test of comprehension rather than speed, make sure you understand what you read. Read actively, not passively.

As You Read, Ask Yourself: What Is the Main Theme of This Passage? How Do the Specific Ideas Relate to the Main Theme? What Is the Author's Attitude Toward the Subject?

But don't get stuck on specific details. This is particularly true if there is some technical point in the selection that you don't understand. Even if you don't understand a technicality, you can still answer most of the questions so long as you do understand *why* the technical point is in the selection.

Using Your Pencil, Draw a Box Around Points That Are Difficult to Understand.

Don't spend a lot of time trying to figure out a technical idea that may not even be the basis of a question.

Finally, once you have completed your reading of the selection, pause briefly and ask yourself about what you have just read.

Before Attacking the Questions, Summarize in Your Own Words the Main Idea and General Development of the Passage.

Ask yourself about what you have just read. If you are clear in your own mind about the passage, the wrong answer choices will be less likely to distract your attention from the correct answer.

At the bottom of this page you will find the selection you have been waiting for (about snakes). But before you read it, review these two Test Busters:

As You Read, Ask Yourself: What Is the Main Theme of this Passage? How Do the Specific Ideas Relate to the Main Theme? What Is the Author's Attitude Toward the Subject? Using Your Pencil, Draw a Box Arround Points That Are Difficult to Understand.

Now read the passage:

J. Hector St. John Crèvecoeur wrote a long series of letters to a friend in England, describing his life as a frontier farmer in the colony of Pennsylvania. These letters were collected and printed in 1782 as Letters from an American Farmer. *They remain a fascinating record of the natural history, politics, and customs of the colonial era.*

You insist on my saying something about our snakes; and relating what I know concerning them, were it not for two singularities, the one of which I saw, and the other I received from an eyewitness, I should have but very little to observe. The southern provinces are the countries where nature has formed the greatest variety of alligators, snakes, serpents; and scorpions, from the smallest size, up to the *pine barren*, the largest species known here. We have but two, whose stings are mortal, which deserve to be mentioned; as for the black one, it is remarkable for nothing but its industry, agility, beauty, and the art of inticing birds by the power of its eyes. I admire it much and never kill it, though its formidable length and appearance often get the better of the philosophy of some people, particularly the Europeans. The most dangerous one is the *pilot*, or *copperhead*; for the poison of which no remedy has yet been discovered. It bears the first name because it always preceeds the rattlesnake; that is, quits its state of torpidity in the spring a week before the other. It bears the second name on account of its head being adorned with many copper-coloured spots. It lurks in rocks near the water, and is extremely active and dangerous. Let man beware of it! I have heard of only one person who was stung by a copperhead in this country. The poor wretch instantly swelled in a most dreadful manner; a multitude of different spots of different hues alternately appeared and vanished, on different parts of his body; his eyes were filled with madness and rage, he cast them on all present with the most vindictive looks: he thrust out his tongue as the snakes do; he hissed through his teeth with inconceivable strength, and became an object of terror to all bye-standers. To the lividness of a corpse he united the desperate force of a hardly maniac; they hardly were able to fasten him, so as to guard themselves from his attacks; when in the space of two hours death relieved the poor wretch from his struggles, and the spectators from their apprehensions. The poison of the rattlesnake is not mortal in so short a space, and hence there is more time to procure relief; we are aquainted with several antidotes with which almost every family is provided. They are extremely inactive, and if not touched, are perfectly inoffensive. I once saw, as I was travelling, a great cliff which was full of them; I handled several, and they appeared to be dead; they were all entwined together, and thus they remained until the return of the sun. I found them out, by following the track of some wild hogs which had fed on them; and even the Indians often regale on them. When they find them asleep, they put a small forked stick over their necks, which they keep immoveably fixed on the ground; giving the snake a piece of leather to bite: and this they pull back several times with great force, until they observe their two poisonous fangs torne out. Then they cut off the head, skin the body, and cook it as we do eels; and their flesh is extremely sweet and white. I once saw a *tamed one*, as gentle as you can possibly conceive a reptile to be; it took to the water and swam whenever it pleased; and when the boys to who it belonged called it back, their summons was readily obeyed.

Did you read actively? Did you box material? To illustrate the Test Buster concerning technical material, look back at lines 12–16. What did you learn about *copperhead* snakes? How has the author used the word *bears*? What is a "state of torpidity"? You don't need to answer these questions in order to understand most of the material. To prove this, try reading those lines with that material deleted:

> The most dangerous one is the *pilot*, or xxxxxxxxxx; for the poison of which no remedy has yet been discovered. It xxxxx the first name because it always preceeds the rattlesnake; that is, quits its xxxxxxxxx in the spring a week before the other.

You can understand the gist of the material even without all the detail.

Now you can attack the questions based on the passage:

1. In line 7, the word *mortal* is used to mean
   (A) human
   (B) imperfect
   (C) deadly
   (D) perishable
   (E) individual

This is a vocabulary-in-context question.

Be Aware That the Answer Choices for a Vocabulary-in-Context Question May All Be Synonyms for the Original Word.

In this case, *mortal* has a variety of meanings, several of which are represented by the answer choices. You must look for the correct shade of meaning by plugging the choices into the original context.

For a Vocabulary-in-Context Question, Plug Choices into the Original Sentence.

"We have but two, whose stings are *mortal*, which deserve to be mentioned . . . "

Trying out the choices one by one in place of the word *mortal* proves that the answer must be (C), *deadly*. The stings of the two snakes are *mortal*, or *deadly*.

The second question is an interpretation question.

2. What does the author mean when he says that "particularly the Europeans" are fearful of the black snake's appearance (lines 10–12)?
   (A) People who are not familiar with these snakes expect them to be dangerous.
   (B) Europeans fear snakes of all kinds.
   (C) The snakes are meant to scare Europeans.
   (D) European snakes are more unnerving than these black snakes.
   (E) Black snakes can frighten even people who know them well.

Notice that this question refers you to a specific part of the selection, lines 10–12.

The Answer to an Interpretation Question Is Found by Looking Closely at the Context in Which the Excerpt Occurs.

Many interpretation questions require you to paraphrase an author's words, to restate a phrase in different, often more modern-sounding words.

When Rereading Part of the Passage, Make Sure to Identify Antecedents for Any Mysterious Pronouns.

"I admire it much, and never kill it, though its formidable length and appearance often get the better of the philosophy of some people, particularly the Europeans."

As you look back at lines 10–12, you must understand the antecedent to which the word *it* refers. To do this, you may need to read a sentence or two before the cited lines. Here, the author is referring to the black snake.

In Answering an Interpretation Question, Try to Restate the Cited Lines in Your Own Words.

The black snake's "formidable length and appearance" often "get the better of the philosophy of some people." In other words, the snake is really big and it scares certain people, "particularly the Europeans." In other words, especially Europeans are nervous around this snake.

Think About Why the Author Used a Particular Phrase or Word.

If you compare your restatement to the answer choices, you will see that several answers mention scariness and snakes. Consider the author's intent: Why did he bring up Europeans? After all, he is discussing snakes in the Colonies. Europeans would not be familiar with such snakes. Look back at the answer choices. Can you see that (A) is the correct choice?

The next question is an evaluation question.

3. To support his statement that copperhead snakes are very dangerous to humans, the author cites

   (A) a scientific study
   (B) personal observation
   (C) a case history
   (D) a textbook on natural history
   (E) the experiences of a close friend

All Evaluation Questions Ask You to Make a Judgment About the Passage.

To find the correct answer, you first need to locate in the passage the point covered by the question. In this case, the author supports his claim that copperheads are very dangerous by recounting the gruesome story of a man who was bitten by one and died. Then you must make a judgment. Which of the answer choices best describes the kind of evidence that the author is presenting? In this case, clearly the author is using a case history, choice (C), to prove his point. The purpose of this kind of question is to test your knowledge of the different kinds of evidence used to support an argument, and your ability to differentiate among them.

The last question is a synthesis/analysis question.

4. Why does the author mention handling the rattlesnakes?

   (A) To show his bravery
   (B) To show the contrast between rattlesnakes and the more dangerous copperheads
   (C) To introduce information on nonpoisonous snakes
   (D) To explain how Indians capture rattlesnakes
   (E) Because rattlesnakes may be handled safely when they are very cold and torpid

A Synthesis/Analysis Question Requires You to Understand the Structure and Logic of a Passage.

To answer this question, you should look at what comes before and after the section of the passage in question. If you have read actively, you will recognize that the author moves from a discussion of very poisonous snakes to a discussion of less poisonous snakes. Choices (A), (D), and (E) are not supported by the text, and choice (C) is simply incorrect. The author is setting up a contrast, which is a typical kind of logical structure for a written work. The answer is (B).

Just Because an Answer Is Factually True Does Not Necessarily Make It the Correct Choice.

Sometimes you will know through your own experience or reading that a particular answer choice is true. However, that is not reason enough to select it automatically as the correct answer for a question.

For example, in the question above, choice (E), "Because rattlesnakes may be handled safely when they are very cold and torpid," is factually true. However, it is not the correct answer to the question, which asks *why* the author mentions his experience with rattlesnakes.

In Critical Reading Sections, Do Not Go on from One Passage to the Next Until You Are Certain You Have Answered Every Question You Can.

This Test Buster will help you save time in critical reading sections. If you leave a reading passage before tackling all the questions in hopes of returning to it later, you will surely have to reread the entire selection—and this will cost you precious test-taking minutes.

There is one final point to be made about critical reading.

In Verbal Sections, Save Critical Reading For Last.

Analogy questions and sentence completion questions are short and take much less time to answer than critical reading questions. Reading questions are based on passages—and sometimes those passages are long. Make sure you get to all of the short questions first. Save the long hard ones until last.

ANALOGIES

As you learned in your review of SAT subject areas, analogy items require that you find a pair of words that express a certain relationship.

Create a Sentence That Summarizes the Connection Between the Capitalized Words.

Example➤ SCRIBBLE : WRITE::

(A) inform : supply
(B) mutter : listen
(C) nuzzle : feel
(D) ramble : play
(E) stagger : walk

Solution➤ You can summarize the connection between the capitalized words as "Scribbling is a bad kind of writing." (It doesn't matter that *scribbling* is a noun and *scribble* is a verb. The ideas haven't been changed.) Use this sentence to test answer choices:

(A) *Informing* is a bad kind of *supplying.*
(B) *Muttering* is a bad kind of *listening.*
(C) *Nuzzling* is a bad kind of *feeling.*
(D) *Rambling* is a bad kind of *playing.*
(E) *Staggering* is a bad kind of *walking.*

As you can see, the correct answer must be (E). Of course, the connection "is a bad kind of" is fairly vague.

If Necessary, Make Your Summary Sentence More Precise.

Example➤ CHORUS : SING::

(A) faculty : dance
(B) judge : testify
(C) duck : swim
(D) troupe : act
(E) business : hire

Solution➤ You might start with a sentence like "The purpose of a chorus is to sing." Your other sentences would then be:

(A) The purpose of a *faculty* is to *dance.*
(B) The purpose of a *judge* is to *testify.*
(C) The purpose of a *duck* is to *swim.*
(D) The purpose of a *troupe* is to *act.*
(E) The purpose of a *business* is to *hire.*

Using that sentence, you can confidently eliminate (A) and (B), but not the other possibilities. This indicates that the first sentence wasn't precise enough. Now ask "What is a special feature of a chorus?" It is a group of people who get together to sing. Try this with the remaining choices.

(C) A *duck* is a group that gets together to *swim.*
(D) A *troupe* is a group that gets together to *act.*
(E) A *business* is a group that gets together to *hire.*

The more precise description shows that the correct answer is (D).

You should be alert for certain analogy relationships that appear over and over on the SAT.

"Type of" Analogies

Examples➤ Here are some examples of the "type of" analogies:

SWORD : WEAPON   A sword is a type of weapon.

GRIMACE : EXPRESSION   A grimace is a type of expression.

OAK : TREE   An oak is a type of tree.

WATERCOLOR : PAINTING   A watercolor is a type of painting.

"Part of the Definition of" Analogies

Examples➤ Here are some examples of the "part of the definition of" kind of analogy:

GENEROSITY : PHILANTHROPIST   Generosity is part of the definition of a philanthropist.

BRAVERY : HERO   Bravery is part of the definition of a hero.

FALSE : LIE   It is part of the definition of a lie that it is false.

INVENTION : ORIGINAL   It is part of the definition of an invention that it is original.

FACULTY : TEACH   It is part of the definition of a faculty that it is supposed to teach.

"Lack of Something Is a Part of the Definition" Analogies

Examples➤ TRAITOR : LOYALTY   Lack of loyalty is part of the definition of a traitor.

NEGLIGENT : CARE   It is part of the definition of being negligent that someone lacks care.

ARID : MOISTURE   Lacking moisture is part of the definition of an arid region.

IGNORANCE : KNOWLEDGE   Lack of knowledge is part of the definition of ignorance.

POVERTY : FUNDS   Part of the definition of poverty is a lack of funds.

"Is a Part Of" Analogies

Examples➤ MOVEMENT : SONATA   A movement is a part of a sonata.

CHAPTER : BOOK   A chapter is a part of a book.

ACTOR : TROUPE   An actor is part of a troupe.

LION : PRIDE   A lion is part of a pride.

FINISH : RACE   The finish is part of a race.

"A Place for" Analogies

Examples➤ WITNESS : COURTROOM A courtroom is the place for a witness.

ACTOR : STAGE A stage is the place for an actor.

GRAIN : SILO A silo is a place for storing grain.

PILOT : AIRPLANE An airplane is a place where you would find a pilot.

ORE : MINE A mine is the place where you would find ore.

Of course, you cannot expect to apply these categories without thinking.

Examples➤ GRAIN : SILO::

(A) pilot : plane
(B) judge : courtroom
(C) water : reservoir
(D) clock : time
(E) automobile : highway

If you apply the "place where" idea without thinking, here is what happens.

A silo is a place where you would find grain.

(A) A plane is a place where you would find a pilot.
(B) A courtroom is a place where you would find a judge.
(C) A reservoir is a place where you would find water.
(D) A clock is a place where you would find time.
(E) A highway is a place where you would find automobiles.

You can eliminate (D), but that still leaves you with four choices. So apply the Test Buster that says you should make your sentence more precise:

A silo is a place where grain is stored.

(A) A plane is a place where a pilot is stored.
(B) A courtroom is a place where a judge is stored.
(C) A reservoir is a place where water is stored.
(E) A highway is a place where automobiles are stored.

Now it is easy to see that the correct answer is (C).

One important aspect of analogies is that the capitalized words and the correct answers all exhibit a clear-cut connection.

Eliminate Any Choice in Which the Words Do Not Exhibit a Clear-Cut Connection.

For example, the pair "career : descriptive" could not possibly be a correct answer choice to an SAT analogy because the words do not exhibit a clear-cut connection. (Try making up a sentence that describes the connection between those words.)

Eliminating wrong choices is an important strategy for attacking analogies. Remember, if you can eliminate even one answer choice using the "clear-cut" test, then you must make an educated guess.

Example➤ XXXXX : XXXXX

(A) note : scale
(B) ocean : merchandise
(C) expert : automobile
(D) victory : farmland
(E) teacher : classroom

Solution➤ You don't know what the capitalized words are in this analogy, but you can still eliminate choices (B), (C), and (D). There is no clear-cut connection between the words of those choices. (The actual analogy above is LETTER : ALPHABET : : note : scale.)

The strategy of eliminating choices that do not show a clear-cut connection is very important. Here is an exercise that will help you get used to this idea.

Directions: Of the 30 pairs of words below, only ten are possible correct answers because they exhibit a clear-cut connection. The other pairs are NOT possible right answers. Place a check mark by those that could be correct answers and an "x" by those that could not be correct.

1. DISTRACT : IGNORANCE
2. ENFEEBLE : DESCRIBE
3. COURTESY : CHILD
4. PROSECUTION : DIRECTOR
5. SHOVEL : EXCAVATE
6. PENCIL : POCKET
7. SCALES : JUSTICE
8. CANDLE : POVERTY
9. SIMPLIFY : VALUABLE
10. NULLIFY : VALIDITY
11. SNIP : SCISSORS
12. PRECIOUS : WORRIED
13. TIME : CLOCK
14. ACCESSIBLE : VOYAGE
15. CONTRITE : FAVORITE
16. WHISPER : SHOUT
17. TOTAL : APPLICATION
18. AIR : SUFFOCATION
19. DISMANTLE : EVEN
20. ILLUMINATE : PALE
21. SHREWD : RESENT
22. PARAGRAPH : ESSAY
23. BAFFLE : ANGER
24. UNIFORM : ERRONEOUS
25. ANTHOLOGY : DESCRIPTIVE
26. ILLNESS : VISION
27. DESTITUTE : MONEY
28. RANDOM : SINCERE
29. CREDULOUS : TRUST
30. PREPARE : DELIGHT

The correct answers are:

5. A shovel is a tool used to excavate.
7. Scales are the symbols of justice.
10. To nullify something is to take away its validity.
11. Scissors are a tool used to snip.
13. A clock is a device used to measure time.
16. A shout is a louder form of communication than a whisper.
18. Suffocation occurs from lack of air.
22. A paragraph is a part of an essay.
27. To be destitute is to lack money.
29. To be credulous is more extreme than to be trusting.

SENTENCE COMPLETIONS

The basic idea of a sentence completion item is simply "fill in the blank." You must determine what the sentence means without having read every word.

Robert was extremely ---- when he received a B on the exam, for he was almost certain he had gotten an A.

Although you may not know exactly what word is missing, you can tell from the rest of the sentence that Robert must have been disappointed or upset.

Since the idea of sentence completion is "fill in the blank," the basic strategy is read, predict, and choose.

Read Through the Entire Sentence Completion, Try to Predict an Appropriate Completion, and Then Select the Answer That Best Matches Your Prediction.

Example➤ Robert was extremely ---- when he received a B on the exam, for he was almost certain he had gotten an A.

(A) elated
(B) dissatisfied
(C) fulfilled
(D) harmful
(E) victorious

Solution➤ The anticipated completion for this sentence would be a word like "upset" or "disappointed." Neither of those words appears in the choices, but "dissatisfied" does. And "dissatisfied" is a good match for the words previously predicted.

Sometimes predicting a completion will not be so easy. If you can't just read through the sentence and arrive at a prediction, then examine more carefully the logical structure of the sentence.

Ask Yourself Whether the Word That Will Fill the Blank Must Sustain Some Other Thought in the Sentence.

Example➤ The service at the restaurant was so slow that by the time the salad had arrived we were ----.

(A) ravenous
(B) excited
(C) incredible
(D) forlorn
(E) victorious

Solution➤ The correct answer to this item is (A). The word that fills the blank must explain the consequence of waiting a long time for a meal. The consequences of such a delay, is, of course, great hunger. And (A) provides a word that means great hunger.

Example➤ As a teenager, John was withdrawn, preferring the company of books to that of people; consequently, as a young adult John was socially ----.

(A) successful
(B) uninhibited
(C) intoxicating
(D) inept
(E) tranquil

Solution➤ The "consequently" in this sentence signals that the second idea is an outcome of the first idea. What would be the likely outcome of an adolescence spent with books rather than with people? The person would probably be ill at ease with others, and (D) provides this idea.

Example➤ A decision that is made before all of the relevant data are collected can only be called ----.

(A) calculated
(B) insincere
(C) laudable
(D) unbiased
(E) premature

Solution➤ The correct answer to this item is (E). The blank must be filled by a word that extends the idea of a decision made before it should be. (E), "premature," is the best description of such a decision.

Ask Yourself Whether the Word That Will Fill the Blank Must Reverse Some Other Thought in the Sentence.

Example➤ The advance of science has demonstrated that a fact that appears to be inconsistent with a certain theory may actually be ---- a more advanced formulation of that theory.

(A) incompatible with
(B) in opposition to
(C) reconcilable with
(D) eliminated by
(E) foreclosed by

Solution➤ The correct answer to this item is (C). The sentence has a logical structure.

It seems to be inconsistent, but it is actually ----.

So the correct completion sounds like "is not inconsistent with," and (C) provides this meaning.

Example➤ Although she knew that the artist's work was considered by some critics to be ----, the curator of the museum was anxious to acquire several of his paintings for the museum's collection.

(A) insignificant
(B) important
(C) desirable
(D) successful
(E) retroactive

Solution➤ Here the correct answer is (A). The "although" signals a reversal: The critics had one opinion, but the curator had another. Since the curator wanted to acquire works by the artist, you can anticipate that the critics did not like his works. Therefore, the blank requires a word with negative connotations, and (A) provides this.

Example➤ After witnessing several violent altercations between natives, the anthropologist was forced to revise her earlier opinion that the tribes people were ----.

(A) peaceable
(B) quarrelsome
(C) insensitive
(D) prosperous
(E) unfriendly

Solution➤ The correct answer to this item is (A). The phrasing "was forced to revise" signals a reversal of ideas. So the word that fills the blank must contrast with "violent altercations," and "peaceful" or "friendly" immediately comes to mind. Choice (A) provides this idea.

Sometimes the logical structure of the sentence may not be entirely clear to you. Even so, you may be able to eliminate some answer choices.

Eliminate Any Choice That Results in a Phrase That Is Not Idiomatic.

Example➤ An advocate of consumer rights, Nader has spent much of his professional career attempting to ---- the fraudulent claims of American business.

(A) debunk
(B) immortalize
(C) reprove
(D) construe
(E) import

Solution➤ The correct answer to this item is (A). None of the other answer choices makes an idiomatic statement:

(A) debunk a claim(!)
(B) immortalize a claim(?)
(C) reprove a claim(?)
(D) construe a claim(?)
(E) import a claim(?)

Sentence completions are primarily a test of reading skills (understanding sentence structure), but they are also a test of vocabulary. This is particularly true of the last one or two items in a group.

For a Difficult Sentence Completion, Guess by Selecting a Difficult Vocabulary Word.

Example➤ Because of the ---- of the president of the company, the purchasing department was instructed to order furniture that had been specially reinforced.

(A) modesty
(B) corpulence
(C) inventiveness
(D) rationality
(E) imperiousness

Solution➤ If this is the last item in a group of sentence completions, you know that it is difficult item. And, as has been said, difficult items require difficult solutions. So it is not likely that the correct answer is (A), (C), or (D). The correct answer is almost surely (B) or (E). In fact, the correct response is (B): *Corpulence* means the condition of being excessively fat or obese.

PART

FIVE

Six Full-Length Practice Examinations

CONTENTS

Practice Examination 1

Answer Sheet

If a section has fewer questions than answer ovals, leave the extra ovals blank.

Section 1

1	A	B	C	D	E	11	A	B	C	D	E	21	A	B	C	D	E	31	A	B	C	D	E
2	A	B	C	D	E	12	A	B	C	D	E	22	A	B	C	D	E	32	A	B	C	D	E
3	A	B	C	D	E	13	A	B	C	D	E	23	A	B	C	D	E	33	A	B	C	D	E
4	A	B	C	D	E	14	A	B	C	D	E	24	A	B	C	D	E	34	A	B	C	D	E
5	A	B	C	D	E	15	A	B	C	D	E	25	A	B	C	D	E	35	A	B	C	D	E
6	A	B	C	D	E	16	A	B	C	D	E	26	A	B	C	D	E	36	A	B	C	D	E
7	A	B	C	D	E	17	A	B	C	D	E	27	A	B	C	D	E	37	A	B	C	D	E
8	A	B	C	D	E	18	A	B	C	D	E	28	A	B	C	D	E	38	A	B	C	D	E
9	A	B	C	D	E	19	A	B	C	D	E	29	A	B	C	D	E	39	A	B	C	D	E
10	A	B	C	D	E	20	A	B	C	D	E	30	A	B	C	D	E	40	A	B	C	D	E

Section 2

1	A	B	C	D	E	11	A	B	C	D	E	21	A	B	C	D	E	31	A	B	C	D	E
2	A	B	C	D	E	12	A	B	C	D	E	22	A	B	C	D	E	32	A	B	C	D	E
3	A	B	C	D	E	13	A	B	C	D	E	23	A	B	C	D	E	33	A	B	C	D	E
4	A	B	C	D	E	14	A	B	C	D	E	24	A	B	C	D	E	34	A	B	C	D	E
5	A	B	C	D	E	15	A	B	C	D	E	25	A	B	C	D	E	35	A	B	C	D	E
6	A	B	C	D	E	16	A	B	C	D	E	26	A	B	C	D	E	36	A	B	C	D	E
7	A	B	C	D	E	17	A	B	C	D	E	27	A	B	C	D	E	37	A	B	C	D	E
8	A	B	C	D	E	18	A	B	C	D	E	28	A	B	C	D	E	38	A	B	C	D	E
9	A	B	C	D	E	19	A	B	C	D	E	29	A	B	C	D	E	39	A	B	C	D	E
10	A	B	C	D	E	20	A	B	C	D	E	30	A	B	C	D	E	40	A	B	C	D	E

TEAR HERE

Section 3

1	A	B	C	D	E	6	A	B	C	D	E	11	A	B	C	D	E	16	A	B	C	D	E
2	A	B	C	D	E	7	A	B	C	D	E	12	A	B	C	D	E	17	A	B	C	D	E
3	A	B	C	D	E	8	A	B	C	D	E	13	A	B	C	D	E	18	A	B	C	D	E
4	A	B	C	D	E	9	A	B	C	D	E	14	A	B	C	D	E	19	A	B	C	D	E
5	A	B	C	D	E	10	A	B	C	D	E	15	A	B	C	D	E	20	A	B	C	D	E

Section 4

1	A	B	C	D	E	6	A	B	C	D	E	11	A	B	C	D	E	16	A	B	C	D	E
2	A	B	C	D	E	7	A	B	C	D	E	12	A	B	C	D	E	17	A	B	C	D	E
3	A	B	C	D	E	8	A	B	C	D	E	13	A	B	C	D	E	18	A	B	C	D	E
4	A	B	C	D	E	9	A	B	C	D	E	14	A	B	C	D	E	19	A	B	C	D	E
5	A	B	C	D	E	10	A	B	C	D	E	15	A	B	C	D	E	20	A	B	C	D	E

Section 5

1 (A) (B) (C) (D) (E)	6 (A) (B) (C) (D) (E)	11 (A) (B) (C) (D) (E)
2 (A) (B) (C) (D) (E)	7 (A) (B) (C) (D) (E)	12 (A) (B) (C) (D) (E)
3 (A) (B) (C) (D) (E)	8 (A) (B) (C) (D) (E)	13 (A) (B) (C) (D) (E)
4 (A) (B) (C) (D) (E)	9 (A) (B) (C) (D) (E)	14 (A) (B) (C) (D) (E)
5 (A) (B) (C) (D) (E)	10 (A) (B) (C) (D) (E)	15 (A) (B) (C) (D) (E)

Note: ONLY the answers entered on the grid are scored.
Handwritten answers at the top of the column are NOT scored.

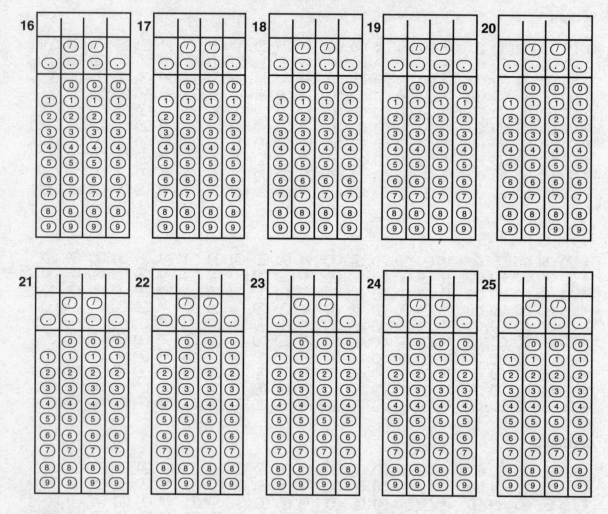

Grid-in items 16, 17, 18, 19, 20, 21, 22, 23, 24, 25 — each grid:

	(/)	(/)	
(.)	(.)	(.)	(.)
	(0)	(0)	(0)
(1)	(1)	(1)	(1)
(2)	(2)	(2)	(2)
(3)	(3)	(3)	(3)
(4)	(4)	(4)	(4)
(5)	(5)	(5)	(5)
(6)	(6)	(6)	(6)
(7)	(7)	(7)	(7)
(8)	(8)	(8)	(8)
(9)	(9)	(9)	(9)

Section 6

1 (A) (B) (C) (D) (E)	11 (A) (B) (C) (D) (E)	21 (A) (B) (C) (D) (E)	31 (A) (B) (C) (D) (E)
2 (A) (B) (C) (D) (E)	12 (A) (B) (C) (D) (E)	22 (A) (B) (C) (D) (E)	32 (A) (B) (C) (D) (E)
3 (A) (B) (C) (D) (E)	13 (A) (B) (C) (D) (E)	23 (A) (B) (C) (D) (E)	33 (A) (B) (C) (D) (E)
4 (A) (B) (C) (D) (E)	14 (A) (B) (C) (D) (E)	24 (A) (B) (C) (D) (E)	34 (A) (B) (C) (D) (E)
5 (A) (B) (C) (D) (E)	15 (A) (B) (C) (D) (E)	25 (A) (B) (C) (D) (E)	35 (A) (B) (C) (D) (E)
6 (A) (B) (C) (D) (E)	16 (A) (B) (C) (D) (E)	26 (A) (B) (C) (D) (E)	36 (A) (B) (C) (D) (E)
7 (A) (B) (C) (D) (E)	17 (A) (B) (C) (D) (E)	27 (A) (B) (C) (D) (E)	37 (A) (B) (C) (D) (E)
8 (A) (B) (C) (D) (E)	18 (A) (B) (C) (D) (E)	28 (A) (B) (C) (D) (E)	38 (A) (B) (C) (D) (E)
9 (A) (B) (C) (D) (E)	19 (A) (B) (C) (D) (E)	29 (A) (B) (C) (D) (E)	39 (A) (B) (C) (D) (E)
10 (A) (B) (C) (D) (E)	20 (A) (B) (C) (D) (E)	30 (A) (B) (C) (D) (E)	40 (A) (B) (C) (D) (E)

Practice Examination 1

SECTION 1

25 Questions • Time—30 minutes

Directions: Solve the following problems using any available space on the page for scratchwork. On your answer sheet fill in the choice which best corresponds to the correct answer.

Notes: The figures accompanying the problems are drawn as accurately as possible unless otherwise stated in specific problems. Again, unless otherwise stated, all figures lie in the same plane. All numbers used in these problems are real numbers. Calculators are permitted for this test.

Reference Information

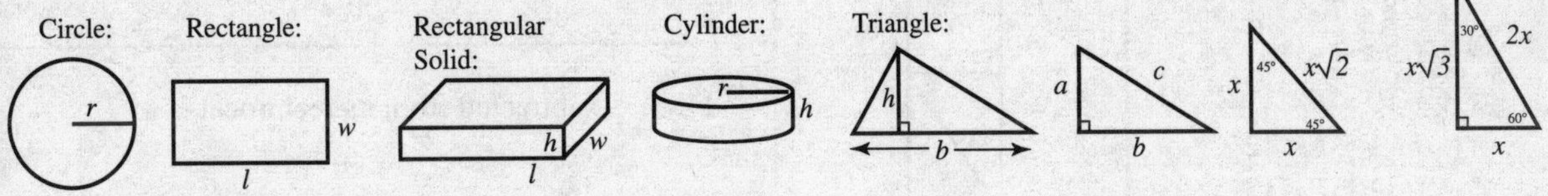

$C = 2\pi r$ $A = \pi r^2$ | $A = lw$ | $V = lwh$ | $V = \pi r^2 h$ | $A = \frac{1}{2}bh$ | $a^2 + b^2 = c^2$

The number of degrees of arc in a circle is 360.
The measure in degrees of a straight angle is 180.
The sum of the measures in degrees of the angles of a triangle is 180.

1. $0.2 \times 0.02 \times 0.002 =$

(A) .08
(B) .008
(C) .0008
(D) .00008
(E) .000008

2. If it costs \$1.30 a square foot to lay linoleum, what will be the cost of laying 20 square yards of linoleum? (3 ft. = 1 yd.)

(A) \$47.50
(B) \$49.80
(C) \$150.95
(D) \$249.00
(E) \$234.00

3. In a family of five, the heights of the members are 5 feet 1 inch, 5 feet 7 inches, 5 feet 2 inches, 5 feet, and 4 feet 7 inches. The average height is

(A) 4 feet $4\frac{1}{5}$ inches
(B) 5 feet
(C) 5 feet 1 inch
(D) 5 feet 2 inches
(E) 5 feet 3 inches

4. Three times the first of three consecutive odd integers is 3 more than twice the third. Find the third integer.

(A) 7
(B) 9
(C) 11
(D) 13
(E) 15

GO ON TO THE NEXT PAGE

5. In the figure below, the largest possible circle is cut out of a square piece of tin. The area, in square inches, of the remaining piece of tin is approximately

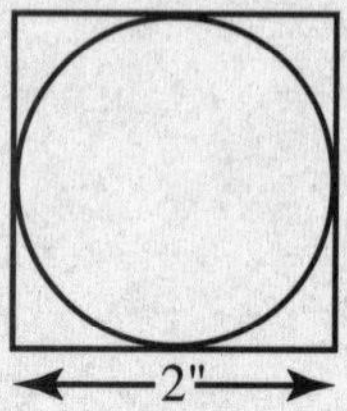

(A) .14
(B) .75
(C) .86
(D) 1.0
(E) 3.14

6. The figure shows one square inside another and a rectangle of diagonal T. The best approximation to the value of T, in inches, is given by which of the following inequalities?

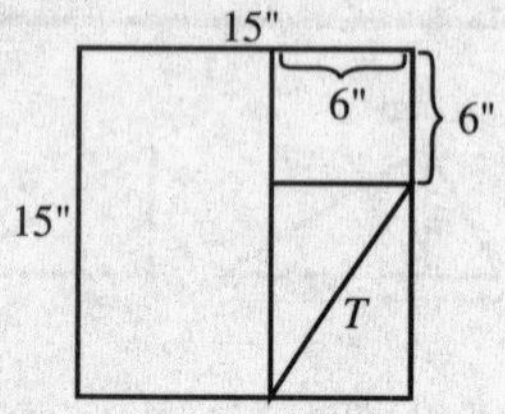

(A) $8 < T < 9$
(B) $9 < T < 10$
(C) $10 < T < 11$
(D) $11 < T < 12$
(E) $12 < T < 13$

7. If nails are bought at 35 cents per dozen and sold at 3 for 10 cents, the total profits on $5\frac{1}{2}$ dozen is

(A) 25 cents
(B) $27\frac{1}{2}$ cents
(C) $28\frac{1}{2}$ cents
(D) $31\frac{1}{2}$ cents
(E) 35 cents

8. The total number of eighths in $2\frac{3}{4}$ is

(A) 11
(B) 14
(C) 19
(D) 22
(E) 24

9. What is the difference when $-x-y$ is subtracted from $-x^2+2y$?

(A) x^2-x-3y
(B) $-3x+y$
(C) x^2+3y
(D) $-x^2+x-3y$
(E) $-x^2+x+3y$

10. If $2^m = 4x$ and $2^w = 8x$, what is m in terms of w?

(A) $w-1$
(B) $w+1$
(C) $2w-1$
(D) $2w+1$
(E) w^2

11. $1\frac{1}{4}$ subtracted from its reciprocal is

(A) $\frac{9}{20}$
(B) $\frac{1}{5}$
(C) $-\frac{1}{20}$
(D) $-\frac{1}{5}$
(E) $-\frac{9}{20}$

12. The total number of feet in x yards, y feet, and z inches is

(A) $3x+y+\frac{z}{12}$
(B) $12(x+y+z)$
(C) $x+y+z$
(D) $\frac{x}{36}+\frac{y}{12}+z$
(E) $x+3y+36z$

13. If five triangles are constructed having sides of the lengths indicated below, the triangle that will NOT be a right triangle is:

(A) 5, 12, 13
(B) 3, 4, 5
(C) 8, 15, 17
(D) 9, 40, 41
(E) 12, 15, 18

14. Of the following, the one that may be used correctly to compute $26 \times 3\frac{1}{2}$ is

(A) $(26 \times 30) + (26 \times \frac{1}{2})$
(B) $(20 \times 3) + (6 \times 3\frac{1}{2})$
(C) $(20 \times 3\frac{1}{2}) + (6 \times 3)$
(D) $(20 \times 3) + (26 \times \frac{1}{2}) + (6 \times 3\frac{1}{2})$
(E) $(26 \times \frac{1}{2}) + (20 \times 3) + (6 \times 3)$

15. In the figure, *ST* is tangent to the circle at *T*. *RT* is a diameter. If *RS* = 12, and *ST* = 8, what is the area of the circle?

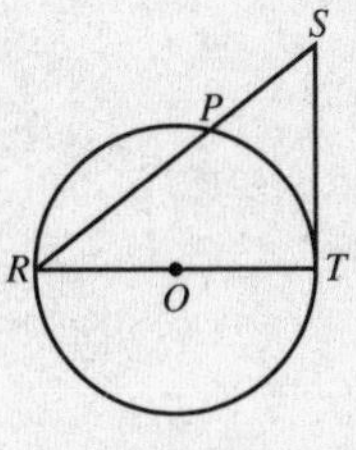

(A) 5π
(B) 8π
(C) 9π
(D) 20π
(E) 40π

16. What would be the marked price of an article if the cost was $12.60 and the gain was 10% of the selling price?

(A) $11.34
(B) $12.48
(C) $13.66
(D) $13.86
(E) $14.00

17. If the average weight of boys who are John's age and height is 105 lbs., and if John weighs 110% of the average, then how many pounds does John weigh?

(A) 110
(B) 110.5
(C) 112
(D) 114.5
(E) 115.5

18. The radius of a circle that has a circumference equal to the perimeter of a hexagon whose sides are each 22 inches long is closest in length to which of the following?

(A) 7
(B) 14
(C) 21
(D) 24
(E) 28

19. In the first year of the United States Stickball League, the Bayonne Bombers won 50% of their games. During the second season of the league the Bombers won 65% of their games. If there were twice as many games played in the second season as in the first, what percentage of the games did the Bombers win in the first two years of the league?

(A) 115%
(B) 60%
(C) 57.5%
(D) 55%
(E) It cannot be determined from the information given.

20. If the total weight of an apple is $\frac{4}{5}$ of its weight plus $\frac{4}{5}$ of an ounce, what is its weight in ounces?

(A) $1\frac{3}{5}$
(B) $3\frac{1}{2}$
(C) 4
(D) $4\frac{4}{5}$
(E) 5

GO ON TO THE NEXT PAGE

21. Nine playing cards from the same deck are placed as shown in the figure below to form a large rectangle of area 180 sq. in. How many inches are there in the perimeter of this large rectangle?

(A) 29
(B) 58
(C) 64
(D) 116
(E) 210

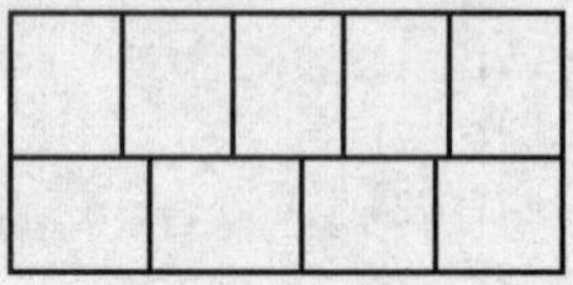

22. If each of the dimensions of a rectangle is increased 100%, the area is increased

(A) 100%
(B) 200%
(C) 300%
(D) 400%
(E) 500%

23. A recipe for a cake calls for $2\frac{1}{2}$ cups of milk and 3 cups of flour. With this recipe, a cake was baked using 14 cups of flour. How many cups of milk were required?

(A) $10\frac{1}{3}$

(B) $10\frac{3}{4}$

(C) 11

(D) $11\frac{3}{5}$

(E) $11\frac{2}{3}$

24. In the figure below, M and N are midpoints of the sides PR and PQ, respectively, of ΔPQR. What is the ratio of the area of ΔMNS to that of ΔPQR?

(A) 2 : 5
(B) 2 : 9
(C) 1 : 4
(D) 1 : 8
(E) 1 : 12

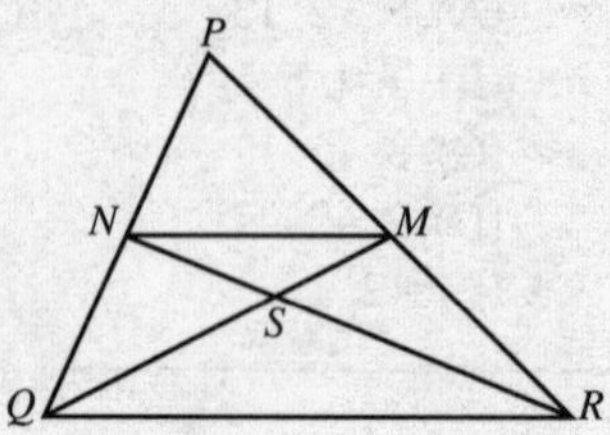

25. What is 10% of $\frac{1}{3}x$ if $\frac{2}{3}x$ is 10% of 60?

(A) .1
(B) .2
(C) .3
(D) .4
(E) .5

STOP

END OF SECTION 1. IF YOU HAVE ANY TIME LEFT, GO OVER YOUR WORK IN THIS SECTION ONLY. DO NOT WORK IN ANY OTHER SECTION OF THE TEST.

SECTION 2

30 Questions • Time—30 Minutes

Directions: Each of the following questions consists of an incomplete sentence followed by five words or pairs of words. Choose that word or pair of words which, when substituted for the blank space or spaces, *best* completes the meaning of the sentence and mark the letter of your choice on your answer sheet.

Example:

In view of the extenuating circumstances and the defendant's youth, the judge recommended ----.

(A) conviction (B) a defense
(C) a mistrial (D) leniency
(E) life imprisonment Ⓐ Ⓑ Ⓒ ● Ⓔ

1. Because the elder Johnson was regarded with much ---- by an appreciative public, the younger quite naturally received ----.

   (A) disdain..kudos
   (B) awe..respect
   (C) curiosity..familiarity
   (D) contemplation..abandonment
   (E) pleasantry..laughs

2. Her temperament was exceedingly ----, angry one minute but serene the next.

   (A) mercurial
   (B) steadfast
   (C) distraught
   (D) archetypal
   (E) circumspect

3. Traveling by automobile was ---- to him, but he thought nothing of bobsledding, which had been his ---- for many years.

   (A) tiresome..profession
   (B) tiring..outlet
   (C) harrowing..hobby
   (D) a threat..relief
   (E) exciting..fun

4. Perennial flowers such as irises remain ---- every winter, but they ---- in the spring.

   (A) fertile..wither
   (B) arable..congeal
   (C) dormant..burgeon
   (D) distended..contract
   (E) attenuated..rebound

5. The ---- customer was ---- by the manager's prompt action and apology.

   (A) pecuniary..appalled
   (B) weary..enervated
   (C) sedulous..consoled
   (D) intrepid..mortified
   (E) irate..mollified

GO ON TO THE NEXT PAGE

Directions: Each of the following questions consists of a capitalized pair of words followed by five pairs of words lettered A to E. The capitalized words bear some meaningful relationship to each other. Choose the lettered pair of words whose relationship is most similar to that expressed by the capitalized pair and mark its letter on your answer sheet.

Example:

DAY : SUN : :

(A) sunlight : daylight (B) ray : sun
(C) night : moon (D) heat : cold
(E) moon : star

Ⓐ Ⓑ ● Ⓓ Ⓔ

---

6. NOSE : HEAD : :

(A) hand : arm
(B) foot : toe
(C) eye : lid
(D) wrist : finger
(E) teeth : gums

7. WHEAT : GRAIN : :

(A) cow : beef
(B) orange : lime
(C) carrot : vegetable
(D) coconut : palm
(E) hamburger : steak

8. COTTAGE : CASTLE : :

(A) house : apartment
(B) puppy : dog
(C) dory : liner
(D) man : family
(E) poet : gentleman

9. OLD : ANTIQUE : :

(A) new : modern
(B) cheap : expensive
(C) useless : useful
(D) wanted : needed
(E) rich : valuable

10. POSSIBLE : PROBABLE : :

(A) likely : unlikely
(B) best : better
(C) willing : eager
(D) quick : fast
(E) frightened : worried

11. DIGRESS : RAMBLE : :

(A) muffle : stifle
(B) rust : weld
(C) introduce : conclude
(D) rest : stir
(E) find : explain

12. TIME : MINUTES : :

(A) month : calendar
(B) clock : faces
(C) race : laps
(D) yard : square
(E) arms : legs

13. MOUNTAIN : TUNNEL : :

(A) window : frame
(B) river : bridge
(C) door : handle
(D) charcoal : fire
(E) wall : window

Directions: Each passage below is followed by a set of questions. Read each passage, then answer the accompanying questions, basing your answers on what is stated or implied in the passage and in any introductory material provided. Mark the letter of your choice on your answer sheet.

Questions 14–21 are based on the following passage.

This passage is taken from the first book of short stories published by Willa Cather (1873–1947), better known for her novels of the western past such as O Pioneers! *For obvious reasons, "Paul's Case" is subtitled "A Study in Temperament."*

It was Paul's afternoon to appear before the faculty of the Pittsburgh High School to account for his various misdemeanors. He had been suspended a week ago, and his father had called at the Principal's office and confessed his perplexity about his son. Paul entered the faculty room suave and smiling. His clothes were a trifle outgrown, and the tan velvet on the collar of his open overcoat was frayed and worn; but for all that there was something of the dandy in him, and he wore an opal pin in his neatly knotted black four-in-hand, and a red carnation in his buttonhole. This latter adornment the faculty somehow felt was not properly significant of the contrite spirit befitting a boy under the ban of suspension.

Paul was tall for his age and very thin, with high, cramped shoulders and a narrow chest. His eyes were remarkable for a certain hysterical brilliancy, and he continually used them in a conscious, theatrical sort of way, peculiarly offensive in a boy. The pupils were abnormally large, as though he was addicted to belladonna, but there was a glassy glitter about them which that drug does not produce.

When questioned by the Principal as to why he was there Paul stated, politely enough, that he wanted to come back to school. This was a lie, but Paul was quite accustomed to lying; found it, indeed, indispensable for overcoming friction. His teachers were asked to state their respective charges against him, which they did with such a rancor and aggrievedness as evinced that this was not a usual case. Disorder and impertinence were among the offenses named, yet each of his instructors felt that it was scarcely possible to put into words the cause of the trouble, which lay in a sort of hysterically defiant manner of the boy's; in the contempt which they all knew he felt for them, and which he seemingly made not the least effort to conceal. Once, when he had been making a synopsis of a paragraph at the blackboard, his English teacher had stepped to his side and attempted to guide his hand. Paul had started back with a shudder and thrust his hands violently behind him. The astonished woman could scarcely have been more hurt and embarrassed had he struck at her. The insult was so involuntary and definitely personal as to be unforgettable. In one way and another he had made all of his teachers, men and women alike, conscious of the same feeling of physical aversion. In one class he habitually sat with his hand shading his eyes; in another he always looked out the window during the recitation; in another he made a running commentary on the lecture, with humorous intention.

His teachers felt this afternoon that his whole attitude was symbolized by his shrug and his flippantly red carnation flower, and they fell upon him without mercy, his English teacher leading the pack. He stood through it smiling, his pale lips parted over his white teeth. (His lips were constantly twitching, and he had a habit of raising his eyebrows that was contemptuous and irritating to the last degree.) Older boys than Paul had broken down and shed tears under that baptism of fire, but his set smile did not once desert him, and his only sign of discomfort was the nervous trembling of the fingers that toyed with the buttons of his overcoat, and an occasional jerking of the other hand that held his hat. Paul was always smiling, always glancing about him, seeming to feel that people might be watching him and trying to detect something. This conscious expression, since it was as far as possible from boyish mirthfulness, was usually attributed to insolence or "smartness."

14. The subtitle "A Study in Temperament" suggests that Cather wants to examine

(A) a certain type of character
(B) reactions under pressure
(C) how people change over time
(D) people and their settings
(E) inner rage

GO ON TO THE NEXT PAGE

15. Cather makes it clear in the first paragraph that the faculty of the high school

(A) are perplexed by Paul's actions
(B) find Paul's demeanor inappropriate
(C) cannot understand Paul's words
(D) want only the best for Paul
(E) are annoyed at Paul's disruption of their day

16. As it is used in lines 17 and 33–34, *hysterical* seems to imply

(A) hilarious
(B) raving
(C) uncontrolled
(D) frothing
(E) delirious

17. Cather implies that the most serious flaw Paul has is his

(A) refusal to sit up straight
(B) flippant sense of humor
(C) drug use
(D) failure to hide his contempt for others
(E) inability to complete his work

18. To keep the reader from sympathizing with the faculty, Cather compares them metaphorically to

(A) rabbits
(B) wolves
(C) dictators
(D) comedians
(E) warships

19. The word *smartness* (line 68) is used to mean

(A) wit
(B) intelligence
(C) impudence
(D) reasonableness
(E) resoucefulness

20. Which adjective does *not* describe Paul as Cather presents him here?

(A) paranoid
(B) defiant
(C) proud
(D) flippant
(E) candid

21. By the end of the selection, we find that the faculty

(A) resent and loathe Paul
(B) admire and trust Paul
(C) struggle to understand Paul
(D) are physically revolted by Paul
(E) may learn to get along with Paul

Questions 22–30 are based on the following passage.

Thomas Jefferson wrote in 1787 to his nephew, Peter Carr, a student at the College of William and Mary. Here, Jefferson gives advice about Peter's proposed course of study.

Paris, August 10, 1787

Dear Peter, ______ I have received your two letters of Decemb. 30. and April 18. and am very happy to find by them, as well as by letters from Mr. Wythe, that you have been so fortunate as to attract his notice and good will: I am sure you will find this to have been one of the more fortunate events of your life, as I have ever been sensible it was of mine. I inclose you a sketch of the sciences to which I would wish you to apply in such order as Mr. Wythe shall advise: I mention also the books in them worth your reading, which submit to his correction. Many of these are among your father's books, which you should have brought to you. As I do not recollect those of them not in his library, you must write to me for them, making out a catalogue of such as you think you shall have occasion for in 18 months from the date of your letter, and consulting Mr. Wythe on the subject. To this sketch I will add a few particular observations.

1. Italian. I fear the learning of this language will confound your French and Spanish. Being all of them degenerated dialects of the Latin, they are apt to mix in conversation. I have never seen a person speaking the three languages who did not mix them. It is a delightful language, but late events having rendered the Spanish more useful, lay it aside to prosecute that.

2. Spanish. Bestow great attention on this, and endeavor to acquire an accurate knowledge of it. Our future connections with Spain and Spanish America will render that language a valuable acquisition. The ancient history of a great part of America too is written in that language. I send you a dictionary.

3. Moral philosophy. I think it lost time to attend lectures in this branch. He who made us would have been a pitiful bungler if he had made the rules of our moral conduct a matter of science. For one man of science, there are thousands who are not. What would have become of them? Man was destined for society. His morality therefore was to be formed to this object. He was endowed with a sense of right and wrong merely relative to this. This sense is as much a part of his nature as the sense of hearing, seeing, feeling; it is the true foundation of morality. . . . The moral sense, or conscience, is as much a part of man as his leg or arm. It is given to all human beings in a stronger or weaker degree, as force of members is given them in a greater or less degree. . . .State a moral case to a ploughman and a professor. The former will decide it as well, and often better than the latter, because he has not been led astray by artificial rules. . . .

22. As he refers to Mr. Wythe, Jefferson seems to

(A) affect an air of condescension
(B) reject many of that man's opinions
(C) warn his nephew not to repeat his mistakes
(D) relive pleasant memories from his youth
(E) dispute his nephew's preconceived notions

23. Jefferson uses the word *sciences* (line 8) to mean

(A) Italian and Spanish only
(B) moral philosophy and the physical sciences
(C) school subjects in general
(D) the subjects treated in his father's books
(E) biology and chemistry

24. Jefferson's numbered points refer to

(A) subjects in order of importance
(B) academic courses
(C) languages of the world
(D) topics discussed in an earlier letter
(E) items from a catalogue

25. Jefferson uses the word *confound* (line 20) to mean

(A) fluster
(B) misunderstand
(C) curse
(D) muddle
(E) clarify

26. Jefferson encourages his nephew to study Spanish because

(A) it is related to Latin
(B) it will prove useful in international relations
(C) there are many good dictionaries available
(D) it will prove helpful in learning Italian
(E) it is the language of history

27. By "lost time" (line 32), Jefferson means

(A) wasted time
(B) the past
(C) missing time
(D) youth
(E) about time

28. Jefferson's main objection to attending lectures in moral philosophy is that

(A) it could be taught as well by farmers
(B) it is innate and cannot be taught
(C) it is better practiced outside school
(D) very few people understand what it means
(E) parents, not professors, should be the instructors

29. The example of the ploughman and the professor is used to

(A) illustrate the uselessness of education
(B) demonstrate the path to true knowledge
(C) explain the universality of morality
(D) define the nature of conscience
(E) disprove Mr. Wythe's theory of moral conduct

GO ON TO THE NEXT PAGE

30. Jefferson compares conscience to a physical limb of the body to show

(A) that it is natural and present in all human beings
(B) how easily we take it for granted
(C) that without it, men are powerless
(D) how mental and physical states are integrated
(E) what is meant by "the arm of the law."

STOP

END OF SECTION 2. IF YOU HAVE ANY TIME LEFT, GO OVER YOUR WORK IN THIS SECTION ONLY. DO NOT WORK IN ANY OTHER SECTION OF THE TEST.

SECTION 3

10 Questions • Time—15 Minutes

Directions: Solve the following problems using any available space on the page for scratchwork. On your answer sheet fill in the choice which best corresponds to the correct answer.

Notes: The figures accompanying the problems are drawn as accurately as possible unless otherwise stated in specific problems. Again, unless otherwise stated, all figures lie in the same plane. All numbers used in these problems are real numbers. Calculators are permitted for this test.

Reference Information

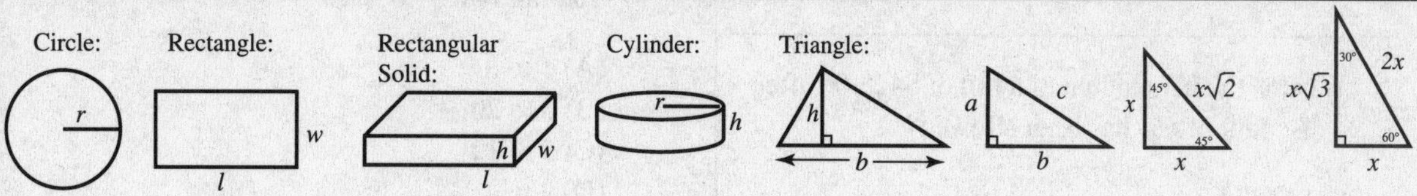

$C = 2\pi r$ $\quad A = lw \quad V = lwh \quad V = \pi r^2 h \quad A = \frac{1}{2}bh \quad a^2 + b^2 = c^2$

$A = \pi r^2$

The number of degrees of arc in a circle is 360.
The measure in degrees of a straight angle is 180.
The sum of the measures in degrees of the angles of a triangle is 180.

1. The total savings in purchasing thirty 13-cent lollipops for a class party at a reduced rate of \$1.38 per dozen is

   (A) \$.35
   (B) \$.38
   (C) \$.40
   (D) \$.45
   (E) \$.50

2. A gallon of water is equal to 231 cubic inches. How many gallons of water are needed to fill a fish tank that measures 11" high, 14" long, and 9" wide?

   (A) 6
   (B) 8
   (C) 9
   (D) 14
   (E) 16

3. The area of a right triangle is 12 square inches. The ratio of its legs is 2:3. Find the number of inches in the hypotenuse of this triangle.

   (A) $\sqrt{13}$
   (B) $\sqrt{26}$
   (C) $3\sqrt{13}$
   (D) $\sqrt{52}$
   (E) $4\sqrt{13}$

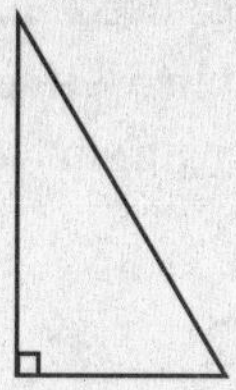

4. A rectangular block of metal weighs 3 ounces. How many pounds will a similar block of the same metal weigh if the edges are twice as large?

   (A) $\frac{3}{8}$
   (B) $\frac{3}{4}$
   (C) $1\frac{1}{2}$
   (D) 3
   (E) 24

GO ON TO THE NEXT PAGE

5. A college graduate goes to work for x dollars per week. After several months the company gives all the employees a 10% pay cut. A few months later the company gives all the employees a 10% raise. What is the college graduate's new salary?

(A) $.90x$
(B) $.99x$
(C) x
(D) $1.01x$
(E) $1.11x$

6. What is the net amount of a bill of $428.00 after a discount of 6% has been allowed?

(A) $432.62
(B) $430.88
(C) $414.85
(D) $412.19
(E) $402.32

7. A certain type of board is sold only in lengths of multiples of 2 feet, from 6 feet to 24 feet. A builder needs a larger quantity of this type of board in $5\frac{1}{2}$-foot lengths. For minimum waste, the lengths in feet to be ordered should be

(A) 6
(B) 12
(C) 18
(D) 22
(E) 24

8. A cube has an edge which is four inches long. If the edge is increased by 25%, then the volume is increased by approximately

(A) 25%
(B) 48%
(C) 73%
(D) 95%
(E) 122%

9. The ratio of $\frac{1}{4}$ to $\frac{3}{5}$ is

(A) 1 to 3
(B) 3 to 20
(C) 5 to 12
(D) 3 to 4
(E) 5 to 4

10. Which of the following numbers is the smallest?

(A) $\sqrt{3}$

(B) $\frac{1}{\sqrt{3}}$

(C) $\frac{\sqrt{3}}{3}$

(D) $\frac{1}{3}$

(E) $\frac{1}{3\sqrt{3}}$

STOP

END OF SECTION 3. IF YOU HAVE ANY TIME LEFT, GO OVER YOUR WORK IN THIS SECTION ONLY. DO NOT WORK IN ANY OTHER SECTION OF THE TEST.

SECTION 4

10 Questions • Time—15 Minutes

Directions: The two passages given below deal with a related topic. Following the passages are questions about the content of each passage or about the relationship between the two passages. Answer the questions based upon what is stated or implied in the passages and in any introductory material provided. Mark the letter of your choice on your answer sheet.

Questions 1–10 are based on the following passages:

It was long thought that an American could not be truly educated who had not been abroad. Nevertheless, by the nineteenth century, some writers were questioning this. These passages are by Henry David Thoreau (1817–1862), the transcendental philosopher best known for Walden; *and by Washington Irving (1783–1859), writer and humorist, who lived in Europe from 1815 until 1832.*

Passage 1—from Thoreau's* Journal *(1856)

When it was proposed to me to go abroad, rub off some rust, and *better my condition* in a worldly sense, I fear lest my life will lose some of its homeliness. If these fields and streams and woods, the phenomena of nature here, and the simple occupations of the inhabitants should cease to interest and inspire me, no culture or wealth would atone for the loss. I fear the dissipation that travelling, going into society, even the best, the enjoyment of intellectual luxuries, imply. If Paris is much in your mind, if it is more and more to you, Concord is less and less, and yet it would be a wretched bargain to accept the proudest Paris in exchange for my native village. At best, Paris could only be a school in which to learn to live here, a stepping-stone to Concord, a school in which to fit for this university. I wish so to live ever as to derive my satisfactions and inspirations from the commonest events, every-day phenomena, so that what my senses hourly perceive, my daily walk, the conversation of my neighbors, may inspire me, and I may dream of no heaven but that which lies about me. A man may acquire a taste for wine or brandy, and so lose his love for water, but should we not pity him?

Passage 2—from Irving's* The Sketch Book *(1820)

I visited parts of my own country; and had I been merely a lover of fine scenery, I should have felt little desire to seek elsewhere its gratification, for on no country have the charms of nature been more prodigally lavished. Her mighty lakes, like oceans of liquid silver, her mountains, with their bright aerial tints; her valleys, teeming with wild fertility; her tremendous cataracts, thundering in their solitudes; her boundless plains, waving with spontaneous verdure; her broad deep rivers, rolling in solemn silence to the ocean; her trackless forests, where vegetation puts forth all its magnificence; her skies, kindling with the magic of summer clouds and glorious sunshine;—no, never need an American look beyond his own country for the sublime and beautiful of natural scenery.

But Europe held forth the charms of storied and poetical association. There were to be seen the masterpieces of art, the refinements of highly cultivated society, the quaint peculiarities of ancient and local custom. My native country was full of youthful promise: Europe was rich in the accumulated treasures of age. Her very ruins told the history of times gone by, and every mouldering stone was a chronicle. I longed to wander over the scenes of renowned achievement, — to tread, as it were, in the footsteps of antiquity, — to loiter about the ruined castle, — to meditate on the falling tower, — to escape, in short, from the commonplace realities of the present, and lose myself among the shadowy grandeurs of the past.

I had, beside all this, an earnest desire to see the great men of the earth. We have, it is true, our great men in America: not a city but has an ample share of them. I have mingled among them in my time, and been almost withered by the shade into which they cast me; for there is nothing so baleful to a small man as the shade of a great one, particularly the great man of a city. But I was anxious to see the great men of Europe; for I had read in the works of great philosophers, that all animals degenerated in America, and man among the number. A great man in Europe, thought I, must therefore be as superior to a great man of America, as a peak of the Alps to a

GO ON TO THE NEXT PAGE

highland of the Hudson; and in this idea I was confirmed, by observing the comparative importance and swelling magnitude of many English travellers among us, who, I was assured, were very little people in their own country. I will visit this land of wonders, thought I, and see the gigantic race from which I am degenerated.

It has been either my good or evil lot to have my roving passion gratified. I have wandered through different countries, and witnessed many of the shifting scenes of life. I cannot say that I have studied them with the eye of a philosopher, but rather with the sauntering gaze with which humble lovers of the picturesque stroll from the window of one print-shop to another, caught sometimes by the delineations of beauty, sometimes by the distortions of caricature, and sometimes by the loveliness of landscape. As it is the fashion for modern tourists to travel pencil in hand, and bring home their portfolios filled with sketches, I am disposed to get up a few for the entertainment of my friends.

1. Thoreau uses the phrase "rub off some rust" (lines 1–2) to mean

   (A) rid himself of outdated conduct
   (B) shine up his coach-and-four
   (C) add sparkle to his life
   (D) improve his health
   (E) polish his manners

2. Thoreau's main objection to going abroad is that it

   (A) would interfere with his work
   (B) is something his neighbors cannot do
   (C) does not interest him
   (D) might reduce his enjoyment of home
   (E) could drive him to depravity

3. Thoreau uses the image of brandy and water to show

   (A) that excess drink is a hazard of travel abroad
   (B) that one is merely an amalgam of the other
   (C) how love of the exotic may destroy everyday pleasures
   (D) how easy it is to lose sight of the truth
   (E) that Americans are drunk on foreign travel

4. A reasonable title for Thoreau's paragraph might be

   (A) "Among the Fields and Streams"
   (B) "Society in Paris"
   (C) "Improving My Life"
   (D) "The Joys of Travel"
   (E) "A Simple Life is Best"

5. When Irving remarks on America's "spontaneous verdure" (line 31), he means that

   (A) the virtue of America lies in its impetuousness
   (B) the plains are carefully tended
   (C) wheatfields wave farewell
   (D) people in the Midwest are candid and friendly
   (E) vegetation grows wild

6. When Irving refers to "the gigantic race" (line 69), he is being

   (A) condescending
   (B) sympathetic
   (C) respectful
   (D) sarcastic
   (E) straightforward

7. The main idea of Irving's third paragraph can be stated,

   (A) "America has no great men"
   (B) "Europeans think they're great, and I want proof"
   (C) "Europeans are superior in all ways to Americans"
   (D) "Americans are just degenerated Europeans"
   (E) "Urban dwellers are influential"

8. Irving compares his jaunts through Europe to

   (A) a photographer snapping portraits
   (B) stones rotting in a monument
   (C) the words of a philosopher
   (D) an art-lover in a print shop
   (E) a cloud on a summer's day

9. Unlike Thoreau, Irving sees some value in

   (A) escaping the commonplace
   (B) contemplating everyday scenes of life
   (C) observing beautiful landscapes
   (D) studying the classics
   (E) sketching fellow tourists

10. Both Thoreau and Irving agree on the

   (A) need for European adventures
   (B) beauty of American scenery
   (C) richness of European history
   (D) both A and B
   (E) both B and C

STOP

END OF SECTION 4. IF YOU HAVE ANY TIME LEFT, GO OVER YOUR WORK IN THIS SECTION ONLY. DO NOT WORK IN ANY OTHER SECTION OF THE TEST.

SECTION 5

25 Questions • Time—30 Minutes

Directions: Solve the following problems using any available space on the page for scratchwork. On your answer sheet fill in the choice which best corresponds to the correct answer.

Notes: The figures accompanying the problems are drawn as accurately as possible unless otherwise stated in specific problems. Again, unless otherwise stated, all figures lie in the same plane. All numbers used in these problems are real numbers. Calculators are permitted for this test.

Reference Information

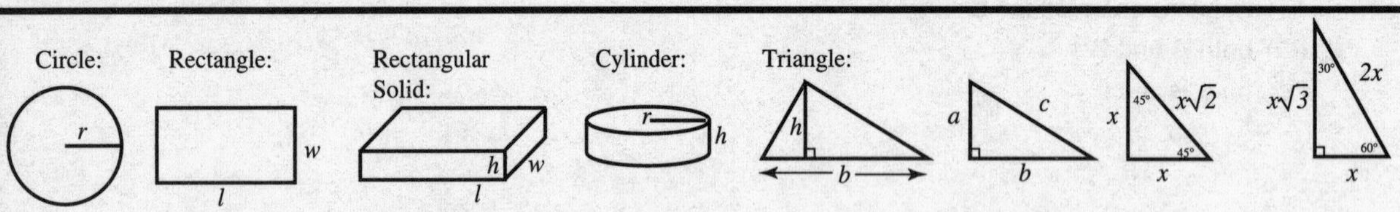

$C = 2\pi r$ $A = lw$ $V = lwh$ $V = \pi r^2 h$ $A = \frac{1}{2}bh$ $a^2 + b^2 = c^2$

$A = \pi r^2$

The number of degrees of arc in a circle is 360.
The measure in degrees of a straight angle is 180.
The sum of the measures in degrees of the angles of a triangle is 180.

Part 1: Quantitative Comparison Questions

Directions: For each of the following questions, two quantities are given—one in Column A, and the other in Column B. Compare the two quantities and mark your answer sheet as follows:

(A) if the quantity in Column A is greater
(B) if the quantity in Column B is greater
(C) if the two quantities are equal
(D) if the relationship cannot be determined from the information given.

Notes:

(1) Information concerning one or both of the compared quantities will be centered above the two columns for some items.
(2) Symbols that appear in both columns represent the same thing in Column A as in Column B.
(3) Letters such as *x*, *n*, and *k* are symbols for real numbers.

Examples

	Column A	*Column B*	*Answers*
	$a > 0$, $x > 0$		
E1.	$a - x$	$a + x$	(A) ● (C) (D)
E2.	The average of 17, 19, 21, 23	The average of 16, 18, 20, 22	● (B) (C) (D)

DO NOT MARK CHOICE (E) FOR THESE QUESTIONS. THERE ARE ONLY FOUR ANSWER CHOICES.

	Column A	Column B
1.	The number of sides in a polygon	The number of sides in a quadrilateral

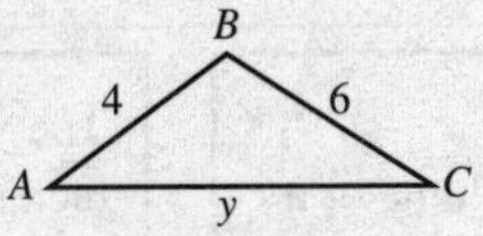

	Column A	Column B
2.	Length of side AC	10

$x(y + z) = 0$

$y = -z$

	Column A	Column B
3.	x	$y + z$

	Column A	Column B
4.	Area of a circle with a radius of $\frac{2r}{3}$	Area of a circle with a diameter of $\frac{4r}{3}$

$a \phi b = (a + b)(a - b)$

	Column A	Column B
5.	$2 \phi 2$	$-2 \phi -2$

p is an integer

	Column A	Column B
6.	The ratio of p to $(p + 1)$ if $5 < p < 10$	The ratio of p to $(p + 1)$ if $10 < p < 15$

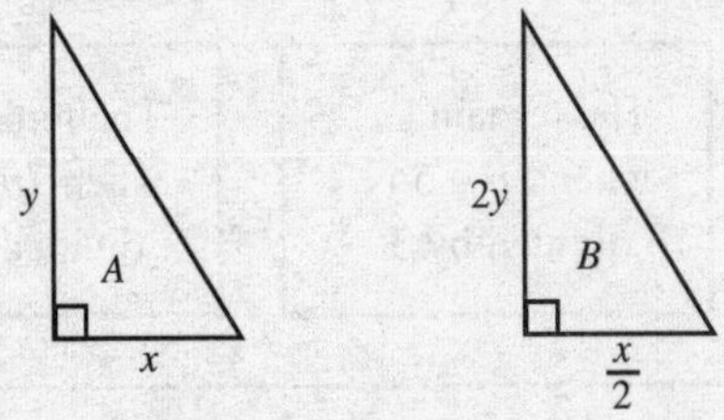

	Column A	Column B
7.	Area of triangle A	Area of triangle B

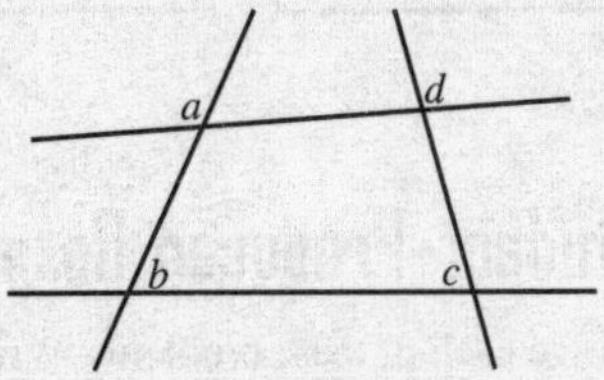

	Column A	Column B
8.	$\frac{a+b+c+d}{4}$	90

Questions 9 and 10 refer to the statement below.

In a sequence of N numbers the first is –1, the second is 1, the third is –2, the fourth is 2, and so on.

	Column A	Column B
9.	The ninth number times the eleventh number	The tenth number times the twelfth number
10.	The sum of the first through the fifth numbers	The sum of the sixth through the tenth numbers

$0 < k < 1$

	Column A	Column B
11.	$2k$	k^2

GO ON TO THE NEXT PAGE

	Column A	Column B
	p is a positive integer	
12.	The remainder when $3p + 5$ is divided by 3	The remainder when $7p + 8$ is divided by 7
13.	The number of prime numbers between 1 and 25	9

	Column A	Column B
	$\frac{m^4}{3} = 27$	
14.	m	4
	$s > 1$	
15.	The volume of a cube with a side of s	The volume of a rectangular solid with sides of s, $s + 1$, and $s - 1$

Part 2: Student-Produced Response Questions

Directions: Solve each of these problems. Write the answer in the corresponding grid on the answer sheet and fill in the ovals beneath each answer you write. Here are some examples.

Answer: $\frac{3}{4}$ (= .75; show answer either way)

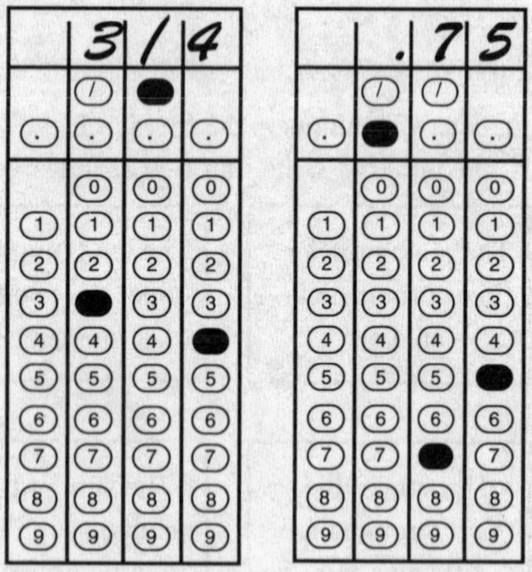

Note: A mixed number such as $3\frac{1}{2}$ must be gridded as 7/2 or as 3.5. If gridded as "3 1/2," it will be read as "thirty-one halves."

Answer: 325

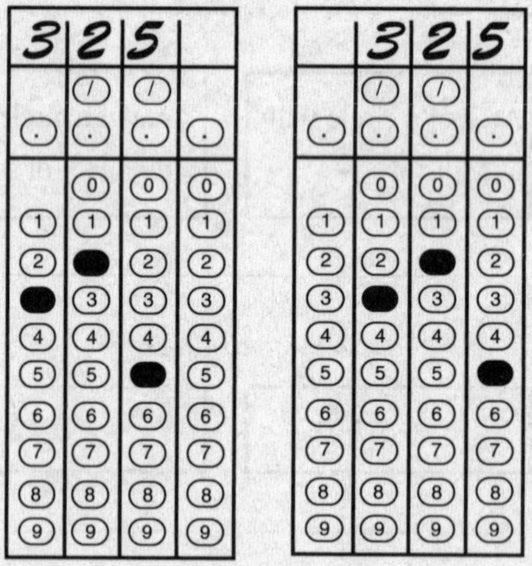

Note: Either position is correct.

16. The average temperatures for five days were 82°, 86°, 91°, 79°, and 91°. What is the mode for these temperatures?

17. If $-2x + 5 = 2 - (5 - 2x)$, what is the value of x?

18. In the figure below, $BA \perp AD$ and $CD \perp AD$. Using the values indicated in the figure, what is the area of polygon $ABCD$?

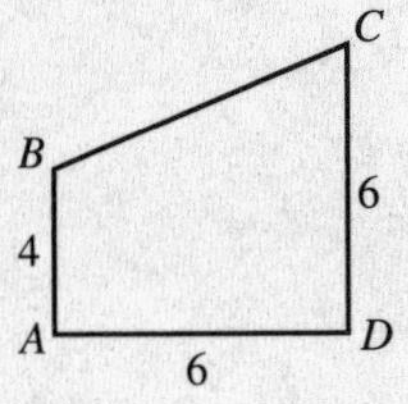

19. In the figure below, $AC = BC$. If $m\angle B = 50°$, what is the measure of $\angle ECD$? (Do not grid the degree symbol.)

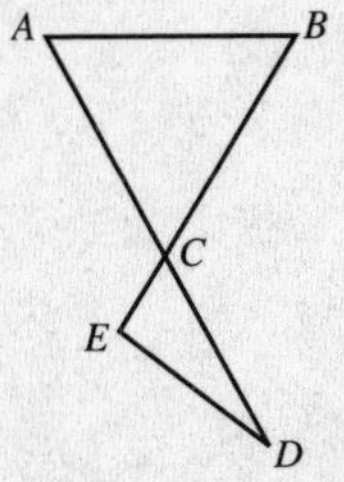

20. What is the value of $-m^2n^3$, when m = –2 and $n = -1$?

21. Given a square, a rectangle, a trapezoid, and a circle, if one of these figures is selected at random, what is the probability that the figure has four right angles?

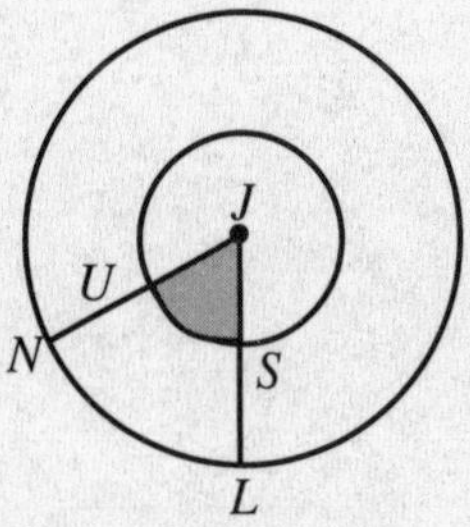

22. Given the concentric circles above, if radius JN is 3 times JU, then the ratio of the shaded area to the area of sector NJL is $1{:}b$. What is the value of b?

23. In a three-hour examination of 350 questions, there are 50 mathematical problems. If twice as much time should be allowed for each problem as for each of the other questions, how many minutes should be spent on the mathematical problems?

GO ON TO THE NEXT PAGE

24. In a pantry there are 28 cans of vegetables. Eight of these have labels with white lettering, 18 have labels with green lettering, and 8 have labels with neither white nor green lettering. How many cans have both white and green lettering?

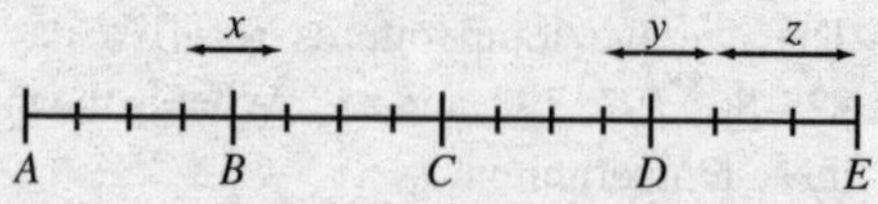

25. B, C and D divide AE into 4 equal parts. AB, BC, CD are divided into 4 equal parts as shown.

DE is divided into 3 equal parts as shown.

$$\frac{x+z}{y} =$$

STOP

END OF SECTION 5. IF YOU HAVE ANY TIME LEFT, GO OVER YOUR WORK IN THIS SECTION ONLY. DO NOT WORK IN ANY OTHER SECTION OF THE TEST.

SECTION 6

35 Questions • Time—30 Minutes

Directions: Each of the following questions consists of an incomplete sentence followed by five words or pairs of words. Choose that word or pair of words which, when substituted for the blank space or spaces, *best* completes the meaning of the sentence and mark the letter of your choice on your answer sheet.

Example:

In view of the extenuating circumstances and the defendant's youth, the judge recommended ----.

(A) conviction (B) a defense
(C) a mistrial (D) leniency
(E) life imprisonment Ⓐ Ⓑ Ⓒ ● Ⓔ

1. He dashed into the house, ran for the phone, and answered ----, tripping over the cord.

(A) hesitantly
(B) nobly
(C) soothingly
(D) distantly
(E) breathlessly

2. The criminal record of the witness caused the jury to ---- his testimony.

(A) affirm
(B) belie
(C) retract
(D) acquit
(E) discredit

3. Although the storm left the family ----, it could not ---- their spirits.

(A) discordant..raise
(B) moribund..drench
(C) destitute..dampen
(D) sodden..excite
(E) indolent..inhibit

4. By a stroke of luck the troops ----, avoiding a crushing ----.

(A) converged..blow
(B) prevailed..defeat
(C) diverged..siege
(D) retrenched..retreat
(E) interceded..assault

5. You must act with ---- if you want to buy your airline ticket before tomorrow's price increase.

(A) celerity
(B) clemency
(C) facility
(D) lassitude
(E) laxity

6. The ---- background music hinted of the dangers threatening the movie's heroine.

(A) trenchant
(B) ebullient
(C) sardonic
(D) portentous
(E) precocious

7. Nineteenth-century advances in women's rights were gradual and ----; years might separate one advance from the next.

(A) reticent
(B) onerous
(C) incumbent
(D) docile
(E) sporadic

8. Since several offices have been ---- across the street, the old directory is now ----.

(A) refurbished..adequate
(B) relocated..obsolete
(C) deployed..reserved
(D) transmuted..oblivious
(E) removed..upgraded

GO ON TO THE NEXT PAGE

9. The junta's promise of free elections was ----, a mere sop to world opinion.

(A) spurious
(B) contentious
(C) unctuous
(D) lucid
(E) presumptuous

10. The woman acted in a ---- manner, pretending not to notice the nearby celebrities.

(A) convivial
(B) doleful
(C) nonchalant
(D) cogent
(E) vicarious

11. His ---- manner served to hide the fact that he secretly indulged in the very vices he publicly ----.

(A) sedulous..dispelled
(B) sanctimonious..condemned
(C) dogmatic..espoused
(D) stentorian..prescribed
(E) candid..promulgated

12. Because of the ---- caused by the flood, living conditions in the area have ----; many people have lost all their belongings.

(A) trepidation..augmented
(B) morass..careened
(C) censure..abated
(D) devastation..deteriorated
(E) vertigo..ameliorated

13. Propaganda is a(n) ---- of truth, a mixture of half-truths and half-lies calculated to deceive.

(A) revision
(B) perversion
(C) dissension
(D) perception
(E) invasion

14. Though brilliantly presented, the report was ---- since the information on which it was based was erroneous.

(A) informative
(B) erudite
(C) laudable
(D) worthless
(E) verbose

Directions: Each of the following questions consists of a capitalized pair of words followed by five pairs of words lettered A to E. The capitalized words bear some meaningful relationship to each other. Choose the lettered pair of words whose relationship is most similar to that expressed by the capitalized pair and mark its letter on your answer sheet.

Example:

DAY : SUN ::

(A) sunlight : daylight
(B) ray : sun
(C) night : moon
(D) heat : cold
(E) moon : star

Ⓐ Ⓑ ● Ⓓ Ⓔ

15. LIBRARY : BOOKS : :

(A) hotel : children
(B) zoo : animals
(C) office : sales
(D) park : cars
(E) school : buses

16. TINY : HUGE : :

(A) small : little
(B) great : grand
(C) weak : strong
(D) sad : gloomy
(E) chaotic : confused

17. FRIGHTEN : SCARE : :

(A) question : ask
(B) look : see
(C) terrorize : startle
(D) brave : fear
(E) upset : calm

18. SEARCH : FIND : :

(A) fight : win
(B) obey : believe
(C) look : seek
(D) write : read
(E) listen : talk

19. DOOR : OPEN : :

(A) cap : remove
(B) knife : cut
(C) blackboard : erase
(D) gift : take
(E) car : speed

20. DASTARD : COWARDICE : :

(A) cipher : importance
(B) scoundrel : immorality
(C) native : intimacy
(D) refugee : nationality
(E) client : independence

21. TOE : FOOT : :

(A) elbow : wrist
(B) fist : hand
(C) shoe : sock
(D) pupil : eye
(E) arm : leg

22. STRUM : GUITAR : :

(A) tune : instrument
(B) tighten : drum
(C) polish : bugle
(D) pedal : organ
(E) hum : song

23. PUERILE : MATURITY : :

(A) pungent : poignancy
(B) poised : serenity
(C) obscure : clarity
(D) ostentatious : pretension
(E) profuse : extravagance

24. HURTLE : TOSS : :

(A) strike : tap
(B) throw : bite
(C) squelch : crush
(D) quarrel : squabble
(E) murmur : mumble

25. INFINITE : BOUNDS : :

(A) intangible : property
(B) kinetic : motion
(C) nebulous : clarity
(D) ponderous : bulk
(E) propitious : favor

GO ON TO THE NEXT PAGE

Directions: The reading passage below is followed by a set of questions. Read the passage and answer the accompanying questions, basing your answers on what is stated or implied in the passage. Mark the letter of your choice on your answer sheet.

Questions 26–35 are based on the following passage.

A major step forward in the history of the novel, Don Quixote *was penned by Miguel de Cervantes and first published in Spain in 1605. Driven mad by his constant perusal of tales of chivalry, Alonso Quijano changes his name to Don Quixote and rides off to seek adventure. This passage describes his First Expedition.*

Once these preparations were completed, he was anxious to wait no longer before putting his ideas into effect, impelled to this by the thought of the loss the world suffered by his delay, seeing the grievances there were to redress, the wrongs to right, the injuries to amend, and the debts to discharge. So, telling nobody of his intentions, and quite unobserved, one morning before dawn—it was on one of those sweltering July days—he armed himself completely, mounted Rocinante, put on his badly-mended headpiece, slung on his shield, seized his lance and went out into the plain through the back gate of his yard, pleased and delighted to see with what ease he had started on his fair design. But scarcely was he in open country when he was assailed by a thought so terrible that it almost made him abandon the enterprise he had just begun. For he suddenly remembered that he had never received the honor of knighthood, and so, according to the laws of chivalry, he neither could nor should take arms against any knight, and even if he had been knighted he was bound, as a novice, to wear plain armour without a device on his shield until he should gain one by his prowess. These reflections made him waver in his resolve, but as his madness outweighed any other argument, he made up his mind to have himself knighted by the first man he met, in imitation of many who had done the same, as he had read in the books which had so influenced him. As to plain armor, he decided to clean his own, when he had time, till it was whiter than ermine. With this he quieted his mind and went on his way, taking whatever road his horse chose, in the belief that in this lay the essence of adventure.

As our brand-new adventurer journeyed along, he talked to himself, saying: "Who can doubt that in ages to come, when the authentic story of my famous deeds comes to light, the sage who writes of them will say, when he comes to tell of my first expedition so early in the morning: 'Scarce had the ruddy Apollo spread the golden threads of his lovely hair over the broad and spacious face of the earth, and scarcely had the forked tongues of the little painted birds greeted with mellifluous harmony the coming of the rosy Aurora who, leaving the soft bed of her jealous husband, showed herself at the doors and balconies of the Manchegan horizon, when the famous knight, Don Quixote de la Mancha, quitting the slothful down, mounted his famous steed Rocinante and began to journey across the ancient and celebrated plain of Montiel'?" That was, in fact, the road that our knight actually took, as he went on: "Fortunate the age and fortunate the times in which my famous deeds will come to light, deeds worthy to be engraved in bronze, carved in marble and painted on wood, as a memorial for posterity. And you, sage enchanter, whoever you may be, to whose lot it falls to be the chronicler of this strange history, I beg you not to forget my good Rocinante, my constant companion on all my rides and journeys!" And presently he cried again, as if he had really been in love: "O Princess Dulcinea, mistress of this captive heart! You did me great injury in dismissing me and inflicting on me the cruel rigour of your command not to appear in your beauteous presence. Deign, lady, to be mindful of your captive heart, which suffers such griefs for love of you."

He went on stringing other nonsense on to this, all after the fashion he had learnt in his reading, and imitating the language of his books as best he could. And all the while he rode so slowly and the sun's heat increased so fast that it would have been enough to turn his brain, if he had had any.

26. The word *device* in line 21 probably means

(A) emblem
(B) tool
(C) gadget
(D) trick
(E) metal

27. The words that best describe the first speech Cervantes has Don Quixote make (lines 34–48) might be

(A) informative and deliberate
(B) profound and resolute
(C) dull and ill-conceived
(D) shocking and defamatory
(E) flowery and overwrought

28. What does Don Quixote mean when he says "quitting the slothful down" (line 46)?

(A) leaving the farm
(B) climbing into the saddle
(C) feeling happier and more energetic
(D) recovering from illness
(E) getting out of bed

29. The phrase "as if he had really been in love" (line 58) is used to illuminate Don Quixote's

(A) need for attention
(B) starved spirit
(C) dementia
(D) unhappy childhood
(E) inability to emote

30. Cervantes has his hero address his remarks to

(A) God
(B) the reader
(C) his horse
(D) a mythical historian and a princess
(E) an unknown knight

31. The last line of the selection reminds us that

(A) the story takes place in Spain
(B) Don Quixote is mad
(C) Rocinante has no destination in mind
(D) other knights have taken this same route
(E) the long day is about to end

32. We first suspect that Don Quixote is not quite the hero he seems when he recalls that

(A) he left his armor at home
(B) his horse is named Rocinante
(C) he is not a real knight
(D) Dulcinea holds him captive
(E) he started his journey with ease

33. According to the author, Don Quixote's speech is affected by

(A) romantic books he has read
(B) the language of seventeenth-century Spain
(C) letters received from Dulcinea
(D) the speeches of Alfonso X
(E) his night visions

34. Cervantes's opinion of the literature of his day seems to be that it is

(A) written by madmen
(B) argumentative and controversial
(C) not up to the standards of the previous century
(D) sentimental drivel
(E) derivative

35. The best word to describe Cervantes's feeling toward his hero might be

(A) disdainful
(B) revolted
(C) indifferent
(D) mocking
(E) appreciative

STOP

END OF SECTION 6. IF YOU HAVE ANY TIME LEFT, GO OVER YOUR WORK IN THIS SECTION ONLY. DO NOT WORK IN ANY OTHER SECTION OF THE TEST.

Practice Examination 1

Answer Key

Section 1: MATH

1. E	6. C	11. E	16. E	21. B
2. E	7. B	12. A	17. E	22. C
3. C	8. D	13. E	18. C	23. E
4. E	9. E	14. E	19. B	24. E
5. C	10. A	15. D	20. C	25. C

Section 2: VERBAL

1. B	7. C	13. B	19. C	25. D
2. A	8. C	14. A	20. E	26. B
3. C	9. A	15. B	21. A	27. A
4. C	10. C	16. C	22. D	28. B
5. E	11. A	17. D	23. C	29. C
6. A	12. C	18. B	24. B	30. A

Section 3: MATH

1. D	3. D	5. B	7. D	9. C
2. A	4. C	6. E	8. D	10. E

Section 4: VERBAL

1. C	3. C	5. E	7. B	9. A
2. D	4. E	6. D	8. D	10. B

Section 5: MATH

Part 1

1. D	4. C	7. C	10. B	13. C
2. B	5. C	8. C	11. A	14. B
3. D	6. B	9. C	12. A	15. A

Part 2

16. 91	18. 30	20. 4	22. 9	24. 6
17. 2	19. 80	21. $\frac{1}{2} = .5$	23. 45	25. 2

Section 6: VERBAL

1. E	8. B	15. B	22. D	29. C
2. E	9. A	16. C	23. C	30. D
3. C	10. C	17. A	24. A	31. B
4. B	11. B	18. A	25. C	32. C
5. A	12. D	19. B	26. A	33. A
6. D	13. B	20. B	27. E	34. D
7. E	14. D	21. D	28. E	35. D

Practice Examination 1

Explanatory Answers

Note: A [calculator icon] following a math answer explanation indicates that a calculator could be helpful in solving that particular problem.

Section 1

1. **(E)** Count the number of decimal places in the terms to be multiplied; this adds up to 6. It should be clear that the last number must be 8. There must be six decimal places accounted for and thus there must be five zeros in front of the 8.

2. **(E)** 20 square yards = 180 square feet. At \$1.30 per square foot, it will cost \$234.00.

3. **(C)**
   5 ft. 1 in.
   5 ft. 7 in.
   5 ft. 2 in.
   5 ft.
   4 ft. 7 in.
   24 ft. 17 in., or 25 ft. 5 in.

   Average = $\frac{25 \text{ ft. } 5 \text{ in.}}{5}$ = 5 ft. 1 in.

4. **(E)** Let x = first integer
   $x + 2$ = second integer
   $x + 4$ = third integer
   $3(x) = 3 + 2(x + 4)$
   $3x = 3 + 2x + 8$
   $x = +11$
   The third integer is 15.

5. **(C)** Area of square = $2^2 = 4$
   Area of circle = $\pi \cdot 1^2 = \pi$
   Difference = $4 - \pi = 4 - 3.14 = .86$

6. **(C)** The right triangle of which T is the hypotenuse has legs that are obviously 6 inches and 9 inches.
   Hence, $T^2 = 6^2 + 9^2$
   $T^2 = 36 + 81 = 117$
   $T = \sqrt{117}$
   or $10 < T < 11$

7. **(B)** $5\frac{1}{2}$ dozen nails are bought for $5\frac{1}{2}$ dozen × 35 cents per dozen = 192.5 cents. There are 66 nails in $5\frac{1}{2}$ dozen and 66 ÷ 3 = 22 sets sold at 10 cents per set, so 22 sets × 10 cents per set = 220 cents. The profit is 220 – 192.5 = $27\frac{1}{2}$ cents.

8. **(D)** $2\frac{3}{4} \div \frac{1}{8} = \frac{11}{4} \div \frac{1}{8} = \frac{11}{4} \times 8 = 22.$

9. **(E)** $-x^2 + 2y - (-x-y)$
   $= -x^2 + 2y + x + y$
   $= -x^2 + x + 3y$

10. **(A)** Multiply the equation $2^m = 4x$ by 2
    $2(2^m) = 2(4x)$
    $2^{m+1} = 8x = 2^w$
    $\therefore w = m + 1$ and $m = w - 1$

11. **(E)** The reciprocal of $1\frac{1}{4}$ is $\frac{4}{5}$. $\frac{4}{5} - \frac{5}{4} = \frac{16}{20} - \frac{25}{20} = -\frac{9}{20}$

12. **(A)** x yards = $3x$ feet; y feet = y feet; z inches = $\frac{z}{12}$ feet. Therefore, x yards + y feet + z inches = $3x$ feet + y feet + $\frac{z}{12}$ feet, or $3x + y + \frac{z}{12}$ feet.

13. **(E)** If a triangle is a right triangle, then the squares of two sides will add up to the square of the hypotenuse. $12^2 = 144$. $15^2 = 225$. $18^2 = 324$. $144 + 225 \neq 324$.

14. **(E)** $26 \times 3\frac{1}{2} = (26 \times 3) + (26 \times \frac{1}{2})$ by the distributive law. $26 \times 3 = (20 \times 3) + (6 \times 3)$ by the distributive law. Therefore, $26 \times 3\frac{1}{2} = (26 \times \frac{1}{2}) + (20 \times 3) + (6 \times 3)$.

15. **(D)** Angle T is a right angle. By the Phythagorean Theorem, $RT^2 + ST^2 = RS^2$. Since $RS = 12$ and $ST = 8$, RT must equal $\sqrt{80}$ so, $OT = \frac{1}{2}\sqrt{80}$. By the formula for the area of a circle ($A = \pi r^2$),

area equals (π) $\left(\frac{1}{2}\right)^2$ $\left(\sqrt{80}\right)^2$, or (π) $\left(\frac{1}{4}\right)$ (80), which equals 20π.

16. **(E)** If the gain was 10% of the selling price, then \$12.60 was 90%. Therefore, 100% was equal to \$14.00.

17. **(E)** If John weighs 110% of the average, he weighs 10% more than the average weight of 105 lbs., or $.10 \times 105 = 10.5$ lbs. John weighs $105 + 10.5 = 115.5$ lbs.

18. **(C)** A hexagon with 22-inch sides has a perimeter of 6×22, or 132 inches.
$$C = 2\pi r$$
$$132 = 2\pi r$$
$$132 = 2(3.14)r$$
$$132 = 6.28r$$
$$21.02 = r$$

19. **(B)** We are not told how many games the Bombers played, but we know that the ratio of the number of games played in the 2nd year to that in the first is 2 : 1. Problems like this can be solved by plugging in real numbers. Let's say that there were 50 games in the first year, so they won 25. In the second year there were 100 games, so they won 65 games. Altogether they won 90 out of 150 games, and this fraction can be reduced to 3 out of 5, or 60%.

20. **(C)** Let x = weight in ounces of the apple.
Then $x = \frac{4}{5}x + \frac{4}{5}$
$$5x = 4x + 4$$
$$x = 4$$

21. **(B)** Let L = length of each card and W = width of each card. Then $5W$ = length of large rectangle and $L + W$ = width of large rectangle. Length of large rectangle = $4L$. Thus, $5W = 4L$.
$$5W(L + W) = 180, \text{ also}$$
$$9LW = 180 \text{ or } LW = 20$$
$$5LW + 5W^2 = 180$$
$$LW + W^2 = 36$$
$$20 + W^2 = 36$$
$$W^2 = 16$$
$$W = 4 \text{ and } L = 5$$
Thus, perimeter $= 2[5W + (L + W)]$
$= 2\,(20 + 9) = 58$

22. **(C)** If each of the dimensions is doubled, the area of the new rectangle is four times the size of the original one. The increase is three times, or 300%.

23. **(E)** This is a proportion of $2\frac{1}{2} : 3 = x : 14$; $x = \frac{35}{3}$, or $11\frac{2}{3}$.

24. **(E)** $MN = \frac{1}{2}QR$ and MN is parallel to QR. Since $\Delta MNS \sim \Delta QSR$, it follows that the altitude from S to $NM = \frac{1}{2}$ the altitude from S to QR. Hence, the altitude from S to $NM = \frac{1}{3}$ of $\frac{1}{2}$ the altitude from P to QR, or $\frac{1}{6}$ of this altitude (h).
Thus $\Delta NMS = \frac{1}{2} \bullet MN \bullet$ alt. from S to MN
$= \frac{1}{2}(\frac{1}{2}QR)(\frac{1}{6}h)$
$= \frac{1}{2}(\frac{1}{12}\ QR \bullet h) = \frac{1}{12}(\frac{1}{2} \bullet QR \bullet h)$.
But $\frac{1}{2} \bullet QR \bullet h = \Delta PQR$
Hence, $\Delta NMS = \frac{1}{12} \bullet \Delta PQR$
Ratio is 1:12

25. **(C)** Given $\frac{2}{3}x = \frac{1}{10}(60) = 6$
$$\therefore x = 9$$
Find $\frac{1}{10}\left(\frac{1}{3}x\right) = \frac{1}{30}(9) = \frac{3}{10} = .3$

Section 2

1. **(B)** An "appreciative public" is likely to give the elder Johnson's son *respect.*

2. **(A)** A person who is angry one minute but serene the next is said to be *mercurial* (changeable).

3. **(C)** Irony or paradox is indicated by the phrase "but he thought nothing of." It is ironic that automobile travel should be *harrowing,* or frightening, to someone used to bobsledding, a dangerous sport.

4. **(C)** A perennial flower is one that blooms every year. In the winter it lies *dormant* (inactive), but the following spring it *burgeons* (sprouts) anew.

5. **(E)** A manager who apologizes must be dealing with an *irate* (angry) customer. As a result of the apology, the customer was *mollified* (soothed and pacified).

6. **(A)** The *nose* is part of the *head,* and the *hand* a part of the *arm.*

7. **(C)** *Wheat* is a type of *grain; carrot* is a type of *vegetable.* Both are foodstuffs.

8. **(C)** A *cottage* is a small house; a *castle* is a large and luxurious one. A *dory* is a modest rowboat; a *liner* is a large and luxurious passenger ship.

9. **(A)** Something *antique* is necessarily *old*, and something *modern* is necessarily *new.*

10. **(C)** Something that is *possible* might be, but is not necessarily, *probable.* Someone who is *willing* might be, but is not necessarily *eager.*

11. **(A)** To *digress* from a topic is to *ramble,* and to *muffle* a sound is to *stifle* it. The relationship is one of synonyms.

12. **(C)** *Time* is measured in *minutes* as a *race* is measured in *laps.*

13. **(B)** A *tunnel* is a roadway through a *mountain* and a *bridge* is a roadway over a *river.*

14. **(A)** Only the first choice explains the subtitle. The other choices may be included under the idea "A Study in Temperament," but they are not the main idea.

15. **(B)** The faculty may be perplexed (A), but the first paragraph focuses on their feeling that Paul's dress and behavior are not properly contrite.

16. **(C)** Paul seems to be unable to control his odd mannerisms, but he is not actually frenzied, as (B), (D), or (E) would suggest.

17. **(D)** It is this flaw that has landed Paul in trouble, as evidenced in lines 36 and 46–50.

18. **(B)** The faculty "fell upon him without mercy, his English teacher leading the pack" (lines 53–54). The comparison is to a pack of wolves.

19. **(C)** All of these choices could mean "smartness," but only *impudence* makes sense in context.

20. **(E)** There is evidence for every other choice in the descriptions of Paul's actions. The point is made in lines 25–26 that Paul often lies; he cannot be called "candid."

21. **(A)** Paul is physically revolted by the faculty, not *vice versa* (D). The faculty's attack on Paul indicates their hatred for him.

22. **(D)** Jefferson is "ever sensible" that meeting and attracting the good will of Mr. Wythe was "one of the most fortunate events" of his life (lines 5–7).

23. **(C)** Jefferson uses the word *sciences* as a general term covering Italian, Spanish, and moral philosophy. Clearly, he is referring to school subjects in general.

24. **(B)** The numbered points are (1) Italian, (2) Spanish, and (3) Moral philosophy—courses that Peter proposes taking.

25. **(D)** This is part of Jefferson's argument that since Italian, French, and Spanish are related, people mix or muddle them in conversation.

26. **(B)** Jefferson says "Our future connections with Spain and Spanish America will render that language a valuable acquisition."

27. **(A)** Point 3 is all about the fact that no one needs to study moral philosophy. In other words, to study it is a waste of time.

28. **(B)** Lines 33–35 explain this reasoning.

29. **(C)** Jefferson's point is that either one is as likely to decide a moral argument fairly; morality is bred into everyone and does not require an advanced degree.

30. **(A)** Choices (B), (C), and (D) may be true, but Jefferson only covers the first point, that morality is as natural as an arm or leg, and is given to all "in a stronger or weaker degree" (lines 44–45).

Section 3

1. **(D)** Buying the lollipops singly would cost: $30 \text{ pops} \times \$.13 \text{ per pop} = \$3.90$. The reduced rate is \$1.38 per dozen. Thirty pops is $2\frac{1}{2}$ dozen, so the cost for 30 pops is $\$1.38 \times 2.5 = \$3.45$. The savings with this reduced rate is $\$3.90 - \$3.45 = \$.45$.

2. **(A)** The volume of the fish tank is 11" × 14" × 9" = 1,386 cu. in. The amount needed to fill the tank is 1,386 cu. in ÷ 231 cu. in./gal. = 6 gallons.

3. **(D)** Let legs be $2x$ and $3x$.
Then $(2x)^2 + (3x)^2 = (\text{hypotenuse})^2$ and

$$\tfrac{1}{2} \bullet 2x \bullet 3x = 12$$
$$3x^2 = 12$$
$$x^2 = 4$$
$$x = 2$$

Thus, $4^2 + 6^2 = (\text{hypotenuse})^2$

$$16 + 36 = 52$$
$$\text{hypotenuse} = \sqrt{52}$$

4. **(C)** The weights are proportional to the volumes, and the volumes vary as the cubes of their dimensions. If the edges are doubled, the volume becomes $2^3 = 8$ times as large. Hence, the weight $= 8 \times 3 = 24$ ounces $= 1\frac{1}{2}$ lbs.

5. **(B)** The graduate starts at x dollars per week. After the pay cut the graduate receives 90% of the original salary. The 10% raise adds 9% to the salary (10% of 90%), so the new salary is $.99x$.

6. **(E)** \$428.00 – (.06) \$428.00 = \$402.32

7. **(D)** There will be no waste if the lengths are multiples of $5\frac{1}{2}$ feet. This occurs between 6 and 24 feet only for 22 feet.

8. **(D)** A cube with an edge of 4 has a volume of 64 cubic inches. A cube with an edge of 5 has a volume of 125 cubic inches. The percentage increase is $\frac{61}{64}$, or approximately 95%.

9. **(C)** $\frac{1}{4} : \frac{3}{5} = \frac{1}{4} \div \frac{3}{5}$

$$= \frac{1}{4} \times \frac{5}{3}$$
$$= \frac{5}{12}$$
$$= 5 : 12$$

10. **(E)** $\sqrt{3} = 1.73$ (approx.)

$$\frac{1}{\sqrt{3}} = \frac{\sqrt{3}}{3} = \frac{1.73}{3} = .57$$
$$\frac{\sqrt{3}}{3} = \frac{1.73}{3} = .57$$
$$\frac{1}{3} = .3333.....$$
$$\frac{1}{3\sqrt{3}} = \frac{\sqrt{3}}{3 \times 3} = \frac{\sqrt{3}}{9} = \frac{1.73}{9} = .19$$

Thus, the smallest is $\frac{1}{3\sqrt{3}}$

Section 4

1. **(C)** This phrase is used to show that those who urge Thoreau to go abroad mean that he has become rusted in some place; he needs to add some excitement to his life.

2. **(D)** This is the main idea of the passage.

3. **(C)** The last sentence of Thoreau's entry contains the thought that we should pity a man who loses his love for water as he acquires a taste for brandy; in other words, that one who gives up the everyday pleasures of life is to be pitied.

4. **(E)** This is a fairly accurate summary of Thoreau's main themes.

5. **(E)** The paragraph deals with the wild beauty of the American landscape. The word *spontaneous* connotes a wildness in the "verdure" of the plains.

6. **(D)** Irving is poking fun at those Europeans who believe that Americans are merely degenerated Europeans.

7. **(B)** This paragraph is tongue-in-cheek. Irving has met "many English travellers" who acted pompous and important but really were undistinguished at home; this makes him think that great men of Europe must be truly amazing.

8. **(D)** This comparison comes in lines 74–76. Irving gives the impression of wandering aimlessly through Europe, being delighted by anything that catches his eye.

9. **(A)** Whereas Thoreau longs to cling to the commonplace, Irving wishes at times to "escape. . . from the commonplace realities of the present, and lose myself among the shadowy grandeurs of the past" (lines 49–51).

10. **(B)** See lines 4–8 in Thoreau and paragraph 1 in Irving.

Section 5

Part 1

1. **(D)** Since a polygon can have three or more sides, an answer is not possible.

2. **(B)** No one side of a triangle can be greater than or equal to the sum of the other two sides.

3. **(D)** If y is the opposite of z, then we know that $y + z$ is equal to 0. We do not, however, know the value of x.

4. **(C)** The radius is equal to one-half the diameter. The circle in Column B has a diameter of $\frac{4r}{3}$, and $\frac{1}{2}$ of that is $\frac{2r}{3}$. Therefore, the columns are equal.

5. **(C)** Both columns are equal to 0.

6. **(B)** The largest fraction that Column A could be is $\frac{9}{10}$. The smallest fraction that Column B could be is $\frac{11}{12}$. Thus, Column B is always bigger.

7. **(C)** Triangle *B* has a height that is double that of Triangle *A*; it has a base that is half that of Triangle *A*. This will result in the two triangles having the same area.

8. **(C)** Since the opposite angles are equal, angles *a* and *d* can be moved inside the quadrilateral. All quadrilaterals contain 360 degrees. 360 divided by 4 is 90.

9. **(C)** In this problem it is easy to figure out that the ninth through twelfth numbers would be −5, 5, −6, and 6. $(-5) \times (-6) = 30$ and $5 \times 6 = 30$.

10. **(B)** Column A would equal −3. Column B would equal 3.

11. **(A)** If a fraction between 0 and 1 is squared, the result is always smaller than the original number.

12. **(A)** The question can be simplified. When you divide 5 by 3 the remainder is 2. When you divide 8 by 7, the remainder is 1.

13. **(C)** The prime numbers would be 2, 3, 5, 7, 11, 13, 17, 19, and 23.

14. **(B)** If you multiply both sides by 3, you find that $m^4 = 81$. Therefore, m can equal 3 or −3. In either case, m is less than 4.

15. **(A)** This is easily solved by substitution. Make s equal to 2. The volume of a cube with a side of 2 is 8. The volume of the rectangular block in Column B is $2 \times 1 \times 3 = 6$.

Part 2

16. The mode is the data element with the greatest frequency.
mode = 91

17.
$$\begin{aligned} -2x + 5 &= 2 - (5 - 2x) \\ &= 2 - 5 + 2x \\ &= -3 + 2x \\ -2x + 5 &= -3 + 2x \\ +2x \quad &= \quad +2x \\ \hline 5 &= -3 + 4x \\ +3 &= +3 \\ \hline 8 &= 4x \\ x &= 2 \end{aligned}$$

18.

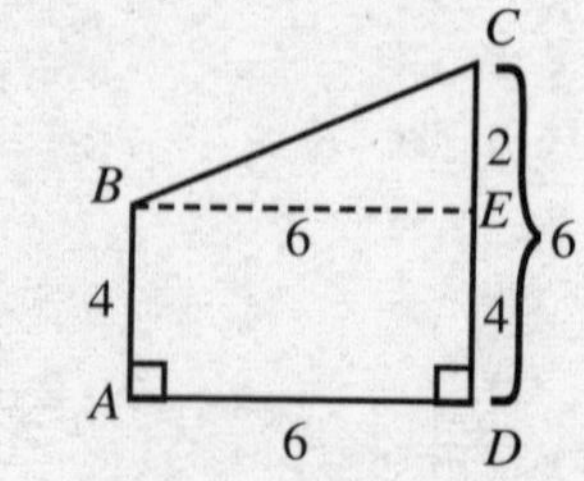

Area of rectangle *ABED*:
$bh = 6(4) = 24$

Area of ΔBEC:

$\frac{1}{2}bh = \frac{1}{2}(6)(2) = 6$

Area of polygon = 24 + 6 = 30

19. 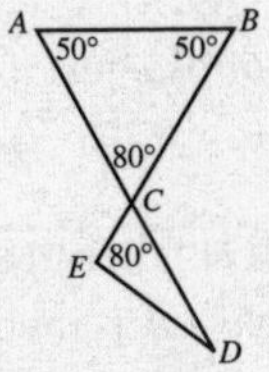

If $AC = BC$

then $m\angle A = m\angle B = 50°$

In ΔABC

$m\angle ACB = 180° - (m\angle A + m\angle B)$

$m\angle ACB = 80°$

$m\angle ACB = m\angle ECD$ (vertical angles)

$m\angle ECD = 80°$

20. $-m^2n^3 = -(-2)^2(-1)^3$

$= -(4)(-1) = 4$

21.

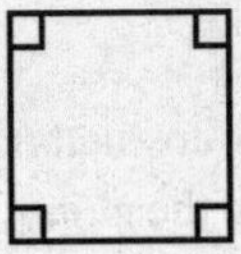

The square has four right angles.

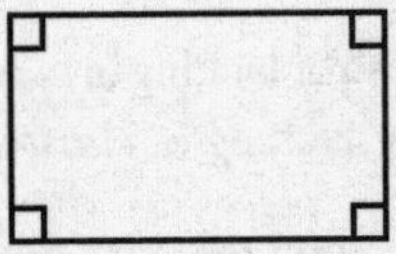

The rectangle has four right angles.

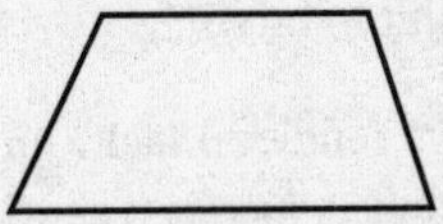

The trapezoid does not have four right angles.

The circle does not have four right angles.

Probability of four right angles

$= \frac{\text{number of successes}}{\text{number of possibilities}} = \frac{2}{4} = \frac{1}{2} = .5$

22. 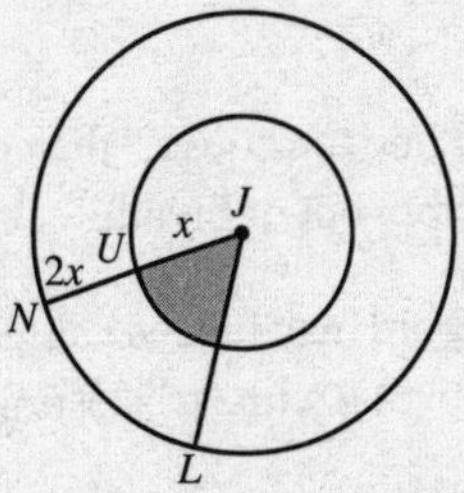

If $JU = x$, then $JN = 3x \therefore NU = 2x$. The area of the smaller circle $= \pi(x)^2 = \pi x^2$. The area of the larger circle $= \pi(3x)^2 = 9x^2(\pi)$
$= 9\pi x^2$.

$\frac{\text{Area } JUS}{\text{Area } NJL} = \frac{\pi x^2}{9\pi x^2} = \frac{1}{9} = 1{:}9 = 1{:}b$

$\therefore b = 9$

23. Letting m be the time per regular question, $2m$ is the time per math problem. $300m$ is the total time for all the regular questions and $50(2m)$ is the total time for all the math problems. Since the exam is 3 hours, or 180 minutes, $300m + 100m = 180$ minutes, $400m = 180$, and $m = \frac{180}{400} = \frac{9}{20}$. The time to do a math problem is $2\left(\frac{9}{20}\right) = \left(\frac{9}{10}\right)$. All 50 math problems can be done in $50\left(\frac{9}{10}\right) = 45$ minutes.

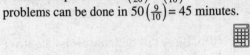

24. 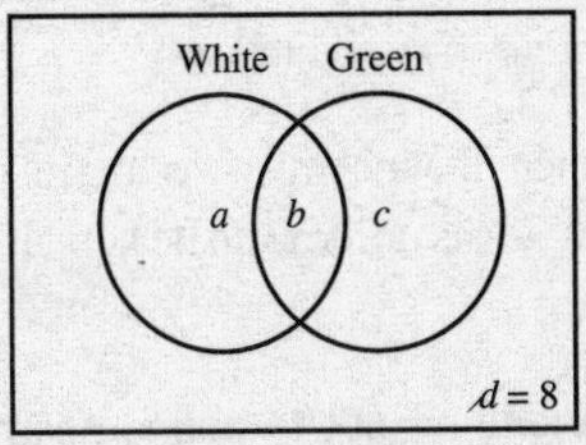

$a + b = 8,\ b + c = 18,\ d = 8$

$\underbrace{\text{Total}}_{28} = \underbrace{a + b}_{8} + c + \underbrace{d}_{8}$

$28 = 8 + c + 8$

$\therefore c = 12$

Since $b + c = 18$ and $c = 12$

$\therefore b = 6$

25. $x = \frac{2}{4},\ y = \frac{1}{4} + \frac{1}{3},\ z = \frac{2}{3}$

$\frac{x + z}{y} = \frac{\left(\frac{2}{4}\right) + \left(\frac{2}{3}\right)}{\frac{1}{4} + \frac{1}{3}} = \frac{2\left(\frac{1}{4} + \frac{1}{3}\right)}{\left(\frac{1}{4} + \frac{1}{3}\right)} = 2$

Section 6

1. **(E)** If he "dashed into the house," then he was in a hurry and probably out of breath.

2. **(E)** A criminal record may indeed cause a jury to *discredit* (disbelieve) a witness's testimony.

3. **(C)** A catastrophic storm might leave a family *destitute* (living in poverty). For the second blank, the word *although* indicates a shift in mood from negative to positive; poverty could not *dampen* (depress) the family's spirits.

4. **(B)** "By a stroke of luck" implies good fortune; the troops likely *prevailed* (were victorious), thereby avoiding a crushing *defeat.*

5. **(A)** If the price is going up tomorrow, you must do your buying with *celerity* (swiftness).

6. **(D)** If danger threatens, the music would likely be *portentous* (ominous).

7. **(E)** If years separated one advance from the next, progress in women's rights was *sporadic* (occasional or scattered over time).

8. **(B)** Offices that are now across the street have been *relocated* (moved). As a result, the directory is *obsolete* (out of date).

9. **(A)** Since the promise—a mere sop to world opinion—was unlikely to be kept, it was *spurious* (false).

10. **(C)** Pretending not to notice nearby celebrities is acting in a *nonchalant* (casually indifferent) manner.

11. **(B)** Normally, vices are publically *condemned.* Secret indulgence in them might, however, be hidden by a *sanctimonious* (excessively righteous) manner.

12. **(D)** A flood that destroys people's belongings causes *devastation.* Living conditions in the area can be said to have *deteriorated* (worsened).

13. **(B)** A *perversion* of the truth is a deviation from the truth, or the half-truths and half-lies mentioned in the second half of the sentence.

14. **(D)** As indicated by the word *though,* the sentence requires a contrast. Since the presentation was positive, the blank should be filled by a negative; *worthless* is the best choice to describe a report full of errors.

15. **(B)** A *library* is a place for *books*, just as a *zoo* is a place for *animals.*

16. **(C)** Something *tiny* is much smaller in size than something *huge*. Something *weak* is much less in strength than something *strong.*

17. **(A)** To *frighten* someone is to *scare* that person; to *question* someone is to *ask* that person.

18. **(A)** *Finding* is a result of *searching*, and *winning* is a result of *fighting.*

19. **(B)** By means of a *door*, we can *open* something. By means of a *knife*, we can *cut* into something.

20. **(B)** A *dastard* is characterized by *cowardice,* just as a *scoundrel* is characterized by *immorality.*

21. **(D)** A *toe* is part of the *foot*, and the *pupil* is part of the eye.

22. **(D)** *Strumming* and *pedaling* are methods of playing an instrument. We strum the *guitar* and pedal the *organ.*

23. **(C)** *Puerile* means childish or lacking in *maturity. Obscure* means vague or lacking in *clarity.*

24. **(A)** To *hurtle* is to throw with force; to *toss* is to throw lightly. Similarly, to *strike* is to hit with force and to *tap* is to hit lightly.

25. **(C)** Something *infinite* (endless) lacks limits or *bounds,* just as something *nebulous* (vague) lacks *clarity.*

26. **(A)** Don Quixote is worried that he cannot wear armor with a *device* on his shield that denotes his knighthood. The only appropriate choice is (A).

27. **(E)** With such malapropisms as "forked tongues" of birds, Cervantes imbues his hero with language that mimics the flowery language of the romances he reads.

28. **(E)** In his florid, overblown language, Don Quixote tells of getting out of bed to ride off on his adventure. "The slothful down" seems to refer to the down mattress on which he sleeps.

29. **(C)** Don Quixote is talking to himself and calling on a woman who may or may not exist. His speech cries out for his love for Dulcinea, but Cervantes pulls the reader back with this line to show that Quixote is mad.

30. **(D)** Don Quixote speaks first to the "sage enchanter" who might chronicle his tale (lines 53–57) and then to Dulcinea, "mistress of this captive heart" (lines 58–63).

31. **(B)** The sun's heat "would have been enough to turn his brain, if he had had any." Cervantes is again reminding the reader that Don Quixote is out of his mind.

32. **(C)** The story up to this point might be the tale of any knight somewhat down on his luck, but in lines 16–18, Cervantes jolts the reader into realizing that Don Quixote is out of his mind—he is not even a real knight.

33. **(A)** Cervantes refers to the romantic books that fill Don Quixote's head in lines 27 and 66.

34. **(D)** Although he never comes right out and says so, Cervantes's mocking reproduction of the language of romantic books makes it clear that he does not think much of the writing styles he imitates. The fact that the hero who speaks the way such writers write is completely mad is another ironic twist that reveals Cervantes's opinion.

35. **(D)** Throughout, Cervantes uses a gently mocking tone to show Don Quixote's ridiculousness. Examples such as lines 17–18, 25–26, and 64 show that Cervantes is amused by his hero but not contemptuous as (A) would suggest.

Evaluating Practice Examination 1

To determine your Verbal Reasoning Score:

1. Using the Analysis Worksheet, enter the number of correct answers for each verbal reasoning section on the appropriate line in Column A of the Verbal Reasoning grid.

2. Enter the number of incorrect answers for each verbal reasoning section on the appropriate line in Column B of the Verbal Reasoning grid.

3. Total Columns A and B and enter these totals in boxes A and B, respectively.

4. Perform the indicated calculation to find your Raw Score: (value in box A) minus (one-quarter of the value in box B) = Raw Score.

5. Consult the Conversion Chart to find your approximate Scaled Score.

To determine your Mathematical Reasoning Score:

1. Enter the number of correct answers for each mathematical reasoning section on the appropriate line in Column C of the Mathematical Reasoning grid.

2. Enter the number of incorrect answers for each mathematical reasoning section on the appropriate line in Column D, E, or F of the Mathematical Reasoning grid.

3. Total Columns C, D, E, and F and enter these totals in boxes C, D, E, and F, respectively.

4. Perform the indicated calculation to find your Raw Score: (value in box C) minus (one-quarter of the value in box D) minus (one-third of the value in box E) = Raw Score.

5. Consult the Conversation Chart to find your approximate Scaled Score.

Note: Box F is not used in this calculation.

Analysis Worksheet

VERBAL REASONING

Section	Number of Questions	Column A Number of Correct Answers	Column B Number of Incorrect Answers
2	30		
4	10		
6	35		
	Total	A	B

A $- \frac{1}{4}$ B = Raw Score → Use Conversion Chart → Scaled Score

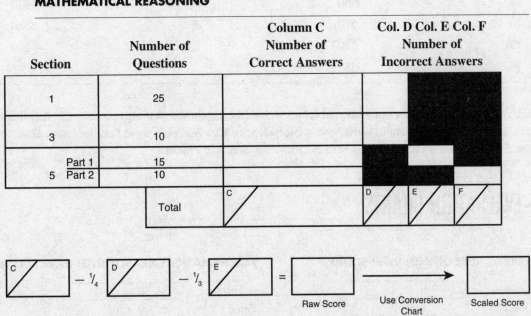

MATHEMATICAL REASONING

Section	Number of Questions	Column C Number of Correct Answers	Col. D Number of Incorrect Answers	Col. E	Col. F
1	25				
3	10				
5 Part 1	15				
5 Part 2	10				
	Total	C	D	E	F

C $- \frac{1}{4}$ D $- \frac{1}{3}$ E = Raw Score → Use Conversion Chart → Scaled Score

Conversion Scales for Practice Examination I

VERBAL REASONING:

Raw Score	Scaled Score	Raw Score	Scaled Score
75	800	40	550
70	800	35	520
65	760	30	480
60	710	25	440
55	670	20	410
50	620	15	370
45	590	10	340
		5	290
		0	230

MATHEMATICAL REASONING:

Raw Score	Scaled Score	Raw Score	Scaled Score
60	800	25	510
55	760	20	480
50	690	15	440
45	650	10	410
40	610	5	340
35	580	0	200
30	550		

Although you now have some idea of what your scores would like had they been scaled according to unofficial ETS standards, you will probably want to know how to interpret your Raw Scores in more familiar terms. If so, use the following Self-Evaluation Charts to see what your Raw Scores actually mean.

SELF-EVALUATION CHARTS

VERBAL REASONING: RAW SCORE

Excellent	60 – 75
Good	50 – 60
Average	30 – 50
Fair	20 – 30
Poor	0 – 20

MATHEMATICAL REASONING: RAW SCORE

Excellent	50 – 60
Good	40 – 50
Average	20 – 40
Fair	10 – 20
Poor	0 – 10

TEAR HERE

Practice Examination 2

Answer Sheet

If a section has fewer questions than answer ovals, leave the extra ovals blank.

Section 1

1 (A) (B) (C) (D) (E)	11 (A) (B) (C) (D) (E)	21 (A) (B) (C) (D) (E)	31 (A) (B) (C) (D) (E)
2 (A) (B) (C) (D) (E)	12 (A) (B) (C) (D) (E)	22 (A) (B) (C) (D) (E)	32 (A) (B) (C) (D) (E)
3 (A) (B) (C) (D) (E)	13 (A) (B) (C) (D) (E)	23 (A) (B) (C) (D) (E)	33 (A) (B) (C) (D) (E)
4 (A) (B) (C) (D) (E)	14 (A) (B) (C) (D) (E)	24 (A) (B) (C) (D) (E)	34 (A) (B) (C) (D) (E)
5 (A) (B) (C) (D) (E)	15 (A) (B) (C) (D) (E)	25 (A) (B) (C) (D) (E)	35 (A) (B) (C) (D) (E)
6 (A) (B) (C) (D) (E)	16 (A) (B) (C) (D) (E)	26 (A) (B) (C) (D) (E)	36 (A) (B) (C) (D) (E)
7 (A) (B) (C) (D) (E)	17 (A) (B) (C) (D) (E)	27 (A) (B) (C) (D) (E)	37 (A) (B) (C) (D) (E)
8 (A) (B) (C) (D) (E)	18 (A) (B) (C) (D) (E)	28 (A) (B) (C) (D) (E)	38 (A) (B) (C) (D) (E)
9 (A) (B) (C) (D) (E)	19 (A) (B) (C) (D) (E)	29 (A) (B) (C) (D) (E)	39 (A) (B) (C) (D) (E)
10 (A) (B) (C) (D) (E)	20 (A) (B) (C) (D) (E)	30 (A) (B) (C) (D) (E)	40 (A) (B) (C) (D) (E)

Section 2

1 (A) (B) (C) (D) (E)	11 (A) (B) (C) (D) (E)	21 (A) (B) (C) (D) (E)	31 (A) (B) (C) (D) (E)
2 (A) (B) (C) (D) (E)	12 (A) (B) (C) (D) (E)	22 (A) (B) (C) (D) (E)	32 (A) (B) (C) (D) (E)
3 (A) (B) (C) (D) (E)	13 (A) (B) (C) (D) (E)	23 (A) (B) (C) (D) (E)	33 (A) (B) (C) (D) (E)
4 (A) (B) (C) (D) (E)	14 (A) (B) (C) (D) (E)	24 (A) (B) (C) (D) (E)	34 (A) (B) (C) (D) (E)
5 (A) (B) (C) (D) (E)	15 (A) (B) (C) (D) (E)	25 (A) (B) (C) (D) (E)	35 (A) (B) (C) (D) (E)
6 (A) (B) (C) (D) (E)	16 (A) (B) (C) (D) (E)	26 (A) (B) (C) (D) (E)	36 (A) (B) (C) (D) (E)
7 (A) (B) (C) (D) (E)	17 (A) (B) (C) (D) (E)	27 (A) (B) (C) (D) (E)	37 (A) (B) (C) (D) (E)
8 (A) (B) (C) (D) (E)	18 (A) (B) (C) (D) (E)	28 (A) (B) (C) (D) (E)	38 (A) (B) (C) (D) (E)
9 (A) (B) (C) (D) (E)	19 (A) (B) (C) (D) (E)	29 (A) (B) (C) (D) (E)	39 (A) (B) (C) (D) (E)
10 (A) (B) (C) (D) (E)	20 (A) (B) (C) (D) (E)	30 (A) (B) (C) (D) (E)	40 (A) (B) (C) (D) (E)

Section 3

1 (A) (B) (C) (D) (E)	6 (A) (B) (C) (D) (E)	11 (A) (B) (C) (D) (E)	16 (A) (B) (C) (D) (E)
2 (A) (B) (C) (D) (E)	7 (A) (B) (C) (D) (E)	12 (A) (B) (C) (D) (E)	17 (A) (B) (C) (D) (E)
3 (A) (B) (C) (D) (E)	8 (A) (B) (C) (D) (E)	13 (A) (B) (C) (D) (E)	18 (A) (B) (C) (D) (E)
4 (A) (B) (C) (D) (E)	9 (A) (B) (C) (D) (E)	14 (A) (B) (C) (D) (E)	19 (A) (B) (C) (D) (E)
5 (A) (B) (C) (D) (E)	10 (A) (B) (C) (D) (E)	15 (A) (B) (C) (D) (E)	20 (A) (B) (C) (D) (E)

Section 4

1 (A) (B) (C) (D) (E)	6 (A) (B) (C) (D) (E)	11 (A) (B) (C) (D) (E)	16 (A) (B) (C) (D) (E)
2 (A) (B) (C) (D) (E)	7 (A) (B) (C) (D) (E)	12 (A) (B) (C) (D) (E)	17 (A) (B) (C) (D) (E)
3 (A) (B) (C) (D) (E)	8 (A) (B) (C) (D) (E)	13 (A) (B) (C) (D) (E)	18 (A) (B) (C) (D) (E)
4 (A) (B) (C) (D) (E)	9 (A) (B) (C) (D) (E)	14 (A) (B) (C) (D) (E)	19 (A) (B) (C) (D) (E)
5 (A) (B) (C) (D) (E)	10 (A) (B) (C) (D) (E)	15 (A) (B) (C) (D) (E)	20 (A) (B) (C) (D) (E)

Section 5

1	A	B	C	D	E	11	A	B	C	D	E	21	A	B	C	D	E	31	A	B	C	D	E
2	A	B	C	D	E	12	A	B	C	D	E	22	A	B	C	D	E	32	A	B	C	D	E
3	A	B	C	D	E	13	A	B	C	D	E	23	A	B	C	D	E	33	A	B	C	D	E
4	A	B	C	D	E	14	A	B	C	D	E	24	A	B	C	D	E	34	A	B	C	D	E
5	A	B	C	D	E	15	A	B	C	D	E	25	A	B	C	D	E	35	A	B	C	D	E
6	A	B	C	D	E	16	A	B	C	D	E	26	A	B	C	D	E	36	A	B	C	D	E
7	A	B	C	D	E	17	A	B	C	D	E	27	A	B	C	D	E	37	A	B	C	D	E
8	A	B	C	D	E	18	A	B	C	D	E	28	A	B	C	D	E	38	A	B	C	D	E
9	A	B	C	D	E	19	A	B	C	D	E	29	A	B	C	D	E	39	A	B	C	D	E
10	A	B	C	D	E	20	A	B	C	D	E	30	A	B	C	D	E	40	A	B	C	D	E

Section 6

1	A	B	C	D	E	6	A	B	C	D	E	11	A	B	C	D	E
2	A	B	C	D	E	7	A	B	C	D	E	12	A	B	C	D	E
3	A	B	C	D	E	8	A	B	C	D	E	13	A	B	C	D	E
4	A	B	C	D	E	9	A	B	C	D	E	14	A	B	C	D	E
5	A	B	C	D	E	10	A	B	C	D	E	15	A	B	C	D	E

Note: ONLY the answers entered on the grid are scored.
Handwritten answers at the top of the column are NOT scored.

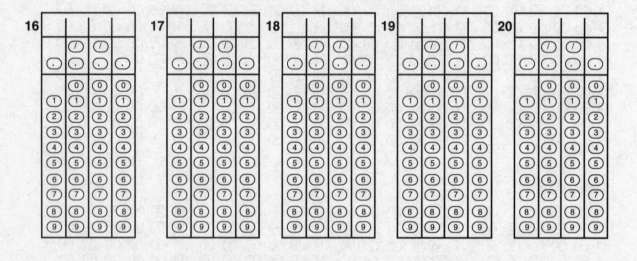

16

	/	/	
.	.	.	.
	0	0	0
1	1	1	1
2	2	2	2
3	3	3	3
4	4	4	4
5	5	5	5
6	6	6	6
7	7	7	7
8	8	8	8
9	9	9	9

17

	/	/	
.	.	.	.
	0	0	0
1	1	1	1
2	2	2	2
3	3	3	3
4	4	4	4
5	5	5	5
6	6	6	6
7	7	7	7
8	8	8	8
9	9	9	9

18

	/	/	
.	.	.	.
	0	0	0
1	1	1	1
2	2	2	2
3	3	3	3
4	4	4	4
5	5	5	5
6	6	6	6
7	7	7	7
8	8	8	8
9	9	9	9

19

	/	/	
.	.	.	.
	0	0	0
1	1	1	1
2	2	2	2
3	3	3	3
4	4	4	4
5	5	5	5
6	6	6	6
7	7	7	7
8	8	8	8
9	9	9	9

20

	/	/	
.	.	.	.
	0	0	0
1	1	1	1
2	2	2	2
3	3	3	3
4	4	4	4
5	5	5	5
6	6	6	6
7	7	7	7
8	8	8	8
9	9	9	9

21

	/	/	
.	.	.	.
	0	0	0
1	1	1	1
2	2	2	2
3	3	3	3
4	4	4	4
5	5	5	5
6	6	6	6
7	7	7	7
8	8	8	8
9	9	9	9

22

	/	/	
.	.	.	.
	0	0	0
1	1	1	1
2	2	2	2
3	3	3	3
4	4	4	4
5	5	5	5
6	6	6	6
7	7	7	7
8	8	8	8
9	9	9	9

23

	/	/	
.	.	.	.
	0	0	0
1	1	1	1
2	2	2	2
3	3	3	3
4	4	4	4
5	5	5	5
6	6	6	6
7	7	7	7
8	8	8	8
9	9	9	9

24

	/	/	
.	.	.	.
	0	0	0
1	1	1	1
2	2	2	2
3	3	3	3
4	4	4	4
5	5	5	5
6	6	6	6
7	7	7	7
8	8	8	8
9	9	9	9

25

	/	/	
.	.	.	.
	0	0	0
1	1	1	1
2	2	2	2
3	3	3	3
4	4	4	4
5	5	5	5
6	6	6	6
7	7	7	7
8	8	8	8
9	9	9	9

Practice Examination 2

SECTION 1

30 Questions • Time—30 Minutes

Directions: Each of the following questions consists of an incomplete sentence followed by five words or pairs of words. Choose that word or pair or words which, when substituted for the blank space or spaces, *best* completes the meaning of the sentence and mark the letter of your choice on your answer sheet.

Example:

In view of the extenuating circumstances and the defendant's youth, the judge recommended ----.

(A) conviction
(B) a defense
(C) a mistrial
(D) leniency
(E) life imprisonment

Ⓐ Ⓑ Ⓒ ● Ⓔ

1. An audience that laughs in all the wrong places can ---- even the most experienced actor.

   (A) disparage
   (B) allay
   (C) disconcert
   (D) upbraid
   (E) satiate

2. Their assurances of good faith were hollow; they ---- on the agreement almost at once.

   (A) conferred
   (B) expiated
   (C) recapitulated
   (D) obtruded
   (E) reneged

3. If we ---- our different factions, then together we can gain the majority in their legislature.

   (A) amalgamate
   (B) manifest
   (C) preclude
   (D) alienate
   (E) deviate

4. The Eighteenth Amendment, often called the Prohibition Act, ---- the sale of alcoholic beverages.

   (A) prolonged
   (B) preempted
   (C) sanctioned
   (D) proscribed
   (E) encouraged

5. The police received a(n) ---- call giving them valuable information, but the caller would not give his name out of fear of ----.

   (A) private..impunity
   (B) anonymous..reprisals
   (C) professional..dissension
   (D) enigmatic..refusal
   (E) adamant..transgression

GO ON TO THE NEXT PAGE

Directions: Each of the following questions consists of a capitalized pair of words followed by five pairs of words lettered A to E. The capitalized words bear some meaningful relationship to each other. Choose the lettered pair of words whose relationship is most similar to that expressed by the capitalized pair and mark its letter on your answer sheet.

Example:

DAY : SUN : :

(A) sunlight : daylight (B) ray : sun
(C) night : moon (D) heat : cold
(E) moon : star Ⓐ Ⓑ ● Ⓓ Ⓔ

6. THROAT : SWALLOW : :

(A) teeth : chew
(B) eyelid : wink
(C) nose : point
(D) ear : absorb
(E) mouth : smile

7. GARNET : RED : :

(A) pearl : round
(B) diamond : solid
(C) emerald : green
(D) ivory : living
(E) silver : shining

8. PATIENCE : VIRTUES : :

(A) prudence : skills
(B) sailing : crafts
(C) grief : traits
(D) temerity : vices
(E) literature : arts

9. SOAR : ALIGHT : :

(A) hop : stumble
(B) crawl : run
(C) lift : carry
(D) walk : hike
(E) sail : moor

10. OASIS : DESERT : :

(A) canyon : gorge
(B) savanna : steppe
(C) island : ocean
(D) tundra : icecap
(E) channel : reef

11. COTTON : SOFT : :

(A) wool : warm
(B) iron : hard
(C) nylon : strong
(D) wood : polished
(E) silk : expensive

12. YEAR : CENTURY : :

(A) inch : yard
(B) mile : speed
(C) week : month
(D) cent : dollar
(E) day : year

13. MULE : INTRACTABLE : :

(A) horse : turbulent
(B) fox : wily
(C) dog : candid
(D) wolf : fickle
(E) tiger : inexorable

14. STUMBLE : WALK : :

(A) creep : run
(B) pain : hurt
(C) stammer : speak
(D) pitch : throw
(E) smile : frown

Directions: Each passage below is followed by a set of questions. Read each passage, then answer the accompanying questions, basing your answers on what is stated or implied in the passage and in any introductory material provided. Mark the letter of your choice on your answer sheet.

Questions 15–22 are based on the following passage.

One of the most frequently read political treatises of all time is The Prince *by Niccolò Machiavelli (1469-1527). The word* Machiavellian *is now used to mean diabolical, but Machiavelli's work, although sometimes used to justify dictatorship, is thoughtful, original, and often brilliant.*

I say that every Prince should desire to be accounted merciful and not cruel. Nevertheless, he should be on his guard against the abuse of this quality of mercy. Cesare Borgia was reputed cruel, yet his cruelty restored Romagna, united it, and brought it to order and obedience; so that if we look at things in their true light, it will be seen that he was in reality far more merciful than the people of Florence, who, to avoid the imputation of cruelty, suffered Pistoja to be torn to pieces by factions.

A Prince should therefore disregard the reproach of being thought cruel where it enables him to keep his subjects united and obedient. For he who quells disorder by a very few signal examples will in the end be more merciful than he who from too great leniency permits things to take their course and so to result in rapine and bloodshed; for these hurt the whole State, whereas the severities of the Prince injure individuals only.

And for a new Prince, of all others, it is impossible to escape a name for cruelty, since new States are full of dangers. Wherefore Virgil, by the mouth of Dido, excuses the harshness of her reign on the plea that it was new, saying:

A fate unkind, and newness in my reign
Compel me thus to guard a wide domain.

Nevertheless, the new Prince should not be too ready of belief, nor too easily set in motion; nor should he himself be the first to raise alarms; but should so temper prudence with kindliness that too great confidence in others shall not throw him off his guard, nor groundless distrust render him insupportable.

And here comes the question whether it is better to be loved rather than be feared, or feared rather than loved. It might perhaps be answered that we should wish to be both; but since love and fear can hardly exist together, if we must choose between them, it is far safer to be feared than loved. For of men it may generally be affirmed that they are thankless, fickle, false, studious to avoid danger, greedy of gain, devoted to you while you are able to confer benefits upon them, and ready, as I said before, while danger is distant, to shed their blood, and sacrifice their property, their lives, and their children for you; but in the hour of need they turn against you. The Prince, therefore, who without otherwise securing himself builds wholly on their professions is undone. For the friendships which we buy with a price, and do not gain by greatness and nobility of character, though they may be fairly earned are not made good, but fail us when we have occasion to use them.

15. Cesare Borgia (line 4) is held up as an example of

(A) an unnecessarily cruel Prince
(B) someone who drew strength from cruel actions
(C) a leader loved by his people and feared by foreigners
(D) a compassionate man with a bad reputation
(E) a model of obedience and duty

16. "A very few signal examples" (line 14) would most likely imply

(A) commutations of sentences
(B) censures
(C) fines
(D) executions
(E) imprisonments

17. The main point of paragraph 4 seems to be that a Prince

(A) cannot escape being cruel
(B) is in constant danger of being unseated
(C) should not trust anyone
(D) needs to be kind to his subjects
(E) must balance trust with caution

Practice Exam 2 • Section 1

GO ON TO THE NEXT PAGE

18. Machiavelli asserts in this passage that

(A) the people of Florence overreacted cruelly against Pistoja
(B) Cesare Borgia was just as cruel as the people in Florence
(C) the subjects of a ruler remain loyal to him only as long as he continues to make them happy
(D) it is better to be loved than feared
(E) fear without love is better than love without fear

19. According to Machiavelli, a ruler should

(A) keep his subjects in constant fear of himself
(B) resign if he has any reputation for cruelty
(C) depend wholly on the unswerving loyalty of his subjects
(D) take care not to have his generosity abused
(E) do none of the above

20. According to this passage, the *least* important criterion for a successful ruler would be his

(A) nobility of character
(B) popularity
(C) severity
(D) greatness
(E) prudence

21. Machiavelli's view of mankind seems to be

(A) largely positive
(B) changeable
(C) pessimistic
(D) compassionate
(E) heartless

22. The most suitable title for this selection would be

(A) "Problems for Princes"
(B) "I'd Rather Be Right than President"
(C) "Criteria for Leadership"
(D) "Whether It Is Better to Be Loved or Feared"
(E) "Democracy *versus* Anarchy"

Questions 23–30 are based on the following passage.

Thomas Bulfinch (1796–1867) was a teacher and writer known for his popularization of myths and legends. In this excerpt from Bulfinch's Mythology, *he tells the story behind the Trojan War.*

Minerva was the goddess of wisdom, but on one occasion she did a very foolish thing; she entered into competition with Juno and Venus for the prize of beauty. It happened thus: At the nuptials of Peleus and Thetis all the gods were invited with the exception of Eris, or Discord. Enraged at her exclusion, the goddess threw a golden apple among the guests, with the inscription, "For the fairest." Thereupon Juno, Venus, and Minerva each claimed the apple. Jupiter, not willing to decide in so delicate a matter, sent the goddesses to Mount Ida, where the beautiful shepherd Paris was tending his flocks, and to him was committed the decision. The goddesses accordingly appeared before him. Juno promised him power and riches, Minerva glory and renown in war, and Venus the fairest of women for his wife, each attempting to bias his decision in her own favor. Paris decided in favour of Venus and gave her the golden apple, thus making the two other goddesses his enemies. Under the protection of Venus, Paris sailed to Greece, and was hospitably received by Menelaus, king of Sparta. Now Helen, the wife of Menelaus, was the very woman whom Venus had destined for Paris, the fairest of her sex. She had been sought as a bride by numerous suitors, and before her decision was made known, they all, at the suggestion of Ulysses, one of their number, took an oath that they would defend her from all injury and avenge her cause if necessary. She chose Menelaus, and was living with him happily when Paris became their guest. Paris, aided by Venus, persuaded her to elope with him, and carried her to Troy, whence arose the famous Trojan war, the theme of the greatest poems of antiquity, those of Homer and Virgil.

Menelaus called upon his brother chieftains of Greece to fulfill their pledge, and join him in his efforts to recover his wife. They generally came forward, but Ulysses, who had married Penelope, and was very happy in his wife and child, had no disposition to embark in such a troublesome affair. He therefore hung back and Palamedes was sent to urge him. When Palamedes arrived at Ithaca Ulysses pretended to be mad. He yoked an ass and an ox together to the plough and began to sow salt. Palamedes, to try him, placed the infant Telemachus before the plough, whereupon the father turned the plough aside, showing plainly that he was no madman, and after that could no longer refuse to fulfill his promise. Being now himself gained for the undertaking, he lent his aid to bring in other reluctant chiefs, especially Achilles. This hero was the son of that Thetis at whose marriage the apple of Discord had been thrown among the goddesses. Thetis was herself one of the immortals, a sea-nymph, and knowing that her son was fated to perish before Troy if he went on the expedition, she endeavoured to prevent his going. She sent him away to the court of King Lycomedes, and induced him to conceal himself in the disguise of a maiden among the daughters of the king. Ulysses, hearing he was there, went disguised as a merchant to the palace and offered for sale female ornaments, among which he had placed some arms. While the king's daughters were engrossed with the other contents of the merchant's pack, Achilles handled the weapons and thereby betrayed himself to the keen eye of Ulysses, who found no great difficulty in persuading him to disregard his mother's prudent counsels and join his countrymen in the war.

23. Bulfinch describes Jupiter as unwilling to "decide in so delicate a matter" (lines 9–10), implying that

(A) Jupiter is usually heavy-handed
(B) any decision is bound to offend someone
(C) Jupiter is overly sensitive
(D) the problems are so obscure that no one can judge them
(E) all three goddesses are fragile and dainty

24. The word *disposition* (line 38) is used to mean

(A) inclination
(B) nature
(C) integrity
(D) value
(E) habit

25. The sowing of salt is used by Bulfinch to show

(A) Ulysses's attempt to be found insane
(B) the difficulty of cultivating in rocky soil
(C) how the tears of the gods created the sea
(D) the gods' punishment of those who disobey them
(E) Ulysses's talent as a soldier rather than a farmer

26. When Palamedes "tries" Ulysses (line 43), he

(A) finds him guilty
(B) judges him
(C) tests him
(D) attempts to help him
(E) taxes his patience

27. Bulfinch reveals that Thetis is a sea-nymph in order to explain

(A) why she married Peleus
(B) why she dislikes the idea of war
(C) the effect of the apple of Discord
(D) her love for Achilles
(E) her ability to predict the future

28. Among the chieftains of Greece apparently are

(A) Juno, Venus, and Minerva
(B) Paris and Lycomedes
(C) Ulysses, Achilles, and Menelaus
(D) Eris and Thetis
(E) Homer and Virgil

29. Why does Ulysses display arms among the ornaments?

(A) to test Achilles into revealing himself
(B) as a declaration of war
(C) to mislead the daughters of the king
(D) to complete his disguise as a merchant
(E) because he wants to start an altercation

GO ON TO THE NEXT PAGE

30. A reasonable title for this narrative might be

(A) "Disputes and Deceit"
(B) "Achilles and Ulysses"
(C) "Beauty and the Beast"
(D) "The Pettiness of the Gods"
(E) "The Apple of Discord Leads to War"

STOP

END OF SECTION 1. IF YOU HAVE ANY TIME LEFT, GO OVER YOUR WORK IN THIS SECTION ONLY. DO NOT WORK IN ANY OTHER SECTION OF THE TEST.

SECTION 2

25 Questions • Time—30 Minutes

Directions: Solve the following problems using any available space on the page for scratchwork. On your answer sheet fill in the choice which best corresponds to the correct answer.

Notes: The figures accompanying the problems are drawn as accurately as possible unless otherwise stated in specific problems. Again, unless otherwise stated, all figures lie in the same plane. All numbers used in these problems are real numbers. Calculators are permitted for this test.

Reference Information

Circle: Rectangle: Rectangular Solid: Cylinder: Triangle:

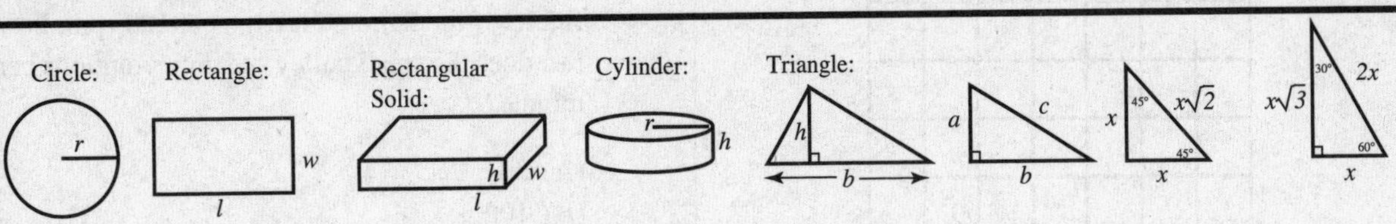

$C = 2\pi r$ $A = lw$ $V = lwh$ $V = \pi r^2 h$ $A = \frac{1}{2}bh$ $a^2 + b^2 = c^2$

$A = \pi r^2$

The number of degrees of arc in a circle is 360.
The measure in degrees of a straight angle is 180.
The sum of the measures in degrees of the angles of a triangle is 180.

1. One angle of a triangle is 82°. The other two angles are in the ratio 2 : 5. Find the number of degrees in the smallest angle of the triangle.

(A) 14
(B) 25
(C) 28
(D) 38
(E) 82

2. Village A has a population of 6,800, which is decreasing at a rate of 120 per year. Village B has a population of 4,200, which is increasing at a rate of 80 per year. In how many years will the population of the two villages be equal?

(A) 9
(B) 11
(C) 13
(D) 14
(E) 16

3. If $*x$ is defined such that $*x = x^2 - 2x$, the value of $*2 - *1$ is

(A) –1
(B) 0
(C) 1
(D) 2
(E) 4

4. In a right triangle, the ratio of the legs is 1 : 2. If the area of the triangle is 25 square units, what is the length of the hypotenuse?

(A) $\sqrt{5}$
(B) $5\sqrt{5}$
(C) $5\sqrt{3}$
(D) $10\sqrt{3}$
(E) $25\sqrt{5}$

GO ON TO THE NEXT PAGE

5. In the graph below, the axes and the origin are not shown. If point P has coordinates (3,7), what are the coordinates of point Q, assuming each box is one unit?

(A) (5, 6)
(B) (1, 10)
(C) (6, 9)
(D) (6, 5)
(E) (5, 10)

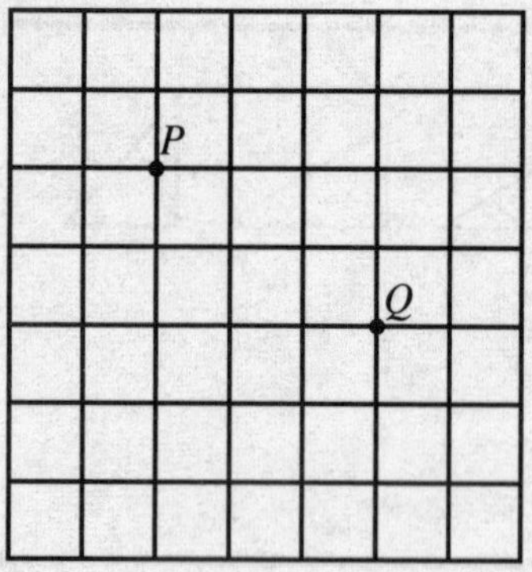

6. If $r = 5x$, how many tenths of r does $\frac{1}{2}$ of x equal?

(A) 1
(B) 2
(C) 3
(D) 4
(E) 5

7. $ABCD$ is a parallelogram, and $DE = EC$.

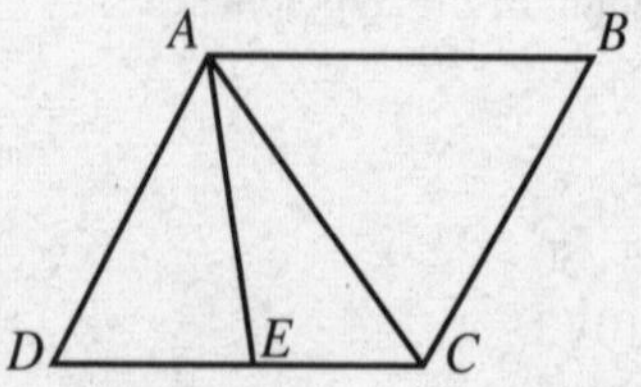

What is the ratio of triangle ADE to the area of the parallelogram?

(A) 2 : 5
(B) 1 : 2
(C) 1 : 3
(D) 1 : 4
(E) It cannot be determined from the information given.

8. In any square, the length of one side is

(A) one-half the diagonal of the square
(B) the square root of the perimeter of the square
(C) about .7 the length of the diagonal of the square
(D) the square root of the diagonal
(E) one-fourth the area

9. A pulley having a 9-inch diameter is belted to a pulley having a 6-inch diameter, as shown in the figure. If the large pulley runs at 120 rpm, how fast does the small pulley run, in revolutions per minute?

(A) 80
(B) 100
(C) 160
(D) 180
(E) 240

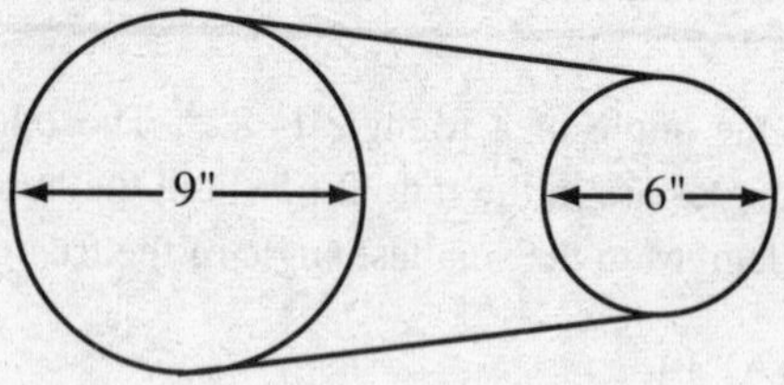

10. The number of degrees through which the hour hand of a clock moves in 2 hours and 12 minutes is

(A) 66
(B) 72
(C) 126
(D) 732
(E) 792

11. The average of 8 numbers is 6; the average of 6 other numbers is 8. What is the average of all 14 numbers?

(A) 6
(B) $6\frac{6}{7}$
(C) 7
(D) $7\frac{2}{7}$
(E) $8\frac{1}{7}$

12. If x is between 0 and 1, which of the following increases as x increases?

I. $1-x^2$
II. $x-1$
III. $\frac{1}{x^2}$

(A) I and II
(B) II and III
(C) I and III
(D) II only
(E) I only

13. In the series 3, 7, 12, 18, 25, ... the 9th term is

(A) 50
(B) 63
(C) 75
(D) 86
(E) 88

14. Simplify $\frac{x^2-y^2}{x-y}$

(A) $\frac{xy}{x+y}$

(B) $\frac{x+y}{xy}$

(C) $x+y$

(D) xy

(E) x^2+y^2-1

15. The front wheels of a wagon are 7 feet in circumference and the back wheels are 9 feet in circumference. When the front wheels have made 10 more revolutions than the back wheels, what distance, in feet, has the wagon gone?

(A) 126
(B) 180
(C) 189
(D) 315
(E) 630

16. A rectangular flower bed, dimensions 16 yards by 12 yards, is surrounded by a walk 3 yards wide. The area of the walk in square yards is

(A) 78
(B) 93
(C) 132
(D) 204
(E) 396

17. Doreen can wash her car in 15 minutes, while her younger brother Dave takes twice as long to do the same job. If they work together, how many minutes will the job take them?

(A) 5
(B) $7\frac{1}{2}$
(C) 10
(D) $22\frac{1}{2}$
(E) 30

18. A circle is inscribed in a given square and another circle is circumscribed about the same square. What is the ratio of the area of the inscribed to the circumscribed circle?

(A) 1:4
(B) 4:9
(C) 1:2
(D) 2:3
(E) 3:4

19. If $\frac{3}{7}$ of a bucket can be filled in 1 minute, how many minutes will it take to fill the rest of the bucket?

(A) $\frac{7}{3}$

(B) $\frac{4}{3}$

(C) 1

(D) $\frac{3}{4}$

(E) $\frac{4}{7}$

GO ON TO THE NEXT PAGE

20. In the figure below, the side of the large square is 14. The four smaller squares are formed by joining the midpoints of opposite sides. Find the value of Y.

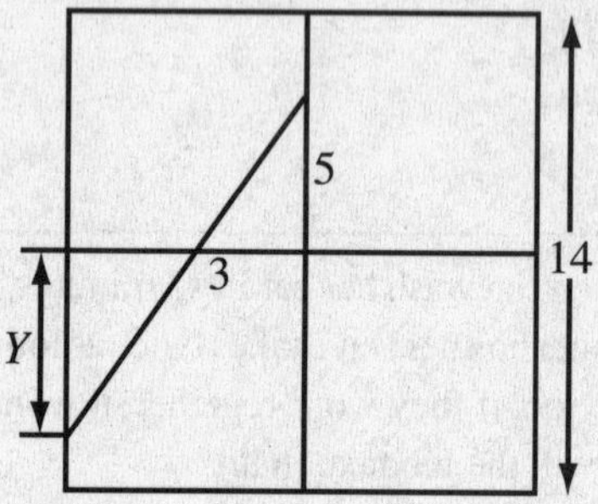

(A) 5

(B) 6

(C) $6\frac{5}{8}$

(D) $6\frac{2}{3}$

(E) 6.8

21. If the base of a rectangle is increased by 30% and the altitude is decreased by 20%, the area is increased by

(A) 4%
(B) 5%
(C) 10%
(D) 25%
(E) 104%

22. Using a 9×12-inch sheet of paper lengthwise, a typist leaves a 1-inch margin on each side and a $1\frac{1}{2}$-inch margin on top and bottom. What fractional part of the page is used for typing?

(A) $\frac{5}{12}$

(B) $\frac{7}{12}$

(C) $\frac{5}{9}$

(D) $\frac{3}{4}$

(E) $\frac{21}{22}$

23. In the figure, $PQRS$ is a parallelogram, and $ST = TV = VR$. What is the ratio of the area of triangle SPT to the area of the parallelogram?
Note: Figure is not drawn to scale.

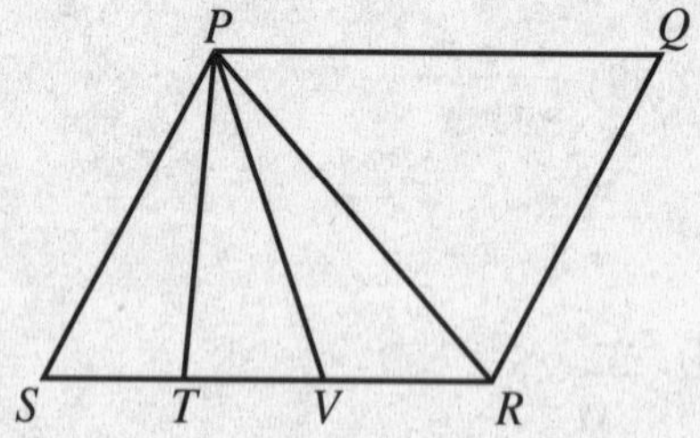

(A) $\frac{1}{6}$

(B) $\frac{1}{5}$

(C) $\frac{2}{7}$

(D) $\frac{1}{3}$

(E) It cannot be determined from the information given.

24. Given formula $A = P(1 + rt)$, then $t =$

(A) $A - P - Pr$

(B) $\frac{A + P}{Pr}$

(C) $\frac{A}{P} - r$

(D) $\frac{A - P}{Pr}$

(E) $\frac{A - r}{Pr}$

25. If $p > q$ and $r < 0$, which of the following is (are) true?

I. $pr < qr$
II. $p + r > q + r$
III. $p - r < q - r$

(A) I only
(B) II only
(C) I and III only
(D) I and II only
(E) I, II and III

STOP

END OF SECTION 2. IF YOU HAVE ANY TIME LEFT, GO OVER YOUR WORK IN THIS SECTION ONLY. DO NOT WORK IN ANY OTHER SECTION OF THE TEST.

SECTION 3

12 Questions • Time—15 Minutes

Directions: The two passages given below deal with a related topic. Following the passages are questions about the content of each passage or about the relationship between the two passages. Answer the questions based upon what is stated or implied in the passages and in any introductory material provided. Mark the letter of your choice on your answer sheet.

Questions 1–12 are based on the following passages.

Writing in eighteenth-century England, essayist William Shenstone and his more famous compatriot, Horace Walpole, spent some time preoccupied with the question of good taste in landscape architecture.

Passage 1—William Shenstone, from "Unconnected Thoughts on Gardening" (1764)

The eye should always look rather down upon water: customary nature makes this requisite. I know nothing more sensibly displeasing than Mr. T—'s flat ground twixt terrace and his water.

It is not easy to account for the fondness of former times for straight-lined avenues to their houses: straight-lined walks through their woods, and, in short, every kind of straight line where the foot is to travel over what the eye has done before. This circumstance is one objection. Another, somewhat of the same kind, is the repetition of the same object, tree after tree for a length of way together . . . . To stand still and survey such avenues may afford some slender satisfaction through the change derived from perspective; but to move on continually and find no change of scene in the last attendant on our change of place must give actual pain to a person of taste. For such an one to be condemned to pass along the famous vista from Moscow to Petersburg or that other from Agra to Lahore in India, must be as disagreeable a sentence as to be condemned to labor at the galleys. I conceived some ideas of the sensation he must feel from walking but a few minutes, immured, betwixt Lord D—'s high shorn yew hedges, which run exactly parallel at a distance of about ten feet and are contrived perfectly to exclude all kinds of objects whatsoever.

When a building or other object has been once viewed from its proper point, the foot should never travel to it by the same path which the eye has traveled over before. Lose the object, and draw nigh obliquely . . . .

Water should ever appear as an irregular lake or winding stream.

Passage 2—Horace Walpole, from "Essay on Modern Gardening" (1771)

. . . At that moment appeared Kent, painter enough to taste the charms of landscape, bold and opinionative enough to dare and to dictate, and born with a genius to strike out a great system from the twilight of imperfect essays. He leaped the fence, and saw that all nature was a garden. He felt the delicious contrast of hill and valley, changing imperceptibly into each other, tasted the beauty of the gentle swell or concave scoop, and remarked how loose groves crowned an easy eminence with happy ornament, and while they called in the distant view between their graceful stems, removed and extended the perspective by delusive comparison.

Thus the pencil of his imagination bestowed all the arts of landscape on the scenes he handled. The great principles on which he worked were perspective, and light and shade. Groups of trees broke too uniform or too extensive a lawn; evergreens and woods were opposed to the glare of the champaign, and where the view was less fortunate, or so much exposed as to be beheld at once, he blotted out some parts by thick shades, to divide it into variety, or to make the richest scene more enchanting by reserving it to a farther advance of the spectator's steps. Thus . . . he realized the compositions of the greatest masters in painting. Where objects were wanting to animate his horizon, his taste as an architect could bestow immediate termination. His buildings, his seats, his temples were more the works of his pencil than of his compasses. We owe the restoration of Greece and the diffusion of architecture to his skill in landscape.

But of all the beauties he added to the face of this beautiful country, none surpassed his management of water. Adieu to canals, circular basins, and cascades tumbling down marble steps, that last absurd magnificence of Italian and French villas. The forced elevation of cataracts was no more. The gentle stream was taught to serpentize seemingly at its pleasure, and where discontinued by different levels, its course appeared to be concealed by thickets properly interspersed, and glittered again at a distance where it might be supposed naturally to arrive. Its borders were smoothed, but preserved their waving irregularity. A few trees scattered here and there on its edges sprinkled the tame bank that accompanied its meanders; and when it disappeared among the hills, shades descending from the heights leaned towards its progress, and framed the distant point of light under which it was lost, as it turned aside to either hand of the blue horizon.

1. The phrase "sensibly displeasing" in Passage 1 (line 3) is used to mean

   (A) rationally provoking
   (B) reasonably unpleasant
   (C) wisely disturbing
   (D) nonsensically pleasing
   (E) annoying to the senses

2. How does the author of Passage 1 feel about straight lines?

   (A) They are painfully boring.
   (B) They are necessary evils.
   (C) They are used to good effect in India.
   (D) They are satisfyingly attractive.
   (E) They are appropriate for the banks of streams.

3. The word *immured* (line 22) in Passage 1 means

   (A) enclosed
   (B) free
   (C) invulnerable
   (D) enduring
   (E) spontaneous

4. The phrase "lose the object" (line 30) in Passage 1 means

   (A) rid yourself of the burden
   (B) let the object be hidden from view
   (C) abandon your goal
   (D) remove the objective
   (E) free the element

5. As illustrations of unattractive landscaping, the author of Passage 1 cites all of the following EXCEPT

   (A) a uniform expanse of lawn
   (B) straight paths through forests
   (C) trees of the same species aligned in a row
   (D) Lord D—'s yew hedges
   (E) the road from Moscow to Petersburg

6. In Passage 2, the author uses the phrase "he leaped the fence" (line 38) to indicate

   (A) Kent's agility
   (B) the author's quest for freedom
   (C) Kent's ingenuity
   (D) the reader's new way of looking at things
   (E) Kent's building know-how

7. In paragraph 2 of Passage 2, the author's main purpose is to

   (A) discuss the use of plantings to improve vistas
   (B) analyze the black-and-white drawings of a master
   (C) examine light and shadow in architecture
   (D) encourage the reader to look for art in nature
   (E) show how artistic principles influenced Kent's landscaping

8. The word *serpentize* in Passage 2 (line 69) seems to mean

   (A) shed
   (B) poison
   (C) hiss
   (D) twist
   (E) drop

9. Why does the author of Passage 2 mention Italian and French villas?

   (A) To provide an example of unattractive landscaping
   (B) To liken their landscaping to Kent's work in England
   (C) To give an illustration of one of Kent's works
   (D) To show the influence of English landscaping in Europe
   (E) To describe an alternative type of attractive landscaping

GO ON TO THE NEXT PAGE

10. The author of Passage 2 would most likely find which of the following an example of good taste in landscaping?

    (A) A marble fountain shooting jets of water in the air
    (B) Formally arranged flowerbeds bordering a drive
    (C) A winding stream with trees and bushes scattered along its bank
    (D) An uninterrupted vista across a broad, straight canal
    (E) Lawns divided into ordered squares by hedges

11. How do both authors feel about water in parks?

    (A) The eye should look down on it.
    (B) It should be used sparingly.
    (C) It should look natural.
    (D) It should follow straight lines.
    (E) It should be lined with trees.

12. With which statement would both authors clearly agree?

    (A) Kent was one of the country's best landscapers.
    (B) Repetition of trees or objects can lead the eye naturally along an avenue.
    (C) Vistas should be broken up so that they cannot be viewed all at once.
    (D) High hedges are always disagreeable.
    (E) Bad taste is painful to the beholder.

STOP

END OF SECTION 3. IF YOU HAVE ANY TIME LEFT, GO OVER YOUR WORK IN THIS SECTION ONLY. DO NOT WORK IN ANY OTHER SECTION OF THE TEST.

SECTION 4

10 Questions • Time—15 Minutes

Directions: Solve the following problems using any available space on the page for scratchwork. On your answer sheet fill in the choice which best corresponds to the correct answer.

Notes: The figures accompanying the problems are drawn as accurately as possible unless otherwise stated in specific problems. Again, unless otherwise stated, all figures lie in the same plane. All numbers used in these problems are real numbers. Calculators are permitted for this test.

Reference Information

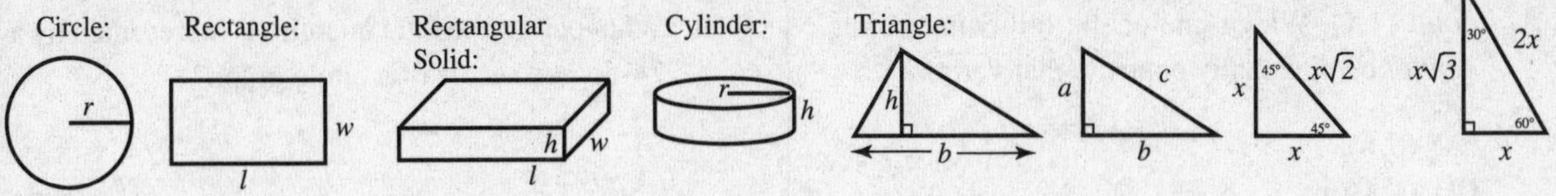

$C = 2\pi r$, $A = \pi r^2$ | $A = lw$ | $V = lwh$ | $V = \pi r^2 h$ | $A = \frac{1}{2}bh$ | $a^2 + b^2 = c^2$

The number of degrees of arc in a circle is 360.
The measure in degrees of a straight angle is 180.
The sum of the measures in degrees of the angles of a triangle is 180.

1. Which one of the following quantities has the lowest numerical value?

(A) $\frac{4}{5}$
(B) $\frac{7}{9}$
(C) .76
(D) $\frac{5}{7}$
(E) $\frac{9}{11}$

2. A salesperson earns twice as much in December as in each of the other months of a year. What part of this salesperson's entire year's earnings are earned in December?

(A) $\frac{1}{7}$
(B) $\frac{2}{13}$
(C) $\frac{1}{6}$
(D) $\frac{2}{11}$
(E) $\frac{3}{14}$

3. If $x = -1$, then $3x^3 + 2x^2 + x + 1 =$

(A) –5
(B) –1
(C) 1
(D) 2
(E) 5

4. $.03\% \times .21 =$

(A) .63
(B) .063
(C) .0063
(D) .00063
(E) .000063

GO ON TO THE NEXT PAGE

5. An equilateral triangle 3 inches on a side is cut up into smaller equilateral triangles one inch on a side. What is the greatest number of such triangles that can be formed?

(A) 3
(B) 6
(C) 9
(D) 12
(E) 15

6. A square 5 units on a side has one vertex at the point (1,1). Which one of the following points *cannot* be diagonally opposite that vertex?

(A) (6, 6)
(B) (– 4, 6)
(C) (– 4, – 4)
(D) (6, – 4)
(E) (4, – 6)

7. Five equal squares are placed side by side to make a single rectangle whose perimeter is 372 inches. Find the number of square inches in the area of one of these squares.

(A) 72
(B) 324
(C) 900
(D) 961
(E) 984

8. The water level of a swimming pool, 75 feet by 42 feet, is to be raised four inches. How many gallons of water must be added to accomplish this?
(7.48 gal. = 1 cubic ft.)

(A) 140
(B) 7,854
(C) 31,500
(D) 94,500
(E) 727,650

9. What part of the total quantity is represented by a 24-degree sector of a circle graph?

(A) $6\frac{2}{3}\%$

(B) 12%

(C) $13\frac{1}{3}\%$

(D) 15%

(E) 24%

10. The square of a fraction between 0 and 1 is

(A) less than the original fraction
(B) greater than the original fraction
(C) twice the original fraction
(D) less than the cube of the fraction
(E) not necessarily any of the preceding

STOP

END OF SECTION 4. IF YOU HAVE ANY TIME LEFT, GO OVER YOUR WORK IN THIS SECTION ONLY. DO NOT WORK IN ANY OTHER SECTION OF THE TEST.

SECTION 5

35 Questions • Time—30 Minutes

Directions: Each of the following questions consists of an incomplete sentence followed by five words or pairs of words. Choose that word or pair of words which, when substituted for the blank space or spaces, *best* completes the meaning of the sentence and mark the letter of your choice on your answer sheet.

Example:

In view of the extenuating circumstances and the defendant's youth, the judge recommended ----.

(A) conviction (B) a defense
(C) a mistrial (D) leniency
(E) life imprisonment Ⓐ Ⓑ Ⓒ ● Ⓔ

1. The ---- was greatest when the pitcher paused before delivering the last strike.

(A) game
(B) crowd
(C) cheering
(D) sportsmanship
(E) tension

2. Her ---- instincts led her to fund the construction of a hospital for the poor.

(A) far-ranging
(B) humanitarian
(C) humble
(D) popular
(E) eclectic

3. After years of ---- war, the Great Wall was constructed to ---- the Chinese people.

(A) internecine..instigate
(B) destructive..resurrect
(C) unceasing..protect
(D) amicable..unite
(E) pitiable..win

4. His remarks were so ---- that we could not decide which of the possible meanings was correct.

(A) facetious
(B) ambiguous
(C) cogent
(D) impalpable
(E) congruent

5. In an attempt to ---- a strike, the two sides agreed to negotiate through the night.

(A) arbitrate
(B) herald
(C) trigger
(D) transmute
(E) avert

6. Elder statesmen used to be ---- for their wisdom when respect for age was part of every person's upbringing.

(A) deplored
(B) exonerated
(C) rebuked
(D) venerated
(E) exiled

7. Being less than perfectly prepared, she approached the exam with ----.

(A) aplomb
(B) trepidation
(C) indifference
(D) confidence
(E) duplicity

8. As citizens, we would be ---- if we did not make these facts public.

(A) derelict
(B) pejorative
(C) impersonal
(D) private
(E) derogatory

GO ON TO THE NEXT PAGE

9. She was usually a model of ----, so her sudden burst of temper was atypical.

(A) veracity
(B) lucidity
(C) facility
(D) equanimity
(E) hostility

10. The ---- attitudes politicians have today cause them to ---- at the slightest hint of controversy.

(A) dauntless..recoil
(B) craven..cower
(C) pusillanimous..prevail
(D) undaunted..quail
(E) fractious..grovel

11. A person who is ---- is slow to adapt to a new way of life.

(A) nonchalant
(B) intractable
(C) rabid
(D) insolent
(E) doughty

12. Though they came from ---- social backgrounds, the newly married couple shared numerous interests and feelings.

(A) desultory
(B) obsolete
(C) malleable
(D) disparate
(E) deleterious

13. The ---- was a ---- of gastronomic delights.

(A) internist..progeny
(B) gourmet..connoisseur
(C) scientist..facilitator
(D) xenophobe..promotor
(E) tyro..master

14. Mrs. Jenkins, upon hearing that her arm was broken, looked ---- at the doctor.

(A) jovially
(B) plaintively
(C) fortuitously
(D) serendipitously
(E) opportunely

15. Even ---- pleasures may leave ---- memories.

(A) ephemeral..lasting
(B) emphatic..stalwart
(C) transitory..fleeting
(D) surreptitious..secret
(E) enigmatic..mysterious

Directions: Each of the following questions consists of a capitalized pair of words followed by five pairs of words lettered A to E. The capitalized words bear some meaningful relationship to each other. Choose the lettered pair of words whose relationship is most similar to that expressed by the capitalized pair and mark its letter on your answer sheet.

Example:

DAY : SUN : :

(A) sunlight : daylight (B) ray : sun
(C) night : moon (D) heat : cold
(E) moon : star

Ⓐ Ⓑ ● Ⓓ Ⓔ

16. FEEL : TOUCH : :

(A) tickle : hurt
(B) see : look
(C) sprint : lift
(D) giggle : laugh
(E) shed : grow

17. CIRCLE : SQUARE : :

(A) ball : bat
(B) oval : rectangle
(C) sphere : globe
(D) angular : straight
(E) volume : area

18. CHICKEN : ROOSTER : :

(A) deer : doe
(B) duck : drake
(C) flock : hen
(D) ewe : ram
(E) pig : piglet

19. TRIGGER : PISTOL : :

(A) bullet : gun
(B) rifle : revolver
(C) guard : police
(D) switch : motor
(E) fire : shoot

20. GOOD : ANGELIC : :

(A) bad : poor
(B) glad : joyous
(C) mean : human
(D) sweet : musty
(E) correct : incorrect

21. CLARINET : WOODWIND : :

(A) piano : key
(B) symphony : composer
(C) banjo : guitar
(D) trumpet : brass
(E) horn : tuba

22. GRIEF : DOLEFUL : :

(A) melancholy : hopeful
(B) greed : successful
(C) anger : wrathful
(D) fear : unintentional
(E) reaction : involuntary

23. PAIL : WATER : :

(A) milk : quart
(B) eggs : dozen
(C) gallon : container
(D) river : ocean
(E) shaker : salt

24. FISH : AQUARIUM : :

(A) birds : aviary
(B) car : garage
(C) insects : ground
(D) lightning : sky
(E) dogs : pets

25. DISAGREEMENT : CONCORD : :

(A) limitation : restriction
(B) impartiality : bias
(C) advantage : agreement
(D) predicament : dilemma
(E) predictability : routine

Directions: The reading passage below is followed by a set of questions. Read the passage and answer the accompanying questions, basing your answers on what is stated or implied in the passage. Mark the letter of your choice on your answer sheet.

Questions 26–35 are based on the following passage.

Louisa May Alcott (1832–1888) was a beloved author of books for children, but she also wrote gothic tales and short stories for adults. This excerpt is from "Mrs. Gay's Prescription."

The poor little woman looked as if she needed rest but was not likely to get it; for the room was in a chaotic state, the breakfast table presented the appearance of having been devastated by a swarm of locusts, the baby began to fret, little Polly set up her usual whine of "I want sumpin to do," and a pile of work loomed in the corner waiting to be done.

"I don't see how I ever shall get through it all," sighed the despondent matron as she hastily drank a last cup of tea, while two great tears rolled down her cheeks, as she looked from one puny child to the other, and felt the weariness of her own tired soul and body more oppressive than ever.

"A good cry" was impending, when there came a brisk ring at the door, a step in the hall, and a large, rosy woman came bustling in, saying in a cheery voice as she set a flower-pot down upon the table, "Good morning! Nice day, isn't it? Came in early on business and brought you one of my Lady Washingtons, you are so fond of flowers."

"Oh, it's lovely! How kind you are. Do sit down if you can find a chair; we are all behind hand today, for I was up half the night with poor baby, and haven't energy enough to go to work yet," answered Mrs. Bennet, with a sudden smile that changed her whole face, while baby stopped fretting to stare at the rosy clusters, and Polly found employment in exploring the pocket of the new comer, as if she knew her way there.

"Let me put the pot on your stand first, girls are so careless, and I'm proud of this. It will be an ornament to your parlor for a week," and opening a door Mrs. Gay carried the plant to a sunny bay window where many others were blooming beautifully.

Mrs. Bennet and the children followed to talk and admire, while the servant leisurely cleared the table.

"Now give me that baby, put yourself in the easy chair, and tell me all about your worries," said Mrs. Gay, in the brisk, commanding way which few people could resist.

"I'm sure I don't know where to begin," sighed Mrs. Bennet, dropping into the comfortable seat while baby changed bearers with great composure.

"I met your husband and he said the doctor had ordered you and these chicks off to Florida for the winter. John said he didn't know how he should manage it, but he meant to try."

"Isn't it dreadful? He can't leave his business to go with me, and we shall have to get Aunt Miranda to come and see to him and the boys while I'm gone, and the boys can't bear her strict, old-fashioned ways, and I've got to go that long journey all alone and stay among strangers, and these heaps of fall work to do first, and it will cost an immense sum to send us, and I don't know what is to become of me."

Here Mrs. Bennet stopped for breath, and Mrs. Gay asked briskly, "What is the matter with you and the children?"

"Well, baby is having a hard time with his teeth and is croupy, Polly doesn't get over scarlet fever well, and I'm used up; no strength or appetite, pain in my side and low spirits. Entire change of scene, milder climate, and less work for me, is what we want, the doctor says. John is very anxious about us, and I feel regularly discouraged."

"I'll spend the day and cheer you up a bit. You just rest and get ready for a new start to-morrow; it is a saving of time to stop short now and then and see where to begin next. Bring me the most pressing job of work. I can sew and see to this little rascal at the same time."

26. The "little woman" referred to in line 1 is

(A) Lady Washington
(B) Alcott's mother
(C) a servant
(D) Mrs. Bennet
(E) Mrs. Gay

27. When Alcott compares the breakfast table to something "devastated by a swarm of locusts" (line 4), she means

(A) that it is a mess left by an uncaring mob
(B) that children are no more meaningful than insects to Mrs. Bennet
(C) to indicate Mrs. Bennet's flightiness
(D) to illustrate the horror of Mrs. Bennet's life
(E) that the Bennets are pests

28. Had Mrs. Gay not arrived when she did, Alcott leads us to suspect that

(A) Mrs. Bennet would have gone back to bed
(B) the children would have continued to cry
(C) Mrs. Bennet would have accomplished little all day
(D) sickness would have overtaken the entire family
(E) the servant would have left the dishes untended

29. The "rosy clusters" in lines 26–27 are

(A) Mrs. Gay's cheeks
(B) Mrs. Bennet's cheeks
(C) flowers
(D) candies from Mrs. Gay's pockets
(E) embroidered pockets

30. In lines 31–33 Alcott

(A) reveals Mrs. Bennet's only talent
(B) uses the sunny parlor as a symbol of hope
(C) contrasts Mrs. Gay's sunniness with Mrs. Bennet's dullness
(D) contrasts Mrs. Bennet's plants with her children
(E) opens the door to Mrs. Bennet's despair

31. When Mrs. Bennet says that she's "used up" (line 60), she means that she

(A) has no energy
(B) is abused
(C) is exploited
(D) has spent all her money
(E) has given up

32. The word *pressing* (line 68) means

(A) heavy
(B) ardent
(C) forceful
(D) important
(E) concentrated

33. Mrs. Bennet's friend's disposition is indicated by

(A) her name
(B) her speech
(C) her clothing
(D) both A and B
(E) both B and C

34. Alcott implies that Mrs. Bennet's real problem is

(A) her inability to cope
(B) a touch of fever
(C) the cold winter weather
(D) unsympathetic children
(E) a lack of common sense

35. Mrs. Gay's primary quality seems to be her

(A) lethargy
(B) obliviousness
(C) anxiety
(D) dignity
(E) practical nature

STOP

END OF SECTION 5. IF YOU HAVE ANY TIME LEFT, GO OVER YOUR WORK IN THIS SECTION ONLY. DO NOT WORK IN ANY OTHER SECTION OF THE TEST.

SECTION 6

25 Questions • Time—30 Minutes

Directions: Solve the following problems using any available space on the page for scratchwork. On your answer sheet fill in the choice which best corresponds to the correct answer.

Notes: The figures accompanying the problems are drawn as accurately as possible unless otherwise stated in specific problems. Again, unless otherwise stated, all figures lie in the same plane. All numbers used in these problems are real numbers. Calculators are permitted for this test.

Reference Information

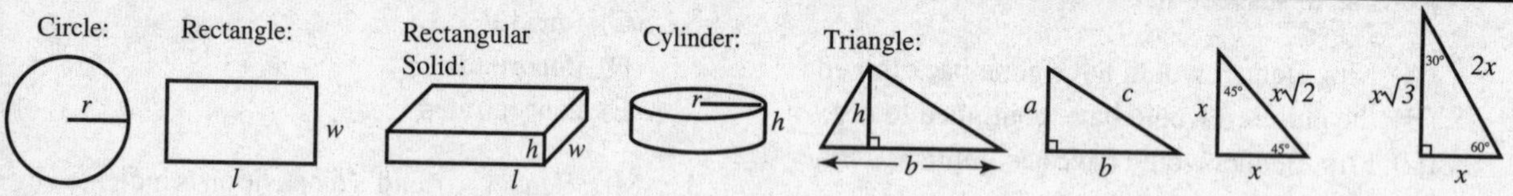

$C = 2\pi r$
$A = \pi r^2$

$A = lw$

$V = lwh$

$V = \pi r^2 h$

$A = \frac{1}{2}bh$

$a^2 + b^2 = c^2$

The number of degrees of arc in a circle is 360.
The measure in degrees of a straight angle is 180.
The sum of the measures in degrees of the angles of a triangle is 180.

Part I: Quantitative Comparison Questions

Directions: For each of the following questions, two quantities are given—one in Column A, the other in Column B. Compare the two quantities and mark your answer sheet as follows:

(A) if the quantity in Column A is greater
(B) if the quantity in Column B is greater
(C) if the quantities are equal
(D) if the relationship cannot be determined from the information given

Notes:

(1) Information concerning one or both of the compared quantities will be centered above the two columns for some items.
(2) Symbols that appear in both columns represent the same thing in Column A as in Column B.
(3) Letters such as *x*, *n*, and *k* are symbols for real numbers.

Examples

	Column A	Column B	Answers
	$a > 0$ $x > 0$		
E1.	$a - x$	$a + x$	Ⓐ ● Ⓒ Ⓓ
E2.	The average of 17, 19, 21, 23	The average of 16, 18, 20, 22	● Ⓑ Ⓒ Ⓓ

DO NOT MARK CHOICE (E) FOR THESE QUESTIONS. THERE ARE ONLY FOUR ANSWER CHOICES.

	Column A	Column B
1.	$\dfrac{a^2+b}{2}$	$.5(a^2+b)$

Note: Figure not drawn to scale.

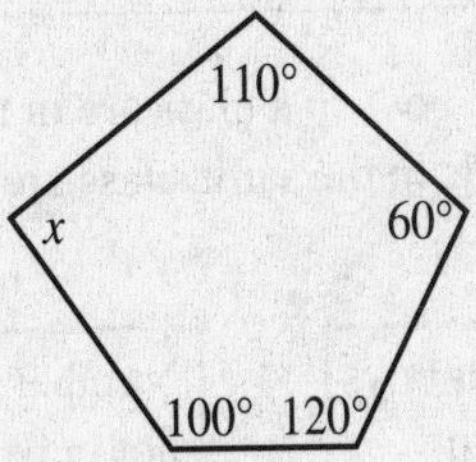

2.	x	90°

$$\frac{m}{n}=\frac{7}{10}$$

3.	mn	70

For all real numbers x and y, let Δ be defined as $x\Delta y = \dfrac{xy}{x-y}$.

4.	$-3\Delta -2$	$-2\Delta -3$

Note: Figure not drawn to scale.

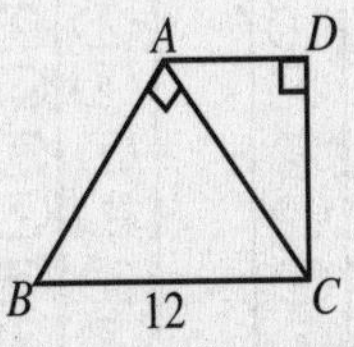

5.	12	side *CD*

	Column A	Column B

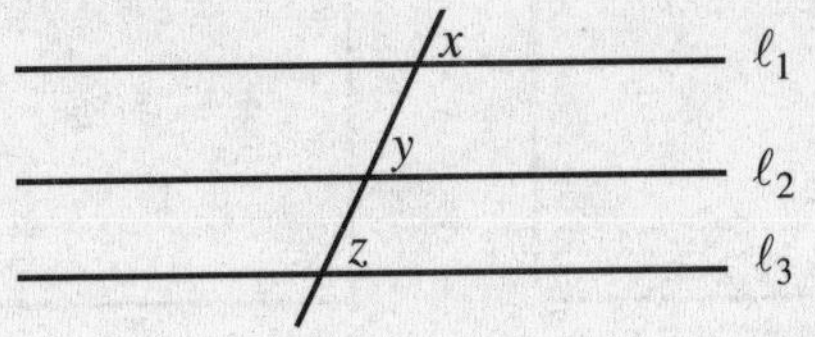

$\ell_1 \| \ell_2 \| \ell_3$

6.	$x+y$	$y+z$
7.	3% of 4%	.0012

A two-pound box of Brand A costs $7.88.
A three-pound box of Brand B costs $11.79.

8.	Cost per pound of Brand A	Cost per pound of Brand B

Note: Figure not drawn to scale.

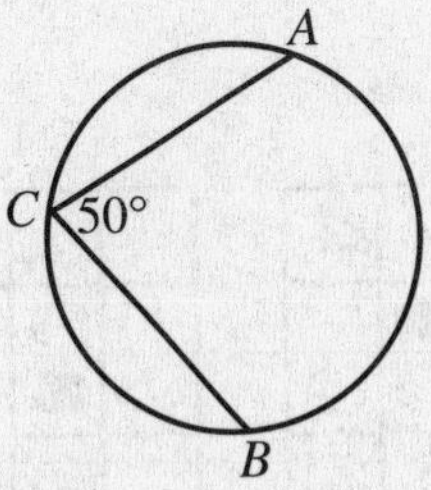

9.	90	Degree measure of arc *AB*
10.	$\sqrt{8}+\sqrt{24}$	$\sqrt{32}$

GO ON TO THE NEXT PAGE

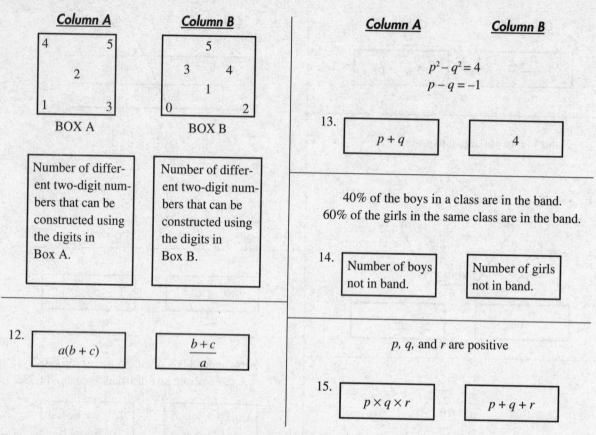

Column A	Column B
BOX A: 4, 5, 2, 1, 3	BOX B: 5, 3, 4, 1, 0, 2
Number of different two-digit numbers that can be constructed using the digits in Box A.	Number of different two-digit numbers that can be constructed using the digits in Box B.

12.

Column A	Column B
$a(b+c)$	$\frac{b+c}{a}$

$$p^2 - q^2 = 4$$
$$p - q = -1$$

13.

Column A	Column B
$p+q$	4

40% of the boys in a class are in the band.
60% of the girls in the same class are in the band.

14.

Column A	Column B
Number of boys not in band.	Number of girls not in band.

p, q, and r are positive

15.

Column A	Column B
$p \times q \times r$	$p + q + r$

Part 2: Student-Produced Response Questions

Directions: Solve each of these problems. Write the answer in the corresponding grid on the answer sheet and fill in the ovals beneath each answer you write. Here are some examples.

Answer: $\frac{3}{4}$ (= .75; show answer either way)

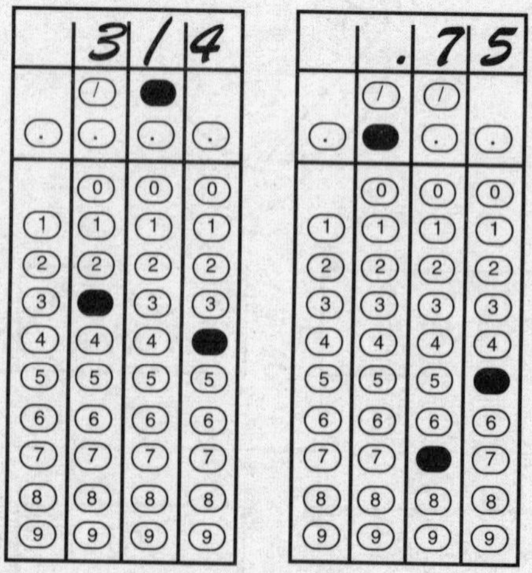

Note: A mixed number such as $3\frac{1}{2}$ must be gridded as 7/2 or as 3.5. If gridded as "3 1/2," it will be read as "thirty-one halves."

Answer: 325

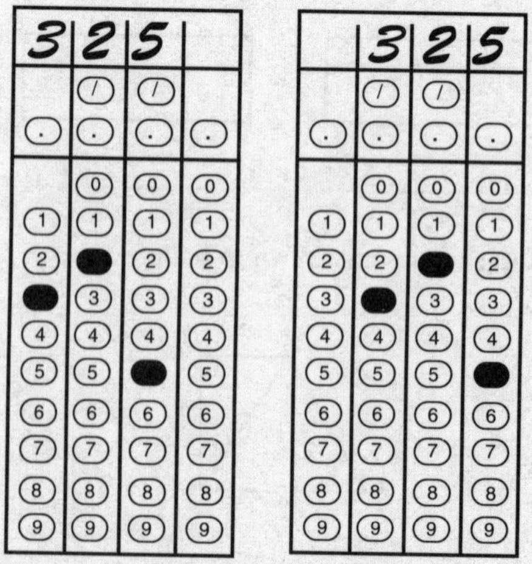

Note: Either position is correct.

16. $\left(\sqrt{18}-\sqrt{8}\right)^2 =$

17. The distance from the center of a circle to a chord is 5. If the length of the chord is 24, what is the length of the radius of the circle?

18. If the cost of a party is to be split equally among 11 friends, each would pay \$15.00. If 20 persons equally split the same cost, how much would each person pay?

19. In the figure below, $m\angle N = (9x - 40)°$, $m\angle J = (4x + 30)°$ and $m\angle JLR = (8x + 40)°$. What is the measure of $\angle J$? (Do not grid the degree symbol.)

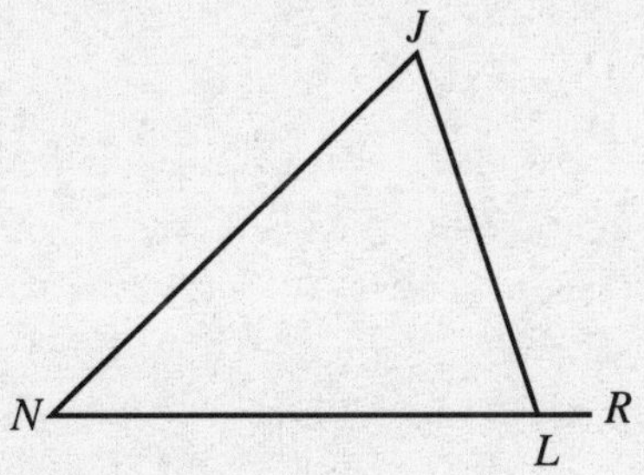

20. $\dfrac{2^2 + 3^2}{5^2} + \dfrac{1}{10} =$

21. In the figure below two circles are tangent to each other and each is tangent to three sides of the rectangle. If the radius of each circle is 3, then the area of the shaded portion is $a - b\pi$. What is the value of a?

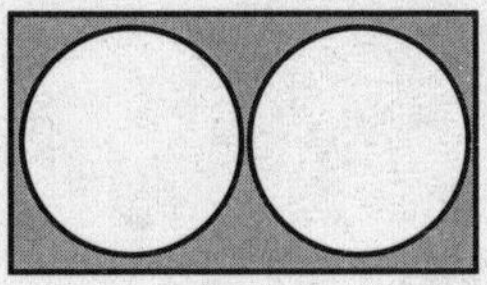

22. The measures of the angles of a triangle are in the ratio of 3:5:7. What is the measure, in degrees, of the smallest angle? (Do not grid the degree symbol.)

23. The length of the line segment whose end points are (3, –2) and (–4,5) is $b\sqrt{2}$. What is the value of b?

24. Jessica caught five fish with an average weight of 10 pounds. If three of the fish weigh 9, 9, and 10 pounds, respectively, what is the average (arithmetic mean) weight of the other two fish?

25. In the figure below, what is the area of ΔNKL?

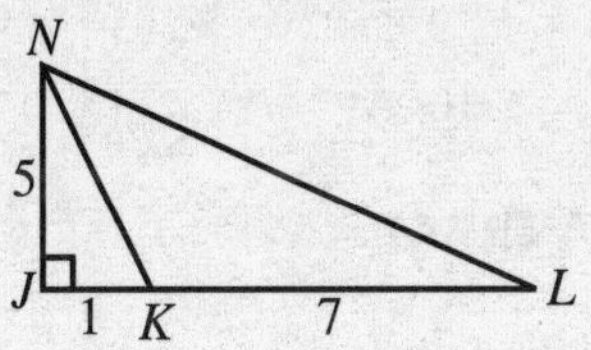

STOP

END OF SECTION 6. IF YOU HAVE ANY TIME LEFT, GO OVER YOUR WORK IN THIS SECTION ONLY. DO NOT WORK IN ANY OTHER SECTION OF THE TEST.

Pratice Examination 2

Answer Key

Section 1: VERBAL

1. C	7. C	13. B	19. D	25. A
2. E	8. E	14. C	20. B	26. C
3. A	9. E	15. B	21. C	27. E
4. D	10. C	16. D	22. D	28. C
5. B	11. B	17. E	23. B	29. A
6. A	12. D	18. C	24. A	30. E

Section 2: MATH

1. C	6. A	11. B	16. D	21. A
2. C	7. D	12. D	17. C	22. B
3. C	8. C	13. B	18. C	23. A
4. B	9. D	14. C	19. B	24. D
5. D	10. A	15. D	20. D	25. D

Section 3: VERBAL

1. E	4. B	7. E	10. C
2. A	5. A	8. D	11. C
3. A	6. C	9. A	12. C

Section 4: MATH

1. D	3. B	5. C	7. D	9. A
2. B	4. E	6. E	8. B	10. A

Section 5: VERBAL

1. E	8. A	15. A	22. C	29. C
2. B	9. D	16. B	23. E	30. B
3. C	10. B	17. B	24. A	31. A
4. B	11. B	18. B	25. B	32. D
5. E	12. D	19. D	26. D	33. D
6. D	13. B	20. B	27. A	34. A
7. B	14. B	21. D	28. C	35. E

Section 6: MATH

Part 1

1. C	4. B	7. C	10. A	13. B
2. A	5. A	8. A	11. B	14. D
3. D	6. C	9. B	12. D	15. D

Part 2

16. 2	18. 8.25	20. $\frac{31}{50} = .62$	22. 36	24. 11
17. 13	19. 70	21. 72	23. 7	25. $17.5 = \frac{35}{2}$

Practice Examination 2

Explanatory Answers

Note: A following a math answer explanation indicates that a calculator could be helpful in solving that particular problem.

Section 1

1. **(C)** Audience laughter at the wrong moment can easily *disconcert* (upset or confuse) an actor.

2. **(E)** Since the assurances of good faith were "hollow," it is not surprising that those who made them *reneged* on (went back on) their agreement.

3. **(A)** To win the majority, we must unite, or *amalgamate,* the different factions.

4. **(D)** A law known as the Prohibition Act would naturally be expected to *proscribe* (outlaw) something.

5. **(B)** A caller who will not give his name is by definition *anonymous.* Since he is giving information to the police, he may well fear *reprisals* (retaliation) by a criminal.

6. **(A)** A primary function of the *throat* is to *swallow*, and a primary function of the *teeth* is to *chew.*

7. **(C)** A *garnet* has the color *red,* and an *emerald* has the color *green.*

8. **(E)** *Patience* is considered one of the virtues, just as *literature* is considered one of the *arts.*

9. **(E)** An airplane that can *soar* will eventually *alight* on the ground. A boat that can *sail* will eventually *moor* at a dock.

10. **(C)** An *oasis* is a place of refuge in the middle of the *desert.* An *island* is a place of refuge in the middle of the *ocean.*

11. **(B)** *Cotton* is *soft* to the touch, as an *iron* is *hard* to the touch.

12. **(D)** A *year* is a hundredth of a *century*, and a *cent* is a hundredth of a *dollar.*

13. **(B)** A well-known characteristic of a *mule* is that it is *intractable* (stubborn). Likewise, the *fox* is known for being *wily* (sly and crafty).

14. **(C)** If we *stumble,* our *walking* is impeded, and if we *stammer,* our *speaking* is impeded.

15. **(B)** Although Borgia was "reputed cruel," "his cruelty restored Romagna, united it, and brought it to order . . ." (lines 4–5). He used cruelty to good effect, according to Machiavelli.

16. **(D)** In this passage, *signal* means out of the ordinary, or remarkable, as used in "For he who quells disorder by a very few signal examples will be in the end more merciful than he who from too great leniency permits things to take their course and so to result in rapine and bloodshed." One can infer from this that capital punishment as a preventive measure can inhibit capital crimes later, if judiciously applied.

17. **(E)** The idea of balance is presented through parallel and contrasting clauses in this paragraph. A Prince should "temper prudence with kindliness" (lines 28–29).

18. **(C)** The last paragraph avers that ". . . it is far safer to be feared than loved. For of men it may be generally affirmed that they are thankless, fickle, false, studious to avoid danger, greedy of gain, devoted to you while you are able to confer benefits upon them, and ready, as I said before, while danger is distant, to shed their blood and sacrifice their property, their lives, and their children for you; but in the hour of need they turn against you."

19. **(D)** This is made clear in the first paragraph, "I say that every Prince should desire to be accounted merciful and not cruel. Nevertheless, he should be on his guard against the abuse of this quality of mercy."

20. **(B)** *Greatness* and *nobility of character* were singled out in the last paragraph as essentials for maintaining loyalty and friendship; *prudence,* according to the fourth paragraph, is essential to prevent being thrown off guard. As for *severity,* which inspires fear, ". . . it is far safer to be feared than loved." *Popularity,* it is implied throughout the passage, can be dispensed with up to a point, but the other criteria are shown to be indispensable.

21. **(C)** Machiavelli uses the words "thankless, fickle, false, studious to avoid danger, greedy of gain . . ." to describe men in general—a pessimistic view of human nature, but one he feels is realistic and should be taken into account by any Prince.

22. **(D)** In every paragraph, the merits of being popular (i.e., *loved*) as opposed to being firm (i.e., *feared*) are discussed. In the second, fourth, and fifth paragraphs the writer discusses these merits in terms of rulers in general; in the first and third paragraphs he cites the examples of Borgia and Dido as implementers of his ideas on love and fear in rulers.

23. **(B)** Jupiter is being asked to decide which of three goddesses is the fairest—it is a no-win decision, since it is bound to anger two of the three.

24. **(A)** Ulysses has no inclination to embark on the adventure, since he is happy at home with his family.

25. **(A)** "Ulysses pretended to be mad" (lines 41–42), and one of the methods he chose was to hitch up a mismatched team and sow something that could not grow.

26. **(C)** Palamedes doesn't buy Ulysses's mad act, and he thinks up a way to test him. Since Ulysses is unwilling to run over his own son, he is obviously not as mad as he pretends to be.

27. **(E)** Rather than say that Thetis, being a sea-nymph, can read the future, Bulfinch merely mentions her immortal status and expects the reader to understand that this means that she knows "her son was fated to perish."

28. **(C)** The names in (A) are those of goddesses. Paris is a "beautiful shepherd" (line 11). Eris is a goddess (line 6). Thetis is a sea-nymph (lines 51–52). Homer and Virgil are poets (lines 32–33). Only choice (C) names three chieftains of Greece.

29. **(A)** Again, Bulfinch expects his readers to understand Ulysses's clever ploy without its being spelled out. Achilles is disguised as a woman, but he is inappropriately interested in manly objects.

30. **(E)** This is an accurate summary of the main themes in the passage.

Section 2

1. **(C)** Let the other two angles be $2x$ and $5x$.

$$\text{Thus, } 2x + 5x + 82 = 180$$
$$7x = 98$$
$$x = 14$$
$$2x = 28$$
$$5x = 70$$

Smallest angle = 28°

2. **(C)** Let x = no. of years for 2 populations to be equal.

$$\text{Then } 6800 - 120x = 4200 + 80x$$
$$2600 = 200x$$
$$x = 13$$

3. **(C)** Simply plug the two values into the formula.

$2^2 - 2(2) = 0$ and $1^2 - 2(1) = -1$
$*2 - *1 = 0 - (-1) = 1.$

4. **(B)**

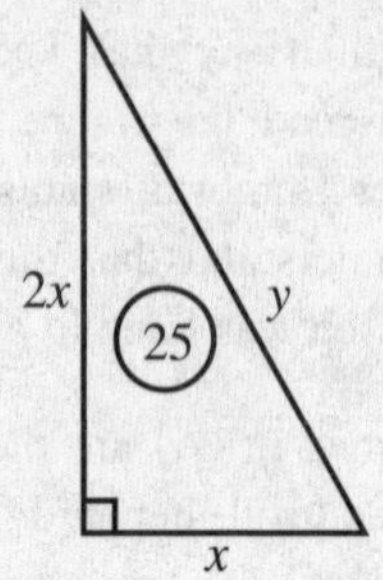

$$\frac{1}{2} \cdot x \cdot 2x = 25$$

$$x^2 = 25$$

$$x = 5$$

$$2x = 10$$

$$y^2 = 5^2 + 10^2$$

$$y^2 = 25 + 100$$

$$y^2 = 125$$

$$y = \sqrt{125} = \sqrt{25 \times 5}$$

$$y = 5\sqrt{5}$$

5. **(D)** The abscissa of Q is 3 more than that of P. The ordinate of Q is 2 less than that of P. Hence, coordinates of Q are $(3 + 3, 7–2) = (6, 5)$

6. **(A)** $r = 5x$
   Divide both sides by 10

$$\frac{r}{10} = \frac{5}{10}x$$

or $$\frac{1}{10}r = \frac{1}{2}x$$

Hence, 1 is the answer.

7. **(D)** The area of triangle ADE equals the area of triangle AEC, since they have the same base and altitude. The area of triangle ABC equals that of triangle ADC, since the diagonal of a parallelogram divides it equally.

8. **(C)** If the side of a square is s, its diagonal is the hypotenuse of a right triangle with two sides as its legs. The length of the diagonal is $\sqrt{s^2 + s^2} = \sqrt{2}s$

$$0.7(\sqrt{2}s) \approx (0.7)(1.4)s \approx 1s = s.$$

9. **(D)** This is an inverse proportion; that is:

$$\frac{9}{6} = \frac{x}{120}$$

$$6x = 1080$$

$$x = 180$$

10. **(A)** Thinking of a clock in terms of degrees, there are 360 degrees from 12 noon to 12 midnight. In one hour there are 360 degrees ÷ 12 hours = 30 degrees per hour. In two hours the hour hand moves 2 hours × 30 degrees per hour = 60 degrees. Therefore, in 2 hours and 12 minutes the hour hand moves 66 degrees.

11. **(B)** $8 \times 6 = 48$

$$6 \times 8 = 48$$

$48 + 48 = 96$ (sum of all 14 numbers)

$$\text{Average} = \frac{96}{14} = 6\frac{6}{7}$$

12. **(D)** I. As x increases, $(1 - x^2)$ decreases.
    II. As x increases, $(x - 1)$ increases
    III. As x increases, $\frac{1}{x^2}$ decreases.
    Hence, only II increases.

13. **(B)** 3, 7, 12, 18, 25,

    Differences are 4, 5, 6, 7, 8, . . . etc.
    Thus the series progresses as follows: 3, 7, 12, 18, 25, 33, 42, 52, 63

14. **(C)** The numerator is the difference between perfect squares. $x^2 - y^2$ is equal to the product of $(x + y)$ and $(x - y)$. Therefore,

$$\frac{x^2 - y^2}{x - y} = \frac{(x + y)(x - y)}{x - y} = x + y$$

15. **(D)** The distance traveled is the circumference of the wheel times the number of revolutions. If r is the number of revolutions of the back wheel, $r + 10$ will be the number of revolutions of the front wheel. They will have traveled the same distance, so 7 ft. × $(r + 10)$ = 9ft. × r, and $r = 35$. The wagon has gone 9 ft. × 35 revolutions = 315 ft.

16. **(D)** The dimensions of the flower bed including the walk are (12 + 6) and (16 + 6). Thus, the area is 18 yds. × 22 yds = 396 square yards. The area of the flower bed alone is 12 × 16 = 192 square yds. Therefore, the area of the walk is 396 square yds – 192 square yds. = 204 square yds.

17. **(C)** Dave takes 30 minutes to wash the car alone.

$$\frac{x}{15}+\frac{x}{30}=1$$
$$2x + x = 30$$
$$3x = 30$$
$$x = 10$$

18. **(C)** Let r = radius of inscribed circle and s = radius of circumscribed circle. Then in right triangle OPQ, $PQ = OQ = r$ and $s = OP = r\sqrt{2}$.

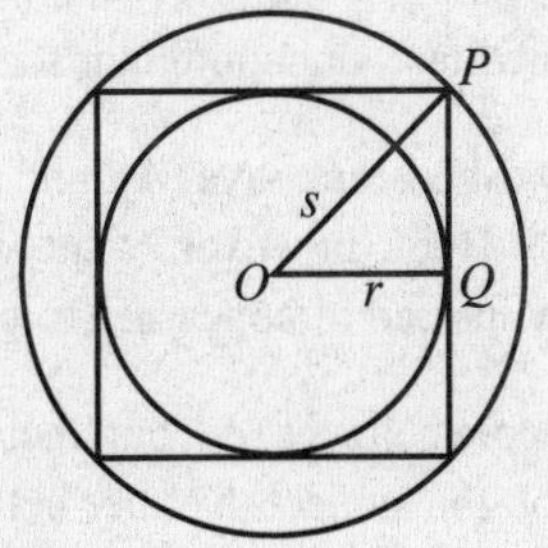

Area of inscribed circle = πr^2

Area of circumscribed circle = $\pi s^2 = \pi\left(r\sqrt{2}\right)^2 = 2\pi r^2$

Ratio = $\frac{\pi r^2}{2\pi r^2} = 1{:}2$

19. **(B)** Let x = no. of minutes to fill $\frac{4}{7}$ of bucket.

Then $\frac{\frac{3}{7}}{1}=\frac{\frac{4}{7}}{x}$, or $\frac{3}{1}=\frac{4}{x}$

$3x = 4 \qquad x=\frac{4}{3}$

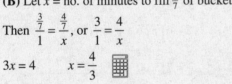

20. **(D)** The similar triangles in the configuration produce the proportion

$$\frac{3}{5}=\frac{4}{Y}$$
$$3Y = 20$$
$$Y = 6\frac{2}{3}$$

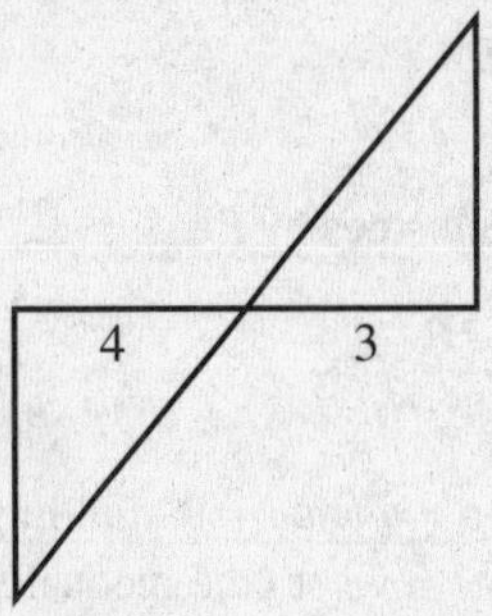

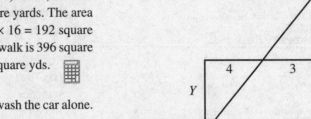

21. **(A)** An increase of 30% in the base b means that the new base will be $b + .30b$. A 20% decrease in the new altitude a means that the new altitude will be $a - .20a$. The new area is $(b + .30b)(a - .20a) = 1.04ba$. The new area is 104% of the old, an increase of 104% – 100% = 4%.

22. **(B)** Typing space is 12 – 3 = 9 inches long and 9 – 2 = 7 inches wide. Part used =

$$\frac{9\times7}{9\times12}=\frac{7}{12}$$

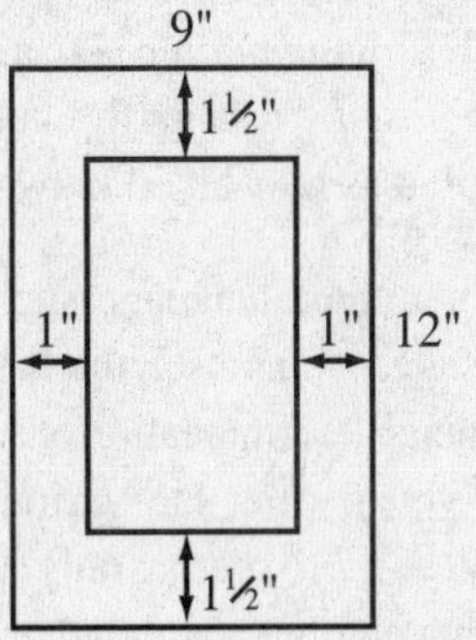

23. **(A)** $\Delta SPT = \frac{1}{3}\Delta PSR$ since they have common altitude and the base $ST = \frac{1}{3}SR$.

But $\Delta PSR = \frac{1}{2}\square\ PQRS$

Hence $\Delta SPT = \frac{1}{3}\bullet\frac{1}{2}\square = \frac{1}{6}\square$

24. **(D)** $A = P(1+rt)$

$A = P + Prt$

$A - P = Prt$

Divide both sides by *Pr*.

$$t = \frac{A-P}{Pr}$$

25. **(D)** I. If $p > q$ and $r < 0$, multiplying both sides by r reverses the inequality $pr < qr$

II. Also $p + r > q + r$

III. However, subtracting r from both sides leaves inequality in same order.

Hence I and II only.

Section 3

1. **(E)** Try out other choices in the context of the sentence, and you will see that only one choice works.

2. **(A)** This is the main idea of paragraph 2, and the author goes so far in lines 16–17 to say that these straight avenues "must give actual pain to a person of taste."

3. **(A)** The other choices are synonyms for *immune* [(B) and (C)], *immutable* (D), and *impulsive* (E). Only *enclosed* explains the author's feeling of being jailed as he walked between the hedges.

4. **(B)** With archaic language such as that in these two passages, you must work harder than usual to comprehend the connotation of each phrase. However, if you try out the various choices in the sentence, you will see that only (B) fits the context of viewing an object and then traveling to it by a different path.

5. **(A)** The author of Passage 1 cites all of the answer choices except for (A) as illustrations of unattractive landscaping. Choice (A), a "uniform expanse of lawn," is referred to by the author of Passage 2, who cites "too uniform or too extensive a lawn" as a feature that Kent sought to eliminate by adding trees.

6. **(C)** This figure of speech refers to Kent's ability to look beyond the traditional fenced-in garden and see, as the author says, "that all nature was a garden."

7. **(E)** The author touches on (A) and hints at (B), but neither of these is his main purpose. You must look at the paragraph as a whole to understand that every sentence has to do with Kent's application of artistic principles to landscaping.

8. **(D)** The root *serpent* helps, but the context of the sentence helps more. The author is contrasting forced canals and waterfalls to a more natural, winding motion of streams.

9. **(A)** The villas in question relied on forced cataracts and other unnatural uses of water, all of which the author considers "absurd." Hence, he clearly considers their landscaping to be unattractive.

10. **(C)** The only answer choice of which the author of Passage 2 would likely approve is (C), "a winding stream with trees and bushes scattered along its banks." The others are all examples of overly artificial, unnatural landscapes.

11. **(C)** Only Shenstone says (A), and neither author says (B). Both, however, want water to wind naturally instead of appearing forced.

12. **(C)** Walpole believes (A), but Shenstone is never quoted on the subject. Neither believes (B), and only Shenstone gives any opinion on (D) or (E). Both authors talk about breaking up vistas, Shenstone in paragraphs 2 and 3, and Walpole in paragraph 2.

Section 4

1. **(D)** $\frac{4}{5} = .8$

$$\frac{7}{9} = \begin{array}{r} .78 \\ 9\overline{)7.00} \end{array}$$

$$\frac{5}{7} = \begin{array}{r} .71 \\ 7\overline{)5.00} \end{array}$$

$$\frac{9}{11} = \begin{array}{r} .82 \\ 11\overline{)9.00} \end{array}$$

Thus, $\frac{5}{7}$ is the smallest quantity.

2. **(B)** Let x = amount earned each month. $2x$= amount earned in December.

Then $11x + 2x = 13x$ (entire earnings).

$$\frac{2x}{13x} = \frac{2}{13}$$

3. **(B)** $3x^3+2x^2+x+1$

$=3(-1)^3+2(-1)^2+(-1)+1$

$=3(-1)+2(1)-1+1$

$=-3+2+0$

$=-1$

4. **(E)** Convert the percent to decimal form before multiplying. .03% = .0003

$.0003\times.21=.000063$

The number of decimal places in the product must be equal to the sum of the number of decimal places in the terms to be multiplied.

5. **(C)** Since the ratio of the sides is 3:1, the ratio of the areas is 9:1.
The subdivision into 9Δ is shown.

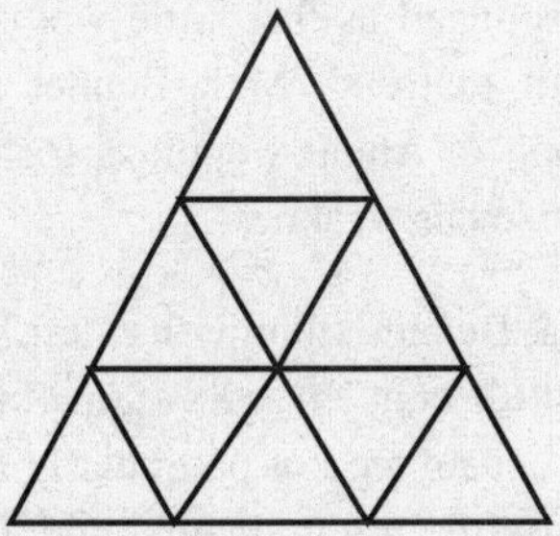

6. **(E)** The opposite vertices may be any of the number pairs $(1\pm5,\ 1\pm5)$, or (6, 6), (– 4, – 4), (– 4, 6), and (6, – 4).

Thus, (4, – 6) is not possible.

7. **(D)**

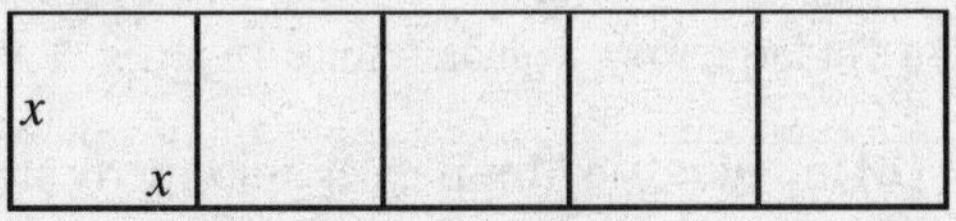

Perimeter of rectangle $=x+5x+x+5x$

Thus, $12x=372$

$x=31$

Area of square $=31^2=961$

8. **(B)** 4 inches is $\frac{1}{3}$ ft. The volume of the added level is $75\times42\times\frac{1}{3}=1050$ cubic ft. There are 7.48 gallons in 1 cubic ft., so 1050 cubic ft. × 7.48 gal./cubic ft. = 7,854 gallons.

9. **(A)** There are 360 degrees in a circle. A 24-degree sector is $\frac{24}{360}=.067$, or about $6\frac{2}{3}\%$ of a circle.

10. **(A)** In these fractions the numerator n is always less than the denominator d. After squaring the fraction $(\frac{n}{d})^2=\frac{n^2}{d^2}$, the new fraction is less than the original since the denominator is getting larger faster than the numerator.

Section 5

1. **(E)** *Tension* is likely to mount before a pitcher delivers the last strike of a game—especially during a pause.

2. **(B)** Funding a hospital for the poor may properly be called a *humanitarian* act. It may or may not be popular.

3. **(C)** This is the only answer in which both words are correct in relation to each other as well as to the sense of the sentence.

4. **(B)** The word that means "having more than one meaning" is *ambiguous*.

5. **(E)** The two sides might negotiate, or bargain, through the night in an attempt to *avert*, or prevent, a strike.

6. **(D)** The missing word must mean the same as "respect for age." The correct choice is *venerated.*

7. **(B)** It is likely that someone who is unprepared would approach an exam with *trepidation,* or apprehension, not with *aplomb* (self-assurance), *indifference* (lack of concern), *confidence,* or *duplicity* (hypocrisy).

8. **(A)** The only word that makes sense in this context is *derelict,* meaning neglectful of duty, or remiss.

9. **(D)** If a show of temper is atypical or unusual, she must be something opposite in meaning. *Equanimity,* or calmness, is the correct choice.

10. **(B)** In this sentence, two negative words are needed, thus eliminating choices (A), (C) and (D), which have at least one positive response. Choice (E) makes no sense. The correct answer is

(B), which includes two evidently negative responses. The *craven,* or cowardly, attitudes of politicians may cause them to *cower*, or shrink back, when there is controversy.

11. **(B)** An *intractable,* or stubborn, individual is likely to have trouble adapting to a new way of life. Choice (A), *nonchalant,* means unconcerned. Choice (C), *rabid*, means furious. Choice (D), *insolent,* means rude. And choice (E), *doughty,* means valiant.

12. **(D)** The key word *though* indicates that the word in the blank should be opposite in meaning from *shared.* The only choice that satisfies this condition is *disparate* (very different; having nothing in common).

13. **(B)** If you understand that *gastronomic* is an adjective having to do with eating, the only possible choice is (B). A *gourmet* (person who appreciates good food) is a *connoisseur,* or expert, in food.

14. **(B)** The phrase "her arm was broken" points to a negative word choice for this sentence. The only negative word is *plaintively,* which means sadly. All other choices are positive.

15. **(A)** The word *even* indicates that the sentence is completed by opposites. Only *ephemeral* (temporary or short-lived) and *lasting* satisfy this condition.

16. **(B)** When you *touch* something, you *feel* it. Similarly, when you *look* at something, you *see* it.

17. **(B)** The contrast in shape between a *circle* and a *square* is not unlike that between an *oval* and a *rectangle.*

18. **(B)** The male *chicken* is a *rooster*, and the male *duck* is a *drake.*

19. **(D)** A *trigger* activates a *pistol* and a *switch* a *motor.*

20. **(B)** *Angelic* is a greater degree of *good*, just as *joyous* is a greater degree of *glad.*

21. **(D)** The *clarinet* is a member of the *woodwind* family of instruments. The *trumpet* is a member of the *brass* family of instruments.

22. **(C)** To be *doleful* is to be full of *grief*, just as to be *wrathful* is to be full of *anger.* No other pair reflects a similar relationship.

23. **(E)** A *pail* holds *water* and water can be poured from a pail. A *shaker* holds *salt* and salt can be poured from a shaker.

24. **(A)** *Fish* kept in an artificial environment in captivity live in an *aquarium.* When *birds* are kept in captivity they live in an *aviary.* (B) is not a bad answer but it is not as good as (A) because a car is not alive.

25. **(B)** *Disagreement* is characterized by a lack of *concord* (harmony). Similarly, *impartiality* is characterized by a lack of *bias* (prejudice).

26. **(D)** Introduced as the "little woman" and "despondent matron," Mrs. Bennet is named in paragraph 4. Alcott's epithets for Mrs. Bennet emphasize her weakness.

27. **(A)** Mrs. Bennet's family has left her this mess with as little concern as a swarm of insects might have. Locusts are not particularly horrible; had Alcott used a more potent simile, (D) might be correct.

28. **(C)** Before Mrs. Gay's arrival, Mrs. Bennet was about to have "a good cry" (line 14). There is no indication that she would have been able to cope with her household duties.

29. **(C)** The flowers Mrs. Gay brings echo the rosiness of Mrs. Gay herself—she is earlier described as "a large rosy woman" (lines 15–16).

30. **(B)** In contrast to Mrs. Bennet's disorderly breakfast room, her front parlor is sunny and filled with blooming flowers, which contrast with her sickly children (D). (D) is not the correct response, however, because it only tells part of the story.

31. **(A)** Mrs. Bennet's lack of energy is her primary quality.

32. **(D)** Mrs. Gay, in her practical way, requests the job that is most vital, knowing that to get that job out of the way will improve Mrs. Bennet's spirits.

33. **(D)** Mrs. Gay has a name that suits her, and every speech she makes reveals her good humor and energy.

34. **(A)** Mrs. Bennet seems paralyzed by her situation. The "weariness of her own tired soul and body" oppresses her (line 12), and she surveys her household with despair.

35. **(E)** The last paragraph of the passage best expresses this quality. Mrs. Gay's get-things-done attitude is contrasted with Mrs. Bennet's ineffectiveness.

Section 6

Part 1

1. **(C)** Since dividing by 2 and multiplying by .5 have the same results, the quantities must be equal.

2. **(A)** Since the figure has 5 sides, it contains

$180(5-2)=540$ degrees
$540=x+110+60+120+100$
$540=x+390$
$150=x$

3. **(D)** The problem tells us only that the ratio of m to n is 7 to 10. It is possible, for example, that m is 700 and n is 1000.

4. **(B)** Simply plug the values into the formula.

$$\text{Column A} = \frac{(-3)(-2)}{-3-(-2)} = \frac{6}{-1} = -6$$

$$\text{Column B} = \frac{(-2)(-3)}{-2-(-3)} = \frac{6}{1} = 6$$

5. **(A)** Notice the right angle at $\angle BAC$. Side BC must be the longest side since it is opposite the largest angle. Since $\angle ADC$ is also a right angle, side AC must be longer than CD.

6. **(C)** Since there are three parallel lines, the corresponding angles are equal. If x, y and z are all the same, then $x + y$ must equal $y + z$.

7. **(C)** Since 3% = .03 and 4% = .04, then .03 × .04 = .0012.

8. **(A)** \$7.88 divided by 2 equals \$3.94. \$11.79 divided by 3 equals \$3.93.

9. **(B)** When an angle is inscribed in a circle, the arc is twice the angle. Arc AB equals 2 times 50, which is 100.

10. **(A)** $\sqrt{8}$ is almost 3. $\sqrt{24}$ is almost 5. Thus, Column A is close to 8. This is larger than $\sqrt{32}$ which is less than 6.

11. **(B)** Since there are more digits in Box B, it must contain more possibilities.

12. **(D)** There is no way to determine the relative values of a, b, and c.

13. **(B)** $p^2-q^2=(p+q)(p-q)=4$. We can substitute –1 for $(p-q)$.
$(p+q)(-1)=4$
$(p+q)=-4$

14. **(D)** The information tells us about percents only. We do not know how many boys or girls are in the class.

15. **(D)** While p, q, and r are positive, we do not know whether they are fractions. If the three variables were $\frac{1}{2}$, $\frac{1}{3}$ and $\frac{1}{4}$, the sum of the variables would be greater than the product.

Part 2

16. $(\sqrt{18}-\sqrt{8})^2$
$=(3\sqrt{2}-2\sqrt{2})^2$
$=(\sqrt{2})^2=2$

17.

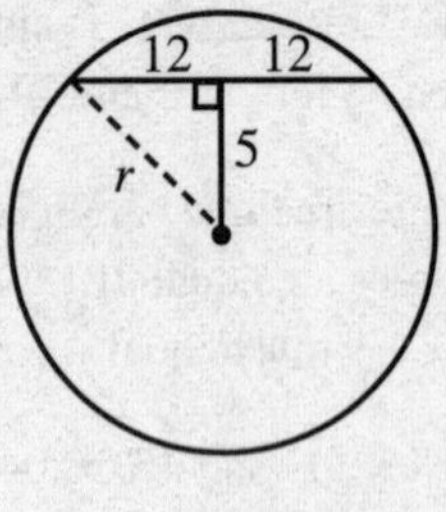

A radius drawn perpendicular to a chord bisects the chord. Construct the radius as shown above.

$$5^2+12^2=r^2$$
$$25+144=r^2$$
$$r^2=169$$
$$r=13$$

18. $\frac{x}{11}=15$

$x=165$

$\frac{165}{20}=8.25$

19.

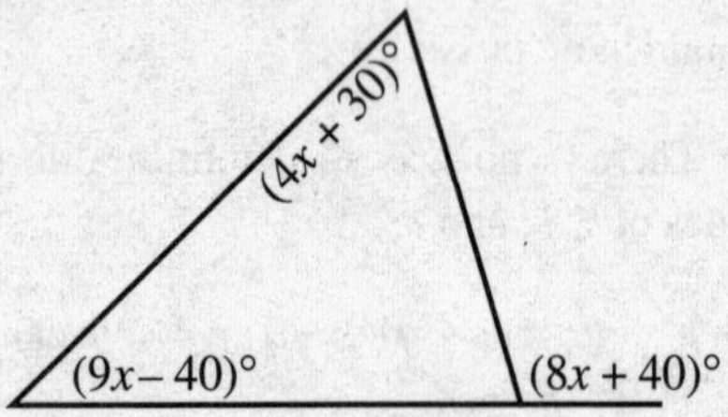

An exterior angle of a triangle is equal to the sum of the two remote interior angles.

$$8x+40=(9x-40)+(4x+30)$$
$$8x+40=13x-10$$
$$5x=50$$
$$x=10$$
$$m\angle J=(4x+30)°=(40+30)°=70°$$

20. $\frac{2^2+3^2}{5^2}+\frac{1}{10}=\frac{4+9}{25}+\frac{1}{10}$

$=\frac{13}{25}+\frac{1}{10}$

The lowest common denominator is 50.

$=\frac{26}{50}+\frac{5}{50}=\frac{31}{50}=.62$

21. The shaded area is the area of the rectangle minus the area of the two circles.

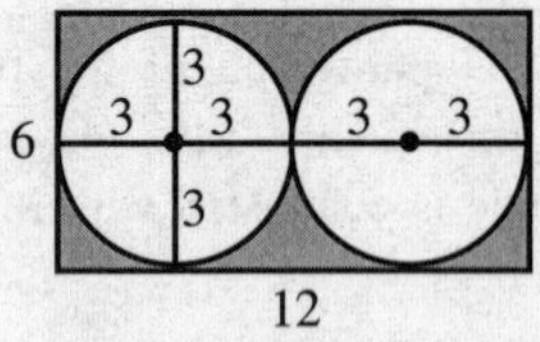

Area of the rectangle = 6(12) = 72

Area of circle $=\pi r^2=9\pi$

Shaded area $=72-2(9\pi)$

$=72-18\pi$

$=a-b\pi$

$\therefore a=72$ and $b=18$

22.

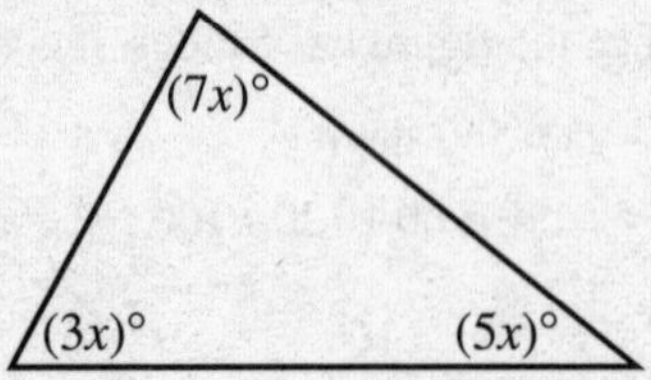

Let $3x$ = the measure of one of the angles

$5x$ = the measure of the 2nd angle

$7x$ = the measure of the 3rd angle

$$3x+5x+7x=180$$
$$15x=180$$
$$x=12$$

The smallest angle = $3x$ = 36°

23. $d = \sqrt{(x_2 - x_1)^2 + (y_2 - y_1)^2}$

$= \sqrt{(3-(-4))^2 + (-2-5)^2}$

$= \sqrt{7^2 + (-7)^2}$

$= \sqrt{49+49} = \sqrt{98} = \sqrt{49}\sqrt{2}$

$= 7\sqrt{2} = b\sqrt{2}$

$\therefore b = 7$

24. $\dfrac{9+9+10+x+y}{5} = 10$

$28 + x + y = 50$

$x + y = 22$

the average of x and y is

$\dfrac{x+y}{2} = \dfrac{22}{2} = 11$

25.

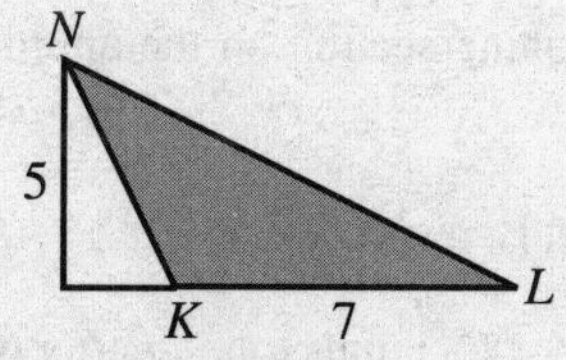

Area $\Delta NKL = \dfrac{1}{2}(b)(h)$

$= \dfrac{1}{2}(7)(5) = 17.5 = \dfrac{35}{2}$

Evaluating Practice Examination 2

To determine your Verbal Reasoning Score:

1. Using the Analysis Worksheet, enter the number of correct answers for each verbal reasoning section on the appropriate line in Column A of the Verbal Reasoning grid.

2. Enter the number of incorrect answers for each verbal reasoning section on the appropriate line in Column B of the Verbal Reasoning grid.

3. Total Columns A and B and enter these totals in boxes A and B, respectively.

4. Perform the indicated calculation to find your Raw Score: (value in box A) minus (one-quarter of the value in box B) = Raw Score.

5. Consult the Conversion Chart to find your approximate Scaled Score.

To determine your Mathematical Reasoning Score:

1. Enter the number of correct answers for each mathematical reasoning section on the appropriate line in Column C of the Mathematical Reasoning grid.

2. Enter the number of incorrect answers for each mathematical reasoning section on the appropriate line in Column D, E, or F of the Mathematical Reasoning grid.

3. Total Columns C, D, and E, and enter these totals in boxes C, D, and E, respectively.

4. Perform the indicated calculation to find your Raw Score: (value in box C) minus (one-quarter of the value in box D) minus (one-third of the value in box E) = Raw Score.

5. Consult the Conversion Chart to find your approximate Scaled Score.

Note: Box F is not used in this calculation.

Analysis Worksheet

VERBAL REASONING

Section	Number of Questions	Column A Number of Correct Answers	Column B Number of Incorrect Answers
1	30		
3	12		
5	35		
	Total	A	B

A – ¼ B = Raw Score → Use Conversion Chart → Scaled Score

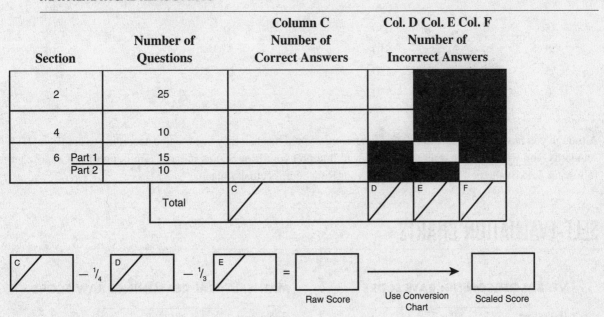

MATHEMATICAL REASONING

Section	Number of Questions	Column C Number of Correct Answers	Col. D Number of Incorrect Answers	Col. E	Col. F
2	25				
4	10				
6 Part 1	15				
Part 2	10				
	Total	C	D	E	F

C – ¼ D – ⅓ E = Raw Score → Use Conversion Chart → Scaled Score

Conversion Scales for Practice Examination 2

VERBAL REASONING:

Raw Score	Scaled Score	Raw Score	Scaled Score
75	800	40	550
70	800	35	520
65	760	30	480
60	710	25	440
55	670	20	410
50	620	15	370
45	590	10	340
		5	290
		0	230

MATHEMATICAL REASONING:

Raw Score	Scaled Score	Raw Score	Scaled Score
60	800	25	510
55	760	20	480
50	690	15	440
45	650	10	410
40	610	5	340
35	580	0	200
30	550		

Although you now have some idea of what your scores would like had they been scaled according to unofficial ETS standards, you will probably want to know how to interpret your Raw Scores in more familiar terms. If so, use the following Self-Evaluation Charts to see what your Raw Scores actually mean.

SELF-EVALUATION CHARTS

VERBAL REASONING: RAW SCORE

Excellent	60 – 75
Good	50 – 60
Average	30 – 50
Fair	20 – 30
Poor	0 – 20

MATHEMATICAL REASONING: RAW SCORE

Excellent	50 – 60
Good	40 – 50
Average	20 – 40
Fair	10 – 20
Poor	0 – 10

Practice Examination 3

Answer Sheet

If a section has fewer questions than answer ovals, leave the extra ovals blank.

Section 1

1 (A) (B) (C) (D) (E)	11 (A) (B) (C) (D) (E)	21 (A) (B) (C) (D) (E)	31 (A) (B) (C) (D) (E)
2 (A) (B) (C) (D) (E)	12 (A) (B) (C) (D) (E)	22 (A) (B) (C) (D) (E)	32 (A) (B) (C) (D) (E)
3 (A) (B) (C) (D) (E)	13 (A) (B) (C) (D) (E)	23 (A) (B) (C) (D) (E)	33 (A) (B) (C) (D) (E)
4 (A) (B) (C) (D) (E)	14 (A) (B) (C) (D) (E)	24 (A) (B) (C) (D) (E)	34 (A) (B) (C) (D) (E)
5 (A) (B) (C) (D) (E)	15 (A) (B) (C) (D) (E)	25 (A) (B) (C) (D) (E)	35 (A) (B) (C) (D) (E)
6 (A) (B) (C) (D) (E)	16 (A) (B) (C) (D) (E)	26 (A) (B) (C) (D) (E)	36 (A) (B) (C) (D) (E)
7 (A) (B) (C) (D) (E)	17 (A) (B) (C) (D) (E)	27 (A) (B) (C) (D) (E)	37 (A) (B) (C) (D) (E)
8 (A) (B) (C) (D) (E)	18 (A) (B) (C) (D) (E)	28 (A) (B) (C) (D) (E)	38 (A) (B) (C) (D) (E)
9 (A) (B) (C) (D) (E)	19 (A) (B) (C) (D) (E)	29 (A) (B) (C) (D) (E)	39 (A) (B) (C) (D) (E)
10 (A) (B) (C) (D) (E)	20 (A) (B) (C) (D) (E)	30 (A) (B) (C) (D) (E)	40 (A) (B) (C) (D) (E)

Section 2

1 (A) (B) (C) (D) (E)	11 (A) (B) (C) (D) (E)	21 (A) (B) (C) (D) (E)	31 (A) (B) (C) (D) (E)
2 (A) (B) (C) (D) (E)	12 (A) (B) (C) (D) (E)	22 (A) (B) (C) (D) (E)	32 (A) (B) (C) (D) (E)
3 (A) (B) (C) (D) (E)	13 (A) (B) (C) (D) (E)	23 (A) (B) (C) (D) (E)	33 (A) (B) (C) (D) (E)
4 (A) (B) (C) (D) (E)	14 (A) (B) (C) (D) (E)	24 (A) (B) (C) (D) (E)	34 (A) (B) (C) (D) (E)
5 (A) (B) (C) (D) (E)	15 (A) (B) (C) (D) (E)	25 (A) (B) (C) (D) (E)	35 (A) (B) (C) (D) (E)
6 (A) (B) (C) (D) (E)	16 (A) (B) (C) (D) (E)	26 (A) (B) (C) (D) (E)	36 (A) (B) (C) (D) (E)
7 (A) (B) (C) (D) (E)	17 (A) (B) (C) (D) (E)	27 (A) (B) (C) (D) (E)	37 (A) (B) (C) (D) (E)
8 (A) (B) (C) (D) (E)	18 (A) (B) (C) (D) (E)	28 (A) (B) (C) (D) (E)	38 (A) (B) (C) (D) (E)
9 (A) (B) (C) (D) (E)	19 (A) (B) (C) (D) (E)	29 (A) (B) (C) (D) (E)	39 (A) (B) (C) (D) (E)
10 (A) (B) (C) (D) (E)	20 (A) (B) (C) (D) (E)	30 (A) (B) (C) (D) (E)	40 (A) (B) (C) (D) (E)

Section 3

Answer spaces for Section 3 are on the back of this Answer Sheet.

Section 4

1 (A) (B) (C) (D) (E)	11 (A) (B) (C) (D) (E)	21 (A) (B) (C) (D) (E)	31 (A) (B) (C) (D) (E)
2 (A) (B) (C) (D) (E)	12 (A) (B) (C) (D) (E)	22 (A) (B) (C) (D) (E)	32 (A) (B) (C) (D) (E)
3 (A) (B) (C) (D) (E)	13 (A) (B) (C) (D) (E)	23 (A) (B) (C) (D) (E)	33 (A) (B) (C) (D) (E)
4 (A) (B) (C) (D) (E)	14 (A) (B) (C) (D) (E)	24 (A) (B) (C) (D) (E)	34 (A) (B) (C) (D) (E)
5 (A) (B) (C) (D) (E)	15 (A) (B) (C) (D) (E)	25 (A) (B) (C) (D) (E)	35 (A) (B) (C) (D) (E)
6 (A) (B) (C) (D) (E)	16 (A) (B) (C) (D) (E)	26 (A) (B) (C) (D) (E)	36 (A) (B) (C) (D) (E)
7 (A) (B) (C) (D) (E)	17 (A) (B) (C) (D) (E)	27 (A) (B) (C) (D) (E)	37 (A) (B) (C) (D) (E)
8 (A) (B) (C) (D) (E)	18 (A) (B) (C) (D) (E)	28 (A) (B) (C) (D) (E)	38 (A) (B) (C) (D) (E)
9 (A) (B) (C) (D) (E)	19 (A) (B) (C) (D) (E)	29 (A) (B) (C) (D) (E)	39 (A) (B) (C) (D) (E)
10 (A) (B) (C) (D) (E)	20 (A) (B) (C) (D) (E)	30 (A) (B) (C) (D) (E)	40 (A) (B) (C) (D) (E)

Section 5

1 (A) (B) (C) (D) (E)	6 (A) (B) (C) (D) (E)	11 (A) (B) (C) (D) (E)	16 (A) (B) (C) (D) (E)
2 (A) (B) (C) (D) (E)	7 (A) (B) (C) (D) (E)	12 (A) (B) (C) (D) (E)	17 (A) (B) (C) (D) (E)
3 (A) (B) (C) (D) (E)	8 (A) (B) (C) (D) (E)	13 (A) (B) (C) (D) (E)	18 (A) (B) (C) (D) (E)
4 (A) (B) (C) (D) (E)	9 (A) (B) (C) (D) (E)	14 (A) (B) (C) (D) (E)	19 (A) (B) (C) (D) (E)
5 (A) (B) (C) (D) (E)	10 (A) (B) (C) (D) (E)	15 (A) (B) (C) (D) (E)	20 (A) (B) (C) (D) (E)

Section 6

1 Ⓐ Ⓑ Ⓒ Ⓓ Ⓔ 6 Ⓐ Ⓑ Ⓒ Ⓓ Ⓔ 11 Ⓐ Ⓑ Ⓒ Ⓓ Ⓔ 16 Ⓐ Ⓑ Ⓒ Ⓓ Ⓔ
2 Ⓐ Ⓑ Ⓒ Ⓓ Ⓔ 7 Ⓐ Ⓑ Ⓒ Ⓓ Ⓔ 12 Ⓐ Ⓑ Ⓒ Ⓓ Ⓔ 17 Ⓐ Ⓑ Ⓒ Ⓓ Ⓔ
3 Ⓐ Ⓑ Ⓒ Ⓓ Ⓔ 8 Ⓐ Ⓑ Ⓒ Ⓓ Ⓔ 13 Ⓐ Ⓑ Ⓒ Ⓓ Ⓔ 18 Ⓐ Ⓑ Ⓒ Ⓓ Ⓔ
4 Ⓐ Ⓑ Ⓒ Ⓓ Ⓔ 9 Ⓐ Ⓑ Ⓒ Ⓓ Ⓔ 14 Ⓐ Ⓑ Ⓒ Ⓓ Ⓔ 19 Ⓐ Ⓑ Ⓒ Ⓓ Ⓔ
5 Ⓐ Ⓑ Ⓒ Ⓓ Ⓔ 10 Ⓐ Ⓑ Ⓒ Ⓓ Ⓔ 15 Ⓐ Ⓑ Ⓒ Ⓓ Ⓔ 20 Ⓐ Ⓑ Ⓒ Ⓓ Ⓔ

Section 3

1 Ⓐ Ⓑ Ⓒ Ⓓ Ⓔ 6 Ⓐ Ⓑ Ⓒ Ⓓ Ⓔ 11 Ⓐ Ⓑ Ⓒ Ⓓ Ⓔ
2 Ⓐ Ⓑ Ⓒ Ⓓ Ⓔ 7 Ⓐ Ⓑ Ⓒ Ⓓ Ⓔ 12 Ⓐ Ⓑ Ⓒ Ⓓ Ⓔ
3 Ⓐ Ⓑ Ⓒ Ⓓ Ⓔ 8 Ⓐ Ⓑ Ⓒ Ⓓ Ⓔ 13 Ⓐ Ⓑ Ⓒ Ⓓ Ⓔ
4 Ⓐ Ⓑ Ⓒ Ⓓ Ⓔ 9 Ⓐ Ⓑ Ⓒ Ⓓ Ⓔ 14 Ⓐ Ⓑ Ⓒ Ⓓ Ⓔ
5 Ⓐ Ⓑ Ⓒ Ⓓ Ⓔ 10 Ⓐ Ⓑ Ⓒ Ⓓ Ⓔ 15 Ⓐ Ⓑ Ⓒ Ⓓ Ⓔ

Note: ONLY the answers entered on the grid are scored.
Handwritten answers at the top of the column are NOT scored.

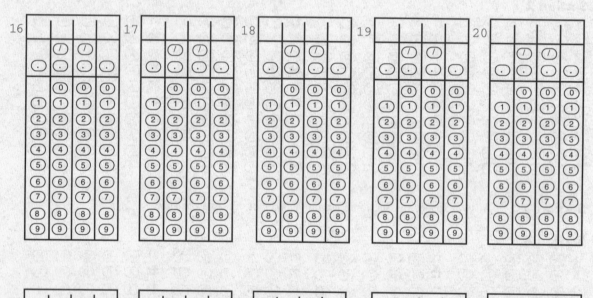

16 17 18 19 20

21 22 23 24 25

Practice Examination 3

SECTION 1

25 Questions • Time—30 Minutes

Directions: Solve the following problems using any available space on the page for scratchwork. On your answer sheet fill in the choice which best corresponds to the correct answer.

Notes: The figures accompanying the problems are drawn as accurately as possible unless otherwise stated in specific problems. Again, unless otherwise stated, all figures lie in the same plane. All numbers used in these problems are real numbers. Calculators are permitted for this test.

Reference Information

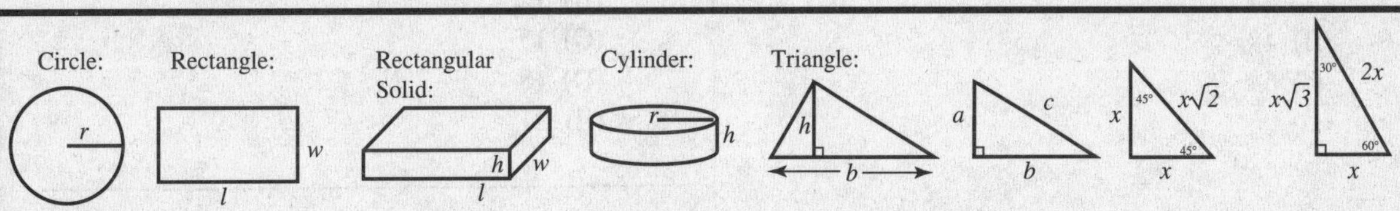

$C = 2\pi r$, $A = \pi r^2$ | $A = lw$ | $V = lwh$ | $V = \pi r^2 h$ | $A = \frac{1}{2}bh$ | $a^2 + b^2 = c^2$

The number of degrees of arc in a circle is 360.
The measure in degrees of a straight angle is 180.
The sum of the measures in degrees of the angles of a triangle is 180.

1. If $9x + 5 = 23$, what is the numerical value of $18x + 5$?

   (A) 46
   (B) 41
   (C) 36
   (D) 32
   (E) It cannot be determined from the information given.

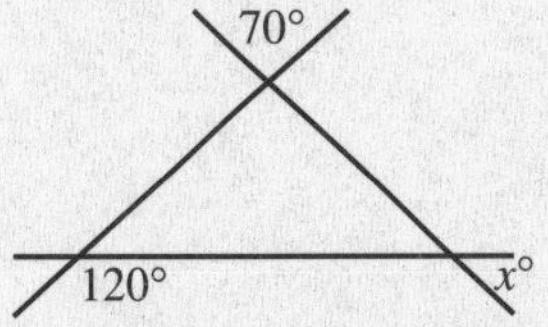

Note: Figure not drawn to scale.

2. In the figure above, $x =$

   (A) 35
   (B) 50
   (C) 70
   (D) 90
   (E) 110

GO ON TO THE NEXT PAGE

3. If $2y = \frac{1}{3}$, then $\frac{1}{4y} =$

(A) $\frac{3}{2}$
(B) $\frac{3}{4}$
(C) $\frac{2}{5}$
(D) $\frac{1}{5}$
(E) $\frac{4}{3}$

4. Pieces of wire are soldered together so as to form the edges of a cube, whose volume is 64 cubic inches. The number of inches of wire used is

(A) 24
(B) 48
(C) 64
(D) 96
(E) 120

5. If a box of note paper costs $4.20 after a 40% discount, what was its original price?

(A) $2.52
(B) $4.60
(C) $5.33
(D) $7.00
(E) $10.50

6. *A* is 15 years old. *B* is one-third older. How many years ago was *B* twice as old as *A*?

(A) 3
(B) 5
(C) 7.5
(D) 8
(E) 10

7. The distance, *s*, in feet that an object falls in *t* seconds when dropped from a height is obtained by use of the formula $s = 16t^2$. How many feet will an object fall in 8 seconds?

(A) 256
(B) 1,024
(C) 2,048
(D) 15,384
(E) 16,000

8. Three circles are tangent externally to each other and have radii of 2 inches, 3 inches, and 4 inches, respectively. How many inches are in the perimeter of the triangle formed by joining the centers of the three circles?

(A) 9
(B) 12
(C) 15
(D) 18
(E) 21

9. One-tenth is what part of three-fourths?

(A) $\frac{3}{40}$
(B) $\frac{1}{8}$
(C) $\frac{2}{15}$
(D) $\frac{15}{2}$
(E) $\frac{40}{3}$

10. The area of square *PQRS* is 49. What are the coordinates of *Q*?

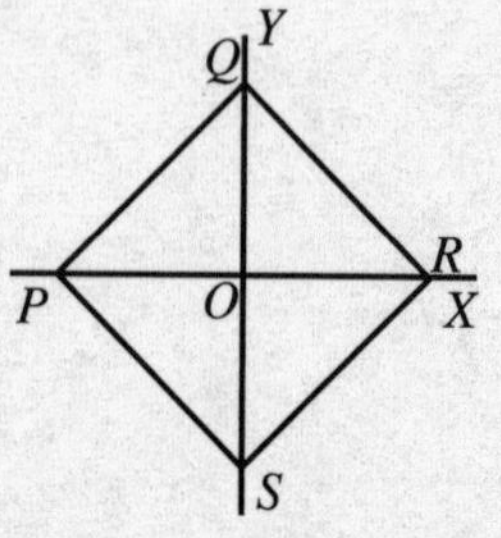

(A) $(\frac{7}{2}\sqrt{2}, 0)$
(B) $(0, \frac{7}{2}\sqrt{2})$
(C) $(0, 7)$
(D) $(7, 0)$
(E) $(0, 7\sqrt{2})$

11. If one-half of the female students in a certain college eat in the cafeteria and one-third of the male students eat there, what fractional part of the student body eats in the cafeteria?

(A) $\frac{5}{12}$
(B) $\frac{2}{5}$
(C) $\frac{3}{4}$
(D) $\frac{5}{6}$
(E) It cannot be determined from the information given.

12. A recent report states that if you were to eat each meal in a different restaurant in New York City, it would take you more than 19 years to cover all of New York City's eating places, assuming that you eat three meals a day. On the basis of this information, the number of restaurants in New York City

(A) exceeds 20,500
(B) is closer to 20,000 than 21,000
(C) exceeds 21,000
(D) exceeds 21,000 but does not exceed 21,500
(E) is less than 20,500

13. In the figure below, $AB = BC$ and angle BEA is a right angle. If the length of DE is four times the length of BE, then what is the ratio of the area of ΔACD to the area of ΔABC?

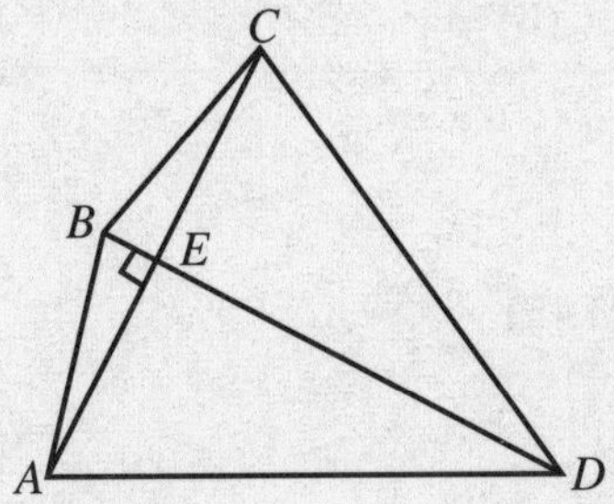

(A) 1:4
(B) 1:2
(C) 2:1
(D) 4:1
(E) It cannot be determined from the information given.

14. A pound of water is evaporated from 6 pounds of sea water containing 4% salt. The percentage of salt in the remaining solution is

(A) 3.6%
(B) 4%
(C) 4.8%
(D) 5.2%
(E) 6%

15. The product of 75^3 and 75^7 is

(A) $(75)^5$
(B) $(75)^{10}$
(C) $(150)^{10}$
(D) $(5625)^{10}$
(E) $(75)^{21}$

16. The distance from City A to City B is 150 miles and the distance from City A to City C is 90 miles. Therefore, it is necessarily true that

(A) the distance between B to C is 60 miles
(B) six times the distance from A to B equals 10 times the distance from A to C.
(C) the distance from B to C is 240 miles
(D) the distance from A to B exceeds by 30 miles twice the distance from A to C
(E) three times the distance from A to C exceeds by 30 miles twice the distance from A to B

17. If $a+b=3$ and $ab=4$, then $\frac{1}{a}+\frac{1}{b}=$

(A) $\frac{3}{4}$
(B) $\frac{3}{7}$
(C) $\frac{4}{7}$
(D) $\frac{1}{7}$
(E) $\frac{1}{12}$

18. $(x)^6+(2x^2)^3+(3x^3)^2=$

(A) $5x^5+x^6$
(B) $17x^5+x^6$
(C) $6x^6$
(D) $18x^6$
(E) $6x^{18}$

19. The scale of a map is $\frac{3}{4}$ inch = 10 miles. If the distance on the map between two towns is 6 inches, the actual distance in miles is

(A) 45
(B) 60
(C) 75
(D) 80
(E) 90

20. If $d=m-\frac{50}{m}$, and m is a positive number, then as m increases in value, d

(A) increases in value
(B) decreases in value
(C) remains unchanged
(D) increases, then decreases
(E) decreases, then increases

21. If a cubic inch of metal weighs 2 pounds, a cubic foot of the same metal weighs how many pounds?

(A) 8
(B) 24
(C) 96
(D) 288
(E) 3,456

22. If the number of square inches in the area of a circle is equal to the number of inches in its circumference, the diameter of the circle in inches is

(A) 4
(B) π
(C) 2
(D) $\frac{\pi}{2}$
(E) 1

23. John is now three time Pat's age. Four years from now John will be x years old. In terms of x, how old is Pat now?

(A) $\frac{x+4}{3}$
(B) $3x$
(C) $x+4$
(D) $x-4$
(E) $\frac{x-4}{3}$

24. When the fractions $\frac{2}{3}$, $\frac{5}{7}$, $\frac{8}{11}$, and $\frac{9}{13}$ are arranged in ascending order of size, the result is

(A) $\frac{8}{11}, \frac{5}{7}, \frac{9}{13}, \frac{2}{3}$
(B) $\frac{5}{7}, \frac{8}{11}, \frac{2}{3}, \frac{9}{13}$
(C) $\frac{2}{3}, \frac{8}{11}, \frac{5}{7}, \frac{9}{13}$
(D) $\frac{2}{3}, \frac{9}{13}, \frac{5}{7}, \frac{8}{11}$
(E) $\frac{9}{13}, \frac{2}{3}, \frac{8}{11}, \frac{5}{7}$

25. In a certain course a student takes eight tests, all of which count equally. When figuring out the final grade, the instructor drops the best and the worst grade and averages the other six. The student calculates that his average for all eight tests is 84%. After dropping the best and the worst grade the student averages 86%. What was the average of the best and the worst test?

(A) 68
(B) 72
(C) 78
(D) 88
(E) It cannot be determined from the information given.

STOP

END OF SECTION 1. IF YOU HAVE ANY TIME LEFT, GO OVER YOUR WORK IN THIS SECTION ONLY. DO NOT WORK IN ANY OTHER SECTION OF THE TEST.

SECTION 2

30 Questions • Time—30 minutes

Directions: Each of the following questions consists of an incomplete sentence followed by five words or pairs of words. Choose that word or pair of words which, when substituted for the blank space or spaces, *best* completes the meaning of the sentence and mark the letter of your choice on your answer sheet.

Example:

In view of the extenuating circumstances and the defendant's youth, the judge recommended ---- .

(A) conviction
(B) a defense
(C) a mistrial
(D) leniency
(E) life imprisonment

Ⓐ Ⓑ Ⓒ ● Ⓔ

1. Unsure of her skills in English , the young girl was ---- when called on to speak in class.

(A) remunerative
(B) transient
(C) reticent
(D) sartorial
(E) resilient

2. Anyone familiar with the facts could ---- his arguments, which seemed logical but were actually ---- .

(A) refute..specious
(B) support..protracted
(C) repeat..recumbent
(D) review..cogent
(E) elicit..prodigious

3. Each spring the ---- tree put out fewer and fewer leaves.

(A) ambient
(B) malignant
(C) desultory
(D) moribund
(E) reclusive

4. The building had been ---- ; she could not even be sure exactly where it had stood.

(A) jettisoned
(B) debilitated
(C) mitigated
(D) berated
(E) obliterated

5. The bully's menacing, ---- manner was actually just for show; in reality it was entirely ---- .

(A) imperturbable..vapid
(B) truculent..affected
(C) stringent..credulous
(D) supercilious..blatant
(E) parsimonious..contentious

Directions: Each of the following questions consists of a capitalized pair of words followed by five pairs of words lettered A to E. The capitalized words bear some meaningful relationship to each other. Choose the lettered pair of words whose relationship is most similar to that expressed by the capitalized pair and mark its letter on your answer sheet.

Example:

DAY : SUN : :

(A) sunlight : daylight (B) ray: sun
(C) night : moon (D) heat : cold
(E) moon : star Ⓐ Ⓑ ● Ⓓ Ⓔ

6. PEEL : APPLE : :

(A) skin : knee
(B) sail : boat
(C) shell : lobster
(D) pit : grape
(E) coat : fur

7. FINGER : RING : :

(A) neck : necklace
(B) bandage : wound
(C) bracelet : wrist
(D) glove : hand
(E) lip : tune

8. ADULT : CHILD : :

(A) mother : baby
(B) sheep : lamb
(C) cow : calf
(D) puppy : baby
(E) buck : fawn

9. PEPPER : SEASON : :

(A) cinnamon : prepare
(B) sugar : sweeten
(C) celery : plant
(D) accent : cook
(E) salt : taste

10. BEEF : JERKY : :

(A) corn : flake
(B) ham : pork
(C) grape : raisin
(D) meat : sausage
(E) flesh : bone

11. SCHOOL : FISH : :

(A) herd : cows
(B) cars : traffic
(C) dog : puppy
(D) bird : wing
(E) pig : barn

12. AUTHOR : NOVEL : :

(A) composer : piano
(B) artist : easel
(C) sculptor : statue
(D) painter : color
(E) mechanic : oil

13. MAGNANIMOUS : PETTY : :

(A) arrogant : insolent
(B) valiant : belligerent
(C) passionate : blasé
(D) munificent : generous
(E) circumspect : prudent

GO ON TO THE NEXT PAGE

Directions: Each passage below is followed by a set of questions. Read each passage, then answer the accompanying questions, basing your answers on what is stated or implied in the passage and any introductory material provided. Mark the letter of your choice on your answer sheet.

Questions 14–21 are based on the following passage.

The following speech was delivered at the height of the 1960s civil rights movement by Dr. Martin Luther King, head of the Southern Christian Leadership Conference and the movement's most eloquent spokesperson.

We have come to this hallowed spot to remind America of the fierce urgency of now. This is no time to engage in the luxury of cooling off or to take the tranquilizing drug of gradualism. Now is the time to make real the promises of democracy. Now is the time to rise from the dark and desolate valley of segregation to the sunlit path of racial justice. Now is the time to lift our nation from the quicksand of racial injustice to the solid rock of brotherhood. Now is the time to make justice a reality for all of God's children.

It would be fatal for the nation to overlook the urgency of the moment. This sweltering summer of the Negro's legitimate discontent will not pass until there is an invigorating autumn of freedom and equality. Those who hope that the Negro needed to blow off steam and will now be content will have a rude awakening if the nation returns to business as usual. There will be neither rest nor tranquility in America until the Negro is granted his citizenship rights. The whirlwinds of revolt will continue to shake the foundations of our nation until the bright day of justice emerges.

But that is something that I must say to my people who stand on the warm threshold which leads into the palace of justice. In the process of gaining our rightful place we must not be guilty of wrongful deeds. Let us not seek to satisfy our thirst for freedom by drinking from the cup of bitterness and hatred.

We must forever conduct our struggle on the high plane of dignity and discipline. We must not allow our creative protest to degenerate into physical violence. Again and again we must rise to the majestic heights of meeting physical force with soul force. The marvelous new militancy which has engulfed the Negro community must not lead us to a distrust of all white people, for many of our white brothers, as evidenced by their presence here today, have come to realize that their destiny is tied up with our destiny. And they have come to realize that their freedom is inextricably bound to our freedom. We cannot walk alone.

As we walk, we must make the pledge that we shall always march ahead. We cannot turn back. There are those who are asking the devotees of civil rights, "When will you be satisfied?" We can never be satisfied as long as the Negro is the victim of the unspeakable horrors of police brutality. We can never be satisfied as long as the Negro's basic mobility is from a smaller ghetto to a larger one. We can never be satisfied as long as our children are stripped of their selfhood and robbed of their dignity by signs stating "For Whites Only." We cannot be satisfied as long as a Negro in Mississippi cannot vote and a Negro in New York believes he has nothing for which to vote. No, no, we are not satisfied, and we will not be satisfied until justice rolls down like waters and righteousness like a mighty stream.

I am not unmindful that some of you have come out of great trials and tribulations. Some of you have come fresh from narrow jail cells. Some of you have come from areas where your quest for freedom left you battered by the storms of persecution and staggered by the winds of police brutality. You have been the veterans of creative suffering. Continue to work with the faith that unearned suffering is redemptive.

Go back to Mississippi, go back to Alabama, go back to South Carolina, go back to Louisiana, go back to the slums and ghettos of our Northern cities, knowing that somehow this situation can and will be changed. Let us not wallow in the valley of despair.

14. When King says in line 62 that "unearned suffering is redemptive," he means that it

    (A) provokes police brutality
    (B) confers sanctity, or holiness, upon the sufferer
    (C) is bound to continue forever
    (D) strips children of their dignity or self-worth
    (E) will never be repaid

15. In the passage, King's attitude is generally

    (A) prejudiced
    (B) cynical
    (C) fearful
    (D) optimistic
    (E) neutral

16. Which quotation best suggests the main idea of the speech?

    (A) ". . . we must not be guilty of wrongful deeds."
    (B) "We cannot walk alone."
    (C) "We can never be satisfied as long as the Negro's basic mobility is from a smaller ghetto to a larger one."
    (D) ". . . to remind America of the fierce urgency of now."
    (E) ". . . this situation can and will be changed."

17. The tone of this speech can best be described as

    (A) inspirational
    (B) boastful
    (C) defiant
    (D) sad
    (E) buoyant

18. King's attitude toward white Americans appears to be based on

    (A) noncommitment
    (B) contempt for authority
    (C) mutual distrust
    (D) mutual respect
    (E) negativism

19. King's remarks indicate that he considers the racial problem a national problem because

    (A) all white Americans are prejudiced
    (B) African-Americans are moving to the suburbs
    (C) all areas of American life are affected
    (D) the United States Constitution supports segregation
    (E) laws will be broken if the problem is left unattended

20. In the passage, King implies that the struggle for racial justice can be best won through

    (A) marching on Washington
    (B) civil disorder
    (C) creative protest
    (D) challenging unjust laws
    (E) doing nothing

21. In this speech, King specifically recommends

    (A) nonviolent resistance
    (B) faith in God
    (C) Communist ideas
    (D) social turmoil
    (E) turbulent revolt

Questions 22–30 are based on the following passage.

Agustín Yáñez was the author of many short stories, most of them based in or around Guadalajara, Mexico, his hometown. "Alda," from which this passage is excerpted, is from a collection entitled Archipiélago de mujeres.

I never met my first love. She must have been a sweet and sad child. Her photographs inspire my imagination to reconstruct the outlines of her soul, simple and austere as a primitive church, extensive as a castle, stately as a tower, deep as a well. Purity of brow, which, like the throat, the hands, the entire body, must have been carved in crystal or marble; the very soft lines of the face; the deep-set eyes with a look of surprise, sweet and sad, beneath the veil of the eyelashes; a brief mouth with fine lips, immune to sensuality; docile hair, harmonious and still; simply dressed in harmony with the obvious distinction and nobility of her bearing; all of her, aglow with innocence and a certain gravity in which are mixed the delights of childhood and the reverie of first youth. Her photographs invite one to try to imagine the timbre and rhythm of her voice, the ring of her laughter, the depth of her silences, the cadence of her movements, the direction and intensity of her glances. Her arms must have moved like the wings of a musical and tranquil bird; her figure must have yielded with the gentleness of a lily in an April garden. How many times her translucent hands must have trimmed the lamps of the vigilant virgins who know not the day or the hour; in what moments of rapture did her mouth and eyes accentuate their sadness? When did they emphasize her sweet smile?

No, I never met her. And yet, even her pictures were with me for a long time after she died. Long before then, my life was filled with her presence, fashioned of unreal images, devoid of all sensation; perhaps more faithful, certainly more vivid, than these almost faded

GO ON TO THE NEXT PAGE

photographs. Hers was a presence without volume, line or color; an elusive phantom, which epitomized the beauty of all faces without limiting itself to any one, and embodied the delicacy of the best and loftiest spirits, indefinitely.

I now believe that an obscure feeling, a fear of reality, was the cause of my refusal to exchange the formless images for a direct knowledge of her who inspired them. How many times, just when the senses might have put a limit to fancy did I avoid meeting her; and how many others did Fate intervene! On one of the many occasions that I watched the house in which my phantom lived, I decided to knock; but the family was out.

22. What does Yáñez mean when he says "I never met my first love" (line 1)?

(A) He loved unconditionally.
(B) His first love died young.
(C) He never fell in love.
(D) He fell in love with someone he never really knew.
(E) His first love was not a human being.

23. The description in paragraph 1 moves from

(A) sound to sight
(B) smell to sight to sound
(C) sight to touch
(D) sight to sound to movement
(E) touch to sound to sight

24. The word *docile* (line 10) is used to imply

(A) wildness
(B) conformity
(C) manageability
(D) indifference
(E) willingness

25. In paragraph 1, to what does Yáñez compare Alda's soul?

(A) A series of buildings
(B) Crystal and marble
(C) The wings of a bird
(D) A flower in a garden
(E) A photograph

26. When Yáñez says he is "devoid of all sensation" (line 30), he means that he

(A) has no sense of who Alda might be
(B) does not see, hear, or touch Alda
(C) cannot be sensible where Alda is concerned
(D) has little judgment
(E) feels nothing for Alda

27. The word *faithful* (line 31) is used to mean

(A) loyal
(B) constant
(C) devoted
(D) firm
(E) reliable

28. Unlike the previous paragraphs, paragraph 3

(A) suggests an explanation for the author's behavior
(B) describes the author's photographs of Alda
(C) mentions the elusive qualities of Alda
(D) compares Alda to someone the author loved later
(E) expresses regret for losing Alda's love

29. How might you reword the phrase "the senses might have put a limit to fancy" (lines 40–41)?

(A) if I were sensible, I would not have fantasized
(B) my good taste enabled me to dream without limits
(C) good sense would have made things plainer
(D) I could sense that she wanted to end my dreams
(E) seeing her might have stopped my fantasies

30. Which of these might be a good title for this excerpt?

(A) "A Tragic Love Affair"
(B) "First and Only Love"
(C) "My Dead Sweetheart"
(D) "Remembrance of a Phantom Love"
(E) "Love and Photography"

STOP

END OF SECTION 2. IF YOU HAVE ANY TIME LEFT, GO OVER YOUR WORK IN THIS SECTION ONLY. DO NOT WORK IN ANY OTHER SECTION OF THE TEST.

SECTION 3

25 Questions • Time—30 Minutes

Directions: Solve the following problems using any available space on the page for scratchwork. On your answer sheet fill in the choice which best corresponds to the correct answer.

Notes: The figures accompanying the problems are drawn as accurately as possible unless otherwise stated in specific problems. Again, unless otherwise stated, all figures lie in the same plane. All numbers used in these problems are real numbers. Calculators are permitted for this test.

Reference Information

Circle: Rectangle: Rectangular Solid: Cylinder: Triangle:

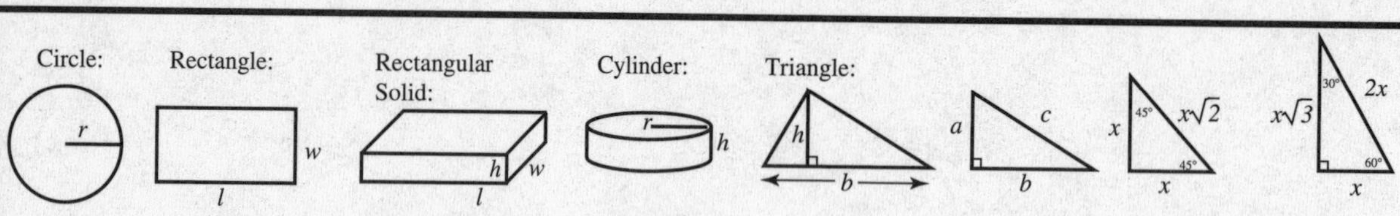

$C = 2\pi r$ $A = \pi r^2$ | $A = lw$ | $V = lwh$ | $V = \pi r^2 h$ | $A = \frac{1}{2}bh$ | $a^2 + b^2 = c^2$

The number of degrees of arc in a circle is 360.
The measure in degrees of a straight angle is 180.
The sum of the measures in degrees of the angles of a triangle is 180.

Part 1: Quantitative Comparison Questions

Directions: For each of the following questions, two quantities are given—one in Column A, the other in Column B. Compare the two quantities and mark your answer sheet as follows:

(A) if the quantity in Column A is greater
(B) if the quantity in Column B is greater
(C) if the quantities are equal
(D) if the relationship cannot be determined from the information given

Notes:

(1) Information concerning one or both of the compared quantities will be centered above the two columns for some items.
(2) Symbols that appear in both columns represent the same thing in Column A as in Column B.
(3) Letters such as x, n, and k are symbols for real numbers.

Examples

$a > 0$
$x > 0$

	Column A	Column B	Answers
E1.	$a - x$	$a + x$	(A) ● (C) (D)
E2.	The average of 17, 19, 21, 23	The average of 16, 18, 20, 22	● (B) (C) (D)

DO NOT MARK CHOICE (E) FOR THESE QUESTIONS. THERE ARE ONLY FOUR ANSWER CHOICES.

	Column A	Column B

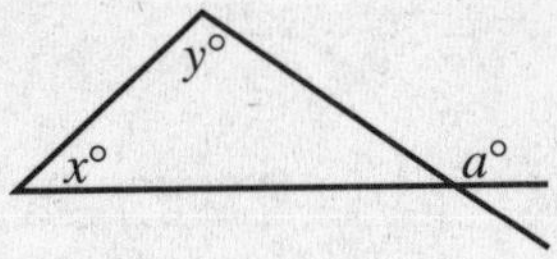

	Column A	Column B
1.	$a - y$	x

Questions 2–3 refer to the following definition.

$\boxed{u} = u^2 - u$

	Column A	Column B
2.	$\boxed{3}$	$\boxed{-3}$
3.	$\boxed{u+1}$	$\boxed{u-1}$

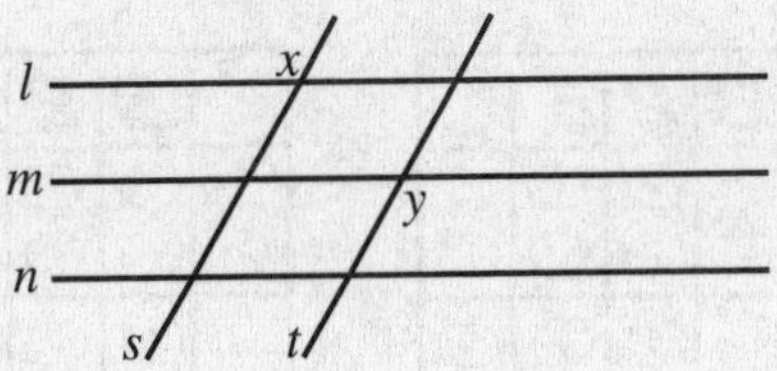

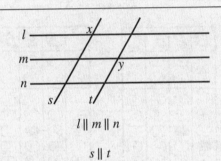

$l \parallel m \parallel n$

$s \parallel t$

	Column A	Column B
4.	$\angle x$	$\angle y$
5.	Area of square with side 4	Twice the area of a triangle with base 4 and height 4

	Column A	Column B

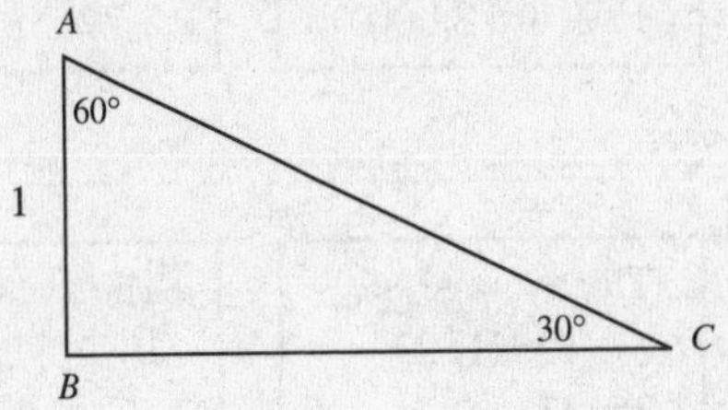

	Column A	Column B
6.	$\sqrt{3}$	BC

$3x + 4 = y$

x is a positive integer less than or equal to 7

	Column A	Column B
7.	The number of values for y which are prime numbers	2

r is the radius of a given circle.

	Column A	Column B
8.	r^2	r^3
9.	9 + 3 (–2) (4–5) + 1	(3–6) [2–5 (3–4)]
10.	The average of the degrees in all the angles in a quadrilateral	The average of the degrees in all the angles of *two* triangles

$s = 1$
$t = 4$
$r = -3$

	Column A	Column B
11.	$4s + 3t$	$2t - 2r$

GO ON TO THE NEXT PAGE

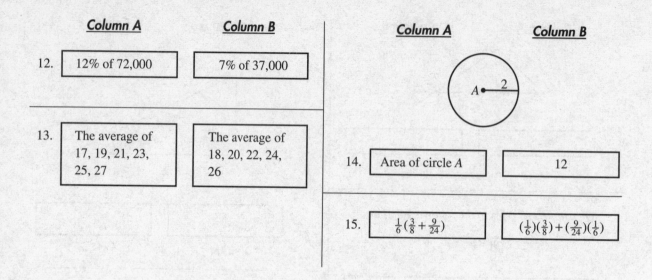

	Column A	Column B
12.	12% of 72,000	7% of 37,000
13.	The average of 17, 19, 21, 23, 25, 27	The average of 18, 20, 22, 24, 26

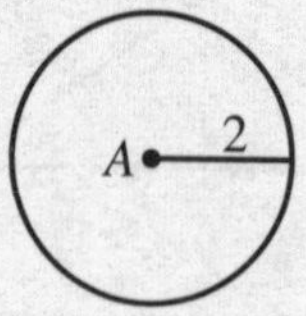

	Column A	Column B
14.	Area of circle A	12
15.	$\frac{1}{6}\left(\frac{3}{8}+\frac{9}{24}\right)$	$\left(\frac{1}{6}\right)\left(\frac{3}{8}\right)+\left(\frac{9}{24}\right)\left(\frac{1}{6}\right)$

Part 2: Student-Produced Response Questions

Directions: Solve each of these problems. Write the answer in the corresponding grid on the answer sheet and fill in the ovals beneath each answer you write. Here are some examples.

Answer: $\frac{3}{4}$ (= .75; show answer either way)

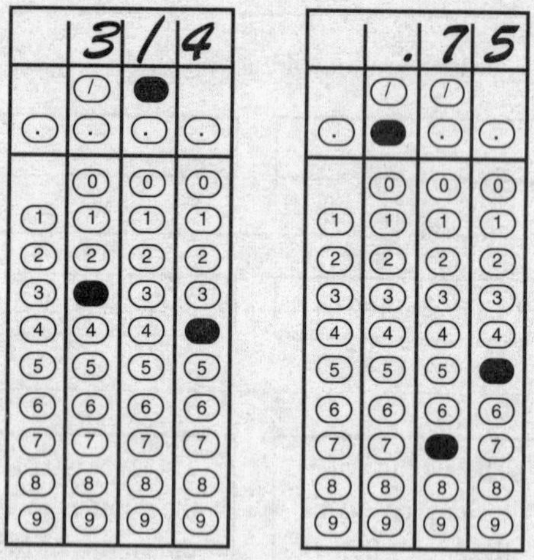

Note: A mixed number such as $3\frac{1}{2}$ must be gridded as 7/2 or as 3.5. If gridded as "$3\ \frac{1}{2}$," it will be read as "thirty-one halves."

Answer: 325

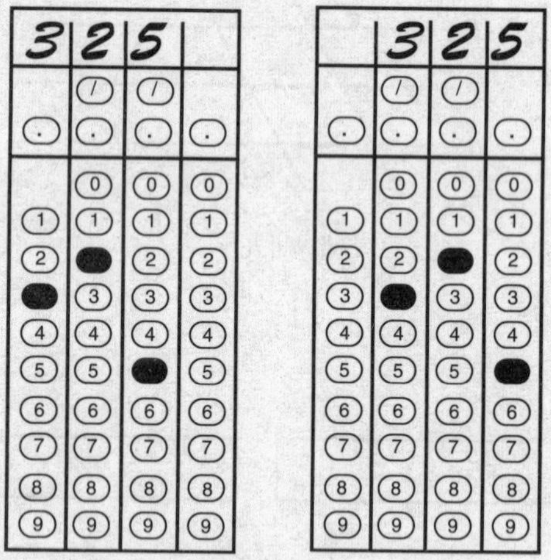

Note: Either position is correct.

16. Joshua bought two dozen apples for 3 dollars. At this rate, how much will 18 apples cost? (Do not grid the dollar sign.)

17. What is $\frac{1}{10}\%$ of $\frac{1}{10}$ of 10?

18. $\dfrac{\frac{-1}{3}}{3} - \dfrac{3}{-\frac{1}{3}} =$

19. Dawn's average for four math tests is 80. What score must she receive on her next exam to increase her average by three points?

20. In the figure below, square *WXYZ* is formed by connecting the midpoints of the sides of square *ABCD*. If the length of $AB = 6$, what is the area of the shaded region?

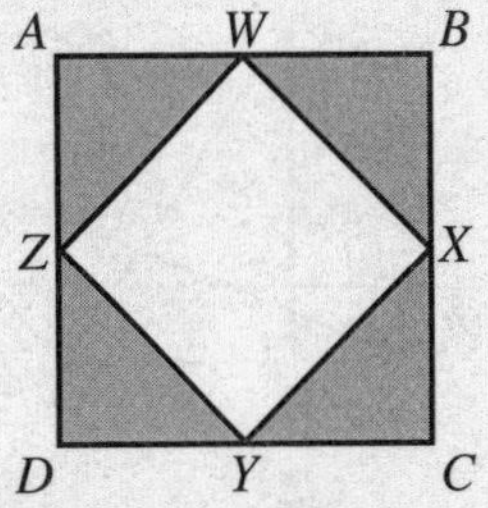

21. Thirty thousand two hundred and forty minutes is equivalent to how many weeks?

22. In the figure below, line l_1 is parallel to l_2. Transversals t_1 and t_2 are drawn. What is the value of $a + b + c + d$? (Do not grid the degree symbol.)

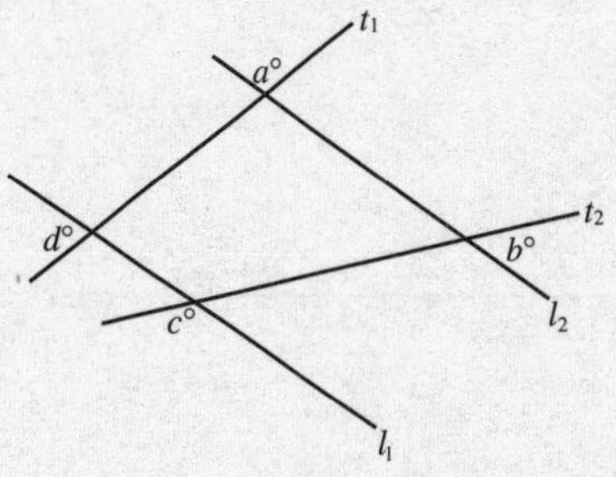

23. A car travels from town A to town B, a distance of 360 miles, in 9 hours. How many hours would the same trip have taken had the car travelled 5 mph faster?

GO ON TO THE NEXT PAGE

24. In the figure below, KJ bisects $\angle J$. The measure of $\angle K$ is 40° and the measure of $\angle L$ is 20°. What is the measure of $\angle N$? (Do not grid the degree symbol.)

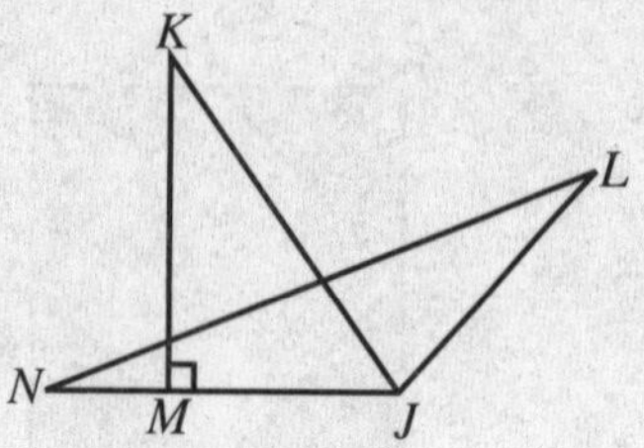

25. The area of a circle that is inscribed in a square with a diagonal of 8 is $a\pi$. What is the value of a?

STOP

END OF SECTION 3. IF YOU HAVE ANY TIME LEFT, GO OVER YOUR WORK IN THIS SECTION ONLY. DO NOT WORK IN ANY OTHER SECTION OF THE TEST.

SECTION 4

35 Questions • Time—30 minutes

Directions: Each of the following questions consists of an incomplete sentence followed by five words or pairs of words. Choose that word or pair of words which, when substituted for the blank space or spaces, *best* completes the meaning of the sentence and mark the letter of your choice on your answer sheet.

Example:

In view of the extenuating circumstances and the defendant's youth, the judge recommended ---- .

(A) conviction
(B) a defense
(C) a mistrial
(D) leniency
(E) life imprisonment

Ⓐ Ⓑ Ⓒ ● Ⓔ

1. Her clear ---- of the situation kept the meeting from breaking up into ----.

(A) grasp..chaos
(B) vision..anarchy
(C) knowledge..uproar
(D) control..harmony
(E) idea..laughter

2. The mayor remained ---- in her commitment to ---- the rise of unemployment among her constituents.

(A) firm..uphold
(B) wavering..identify
(C) steadfast..stem
(D) uncertain..staunch
(E) alone..approach

3. A ---- old stone farmhouse, it had been a landmark since before the Civil War.

(A) corrupt
(B) sturdy
(C) rickety
(D) ramshackle
(E) vital

4. Because she thought her hateful cousin's behavior was ----, it ---- her to hear the adults praise him.

(A) intangible..thrilled
(B) putative..baffled
(C) laconic..encouraged
(D) insipid..demeaned
(E) obnoxious..galled

5. A public official must be ---- in all his or her actions to avoid even the appearance of impropriety.

(A) redolent
(B) unctuous
(C) baleful
(D) circumspect
(E) propitious

6. So many people turned out for the meeting that there were not enough seats to ---- them all.

(A) count
(B) ascertain
(C) accommodate
(D) delineate
(E) delegate

7. The editorial accused the mayor of ---- for making promises he knew he could not ----.

(A) hypocrisy..fulfill
(B) revulsion..condone
(C) impunity..reprise
(D) liability..improve
(E) petulance..verify

GO ON TO THE NEXT PAGE

8. She was ---- as a child, accepting without question everything she was told.

(A) obstreperous
(B) recalcitrant
(C) credulous
(D) truculent
(E) tearful

9. Warned by an anonymous phone call that an explosion was ----, the police ---- the building immediately.

(A) expected..filled
(B) ubiquitous..purged
(C) eminent..checked
(D) imminent..evacuated
(E) insidious..obviated

10. Route 71 has always been known to wind its ---- way through steep mountain passes and coarse terrain.

(A) neat
(B) indirect
(C) evasive
(D) tortuous
(E) deceitful

11. The municipality attracted the country's scientific elite and ---- them, insulating them entirely from the problems of ordinary civilian life.

(A) cajoled
(B) muted
(C) mused
(D) cosseted
(E) impeded

12. Although the bank executive gave the appearance of a ---- businessman, he was really a ----.

(A) dedicated..capitalist
(B) respectable..reprobate
(C) depraved..profligate
(D) empathetic..philanthropist
(E) churlish..miscreant

13. During a campaign, politicians often engage in ---- debate, attacking each other's proposals in a torrent of ---- words.

(A) acerbic..amiable
(B) acrimonious..angry
(C) intensive..nebulous
(D) garrulous..inarticulate
(E) impassioned..vapid

14. He was uneven in his approach to the problem, at once ---- and ----.

(A) surly..unwilling
(B) sincere..well-meaning
(C) harmonious..foolhardy
(D) conscientious..frivolous
(E) careless..insouciant

Directions: Each of the following questions consists of a capitalized pair of words followed by five pairs of words lettered A to E. The capitalized words bear some meaningful relationship to each other. Choose the lettered pair of words whose relationship is most similar to that expressed by the capitalized pair and mark its letter on your answer sheet.

Example:

DAY : SUN : :

(A) sunlight : daylight (B) ray : sun
(C) night : moon (D) heat : cold
(E) moon : star Ⓐ Ⓑ ● Ⓓ Ⓔ

15. CRACK : SMASH : :

(A) merge : break
(B) run : hover
(C) whisper : scream
(D) play : work
(E) tattle : tell

16. SURGEON : DEXTEROUS : :

(A) clown : fat
(B) actress : beautiful
(C) athlete : tall
(D) acrobat : agile
(E) man : strong

17. SPECTATOR : SPORT : :

(A) jury : trial
(B) witness : crime
(C) soloist : music
(D) player : team
(E) fan : grandstand

18. WALK : AMBLE : :

(A) work : tinker
(B) play : rest
(C) run : jump
(D) jog : trot
(E) go : come

19. HILT : BLADE : :

(A) holster : gun
(B) sheath : knife
(C) leash : dog
(D) stem : leaf
(E) petal : branch

20. RULER : DISTANCE : :

(A) king : country
(B) yardstick : dimension
(C) barometer : weather
(D) microscope : size
(E) thermometer : temperature

21. HAMMER : TOOL : :

(A) tire : wheel
(B) wagon : vehicle
(C) nail : screw
(D) stick : drum
(E) saw : wood

22. FLIPPERS : DIVER : :

(A) baton : runner
(B) cap : ballplayer
(C) gloves : skater
(D) tights : dancer
(E) spikes : golfer

23. BRAGGART : DIFFIDENCE : :

(A) benefactor : generosity
(B) pariah : esteem
(C) partisan : partiality
(D) savant : wisdom
(E) sycophant : flattery

24. DIATRIBE : BITTERNESS : :

(A) dictum : injury
(B) critique : even-handedness
(C) polemic : consonance
(D) encomium : praise
(E) concordance : disagreement

25. TRAVESTY : RIDICULE : :

(A) reproduction : provoke
(B) forgery : deceive
(C) imitation : feign
(D) treachery : reprieve
(E) poetry : comprehend

GO ON TO THE NEXT PAGE

Directions: The reading passage below is followed by a set of questions. Read the passage and answer the accompanying questions, basing your answers on what is stated or implied in the passage. Mark the letter of your choice on your answer sheet.

Questions 26–35 are based on the following passage.

Alexander Wilson was a poet and a naturalist. Born in Scotland in 1766, he emigrated to Pennsylvania in 1794 and soon became a full-time naturalist. This excerpt on hummingbird nests is from a nine-volume work titled American Ornithology, *published in 1808–1814.*

About the twenty-fifth of April the Hummingbird usually arrives in Pennsylvania; and about the tenth of May begins to build its nest. This is generally fixed on the upper side of a horizontal branch, not among the twigs, but on the body of the branch itself. Yet I have known instances where it was attached by the side to an old moss-grown trunk; and others where it was fastened on a strong rank stalk, or weed, in the garden; but these cases are rare. In the woods it very often chooses a white oak sapling to build on; and in the orchard, or garden, selects a pear tree for that purpose. The branch is seldom more than ten feet from the ground. The nest is about an inch in diameter, and as much in depth. A very complete one is now lying before me, and the materials of which it is composed are as follows: —The outward coat is formed of small pieces of bluish grey lichen that vegetates on old trees and fences, thickly glued on with the saliva of the bird, giving firmness and consistency to the whole, as well as keeping out moisture. Within this are thick matted layers of the fine wings of certain flying seeds, closely laid together; and lastly, the downy substance from the great mullein, and from the stalks of the common fern, lines the whole. The base of the nest is continued round the stem of the branch, to which it closely adheres; and, when viewed from below, appears a mere mossy knot or accidental protuberance. The eggs are two, pure white, and of equal thickness at both ends. . . . On a person's approaching their nest, the little proprietors dart around with a humming sound, passing frequently within a few inches of one's head; and should the young be newly hatched, the female will resume her place on the nest even while you stand within a yard or two of the spot. The precise period of incubation I am unable to give; but the young are in the habit, a short time before they leave the nest, of thrusting their bills into the mouths of their parents, and sucking what they have brought them. I never could perceive that they carried them any animal food; tho, from circumstances that will presently be mentioned, I think it highly probable they do. As I have found their nest with eggs so late as the twelfth of July, I do not doubt but that they frequently, and perhaps usually, raise two broods in the same season.

26. Why does Wilson mention the "old moss-grown trunk" and "strong rank stalk" (lines 7–8)?

(A) To compare relative sizes of birds
(B) To establish the birds' eating patterns
(C) To illustrate nontypical nesting behaviors
(D) To delineate plant life in Pennsylvania
(E) To complete a list of related flora

27. When Wilson remarks that the birds' nests resemble "an accidental protuberance" (line 26), he implies that

(A) the nests are messily constructed
(B) nests may be destroyed accidently
(C) the nests are usually invisible
(D) the nests are designed to blend into their surroundings
(E) most nests resemble the beak of the bird itself

28. The phrase "little proprietors" (line 29) refers to

(A) children in the orchard
(B) eggs
(C) naturalists
(D) shopowners
(E) nesting pairs of hummingbirds

29. When Wilson remarks that he "never could perceive" hummingbirds feeding their nestlings animal food (lines 37–38), he is suggesting

(A) that his eyesight is failing
(B) his limitations as an observer
(C) that animal food may, in fact, be eaten
(D) that no animal food is eaten
(E) that hummingbirds eat only at night

30. The fact that Wilson has found nests with eggs "so late as the twelfth of July" indicates that

(A) birds do not lay eggs before June
(B) most eggs are found earlier than July 12
(C) the eggs are not likely to hatch
(D) the birds began nesting late in the season
(E) some birds abandon their nests

31. The hummingbirds' nest is composed of all of the following EXCEPT

(A) moss
(B) lichen
(C) the wings of flying seeds
(D) a downy substance from fern stalks
(E) hummingbird saliva

32. How does Wilson reconstruct the makeup of the nest?

(A) By taking apart a nest that hangs in the orchard
(B) By watching a hummingbird build a nest in the stable
(C) By reading a report by John Audubon
(D) By inspecting a nest that lies on his desk
(E) By making a copy of a nest he has observed

33. Which of the following can be inferred about the hummingbirds' habits?

(A) They flourish only in Pennsylvania.
(B) Their broods each consist of a single egg.
(C) They migrate in the spring.
(D) They always raise two broods in a season.
(E) They spend the winter in Pennsylvania.

34. The main purpose of this passage is to describe

(A) the nesting behavior of the hummingbird
(B) the mating behavior of the hummingbird
(C) the relative size of the hummingbird
(D) hummingbirds in Pennsylvania
(E) young hummingbird fledglings

35. If Wilson were to study crows, he would be likely to

(A) stuff and mount them
(B) observe them in the wild
(C) read all about them
(D) mate them in a laboratory
(E) dissect them

STOP

END OF SECTION 4. IF YOU HAVE ANY TIME LEFT, GO OVER YOUR WORK IN THIS SECTION ONLY. DO NOT WORK IN ANY OTHER SECTION OF THE TEST.

SECTION 5

10 Questions • Time—15 Minutes

Directions: Solve the following problems using any available space on the page for scratchwork. On your answer sheet fill in the choice which best corresponds to the correct answer.

Notes: The figures accompanying the problems are drawn as accurately as possible unless otherwise stated in specific problems. Again, unless otherwise stated, all figures lie in the same plane. All numbers used in these problems are real numbers. Calculators are permitted for this test.

Reference Information

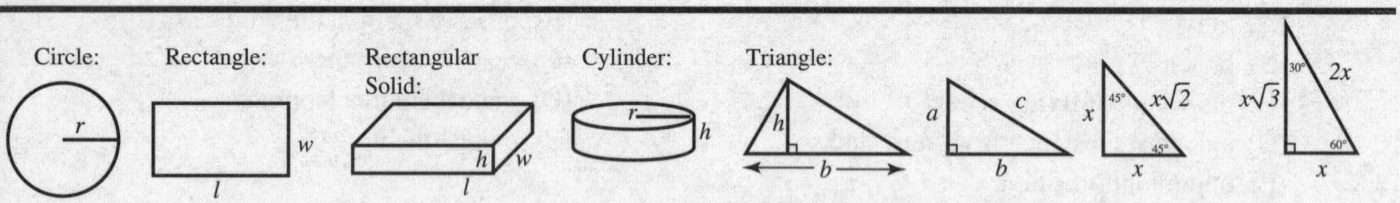

$C = 2\pi r$ $A = \pi r^2$ $A = lw$ $V = lwh$ $V = \pi r^2 h$ $A = \frac{1}{2}bh$ $a^2 + b^2 = c^2$

The number of degrees of arc in a circle is 360.
The measure in degrees of a straight angle is 180.
The sum of the measures in degrees of the angles of a triangle is 180.

1. In the figure, what percent of the area of rectangle *PQRS* is shaded?

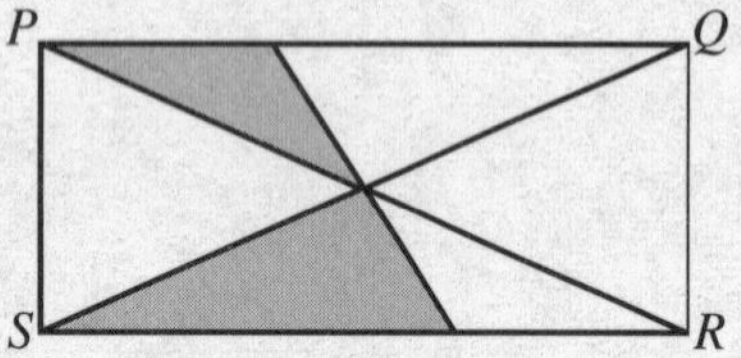

(A) 20
(B) 25
(C) 30
(D) $33\frac{1}{3}$
(E) 35

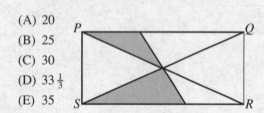

2. One wheel has a diameter of 30 inches and a second wheel has a diameter of 20 inches. The first wheel traveled a certain distance in 240 revolutions. In how many revolutions did the second wheel travel the same distance?

(A) 120
(B) 160
(C) 360
(D) 420
(E) 480

3. The one of the following to which 1.86×10^5 is equivalent is

(A) 18,600
(B) 186,000
(C) 18,600,000
(D) $186 \times 500{,}000$
(E) 1,860,000

4. How many of the numbers between 100 and 300 begin or end with 2?

(A) 20
(B) 40
(C) 100
(D) 110
(E) 180

5. The area of a square is $49x^2$. What is the length of a diagonal of the square?

(A) $7x$
(B) $7x\sqrt{2}$
(C) $14x$
(D) $7x^2$
(E) $\frac{7x}{\sqrt{2}}$

6. If shipping charges to a certain point are 62 cents for the first five ounces and 8 cents for each additional ounce, the weight of a package, in pounds, for which the charges are $1.66 is

(A) $\frac{7}{8}$
(B) 1
(C) $1\frac{1}{8}$
(D) $1\frac{1}{4}$
(E) $1\frac{1}{2}$

7. If 15 cans of food are needed for seven adults for two days, the number of cans needed to feed four adults for seven days is

(A) 15
(B) 20
(C) 25
(D) 30
(E) 35

8. A rectangular sign is cut down by 10% of its height and 30% of its width. What percent of the original area remains?

(A) 30
(B) 37
(C) 57
(D) 63
(E) 70

9. If the average (arithmetic mean) of a series of numbers is 20 and their sum is 160, how many numbers are in the series?

(A) 8
(B) 16
(C) 32
(D) 48
(E) 80

10. If the result of squaring a number is less than the number, the number is

(A) negative and greater than –1
(B) negative and less than –1
(C) a positive fraction greater than 1
(D) positive and less than 1
(E) 1 and only 1

STOP

END OF SECTION 5. IF YOU HAVE ANY TIME LEFT, GO OVER YOUR WORK IN THIS SECTION ONLY. DO NOT WORK IN ANY OTHER SECTION OF THE TEST.

SECTION 6

10 Questions • Time—15 minutes

Directions: The two passages below deal with a related topic. Following the passages are questions about the content of each passage or about the relationship between the two passages. Answer the questions based upon what is stated or implied in the passages and in any introductory material provided. Mark the letter of your choice on your answer sheet.

Questions 1–10 are based on the following passages.

The treatment of prisoners is the theme of both passages below. The first is testimony from a British prisoner of war who was held in a Scottish prison during the second Jacobite rebellion. The second is from a magazine piece written by a reporter about prison-farms in Australia in the nineteenth century.

Passage 1—James Bradshaw's Testimony before the Sheriffs of Surrey (1746)

I was put into one of the Scotch kirks, together with a great number of wounded prisoners, who were stripped naked, and then left to die of their wounds without the least assistance; and though we had a surgeon of our own, a prisoner in the same place, yet he was not permitted to dress their wounds, but his instruments were taken from him on purpose to prevent it, and in consequence of this many expired in the utmost agonies. Several of the wounded were put on board the *Jean* of Leith, and there died in lingering tortures. Our general allowance, while we were prisoners there, was half a pound of meal a day, which was sometimes increased to a pound, but never exceeded it; and I myself was an eyewitness that great numbers were starved to death. Their barbarity extended so as not to suffer the men who were put on board the *Jean* to lie down even on planks, but they were obliged to sit on large stones, by which means their legs swelled as big almost as their bodies. These are some few of the cruelties exercised, which being almost incredible in a Christian country, I am obliged to add an asseveration to the truth of them; and I do assure you, upon the word of a dying man, as I hope for mercy at the day of judgment, I assert nothing but what I know to be true.

Passage 2—P. Cunningham on the Treatment of Convicts in Australia (1827)

The convict-servants are accommodated upon the farms in huts walled round and roofed with bark, or built of split wood and plaster, with thatched roofs. About four of them generally sleep and mess in each hut, drawing their provisions every Saturday, and being generally allowed the afternoon of that day, whereupon to wash their clothes and grind their wheat. Their usual allowance I have already stated to be a peck of wheat; seven pounds of beef, or four and a half of pork; two ounces of tea, two ounces of tobacco, and a pound of sugar, weekly; the majority of settlers permitting them to raise vegetables in little gardens allotted for their use, or supplying them occasionally from their own gardens. Wages are only allowed at the option of the master; but you are obliged to supply them with two full suits of clothes annually; and you also furnish a bed-tick (to be stuffed with grass), and a blanket, to each person, besides a tin-pot and knife; as also an iron-pot and frying pan to each mess. The tea, sugar, and tobacco, are considered bonuses for good conduct, and withheld in default thereof.

To get work done, you must feed well; and when the rations are ultimately raised upon your own farm, you never give their expense a moment's consideration. The farm-men usually bake their flour into flat cakes, which they call dampers, and cook these in the ashes, cutting their salted meats into thin slices, and boiling them in the iron-pot or frying-pan, by which means the salt is, in a great measure, extracted. If tea and sugar are not supplied, milk is allowed as a substitute, tea or milk forming the beverage to every meal. Though not living so comfortably as when everything is cooked and put down before them, yet it is more after their own mind, while the operations of preparing their meals amuse their leisure hours and give a greater zest to the enjoyment of those repasts. When the labour of the day is over, with enlivening chit-chat, singing, and smoking, they chase away *ennui*, and make the evening hours jog merrily by. Indeed, without the aid of that magic care-killer, the pipe, I believe the greater portion of our "pressed men" would "take the bush" in a week after their arrival in our solitudes, before time had attuned their minds to rural prospects and industrious pursuits.

Convicts, when first assigned, if long habituated to a life of idleness and dissipation, commonly soon become restless and dissatisfied; and if failing to provoke you to return them into the government employ, wherein they may again be enabled to idle away their time in the joyous companionship of their old associates, will run off for headquarters, regardless of the flogging that awaits them on being taken or on giving themselves up—the idle ramble they have had fully compensating them for the twenty-five or fifty lashes they may receive, in case they should not be admitted at headquarters . . . If they can be coaxed or compelled to stop, however, for a twelvemonth or so, the greater portion, even of the worst, generally turn out very fair and often good servants; cockneys becoming able ploughmen, and weavers, barbers, and such like soft-fingered gentry, being metamorphosed into good fencers, herdsmen, and shepherds; a little urging and encouragement on the part of the master, and perseverance in enforcing his authority, generally sufficing.

1. The word *asseveration* in Passage 1 (line 21) means

   (A) affirmation
   (B) removal
   (C) solemnity
   (D) denial
   (E) amputation

2. Why might Bradshaw have mentioned that he was dying (line 23)?

   (A) To gain the trust of the sheriffs
   (B) To underscore the barbarity he suffered
   (C) To beg for mercy from the sheriffs
   (D) Both A and B
   (E) Both B and C

3. Bradshaw is trying to convince his listeners

   (A) to try other means of dealing with convicts
   (B) to rehabilitate prisoners in farm-camps
   (C) that Scottish prisoners are treated abominably
   (D) that he himself should be freed
   (E) both C and D

4. To whom does Cunningham refer when he mentions "pressed men" (line 65)?

   (A) Men who are easily influenced
   (B) Weavers and others who work with their hands
   (C) Men impressed into penal servitude
   (D) Depressed and angry men
   (E) Men who work under pressure

5. When Cunningham says that such men might "take the bush" (line 65), he means that they might

   (A) escape
   (B) enjoy the rural life
   (C) scam their way out of working
   (D) relax
   (E) "go native"

6. A word that might describe Cunningham's opinion of the Australian prison farms is

   (A) undignified
   (B) impressive
   (C) barbaric
   (D) ineffectual
   (E) pathetic

7. Cunningham believes that if a prisoner is treated well, he

   (A) can rejoin society in a year
   (B) will give up his wicked ways
   (C) will repay kindness with savagery
   (D) can make a good servant
   (E) will join the opposing cause

8. Unlike Cunningham, Bradshaw is writing from the point of view of

   (A) a keen observer of prison life
   (B) a former prisoner
   (C) an Australian
   (D) a journalist
   (E) a lawman

GO ON TO THE NEXT PAGE

9. Unlike the men referred to by Cunningham, those mentioned by Bradshaw are

   (A) prisoners
   (B) English
   (C) innocent
   (D) tradesmen
   (E) soldiers

10. Neither writer believes that

    (A) prisoners need exercise
    (B) physical punishment is beneficial
    (C) workers should be fed well
    (D) prison guards can be fair
    (E) children should be jailed

STOP

END OF SECTION 6. IF YOU HAVE ANY TIME LEFT, GO OVER YOUR WORK IN THIS SECTION ONLY. DO NOT WORK IN ANY OTHER SECTION OF THE TEST.

Practice Examination 3

Answer Key

Section 1: MATH

1. B	6. E	11. E	16. B	21. E
2. B	7. B	12. A	17. A	22. A
3. A	8. D	13. D	18. D	23. E
4. B	9. C	14. C	19. D	24. D
5. D	10. B	15. B	20. A	25. C

Section 2: VERBAL

1. C	8. B	15. D	22. D	29. E
2. A	9. B	16. E	23. D	30. D
3. D	10. C	17. A	24. C	
4. E	11. A	18. D	25. A	
5. B	12. C	19. C	26. B	
6. C	13. C	20. C	27. E	
7. A	14. B	21. A	28. A	

Section 3: MATH

Part 1

1. C	4. C	7. A	10. A	13. C
2. B	5. C	8. D	11. A	14. A
3. D	6. C	9. A	12. A	15. C

Part 2

16. $2.25 = \frac{9}{4}$	18. $\frac{80}{9} = 8.89$	20. 18	22. 360	24. 60
17. .001	19. 95	21. 3	23. 8	25. 8

Section 4: VERBAL

1. A	8. C	15. C	22. E	29. C
2. C	9. D	16. D	23. B	30. B
3. B	10. D	17. B	24. D	31. A
4. E	11. D	18. A	25. B	32. D
5. D	12. B	19. D	26. C	33. C
6. C	13. B	20. E	27. D	34. A
7. A	14. D	21. B	28. E	35. B

Section 5: MATH

1. B	3. B	5. B	7. D	9. A
2. C	4. D	6. C	8. D	10. D

Section 6: VERBAL

1. A	3. C	5. A	7. D	9. E
2. D	4. C	6. B	8. B	10. B

Practice Examination 3

Explanatory Answers

Note: A [calculator icon] following a math answer explanation indicates that a calculator could be helpful in solving that particular problem.

Section 1

1. **(B)** If $9x + 5 = 23$, $9x = 18$, or $x = 2$. Thus, $18x + 5 = 36 + 5 = 41$.

2. **(B)**

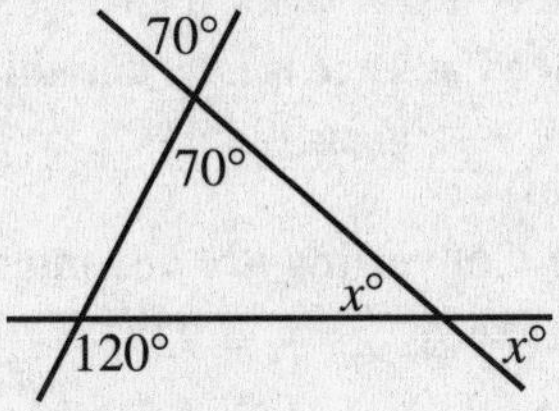

$$120 = 70 + x$$
$$x = 50$$

3. **(A)** $2y = \frac{1}{3}$

$$6y = 1$$
$$y = \frac{1}{6}$$
$$\frac{1}{4y} = \frac{1}{4(\frac{1}{6})} = \frac{1}{\frac{2}{3}} = \frac{3}{2}$$

4. **(B)** The volume of a cube is $V = s^3$ The side s of this cube is $\sqrt[3]{64} = 4$ in. Since there are 12 edges to a cube, the amount of wire needed is 12×4 in., or 48 inches.

5. **(D)** Let x = original price.
Then $.60x = \$4.20$
or $6x = \$42.00$
$x = \$7.00$

6. **(E)** $A = 15$
$B = 15 + \frac{1}{3}(15) = 20$
$15 - n$ is A's age n years ago
$20 - n$ is B's age n years ago
$(20 - n) = 2(15 - n)$
$20 - n = 30 - 2n$
$n = 10$

7. **(B)** By simple substitutions,
$s = 16 \times 8 \times 8$, or 1,024.

8. **(D)** The line of center of two tangent circles passes through the point of tangency. Hence, perimeter of $\Delta = (2 + 3) + (3 + 4) + (4 + 2) = 5 + 7 + 6 = 18$.

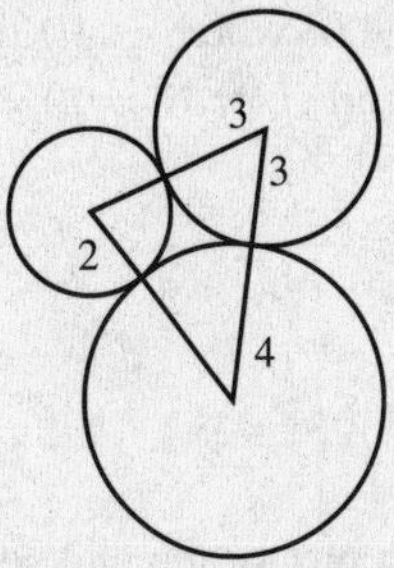

9. **(C)** $\frac{1}{10} = x \bullet \frac{3}{4} = \frac{3x}{4}$

$$30x = 4$$
$$x = \frac{2}{15}$$

10. **(B)** Since $QR = 7$, and QOR is a right isosceles triangle, $OQ = \frac{7}{\sqrt{2}} = \frac{7\sqrt{2}}{2}$.
Hence, coordinates of Q are $(0, \frac{7}{2}\sqrt{2})$.

11. **(E)** There is no indication as to the exact percentage of students who eat in the cafeteria, since we do not know how many boys or girls there are.

12. **(A)** Three meals a day times 365 days per year means there are $3 \times 365 = 1{,}095$ meals in one year. Over 19 years there are $1{,}095 \times 19 = 20{,}805$ meals. Therefore, the number of restaurants in New York City exceeds 20,500.

13. **(D)** Both of the triangles share a common base, line segment *AC*. The difference in their area is accounted for by the difference in their altitudes. Since we are given a right angle we know that *DE* is the altitude of the larger triangle and *BE* is the altitude of the smaller triangle. Since the ratio of those two segments is 4:1, then the areas must be in the ratio of 4:1.

14. **(C)** The original 6 pounds contained .24 pounds of salt. Now, the same .24 pounds are in 5 pounds of solution, so the percentage is $\frac{.24}{5}(100) = 4.8\%$.

15. **(B)** By the Law of Exponents,

$$(75)^3 \times (75)^7 = (75)^{3+7} = (75)^{10}.$$

16. **(B)** Cities *A, B,* and *C* need not be on a straight line; therefore, one cannot add or subtract miles. Six times the distance between *A* and *B* is $150 \times 6 = 900$, which is 10 times the distance between *A* and *C*, or $10 \times 90 = 900$.

17. **(A)** $\frac{1}{a} + \frac{1}{b} = \frac{b+a}{ab} = \frac{3}{4}$

18. **(D)**
$x^6 + (2x^2)^3 + (3x^3)^2 = x^6 + 8x^6 + 9x^6 = 18x^6$

19. **(D)** Set up a proportion and solve for *x*:

$$\frac{\frac{3}{4}\text{ in.}}{6\text{ in.}} = \frac{10\text{ mi.}}{x\text{ mi.}}$$

$$\frac{3}{4}x = 60$$

$$x = 80$$

20. **(A)** If h is any positive quantity, then letting $d' = (m+h) - \frac{50}{m+h}$, we can see that d' is greater than d, since h is greater than zero, and $\frac{50}{m}$ is greater than $\frac{50}{m+h}$. Therefore, d increases as m does.

21. **(E)** One cubic foot equals 12^3 cubic inches, or 1,728. Thus, one cubic foot of the metal would weigh 3,456 pounds.

22. **(A)** The area of the circle is πr^2 and the circumference is $2\pi r$. If the area equals the circumference, solve the equation $\pi r^2 = 2\pi r$, or $r = 2$. The diameter is $2r$, or 4 inches.

23. **(E)** Let's substitute *J* for John and *P* for Pat.

(*J* is 3 times *P*)	$J = 3P$
(J in four years)	$x = J + 4$
(substitute 3*P* for *J*)	$x = 3P + 4$
	$x - 4 = 3P$
	$\frac{x-4}{3} = P$

You can also reason this way: If John will be x years old in 4 years, then he is x–4 years old now. Since Pat's age is now one-third of John's, Pat is now $\frac{x-4}{3}$ years old.

24. **(D)** Converting to decimals, $\frac{2}{3} = .666...$, $\frac{5}{7} = .7142...$, $\frac{8}{11} = .7272...$, $\frac{9}{13} = .6923...$, so the order is $\frac{2}{3}, \frac{9}{13}, \frac{5}{7}, \frac{8}{11}$.

25. **(C)** If the average for the eight tests is 84%, then the sum of the eight tests must be 8 times 84, or 672. For the six tests the sum must be 6 times 86, or 516. The two dropped tests must have accounted for 156 points. 156 divided by 2 is 78.

Section 2

1. **(C)** If the young girl was unsure of her English skills, she was likely to be *reticent* (shy and restrained) when asked to speak.

2. **(A)** Arguments that only seemed logical were likely to be *specious* (false), and anyone familiar with the facts could *refute* (disprove) them.

3. **(D)** A tree that puts out fewer and fewer leaves is probably *moribund* (dying).

4. **(E)** If no trace of the building remained, it had been *obliterated* (destroyed completely).

5. **(B)** A manner that is menacing or threatening is said to be *truculent*. If, however, it is put on only for show, it is merely *affected.*

6. **(C)** The *peel* is the outer layer of an *apple,* just as the *shell* is the outer covering of a *lobster.*

7. **(A)** A *ring* is worn around the *finger* and a *necklace* is worn around the *neck.*

8. **(B)** A *child,* on becoming a fully mature person, is an *adult.* A *lamb* becomes a *sheep* on reaching full maturity. (*Cow* and *buck,* other mature animals, are specifically female and male, respectively.)

9. **(B)** *Pepper* is added to food to *season* it, and *sugar* to *sweeten* it.

10. **(C)** *Beef* can be dried to make *jerky,* and *grapes* can be dried to make *raisins.*

11. **(A)** A group of *fish* is called a *school* and a group of *cows* is called a *herd.*

12. **(C)** The *author* produces a *novel* while a *sculptor* makes a *statue.*

13. **(C)** One who is *magnanimous* (generous) is not *petty* (mean-spirited), just as one who is *passionate* (ardent) is not *blasé* (bored).

14. **(B)** King urges his listeners to "continue to work with the faith that unearned suffering is redemptive." Even if you did not know the meaning of *redemptive,* you could infer that it promised something positive. Of the choices only (B) satisfies this condition.

15. **(D)** The last paragraph gives King's belief that ". . . this situation can and will be changed."

16. **(E)** This is stated in the last paragraph and sums up the point of the entire speech.

17. **(A)** King is attempting to inspire his listeners.

18. **(D)** Lines 34-37 state that this new attitude ". . . must not lead us to a distrust of all white people, for many of our white brothers . . . have come to realize that their destiny is tied up with our destiny."

19. **(C)** King states in lines 17-19: "There will be neither rest nor tranquility in America until the Negro is granted his citizenship rights."

20. **(C)** Paragraph 4 specifically mentions creative protest.

21. **(A)** The second paragraph discusses "the whirlwinds of revolt" that will continue until justice prevails; the third paragraph urges listeners to obey the law, as ". . . we must not be guilty of wrongful deeds." Thus nonviolent resistance is the best response.

22. **(D)** This is a completely literal statement. As the rest of the passage makes clear, the narrator never really knew Alda.

23. **(D)** To answer this synthesis/analysis question will require looking back at the paragraph and tracing its structure. The narrator describes what Alda looked like, speculates on what she sounded like, and guesses what she moved like, in that order.

24. **(C)** *Docile* has several connotations, but a look back at the citation in question will tell you that only two of the choices could easily be applied to hair, and (A) is exactly opposite to the meaning the narrator intends.

25. **(A)** He compares her brow to (B) and he speaks of a flower (D) and a photograph (E). However, he compares her soul to a church, castle, and tower as well as to a well (see lines 4–5).

26. **(B)** Reread the surrounding text to remind yourself of the author's main point. Her presence has no sensation for him, because he has not really met her.

27. **(E)** Each choice is a possible synonym, but only choice (E) suits the idea of memory being more faithful than faded photographs.

28. **(A)** In the first sentence of paragraph 3, the author suggests that his fear of reality was the reason he failed to meet Alda. This is the first time he has made such a suggestion. Paragraph 3 might also be said to support (C), but so do paragraphs 1 and 2. Choices (D) and (E) are not supported anywhere in the passages.

29. **(E)** Here is an example of an oddly worded phrase that cannot be easily deciphered. By testing the choices in place of the phrase in context, however, the reasonable translation is clear.

30. **(D)** When you are asked to choose a title, you are really being asked to summarize the passage. In this case, choice (A) does not work—we don't know that this is tragic. Choice (B) does not work because we have no hint that this was the narrator's only love. Choice (C) does not work—the two were never sweethearts. Choice (E) is clearly irrelevant, but choice (D) accurately reflects the scope and tone of the excerpt.

Section 3

Part 1

1. **(C)** The exterior angle of a triangle is equal to the sum of the two interior nonadjacent angles. Thus, $x + y = a$ and $\therefore x = a - y$. Therefore, Column A and Column B are equal.

2. **(B)** $3^2 - 3 = 6$. $(-3)^2 - (-3) = 12$.

3. **(D)** This type of problem is most easily solved by plugging in small values.
If $u = 0$ then $1^2 - 1 = 0$, while $(-1)^2 - (-1) = 2$.
If $u = 1$ then $2^2 - 2 = 2$ while $(0)^2 - 0 = 0$.
Since Column B is larger than Column A when $u = 0$, but smaller when $u = 1$, the answer must be (D).

4. **(C)** An alternate exterior angle of $\angle x$ is a vertical angle to an alternate exterior angle of $\angle y$. Since alternate exterior angles of two parallel lines cut by a transversal are equal, and vertical angles are always equal, $\angle x = \angle y$. Thus, the two columns are equal.

5. **(C)** The area of a square with side 4 is $4^2 = 16$. The area of the triangle in Column B is $(\frac{1}{2})(4)(4) = 8$. Twice this area is 16. Thus, the two areas are equal.

6. **(C)** Since two of the angles of this triangle total 90°, and there are 180° in a triangle, angle *B* must equal 90°, and this is a right triangle. In a right triangle in which the angles are 90°, 60°, and 30°, the length of the side opposite the 30° angle is one-half the length of the hypotenuse, and the length of the side opposite the 60° angle is one-half the length of the hypotenuse times $\sqrt{3}$. Side *AB* is opposite the 30° angle, and so must be one-half the hypotenuse. *AB* is 1; therefore, *AC* must be 2. *BC*, then, will be one-half the length of the hypotenuse times $\sqrt{3}$. So *BC* will be $\sqrt{3}$. Thus, the two columns are equal.

7. **(A)** x can range in value from 1 to 7. Plugging in each of those values, y can be 7, 10, 13, 16, 19, 22, and 25. Of these, 7, 13, and 19 are prime numbers.

8. **(D)** Since r is the radius of a circle, r cannot be negative. Thus $r^3 > r^2$. But, if $0 < r < 1$, $r^2 > r^3$. Hence, it cannot be determined which is larger.

9. **(A)** The values of Column A and Column B are 16 and -9, respectively. Therefore, Column A is greater than Column B.

10. **(A)** There are 360 degrees and 4 angles in all quadrilaterals and 360 divided by 4 is 90. A triangle contains 180 degrees and 3 angles. For two triangles the average would be 360 divided by 6, or 60.

11. **(A)** Substituting for s and t in Column A, $4(1) + 3(4) = 16$. Substituting t and r in Column B, $2(4) - 2(-3) = 14$. Therefore, Column A is larger than Column B.

12. **(A)** In Column A, 12% of 72,000 is $(.12)(72{,}000) = 8{,}640$. In Column B, 7% of 37,000 is (.07)(37,000) = 2,590. Therefore, Column A is greater than Column B.

13. **(C)** The average can be found by totaling the numbers in each column and dividing that sum by the number of terms.

Column A $\dfrac{132}{6} = 22.$

Column B $\dfrac{110}{5} = 22.$

14. **(A)** The area of circle *A* with radius 2 is $\pi r^2 = 4\pi$. 4π is approximately 12.56, so Column A is bigger.

15. **(C)** The values of Column A and Column B are both $\frac{1}{8}$.

Part 2

16. Use a ratio of apples to dollars.

$$\frac{\text{apples}}{\text{dollars}} \rightarrow \frac{24}{3} = \frac{18}{x}$$

$$8 = \frac{18}{x}$$

$$8x = 18$$

$$x = 2.25 = \frac{9}{4}$$

17. $\frac{1}{10}\% = \frac{1}{1000}$

$$\frac{1}{1000} \bullet \frac{1}{10} \bullet \frac{10}{1} = \frac{1}{1000} = .001$$

18. $\frac{-\frac{1}{3}}{3} - \frac{3}{-\frac{1}{3}} = \frac{-\frac{1}{3}}{\frac{3}{1}} - \frac{\frac{3}{1}}{-\frac{1}{3}}$

$$= -\frac{1}{3}\left(\frac{1}{3}\right) - \frac{3}{1}\left(-\frac{3}{1}\right)$$

$$= -\frac{1}{9} + 9$$

$$= 8\frac{8}{9} = \frac{80}{9} = 8.89$$

19. The sum of Dawn's scores for the first four tests is 80(4) = 320.

$$\frac{320 + x}{5} = 83$$

$$320 + x = 415$$

$$x = 95$$

20.

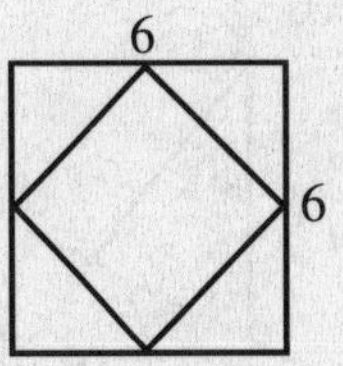

the area of a square = $(\text{side})^2$

or

$$= \frac{(\text{diagonal})^2}{2}$$

Area of $\square$ $ABCD = (\text{side})^2 = 6^2 = 36$

Area of $\square$ $WXYZ = \frac{(\text{diagonal})^2}{2} = \frac{6^2}{2} = 18$

Shaded area $= 36 - 18 = 18$

21. 1 week = 7 days

1 day = 24 hours

1 hour = 60 minutes

$$\frac{30{,}240}{7(24)(60)} = 3$$

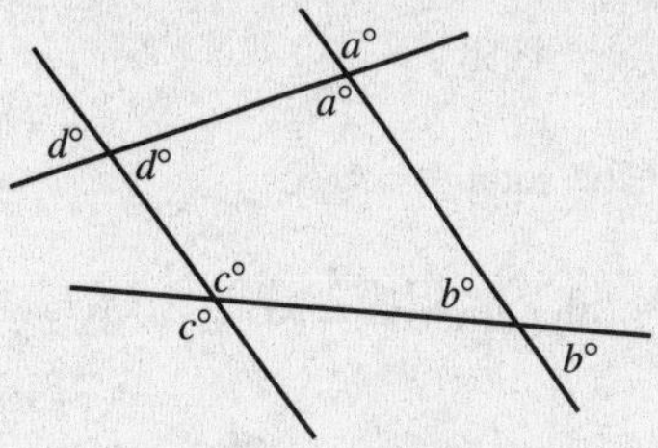

22. The sum of the interior angles of a quadrilateral is 360°.

$\therefore a + b + c + d = 360$

23. Distance = rate × time

$$360 = r(9)$$

$$40 = r$$

If r were 40 + 5 = 45

$$d = rt$$

$$360 = 45t$$

$$t = 8$$

24.

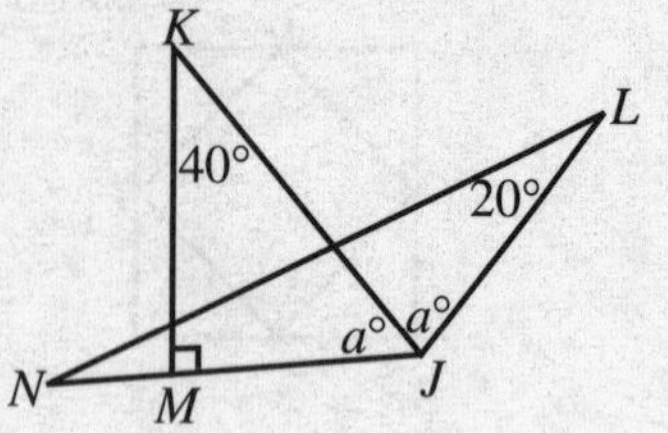

$$40 + 90 + a = 180$$
$$a = 50$$
$$m\angle J = 2(50) = 100°$$
$$m\angle N + m\angle J + m\angle L = 180°$$
$$m\angle N + 100° + 20° = 180°$$
$$m\angle N = 60°$$

25.

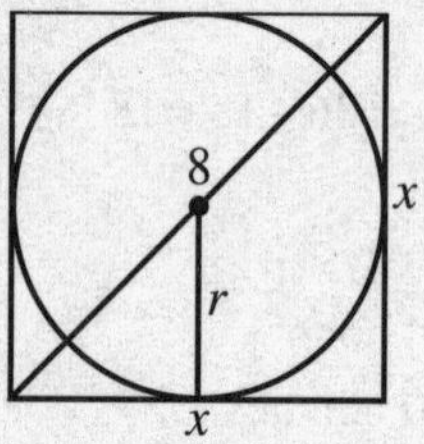

$$x^2 + x^2 = 8^2$$
$$2x^2 = 64$$
$$x = 4\sqrt{2}$$

The side of the square $= 4\sqrt{2}$.

The radius of the circle $= \frac{1}{2}(4\sqrt{2}) = 2\sqrt{2}$.

$$A = \pi r^2$$
$$= \pi(2\sqrt{2})^2 = 8\pi = a\pi \therefore a = 8$$

Section 4

1. **(A)** Keeping a meeting from breaking up requires more than a clear *idea* or *vision*; it requires control, or a *grasp* of the situation.

2. **(C)** The word *commitment* signals the appropriate actions of the mayor; to be *steadfast* in her commitment, she must *stem*, or check, the increase of economic problems for the people who voted her into office.

3. **(B)** For the farmhouse to have been a landmark since before the Civil War, it must have been well built, or *sturdy*.

4. **(E)** If she thought her cousin was hateful, it is most likely that she found his behavior *obnoxious* (offensive) and that she was *galled*, or irritated, to hear him praised.

5. **(D)** *Circumspect*, meaning "watchful or wary," is the only choice that makes sense.

6. **(C)** *Accomodate,* meaning "to provide space for," is the only answer that makes sense.

7. **(A)** To make promises you know you cannot *fulfill* is *hypocrisy.* No other choice correctly fills both blanks.

8. **(C)** One who accepts without question is *credulous* (tending to believe readily).

9. **(D)** If the police know an explosion is *imminent* (about to happen), they are likely to *evacuate* (empty) the building quickly.

10. **(D)** The key word is *wind.* A road that winds is *tortuous* (D). (C) and (E) are wrong because they refer to other meanings of *tortuous.* Choices (A) and (B) make no sense.

11. **(D)** Those who are protected from the harsh world around them are pampered, or *cossetted.* The other choices make no sense.

12. **(B)** The transitional word *although* sets up a contrast suggesting that one choice will be positive and one choice will be negative. The only possible choice is (B). Someone only appearing to be a respectable businessman may in reality be a *reprobate*, or a scoundrel.

13. **(B)** The word *attacking* indicates the need for two strong negative words. Only choice (B) satisfies this requirement with *acrimonious,* meaning harsh or bitter, and *angry.*

14. **(D)** *Conscientious* (extremely careful) and *frivolous* (silly) are opposing characteristics.

15. **(C)** To *smash* something is to do much greater damage than merely *crack* it. To *scream* is to make a much greater noise than to *whisper.*

16. **(D)** A *surgeon* is necessarily *dexterous* (skillful in using the hands), and an *acrobat* is necessarily *agile.*

17. **(B)** A *sport* is viewed by a *spectator,* and a *crime* is viewed by a *witness.*

18. **(A)** To *amble* is to *walk* unhurriedly without a predetermined destination. To *tinker* is to *work* aimlessly without a predetermined direction.

19. **(D)** A *hilt* (handle) is the part of a sword to which the *blade* is attached. Similarly, the *stem* is part of a plant to which a *leaf* is attached.

20. **(E)** A *ruler* is used to measure *distance,* and a *thermometer* is used to measure *temperature.*

21. **(B)** A *hammer* is a *tool,* and a *wagon* is a *vehicle.*

22. **(E)** *Flippers* and *spikes* are each footgear for a sport: *flippers* for the *diver* and *spikes* for the *golfer.*

23. **(B)** A *braggart* (offensively boastful person) lacks *diffidence* (modesty), just as a *pariah* (outcast) lacks *esteem* (regard).

24. **(D)** A *diatribe* is a speech full of *bitterness.* An *encomium* is speech full of *praise.*

25. **(B)** A *travesty* is an imitation intended to *ridicule.* A *forgery* is an imitation intended to *deceive.*

26. **(C)** Wilson states that nests are sometimes attached to such objects, but "these cases are rare" (lines 8–9).

27. **(D)** The nest is not easily seen, but it is not invisible, as (C) suggests. Wilson describes seeing it from below (line 25).

28. **(E)** Wilson refers to the proprietors darting around to protect the nest (line 29).

29. **(C)** Wilson believes that hummingbirds *do* feed their young such food, saying, "I think it highly probable they do" (lines 39–40). However, he has not seen it.

30. **(B)** Since Wilson takes this to mean that hummingbirds may raise two broods (line 42), the only possible answer here is (B).

31. **(A)** According to the passage (lines 15–23), the nest is composed of bluish-grey lichen glued on with hummingbird saliva, the wings of flying seeds, and downy substances from fern stalks and from the great mullein (another kind of plant).

32. **(D)** Line 14 shows that Wilson is looking at something that "is now lying before me."

33. **(C)** It can inferred from the sentence that the hummingbirds migrate into Pennsylvania (presumably from the south) "about the twenty-fifth of April." None of the other choices is supported by the passage.

34. **(A)** Although other details about the hummingbird are included, the passage focuses on hummingbirds' nesting.

35. **(B)** Most of Wilson's observations in this piece happen in the wild; it is safe to assume that he would study crows the same way.

Section 5

1. **(B)**

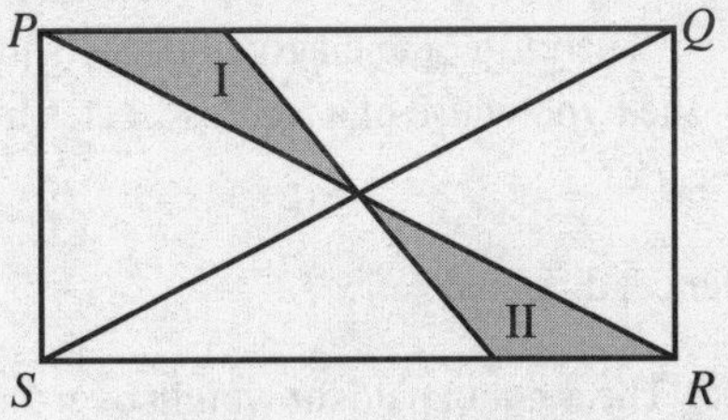

Area of ΔI = Area of ΔII

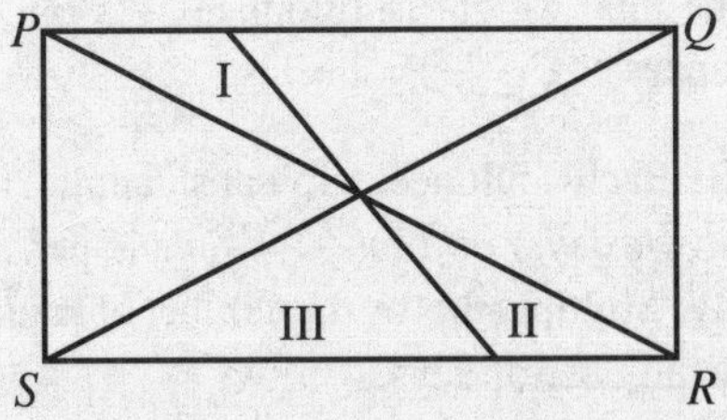

Area of ΔI + ΔIII = Area of ΔIII + ΔII

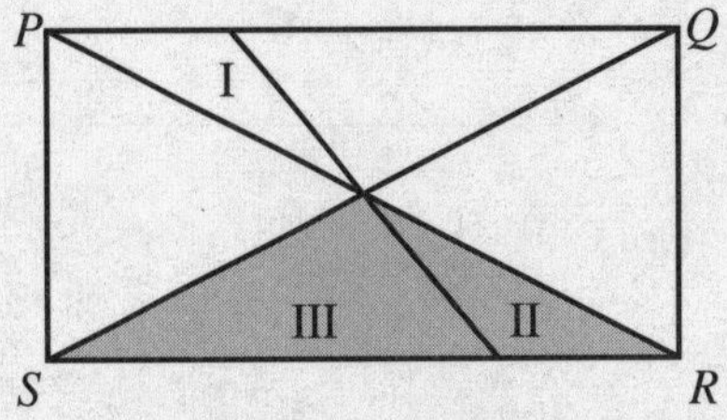

PR and *SQ* are diagonals of rectangle *PQRS.* The diagonals of a rectangle divide the rectangle into four triangles of equal area.

∴ ΔIII + ΔII = 25% of rectangle *PQRS.*

2. **(C)** The number of revolutions is inversely proportional to size of wheel.

Thus, $\frac{30}{20} = \frac{n}{240}$

Where n = no. of revolutions for second wheel,

$20n = 7200$

$n = 360$

3. **(B)** $1.86 \times 10^5 = 1.86 \times 100{,}000 = 186{,}000$

4. **(D)** All the numbers from 200 to 299 begin with 2. There are 100 of these. Then all numbers like 102, 112, . . . , 192 end with 2. There are 10 of these.

Hence, there are 110 such numbers.

5. **(B)** If the area is $49x^2$, the side of the square is $7x$. Therefore, the diagonal of the square must be the hypotenuse of a right isosceles triangle of leg $7x$.

Hence, diagonal = $7x\sqrt{2}$

6. **(C)** The amount paid for weight over 5 ounces is $\$1.66 - \$.62 = \$1.04$. At \$.08 for each additional ounce, $\frac{\$1.04}{\$.08}$ = 13 ounces of additional weight. The total weight is 13 ounces + 5 ounces = 18 ounces × $\left(\frac{1\text{ lb.}}{16\text{ oz.}}\right) = 1\frac{1}{8}$ lbs.

7. **(D)** Each adult needs 15 cans/7adults $= \frac{15}{7}$ cans in two days, or $\left(\frac{1}{2}\right)\left(\frac{15}{7}\right) = \frac{15}{14}$ cans per adult per day. Multiply this by the number of adults and by the number of days.
$\left(\frac{15}{14}\right)$(4 adults)(7 days) = 30 cans of food.

8. **(D)** Let the original sign be 10 by 10.

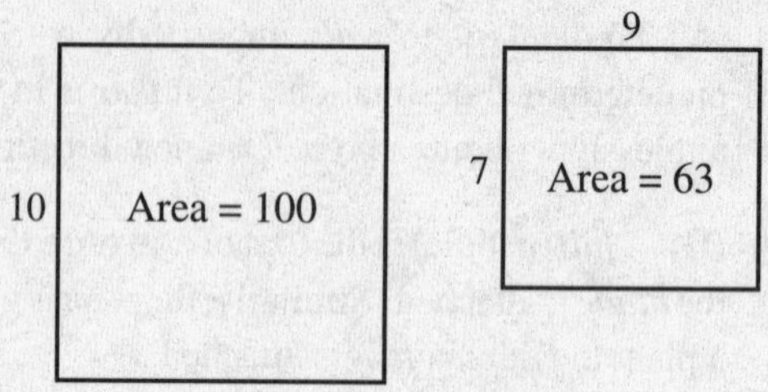

Then the new sign is 9 by 7.

$\frac{63}{100} = 63\%$

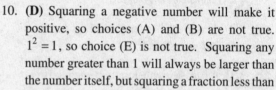

9. **(A)** The average is found by taking the sum of a list of numbers and dividing the sum by the number in the list. If n is the number of numbers in the series, $160 \div n = 20$, so $n = 8$ numbers.

10. **(D)** Squaring a negative number will make it positive, so choices (A) and (B) are not true. $1^2 = 1$, so choice (E) is not true. Squaring any number greater than 1 will always be larger than the number itself, but squaring a fraction less than 1, where the denominator is larger than the numerator, will make the denominator much larger than the numerator, thus making the whole fraction smaller.

Section 6

1. **(A)** Bradshaw wishes desperately to be believed; his entire final sentence is a vow pledging that what he has said is true.

2. **(D)** Bradshaw swears to the truth of what he tells "upon the word of a dying man." He wants the sheriffs to trust him. He may or may not be dying because of the injuries inflicted on him by his imprisonment; either way, such a statement helps his cause by stressing the hardship he endured. He is not looking for mercy (C); he is looking for justice.

3. **(C)** The entire passage deals with the cruel way the Scots treated their prisoners. No mention of other rehabilitative techniques [(A) and (B)] is made, and Bradshaw is not petitioning for freedom (D); he is speaking to the Sheriffs of Surrey, not to his Scottish jailers.

4. **(C)** By this, Cunningham simply means "prisoners."

5. **(A)** Cunningham is making the assertion that without pipe tobacco, prisoners would not be able to bear the solitude of the Australian outback, and would run away to the bush.

6. **(B)** Cunningham paints a fairly positive picture of contented, hard-working inmates. He seems to be impressed by the efficiency of the prison farms.

7. **(D)** Cunningham does mention giving prisoners a year (A), but only means that it will take that long for them to become good, solid workers at the tasks to which they are assigned. He never implies that the prisoners will be cured of further misbehavior (B).

8. **(B)** Bradshaw is writing about tortures and imprisonment he himself endured; his use of the first person throughout his testimony makes it clear that he himself was subjected to these indignities.

9. **(E)** Bradshaw refers to wounded prisoners; it is clear that these are prisoners of war.

10. **(B)** Bradshaw thinks the physical punishment meted out to prisoners is barbaric and cruel. Cunningham makes it clear that prisoners will run away despite the lashing they receive on their return (lines 74–76), and his last sentence proves that he favors gentle encouragement to physical discipline.

Evaluating Practice Examination 3

To determine your Verbal Reasoning Score:

1. Using the Analysis Worksheet, enter the number of correct answers for each verbal reasoning section on the appropriate line in Column A of the Verbal Reasoning grid.
2. Enter the number of incorrect answers for each verbal reasoning section on the appropriate line in Column B of the Verbal Reasoning grid.
3. Total Columns A and B and enter these totals in boxes A and B, respectively.
4. Perform the indicated calculation to find your Raw Score; (value in box A) minus (one-quarter of the value in box B) = Raw Score.
5. Consult the Conversion Chart to find your approximate Scaled Score.

To determine your Mathematical Reasoning Score:

1. Enter the number of correct answers for each mathematical reasoning section on the appropriate line in Column C of the Mathematical Reasoning grid.
2. Enter the number of incorrect answers for each mathematical reasoning section on the appropriate line in Column D, E, or F of the Mathematical Reasoning grid.
3. Total Columns C, D, and E, and enter these totals in boxes C, D, and E respectively.
4. Perform the indicated calculation to find your Raw Score: (value in box C) minus (one-quarter of the value in box D) minus (one-third of the value in box E) = Raw Score.
5. Consult the Conversion Chart to find your approximate Scaled Score.

Note: Box F is not used in this calculation.

Analysis Worksheet

Verbal Reasoning

Section	Number of Questions	Column A Number of Correct Answers	Column B Number of Incorrect Answers
2	30		
4	35		
6	10		
	Total	A	B

A — $\frac{1}{4}$ B = Raw Score → Use Conversion Chart → Scaled Score

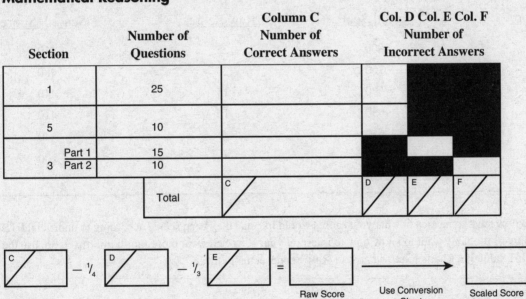

Mathematical Reasoning

Section	Number of Questions	Column C Number of Correct Answers	Col. D Number of Incorrect Answers	Col. E	Col. F
1	25				
5	10				
3 Part 1	15				
3 Part 2	10				
	Total	C	D	E	F

C — $\frac{1}{4}$ D — $\frac{1}{3}$ E = Raw Score → Use Conversion Chart → Scaled Score

Conversion Scales for Practice Examination 3

VERBAL REASONING:

Raw Score	Scaled Score	Raw Score	Scaled Score
75	800	40	550
70	800	35	520
65	760	30	480
60	710	25	440
55	670	20	410
50	620	15	370
45	590	10	340
		5	290
		0	230

MATHEMATICAL REASONING:

Raw Score	Scaled Score	Raw Score	Scaled Score
60	800	25	510
55	760	20	480
50	690	15	440
45	650	10	410
40	610	5	340
35	580	0	200
30	550		

Although you now have some idea of what your scores would like had they been scaled according to unofficial ETS standards, you will probably want to know how to interpret your Raw Scores in more familiar terms. If so, use the following Self-Evaluation Charts to see what your Raw Scores actually mean.

SELF-EVALUATION CHARTS

VERBAL REASONING: RAW SCORE

Excellent	60 – 75
Good	50 – 60
Average	30 – 50
Fair	20 – 30
Poor	0 – 20

MATHEMATICAL REASONING: RAW SCORE

Excellent	50 – 60
Good	40 – 50
Average	20 – 40
Fair	10 – 20
Poor	0 – 10

TEAR HERE

Practice Examination 4

Answer Sheet

If a section has fewer questions than answer ovals, leave the extra ovals blank.

Section 1

1 A B C D E	11 A B C D E	21 A B C D E	31 A B C D E
2 A B C D E	12 A B C D E	22 A B C D E	32 A B C D E
3 A B C D E	13 A B C D E	23 A B C D E	33 A B C D E
4 A B C D E	14 A B C D E	24 A B C D E	34 A B C D E
5 A B C D E	15 A B C D E	25 A B C D E	35 A B C D E
6 A B C D E	16 A B C D E	26 A B C D E	36 A B C D E
7 A B C D E	17 A B C D E	27 A B C D E	37 A B C D E
8 A B C D E	18 A B C D E	28 A B C D E	38 A B C D E
9 A B C D E	19 A B C D E	29 A B C D E	39 A B C D E
10 A B C D E	20 A B C D E	30 A B C D E	40 A B C D E

Section 2

1 A B C D E	11 A B C D E	21 A B C D E	31 A B C D E
2 A B C D E	12 A B C D E	22 A B C D E	32 A B C D E
3 A B C D E	13 A B C D E	23 A B C D E	33 A B C D E
4 A B C D E	14 A B C D E	24 A B C D E	34 A B C D E
5 A B C D E	15 A B C D E	25 A B C D E	35 A B C D E
6 A B C D E	16 A B C D E	26 A B C D E	36 A B C D E
7 A B C D E	17 A B C D E	27 A B C D E	37 A B C D E
8 A B C D E	18 A B C D E	28 A B C D E	38 A B C D E
9 A B C D E	19 A B C D E	29 A B C D E	39 A B C D E
10 A B C D E	20 A B C D E	30 A B C D E	40 A B C D E

Section 3

1 A B C D E	11 A B C D E	21 A B C D E	31 A B C D E
2 A B C D E	12 A B C D E	22 A B C D E	32 A B C D E
3 A B C D E	13 A B C D E	23 A B C D E	33 A B C D E
4 A B C D E	14 A B C D E	24 A B C D E	34 A B C D E
5 A B C D E	15 A B C D E	25 A B C D E	35 A B C D E
6 A B C D E	16 A B C D E	26 A B C D E	36 A B C D E
7 A B C D E	17 A B C D E	27 A B C D E	37 A B C D E
8 A B C D E	18 A B C D E	28 A B C D E	38 A B C D E
9 A B C D E	19 A B C D E	29 A B C D E	39 A B C D E
10 A B C D E	20 A B C D E	30 A B C D E	40 A B C D E

Section 4

1 (A) (B) (C) (D) (E)
2 (A) (B) (C) (D) (E)
3 (A) (B) (C) (D) (E)
4 (A) (B) (C) (D) (E)
5 (A) (B) (C) (D) (E)
6 (A) (B) (C) (D) (E)
7 (A) (B) (C) (D) (E)
8 (A) (B) (C) (D) (E)
9 (A) (B) (C) (D) (E)
10 (A) (B) (C) (D) (E)
11 (A) (B) (C) (D) (E)
12 (A) (B) (C) (D) (E)
13 (A) (B) (C) (D) (E)
14 (A) (B) (C) (D) (E)
15 (A) (B) (C) (D) (E)

Note: ONLY the answers entered on the grid are scored.
Handwritten answers at the top of the column are NOT scored.

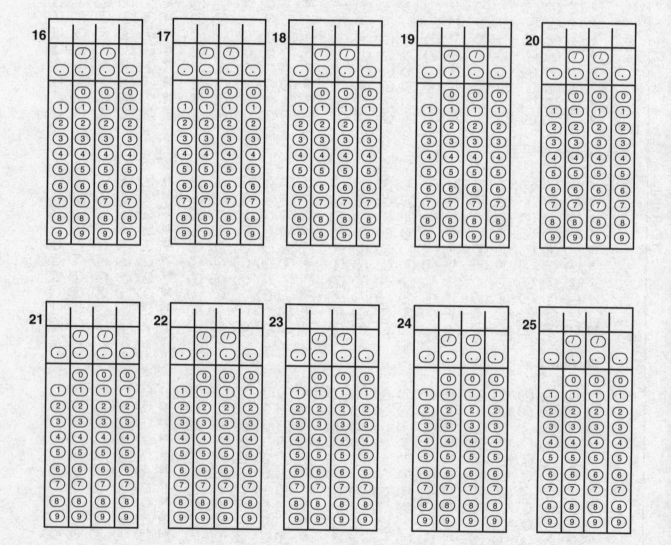

16 17 18 19 20 21 22 23 24 25

(Each grid: columns 2–3 (/); all columns (.); columns 2–4 (0); all columns (1) (2) (3) (4) (5) (6) (7) (8) (9))

TEAR HERE

Section 5

1 (A) (B) (C) (D) (E)	6 (A) (B) (C) (D) (E)	11 (A) (B) (C) (D) (E)	16 (A) (B) (C) (D) (E)
2 (A) (B) (C) (D) (E)	7 (A) (B) (C) (D) (E)	12 (A) (B) (C) (D) (E)	17 (A) (B) (C) (D) (E)
3 (A) (B) (C) (D) (E)	8 (A) (B) (C) (D) (E)	13 (A) (B) (C) (D) (E)	18 (A) (B) (C) (D) (E)
4 (A) (B) (C) (D) (E)	9 (A) (B) (C) (D) (E)	14 (A) (B) (C) (D) (E)	19 (A) (B) (C) (D) (E)
5 (A) (B) (C) (D) (E)	10 (A) (B) (C) (D) (E)	15 (A) (B) (C) (D) (E)	20 (A) (B) (C) (D) (E)

Section 6

1 (A) (B) (C) (D) (E)	6 (A) (B) (C) (D) (E)	11 (A) (B) (C) (D) (E)	16 (A) (B) (C) (D) (E)
2 (A) (B) (C) (D) (E)	7 (A) (B) (C) (D) (E)	12 (A) (B) (C) (D) (E)	17 (A) (B) (C) (D) (E)
3 (A) (B) (C) (D) (E)	8 (A) (B) (C) (D) (E)	13 (A) (B) (C) (D) (E)	18 (A) (B) (C) (D) (E)
4 (A) (B) (C) (D) (E)	9 (A) (B) (C) (D) (E)	14 (A) (B) (C) (D) (E)	19 (A) (B) (C) (D) (E)
5 (A) (B) (C) (D) (E)	10 (A) (B) (C) (D) (E)	15 (A) (B) (C) (D) (E)	20 (A) (B) (C) (D) (E)

Practice Examination 4

SECTION 1

35 Questions • Time—30 Minutes

Directions: Each of the following questions consists of an incomplete sentence followed by five words or pairs of words. Choose that word or pair of words which, when substituted for the blank space or spaces, *best* completes the meaning of the sentence and mark the letter of your choice on your answer sheet.

Example:

In view of the extenuating circumstances and the defendant's youth, the judge recommended ----.

(A) conviction (B) a defense
(C) a mistrial (D) leniency
(E) life imprisonment Ⓐ Ⓑ Ⓒ ● Ⓔ

---

1. ---- by her family, the woman finally agreed to sell the farm.

 (A) Decimated
 (B) Importuned
 (C) Encumbered
 (D) Interpolated
 (E) Designated

2. The ghost of his royal father ---- the young Hamlet to avenge his murder.

 (A) enervates
 (B) parlays
 (C) marauds
 (D) exhorts
 (E) inculcates

3. Concerned for his children's safey, the father tried to ---- in them a ---- attitude toward strangers.

 (A) obviate..hospitable
 (B) ingratiate..assiduous
 (C) insinuate..salubrious
 (D) assimilate..benevolent
 (E) inculcate..wary

4. A life of hardship and poverty has ---- them to petty physical discomforts.

 (A) ascribed
 (B) inured
 (C) remonstrated
 (D) deferred
 (E) impugned

5. Displeased with the ---- of his novel, the author withdrew from the television project.

 (A) adaptation
 (B) compilation
 (C) transliteration
 (D) transfusion
 (E) resurgence

6. Because he changed his mind nearly every day, the governor had a reputation for ----.

 (A) impudence
 (B) impartiality
 (C) perspicuity
 (D) prevarication
 (E) vacillation

GO ON TO THE NEXT PAGE

7. Her ---- smile ---- all those who saw it.

(A) devastating..replenished
(B) penultimate..inured
(C) radiant..obliged
(D) sunny..tanned
(E) bright..dazzled

8. Although he was known as a ---- old miser, his anonymous gifts to charity were always ----.

(A) grasping..tasteless
(B) spendthrift..gracious
(C) gregarious..selfish
(D) penurious..generous
(E) stingy..mangy

9. With one ---- motion, Brian disarmed his assailant and gained his freedom.

(A) maladroit
(B) deft
(C) ponderous
(D) superfluous
(E) brusque

10. The platypus is a biological ----; although it's classed as a mammal, it has a duck-like bill and lays eggs.

(A) euphemism
(B) exemplar
(C) antidote
(D) periphery
(E) anomaly

11. The ---- rites of the fraternity were kept secret by the members and were never ---- to outsiders.

(A) eclectic...delegated
(B) esoteric..divulged
(C) dubious..maligned
(D) inscrutable..traduced
(E) elusive..proscribed

12. The composer was ---- enough to praise the work of a musician he detested.

(A) magnanimous
(B) loquacious
(C) munificient
(D) parsimonious
(E) surreptitious

13. The goodwill of its customers is a genuine but ---- asset for a company.

(A) insensate
(B) redolent
(C) dismissive
(D) intangible
(E) vigilant

14. Though the law's ---- purpose was to curtail false advertising its actual result was to ---- free speech.

(A) potential..preclude
(B) mendacious..eschew
(C) ostensible..circumscribe
(D) illicit..reconcile
(E) recalcitrant..repress

Directions: Each of the following questions consists of a capitalized pair of words followed by five pairs of words lettered A to E. The capitalized words bear some meaningful relationship to each other. Choose the lettered pair of words whose relationship is most similiar to that expressed by the capitalized pair and mark its letter on your answer sheet.

Example:

DAY : SUN : :

(A) sunlight : daylight
(B) ray : sun
(C) night : moon
(D) heat : cold
(E) moon : star

Ⓐ Ⓑ ● Ⓓ Ⓔ

15. TEACHER : INSTRUCTION : :

(A) lawyer : crime
(B) army : regiment
(C) doctor : disease
(D) guard : protection
(E) student : learning

16. USHER : THEATER : :

(A) conductor : train
(B) program : movie
(C) aisle : row
(D) friend : actor
(E) pilot : airplane

17. SKATE : RINK : :

(A) build : arena
(B) sleep : lecture
(C) repose : bed
(D) park : stadium
(E) draw : circle

18. SAPLING : TREE : :

(A) weed : plant
(B) grass : wheat
(C) puppy : dog
(D) seed : vegetable
(E) acorn : oak

19. FRET : RELAX : :

(A) worry : avoid
(B) sob : cry
(C) fight : submit
(D) sing : laugh
(E) frolic : play

20. STUTTER : TALK : :

(A) worry : analyze
(B) stumble : walk
(C) walk : run
(D) hear : understand
(E) trip : fall

21. DAMAGE : DEMOLISH : :

(A) whimper : wail
(B) break : mar
(C) loosen : cinch
(D) punish : accept
(E) plan : act

22. HOSE : WATER : :

(A) lawn : grass
(B) speaker : sound
(C) window : air
(D) vent : flap
(E) chimney : smoke

23. EXERCISE : STRENGTH : :

(A) concern : resource
(B) practice : skill
(C) success : loss
(D) sport : contest
(E) gym : weight

24. SERGEANT : SOLDIERS : :

(A) captain : sports
(B) colonel : tanks
(C) coach : players
(D) director : scripts
(E) teacher : books

25. VOLATILE : STABILITY : :

(A) spontaneous : enthusiasm
(B) voluble : glibness
(C) wanton : restraint
(D) reverent : respect
(E) servile : humility

GO ON TO THE NEXT PAGE

Directions: The reading passage below is followed by a set of questions. Read the passage and answer the accompanying questions, basing your answers on what is stated or implied in the passage. Mark the letter of your choice on your answer sheet.

Questions 26–35 are based on the following passage.

Samuel Pepys worked for the Navy Office in London for many years, but he is known to us today for his diary. First transcribed in 1825, the diary covers the daily life of Pepys in London between the years 1660 and 1669. Occasionally, as here, Pepys's life and London's history became intertwined.

September 2nd, [1666] (Lord's day). Some of our maids sitting up late last night to get things ready against our feast to-day, Jane called us up about three in the morning, to tell us of a great fire they saw in the City. So I rose and slipped on my night-gown, and went to her window, and thought it to be on the back-side of Mark Lane at the farthest; but, being unused to such fires as followed, I thought it far enough off; and so went to bed again and to sleep. About seven rose again to dress myself, and there looked out at the window, and saw the fire not so much as it was and further off. So to my closet to set things to rights after yesterday's cleaning. By and by Jane comes and tells me that she hears that above 300 houses have been burned down tonight by the fire we saw, and that it is now burning down all Fish Street, by London Bridge. So I made myself ready presently, and walked to the Tower, and there got up upon one of the high places, Sir J. Robinson's little son going up with me; and there I did see the houses at that end of the bridge all on fire, and an infinite great fire on this and the other side of the end of the bridge; which, among other people, did trouble me for poor little Michell and our Sarah on the bridge. So down, with my heart full of trouble, to the Lieutenant of the Tower, who tells me that it begun this morning in the King's baker's house in Pudding Lane, and that it hath burned St. Magnus's Church and most part of Fish Street already. So I down to the water-side, and there got a boat and through bridge, and there saw a lamentable fire. Poor Michell's house, as far as the Old Swan, already burned that way, and the fire running further, that in a very little time it got as far as the Steelyard, while I was there. Everybody endeavouring to remove their goods, and flinging into the river or bringing them into lighters that lay off; poor people staying in their houses as long as till the very fire touched them, and then running into boats, or clambering from one pair of stairs by the water-side to another. And among other things, the poor pigeons, I perceive, were loth to leave their houses, but hovered about the windows and balconies till they, some of them, burned their wings, and fell down. Having stayed, and in an hour's time seen the fire rage every way, and nobody, to my sight, endeavouring to quench it, but to remove their goods, and leave all to the fire, and having seen it get as far as the Steelyard, and the wind mighty high and driving it into the City; and everything, after so long a drought, proving combustible, even the very stones of churches, and among other things the poor steeple by which pretty Mrs. ___ lives, and whereof my old school-fellow Elborough is parson, taken fire in the very top, and there burned till it fell down: I to White-hall (with a gentleman with me who desired to go off from the Tower, to see the fire, in my boat); and there up to the King's closet in the Chapel, where people come about me, and I did give them an account dismayed them all, and word was carried in to the King. So I was called for, and did tell the King and Duke of York what I saw, and that unless His Majesty did command houses to be pulled down nothing could stop the fire.

26. Pepys's attitude toward the fire is at first

    (A) astonished
    (B) unconcerned
    (C) terrified
    (D) delighted
    (E) vehement

27. Why does Pepys remark that his heart is "full of trouble" (lines 23-24)?

    (A) He realizes that people he knows may be affected.
    (B) He has seen the fire torch the Tower of London.
    (C) He fears for his life.
    (D) He may know the people who started the fire.
    (E) He is worried about the King's safety.

28. The word *lamentable* (line 29) means

(A) disgraceful
(B) encouraging
(C) mournful
(D) howling
(E) awful

29. The phrase *lighters that lay off* (line 34) probably refers to

(A) flames in the distance
(B) arsonists who set fires
(C) boats offshore
(D) lamps that have been doused
(E) bosses who fire employees

30. To underscore the anguish of people when fire threatens their homes, Pepys writes a parallel statement about

(A) soldiers faced with the brutality of battle
(B) firefighters covering their faces with rags
(C) boats carrying people downriver
(D) pigeons who will not leave their nests
(E) the King sheltered in his chambers

31. Having visited the fire as a sightseer, Pepys seems to end this part of the narrative as a(n)

(A) firefighter
(B) arsonist
(C) royal adviser
(D) robber
(E) guide

32. Pepys expresses concern because

(A) his home is in the path of the fire
(B) the King knows nothing about the fire
(C) the fire is raging across London Bridge
(D) no one is trying to put out the fire
(E) the fire is leaving people homeless

33. Pepys's love of detail is evident in his

(A) mention of landmarks
(B) inclusion of the names of people he met at the fire
(C) list of the clothing he wore to the fire
(D) both A and B
(E) both B and C

34. According to Pepys's account, the fire burned all of the following *except*

(A) the King's baker's house
(B) Whitehall
(C) St. Magnus's Church
(D) Fish Street
(E) Michell's house

35. When Pepys tells how he described the fire to the King, he means the King of

(A) York
(B) Whitehall
(C) England
(D) France
(E) London

STOP

END OF SECTION 1. IF YOU HAVE ANY TIME LEFT, GO OVER YOUR WORK IN THIS SECTION ONLY. DO NOT WORK IN ANY OTHER SECTION OF THE TEST.

SECTION 2

25 Questions • Time—30 Minutes

Directions: Solve the following problems using any available space on the page for scratchwork. On your answer sheet fill in the choice which best corresponds to the correct answer.

Notes: The figures accompanying the problems are drawn as accurately as possible unless otherwise stated in specific problems. Again, unless otherwise stated, all figures lie in the same plane. All numbers used in these problems are real numbers. Calculators are permitted for this test.

Reference Information

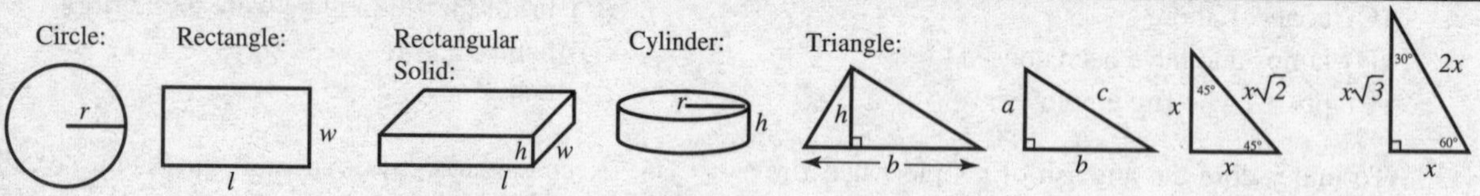

$C = 2\pi r$, $A = \pi r^2$ | $A = lw$ | $V = lwh$ | $V = \pi r^2 h$ | $A = \frac{1}{2}bh$ | $a^2 + b^2 = c^2$

The number of degrees of arc in a circle is 360.
The measure in degrees of a straight angle is 180.
The sum of the measures in degrees of the angles of a triangle is 180.

1. If for all real numbers (a.b.c. – d.e.f.) = (a – d) × (b – e) × (c – f), then (4.5.6. – 1.2.3.) =

   (A) –27
   (B) 0
   (C) 27
   (D) 54
   (E) 108

2. The sum of an odd number and an even number is

   (A) sometimes an even number
   (B) always divisible by 3 or 5 or 7
   (C) always an odd number
   (D) always a prime number (not divisible)
   (E) always divisible by 2

3. If $6x + 12 = 9$, $x^2 =$

   (A) $\frac{21}{6}$
   (B) $-\frac{1}{2}$
   (C) $\frac{9}{12}$
   (D) $\frac{1}{4}$
   (E) $\frac{9}{6}$

4. Under certain conditions, sound travels at about 1,100 ft. per second. If 88 ft. per second is approximately equivalent to 60 miles per hour, the speed of sound in miles per hour under the above conditions is closest to

   (A) 730
   (B) 740
   (C) 750
   (D) 760
   (E) 780

5. If on a blueprint $\frac{1}{4}$ inch equals 12 inches, what is the actual length in feet of a steel bar that is represented on the blueprint by a line $3\frac{3}{8}$ inches long?

(A) $2\frac{1}{2}$
(B) $3\frac{3}{8}$
(C) $6\frac{3}{4}$
(D) 9
(E) $13\frac{1}{2}$

6. If one angle of a triangle is three times a second angle and the third angle is 20 degrees more than the second angle, the second angle, in degrees, is

(A) 64
(B) 50
(C) 40
(D) 34
(E) 32

7. If $x = \frac{3}{2}$ and $y = 2$, then $x + y^2 - \frac{1}{2} =$

(A) 5
(B) 10
(C) $11\frac{1}{2}$
(D) $9\frac{1}{2}$
(E) $\frac{6}{2}$

8. A math class has 27 students in it. Of those students, 14 are also enrolled in history and 17 are enrolled in English. What is the minimum percentage of the students in the math class who are also enrolled in history *and* English?

(A) 15%
(B) 22%
(C) 49%
(D) 63%
(E) 91%

9. A cylindrical container has a diameter of 14 inches and a height of 6 inches. Since one gallon equals 231 cubic inches, the capacity of the tank in gallons is approximately

(A) $\frac{2}{3}$
(B) $1\frac{1}{7}$
(C) $2\frac{2}{7}$
(D) $2\frac{2}{3}$
(E) 4

10. If $\frac{1}{x+y} = 6$ and $x = 2$, then $y =$

(A) $-\frac{11}{6}$
(B) $-\frac{9}{4}$
(C) −2
(D) −1
(E) 4

11. The number of grams in one ounce is 28.35. The number of grams in a kilogram is 1,000. Therefore the number of kilograms in one pound is approximately

(A) 0.045
(B) 0.45
(C) 1.0
(D) 2.2
(E) 4.5

12. Which one of the following numbers is not the square of a rational number?

(A) .0016
(B) .16
(C) 1.6
(D) 16
(E) 1,600

GO ON TO THE NEXT PAGE

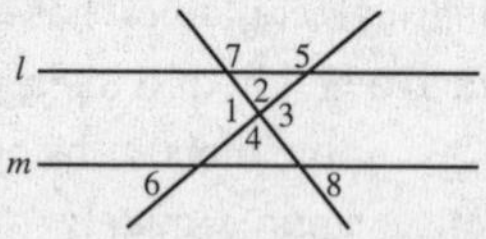

13. In the figure above, lines l and m are parallel. Which of the following must be equal to 180 degrees?

I. 1 plus 3
II. 2 plus 4
III. 5 plus 6
IV. 7 plus 8
V. 8 plus 6

(A) I and II only
(B) III and IV only
(C) V only
(D) I, II, III, IV only
(E) I, II, III, IV, V

14. If x is a fraction which ranges from $\frac{1}{4}$ to $\frac{1}{2}$ and y is a fraction which ranges from $\frac{3}{4}$ to $\frac{11}{12}$, what is the maximum value for $\frac{x}{y}$?

(A) $\frac{3}{16}$
(B) $\frac{11}{48}$
(C) $\frac{3}{8}$
(D) $\frac{11}{24}$
(E) $\frac{2}{3}$

15. These circles share a common center, point 0. The smallest circle has a radius of 2, the next circle a radius of 5, and the largest circle a radius of 9. What fraction of the area of the largest circle is the area of the shaded region?

(A) $\frac{7}{27}$
(B) $\frac{25}{81}$
(C) $\frac{1}{3}$
(D) $\frac{7}{11}$
(E) $\frac{12}{17}$

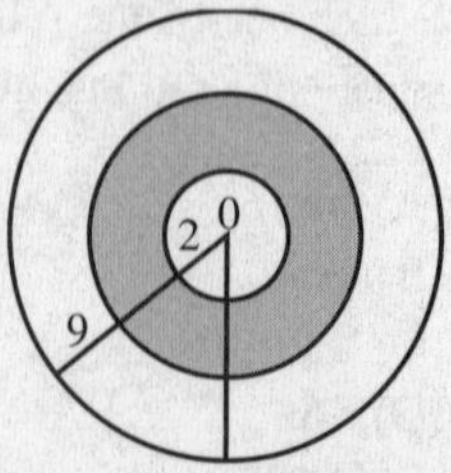

16. If n and d represent positive whole numbers $(n > d > 1)$, the fractions

I. $\frac{d}{n}$
II. $\frac{d+1}{n+1}$
III. $\frac{d-1}{n-1}$
IV. $\frac{n}{d}$
V. $\frac{n-1}{d-1}$

arranged in ascending order of magnitude are represented correctly by

(A) III, II, I, V, IV
(B) IV, V, III, I, II
(C) II, I, IV, III, V
(D) III, V, IV, I, II
(E) III, I, II, IV, V

17. A train running between two towns arrives at its destination 10 minutes late when it goes 40 miles per hour and 16 minutes late when it goes 30 miles per hour. The distance in miles between the towns is

(A) $8\frac{6}{7}$
(B) 12
(C) 192
(D) 560
(E) 720

18. A square has a diagonal of x units. If the diagonal is increased by 2 units, what is the length of the side of the new square?

(A) $x+2$
(B) $(x+2)\sqrt{2}$
(C) $\frac{(x+2)\sqrt{2}}{2}$
(D) $(x+2)2$
(E) $\frac{(x+2)\sqrt{2}}{4}$

19. *PQRS* is a square and *PTS* is an equilateral triangle. How many degrees are there in angle *TRS?*

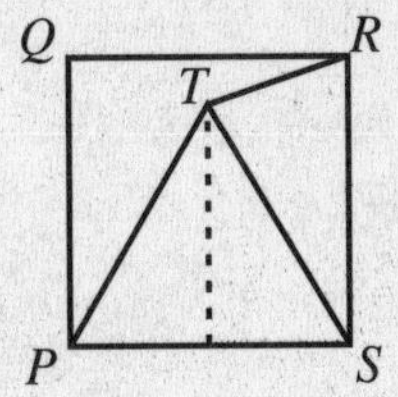

(A) 60
(B) 75
(C) 80
(D) 90
(E) It cannot be determined from the information given.

20. In the figure, line *PQ* is parallel to line *RS*, angle $y = 60°$, and angle $z = 130°$. How many degrees are there in angle *x*?

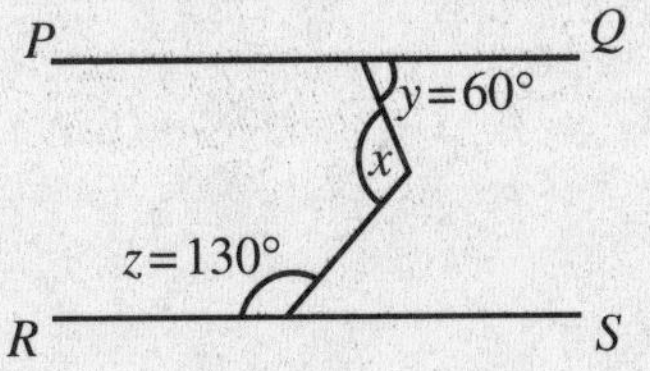

(A) 90°
(B) 100°
(C) 110°
(D) 120°
(E) 130°

21. In the figure below, *QOR* is a quadrant of a circle. *PS* = 6 and *PT* = 8. What is the length of arc *QR*?

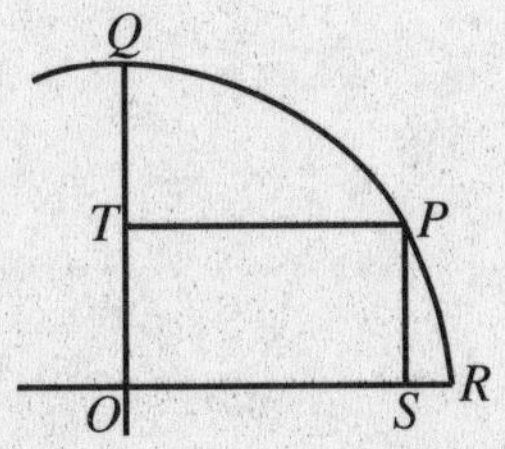

(A) 5π
(B) 10π
(C) 20π
(D) 24
(E) It cannot be determined from the information given.

22. The ice compartment in a refrigerator is 8 inches deep, 5 inches high, and 4 inches wide. How many ice cubes will it hold if each cube is 2 inches on each edge?

(A) 16
(B) 20
(C) 24
(D) 80
(E) 160

23. If Paul can paint a fence in 2 hours and Fred can paint the same fence in 3 hours, Paul and Fred working together can paint the fence in how many hours?

(A) 2.5

(B) $\frac{5}{6}$

(C) 5

(D) 1

(E) 1.2

24. If one-third of the liquid contents of a can evaporates on the first day and three-fourths of the remainder evaporates on the second day, the fractional part of the original contents remaining at the close of the second day is

(A) $\frac{1}{6}$

(B) $\frac{1}{4}$

(C) $\frac{5}{12}$

(D) $\frac{1}{2}$

(E) $\frac{7}{12}$

GO ON TO THE NEXT PAGE

25. A motorist drives 60 miles to her destination at an average speed of 40 miles per hour and makes the return trip at an average rate of 30 miles per hour. Her average speed in miles per hour for the entire trip is

(A) 17

(B) $34\frac{2}{7}$

(C) 35

(D) $43\frac{1}{3}$

(E) 70

STOP

END OF SECTION 2. IF YOU HAVE ANY TIME LEFT, GO OVER YOUR WORK IN THIS SECTION ONLY. DO NOT WORK IN ANY OTHER SECTION OF THE TEST.

SECTION 3

30 Questions • Time—30 Minutes

Directions: Each of the following questions consists of an incomplete sentence followed by five words or pairs of words. Choose that word or pair of words which, when substituted for the blank space or spaces, *best* completes the meaning of the sentence and mark the letter of your choice on the answer sheet.

Example:

In view of the extenuating circumstances and the defendant's youth, the judge recommended ----.

(A) conviction (B) a defense
(C) a mistrial (D) leniency
(E) life imprisonment Ⓐ Ⓑ Ⓒ ● Ⓔ

1. They acted in concert, each ---- for a(n) ---- of the plot.

(A) reliable..source
(B) responsible..element
(C) unavailable..section
(D) appointed..article
(E) agreeable..felony

2. They were unwisely ---- during their education, and ---- was the result.

(A) neglected..ignorance
(B) interrupted..consistency
(C) befriended..alienation
(D) instructed..genius
(E) taught..attendance

3. Most young children are highly conformist and will ---- a classmate whose appearance or manners are ----.

(A) welcome..bizarre
(B) shun..conventional
(C) emulate..unusual
(D) ostracize..different
(E) deride..ordinary

4. The royal astrologers were commanded to determine the most ---- date for the king's coronation.

(A) propitious
(B) ostensible
(C) aberrant
(D) resplendent
(E) obsequious

5. The poem by the great satirist was dripping with venom and was ---- with scorn.

(A) contentious
(B) discordant
(C) redolent
(D) sardonic
(E) vicarious

GO ON TO THE NEXT PAGE

Directions: Each of the following questions consists of a capitalized pair of words followed by five pairs of words lettered A to E. The capitalized words bear some meaningful relationship to each other. Choose the lettered pair of words whose relationship is most similar to that expressed by the capitalized pair and mark its letter on your answer sheet.

Example:

DAY : SUN : :

(A) sunlight : daylight (B) ray : sun
(C) night : moon (D) heat : cold
(E) moon : star

Ⓐ Ⓑ ● Ⓓ Ⓔ

---

6. AWL : PUNCTURE : :

(A) tire : ride
(B) cleaver : cut
(C) plane : soar
(D) throttle : start
(E) axle : steer

7. LUSH : JUNGLE : :

(A) delicious : fruit
(B) diligent : worker
(C) barren : desert
(D) hot : weather
(E) obvious : wealth

8. HAND : GNARLED : :

(A) tree : tall
(B) foot : sore
(C) flower : crushed
(D) brow : creased
(E) tire : round

9. PLANET : ROTATES : :

(A) top : spins
(B) star : shines
(C) moon : glows
(D) toy : plays
(E) rocket : fires

10. MILK : SPOIL : :

(A) metal : bend
(B) water : filter
(C) wood : rot
(D) fish : swim
(E) animal : rest

11. MUNIFICENT : GENEROSITY : :

(A) dolorous : sorrow
(B) domineering : timidity
(C) indisputable : doubt
(D) fortunate : haplessness
(E) beguiled : judiciousness

12. SCIENTIST : LABORATORY : :

(A) chemist : test tube
(B) lawyer : client
(C) dentist : drill
(D) teacher : classroom
(E) actor : playwright

13. JOCULAR : SOLEMNITY : :

(A) latent : visibility
(B) pompous : spectacle
(C) ruined : demolition
(D) vindictive : enmity
(E) lonely : insularity

Directions: Each passage below is followed by a set of questions. Read each passage, then answer the accompanying questions, basing your answers on what is stated or implied in the passage and in any introductory material provided. Mark the letter of your choice on your answer sheet.

Questions 14–21 are based on the following passage.

John Adams Audubon (1785–1851) is known primarily for his bird studies, but as this passage from Ornithological Biography *shows, he was fascinated by the behavior of other animals as well.*

The Black Bear (*Ursus americanus*), however clumsy in appearance, is active, vigilant, and persevering; possesses great strength, courage, and address; and undergoes with little injury the greatest fatigues and hardships in avoiding the pursuit of the hunter. Like the Deer, it changes its haunts with the seasons, and for the same reason, namely, the desire of obtaining suitable food, or of retiring to the more inaccessible parts, where it can pass the time in security, unobserved by man, the most dangerous of its enemies. During the spring months, it searches for food in the low rich alluvial lands that border the rivers, or by the margins of such inland lakes as, on account of their small size, are called by us ponds. There it procures abundance of succulent roots, and of the tender juicy stems of plants, on which it chiefly feeds at that season. During the summer heat, it enters the gloomy swamps, passes much of its time in wallowing in the mud, like a hog, and contents itself with crayfish, roots, and nettles, now and then, when hard pressed by hunger, seizing on a young pig, or perhaps a sow, or even a calf. As soon as the different kinds of berries which grow on the mountain begin to ripen, the Bears betake themselves to the high grounds, followed by their cubs. In such retired parts of the country where there are no hilly grounds, it pays visits to the maize fields, which it ravages for a while. After this, the various species of nuts, acorns, grapes, and other forest fruits, that form what in the western country is called *mast*, attract its attention. The Bear is then seen rambling singly through the woods to gather this harvest, not forgetting to rob every Bee tree it meets with, Bears being, as you well know, expert at this operation. You also know that they are good climbers, and may have been told, or at least may now be told, that the Black Bear now and then houses itself in the hollow trunks of the larger trees for weeks together, when it is said to suck its paws. You are probably not aware of a habit in which it indulges, and which, being curious, must be interesting to you.

At one season, the Black Bear may be seen examining the lower part of the trunk of a tree for several minutes with much attention, at the same time looking around, and snuffing the air, to assure itself that no enemy is near. It then raises itself on its hind legs, approaches the trunk, embraces it with its forelegs, and scratches the bark with its teeth and claws for several minutes in continuance. Its jaws clash against each other, until a mass of foam runs down both sides of the mouth. After this it continues its rambles.

In various portions of our country, many of our woodsmen and hunters who have seen the Bear performing the singular operation just described, imagine that it does so for the purpose of leaving behind an indication of its size and power. They measure the height at which the scratches are made, and in this manner, can, in fact, form an estimate of the magnitude of the individual. My own opinion, however, is different. It seems to me that the Bear scratches on the trees, not for the purpose of showing its size or its strength, but merely for that of sharpening its teeth and claws, to enable it better to encounter a rival of its own species during the amatory season. The Wild Boar of Europe clashes its tusks and scrapes the earth with its feet, and the Deer rubs its antlers against the lower part of the stems of young trees or bushes, for the same purpose.

14. The bear migrates from one habitat to another in order to

(A) teach its cubs to climb
(B) locate a hollow tree
(C) visit every bee tree
(D) escape from the wild boar
(E) find food and security

15. The fact that Audubon calls man the bear's "most dangerous" enemy (line 10) indicates that he

(A) is himself a hunter
(B) has some sympathy for hunted bears
(C) is an animal rights activist
(D) does not believe that bears are dangerous
(E) thinks bears are more dangerous than people

GO ON TO THE NEXT PAGE

16. The word *alluvial* (line 11) refers to

(A) high grounds
(B) rocky shorelines
(C) river-deposited sediment
(D) thick underbrush
(E) maize fields

17. According to the passage, black bears eat all of the following *except*

(A) bark
(B) maize
(C) mast
(D) honey
(E) crayfish

18. Audubon believes that bears scratch trees to

(A) show their power
(B) leave a mark
(C) sharpen their claws
(D) navigate
(E) indicate their size

19. Audubon assumes that his reader knows about bears'

(A) scratching behavior and threatening manner
(B) eating of roots and berries
(C) size and coloring
(D) fear of man
(E) climbing expertise and love of honey

20. Audubon compares the bear with deer twice,

(A) once in relation to its migratory habits, and once in comparing its rubbing behavior
(B) once in relation to its eating habits, and once in comparing its combative behavior
(C) both times having to do with its habitat
(D) both times having to do with hibernation
(E) both times having to do with size and weight

21. From his description, it seems that Audubon's attitude toward black bears is one of

(A) fear
(B) respect
(C) amusement
(D) alarm
(E) bewilderment

Questions 22–30 are based on the following passage.

As the wife of a British ambassador, Lady Mary Wortley Montagu spent many years abroad. She wrote endless amusing letters, focusing particularly on the women she met. Of all of them, she found the women in Turkey the most liberated and the most civil. In this letter to a friend, Lady Montagu tells of her visit to a Turkish bath.

Adrianople, April 1 [1717]

I am now got into a new world, where everything I see appears to me a change of scene; and I write to your ladyship with some content of mind, hoping at least that you will find the charm of novelty in my letters, and no longer reproach me, that I tell you nothing extraordinary. I won't trouble you with a relation of our tedious journey; but I must not omit what I saw remarkable at Sophia, one of the most beautiful towns in the Turkish empire, and famous for its hot baths, that are resorted to both for diversion and health. Designing to go *incognita*, I hired a Turkish coach. These voitures are not at all like ours, but much more convenient for the country, the heat being so great that glasses would be very troublesome. They are made a good deal in the manner of the Dutch coaches, having wooden lattices painted and gilded; the inside being painted with the baskets and nosegays of flowers, intermixed commonly with little poetical mottoes. They are covered all over with scarlet cloth, lined with silk, and very often richly embroidered and fringed. This covering entirely hides the persons in them, but may be thrown back at pleasure, and the ladies peep through the lattices. They hold four people very conveniently, seated on cushions, but not raised.

In one of these covered wagons, I went to the bagnio about ten o'clock. It was already full of women. It is built of stone, in the shape of a dome, with no windows but in the roof, which gives light enough. There were five of these domes joined together, the outmost being less than the rest, and serving only as a hall, where the portress stood at the door. Ladies of quality generally give this woman the value of a crown or ten shillings; and I did not forget that ceremony. The next room is a very large one paved with marble, and all around it, raised, two sofas of marble, one above another. There were four fountains of cold water in this room, falling first into marble basins, and then running on the floor in little channels made for that purpose, which carried the streams into the next room, something less than this, with the same sort of marble sofas, but so hot with teams of sulfur proceeding from the baths joining to it, it was impossible to stay there with one's clothes on. The two other domes were the hot baths, one of which had cocks of cold water turning into it, to temper it to what degree of warmth the bathers have a mind to.

I was in my travelling habit, which is a riding dress, and certainly appeared very extraordinary to them. Yet there was not one of them that shewed the least surprise or impertinent curiosity, but received me with all the obliging civility possible. I know no European court where the ladies would have behaved themselves in so polite a manner to a stranger. I believe in the whole, there were two hundred women, and yet none of those disdainful smiles, or satiric whispers, that never fail in our assemblies when any body appears that is not dressed exactly in fashion. They repeated over and over to me, "Uzelle, pék uzelle," which is nothing but Charming, very charming.—The first sofas were covered with cushions and rich carpets, on which sat the ladies; and on the second, their slaves behind them, but without any distinction of rank by their dress, all being in a state of nature, that is, in plain English, stark naked, without any beauty or defect concealed.

22. When Lady Montagu mentions "a change of scene" (line 2), she refers to Turkey's

    (A) drama
    (B) novelty
    (C) alteration
    (D) trade
    (E) currency

23. The word *relation* (line 6) is used to mean

    (A) affiliation
    (B) retelling
    (C) link
    (D) union
    (E) attachment

24. According to Lady Montagu, Turkish women visit the baths for

    (A) privacy and contemplation
    (B) exercise and fitness
    (C) entertainment and health
    (D) ceremony and ritual
    (E) education and instruction

25. Lady Montagu considers Turkish coaches to be well suited to the climate because

    (A) they are lined with silk
    (B) they conceal the travelers inside them
    (C) their painted interiors are pleasing to the eye
    (D) they hold four passengers comfortably
    (E) they lack glass windows that would make them too hot

26. The main purpose of paragraph 3 is to

    (A) describe the baths
    (B) acquaint the reader with Turkish architecture
    (C) describe Turkish coaches
    (D) reflect on native customs
    (E) tell a story

27. How does Lady Montagu feel about the Turkish women?

    (A) They are unfailingly polite.
    (B) They are extremely wealthy.
    (C) They are impertinent.
    (D) They have no regard for fashion.
    (E) They are disdainful of Europeans.

28. Why does Lady Montagu mention European courts (line 50)?

    (A) To assert her belief in the superiority of European customs
    (B) To contrast Turkish and European dress
    (C) To compare Turkish and European architecture
    (D) To contrast Turkish and European manners
    (E) To offer an example of polite civility

GO ON TO THE NEXT PAGE

29. By "the state of nature" (lines 61-62), Lady Montagu refers to the women's

(A) good manners
(B) natural sweetness
(C) guilelessness
(D) wildness
(E) lack of clothing

30. On the whole, Lady Montagu found her trip to the baths

(A) shocking
(B) irritating
(C) fascinating
(D) disheartening
(E) distressing

STOP

END OF SECTION 3. IF YOU HAVE ANY TIME LEFT, GO OVER YOUR WORK IN THIS SECTION ONLY. DO NOT WORK IN ANY OTHER SECTION OF THE TEST.

SECTION 4

25 Questions • Time—30 Minutes

Directions: Solve the following problems using any available space on the page for scratchwork. On your answer sheet, fill in the choice which best corresponds to the correct answer.

Notes: The figures accompanying the problems are drawn as accurately as possible unless otherwise stated in specific problems. Again, unless otherwise stated, all figures lie in the same plane. All numbers used in these problems are real numbers. Calculators are permitted for this test.

Reference Information

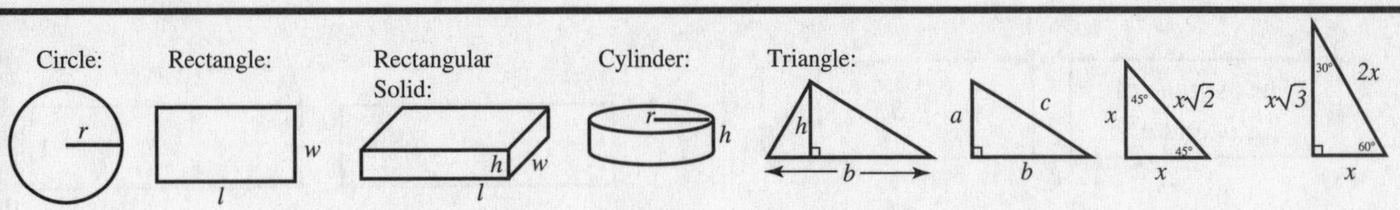

$C = 2\pi r$, $A = \pi r^2$ — $A = lw$ — $V = lwh$ — $V = \pi r^2 h$ — $A = \frac{1}{2}bh$ — $a^2 + b^2 = c^2$

The number of degrees of arc in a circle is 360.
The measure in degrees of a straight angle is 180.
The sum of the measures in degrees of the angles of a triangle is 180.

Part 1: Quantitative Comparison Questions

Directions: For each of the following questions, two quantities are given—one in Column A, the other in Column B. Compare the two quantities and mark your answer sheet as follows:

(A) if the quantity in Column A is greater
(B) if the quantity in Column B is greater
(C) if the quantities are equal
(D) if the relationship cannot be determined from the information given

Notes:
(1) Information concerning one or both of the compared quantities will be centered above the two columns for some items.
(2) Symbols that appear in both columns represent the same thing in Column A as in Column B.
(3) Letters such as *x*, *n,* and *k* are symbols for real numbers.

Examples

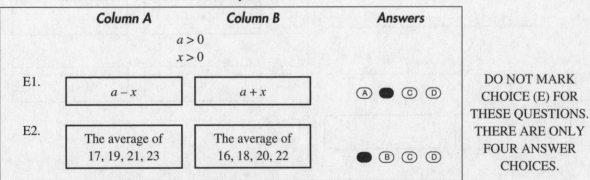

	Column A	Column B	Answers
		$a > 0$ $x > 0$	
E1.	$a - x$	$a + x$	Ⓐ ● Ⓒ Ⓓ
E2.	The average of 17, 19, 21, 23	The average of 16, 18, 20, 22	● Ⓑ Ⓒ Ⓓ

DO NOT MARK CHOICE (E) FOR THESE QUESTIONS. THERE ARE ONLY FOUR ANSWER CHOICES.

GO ON TO THE NEXT PAGE

	Column A	Column B
	$r = -3$	
1.	$r^3 + 5r^2 - 6r + 4$	$3r^2 - 7r - 8$
	$x \neq 0$	
2.	x	$\frac{1}{x}$
3.	The average of a, b, and c	b

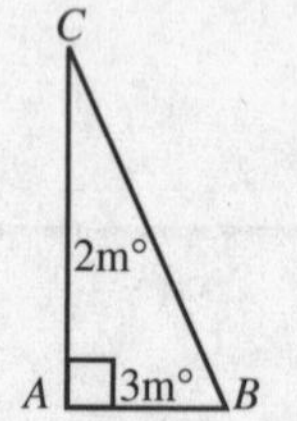

Note: Figure not drawn to scale.

	Column A	Column B
4.	$\angle ABC$	$\angle ACB$

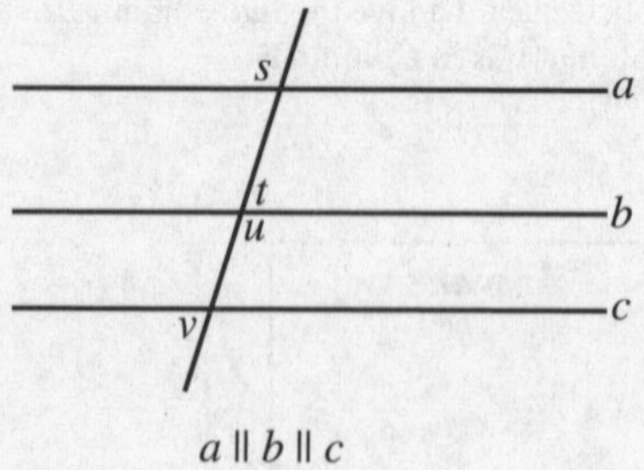

$a \parallel b \parallel c$

$\angle u > \angle v$

	Column A	Column B
5.	s	t

	Column A	Column B
	$R > r$	

	Column A	Column B
6.	Circumference of circle with radius r	Area of circle with radius R
	$s > t$	
7.	s^2	t^2

Questions 8-10 refer to the figure below.

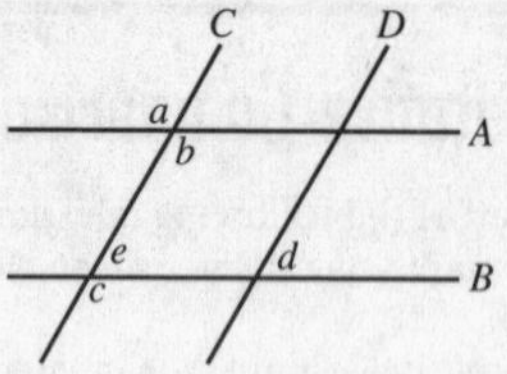

$C \parallel D$

$A \parallel B$

$a = 100°$

	Column A	Column B
8.	$a + b$	$b + d$
9.	180	$b + c$
10.	d	$180 - a$

$$\left(\frac{1}{2}\right)x - \left(\frac{1}{2}\right)a = 4$$

	Column A	Column B
11.	x	a

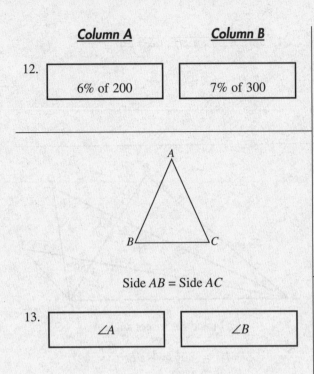

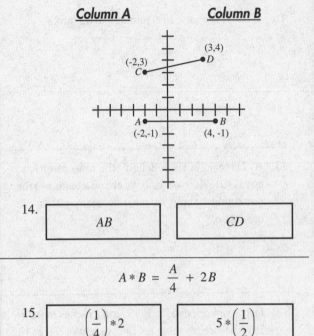

	Column A	Column B
12.	6% of 200	7% of 300

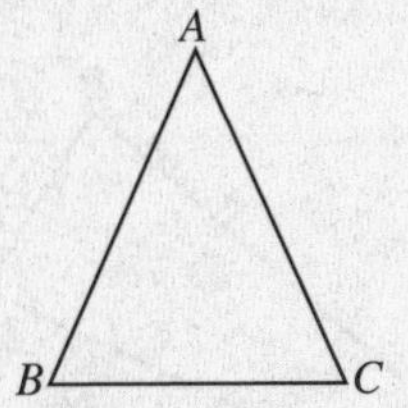

Side AB = Side AC

	Column A	Column B
13.	$\angle A$	$\angle B$

Column A	Column B

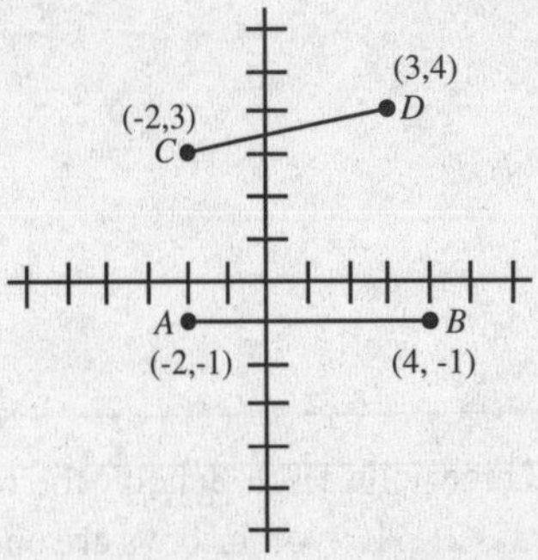

	Column A	Column B
14.	AB	CD

$$A * B = \frac{A}{4} + 2B$$

	Column A	Column B
15.	$\left(\frac{1}{4}\right) * 2$	$5 * \left(\frac{1}{2}\right)$

Part 2: Student-Produced Response Questions

Directions: Solve each of these problems. Write the answer in the corresponding grid on the answer sheet and fill in the ovals beneath each answer you write. Here are some examples.

Answer: $\frac{3}{4}$ (= .75; show answer either way)

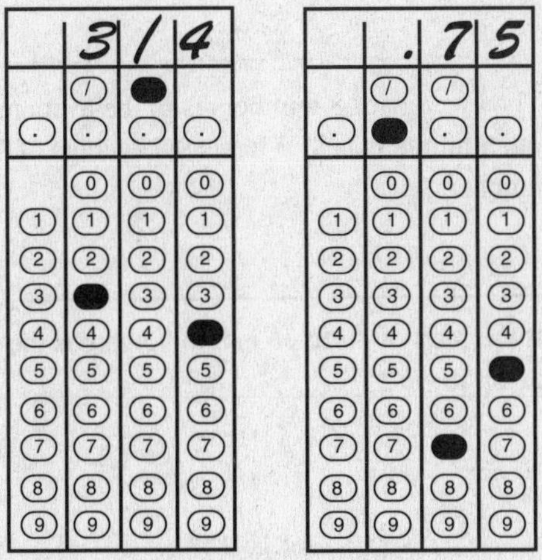

Note: A mixed number such as $3\frac{1}{2}$ must be gridded as 7/2 or as 3.5. If gridded as "3 1/2," it will be read as "thirty-one halves."

Answer: 325

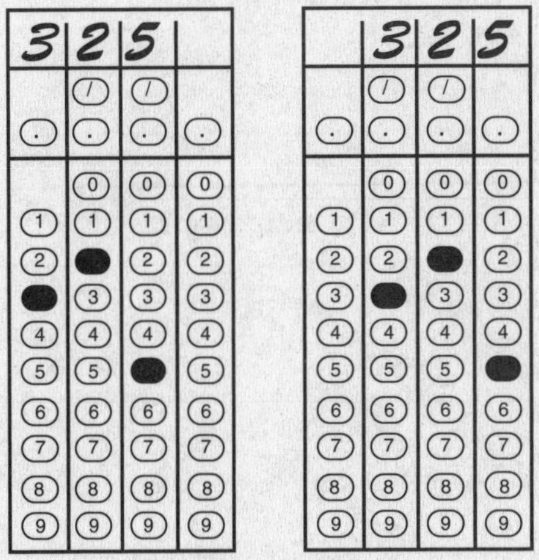

Note: Either position is correct.

GO ON TO THE NEXT PAGE

16. What is the ratio of 6 minutes to 6 hours?

17. At Ungerville High School, the ratio of girls to boys is 2:1. If $\frac{3}{5}$ of the boys are on a team and the remaining 40 boys are not, how many girls are in the school?

18. Jerry grew 5 inches in 1993, and 2 inches more in 1994 before reaching his final height of 5 feet 10 inches. What percentage of his final height did his 1993–1994 growth represent?

19. Seth bought $4\frac{5}{6}$ pounds of peanuts. He gave $\frac{1}{4}$ of his purchase to his sister. How many pounds of peanuts did Seth keep for himself?

20. If $p = 2r = 3s = 4t$, then $\frac{pr}{st} =$

21. $\sqrt{7+9+7+9+7+9+7+9} =$

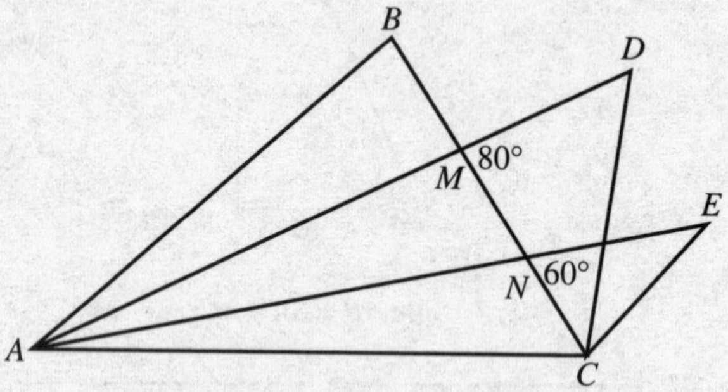

DA and *EA* trisect angle *A*.

22. If $\angle DMC = 80°$ and $\angle ENC = 60°$, then angle A = (Do not grid the degree symbol.)

23. $\dfrac{\frac{7}{8}+\frac{7}{8}+\frac{7}{8}}{\frac{8}{7}+\frac{8}{7}+\frac{8}{7}} =$

24. The average of 8 numbers is 6; the average of 6 other numbers is 8. What is the average of all 14 numbers?

25. If the ratio of $4a$ to $3b$ is 8 to 9, what is the ratio of $3a$ to $4b$?

STOP

END OF SECTION 4. IF YOU HAVE ANY TIME LEFT, GO OVER YOUR WORK IN THIS SECTION ONLY. DO NOT WORK IN ANY OTHER SECTION OF THE TEST.

SECTION 5

10 Questions • Time—15 Minutes

Directions: The two passages given below deal with a related topic. Following the passages are questions about the content of each passage or about the relationship between the two passages. Answer the questions based upon what is stated or implied in the passages and in any introductory material provided. Mark the letter of your choice on your answer sheet.

Questions 1–10 are based on the following passages.

In 1848, a Woman's Rights Convention was held at Seneca Falls, New York. Sponsored by Lucretia Mott, Martha Wright, Elizabeth Cady Stanton, and Mary Ann McClintock, the convention featured the creation of a "Declaration of Sentiments," a document based on American's Declaration of Independence, in which men's unfair dominion over women was described. Crusader for the rights of African-Americans and women, Sojourner Truth was born a slave on a Dutch estate around 1797 and named Isabella. The first edition of her biography was written by Olive Gilbert, a white friend of hers, and published in 1850.

Passage 1—Declaration of Sentiments

The history of mankind is a history of repeated injuries and usurpations on the part of man toward woman, having in direct object the establishment of an absolute tyranny over her. To prove this, let facts be submitted to a candid world.

He has never permitted her to exercise her inalienable right to the elective franchise.

He has compelled her to submit to laws, in the formation of which she had no voice. He has withheld from her rights which are given to the most ignorant and degraded men—both natives and foreigners.

Having deprived her of this first right of a citizen, the elective franchise, thereby leaving her without representation in the halls of legislation, he has oppressed her on all sides.

He has made her, if married, in the eye of the law, civilly dead.

He has taken from her all right in property, even to the wages she earns.

He has made her, morally, an irresponsible being, as she can commit many crimes with impunity, provided they be done in the presence of her husband. In the covenant of marriage, she is compelled to promise obedience to her husband, he becoming, to all intents and purposes, her master—the law giving him power to deprive her of her liberty, and to administer chastisement.

He has so framed the laws of divorce, as to what shall be the proper causes, and in the case of separation, to whom the guardianship of the children shall be given, as to be wholly regardless of the happiness of women—the law, in all cases, going upon a false supposition of the supremacy of man, and giving all power into his hands.

After depriving her of all rights as a married woman, if single, and the owner of property, he has taxed her to support a government which recognizes her only when her property can be made profitable to it.

He has endeavored, in every way that he could, to destroy her confidence in her own powers, to lessen her self-respect, and to make her willing to lead a dependent and abject life.

Passage 2—Sojourner Truth

After emancipation had been decreed by the State, some years before the time fixed for its consummation, Isabella's master told her if she would do well, and be faithful, he would give her "free papers," one year before she was legally free by statute. In the year 1826, she had a badly diseased hand, which greatly diminished her usefulness; but on the arrival of July 4, 1827, the time specified for her receiving her "free papers," she claimed the fulfillment of her master's promise; but he refused granting it, on account (as he alleged) of the loss he had sustained by her hand. She plead that she had worked all the time, and done many things she was not wholly able to do, although she knew she had been less useful than formerly; but her master remained inflexible. Her very faithfulness probably operated against her now, and he found it less easy than he thought to give up the profits of his faithful Bell, who had so long done him efficient service.

But Isabella inwardly determined that she would remain quietly with him only until she had spun his wool—about one hundred pounds—and then she would leave him, taking the rest of the time to herself. "Ah!" she says, with emphasis that cannot be written, "the slaveholders are TERRIBLE for promising to give you this or that, or such and such a privilege, if you will do thus and so; and when the time of fulfillment comes, and one claims the promise, they, forsooth, recollect nothing of the kind; and you are, like as not, taunted with being a LIAR; or, at best, the slave is accused of not having performed *his* part or condition of the contract." "Oh!" said she, "I have felt as if I could not live through the *operation* sometimes. Just think of us! *so* eager for our pleasures, and just foolish enough to keep feeding and feeding ourselves up with the idea that we should get what had been thus fairly promised; and when we think it is almost in our hands, find ourselves flatly denied! Just think! how *could* we bear it?"

1. Both passages concern themselves with a kind of

   (A) tyranny
   (B) liberation
   (C) government
   (D) security
   (E) autonomy

2. The word *injuries* in line 2 of the Declaration of Sentiments might be replaced with the word

   (A) bruises
   (B) prejudice
   (C) mistreatment
   (D) wounds
   (E) shocks

3. When the Declaration of Sentiments states in line 17 that a married woman is "civilly dead," this probably means that

   (A) the law ignores married women
   (B) married women must treat their husbands courteously
   (C) women must give up their lives to their husbands
   (D) a man may kill his wife with impunity
   (E) married women must not show undue emotion

4. The word *her* as used throughout the Declaration of Sentiments refers to

   (A) an emancipated woman
   (B) a married woman
   (C) any woman
   (D) the author of the Declaration
   (E) a woman who is old enough to vote

5. According to the Declaration of Sentiments, women are only seen as useful to the government when they

   (A) promote discord
   (B) can provide it with profit
   (C) vote
   (D) marry
   (E) earn wages

6. The narrative of Sojourner Truth implies that slaveholders' cruelty is based on

   (A) twisted emotions
   (B) desire for profit
   (C) fear of confrontation
   (D) racism
   (E) misunderstanding

7. Truth's main objection to her slaveholder is to his

   (A) harassment
   (B) brutality
   (C) unfairness
   (D) bigotry
   (E) rudeness

8. When Truth refers to "us" in line 74, she means

   (A) African-Americans
   (B) slaveholders
   (C) women
   (D) writers
   (E) slaves

9. The tone of both passages might be described as

   (A) resigned
   (B) calculating
   (C) fierce
   (D) embittered
   (E) hopeful

10. Would you expect Sojourner Truth to approve of the Declaration of Sentiments?

(A) No, because the Declaration clearly represents only white women.
(B) No, because slavery and sexual oppression have little in common.
(C) Yes, because she, too, is taxed to support a government that does not represent her.
(D) Yes, because she, too, is willing to be dependent.
(E) Yes, because she understands as well as anyone what it means to have no rights.

STOP

END OF SECTION 5. IF YOU HAVE ANY TIME LEFT, GO OVER YOUR WORK IN THIS SECTION ONLY. DO NOT WORK IN ANY OTHER SECTION OF THE TEST.

SECTION 6

10 Questions • Time—15 Minutes

Directions: Solve the following problems using any available space on the page for scratchwork. On your answer sheet fill in the choice which best corresponds to the correct answer.

Notes: The figures accompanying the problems are drawn as accurately as possible unless otherwise stated in specific problems. Again, unless otherwise stated, all figures lie in the same plane. All numbers used in these problems are real numbers. Calculators are permitted for this test.

Reference Information

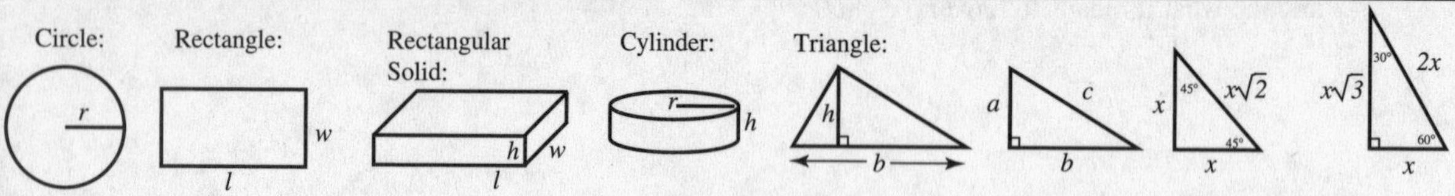

$C = 2\pi r$ $A = \pi r^2$ $A = lw$ $V = lwh$ $V = \pi r^2 h$ $A = \frac{1}{2}bh$ $a^2 + b^2 = c^2$

The number of degrees of arc in a circle is 360.
The measure in degrees of a straight angle is 180.
The sum of the measures in degrees of the angles of a triangle is 180.

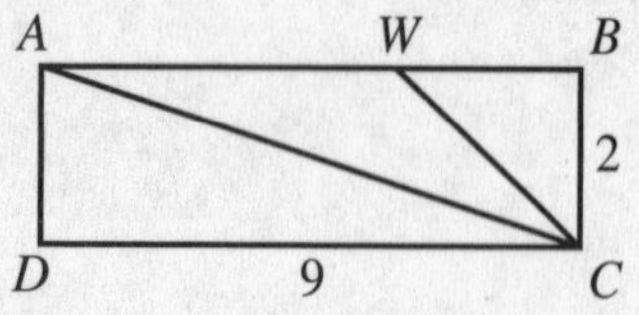

1. In the figure above, BW is one-third the length of AB. What is the area of triangle ACW?

(A) 4
(B) 5
(C) 6
(D) 8
(E) 9

2. Of the following, the one that is *not* equivalent to 376 is

(A) $(3 \times 100) + (6 \times 10) + 16$
(B) $(2 \times 100) + (17 \times 10) + 6$
(C) $(3 \times 100) + (7 \times 10) + 6$
(D) $(2 \times 100) + (16 \times 10) + 6$
(E) $(2 \times 100) + (7 \times 10) + 106$

3. Emily can pack 6 cartons in h days. At this rate she can pack $3h$ cartons in how many days?

(A) 18
(B) $2h$
(C) h^2
(D) $\frac{h^2}{2}$
(E) $2h^2$

4. What is the total length of fencing needed to enclose a rectangular area 46 feet by 34 feet (3 ft. = 1yd.)?

(A) 26 yards 1 foot
(B) $26\frac{2}{3}$ yards
(C) 52 yards 2 feet
(D) $53\frac{1}{3}$ yards
(E) $37\frac{2}{3}$ yards

5. On an income of $15,000 a year, a clerk pays 15% in federal taxes and 10% of the remainder in state taxes. How much is left?

(A) $9,750
(B) $11,475
(C) $12,750
(D) $13,500
(E) $14,125

6. $(x^a)^b =$

(A) $x \bullet a \bullet b$
(B) x^{a+b}
(C) x^{ab}
(D) $(ax)^b$
(E) b^{xa}

7. *A* is 300 miles from *B*. The path of all points equidistant from *A* and *B* can best be described as

(A) a line ǁ to *AB* and 150 miles north of *AB*
(B) a transverse segment cutting through *AB* at a 45° angle
(C) a circle with *AB* as its diameter
(D) the perpendicular bisector of *AB*
(E) the line *AB*

8. If $y = x^2$, $z = x^3$, and $w = xy$ then $y^2 + z^2 + w^2 =$

(A) $x^4 + x^6 + x^{10}$
(B) $x^4 + 2x^5$
(C) $x^4 + 2x^6$
(D) $2x^9$
(E) $2x^{10}$

9. The number missing in the series 2, 6, 12, 20, ?, 42, 56, 72 is

(A) 24
(B) 30
(C) 36
(D) 38
(E) 40

10. The square and the equilateral triangle in the above drawing both have a side of 6. If the triangle is placed inside the square with one side of the triangle directly on one side of the square, what is the area of the shaded region?

(A) $36 - 18\sqrt{3}$
(B) $36 - 9\sqrt{3}$
(C) $36 - 6\sqrt{3}$
(D) $36 + 6\sqrt{3}$
(E) $36 + 9\sqrt{3}$

STOP

END OF SECTION 6. IF YOU HAVE ANY TIME LEFT, GO OVER YOUR WORK IN THIS SECTION ONLY. DO NOT WORK IN ANY OTHER SECTION OF THE TEST.

Practice Examination 4
Answer Key

Section 1: VERBAL

1. B	8. D	15. D	22. E	29. C
2. D	9. B	16. A	23. B	30. D
3. E	10. E	17. C	24. C	31. C
4. B	11. B	18. C	25. C	32. D
5. A	12. A	19. C	26. B	33. D
6. E	13. D	20. B	27. A	34. B
7. E	14. C	21. A	28. E	35. C

Section 2: MATH

1. C	6. E	11. B	16. E	21. A
2. C	7. A	12. C	17. B	22. A
3. D	8. A	13. B	18. C	23. E
4. C	9. E	14. E	19. B	24. A
5. E	10. A	15. A	20. C	25. B

Section 3: VERBAL

1. B	7. C	13. A	19. E	25. E
2. A	8. D	14. E	20. A	26. A
3. D	9. A	15. B	21. B	27. A
4. A	10. C	16. C	22. B	28. D
5. C	11. A	17. A	23. B	29. E
6. B	12. D	18. C	24. C	30. C

Section 4: MATH

Part 1

1. C	4. A	7. D	10. C	13. D
2. D	5. A	8. A	11. A	14. A
3. D	6. D	9. B	12. B	15. A

Part 2

16. $\frac{1}{60}$	18. 10	20. 6	22. 60	24. $\frac{48}{7} = 6.86$
17. 200	19. $\frac{29}{8} = 3.63$	21. 8	23. .766	25. $\frac{1}{2}$

Section 5: VERBAL

1. A	3. A	5. B	7. C	9. D
2. C	4. C	6. B	8. E	10. E

Section 6: MATH

1. C	3. D	5. B	7. D	9. B
2. D	4. D	6. C	8. C	10. B

Practice Examination 4

Explanatory Answers

Note: A  following a math answer explanation indicates that a calculator could be helpful in solving that particular problem.

Section 1

1. **(B)** The word *finally* suggests that the woman agreed to see the farm only after being *importuned*, or repeatedly urged, to do so by her family.

2. **(D)** The ghost urges, or *exhorts,* Hamlet to take revenge.

3. **(E)** Concern for the children's safety would logically lead a father to *inculcate* (teach by constant repetition) in them a *wary* attitude toward strangers.

4. **(B)** With a life full of hardship and poverty, they are surely *inured* (accustomed) to discomfort.

5. **(A)** The author probably withdrew from the project because he was displeased with the novel's *adaptation*, or change required to turn the novel into a television program.

6. **(E)** *Vacillation* means fluctuation of mind or changing from one purpose to another.

7. **(E)** A smile could be *devastating* or *bright,* but it could logically only *dazzle* all those who saw it.

8. **(D)** The word *although* indicates that the blanks will be filled by opposites as in choice (D): *penurious* (stingy) and *generous.*

9. **(B)** To disarm someone in a single motion requires sure and swift, or *deft,* action.

10. **(E)** The platypus, with its curious duckbill and habit of laying eggs, is a biological *anomaly* (abnormality).

11. **(B)** If the rites were kept secret, the members never *divulged* (revealed) them. Furthermore, fraternity rites are very likely to be *esoteric* (known to only a select few).

12. **(A)** A composer who praised the work of a musician he detested would be considered *magnanimous* (extremely generous).

13. **(D)** Goodwill is a genuine asset, but it is necessarily *intangible* (incapable of being touched in the physical sense).

14. **(C)** Clearly, the law's actual result was different from its *ostensible* (apparent) purpose. By curtailing false advertising, it also tended to *circumscribe* (limit) free speech.

15. **(D)** A *teacher* gives *instruction,* and a *guard* gives *protection.*

16. **(A)** An *usher* shows people to their seats in a *theater,* just as a *conductor* shows people to their seats on the *train.*

17. **(C)** A *rink* is a place to *skate;* a *bed* is a place to *repose.*

18. **(C)** A *sapling* is a young *tree,* and a *puppy* is a young *dog.*

19. **(C)** To *fret* is by definition not to *relax,* and to *fight* is necessarily not to *submit.*

20. **(B)** To *stutter* impedes *talking*; to *stumble* impedes *walking.*

21. **(A)** *Damage* is a much less intense degree of destruction than *demolish.* Similarly, *whimper* is much less intense than *wail.*

22. **(E)** A *hose* is used to conduct *water*, just as a *chimney* is used to conduct *smoke.*

23. **(B)** *Exercise* is a way to build *strength. Practice* is a way to build *skill.*

24. **(C)** A *sergeant* trains *soldiers* just as a *coach* trains *players.*

25. **(C)** *Volatile* means lacking in *stability* just as *wanton* means lacking in *restraint.*

26. **(B)** Pepys remarks that he "thought it far enough off; and so went to bed again and to sleep" (lines 8–9). Even when he gets up again, the fire seems even further off. He is unconcerned until he sees the fire from the Tower.

27. **(A)** Pepys's concern is based on what he just saw (lines 22–23)—that houses on the bridge are on fire, which "did trouble me for... Michell and our Sarah."

28. **(E)** (A) and (C) are alternative meanings for *lamentable,* but only *awful* makes sense in context.

29. **(C)** People are flinging their goods into the river or bringing them to these "lighters"; only (C) makes sense in context.

30. **(D)** This description occurs in lines 38 to 41 and is one of the things that makes this narrative so vivid.

31. **(C)** Pepys ends this part of the narrative with his appearance to the King and the Duke of York. He tells them what he has witnessed and recommends action.

32. **(D)** Although the fire is indeed raging across London Bridge (C) and leaving people homeless (E), what sends Pepys finally to see the King is the fact that "nobody, to my sight , [is] endeavouring to quench [the fire]" (lines 42–44).

33. **(D)** Pepys never lists the clothing he wore to the fire (C), but he mentions landmarks throughout and even mentions the name of the boy who goes up the Tower with him.

34. **(B)** Whitehall, where Pepys meets the King, is far from the fire.

35. **(C)** Pepys lives and works in London, which is the capital of England. The King he describes can only be the King of England.

Section 2

1. **(C)** This is easily solved by plugging in the numbers:

$$(4-1)\times(5-2)\times(6-3)=3\times3\times3=27$$

2. **(C)** If $2n$ is an even number, $2n+1$ is odd.

3. **(D)** Solving the equation for x gives x a value of $-\frac{1}{2}$, and $x^2 = \left(-\frac{1}{2}\right)^2 = \frac{1}{4}$.

4. **(C)** Setting up a ratio,

$$\frac{88 \text{ ft./sec.}}{60 \text{ mi./hr.}} = \frac{1100 \text{ ft./sec.}}{x \text{ mi./hr.}}$$
$$88x = (1100)(60)$$
$$x = 750 \text{ mi./hr.}$$

5. **(E)** Setting up a ratio,

$$\frac{\frac{1}{4}\text{ in.}}{12 \text{ in.}} = \frac{3\frac{3}{8}\text{ in.}}{x \text{ in.}}$$
$$\left(\tfrac{1}{4}\right)x = (12)\left(3\tfrac{3}{8}\right)$$
$$x = 162 \text{ in.} = 13\frac{1}{2} \text{ ft.}$$

6. **(E)** Let x be the second angle. The first angle is $3x$, and the third angle is $x + 20$. The angles of a triangle must equal 180°, so $3x + x + (x + 20) = 180$ $5x = 160$, and $x = 32$.

7. **(A)** By substitution, $x + y^2 - \frac{1}{2}$ becomes $\frac{3}{2} + (2)^2 - \frac{1}{2} = \frac{3}{2} + 4 - \frac{1}{2} = \frac{3}{2} + \frac{8}{2} - \frac{1}{2} = \frac{10}{2} = 5.$

8. **(A)** $14 + 17 = 31$ Therefore, there are 4 students who must be enrolled in all three courses. $\frac{4}{27}$ is slightly larger than $\frac{4}{28}$. The answer must be slightly larger than $\frac{1}{7}$, which is $14\frac{2}{7}\%$.

9. **(E)** The volume of the container is the area of the circle at one end times the height. The area of the circle is $A = \pi 7^2 \approx 154$ sq. in. The volume is $154 \times 6 = 924$ cu. in. The capacity of the tank is 924 cu. in. ÷ 231 cu. in./gal. = 4 gallons.

10. **(A)**

$$\frac{1}{x+y} = 6$$
$$\frac{1}{2+y} = 6$$
$$6(2+y) = 1$$
$$12+6y = 1$$
$$6y = -11$$
$$y = -\frac{11}{6}$$

11. **(B)** If there are 28.35 grams per ounce, then 28.35 grams per ounce ÷ 1,000 grams per kilogram= .02835 kilograms per ounce. Since there are 16 ounces to the pound, .02835 kilograms per ounce times 16 ounces per pound = 0.45 kilograms per pound.

12. **(C)** The square root of .16 is .4, so .16 is a perfect square. The square root of 16 is 4, so 16 is a perfect square. The square root of 1,600 is 40, so 1,600 is a perfect square. The square root of .0016 is .04, so .0016 is a perfect square. Only 1.6 is not a perfect square.

13. **(B)** Let's start by pointing out that we do not know the size of angles 1, 2, 3, or 4. We do know that the two lines are parallel and therefore 8 and 6 can be moved to their corresponding locations on the top line. Since all straight lines have 180 degrees, III and IV each equal 180 degrees.

14. **(E)** The maximum value is obtained by making x as large as possible and y as small as possible. Thus, we set up a fraction $\frac{\frac{1}{2}}{\frac{3}{4}} = \frac{1}{2} \times \frac{4}{3} = \frac{4}{6} = \frac{2}{3}$.

15. **(A)** Start by finding the area of the largest circle. The radius of the largest circle is 9, so the area is 81π. The middle circle has a radius of 5, so the area is 25π. The smallest circle has a radius of 2, so the area is 4π. To find the shaded region, subtract the smaller circle from the middle and get 21π. The fraction is thus $\frac{21\pi}{81\pi}$, which can be reduced to $\frac{7}{27}$.

16. **(E)** The answer can quickly be obtained by using a numerical example. Let $n = 5$ and $d = 2$.

I. $\frac{2}{5}$

II. $\frac{3}{6}$

III. $\frac{1}{4}$

IV. $\frac{5}{2}$

V. $\frac{4}{1}$

$$\frac{1}{4} < \frac{2}{5} < \frac{3}{6} < \frac{5}{2} < 4$$

17. **(B)** Let the time the train is scheduled to arrive be t. At 40 mph the train arrives in $t + \frac{10}{60} = t + \frac{1}{6}$ hours. At 30 mph the train takes $t + \frac{16}{60} = t + \frac{4}{15}$ hours. The distance is the speed times the time.

$$40\left(t+\tfrac{1}{6}\right) = 30\left(t+\tfrac{4}{15}\right)$$
$$40t + \tfrac{40}{6} = 30t + 8$$
$$10t = 8 - \tfrac{40}{6}$$
$$10t = 1\tfrac{1}{3} \text{ hr} = 80 \text{ min.}$$
$$t = 8 \text{ min.}$$

The distance between towns is:

$d = (40\text{mph})\left(\frac{8}{60} + \frac{10}{60}\right)\text{hr.}$

$= 40 \times \frac{18}{60}$

$= 12$ miles

18. **(C)** When you are given the diagonal of a square, you can find the length of the side by dividing the diagonal by 2 and multiplying by $\sqrt{2}$.

19. **(B)** $\angle TSP = 60°$
Since $PSR = 90°$, $\angle TSR = 90–60 = 30°$
Since $TS = PS = SR$, $\angle RTS = \angle TRS$. Thus,

$$\angle TRS = \tfrac{1}{2}\left(180° - 30°\right) = \tfrac{1}{2}(150°) = 75°.$$

20. **(C)**

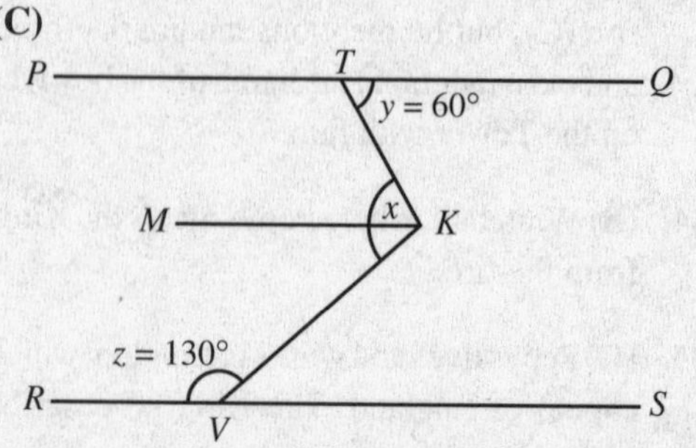

Through point K, draw KM parallel to PQ and RS.

Then

$\angle x = \angle MKV + \angle MKT$

$\angle MKV = \angle KVS = 180 - 130 = 50°$

$\angle MKT = \angle QTK = 60°$

$\angle x = 60° + 50° = 110°$

21. **(A)** Draw OP. Then in right triangle OPS, $OP^2 = PS^2 + OS^2 = 6^2 + 8^2 = 10^2$. $OP = 10$.
Then $\widehat{QR} = \frac{1}{4} \bullet 2\pi r = \frac{1}{4} \bullet 2\pi \bullet 10 = 5\pi$.

22. **(A)**

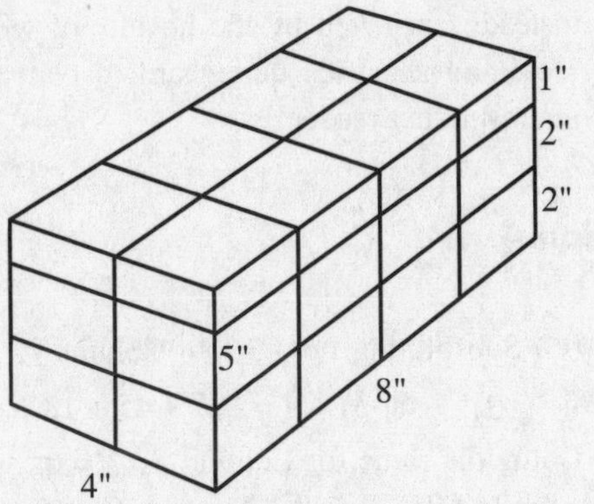

The 2-inch ice cube will fit only in the 8-inch by 4-inch by 4-inch part of the compartment. The upper inch cannot be used.

Hence, $\frac{8 \times 4 \times 4}{2 \times 2 \times 2} = 16$ cubes.

23. **(E)** Since it takes Paul 2 hours to paint 1 fence, he paints $\frac{1}{2}$ of the fence in one hour. Fred paints $\frac{1}{3}$ of the fence per hour. Together their speed is $\frac{1}{2} + \frac{1}{3} = \frac{5}{6}$ fence/hr. The time to paint this fence working together is 1 fence $\div \frac{5}{6}$ fence/hr. = 1.2 hours.

24. **(A)** $\frac{3}{4}$ evaporates the second day, therefore, there is $\frac{1}{4}$ of the $\frac{2}{3}$ of liquid left after evaporation the first day. $\frac{1}{4}$ of $\frac{2}{3} = \frac{1}{6}$, so $\frac{1}{6}$ of the original contents remains after two days.

25. **(B)** The time it takes the driver to arrive at her destination is 60 miles $\div$ 40 miles per hour = $1\frac{1}{2}$ hours. The time it takes to return is 60 miles $\div$ 30 miles per hour = 2 hours, making the total time for this 120-mile trip $1\frac{1}{2} + 2 = 3\frac{1}{2}$ hours. The average speed for the entire trip is 120 miles $\div 3\frac{1}{2}$ hours $= 34\frac{2}{7}$ miles per hour.

Section 3

1. **(B)** Acting together, those involved would each be *responsible* for an *element.*

2. **(A)** Unwise *neglect* during someone's education could result in *ignorance.*

3. **(D)** A conformist is conventional, acting in accordance with the prevailing customs. Children who are conventional are likely to *ostracize* (exclude) classmates who are *different* in behavior or dress.

4. **(A)** The date chosen for a king's coronation would most likely be *propitious* (lucky).

5. **(C)** A poem dripping with venom is apt to be *redolent* with (suggestive of) scorn.

6. **(B)** An *awl* is used to *puncture,* and a *cleaver* is used to *cut.*

7. **(C)** A *jungle* is characteristically *lush;* a *desert* is characteristically *barren.*

8. **(D)** *Hands* may become *gnarled* (knotted and twisted) with age, just as *brows* may become *creased* (wrinkled or ridged) with age.

9. **(A)** A *planet rotates* on its axis just as a *top spins.*

10. **(C)** *Milk* that *spoils* loses its original freshness. *Wood* that *rots* deteriorates from its original condition.

11. **(A)** Something *munificent* is characterized by great *generosity*. Something *dolorous* is characterized by great *sorrow*.

12. **(D)** A *scientist* works in a *laboratory* and a *teacher* works in a *classroom.*

13. **(A)** To be *jocular* is to lack *solemnity*. To be *latent* is to lack *visibility.*

14. **(E)** According to the first paragraph, the bear "changes its haunts with the seasons" in order to obtain "suitable food" and security.

15. **(B)** This is the only possible conclusion one can reach among those listed. Nothing indicates that Audubon hunts (A), and he never denies that bears are dangerous (D).

16. **(C)** Low, rich lands bordering a river are likely to be composed largely of river-deposited sediments.

17. **(A)** The bears scratch bark with their teeth and claws, but they do not eat it. Each of the other choices is specifically mentioned.

18. **(C)** Line 60 puts forth Audubon's theory. Others, he says, believe in theories (A), (B), and (E).

19. **(E)** Audubon draws back and addresses the reader directly in lines 32–33, remarking that "you well know" and "you also know" about bears' honey eating and ability to climb.

20. **(A)** The first comparison comes in lines 6-10 and the second comes at the end of the passage, in lines 58–65.

21. **(B)** Audubon makes much of the positive traits of the bear, focusing on its strength and pragmatism. He brushes over any indications that bears are fearsome (A) or alarming (D).

22. **(B)** Reread the first sentence and you will see that Lady Montagu is struck by the endless newness of Turkey, where everything is a change of scene.

23. **(B)** Each of the choices is a possible synonym for *relation*, but only one makes sense in context.

24. **(C)** As stated in line 10, women resort to the baths "both for diversion and health."

25. **(E)** Every one of the answer choices is mentioned in Lady Montagu's description of the coaches. However, only choice (E), their lack of glass windows, refers to their suitability for the hot Turkish climate. In Lady Montagu's words, "glasses would be very troublesome" (lines 13–14).

26. **(A)** In paragraph 3, Lady Montagu walks her reader through the baths from outside to inside, offering detailed descriptions of everything she sees.

27. **(A)** Lady Montagu is greatly impressed with the women's manners and spends much of paragraph 4 describing their polite reaction to her strange appearance.

28. **(D)** Lady Montagu wants her reader to consider the relatively rude behavior of European women in the presence of unusual behavior or appearances. She is contrasting that behavior with the polite manners of the Turkish women.

29. **(E)** As in question 6, Lady Montagu goes on to define her terms here—"in plain English, stark naked" (line 62).

30. **(C)** As a woman of the world, Lady Montagu cannot bring herself to sound shocked (A), even when she sees dozens of naked women. She is, instead, fascinated by the novelty of what she sees, and she tries quite hard to convey that interest to her reader.

Section 4

Part 1

1. **(C)** Substituting $r = -3$ into Column A, $(-3)^3 + 5(-3)^2 - 6(-3) + 4 = -27 + 45 + 18 + 4 = 40$ Doing the same for Column B, $3(-3)^2 - 7(-3) - 8 = 27 + 21 - 8 = 40$. Therefore, Columns A and B are equal.

2. **(D)** If $x > 1$ or $-1 < x < 0$, then any number $x > \frac{1}{x}$. But if $x < -1$ or $0 < x < 1$ then any number $x < \frac{1}{x}$. Therefore, it is not possible to tell which column is larger.

3. **(D)** Without knowing the value of any of the variables, it is impossible to make a determination.

4. **(A)** The angles of triangle ABC are $2m + 3m + 90° = 180°$. $5m = 90°$ and $m = 18°$. Angle ACB is $2m = 2 \times 18 = 36°$. Angle ABC is $3m = 3 \times 18 = 54°$. Thus, angle ABC is the larger angle.

5. **(A)** Since $a \parallel b \parallel c$ angle t = angle v, being opposite exterior angles. Therefore, since angle $u >$ angle v, angle $u >$ angle t. Also angle s = angle u, since they are opposite exterior angles. Therefore, $u = s > t$. Column A is the larger.

6. **(D)** The circumference of a circle with radius r is $2\pi r$. The area of a circle with radius R is πR^2. If $R > r > \sqrt{2}$, then $\pi R^2 > 2\pi r$. But if $0 < r < R < \sqrt{2}$, then $2\pi r > \pi R^2$. Therefore, it is not possible to tell which column is larger.

7. **(D)** If $s > t > 0$, then $s^2 > t^2$. But if $0 > s > t$, then $s^2 < t^2$. It is not possible to tell which column is the larger.

8. **(A)** a and b are equal, so $a + b = 2a = 2(100°) = 200°$. b and d are supplementary angles, so $b + d = 180°$. Column A is larger than Column B.

9. **(B)** In Column B, $a = b = c$, so $b + c = 100° + 100° = 200°$, which is more than Column A's value of 180°.

10. **(C)** Since a and d are supplementary angles, $d = 180° - a$.

11. **(A)** $\left(\frac{1}{2}\right)x - \left(\frac{1}{2}\right)a = 4$. Multiplying both sides of the equation by 2, $x - a = 8$, and $x = 8 + a$. Adding 8 to any real number will make it larger; therefore, x is the larger number.

12. **(B)** The values of Column A and Column B are 12 and 21 respectively. Therefore, Column B is the larger.

13. **(D)** Since side AB = side Ac, ΔABC is isosceles, and it can be assumed that $\angle B$ and $\angle C$ are equal. This information, though, does not provide any clues as to which is bigger, $\angle A$ or $\angle B$.

14. **(A)** It is obvious that the length of AB is 6. The length of CD is $\sqrt{[3-(-2)]^2 + (4-3)^2} = \sqrt{26}$, or approximately 5.10. Therefore, AB is longer.

15. **(A)** The value of Columns A and B are $4\frac{1}{16}$ and $2\frac{1}{4}$ respectively. Therefore, Column A is larger than Column B.

Part 2

16. $\dfrac{6 \text{ minutes}}{6 \text{ hours}} = \dfrac{6 \text{ minutes}}{6(60) \text{ minutes}} = \dfrac{1}{60}$

17.

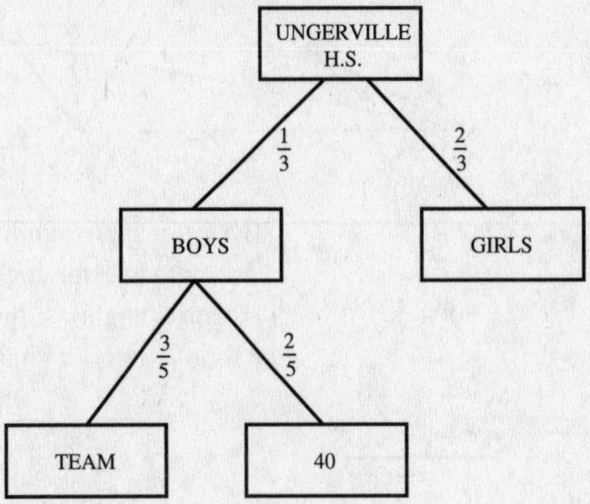

$\frac{2}{5}$(Boys) = 40

$\therefore$ Boys = 100.

There are twice as many girls as boys.

$\therefore$ girls = 200.

18. First convert Jerry's final height to inches:

$5 \times 12 = 60 \qquad 60 + 10 = 70$

Jerry's 7-inch growth is 10% of 70 inches.

19. He kept $\frac{3}{4}$ of his peanuts. $\frac{3}{4}\left(4\frac{5}{6}\right) = \frac{3}{4}\left(\frac{29}{6}\right) = \frac{29}{8} = 3\frac{5}{8} = 3.625$.

Use 3.63.

20. $\dfrac{pr}{st} = \dfrac{p\left(\frac{p}{2}\right)}{\left(\frac{p}{3}\right)\left(\frac{p}{4}\right)} = \dfrac{\frac{p^2}{2}}{\frac{p^2}{12}} = \dfrac{p^2}{2} \bullet \dfrac{12}{p^2} = 6$

21. $\sqrt{7+9+7+9+7+9+7+9} =$

$\sqrt{4(7+9)} = \sqrt{4(16)} = \sqrt{64} = 8$

22.

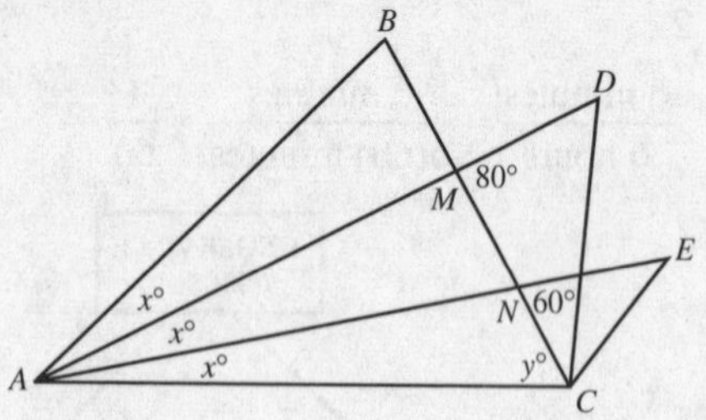

$x + y = 60$ (Exterior angle = sum of the 2 remote interior angles.)

$2x + y = 80$ (Exterior angle = sum of the 2 remote interior angles.)

$$\begin{array}{r} 2x + y = 80 \\ -(x + y = 60) \\ \hline x \quad = 20 \end{array}$$

$\therefore \angle A = 3x = 60$

23. $\dfrac{\frac{7}{8}+\frac{7}{8}+\frac{7}{8}}{\frac{8}{7}+\frac{8}{7}+\frac{8}{7}} = \dfrac{\cancel{3}\left(\frac{7}{8}\right)}{\cancel{3}\left(\frac{8}{7}\right)} = \dfrac{\frac{7}{8}}{\frac{8}{7}}$

$= \frac{7}{8} \bullet \frac{7}{8} = \frac{49}{64} = .766$

24. Average $= \dfrac{\text{Sum}}{\text{Number of items}}$

$\therefore$ Sum = (Avg.)(No. of items)

$$\begin{array}{r} 48 = (8)(6) \\ +\ 48 = (6)(8) \\ \hline 96 \end{array}$$

Average $= \frac{96}{14} = 6\frac{6}{7} = \frac{48}{7} = 6.86$

25. $\dfrac{4a}{3b} = \dfrac{8}{9}$

Multiply each side of the equation by $\frac{9}{16}$.

$$\frac{\overset{1}{\cancel{4}}a}{\underset{1}{\cancel{3}}b} \bullet \frac{\overset{3}{\cancel{9}}}{\underset{4}{\cancel{16}}} = \frac{\overset{1}{\cancel{8}}}{\underset{1}{\cancel{9}}} \bullet \frac{\overset{1}{\cancel{9}}}{\underset{2}{\cancel{16}}}$$

$$\frac{3a}{4b} = \frac{1}{2}$$

Section 5

1. **(A)** The Declaration speaks of the tyranny of men over women; Truth speaks of the tyranny of the slaveholder over his slaves.

2. **(C)** The word *injuries* signifies general mistreatment of women by men. The forms of mistreatment that are listed are primarily legal and social; "bruises," "prejudice," "wounds," and "shocks" are never mentioned.

3. **(A)** "In the eye of the law" is the clue here; a woman who marries is dead in the law's eyes, or ignored by the law.

4. **(C)** Look back at the first paragraph and you will see that the authors of the Declaration are referring to the tyranny of man over woman throughout history. *He* is all men; *her* refers to all women.

5. **(B)** The proof of this is in lines 35-38, wherein the woman is taxed to "support a government which recognizes her only when her property can be made profitable to it."

6. **(B)** This opinion is implied in lines 52–53 ("the loss he had sustained by her hand"); and 58–59 ("to give up the profits of his faithful Bell...")

7. **(C)** We see no signs of brutality (D), but Truth's owner is clearly pictured as unfair. He breaks his promises despite Isabella's faithfulness.

8. **(E)** Truth is referring to those who are eager for freedom but foolish enough to believe that they will get it—slaves, in other words.

9. **(D)** The passages as cited cannot be considered *resigned* (A) or *hopeful* (E). Each is essentially a catalog of sins by an aggrieved victim.

10. **(E)** In fact, Sojourner Truth went on to work hard for the rights of women. Even if you did not know that, however, you could predict her approval based on the fact that her description of slavery parallels so thoroughly the Declaration's description of sexual oppression.

Section 6

1. **(C)** Area $= \frac{1}{2}bh$. The base is AW, which is $\frac{2}{3}$ of AB, or $\frac{2}{3}(9) = 6$. The height is 2. $a = \frac{1}{2}(6)(2) = 6$.

2. **(D)** $(2 \times 100) + (16 \times 10) + 6 = 200 + 160 + 6 = 366$.

3. **(D)** This is a direct proportion $\frac{\text{cartons}}{\text{days}} \Rightarrow \frac{6}{h} = \frac{3h}{x}$

$$6x = 3h^2$$

$$x = \frac{h^2}{2}$$

4. **(D)** The perimeter of a 46' × 34' rectangle is 160 feet, which equals $53\frac{1}{3}$ yards.

5. **(B)** After the 15% deduction, \$12,750 is left. After the 10% is deducted from \$12,750, \$11,475 is left. Note that you cannot simply deduct 25% from the \$15,000.

6. **(C)** By definition, $\left(x^a\right)^b$ is the same as $x^{a\bullet b}$.

7. **(D)** The path of all points equidistant from two points is the perpendicular bisector of the segment which connects the two points. Therefore, the line that is perpendicular to *AB* and intersects it at 150 miles from *A* is the perpendicular bisector of *AB* (Remember, *A* and *B* are 300 miles apart.)

8. **(C)** $w = xy = x(x^2) = x^3$
$y^2 + z^2 + w^2 = (x^2)^2 + (x^3)^2 + (x^3)^2$
$= x^4 + x^6 + x^6 = x^4 + 2x^6$

9. **(B)** The difference between the numbers increases by 2; therefore, ? – 20 = 10, so ? = 30.

10. **(B)** The area of the square is 36. Since the triangle is equilateral, we can use the 30 - 60 - 90 rule to solve. By dropping a perpendicular we find the altitude to be $3\sqrt{3}$. Then the area of the triangle is $9\sqrt{3}$. Thus the shaded area is $36 - 9\sqrt{3}$.

Evaluating Practice Examination 4

To determine your Verbal Reasoning Score:

1. Using the Analysis Worksheet, enter the number of correct answers for each verbal reasoning section on the appropriate line in Column A of the Verbal Reasoning grid.

2. Enter the number of incorrect answers for each verbal reasoning section on the appropriate line in Column B of the Verbal Reasoning grid.

3. Total Columns A and B and enter these totals in boxes A and B, respectively.

4. Perform the indicated calculation to find your Raw Score; (value in box A) minus (one-quarter of the value in box B) = Raw Score.

5. Consult the Conversion Chart to find your approximate Scaled Score.

To determine your Mathematical Reasoning Score:

1. Enter the number of correct answers for each mathematical reasoning section on the appropriate line in Column C of the Mathematical Reasoning grid.

2. Enter the number of incorrect answers for each mathematical reasoning section on the appropriate line in Column D, E, or F of the Mathematical Reasoning grid.

3. Total Columns C, D, and E, and enter these totals in boxes C, D, and E, respectively.

4. Perform the indicated calculation to find your Raw Score: (value in box C) minus (one-quarter of the value in box D) minus (one-third of the value in box E) = Raw Score.

5. Consult the Conversion Chart to find your approximate Scaled Score.

Note: Box F is not used in this calculation.

Analysis Worksheet

VERBAL REASONING

Section	Number of Questions	Column A Number of Correct Answers	Column B Number of Incorrect Answers
1	35		
3	30		
5	10		
	Total	A	B

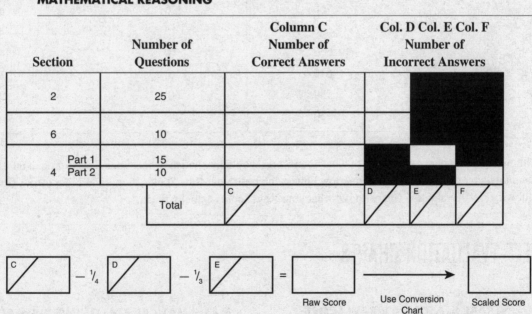

A − $\frac{1}{4}$ B = ____ (Raw Score) → Use Conversion Chart → ____ (Scaled Score)

MATHEMATICAL REASONING

Section		Number of Questions	Column C Number of Correct Answers	Col. D	Col. E	Col. F
				Number of Incorrect Answers		
2		25				
6		10				
4	Part 1	15				
	Part 2	10				
		Total	C	D	E	F

C − $\frac{1}{4}$ D − $\frac{1}{3}$ E = ____ (Raw Score) → Use Conversion Chart → ____ (Scaled Score)

Conversion Scales for Practice Examination 4

VERBAL REASONING:

Raw Score	Scaled Score	Raw Score	Scaled Score
75	800	40	550
70	800	35	520
65	760	30	480
60	710	25	440
55	670	20	410
50	620	15	370
45	590	10	340
		5	290
		0	230

MATHEMATICAL REASONING:

Raw Score	Scaled Score	Raw Score	Scaled Score
60	800	25	510
55	760	20	480
50	690	15	440
45	650	10	410
40	610	5	340
35	580	0	200
30	550		

Although you now have some idea of what your scores would like had they been scaled according to unofficial ETS standards, you will probably want to know how to interpret your Raw Scores in more familiar terms. If so, use the following Self-Evaluation Charts to see what your Raw Scores actually mean.

SELF-EVALUATION CHARTS

VERBAL REASONING: RAW SCORE

Excellent	60 – 75
Good	50 – 60
Average	30 – 50
Fair	20 – 30
Poor	0 – 20

MATHEMATICAL REASONING: RAW SCORE

Excellent	50 – 60
Good	40 – 50
Average	20 – 40
Fair	10 – 20
Poor	0 – 10

Practice Examination 5

Answer Sheet

If a section has fewer questions than answer ovals, leave the extra ovals blank.

Section 1

1	A B C D E	11	A B C D E	21	A B C D E	31	A B C D E
2	A B C D E	12	A B C D E	22	A B C D E	32	A B C D E
3	A B C D E	13	A B C D E	23	A B C D E	33	A B C D E
4	A B C D E	14	A B C D E	24	A B C D E	34	A B C D E
5	A B C D E	15	A B C D E	25	A B C D E	35	A B C D E
6	A B C D E	16	A B C D E	26	A B C D E	36	A B C D E
7	A B C D E	17	A B C D E	27	A B C D E	37	A B C D E
8	A B C D E	18	A B C D E	28	A B C D E	38	A B C D E
9	A B C D E	19	A B C D E	29	A B C D E	39	A B C D E
10	A B C D E	20	A B C D E	30	A B C D E	40	A B C D E

Section 2

Answer spaces for Section 2 are on the back of this Answer Sheet.

Section 3

1	A B C D E	6	A B C D E	11	A B C D E	16	A B C D E
2	A B C D E	7	A B C D E	12	A B C D E	17	A B C D E
3	A B C D E	8	A B C D E	13	A B C D E	18	A B C D E
4	A B C D E	9	A B C D E	14	A B C D E	19	A B C D E
5	A B C D E	10	A B C D E	15	A B C D E	20	A B C D E

Section 4

1	A B C D E	6	A B C D E	11	A B C D E	16	A B C D E
2	A B C D E	7	A B C D E	12	A B C D E	17	A B C D E
3	A B C D E	8	A B C D E	13	A B C D E	18	A B C D E
4	A B C D E	9	A B C D E	14	A B C D E	19	A B C D E
5	A B C D E	10	A B C D E	15	A B C D E	20	A B C D E

Section 5

1	A B C D E	11	A B C D E	21	A B C D E	31	A B C D E
2	A B C D E	12	A B C D E	22	A B C D E	32	A B C D E
3	A B C D E	13	A B C D E	23	A B C D E	33	A B C D E
4	A B C D E	14	A B C D E	24	A B C D E	34	A B C D E
5	A B C D E	15	A B C D E	25	A B C D E	35	A B C D E
6	A B C D E	16	A B C D E	26	A B C D E	36	A B C D E
7	A B C D E	17	A B C D E	27	A B C D E	37	A B C D E
8	A B C D E	18	A B C D E	28	A B C D E	38	A B C D E
9	A B C D E	19	A B C D E	29	A B C D E	39	A B C D E
10	A B C D E	20	A B C D E	30	A B C D E	40	A B C D E

TEAR HERE

Section 6

1 (A) (B) (C) (D) (E)
2 (A) (B) (C) (D) (E)
3 (A) (B) (C) (D) (E)
4 (A) (B) (C) (D) (E)
5 (A) (B) (C) (D) (E)
6 (A) (B) (C) (D) (E)
7 (A) (B) (C) (D) (E)
8 (A) (B) (C) (D) (E)
9 (A) (B) (C) (D) (E)
10 (A) (B) (C) (D) (E)
11 (A) (B) (C) (D) (E)
12 (A) (B) (C) (D) (E)
13 (A) (B) (C) (D) (E)
14 (A) (B) (C) (D) (E)
15 (A) (B) (C) (D) (E)
16 (A) (B) (C) (D) (E)
17 (A) (B) (C) (D) (E)
18 (A) (B) (C) (D) (E)
19 (A) (B) (C) (D) (E)
20 (A) (B) (C) (D) (E)
21 (A) (B) (C) (D) (E)
22 (A) (B) (C) (D) (E)
23 (A) (B) (C) (D) (E)
24 (A) (B) (C) (D) (E)
25 (A) (B) (C) (D) (E)
26 (A) (B) (C) (D) (E)
27 (A) (B) (C) (D) (E)
28 (A) (B) (C) (D) (E)
29 (A) (B) (C) (D) (E)
30 (A) (B) (C) (D) (E)
31 (A) (B) (C) (D) (E)
32 (A) (B) (C) (D) (E)
33 (A) (B) (C) (D) (E)
34 (A) (B) (C) (D) (E)
35 (A) (B) (C) (D) (E)
36 (A) (B) (C) (D) (E)
37 (A) (B) (C) (D) (E)
38 (A) (B) (C) (D) (E)
39 (A) (B) (C) (D) (E)
40 (A) (B) (C) (D) (E)

Section 2

1 (A) (B) (C) (D) (E)
2 (A) (B) (C) (D) (E)
3 (A) (B) (C) (D) (E)
4 (A) (B) (C) (D) (E)
5 (A) (B) (C) (D) (E)
6 (A) (B) (C) (D) (E)
7 (A) (B) (C) (D) (E)
8 (A) (B) (C) (D) (E)
9 (A) (B) (C) (D) (E)
10 (A) (B) (C) (D) (E)
11 (A) (B) (C) (D) (E)
12 (A) (B) (C) (D) (E)
13 (A) (B) (C) (D) (E)
14 (A) (B) (C) (D) (E)
15 (A) (B) (C) (D) (E)

Note: ONLY the answers entered on the grid are scored. Handwritten answers at the top of the column are NOT scored.

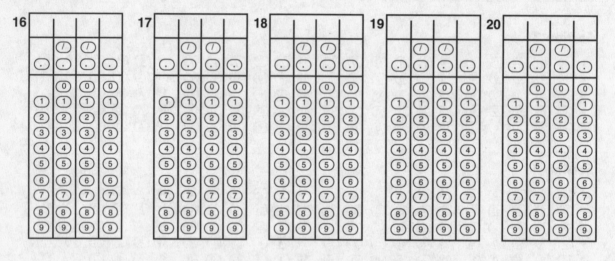

16

	/	/	
.	.	.	.
	0	0	0
1	1	1	1
2	2	2	2
3	3	3	3
4	4	4	4
5	5	5	5
6	6	6	6
7	7	7	7
8	8	8	8
9	9	9	9

17

	/	/	
.	.	.	.
	0	0	0
1	1	1	1
2	2	2	2
3	3	3	3
4	4	4	4
5	5	5	5
6	6	6	6
7	7	7	7
8	8	8	8
9	9	9	9

18

	/	/	
.	.	.	.
	0	0	0
1	1	1	1
2	2	2	2
3	3	3	3
4	4	4	4
5	5	5	5
6	6	6	6
7	7	7	7
8	8	8	8
9	9	9	9

19

	/	/	
.	.	.	.
	0	0	0
1	1	1	1
2	2	2	2
3	3	3	3
4	4	4	4
5	5	5	5
6	6	6	6
7	7	7	7
8	8	8	8
9	9	9	9

20

	/	/	
.	.	.	.
	0	0	0
1	1	1	1
2	2	2	2
3	3	3	3
4	4	4	4
5	5	5	5
6	6	6	6
7	7	7	7
8	8	8	8
9	9	9	9

21

	/	/	
.	.	.	.
	0	0	0
1	1	1	1
2	2	2	2
3	3	3	3
4	4	4	4
5	5	5	5
6	6	6	6
7	7	7	7
8	8	8	8
9	9	9	9

22

	/	/	
.	.	.	.
	0	0	0
1	1	1	1
2	2	2	2
3	3	3	3
4	4	4	4
5	5	5	5
6	6	6	6
7	7	7	7
8	8	8	8
9	9	9	9

23

	/	/	
.	.	.	.
	0	0	0
1	1	1	1
2	2	2	2
3	3	3	3
4	4	4	4
5	5	5	5
6	6	6	6
7	7	7	7
8	8	8	8
9	9	9	9

24

	/	/	
.	.	.	.
	0	0	0
1	1	1	1
2	2	2	2
3	3	3	3
4	4	4	4
5	5	5	5
6	6	6	6
7	7	7	7
8	8	8	8
9	9	9	9

25

	/	/	
.	.	.	.
	0	0	0
1	1	1	1
2	2	2	2
3	3	3	3
4	4	4	4
5	5	5	5
6	6	6	6
7	7	7	7
8	8	8	8
9	9	9	9

Practice Examination 5

SECTION 1

30 Questions • Time—30 Minutes

Directions: Each of the following questions consists of an incomplete sentence followed by five words or pairs of words. Choose that word or pair of words which, when substituted for the blank space or spaces, *best* completes the meaning of the sentence and mark the letter of your choice on your answer sheet.

Example:

In view of the extenuating circumstances and the defendant's youth, the judge recommended ---- .

(A) conviction (B) a defense
(C) a mistrial (D) leniency
(E) life imprisonment Ⓐ Ⓑ Ⓒ ● Ⓔ

1. ---- the activities of her employees, the director refused to ---- their methods.

   (A) Disarming..condone
   (B) Applauding..question
   (C) Repudiating..reward
   (D) Handling..oversee
   (E) Approving..arrogate

2. The ---- soldier ---- at the idea that he was to go to battle.

   (A) luckless..rejoiced
   (B) youthful..retired
   (C) unwilling..recoiled
   (D) frail..relapsed
   (E) vigorous..repined

3. The ---- treatment of the zoo animals resulted in community-wide ---- .

   (A) curious..apathy
   (B) popular..neglect
   (C) critical..distention
   (D) adequate..revulsion
   (E) inhumane..criticism

4. Unlike gold, paper money has no ---- value; it is merely a representation of wealth.

   (A) financial
   (B) inveterate
   (C) economic
   (D) intrinsic
   (E) fiscal

5. His untimely death, at first thought to be due to a ---- fever, was later ---- to poison.

   (A) degenerative..relegated
   (B) debilitating..ascribed
   (C) raging..reduced
   (D) sanguine..abdicated
   (E) pernicious..prescribed

GO ON TO THE NEXT PAGE

Directions: Each of the following questions consists of a capitalized pair of words followed by five pairs of words lettered A to E. The capitalized words bear some meaningful relationship to each other. Choose the lettered pair of words whose relationship is most similar to that expressed by the capitalized pair and mark its letter on your answer sheet.

Example:

DAY : SUN : :

(A) sunlight : daylight
(B) ray : sun
(C) night : moon
(D) heat : cold
(E) moon : star

Ⓐ Ⓑ ● Ⓓ Ⓔ

6. MICROSCOPE : INSTRUMENT : :

(A) autobiography : novel
(B) hammer : metal
(C) necktie : accessory
(D) oar : boat
(E) telescope : stars

7. SKETCH : PAINTING : :

(A) original : replica
(B) camera : photo
(C) scene : play
(D) draft : thesis
(E) illustration : cartoon

8. GATE : PLANE : :

(A) latch : door
(B) fence : yard
(C) track : train
(D) highway : car
(E) driver : bus

9. SWEAR : OATH : :

(A) laugh : smile
(B) grab : boulder
(C) sign : contract
(D) neglect : demand
(E) disregard : notice

10. SPELUNKER : CAVE : :

(A) astronaut : space
(B) teacher : student
(C) miner : ore
(D) pilot : airplane
(E) bear : den

11. LAUGHTER : AMUSEMENT : :

(A) vigor : optimism
(B) squalor : filth
(C) stealth : openness
(D) pride : humility
(E) pallor : illness

12. CURE : PHYSICIAN : :

(A) prescribe : pharmacist
(B) discuss : writer
(C) entertain : comedian
(D) train : athlete
(E) trust : policeman

13. SYMPHONY : MOVEMENT : :

(A) dollar : cent
(B) strings : section
(C) chorus : soloist
(D) play : act
(E) action : reason

Directions: Each passage below is followed by a set of questions. Read each passage, then answer the accompanying questions, basing your answers on what is stated or implied in the passage and in any introductory material provided. Mark the letter of your choice on your answer sheet.

Questions 14–21 are based on the following passage.

The following speech has been adapted from A Citizen is Entitled to Vote *by Susan B. Anthony, a nineteenth-century campaigner for women's rights. At the time of the speech, women were not guaranteed the right to vote.*

Friends and fellow citizens:—I stand before you tonight under indictment for the alleged crime of having voted at the last presidential election, without having a lawful right to vote.

It shall be my work this evening to prove to you that in thus voting, I not only committed no crime, but instead, simply exercised my *citizen's rights,* guaranteed to me and all United States citizens by the National Constitution, beyond the power of any State to deny.

The preamble of the Federal Constitution says: "We, the people of the United States, in order to form a more perfect union, establish justice, insure *domestic* tranquility, provide for the common defense, promote the general welfare, and secure the blessings of liberty to ourselves and our posterity, do ordain and establish this Constitution for the United States of America."

It was we, the people, not we, the white male citizens; but we, the whole people, who formed the Union. And we formed it, not to give the blessings of liberty, but to secure them; not to the half of ourselves and the half of our posterity but to the whole people—women as well as men. And it is a down-right mockery to talk to women of their enjoyment of the blessings of liberty while they are denied the use of the only means of securing them provided by this democratic-republican government—the ballot.

For any State to make sex a qualification that must ever result in the disfranchisement of one entire half of the people is a violation of the supreme law of the land. By it the blessings of liberty are forever withheld from women and their female posterity. To them this government has no just powers derived from the consent of the governed. To them this government is not a democracy. It is not a republic. It is a hateful oligarchy of sex. An oligarchy of learning, where the educated govern the ignorant, might be endured; but this oligarchy of sex, which makes father, brothers, husband, sons, the oligarchs or rulers over the mother and sisters, the wife and daughters of every household—which ordains all men sovereigns, all women subjects, carries dissension, discord and rebellion into every home of the nation.

Webster's Dictionary defines a citizen as a person in the United States, entitled to vote and hold office.

The only question left to be settled now is, Are women persons? And I hardly believe any of our opponents will have the hardihood to say they are not. Being persons, then, women are citizens; and no State has a right to make any law, or to enforce any old law, that shall abridge their privileges or immunities. Hence, every discrimination against women in the constitutions and laws of the several States is today null and void.

14. Anthony talks as if she were a

(A) defendant on trial
(B) chairperson of a committee
(C) legislator arguing for a new law
(D) judge ruling at a trial
(E) lawyer in court

15. Anthony broadens her appeal to her audience by showing how her case could affect all

(A) existing laws
(B) United States citizens
(C) women
(D) uneducated persons
(E) children

16. Anthony quotes the preamble to the Constitution in order to

(A) impress the audience with her intelligence
(B) share common knowledge with her audience
(C) point out which part of the preamble needs to be changed
(D) add force to her argument
(E) utilize a common legalistic trick

GO ON TO THE NEXT PAGE

17. According to this speech, one reason for forming the Union was to

(A) establish an aristocracy
(B) limit the powers of the states
(C) insure domestic harmony
(D) draw up a Constitution
(E) provide an international power

18. Anthony argues that a government that denies women the right to vote is not a democracy because its powers do not come from

(A) the Constitution of the United States
(B) the rights of the states
(C) the consent of the governed
(D) the vote of the majority
(E) both houses of Congress

19. According to this speech, an oligarchy of sex would cause

(A) women to rebel against the government
(B) men to desert their families
(C) poor women to lose hope
(D) problems to develop in every home
(E) the educated to rule the ignorant

20. In this speech, a citizen is *defined* as a person who has the right to vote and also the right to

(A) change laws
(B) acquire wealth
(C) speak publicly
(D) hold office
(E) pay taxes

21. Anthony argues that state laws which discriminate against women are

(A) being changed
(B) null and void
(C) helpful to the rich
(D) supported only by men
(E) supported by the Constitution

Questions 22–30 are based on the following passage.

Daniel Defoe (1660–1731) was an English writer who was influential in the development of the modern novel. In this excerpt from his masterpiece Robinson Crusoe, *young Robinson confronts his parents with his desire to seek adventures abroad.*

. . . My father, a wise and grave man, gave me serious and excellent counsel against what he foresaw was my design. He called me one morning into his chamber, where he was confined by the gout, and expostulated very warmly with me upon this subject: he asked me what reasons, more than a mere wandering inclination, I had for leaving his house, and my native country where I might be well introduced, and had a prospect of raising my fortune, by application and industry, with a life of ease and pleasure. He told me it was men of desperate fortunes, on one hand, or of superior fortunes, on the other, who went abroad upon adventures, aspiring to rise by enterprise, and make themselves famous in undertakings of a nature out of the common road; that these things were all either too far above me, or too far below me; that mine was the middle state, or what might be called the upper station of low life, which he had found, by long experience, was the best state in the world, the most suited to human happiness; not exposed to the miseries and hardships, the labour and sufferings, of the mechanic part of mankind, and not embarrassed with the pride, luxury, ambition, and envy of the upper part of mankind: he told me, I might judge of the happiness of this state by one thing, viz., that this was the state of life which all other people envied; that kings have frequently lamented the miserable consequences of being born to great things, and wished they had been placed in the middle of two extremes, between the mean and the great; that the wise man gave his testimony to this as the just standard of true felicity, when he prayed to have "neither poverty nor riches."

He bade me observe it, and I should always find, that the calamities of life were shared among the upper and lower part of mankind; but that the middle station had the fewest disasters, and was not exposed to so many vicissitudes as the higher or lower part of mankind; nay, they were not subjected to so many distempers and uneasinesses, either of body or mind, as those were who, by vicious living, luxury, extravagancies, on one hand, or by hard labour, want of necessaries, and mean and insufficient diet, on the other hand, bring distempers upon themselves by the natural consequences of their way of living; that the middle station of life was calculated for all kind of virtues, and all kind of enjoyments; that peace and plenty were the handmaids of a middle fortune; that temperance, moderation, quietness, health, society, all agreeable diversions, and all desirable pleasure were the blessings attending the middle station of life; that this way men went silently and smoothly through the world, and comfortably out of it, not embarrassed with the labours of the hands or of the head, not sold to the life of slavery for daily bread, or harassed with perplexed circumstances, which rob the soul of peace, and the body of rest; not enraged with the passion of envy, or secret burning lust of ambition for great things; but, in easy circumstances, sliding gently through the world, and sensibly tasting the sweets of living, without the bitter; feeling that they are happy, and learning by every day's experience, to know it more sensibly. . . .

I was sincerely affected with this discourse, as indeed who could be otherwise? and I resolved not to think of going abroad any more, but to settle at home, according to my father's desire. But, alas! a few days wore it all off; and, in short, to prevent any of my father's farther importunities, in a few weeks after, I resolved to run quite away from him. . . . I took my mother at a time when I thought her a little pleasanter than ordinary, and told her, that my thoughts were so entirely bent upon seeing the world, that I should never settle to anything with resolution enough to go through with it; that I was now eighteen years old, which was too late to go apprentice to a trade, or clerk to an attorney; that I was sure, if I did I should never serve out my time, and I should certainly run away from my master before my time was out, and go to sea; and if she would speak to my father to let me make but one voyage abroad, if I came home again, and did not like it, I would go no more, and I would promise, by a double diligence, to recover the time I had lost.

22. In line 2, the word *counsel* is intended to mean

(A) warning
(B) conceit
(C) foreboding
(D) advice
(E) concern

23. In the first paragraph Defoe implies that

(A) the father knows more than Robinson
(B) Robinson is stubborn
(C) the father is apprehensive about Robinson's leaving
(D) Robinson will not find a good job
(E) Robinson will upset his mother by leaving

24. The "middle state" is best according to the father because it

(A) entails no responsibility
(B) guarantees complete happiness
(C) is free from envy, pride, and want
(D) is the state all wise men aspire to
(E) is a guarantee against all disasters

25. "Desperate fortunes" and "superior fortunes" (lines 10–11), refer to

(A) bad luck and good luck
(B) poverty and wealth
(C) sadness and happiness
(D) hopelessness and hope
(E) humility and pride

26. The father believes that the very wealthy

(A) are always happy
(B) are at peace with themselves
(C) suffer physical and mental distress as a result of their lifestyle
(D) have no ambition
(E) are frugal in their habits

27. Along with choosing the "middle state," the father advocates

(A) making as much money as possible
(B) envying the life of luxury
(C) learning skills and working hard
(D) getting married and starting a family
(E) working with your hands

GO ON TO THE NEXT PAGE

28. Based on this passage you may assume that young Robinson

(A) thinks his father is a fool
(B) has his mother's permission to go abroad
(C) is going to take his father's advice
(D) thinks 18-year-olds should be able to make their own decisions
(E) will soon be on his way

29. Robinson is determined to have

(A) at least one chance to see the world
(B) a job as an attorney's clerk when he gets back
(C) his father's blessing before he goes
(D) fame and great wealth
(E) a career as a ship's captain

30. You may infer from the passage that Robinson's father would most likely admire

(A) a soldier
(B) a hard-working attorney
(C) an explorer
(D) the king
(E) a farmer

STOP

END OF SECTION 1. IF YOU HAVE ANY TIME LEFT, GO OVER YOUR WORK IN THIS SECTION ONLY. DO NOT WORK IN ANY OTHER SECTION OF THE TEST.

SECTION 2

25 Questions • Time—30 Minutes

Directions: Solve the following problems using any available space on the page for scratchwork. On your answer sheet fill in the choice which best corresponds to the correct answer.

Notes: The figures accompanying the problems are drawn as accurately as possible unless otherwise stated in specific problems. Again, unless otherwise stated, all figures lie in the same plane. All numbers used in these problems are real numbers. Calculators are permitted for this test.

Reference Information

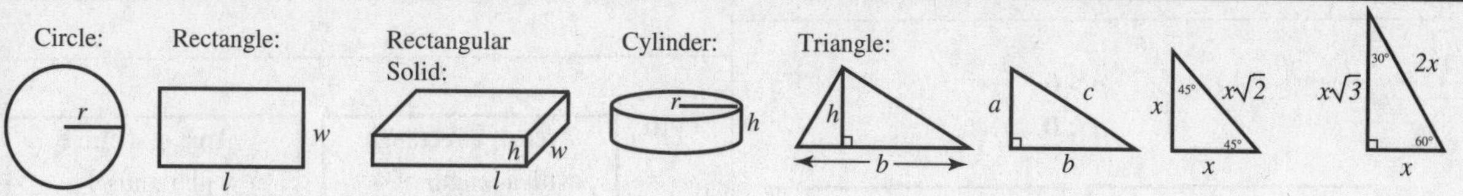

$C = 2\pi r$ $A = \pi r^2$ | $A = lw$ | $V = lwh$ | $V = \pi r^2 h$ | $A = \frac{1}{2}bh$ | $a^2 + b^2 = c^2$

The number of degrees of arc in a circle is 360.
The measure in degrees of a straight angle is 180.
The sum of the measures in degrees of the angles of a triangle is 180.

Part I: Quantitative Comparison Questions

Directions: For each of the following questions, two quantities are given—one in Column A, and the other in Column B. Compare the two quantities and mark your answer sheet as follows:

(A) if the quantity in Column A is greater
(B) if the quantity in Column B is greater
(C) if the two quantities are equal
(D) if the relationship cannot be determined from the information given.

Notes:
(1) Information concerning one or both of the compared quantities will be centered above the two columns for some items.
(2) Symbols that appear in both columns represent the same thing in Column A as in Column B.
(3) Letters such as *x*, *n*, and *k* are symbols for real numbers.

Examples

	Column A	Column B	Answers
	$a > 0$, $x > 0$		
E1.	$a - x$	$a + x$	Ⓐ ● Ⓒ Ⓓ
E2.	The average of 17, 19, 21, 23	The average of 16, 18, 20, 22	● Ⓑ Ⓒ Ⓓ

DO NOT MARK CHOICE (E) FOR THESE QUESTIONS. THERE ARE ONLY FOUR ANSWER CHOICES.

GO ON TO THE NEXT PAGE

	Column A	Column B
	$s > t$	
1.	$s - t$	$t - s$
2.	The cost of a complete stereo system that is discounted 30%	The cost of a pair of speakers that is discounted 30%
	$p > 0$, $q < 0$	
3.	$p + q$	$p - q$
	Distance from *A* to *B* is 12 miles. Distance from *A* to *C* is 10 miles	
4.	Distance from *A* to *B*	Distance from *B* to *C*
5.	The number that 63 is 7% of	7% of 63
	$r = \frac{1}{2}$	
6.	$2r^3 - 12r + 7$	$r^2 + 1$
	$x \neq 0$	
7.	$\frac{1}{x^2}$	x^2
	$m^3 = 64$, $\sqrt{n} = 16$	
8.	m	n

Note: Figure not drawn to scale.

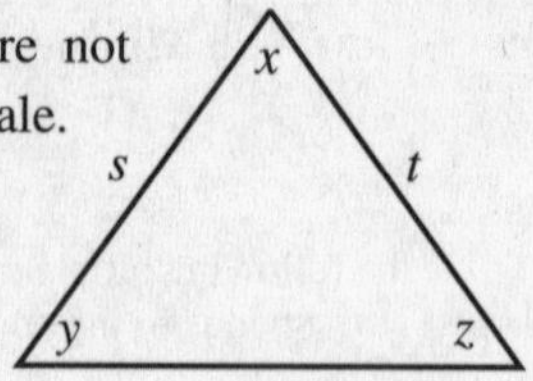

$x = y = z$

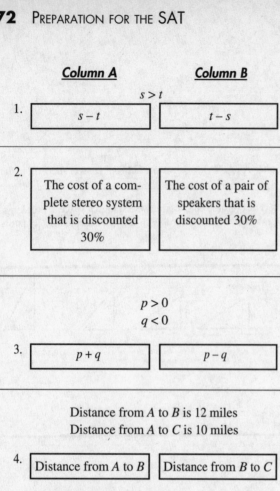

	Column A	Column B
9.	side s	side t
10.	Area of a rectangle with a length of 4 and a width of π	Area of a circle with radius 4

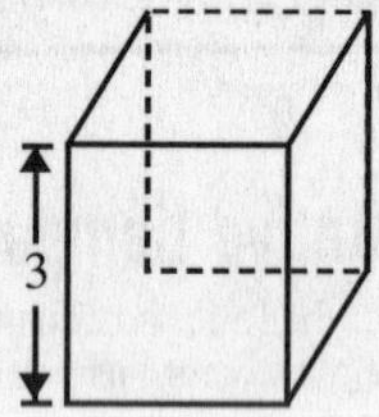

	Column A	Column B
11.	Surface area of the cube	Cutting the cube in half to form 2 smaller boxes: the sum of the surface area of both the boxes
	$r < 0 < s$	
12.	r^5	s^4
	$x^2 = 25$, $2y + 3 = 27$	
13.	x	y

Column A	Column B

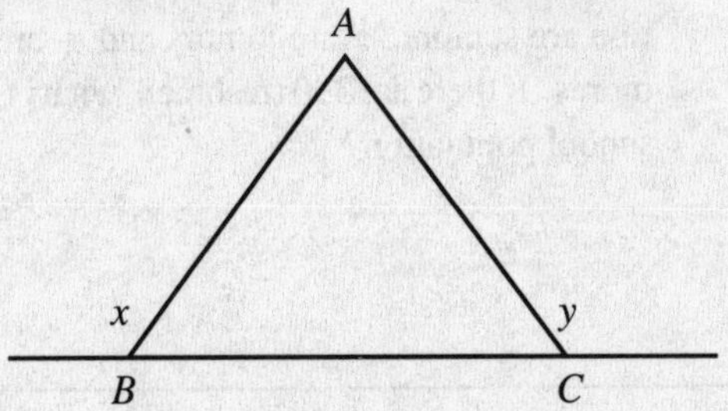

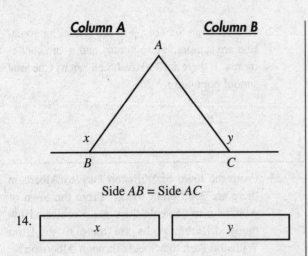

Side AB = Side AC

14.

x	y

Column A	Column B

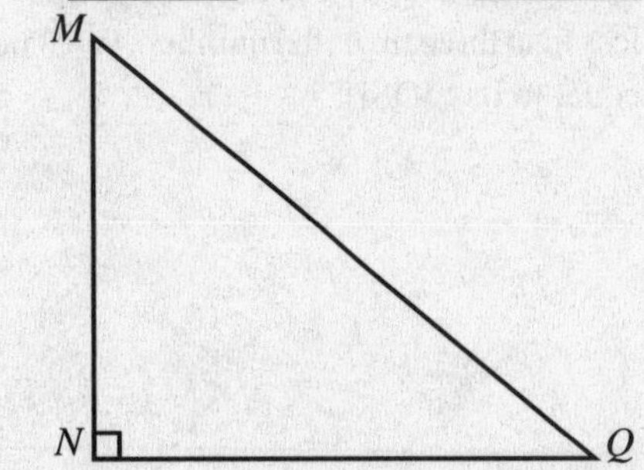

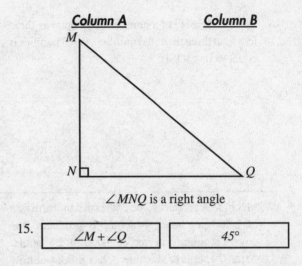

$\angle MNQ$ is a right angle

15.

$\angle M + \angle Q$	$45°$

Part 2: Student-Produced Response Questions

Directions: Solve each of these problems. Write the answer in the corresponding grid on the answer sheet and fill in the ovals beneath each answer you write. Here are some examples.

Answer: *$\frac{3}{4}$ (= .75; show answer either way)*

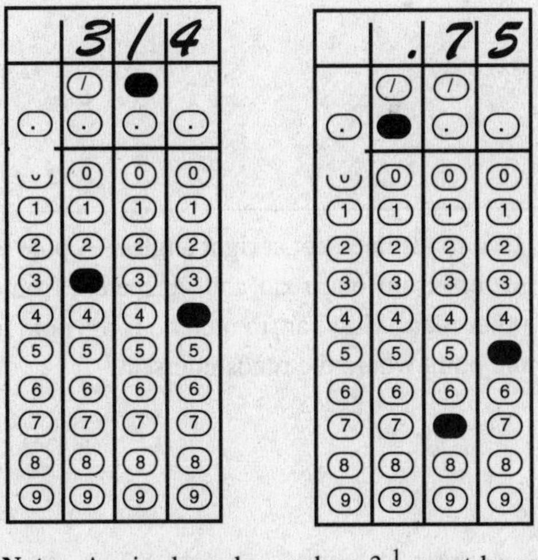

Note: A mixed number such as $3\frac{1}{2}$ must be gridded as 7/2 or as 3.5. If gridded as "3 1/2," it will be read as "thirty-one halves."

Answer: *325*

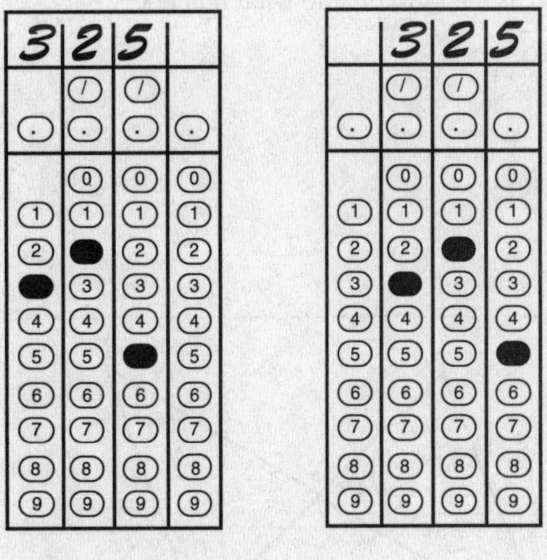

Note: Either position is correct.

16.

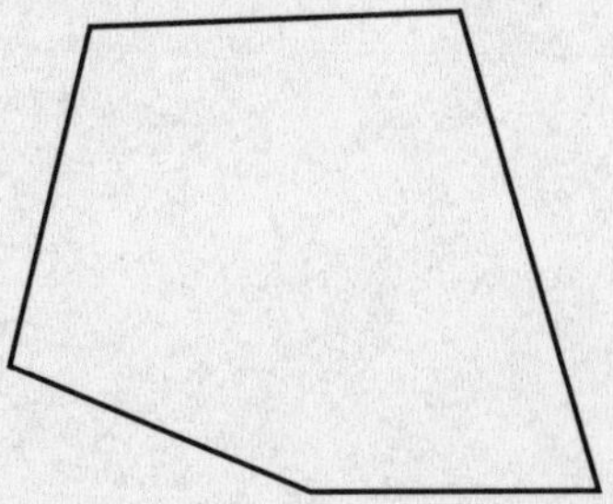

In the pentagon shown, what is the maximum number of different diagonals that can be drawn?

17. If $4x = 2(2 + x)$ and $6y = 3(2 + y)$, then $2x + 3y =$

GO ON TO THE NEXT PAGE

18. Let the "JOSH" of a number be defined as three less than three times the number. What number is equal to its "JOSH"?

19. Machine A produces flue covers at a uniform rate of 2,000 per hour. Machine B produces flue covers at a uniform rate of 5,000 in $2\frac{1}{2}$ hours. After $7\frac{1}{4}$ hours, Machine A has produced how many more flue covers than Machine B?

20. .01 is the ratio of .1 to what number?

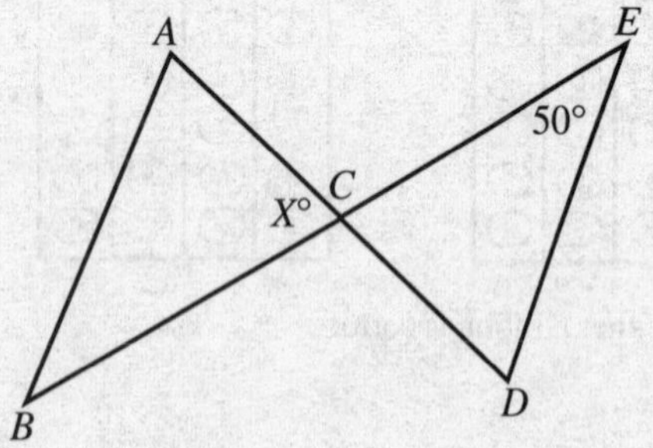

21. In the figure above, AB is parallel to ED and $AC = BC$. If angle E is 50°, then $x =$

22. At NJL High School, $\frac{1}{4}$ of the school's population are seniors, $\frac{1}{5}$ are juniors and $\frac{1}{3}$ are sophomores. If there are 390 freshmen, what is the total school population?

23. From the town of Williston Park to Albertson there are 3 different roads. From the town of Albertson to Mineola there are 5 routes. How many different paths are there to go from Williston Park to Mineola through Albertson?

24. If 12 candies cost $1.70, how many of these candies can be bought for $10.20?

25. Two roads intersect at right angles. A pole is 30 meters from one road and 40 meters from the other road. How far (in meters) is the pole from the point where the roads intersect?

STOP

END OF SECTION 2. IF YOU HAVE ANY TIME LEFT, GO OVER YOUR WORK IN THIS SECTION ONLY. DO NOT WORK IN ANY OTHER SECTION OF THE TEST.

SECTION 3

10 Questions • Time—15 Minutes

Directions: The two passages given below deal with a related topic. Following the passages are questions about the content of each passage or about the relationship between the two passages. Answer the questions based upon what is stated or implied in the passages and in any introductory material provided. Mark the letter of your choice on your answer sheet.

Questions 1–10 are based on the following passages.

President Lincoln referred to Harriet Beecher Stowe as "the little woman who made the great war." Her novel of protest, Uncle Tom's Cabin, *was published in 1852 and became a hit in America and in Europe, where it was reviewed by, among others, the French writer George Sand. In the letter below, she responds to an English admirer's request for information about her life and work. Born Amandine Dupin, George Sand was a prolific writer of romantic novels, essays and letters. Here she gives literary advice to her friend Flaubert, a very different kind of novelist.*

Passage 1—Harriet Beecher Stowe, from a letter to Mrs. Follen (1853)

I had two little curly-headed twin daughters to begin with, and my stock in this line was gradually increased, till I have been the mother of seven children, the most beautiful and the most loved of whom lies buried near my Cincinnati residence. It was at his dying bed and at his grave that I learned what a poor slave mother may feel when her child is torn away from her. In those depths of sorrow which seemed to me immeasurable, it was my only prayer to God that such anguish might not be suffered in vain. There were circumstances about his death of such peculiar bitterness, of what seemed almost cruel suffering, that I felt that I could never be consoled for it unless this crushing of my own heart might enable me to work out some great good to others. . . .

I allude to this here because I have often felt that much that is in that book ("Uncle Tom") had its root in the awful scenes and bitter sorrows of that summer. It has left now, I trust, no trace on my mind except a deep compassion for the sorrowful, especially for mothers who are separated from their children. . . .

I am now writing a work which will contain, perhaps, an equal amount of matter with "Uncle Tom's Cabin." It will contain all the facts and documents upon which that story was founded, and an immense body of facts, reports of trial, legal documents, and testimony of people now living South, which will more than confirm every statement in "Uncle Tom's Cabin."

I must confess that till I began the examination of facts in order to write this book, much as I thought I knew before, I had not begun to measure the depth of the abyss. The law records of courts and judicial proceedings are so incredible as to fill me with amazement whenever I think of them. It seems to me that the book cannot but be felt, and, coming upon the sensibility awaked by the other, do something.

I suffer exquisitely in writing these things. It may be truly said that I suffer with my heart's blood. Many times in writing "Uncle Tom's Cabin" I thought my heart would fail utterly, but I prayed earnestly that God would help me till I got through, and still I am pressed beyond measure and above strength. . . .

Passage 2—George Sand, from a letter to Gustave Flaubert (1876)

This will to paint things as they are, the adventures of life as they present themselves to us, is not well reasoned in my opinion. To paint the inanimate as a realist or as a poet is all one to me, but when one comes to dealing with the human heart it is different. You cannot abstract yourself from this contemplation, for the author is yourself, and other men are readers. However hard you struggle, your story cannot be anything but a conversation between author and readers. If you coldly show him evil without ever showing him good, he will get angry. He will wonder who is evil, you or himself? You may try to move him and attach him to yourself, but you will never succeed unless you are moved yourself, nor will you succeed if you hide your emotions so well that he believes you indifferent. The reader is right. Supreme impartiality is an antihuman thing, and a novel should be human in the first place. If it is not, no

GO ON TO THE NEXT PAGE

one will want to give it credit for being well written, well composed, well observed in detail. The essential quality will be lacking. It will not be interesting. The reader also fails to attach himself to books in which all characters are good without a shade of weakness; he can see perfectly well that it is not human either. I believe the special art of telling a story depends on this opposition of characters; but I want to see goodness triumph in the struggle; events may be allowed to crush the good man, but they must not soil him or belittle him, and if he must be sent to the slaughterhouse let him feel happier there than his butchers.

1. Harriet Beecher Stowe traces her compassion for slave mothers to her

   (A) writing of *Uncle Tom's Cabin*
   (B) hatred of injustice
   (C) meeting a young woman in Cincinnati
   (D) reading of legal documents and testimony
   (E) loss of her own son

2. Stowe is writing a new book that will be

   (A) as long as *Uncle Tom's Cabin*
   (B) fictional, like *Uncle Tom's Cabin*
   (C) more successful than *Uncle Tom's Cabin*
   (D) both A and B
   (E) both B and C

3. By "the depth of the abyss" (lines 30–31), Stowe refers to

   (A) the endless array of documentation
   (B) the cruelty of the judicial process
   (C) the suffering of young mothers
   (D) the horrors of slavery
   (E) the immeasurable intensity of grief

4. Stowe believes that her new book will

   (A) prompt readers to read her last book
   (B) arouse empathy in readers
   (C) cause readers intense suffering
   (D) console readers of *Uncle Tom's Cabin*
   (E) infuriate readers of *Uncle Tom's Cabin*

5. By "abstract" (line 47), George Sand means

   (A) abridge
   (B) summarize
   (C) remove
   (D) conceptualize
   (E) obscure

6. Who is "he" in line 52?

   (A) Flaubert
   (B) the novel's protagonist
   (C) the author
   (D) a poet
   (E) the reader

7. Sand's allusion to the slaughterhouse (line 69) is her way of saying that, in a novel,

   (A) butchers make the best villains
   (B) a good man may die, but must triumph nonetheless
   (C) no one should be allowed to kill off the good man
   (D) a hero should laugh contemptuously in the face of death
   (E) death cannot occur without redemption

8. Sand's main objection to Flaubert's writing is that he

   (A) discusses good and evil too often
   (B) appears impartial and detached
   (C) features weak characters
   (D) describes inhuman events
   (E) writes about inanimate objects

9. Stowe and Sand would probably agree that

   (A) Flaubert is the greatest of French novelists
   (B) slavery is the sign of a corruption in men
   (C) writers may demonstrate evil without showing good
   (D) a writer must be moved by his or her subject
   (E) good will always triumphs in the end

10. Which line from one letter might make a good title for both?

    (A) “To Paint the Inanimate”
    (B) “I Suffer Exquisitely”
    (C) “Bitter Sorrows”
    (D) “The Adventures of Life”
    (E) “A Novel Should Be Human”

STOP

END OF SECTION 3. IF YOU HAVE ANY TIME LEFT, GO OVER YOUR WORK IN THIS SECTION ONLY. DO NOT WORK IN ANY OTHER SECTION OF THE TEST.

SECTION 4

10 Questions • Time—15 Minutes

Directions: Solve the following problems using any available space on the page for scratchwork. On your answer sheet fill in the choice which best corresponds to the correct answer.

Notes: The figures accompanying the problems are drawn as accurately as possible unless otherwise stated in specific problems. Again, unless otherwise stated, all figures lie in the same plane. All numbers used in these problems are real numbers. Calculators are permitted for this test.

Reference Information

Circle: Rectangle: Rectangular Solid: Cylinder: Triangle:

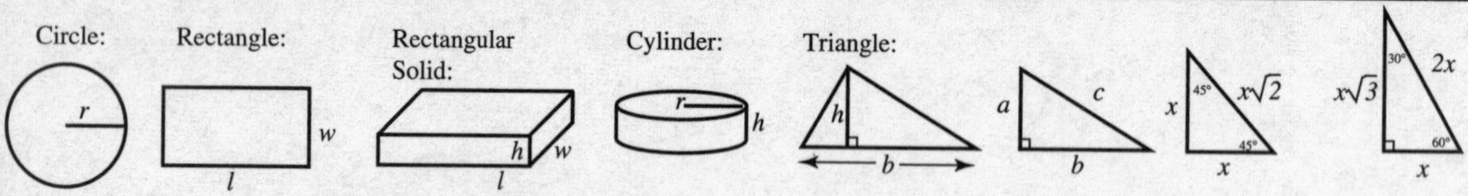

$C=2\pi r$ $A=lw$ $V=lwh$ $V=\pi r^2 h$ $A=\frac{1}{2}bh$ $a^2+b^2=c^2$

$A=\pi r^2$

The number of degrees of arc in a circle is 360.
The measure in degrees of a straight angle is 180.
The sum of the measures in degrees of the angles of a triangle is 180.

1. If a triangle of base 7 is equal in area to a circle of radius 7, what is the altitude of the triangle?

(A) 8π
(B) 10π
(C) 12π
(D) 14π
(E) It cannot be determined from the information given.

2. If the following numbers are arranged in order from the smallest to the largest, what will be their correct order?

I. $\frac{9}{13}$

II. $\frac{13}{9}$

III. 70%

IV. $\frac{1}{.70}$

(A) II, I, III, IV
(B) III, II, I, IV
(C) III, IV, I, II
(D) II, IV, III, I
(E) I, III, IV, II

3. The coordinates of the vertices of quadrilateral *PQRS* are *P*(0,0), *Q*(9,0), *R*(10,3), and *S*(1,3), respectively. What is the area of *PQRS?*

(A) $9\sqrt{10}$
(B) $\frac{9}{2}\sqrt{10}$
(C) $\frac{27}{2}$
(D) 27
(E) It cannot be determined from the information given.

4. If $8x+4=64$, then $2x+1=$

(A) 12
(B) 13
(C) 16
(D) 24
(E) 60

5. A circle whose radius is 7 has its center at the origin. Which of the following points are outside the circle?

I. (4,4)
II. (5,5)
III. (4,5)
IV. (4,6)

(A) I and II only
(B) II and III only
(C) II, III, and IV only
(D) II and IV only
(E) III and IV only

6. What is the difference in surface area between a square with side = 9 and a cube with edge = 3?

(A) 516
(B) 432
(C) 72
(D) 27
(E) 18

7. A set of numbers is "quarked" if the sum of all the numbers in the set is evenly divisible by each of the numbers in the set. Which of the following sets is "quarked"?

(A) (1, 3, 5, 7)
(B) (4, 6, 8)
(C) (6, 7, 8, 9)
(D) (2, 4, 6)
(E) (5, 10, 15, 20)

8. If $x \neq -2$, $\frac{3(x^2-4)}{x+2} =$

(A) $3x^2 + 4$
(B) $3x - 2$
(C) $x - 2$
(D) $3x - 6$
(E) $3x + 6$

9. An ice-cream truck runs down a certain street 4 times a week. This truck carries 5 different flavors of ice-cream bars, each of which comes in 2 different designs. Considering that the truck runs Monday through Thursday, and Monday was the first day of the month, by what day of the month could a person, buying one ice-cream bar each truck run, purchase all the different varieties of ice-cream bars?

(A) 11th
(B) 16th
(C) 21st
(D) 24th
(E) 30th

10. If $N! = N(N-1)(N-2)\ldots[N-(N-1)]$, what does $\frac{N!}{(N-2)!}$ equal?

(A) $N^2 - N$
(B) $N^5 + N^3 - N^2 + \frac{N}{N^2}$
(C) $N + 1$
(D) 1
(E) 6

STOP

END OF SECTION 4. IF YOU HAVE ANY TIME LEFT, GO OVER YOUR WORK IN THIS SECTION ONLY. DO NOT WORK IN ANY OTHER SECTION OF THE TEST.

SECTION 5

35 Questions • Time—30 Minutes

Directions: Each of the following questions consists of an incomplete sentence followed by five words or pairs of words. Choose that word or pair of words which, when substituted for the blank space or spaces, *best* completes the meaning of the sentence and mark the letter of your choice on your answer sheet.

Example:

In view of the extenuating circumstances and the defendant's youth, the judge recommended ----.

(A) conviction (B) a defense
(C) a mistrial (D) leniency
(E) life imprisonment Ⓐ Ⓑ Ⓒ ● Ⓔ

1. The society was not ---- and required much outside aid.

(A) destitute
(B) self-sufficient
(C) democratic
(D) impoverished
(E) benevolent

2. The new regime immediately ---- laws implementing the promised reforms.

(A) vouchsafed
(B) ensconced
(C) augmented
(D) promulgated
(E) parlayed

3. The machines were ----, and because of the below-zero temperature, it was feared they would ----.

(A) frozen..dehydrate
(B) brittle..shatter
(C) frosty..slide
(D) icy..capsize
(E) shiny..expand

4. A long illness can ---- even the strongest constitution.

(A) obviate
(B) inculcate
(C) bolster
(D) enervate
(E) disparage

5. With ---- attention to detail, the careful researcher churned out his reports.

(A) prosaic
(B) painless
(C) meticulous
(D) appealing
(E) atypical

6. A shy look from the beautiful Laura ---- him, and soon they were married.

(A) released
(B) controlled
(C) enchanted
(D) ensconced
(E) jilted

7. The city ---- to the advancing invaders without firing a single shot.

(A) extolled
(B) regressed
(C) equivocated
(D) dissembled
(E) capitulated

8. When the two opposing sides failed to reach a ----, the long-anticipated strike became ----.

(A) consensus..impossible
(B) transition..general
(C) compromise..inevitable
(D) rationale..culpable
(E) precedent..potential

9. Her new neighbor was ---- and charming, the ---- of the bumbling yokel she had expected.

(A) urbane..antithesis
(B) callow..exemplar
(C) provincial..precursor
(D) obtuse..tableau
(E) petulant..delegate

10. If you find peeling potatoes to be ----, perhaps you'd prefer to scrub the floors?

(A) felicitous
(B) remunerative
(C) onerous
(D) vilifying
(E) redundant

11. To strengthen her client's case, the lawyer sought to put the ---- of the witness in doubt.

(A) laxity
(B) posterity
(C) probity
(D) onus
(E) sensitivity

12. During the campaign, the politicians engaged in ---- debate, accusing each other of gross misdeeds.

(A) capricious
(B) acrimonious
(C) altruistic
(D) facetious
(E) chimerical

13. His carelessness produced a(n) ---- report which left everyone ----.

(A) intelligent..inept
(B) ambiguous..confused
(C) complete..mollified
(D) acceptable..angry
(E) insipid..inspired

14. Only a ---- person could be ---- to the suffering of the starving child.

(A) churlish..receptive
(B) dour..disposed
(C) placid..detrimental
(D) pious..uncivil
(E) callous..oblivious

GO ON TO THE NEXT PAGE

Directions: Each of the following questions consists of a capitalized pair of words followed by five pairs of words lettered A to E. The capitalized words bear some meaningful relationship to each other. Choose the lettered pair of words whose relationship is most similiar to that expressed by the capitalized pair and mark its letter on your answer sheet.

Example:

DAY : SUN : :

(A) sunlight : daylight (B) ray : sun
(C) night : moon (D) heat : cold
(E) moon : star

Ⓐ Ⓑ ● Ⓓ Ⓔ

15. OSCILLATE : PENDULUM : :

(A) obligate : promise
(B) float : fish
(C) turn : car
(D) spin : gyroscope
(E) learn : student

16. PREMIERE : MOVIE : :

(A) unveiling : statue
(B) rookie : football
(C) debutante : teenager
(D) ruler : subject
(E) celluloid : film

17. CARPENTER : AWL : :

(A) artist : canvas
(B) computer : disc
(C) film : camera
(D) gardener : hose
(E) miner : pick

18. ROOF : PITCH : :

(A) triangle : side
(B) basement : cement
(C) mountain : grade
(D) tree : sap
(E) ceiling : rafter

19. COG : WATCH : :

(A) plant : biome
(B) piston : engine
(C) scale : fish
(D) handle : pot
(E) leash : dog

20. EQUESTRIAN : HORSE : :

(A) veterinarian : hospital
(B) taxi : cab
(C) cyclist : bicycle
(D) cow : farmer
(E) camel : desert

20. RECLUSE : SOLITARY : :

(A) socialite : gregarious
(B) hermit : old
(C) monk : lowly
(D) soldier : political
(E) hut : squalid

22. DIFFUSE : CONCENTRATION : :

(A) spread : expansion
(B) diffident : shyness
(C) indelicate : coarseness
(D) incongruous : harmony
(E) anger : resentment

23. APPLE : FRUIT : :

(A) dog : bone
(B) tree : bush
(C) sparrow : bird
(D) robin : owl
(E) elm : birch

24. TEN : DECADE : :

(A) score : century
(B) discount : percent
(C) miles : odometer
(D) era : eon
(E) thousand : millennium

25. ZEALOT : FERVOR : :

(A) charlatan : honesty
(B) rogue : sobriety
(C) fledgling : experience
(D) dotard : youth
(E) sage : wisdom

Directions: The reading passage below is followed by a set of questions. Read the passage and answer the accompanying questions, basing your answers on what is stated or implied in the passage. Mark the letter of your choice on your answer sheet.

Questions 26–35 are based on the following passage.

*Anton Chekhov is the Russian playwright responsible for some of our most enduring dramas—*The Sea Gull, The Cherry Orchard, Uncle Vanya, *and others. In this letter he writes to another important playwright, Maxim Gorky, about Gorky's latest work.*

Moscow. Oct. 22, 1901

Five days have passed since I read your play (*The Petty Bourgeois*). I have not written to you till now because I could not get hold of the fourth act; I have kept waiting for it, and—I have still not got it. And so I have read only three acts, but that I think is enough to judge of the play. It is, as I expected, very good, written à la Gorky, original, very interesting; and, to begin by talking of the defects, I have noticed only one, a defect incorrigible as red hair in a red-haired man—the conservatism of the form. You make new and original people sing new songs to an accompaniment that looks second-hand; you have four acts, the characters deliver edifying discourses, there is a feeling of alarm before long speeches, and so on, and so on. But all that is not important, and it is all, so to speak, drowned in the good points of the play. Perchikhin—how living! His daughter is enchanting, Tatyana and Piotr also, and their mother is a splendid old woman. The central figure of the play, Nil, is vigorously drawn and extremely interesting! In fact, the play takes hold of one from the first act. Only, God preserve you from letting anyone act Perchikhin except Artyom, while Alekseyev-Stanislavsky must certainly play Nil. Those two figures will do just what's needed; Piotr—Meierkhold. Only, Nil's part, a wonderful part, must be made two or three times as long. You ought to end the play with it, to make it the leading part. Only, do not contrast him with Piotr and Tatyana, let him be by himself and them by themselves, all wonderful, splendid people independent of one another. When Nil tries to seem superior to Piotr and Tatyana, and says of himself that he is a fine fellow,—the element so characteristic of our decent working man, the element of modesty, is lost. He boasts, he argues, but you know one can see what kind of man he is without that. Let him be merry, let him play pranks through the whole four acts, let him eat a great deal after his work—and that will be enough for him to conquer the audience with. Piotr, I repeat, is good. Most likely you don't even suspect how good he is. Tatyana, too, is a finished figure, only,—(a) she ought really to be a schoolmistress, ought to be teaching children, ought to come home from school, ought to be taken up with her pupils and exercise-books, and—(b) it ought to be mentioned in the first or second act that she has attempted to poison herself; then, after that hint, the poisoning in the third act will not seem so startling and will be more in place. Teterev talks too much: such characters ought to be shown bit by bit among others, for in any case such people are everywhere merely incidental—both in life and on the stage. Make Elena dine with all the rest in the first act, let her sit and make jokes, or else there is very little of her, and she is not clear. . . .

26. By "à la Gorky" (line 6) Chekhov seems to mean

(A) plagiarized from another playwright
(B) in the manner of Maxim's father
(C) quirky
(D) fascinating and creative
(E) full of defects

27. The word *incorrigible* (line 9) means

(A) offensive
(B) irreparable
(C) pessimistic
(D) alarming
(E) impossible

28. When Chekhov states that the "accompaniment looks second-hand" (line 11), he means that

(A) the music should be rewritten
(B) the minor characters are stereotypes
(C) the form of the play is old-fashioned
(D) very few new characters are introduced
(E) the set is shabby

GO ON TO THE NEXT PAGE

29. When Chekhov refers to Perchikhin as "living" (line 16), he means that the character

(A) dies later in the act
(B) seems authentic
(C) is incredibly active
(D) lives well
(E) seethes with rage

30. From the passage you can infer that Nil is most likely a(n)

(A) intellectual
(B) ordinary working man
(C) aristocrat
(D) murderer
(E) revolutionary

31. Chekhov objects to Nil's lack of

(A) willpower
(B) contrast
(C) superiority
(D) modesty
(E) energy

32. Chekhov's advice about Elena (lines 50–53) is meant to

(A) elucidate her character
(B) startle Gorky
(C) remove her from the first act
(D) contrast her behavior with that of Nil
(E) lengthen the play

33. In line 50, the word *incidental* means

(A) insignificant
(B) accidental
(C) coincidental
(D) essential
(E) characteristic

34. Chekhov expresses definite opinions on each of these points EXCEPT

(A) who should play the part of Nil
(B) whose part should be extended
(C) what Tatyana should do for a living
(D) how Teterev's part should be cut
(E) how the third act should end

35. Chekhov suggests change in all of the following characters EXCEPT

(A) Tatyana
(B) Elena
(C) Nil
(D) Teterev
(E) Piotr

STOP

END OF SECTION 5. IF YOU HAVE ANY TIME LEFT, GO OVER YOUR WORK IN THIS SECTION ONLY. DO NOT WORK IN ANY OTHER SECTION OF THE TEST.

SECTION 6

25 Questions • Time—30 Minutes

Directions: Solve the following problems using any available space on the page for scratchwork. On your answer sheet fill in the choice which best corresponds to the correct answer.

Notes: The figures accompanying the problems are drawn as accurately as possible unless otherwise stated in specific problems. Again, unless otherwise stated, all figures lie in the same plane. All numbers used in these problems are real numbers. Calculators are permitted for this test.

Reference Information

Circle: Rectangle: Rectangular Solid: Cylinder: Triangle:

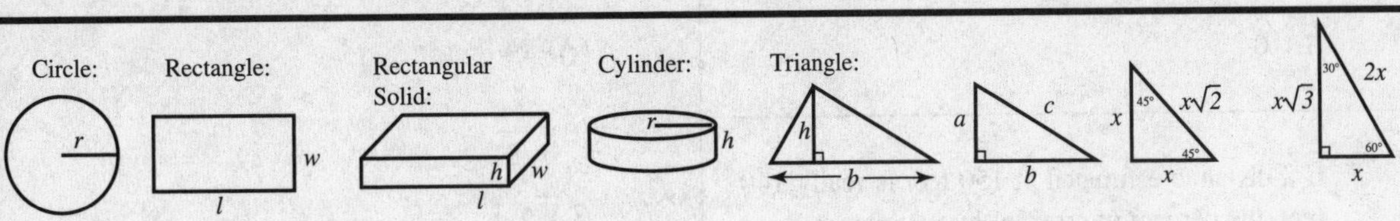

$C = 2\pi r$
$A = \pi r^2$ $A = lw$ $V = lwh$ $V = \pi r^2 h$ $A = \frac{1}{2}bh$ $a^2 + b^2 = c^2$

The number of degrees of arc in a circle is 360.
The measure in degrees of a straight angle is 180.
The sum of the measures in degrees of the angles of a triangle is 180.

1. If $3x + 2 > 2x + 7$, then x is

   (A) 5
   (B) < 5
   (C) > 5
   (D) < 1
   (E) < -1

2. If $x \neq \frac{2}{3}$, then $\frac{6x^2 - 13x + 6}{3x - 2} =$

   (A) $3x - 2$
   (B) $3x - 3$
   (C) $2x - 6$
   (D) $2x - 3$
   (E) $2x^2 + 3x - 3$

3. 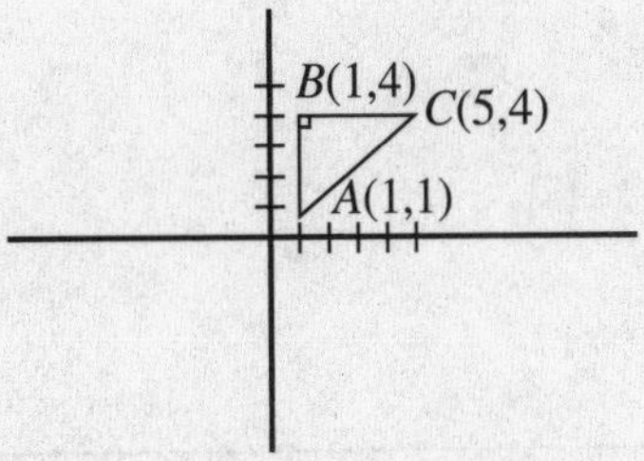

   What is the length of side AC?

   (A) $2\frac{1}{2}$
   (B) 5
   (C) 7
   (D) 11
   (E) 25

GO ON TO THE NEXT PAGE

4. If 3! means $3 \bullet 2 \bullet 1$ and 4! means $4 \bullet 3 \bullet 2 \bullet 1$, then what does $\frac{8!}{9!}$ equal?

(A) 9

(B) $\frac{8}{9}\%$

(C) $\frac{1}{9}\%$

(D) $\frac{1}{89}$

(E) 0

5. If a distance estimated at 150 feet is really 140 feet, the percent of error in this estimate is

(A) 10%

(B) $7\frac{1}{7}\%$

(C) $6\frac{2}{3}\%$

(D) 1%

(E) 0.71%

6. There are x cookies in a cookie jar. One child eats $\frac{1}{4}$ of all the cookies. A second child eats $\frac{1}{3}$ of the remaining cookies. If the remaining cookies are distributed among four other children, what fraction of the original number of cookies did each of the four children receive?

(A) $\frac{7}{12}$

(B) $\frac{1}{2}$

(C) $\frac{5}{12}$

(D) $\frac{1}{6}$

(E) $\frac{1}{8}$

7. $|2y-4|=6$, $y=$

(A) –5, 1
(B) –8
(C) –4, 3
(D) 5, –1
(E) 0

8. Given the system of equations $3x + 2y = 4$ and $6x - 3y = 6$, what does y equal?

(A) 14

(B) $\frac{14}{6}$

(C) 2

(D) $\frac{11}{7}$

(E) $\frac{2}{7}$

9. If the radius of a circle is diminished by 20%, the area is diminished by

(A) 20%
(B) 36%
(C) 40%
(D) 64%
(E) 400%

10. If $x-y=10$ and $x+y=20$ then what is the value of x^2-y^2?

(A) 400
(B) 200
(C) 100
(D) 30
(E) It cannot be determined from the information given.

11. A semicircle surmounts a rectangle whose length a $2a$ and whose width is a, as shown in the diagram. A formula for finding the area of the whole figure is

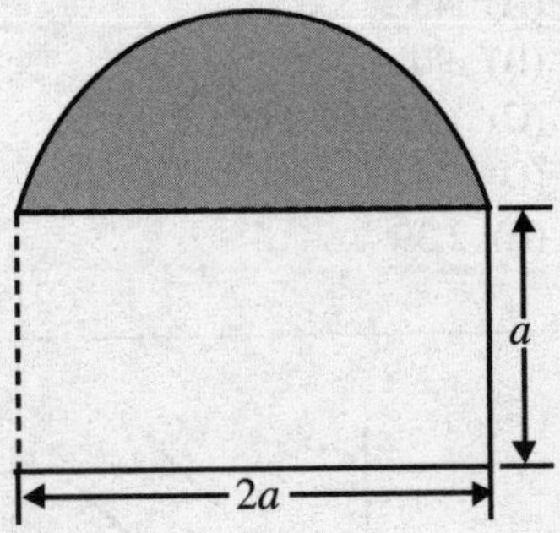

(A) $2a^2 + \frac{\pi a^2}{2}$
(B) $2\pi a^2$
(C) $3\pi a^2$
(D) $2a^2 + \pi a^2$
(E) $2a^2 + 2\pi a^2$

12. An airplane flies 550 yards in 3 seconds. What is the speed of the airplane, expressed in miles per hour? (5,280 ft. = 1 mi.)

(A) 1,125
(B) 375
(C) 300
(D) 125
(E) 90

13. Given that 1 meter = 3.28 ft., the distance run in a 100-meter race approximates most closely

(A) 100 yards
(B) 90 yards
(C) 105 yards
(D) 110 yards
(E) 103 yards

14. Of the following sets of fractions, the set that is arranged in increasing order is

(A) $\frac{7}{12}, \frac{6}{11}, \frac{3}{5}, \frac{5}{8}$
(B) $\frac{6}{11}, \frac{7}{12}, \frac{5}{8}, \frac{3}{5}$
(C) $\frac{6}{11}, \frac{7}{12}, \frac{3}{5}, \frac{5}{8}$
(D) $\frac{3}{5}, \frac{5}{8}, \frac{6}{11}, \frac{7}{12}$
(E) $\frac{7}{12}, \frac{6}{11}, \frac{5}{8}, \frac{3}{5}$

15. If one pipe can fill a tank in $1\frac{1}{2}$ hours and another can fill the same tank in 45 minutes, then how many hours will it take the two pipes to fill the tank if they are working together?

(A) $\frac{1}{3}$
(B) $\frac{1}{2}$
(C) $\frac{5}{6}$
(D) 1
(E) $1\frac{1}{2}$

16. If the sum of the edges of a cube is 48 inches, the volume of the cube in cubic inches is

(A) 64
(B) 96
(C) 149
(D) 512
(E) 1,728

GO ON TO THE NEXT PAGE

17. If the length of each side of a square is $\frac{2x}{3}+1$, the perimeter of the square is

(A) $\frac{8x+4}{3}$

(B) $\frac{8x+12}{3}$

(C) $\frac{2x}{3}+4$

(D) $\frac{2x}{3}+16$

(E) $\frac{4x}{3}+2$

18. Equilateral triangle *ABC* has a perpendicular line drawn from *A* to point *D*. If the triangle is "folded over" on the perpendicular line so that points *B* and *C* meet, the perimeter of the new triangle is approximately what percent of the perimeter of the triangle before the fold?

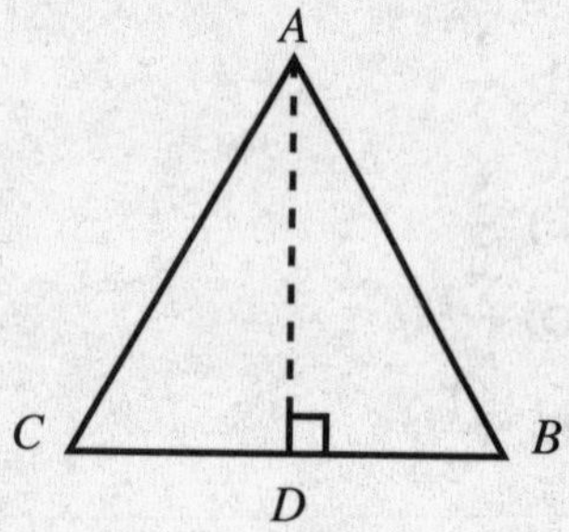

(A) 100%
(B) 78%
(C) 50%
(D) 32%
(E) It cannot be determined from the information given.

19. To find the radius of a circle whose circumference is 60 inches

(A) multiply 60 by π
(B) divide 60 by 2π
(C) divide 30 by 2π
(D) divide 60 by π and extract the square root of the result
(E) multiply 60 by $\frac{\pi}{2}$

20. If the outer diameter of a metal pipe is 2.84 inches and the inner diameter is 1.94 inches, the thickness of the metal in inches is

(A) .45
(B) .90
(C) 1.42
(D) 1.94
(E) 2.39

21.

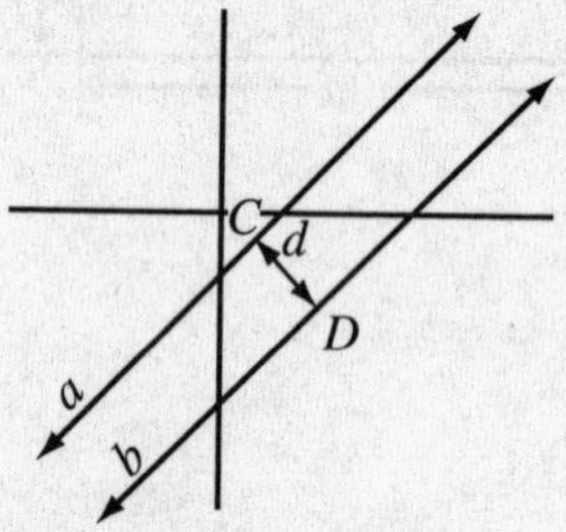

Line $a \| b$, while *d* is the distance between *a* and *b* at points *C* and *D*.

The length of segment *d*

(A) steadily increases as it is moved along lines *a* and *b* to the right
(B) steadily decreases as it is moved toward the left
(C) fluctuates in both directions
(D) remains constant
(E) none of the above

22. $(x + 9)(x + 2) =$

(A) $x^2 + 18$
(B) $11x$
(C) $x^2 + 11$
(D) $x^2 + 11x + 18$
(E) $9(x + 2)+2(x + 9)$

23. The points (3,1) and (5,*y*) are $\sqrt{13}$ units apart. What does *y* equal?

(A) –3
(B) 4
(C) $\sqrt{17}$
(D) 10
(E) 17

24. In a baseball game, a pitcher needs to throw nine strikes to complete an inning. If a pitcher is able to throw strikes on 85% of his pitches, how many pitches to the nearest whole number would it take for him to throw the necessary number of strikes for a nine-inning game?

(A) 95
(B) 97
(C) 103
(D) 105
(E) 111

25. Corner *AFE* is cut from the rectangle as shown in the figure below. The area of the remaining polygon *ABCDE* in square inches is

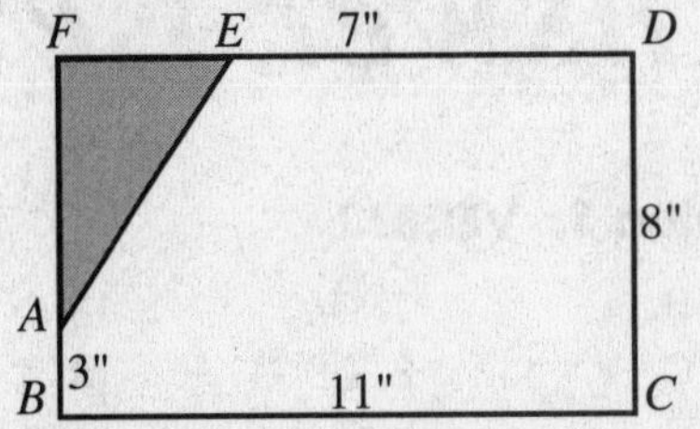

Note: Figure not drawn to scale.

(A) 29
(B) 68
(C) 78
(D) 88
(E) 98

STOP

END OF SECTION 6. IF YOU HAVE ANY TIME LEFT, GO OVER YOUR WORK IN THIS SECTION ONLY. DO NOT WORK IN ANY OTHER SECTION OF THE TEST.

Practice Examination 5

Answer Key

Section 1: VERBAL

1. B	7. D	13. D	19. D	25. B
2. C	8. C	14. A	20. D	26. C
3. E	9. C	15. B	21. B	27. C
4. D	10. A	16. D	22. D	28. E
5. B	11. E	17. C	23. C	29. A
6. C	12. C	18. C	24. C	30. B

Section 2: MATH

Part 1

1. A	4. D	7. D	10. B	13. B
2. D	5. A	8. B	11. B	14. C
3. B	6. C	9. C	12. B	15. A

Part 2

16. 5	18. $1.5 = \frac{3}{2}$	20. 10	22. 1800	24. 72
17. 10	19. 0	21. 80	23. 15	25. 50

Section 3: VERBAL

1. E	3. D	5. C	7. B	9. D
2. A	4. B	6. E	8. B	10. E

Section 4: MATH

1. D	3. D	5. D	7. D	9. B
2. E	4. C	6. D	8. D	10. A

Section 5: VERBAL

1. B	8. C	15. D	22. D	29. B
2. D	9. A	16. A	23. C	30. B
3. B	10. C	17. E	24. E	31. D
4. D	11. C	18. C	25. E	32. A
5. C	12. B	19. B	26. D	33. A
6. C	13. B	20. C	27. B	34. E
7. E	14. E	21. A	28. C	35. E

Section 6: MATH

1. C	6. E	11. A	16. A	21. D
2. D	7. D	12. B	17. B	22. D
3. B	8. E	13. D	18. B	23. B
4. C	9. B	14. C	19. B	24. A
5. B	10. B	15. B	20. A	25. C

Practice Examination 5

Explanatory Answers

Note: A 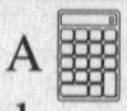 following a math answer explanation indicates that a calculator could be helpful in solving that particular problem.

Section 1

1. **(B)** If the director *applauds* her employees' activities, she is not likely to *question* their methods.

2. **(C)** An *unwilling* soldier would *recoil* at the idea of going to battle.

3. **(E)** The *inhumane* treatment of the zoo animals would result in *criticism.*

4. **(D)** Paper money is merely a representation of wealth; therefore, unlike gold, it has no *intrinsic* (inherent) value.

5. **(B)** The fever could be *degenerative, debilitating, raging,* or *pernicious.* However, only *ascribed* (attributed) makes sense in the second blank.

6. **(C)** A *microscope* is an *instrument,* and a *necktie* is an *accessory.*

7. **(D)** A *sketch* precedes a finished *painting* as a *draft* precedes a finished *thesis.*

8. **(C)** A *plane* arrives at and departs from an assigned *gate,* just as a *train* arrives at and departs from an assigned *track.*

9. **(C)** One *swears* an *oath* and *signs* a *contract.* Both actions show commitment.

10. **(A)** A *spelunker* is a person who explores a *cave.* An *astronaut* is one who explores *space.*

11. **(E)** *Laughter* is a sign of *amusement; pallor* is a sign of *illness.*

12. **(C)** A *physician cures* and a *comedian entertains.*

13. **(D)** Plays and symphonies are performed. A *movement* is a part of a *symphony,* and an *act* is part of a *play.*

14. **(A)** The second sentence of the passage states: "I stand before you tonight under indictment for the alleged crime . . ." A defendant on trial would be under indictment for a supposed crime.

15. **(B)** The fourth paragraph discusses how ". . . not we, the white male citizens; but we, the whole people . . . formed the Union" to secure the blessings of liberty ". . . to the whole people—women as well as men."

16. **(D)** Quoting the preamble of the Constitution adds weight to her argument that all citizens, not merely white, male citizens, should have the right to vote.

17. **(C)** Lines 18–21 state: ". . . we, the whole people, who formed the Union . . . not to give the blessings of liberty, but to secure them . . . to the whole people. . . ."

18. **(C)** Lines 31–34 state: "To them this government has no just powers derived from the consent of the governed. . . . It is a hateful oligarchy of sex."

19. **(D)** Lines 39–41 describe an oligarchy of sex as a government where "all men [are] sovereigns [and] all women subjects, [inciting] dissension, discord and rebellion [in] every home."

20. **(D)** Lines 42–43 present the definition of a citizen ". . . as a person in the United States, entitled to vote and hold office."

21. **(B)** The last sentence of the passage states that ". . . every discrimination against women in the constitutions and laws of the several States is today null and void."

22. **(D)** *Counsel* means "advice," and in this case the father is advising his son against going to sea.

23. **(C)** The father is apprehensive about his son's leaving because the father really believes that only destitute people or very wealthy people go to sea.

24. **(C)** The father believes that in the middle state one is exposed neither to the miseries and hardships of the poor nor to the envy and pride of the rich.

25. **(B)** *Desperate fortunes* implies financial trouble, and *superior fortunes* belong to people who have great money and can do what they want.

26. **(C)** The best answer is found in the statement that the rich bring the distempers (distress) upon themselves by their very way of living (lines 41–43).

27. **(C)** The words "application and industry" in paragraph 1 imply learning skills and working hard. This, in the father's opinion, keeps one in the middle state with all its advantages.

28. **(E)** All suggestions of the son's state of mind in this passage indicate that he probably will soon be on his way to the sea.

29. **(A)** When Robinson says he could never settle with resolution, he means that he can't settle down to work until he has had a chance at the sea.

30. **(B)** The father admires people who apply themselves industriously to their work and would likely approve of Robinson's apprenticing himself to an attorney.

Section 2

Part 1

1. **(A)** For any real numbers s and t, as long as $s > t$, the difference of the smaller from the larger, $s - t$, will always be greater than the larger from the smaller, $t - s$.

2. **(D)** There is no way to determine the cost of the total system or the speakers; therefore, there is no way to determine the discounted price.

3. **(B)** If $p > 0$ and $q < 0$, then $p - q$ is equivalent to $p + |q|$ and $p + q$ is equivalent to $p - |q|$. Since Column B is adding rather than subtracting, Column B is larger.

4. **(D)** Since we know nothing about the placement of A, B, and C, we cannot determine anything about their distances.

5. **(A)** The value of Column A is found by computing $\frac{63}{.07}$, which equals 900. The value of Column B is $(.07)(63) = 4.41$. Hence, Column A is larger.

6. **(C)** Substituting $\frac{1}{2}$ for r in Column A, $2r^3 - 12r + 7 = 2\left(\frac{1}{2}\right)^3 - 12\left(\frac{1}{2}\right) + 7 = 1\frac{1}{4}$. Doing the same in Column B, $r^2 + 1 = \left(\frac{1}{2}\right)^2 + 1 = 1\frac{1}{4}$. The columns are equal.

7. **(D)** We cannot judge which is the larger since if $-1 < x < 1, \frac{1}{x^2} > x^2$, but if $x > 1$ or $x < -1$, $x^2 > \frac{1}{x^2}$.

8. **(B)** Solving the two equations: first, $m^3 = 64, m = \sqrt[3]{64} = 4$, and second, $\sqrt{n} = 16$, $n = (16)^2 = 256$. Therefore, $n > m$, making Column B greater than Column A.

9. **(C)** Since the measures of angles x, y, and z are equivalent, the triangle is an equilateral triangle with all sides equal. Therefore, $s = t$.

10. **(B)** In Column A, the area of the rectangle is $4 \times \pi = 4\pi$. In Column B, the area of the circle is $\pi(4)^2 = 16\pi$. Therefore, the area of the circle is larger, and Column B is the correct choice.

11. **(B)** The surface area of the whole cube is $6(3)^2 = 54$. The new boxes formed by cutting the cube in half have the same surface area as the cube as a whole, but have added surface area on each cube where the cut was made. This is an addition of $3^2 = 9$ for each cube, making the total surface area $54 + 9 + 9 = 72$. Column B is the larger.

12. **(B)** Since r is a negative number, r^5 will also be a negative number. s^4 is always positive and, consequently, larger than r^5.

13. **(B)** If $x^2 = 25, x = \pm 5$. If $2y + 3 = 27, 2y = 24$, so $y = 12$. y is larger whether x is +5 or –5.

14. **(C)** Triangle *ABC* is isosceles with sides *AB* and *AC* equal; therefore, angles *ABC* and *ACB* are equal. Angles *x* and *y* are supplementary angles of angles *ABC* and *ACB*, respectively, and thus must be equal to each other.

15. **(A)** The angles of all triangles add up to 180°. Angle $MNO = 90°$; therefore, the sum of angles *M* and *Q* must also equal 90°. Column A is larger than Column B.

Part 2

16. 5

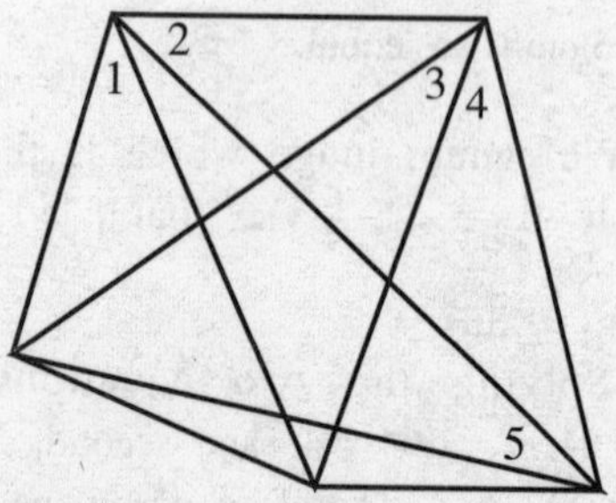

17. $4x = 2(2 + x)$ $\qquad$ $6y = 3(2 + y)$

$4x = 4 + 2x$ $\qquad$ $6y = 6 + 3y$

$2x = 4$ $\qquad$ $3y = 6$

$2x + 3y = 4 + 6 = 10$

18. "JOSH" $= 3n - 3$

$n = 3n - 3$

$-2n = -3$

$n = \frac{3}{2} = 1.5$

19. Machine A produces:

2,000 flue covers/hour

Machine B produces:

$$5{,}000 / \frac{5}{2}\text{ hr.} = 5{,}000\left(\frac{2}{5}\right) = 2{,}000 / \text{hr.}$$

Since the rates are the same, they produce the same amount of flue covers during any period of time.

20. $.01 = \frac{.1}{x}$

$$\frac{1}{100} = \frac{\frac{1}{10}}{x} = \frac{1}{10} \bullet \frac{1}{x} = \frac{1}{10x}$$

$$\frac{1}{100} = \frac{1}{10x}$$

$$10x = 100$$

$$x = 10$$

21.

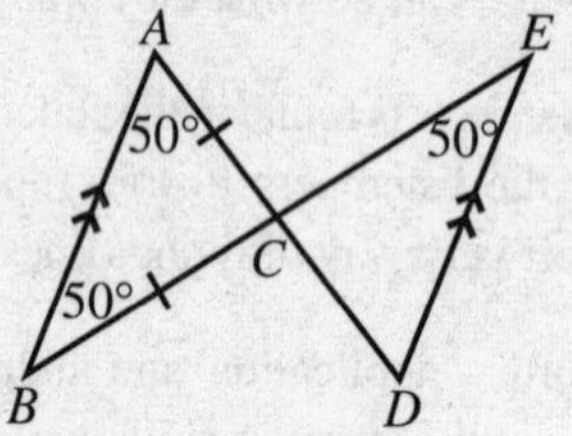

Since $ED \parallel AB$

angle E = angle $B = 50°$

(alternate interior angles)

Since $AC = BC$, angle A = angle $B = 50°$.

(In a triangle opposite equal sides are equal angles.)

In ΔABC

$$50 + 50 + x = 180$$

$$x = 80$$

22. Let p = the school's population

$$\frac{1}{4}p + \frac{1}{5}p + \frac{1}{3}p + 390 = p$$

$$\frac{15p + 12p + 20p}{60} + 390 = p$$

$$60\left(\frac{47p}{60} + 390\right) = p$$

$$47p + 390(60) = 60p$$

$$13p = 390(60)$$

$$p = \frac{\overset{30}{\cancel{390}}(60)}{\cancel{13}} = 30(60) = 1800$$

23.

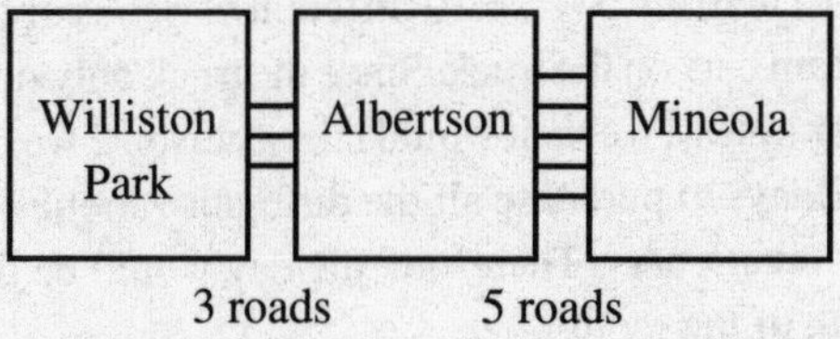

There are $3 \times 5 = 15$ different paths from Williston Park to Mineola through Albertson.

24. Establish a ratio of candies to cents.
Note: \$1.70 = 170 cents and \$10.20 = 1020 cents.

$$\frac{\text{candies}}{\text{cents}} : \frac{12}{170} = \frac{x}{1020}$$

$$170x = 12(1020)$$
$$x = 72$$

25.

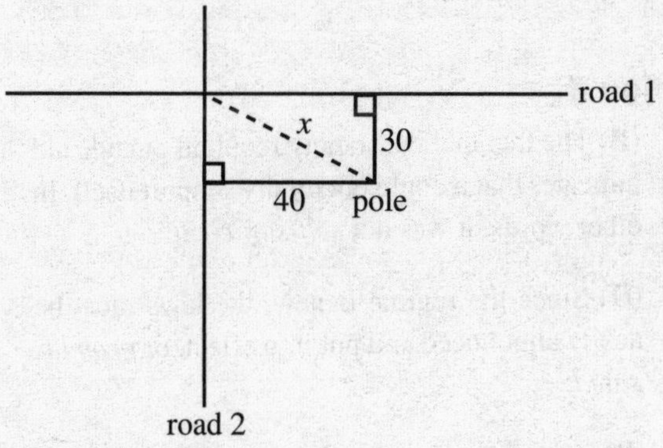

Using the Pythagorean Theorem:

$$(30)^2 + (40)^2 = x^2$$
$$900 + 1{,}600 = x^2$$
$$2{,}500 = x^2$$
$$x = 50$$

Section 3

1. **(E)** Stowe says as much in lines 5–7 and in paragraph 2.

2. **(A)** The book will "contain facts and documents" (line 23), so it will not be fictional (B). It will "contain, perhaps, an equal amount of matter" as the previous book (lines 21–22); in other words, it may be as long.

3. **(D)** Rereading this paragraph and the one before proves that Stowe is referring to the horrors of slavery, which she thought she knew, but now finds she "had not begun to measure."

4. **(B)** "It seems to me that the book cannot but be felt. . . ." (lines 33–34). Stowe thinks that her readers will feel the pain she documents.

5. **(C)** Only this meaning of "abstract" works in context.

6. **(E)** Sand is juxtaposing the author ("you") with the reader ("him").

7. **(B)** Sand does not deny that evil occurs, but she insists that good must triumph. If the hero is butchered, he must end up happier than those who slay him.

8. **(B)** This is the main idea of the letter. Sand wants a writer to be warm and involved.

9. **(D)** Sand says as much; Stowe is clearly moved by her subject and hopes that her work will move her readers.

10. **(E)** This line from Sand's letter (lines 57–58) summarizes her theme. Stowe's discussion of her own sorrow's lending credence to her writing makes it appear that she would share this sentiment.

Section 4

1. **(D)** Since both areas are equal, $\frac{1}{2}bh = \pi r^2$. Thus, knowing the base of the triangle and radius of the circle, $\frac{1}{2}(7)h = \pi(7)^2$, so $h = 14\pi$.

2. **(E)** $70\% = \frac{70}{100} = \frac{7}{10}$. $\frac{1}{.70} = \frac{100}{70} = \frac{10}{7}$. $\frac{13}{9}$ and $\frac{1}{.70}$ are the only fractions larger than 1. Comparing them by finding a common denominator of 63, $\frac{10}{7} = \frac{90}{63}, \frac{13}{9} = \frac{91}{63}$, we find $\frac{10}{7} < \frac{13}{9}$. Comparing $\frac{9}{13}$ and $\frac{7}{10}$, which are both less than 1, we find $\frac{9}{13} = \frac{90}{130}, \frac{7}{10} = \frac{91}{130}$, so $\frac{9}{13} < \frac{7}{10}$. Therefore, $\frac{9}{13} < 70\% < \frac{1}{.70} < \frac{13}{9}$.

3. **(D)** The quadrilateral $PQRS$ is a parallelogram as shown:

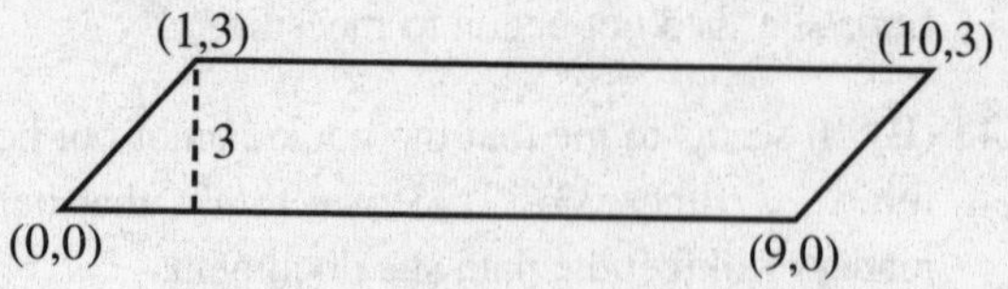

It has a height of 3 and a base of 9. The area is, like that of a rectangle, *bh*, or 27.

4. **(C)** One simple way to solve this problem is to divide each side of the given equation by 4.

$$\frac{8x+4}{4}=\frac{64}{4}$$
$$2x+1=16$$

5. **(D)** Since the center is at the origin, each coordinate point is the length of a leg of a triangle. The hypotenuse of each triangle is the radius of a new circle with its center at the origin. If the hypotenuse of the triangle is greater than 7, the points are outside the circle. (4,4):

$h=\sqrt{4^2+4^2}=5.7$, so (4,4) is inside the circle. (5,5): $h=\sqrt{5^2+5^2}=7.07$, so (5,5) is outside the circle. (4,5): $h=\sqrt{4^2+5^2}=6.4$, so (4,5) is inside the circle. (4,6): $h=\sqrt{4^2+6^2}=7.2$, so (4,6) is outside the circle.

6. **(D)** The surface area of a square with side = 9 is $9\cdot 9=81$. The surface area of a cube with edge = 3 is $3\cdot 3\cdot 6=9\cdot 6=54$ The difference, therefore, is $81-54=27$.

7. **(D)** $2+4+6=12$ and 12 is evenly divisible by all three.

8. **(D)**

$$\frac{3(x^2-4)}{(x+2)}=\frac{3(x+2)(x-2)}{(x+2)}$$
$$=3(x-2)$$
$$=3x-6$$

9. **(B)** There are $5\times 2=10$ different varieties of ice cream bars on the truck. Since the truck only runs four times a week, it would take a person 2 weeks + 2 days to purchase all the different varieties of ice cream bars. Therefore, the day would be the 16th of the month.

10. **(A)**

$$\frac{N!}{(N-2)}=$$
$$\frac{N(N-1)(N-2)(N-3)(N-4)\ldots[N-(N-1)]}{(N-2)(N-3)(N-4)\ldots[N-(N-1)]}$$

Cancelling like factors in the numerator and the denominator leaves only

$$\frac{N(N-1)}{1}=N(N-1)=N^2-N$$

Section 5

1. **(B)** The fact that the society required outside aid indicates that it could not totally support itself. In other words, it was not *self-sufficient*.

2. **(D)** Since the regime is new, the laws must be newly announced and put into effect, or *promulgated*.

3. **(B)** *Brittle* machines might *shatter*.

4. **(D)** When illness strikes, even a person with a strong constitution can be *enervated* (weakened and drained of energy).

5. **(C)** A careful researcher would be *meticulous*.

6. **(C)** A shy look might *enchant* someone into matrimony, but it would not *release*, *control*, *ensconce*, or *jilt* someone to that end.

7. **(E)** A city that has failed to fire a single shot against an invading army has clearly *capitulated* (surrendered).

8. **(C)** A *compromise* (agreement) between two opposing sides might avert a strike, but without one the strike becomes *inevitable* (unavoidable).

9. **(A)** A neighbor who is charming is also likely to be *urbane* (suave and sophisticated). Such a person would be the opposite, or *antithesis*, of a bumbling yokel.

10. **(C)** Peeling potatoes and scrubbing floors are both tasks that are *onerous* (burdensome and unpleasant).

11. **(C)** If the lawyer can cast doubt on the *probity* (honesty or integrity) of the witness, she can probably strengthen her client's case.

12. **(B)** A debate in which candidates fling accusations at each other is likely to be *acrimonious* (harsh or bitter).

13. **(B)** Because they result from *carelessness*, both blanks should be filled by negative words. Carelessness is likely to produce an *ambiguous* (vague or unclear) report, which may leave everyone *confused*.

14. **(E)** Only a *callous* or insensitive person could be *oblivious* to, or unmindful of, the suffering of a starving child.

15. **(D)** A *pendulum* is designed to *oscillate* and a *gyroscope* to *spin*.

16. **(A)** The first showing of a *movie* is its *premiere* and the first showing of a *statue* is its *unveiling*.

17. **(E)** An *awl* is a pointed tool used by a *carpenter* to make holes in wood. A *pick* is a pointed tool used by a *miner* to break up soil or rock.

18. **(C)** The degree of incline of a *roof* is its *pitch*. The degree of incline of a *mountain* is its *grade*.

19. **(B)** A *cog* is a moving part of a *watch* as a *piston* is a moving part of an *engine*.

20. **(C)** An *equestrian* rides a *horse*; a *cyclist* rides a *bicycle*.

21. **(A)** A *recluse* is *solitary*, preferring to be without company. A *socialite* is *gregarious*, or fond of company.

22. **(D)** *Diffuse* means lacking *concentration*. Similarly, *incongruous* means lacking *harmony*.

23. **(C)** An *apple* is a kind of *fruit* and a *sparrow* is a kind of *bird*.

24. **(E)** A *decade* is *ten* years just as a *millennium* is a *thousand* years.

25. **(E)** A *zealot* (ardent supporter of a cause) is characterized by *fervor* (passion) as a *sage* (wise man) is characterized by *wisdom*.

26. **(D)** Chekhov is praising the play. He is presumably familiar with Gorky's style, and thus compares this play to previous plays with this compliment.

27. **(B)** Red hair on a red-haired man cannot be corrected; it is a natural "flaw." Chekhov means that the "defect" in the play is natural and cannot be repaired.

28. **(C)** The play's only defect, according to Chekhov, is "the conservatism of the form" (lines 9–10), which undermines Gorky's new and original characters.

29. **(B)** Chekhov seems concerned throughout with realism. This answer is the only one that makes sense in context.

30. **(B)** As stated in lines 32–33, Nil's modesty is "the element so characteristic of our decent working man."

31. **(D)** Lines 32–33 reveal Chekhov's concern.

32. **(A)** Chekhov is concerned that Elena "is not clear" (lines 52–53); his suggestions attempt to correct that.

33. **(A)** "Both on life and on the stage," Chekhov considers characters such as Teterev unimportant. For this reason, he suggests that Teterev talk less.

34. **(E)** (A) is covered in lines 22–23, (B) in lines 24–26, (C) in lines 39–41, and (D) in lines 47–50. Chekhov has ideas about the ending of the play, which has four acts, but never discusses the ending of the third act.

35. **(E)** Chekhov comments that Piotr "is good. Most likely you don't even suspect how good he is." His only suggestion is that Piotr should be played by the actor Meierkhold.

Section 6

1. **(C)** $3x + 2 > 2x + 7$
$x + 2 > 7$
$x > 5$

2. **(D)** By long division:

$$\begin{array}{r} 2x-3 \\ 3x-2\overline{)6x^2-13x+6} \\ \underline{6x^2-4x} \\ -9x+6 \\ \underline{-9x+6} \\ 0 \end{array}$$

3. **(B)** It can easily be seen that $AB = 3$ and $BC = 4$. By the Pythagorean theorem, $(3)^2 + (4)^2 = (AC)^2$ and $AC = 5$. Also, the distance formula can be used.

$$d = \sqrt{(x - x_1)^2 + (y - y_1)^2}$$
$$= \sqrt{(5-1)^2 + (4-1)^2}$$
$$= \sqrt{(4)^2 + (3)^2} = \sqrt{25} = 5.$$

4. **(C)** $\frac{8!}{9!} = \frac{8\times7\times6\times5\times4\times3\times2\times1}{9\times8\times7\times6\times5\times4\times3\times2\times1}$

Cancelling like terms in the numerator and denominator leaves $\frac{1}{9}$.

5. **(B)** There was an error of 150 ft. – 140 ft. = 10 ft. The percent of error is the error divided by the actual distance, 10 ft. ÷ 140 ft. = .0714 × 100% or about $7\frac{1}{7}$%.

6. **(E)** The first child leaves $\frac{3}{4}$ of the cookies. The second child eats $\frac{1}{3}$ of $\frac{3}{4}$ and that leaves $\frac{1}{2}$. If the $\frac{1}{2}$ is divided among four children, then $\frac{1}{2}$ divided by 4 is $\frac{1}{8}$.

7. **(D)** $|2y - 4| = 6$ means that $2y - 4 = 6$ or $2y - 4 = -6$ Solving the first equation, $y = \frac{10}{2} = 5$, and solving the second equation gives y a value of –1. Therefore, y = both 5 and/or –1

8. **(E)** To solve this system of equations for y, the top equation must be multiplied by 2.

$$3x + 2y = 4 \rightarrow 6x + 4y = 8$$
$$6x - 3y = 6 \rightarrow 6x - 3y = 6$$

Subtracting the two equations on the right gives $7y = 2$. Therefore, $y = \frac{2}{7}$.

9. **(B)** If the radius r of a circle is diminished by 20%, the new radius is $r - .20r$. The new area is $\pi(r - .20r)^2 = \pi(.64r^2)$. The new area is 64% of the old area. Thus, the area was diminished by 100% – 64% = 36%.

10. **(B)** $x^2 - y^2 = (x+y)(x-y) = 10 \times 20 = 200$.

11. **(A)** The area of the rectangle is $(2a) \times a = 2a^2$. The area of a semicircle is $\frac{1}{2}$ the area of a circle. The radius of the semicircle is $\frac{1}{2}(2a) = a$; therefore, the area is $\frac{\pi a^2}{2}$. Add the areas of the rectangle and semicircle to get the total area, $2a^2 + \frac{\pi a^2}{2}$.

12. **(B)** In one second the plane flies about 550 yds. ÷ 3 sec. = 183 yd./sec. There are 3,600 seconds in one hour, so the plane flies 183 yd./sec. × 3,600 sec./hr. = 658,800 yd./hr. There are 1,760 yards in one mile, so the plane flies 658,800 yd./hr. ÷ 1,760 yd./mi. ≈ 375 mi./hr.

13. **(D)** One meter equals approximately 1.10 yards. 100 meters is 100 m. × 1.10 yds. per m. = 110 yards.

14. **(C)** The least common denominator of all the fractions is 1,320. Changing each fraction to have 1,320 as the denominator, we have

$$\frac{6}{11} = \frac{720}{1320}, \frac{7}{12} = \frac{770}{1320}, \frac{3}{5} = \frac{792}{1320}, \text{and } \frac{5}{8} = \frac{825}{1320}.$$

15. **(B)** The first pipe can fill the tank in $1\frac{1}{2}$ or $\frac{3}{2}$ hours, or it can do $\frac{2}{3}$ the work in 1 hour. The second pipe can fill the tank in 45 minutes or $\frac{3}{4}$ hour, doing $\frac{4}{3}$ of the job in 1 hour. Thus, together the two pipes can do $\frac{4}{3} + \frac{2}{3} = \frac{6}{3}$ of the job in 1 hour. Therefore, the pipes working together could fill the entire tank in $\frac{1}{2}$ hour.

16. **(A)** There are 12 edges on a cube, so each edge is 48 in. $\div 12 = 4$ inches. The volume of the cube is $(s)^3 = (4\text{ in.})^3 = 64$ cu. in.

17. **(B)** Since the perimeter of a square is four times the length of a side, it is

$$4\left(\frac{2x}{3}+1\right), \text{ or } \frac{8x+12}{3}$$

18. **(B)** This is more easily solved by using real numbers. If we assign a value of 6 to AB, then we can figure out that the perpendicular AD is $3\sqrt{3}$. The old perimeter was 18 and the new perimeter is $6+3+3\sqrt{3}$, or about 14.1. The fraction $\frac{14}{18}$ can be reduced to $\frac{7}{9}$, which is about 78%.

19. **(B)** If the circumference is 60 inches, since $C = 2\pi r$, substitute $C = 60$; therefore, $r = \frac{60}{2\pi}$.

20. **(A)** The radii of the pipe are 1.42 in. and 0.97 in. The thickness is their difference, or .45 in.

21. **(D)** By definition, parallel lines are everywhere equidistant. Therefore, the length of segment d remains constant.

22. **(D)** By using the foil method, $(x+9)(x+2)$ $= x^2 + 9x + 2x + 18$

By combining like terms, this is shortened to: $x^2 + 11x + 18$.

23. **(B)** If the points (3,1) and (5,y) are $\sqrt{13}$ units apart, then by the distance formula, $\sqrt{13} = \sqrt{(5-3)^2 + (y-1)^2}$.

Solving for y: $13 = (2)^2 + (y-1)^2$
$9 = (y-1)^2$
$y = 4$

24. **(A)** The total number of strikes that a pitcher must throw in a game is 9×9, or 81. Since only 85% of his pitches are strikes, he must throw 81/.85, or 95, pitches a game.

25. **(C)** The area of the rectangle is length $\times$ width = 11" $\times$ 8" = 88 sq. in. The area of the triangle is $\frac{1}{2}$ (base) $\times$ (height). Its base is 8" – 3" = 5"; its height is 11" –7" = 4". The area of the triangle is $\frac{1}{2} \times 5'' \times 4'' = 10$ sq. in. The area of the polygon is 88 – 10 = 78 sq. in.

Evaluating Practice Examination 5

To determine your Verbal Reasoning Score:

1. Using the Analysis Worksheet, enter the number of correct answers for each verbal reasoning section on the appropriate line in Column A of the Verbal Reasoning grid.
2. Enter the number of incorrect answers for each verbal reasoning section on the appropriate line in Column B of the Verbal Reasoning grid.
3. Total Columns A and B and enter these totals in boxes A and B, respectively.
4. Perform the indicated calculation to find your Raw Score: (value in box A) minus (one-quarter of the value in box B) = Raw Score.
5. Consult the Conversion Chart to find your approximate Scaled Score.

To determine your Mathematical Reasoning Score:

1. Enter the number of correct answers for each mathematical reasoning section on the appropriate line in column C of the Mathematical Reasoning grid.
2. Enter the number of incorrect answers for each mathematical reasoning section on the appropriate line in Column D, E, or F of the Mathematical Reasoning grid.
3. Total Columns C, D, and E, and enter these totals in boxes C, D, and E, respectively.
4. Perform the indicated calculation to find your Raw Score: (value in box C) minus (one-quarter of the value in box D) minus (one-third of the value in box E) = Raw Score.
5. Consult the Conversion Chart to find your approximate Scaled Score.

Note: Box F is not used in this calculation.

Analysis Worksheet

VERBAL REASONING

Section	Number of Questions	Column A Number of Correct Answers	Column B Number of Incorrect Answers
1	30		
3	10		
5	35		
	Total	A	B

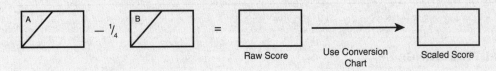

A − 1/4 B = [Raw Score] → Use Conversion Chart → [Scaled Score]

Raw Score — Use Conversion Chart — Scaled Score

MATHEMATICAL REASONING

Section	Number of Questions	Column C Number of Correct Answers	Col. D Number of Incorrect Answers	Col. E	Col. F
4	10				
6	25				
2 Part 1	15				
2 Part 2	10				
	Total	C	D	E	F

C − 1/4 D − 1/3 E = [Raw Score] → Use Conversion Chart → [Scaled Score]

Raw Score — Use Conversion Chart — Scaled Score

Conversion Scales for Practice Examination 5

VERBAL REASONING:

Raw Score	Scaled Score	Raw Score	Scaled Score
75	800	40	550
70	800	35	520
65	760	30	480
60	710	25	440
55	670	20	410
50	620	15	370
45	590	10	340
		5	290
		0	230

MATHEMATICAL REASONING:

Raw Score	Scaled Score	Raw Score	Scaled Score
60	800	25	510
55	760	20	480
50	690	15	440
45	650	10	410
40	610	5	340
35	580	0	200
30	550		

Although you now have some idea of what your scores would like had they been scaled according to unofficial ETS standards, you will probably want to know how to interpret your Raw Scores in more familiar terms. If so, use the following Self-Evaluation Charts to see what your Raw Scores actually mean.

SELF-EVALUATION CHARTS

VERBAL REASONING: RAW SCORE

Excellent	60 – 75
Good	50 – 60
Average	30 – 50
Fair	20 – 30
Poor	0 – 20

MATHEMATICAL REASONING: RAW SCORE

Excellent	50 – 60
Good	40 – 50
Average	20 – 40
Fair	10 – 20
Poor	0 – 10

TEAR HERE

Practice Examination 6

Answer Sheet

If a section has fewer questions than answer ovals, leave the extra ovals blank.

Section 1

1 Ⓐ Ⓑ Ⓒ Ⓓ Ⓔ	6 Ⓐ Ⓑ Ⓒ Ⓓ Ⓔ	11 Ⓐ Ⓑ Ⓒ Ⓓ Ⓔ
2 Ⓐ Ⓑ Ⓒ Ⓓ Ⓔ	7 Ⓐ Ⓑ Ⓒ Ⓓ Ⓔ	12 Ⓐ Ⓑ Ⓒ Ⓓ Ⓔ
3 Ⓐ Ⓑ Ⓒ Ⓓ Ⓔ	8 Ⓐ Ⓑ Ⓒ Ⓓ Ⓔ	13 Ⓐ Ⓑ Ⓒ Ⓓ Ⓔ
4 Ⓐ Ⓑ Ⓒ Ⓓ Ⓔ	9 Ⓐ Ⓑ Ⓒ Ⓓ Ⓔ	14 Ⓐ Ⓑ Ⓒ Ⓓ Ⓔ
5 Ⓐ Ⓑ Ⓒ Ⓓ Ⓔ	10 Ⓐ Ⓑ Ⓒ Ⓓ Ⓔ	15 Ⓐ Ⓑ Ⓒ Ⓓ Ⓔ

Note: ONLY the answers entered on the grid are scored.
Handwritten answers at the top of the column are NOT scored.

16 17 18 19 20

21 22 23 24 25

Section 2

1 A B C D E	11 A B C D E	21 A B C D E	31 A B C D E
2 A B C D E	12 A B C D E	22 A B C D E	32 A B C D E
3 A B C D E	13 A B C D E	23 A B C D E	33 A B C D E
4 A B C D E	14 A B C D E	24 A B C D E	34 A B C D E
5 A B C D E	15 A B C D E	25 A B C D E	35 A B C D E
6 A B C D E	16 A B C D E	26 A B C D E	36 A B C D E
7 A B C D E	17 A B C D E	27 A B C D E	37 A B C D E
8 A B C D E	18 A B C D E	28 A B C D E	38 A B C D E
9 A B C D E	19 A B C D E	29 A B C D E	39 A B C D E
10 A B C D E	20 A B C D E	30 A B C D E	40 A B C D E

Section 3

1 A B C D E	6 A B C D E	11 A B C D E	16 A B C D E
2 A B C D E	7 A B C D E	12 A B C D E	17 A B C D E
3 A B C D E	8 A B C D E	13 A B C D E	18 A B C D E
4 A B C D E	9 A B C D E	14 A B C D E	19 A B C D E
5 A B C D E	10 A B C D E	15 A B C D E	20 A B C D E

Section 4

1 A B C D E	6 A B C D E	11 A B C D E	16 A B C D E
2 A B C D E	7 A B C D E	12 A B C D E	17 A B C D E
3 A B C D E	8 A B C D E	13 A B C D E	18 A B C D E
4 A B C D E	9 A B C D E	14 A B C D E	19 A B C D E
5 A B C D E	10 A B C D E	15 A B C D E	20 A B C D E

Section 5

1 A B C D E	11 A B C D E	21 A B C D E	31 A B C D E
2 A B C D E	12 A B C D E	22 A B C D E	32 A B C D E
3 A B C D E	13 A B C D E	23 A B C D E	33 A B C D E
4 A B C D E	14 A B C D E	24 A B C D E	34 A B C D E
5 A B C D E	15 A B C D E	25 A B C D E	35 A B C D E
6 A B C D E	16 A B C D E	26 A B C D E	36 A B C D E
7 A B C D E	17 A B C D E	27 A B C D E	37 A B C D E
8 A B C D E	18 A B C D E	28 A B C D E	38 A B C D E
9 A B C D E	19 A B C D E	29 A B C D E	39 A B C D E
10 A B C D E	20 A B C D E	30 A B C D E	40 A B C D E

Section 6

1 A B C D E	11 A B C D E	21 A B C D E	31 A B C D E
2 A B C D E	12 A B C D E	22 A B C D E	32 A B C D E
3 A B C D E	13 A B C D E	23 A B C D E	33 A B C D E
4 A B C D E	14 A B C D E	24 A B C D E	34 A B C D E
5 A B C D E	15 A B C D E	25 A B C D E	35 A B C D E
6 A B C D E	16 A B C D E	26 A B C D E	36 A B C D E
7 A B C D E	17 A B C D E	27 A B C D E	37 A B C D E
8 A B C D E	18 A B C D E	28 A B C D E	38 A B C D E
9 A B C D E	19 A B C D E	29 A B C D E	39 A B C D E
10 A B C D E	20 A B C D E	30 A B C D E	40 A B C D E

Practice Examination 6

SECTION 1

25 Questions • Time—30 minutes

Directions: Solve the following problems using any available space on the page for scratchwork. On your answer sheet fill in the choice which best corresponds to the correct answer.

Notes: The figures accompanying the problems are drawn as accurately as possible unless otherwise stated in specific problems. Again, unless otherwise stated, all figures lie in the same plane. All numbers used in these problems are real numbers. Calculators are permitted for this test.

Reference Information

Circle: Rectangle: Rectangular Solid: Cylinder: Triangle:

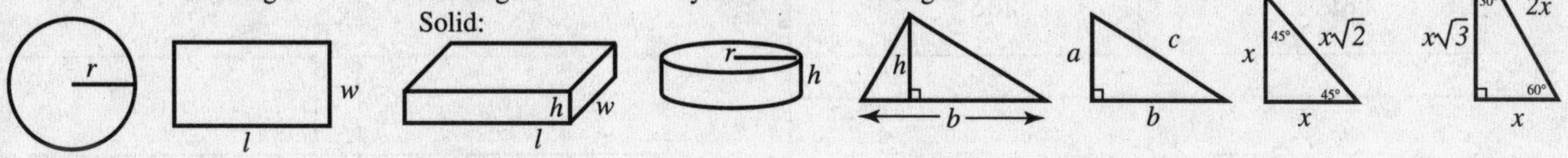

$C = 2\pi r$ $A = \pi r^2$ | $A = lw$ | $V = lwh$ | $V = \pi r^2 h$ | $A = \frac{1}{2}bh$ | $a^2 + b^2 = c^2$

The number of degrees of arc in a circle is 360.
The measure in degrees of a straight angle is 180.
The sum of the measures in degrees of the angles of a triangle is 180.

Part 1: Quantitative Comparison Questions

Directions: For each of the following questions, two quantities are given—one in Column A, the other in Column B. Compare the two and mark your answer sheet as follows:

(A) if the quantity in Column A is greater
(B) if the quantity in Column B is greater
(C) if the quantities are equal
(D) if the relationship cannot be determined from the information given

Notes:

(1) Information concerning one or both of the compared quantities will be centered above the two columns for some items.
(2) Symbols that appear in both columns represent the same thing in Column A as in Column B.
(3) Letters such as *x*, *n*, and *k* are symbols for real numbers.

Examples

	Column A	Column B	Answers
	$a > 0$, $x > 0$		
E1.	$a - x$	$a + x$	Ⓐ ● Ⓒ Ⓓ
E2.	The average of 17, 19, 21, 23	The average of 16, 18, 20, 22	● Ⓑ Ⓒ Ⓓ

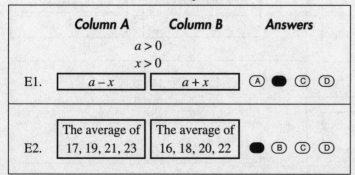

DO NOT MARK CHOICE (E) FOR THESE QUESTIONS. THERE ARE ONLY FOUR ANSWER CHOICES.

GO ON TO THE NEXT PAGE

	Column A	Column B
1.	The sum of all angles of a square	The sum of all angles of a polygon all of whose sides are equal

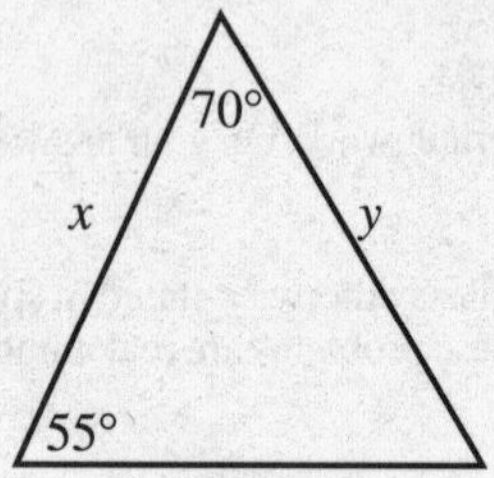

	Column A	Column B
2.	side x	side y

Given $\angle C = 60°$

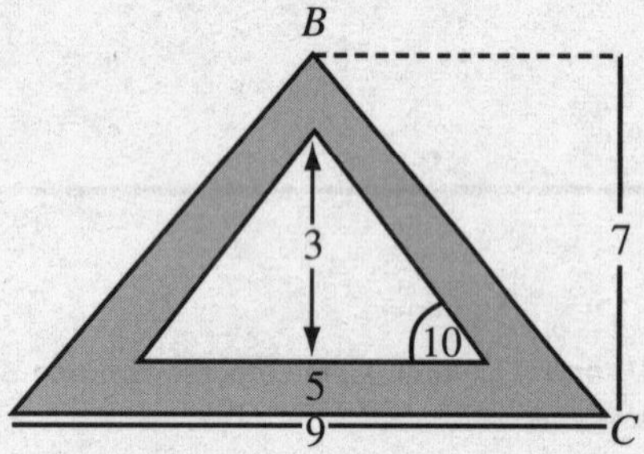

Note: Figure not drawn to scale.

	Column A	Column B
3.	The area of the smaller triangle	The shaded area

$x > 0$

	Column A	Column B
4.	$\frac{1}{x}$	x
5.	$(a+3)(a-4)$	$a^2 - 7a + 12$

	Column A	Column B
6.	Circumference of circle with radius $2r$	Perimeter of square with side πr
7.	$\sqrt{\frac{1}{3} \times \frac{1}{6}}$	$\sqrt{\frac{1}{3} + \frac{1}{6}}$

Questions 8–9 refer to the following definition.

$$\boxed{x} = (x-1)^2 + x$$

	Column A	Column B
8.	-2	2
9.	0	1
10.	$(a+b)(c+d)$	$(d+c)(b+a)$
11.	42% of 165	The number that 80 is 20% of

12. There are eight separate cubes each of which has a side of 1. The eight cubes can be stuck together to make one big cube.

Column A	Column B
Surface area of one small cube	$\frac{\text{Surface area of the big cube}}{8}$

$M > 0$
$N < 0$

	Column A	Column B
13.	MN	$\frac{-M}{N}$

	Column A	Column B

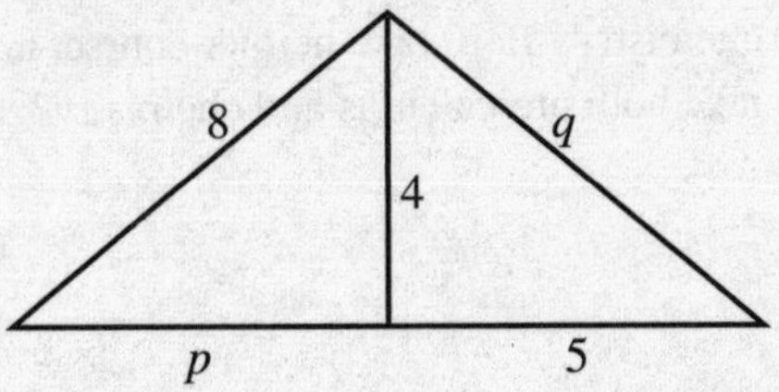

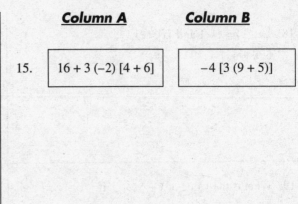

	Column A	Column B
14.	p	q
15.	$16 + 3(-2)[4 + 6]$	$-4[3(9 + 5)]$

Part 2: Student-Produced Response Questions

Directions: Solve each of these problems. Write the answer in the corresponding grid on the answer sheet and fill in the ovals beneath each answer you write. Here are some examples.

Answer: $\frac{3}{4}$ (= .75; show answer either way)

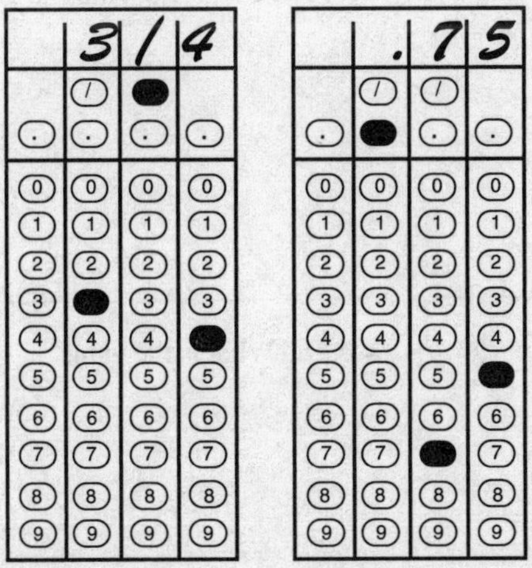

Note: A mixed number such as $3\frac{1}{2}$ must be gridded as 7/2 or as 3.5. If gridded as "31/2," it will be read as "thirty-one halves."

Answer: 325

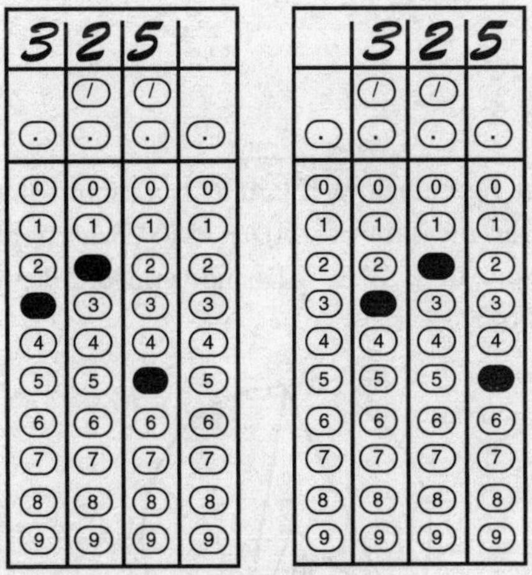

Note: Either position is correct.

16. Two adjacent sides of a rectangle measure 4 and 7. What is the perimeter of the rectangle?

17. Based on the table below, what is the median for the set of data?

Measure	Frequency
70	4
85	3
90	2
95	1

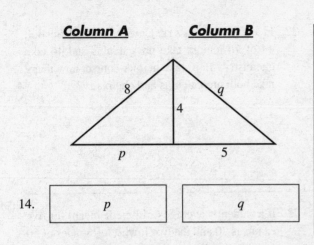

GO ON TO THE NEXT PAGE

18. Let $\textcircled{x} = x - 1$ and $\boxed{x} = 2x$.
$\textcircled{-1} + \boxed{1} =$

19. What is the value of $x + y^2 - z$, if $x = y = z = -1$?

20. The expression $\dfrac{6}{\frac{1}{2} + \frac{1}{3}} =$

21. In the figure below, if $\angle AOC$ is a central angle and the measure of $\angle AOC = 70°$, what is the measure of $\angle ABC$? (Do not grid the degree symbol.)

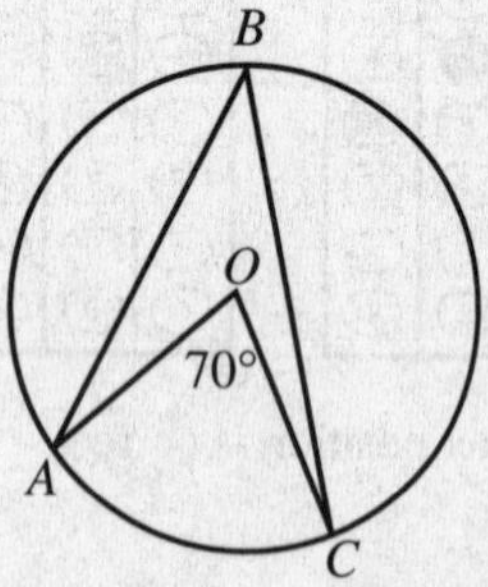

22. In the junior class at Dawnville High School, 44 of 70 juniors take pre-calculus and 46 take chemistry. If 10 take neither course, how many take both pre-calculus and chemistry?

23. If a student's average (arithmetic mean) for five exams is 70 and the two lowest test grades of 50 and 30 are disregarded, what is the student's average for the remaining exams?

24. If $3a + 5b = 10$, and $a - b = 6$, find the value of $7a + 7b$.

25. $a - b = b - c = c - a$. What is the value of $\frac{2a + 3b}{c}$?

STOP

END OF SECTION 1. IF YOU HAVE ANY TIME LEFT, GO OVER YOUR WORK IN THIS SECTION ONLY. DO NOT WORK IN ANY OTHER SECTION OF THE TEST.

SECTION 2

35 Questions • Time—30 Minutes

Directions: Each of the following questions consists of an incomplete sentence followed by five words or pairs of words. Choose that word or pair of words which, when substituted for the blank space or spaces, *best* completes the meaning of the sentence and mark the letter of your choice on your answer sheet.

Example:

In view of the extenuating circumstances and the defendant's youth, the judge recommended ----.

(A) conviction (B) a defense
(C) a mistrial (D) leniency
(E) life imprisonment Ⓐ Ⓑ Ⓒ ● Ⓔ

1. His ---- record collection included everything from Bach to rock.

(A) divisive
(B) effusive
(C) eclectic
(D) intrinsic
(E) laconic

2. The objective may be ----, but the plan presented for achieving it is far from practicable.

(A) compensatory
(B) laudable
(C) insignificant
(D) precarious
(E) subversive

3. Her statements were so ---- that we were left in doubt as to her real intentions.

(A) equitable
(B) equivocal
(C) innocuous
(D) dogmatic
(E) incisive

4. The Senator was under investigation because of accusations that he had filed ---- financial disclosure forms.

(A) veritable
(B) replicated
(C) extraneous
(D) duplicitous
(E) muddled

5. The retiring teacher was ---- for his tireless efforts on behalf of his students.

(A) paraphrased
(B) involved
(C) appointed
(D) commended
(E) directed

6. That particular economist ---- that government regulation ---- leads to higher prices.

(A) teaches..unavailably
(B) knows..insistently
(C) feels..dubiously
(D) sees..blindly
(E) believes..inevitably

7. The teenagers were such ---- followers of the daytime soap opera that they taped every episode.

(A) dexterous
(B) flagrant
(C) assiduous
(D) retentive
(E) adroit

GO ON TO THE NEXT PAGE

8. Scheherazade ---- by spinning tales for the Sultan, thus postponing her execution for a thousand and one nights.

(A) eradicated
(B) temporized
(C) truncated
(D) acclimated
(E) transgressed

9. The supervisor prided herself on her ----, convinced that it was more important to be fair than to be liked by everyone.

(A) cheerfulness
(B) reticence
(C) objectivity
(D) superiority
(E) congeniality

10. That field has become so ---- that researchers on different aspects of the same problem may be ______ each other's work.

(A) secure..bombarded with
(B) partial..surprised at
(C) departmental..inimical to
(D) specialized..unfamiliar with
(E) secretive..knowledgeable of

11. People do not exist in ----, but in functioning ---- which are inseparable from the environment.

(A) isolation..communities
(B) deliberation..actions
(C) prosperity..liberties
(D) houses..homes
(E) destitution..realizations

12. Each political party has traditionally viewed the Constitution in light of its own ---- of government.

(A) denial
(B) deception
(C) philosophy
(D) feeling
(E) reception

13. It takes great ---- to leave a country and ---- a new life in a foreign land.

(A) demands..forget
(B) mandates..regret
(C) courage..establish
(D) conviction..designate
(E) ability..relish

14. The military censors ---- any passages in the letters that they thought might ---- security.

(A) obtruded..malign
(B) impugned..nullify
(C) rebutted..decimate
(D) expunged..jeopardize
(E) divulged..enjoin

Directions: Each of the following questions consists of a capitalized pair of words followed by five pairs of words lettered A to E. The capitalized words bear some meaningful relationship to each other. Choose the lettered pair of words whose relationship is most similar to that expressed by the capitalized pair and mark its letter on your answer sheet.

Example:

DAY : SUN : :

(A) sunlight : daylight (B) ray : sun
(C) night : moon (D) heat : cold
(E) moon : star Ⓐ Ⓑ ● Ⓓ Ⓔ

15. TRUMPET : TUBA : :

(A) piano : keys
(B) violin : bow
(C) drum : cymbal
(D) piccolo : bassoon
(E) music : notes

16. DINGHY : WATER : :

(A) barge : dock
(B) oar : wing
(C) river : boat
(D) glider : air
(E) parachute : plane

17. NAIL : PUNCTURE : :

(A) scalpel : incision
(B) drill : window
(C) saw : tree
(D) cleft : ax
(E) wheel : axle

18. STAR : GALAXY : :

(A) sun : moon
(B) light : dawn
(C) bird : flock
(D) caravan : desert
(E) plane : jet

19. SILVER : METAL : :

(A) gold : alloy
(B) plastic : container
(C) helium : gas
(D) sand : glass
(E) sediment : rock

20. SPRINTER : SPEED : :

(A) athlete : practice
(B) ball : game
(C) soccer : head
(D) weight lifter : strength
(E) gymnast : bars

21. INTERLOPER : MEDDLE : :

(A) stranger : alienate
(B) rogue : repent
(C) avenger : punish
(D) patron : teach
(E) consumer : create

22. METEOROLOGY : WEATHER : :

(A) ornithology : birds
(B) chemistry : test tube
(C) physics : calculus
(D) meteors : earth
(E) clouds : moisture

23. INNOVATION : PRECEDENT : :

(A) inception : reality
(B) illusion : veracity
(C) conservation : simplicity
(D) renovation : antiquity
(E) invention : production

24. ANARCHIST : LAWLESS : :

(A) policeman : cautious
(B) lawyer : ominous
(C) philosopher : escapist
(D) animal : beauty
(E) philistine : uncultured

25. DETRIMENTAL : PERNICIOUS : :

(A) delightful : delicious
(B) cheerful : exuberant
(C) painful : sore
(D) helpful : useful
(E) fearful : timid

GO ON TO THE NEXT PAGE

Directions: The reading passage below is followed by a set of questions. Read the passage and answer the accompanying questions, basing your answers on what is stated or implied in the passage. Mark the letter of your choice on your answer sheet.

Questions 26–35 are based on the following passage.

On July 4, 1852, former slave Frederick Douglass was asked to speak during a commemoration of the Declaration of Independence in Rochester, New York. His speech shocked many listeners and introduced one of the greatest orators of the Civil War era.

What, am I to argue that it is wrong to make men brutes, to rob them of their liberty, to work them without wages, to keep them ignorant of their relations to their fellow men, to beat them with sticks, to flay their flesh with the lash, to load their limbs with irons, to hunt them with dogs, to sell them at auction, to sunder their families, to knock out their teeth, to burn their flesh, to starve them into obedience and submission to their masters? Must I argue that a system thus marked with blood, and stained with pollution, is wrong? No! I will not. I have better employment for my time and strength than such arguments would imply.

What, then, remains to be argued? Is it that slavery is not divine; that God did not establish it; that our doctors of divinity are mistaken? There is blasphemy in the thought. That which is inhuman cannot be divine! Who can reason on such a proposition? They that can, may; I cannot. The time for such argument is past.

At a time like this, scorching iron, not convincing argument, is needed. O! had I the ability, and could I reach the nation's ear, I would today pour out a fiery stream of biting ridicule, blasting reproach, withering sarcasm, and stern rebuke. For it is not light that is needed, but fire; it is not the gentle shower, but thunder. We need the storm, the whirlwind, and the earthquake. The feeling of the nation must be quickened; the conscience of the nation must be roused; the propriety of the nation must be startled; the hypocrisy of the nation must be exposed; and its crimes against God and man must be proclaimed and denounced.

What, to the American slave, is your Fourth of July? I answer: a day that reveals to him, more than all other days in the year, the gross injustice and cruelty to which he is the constant victim. To him, your celebration is a sham; your boasted liberty, an unholy license; your national greatness, swelling vanity; your sounds of rejoicing are empty and heartless; your denunciation of tyrants, brass-fronted impudence; your shouts of liberty and equality, hollow mockery; your prayers and hymns, your sermons and thanksgiving, with all your religious parade and solemnity, are to him, mere bombast, fraud, deception, impiety, and hypocrisy—a thin veil to cover up crimes which would disgrace a nation of savages. There is not a nation on earth guilty of practices more shocking and bloody than are the people of the United States at this very hour.

Go where you may, search where you will, roam through all the monarchies and despotisms of the Old World, travel through South America, search out every abuse, and when you have found the last, lay your facts by the side of the everyday practices of this nation, and you will say with me that, for revolting barbarity and shameless hypocrisy, America reigns without a rival.

26. Douglass opens this section of his speech with a(n)

(A) metaphor
(B) rhetorical question
(C) appeal to the gods
(D) digression
(E) apology

27. The word *lash* (line 5) is used to mean

(A) whip
(B) tie
(C) tether
(D) eyebrow
(E) band

28. In line 6, what is the best definition of *sunder*?

(A) surrender
(B) supply
(C) divide
(D) affix
(E) harbor

29. Which of the following best states Douglass's opinion of the theory that slavery is divinely ordained?

(A) It may or may not be true.
(B) It is blasphemous.
(C) It is a question for the clergy to decide.
(D) It has been proven by doctors of divinity.
(E) The time has come to debate the theory.

30. Why does Douglass list violent natural phenomena in paragraph 3?

(A) To appeal to Heaven for release
(B) To expose the cruelty of man
(C) To show that slavery is unnatural
(D) To stress the need for drastic action
(E) To compare natural and man-made disasters

31. How might you reword the phrase "the feeling of the nation must be quickened" (line 26)?

(A) The opinion of the nation must be expedited.
(B) The nation's approach must be impulsive.
(C) The foreboding in the nation is accelerating.
(D) The nation's beliefs must be perceptive.
(E) The nation's passions must be aroused.

32. How does Douglass feel about the Fourth of July?

(A) It is a fraud.
(B) It is exciting.
(C) It is a time for pride in the nation's heritage.
(D) It is the best day to abolish slavery.
(E) It is the ideal moment for a debate on slavery.

33. With the phrase "a nation of savages" (line 43), Douglass means to compare Americans who condone slavery to

(A) slaves
(B) citizens
(C) barbarians
(D) countrymen
(E) foreigners

34. Why does Douglass mention South America (line 49)?

(A) To contrast slavery in two locales
(B) As an example of a place he considers more barbaric than the United States
(C) To compare two forms of government
(D) As an example of an innocent land
(E) As an example of a place he considers less barbaric than the United States

35. Listeners probably found this speech shocking because of the speaker's

(A) furious denunciation of the celebration
(B) anger at elected officials
(C) profane language and swearing
(D) call for revolt against the government
(E) appeal to rebels to lay down their arms

STOP

END OF SECTION 2. IF YOU HAVE ANY TIME LEFT, GO OVER YOUR WORK IN THIS SECTION ONLY. DO NOT WORK IN ANY OTHER SECTION OF THE TEST.

SECTION 3

10 Questions • Time—15 Minutes

Directions: Solve the following problems using any available space on the page for scratchwork. On your answer sheet fill in the choice which best corresponds to the correct answer.

Notes: The figures accompanying the problems are drawn as accurately as possible unless otherwise stated in specific problems. Again, unless otherwise stated, all figures lie in the same plane. All numbers used in these problems are real numbers. Calculators are permitted for this test.

Reference Information

Circle: Rectangle: Rectangular Solid: Cylinder: Triangle:

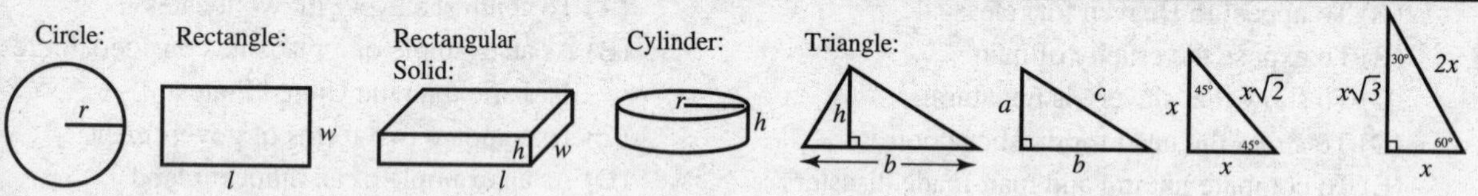

$C = 2\pi r$, $A = \pi r^2$ $A = lw$ $V = lwh$ $V = \pi r^2 h$ $A = \frac{1}{2}bh$ $a^2 + b^2 = c^2$

The number of degrees of arc in a circle is 360.
The measure in degrees of a straight angle is 180.
The sum of the measures in degrees of the angles of a triangle is 180.

1. Which of the following is smaller than $-\frac{1}{2}$?

(A) $-\frac{3}{5}$
(B) $-\frac{3}{7}$
(C) $-\frac{2}{5}$
(D) $-\frac{1}{3}$
(E) $-\frac{1}{4}$

2. $\frac{2}{3}$ of a certain number is 6 more than $\frac{1}{2}$ of the same number. What is the number?

(A) 48
(B) 36
(C) 30
(D) 24
(E) 12

3. What percent is 10 of 2?

(A) 20%
(B) 50%
(C) 200%
(D) 400%
(E) 500%

4. A quart of oil usually sells for $1.39. During a sale, the price is reduced to 59 cents. If a customer buys six quarts at the sale price, how much is she saving off the regular price?

(A) $8.34
(B) $6.40
(C) $4.80
(D) $3.54
(E) $2.88

5. If square $ABCD$ has a side of m, then which of the following represents the shaded area?

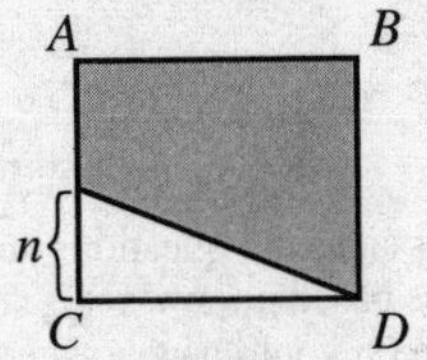

(A) $m^2 - \frac{mn}{2}$

(B) $m^2 + \frac{mn}{2}$

(C) $mn + m^2$

(D) $m^2 - mn$

(E) $m^2 - 2n$

6. John is 6 inches taller than Henry, who is $\frac{3}{4}$ as tall as Mark. Which of the following could be the heights of the three boys?

I. Mark = 4'	John = $3\frac{1}{2}$'	Henry = 3'
II. Mark = 6'	John = $5\frac{1}{2}$'	Henry = $4\frac{1}{2}$'
III. Mark = $5\frac{1}{2}$'	John = $4\frac{1}{2}$'	Henry = 4'

(A) I only
(B) I and II only
(C) II and III only
(D) I and III only
(E) None of the above

7. What is the average of $\frac{2}{3}$, $\frac{3}{4}$, and $\frac{5}{6}$?

(A) $\frac{7}{9}$

(B) $\frac{3}{4}$

(C) $\frac{2}{3}$

(D) $\frac{5}{12}$

(E) $\frac{5}{24}$

8. If $k = \frac{3}{4}j$ and both j and k are positive integers, k could be any of the following *except*

(A) 9
(B) 12
(C) 15
(D) 18
(E) 20

9. If r is an even integer greater than 2, then which of the following must also be even?

(A) $(r-1)^2$

(B) $(r+1)^2$

(C) $\frac{r}{2}+1$

(D) $2r + 1$

(E) $r^2 + r$

10. Segment AB is three times longer than segment BC, which is two times as long as segment CD. If segment BC is removed from the line and the other two segments are joined to form one line, then what is the ratio of the original line AD to the new line AD?

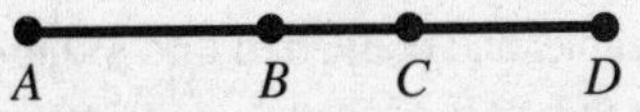

Note: Figure not drawn to scale.

(A) 3 : 2
(B) 9 : 7
(C) 5 : 4
(D) 7 : 6
(E) 11 : 10

STOP

END OF SECTION 3. IF YOU HAVE ANY TIME LEFT, GO OVER YOUR WORK IN THIS SECTION ONLY. DO NOT WORK IN ANY OTHER SECTION OF THE TEST.

SECTION 4

10 Questions • Time—15 Minutes

Directions: The two passages given below deal with a related topic. Following the passages are questions about the content of each passage or about the relationship between the two passages. Answer the questions based upon what is stated or implied in the passages and in any introductory material provided. Mark the letter of your choice on your answer sheet.

Questions 1–10 are based on the two passages that follow.

Passage 1 was written in the Near East during the Middle Ages. In it, the Islamic Usamah ibn Miniqidh narrates an episode that took place about 1140, when the Holy Land was under siege by the Crusaders. He describes what happened to him when his culture clashed with that of the invaders.

Passage 2 is from a much later time. It recounts part of the story of Black Elk, a holy man of the Ogalala Sioux. Black Elk was born in 1863 and lived through the upheavals in the Sioux Nation that culminated in the massacre at Wounded Knee in 1890. In the 1930s, Black Elk told his history orally to a poet named John Neihardt, who took it down and published it. In the passage below, Black Elk recounts the beginning of the end, a time when the whites (Wasichu) would not even allow the Inedians to practice their religion.

Passage 1—from Kitāb al-Iʿtibār

Everyone who is a fresh emigrant from the Frankish lands is ruder in character than those who have become acclimatized and have long association with the Moslems. Here is an illustration of their rude character.

Whenever I visited Jerusalem I always entered the Aqsa Mosque, beside which stood a small mosque which the Franks had converted into a church. When I used to enter the Aqsa Mosque, which was occupied by the Templars . . . who were my friends, the Templars would evacuate the little adjoining mosque so that I might pray in it. One day I entered this mosque, repeated the first formula, "Allah is great," and stood up in the act of praying, upon which one of the Franks rushed on me, got hold of me and turned my face eastward, saying, "This is the way thou shouldst pray!" A group of Templars hastened to him, seized him and repelled him from me. I resumed my prayer.

The same man, while the others were otherwise busy, rushed once more on me and turned my face eastward, saying, "This is the way thou shouldst pray!" The Templars again came in to him and expelled him. They apologized to me, saying, "This is a stranger who has only recently arrived from the land of the Franks and he has never before seen anyone praying except eastward." Thereupon I said to myself, "I have had enough prayer." So I went out, and have ever been surprised at the conduct of this devil of a man, at the change in the color of his face, his trembling, and his sentiment at the sight of one praying towards [the holy city, Mecca].

Passage 2—from Black Elk Speaks*

When Good Thunder and Kicking Bear came back in the spring from seeing the Wanekia, the Wasichus at Pine Ridge put them in prison awhile, and then let them go. This showed the Wasichus were afraid of something. In the Moon of Black Cherries (August) many people were dancing at No Water's Camp on Clay Creek, and the agent came and told them to stop dancing. They would not stop, and they said they would fight for their religion if they had to do it. The agent went away, and they kept on dancing. They called him Young-Man-Afraid-of-Lakotas.

Later, I heard that the Brules were dancing over east of us; and then I heard that Big Foot's people were dancing on the Good River reservation; also that Kicking Bear had gone to Sitting Bull's camp on Grand River, and that people were dancing there too. Word came to us that the Indians were beginning to dance everywhere.

The people were hungry and in despair, and many believed in the good new world that was coming. The Wasichus gave us less than half the beef cattle they promised us in the treaty, and these cattle were very poor. For a while our people would not take the cattle, because there were so few of them and they were so poor. But after a while they had to take them or starve to death. So we got more lies than cattle, and we could not eat lies. When the agent told the people to quit dancing, their hearts were bad. . . .

When I came back from the Brules, the weather was getting cold. Many of the Brules came along when I came back, and joined the Ogalalas in the dancing on Wounded Knee. We heard that there were soldiers at Pine Ridge and that others were coming all the time. Then one morning we heard that the soldiers were marching toward us, so we broke camp and moved west to Grass Creek. From there we went to White Clay and camped awhile and danced.

There came to us Fire Thunder, Red Wound and Young American Horse with a message from the soldiers that this matter of the ghost dance must be looked into, and that there should be rulings over it; and that they did not mean to take the dance away from us. But could we believe anything the Wasichus ever said to us? They spoke with forked tongues.

We moved in closer to Pine Ridge and camped. Many soldiers were there now, and what were they there for?

There was a big meeting with the agent, but I did not go to hear. He made a ruling that we could dance three days every moon, and the rest of the time we should go and make a living for ourselves somehow. He did not say how we could do that. But the people agreed to this.

The next day, while I was sitting in a teepee with Good Thunder, a policeman came to us and said: "I was not sent here, but I came for your good to tell you what I have heard—that they are going to arrest you two."

1. According to Usamah, Franks who have been in Moslem lands longer tend to be more

(A) durable
(B) sophisticated
(C) primitive
(D) spiritual
(E) practical

2. Usamah's refusal to pray the way the Frank wishes is apparently seen by the Frank as a form of

(A) heresy
(B) prejudice
(C) coercion
(D) esteem
(E) domination

3. The tone of Usamah's narrative might be described as

(A) incredulous
(B) paternal
(C) bitter
(D) resigned
(E) apprehensive

4. When Black Elk says that the Indians' "hearts were bad" (line 57), he means that they were

(A) ill and malnourished
(B) sick at heart
(C) afraid
(D) about to die
(E) rotten to the core

5. The Indians' refusal to stop dancing is apparently seen by the Wasichus as a form of

(A) rudeness
(B) brutality
(C) intolerance
(D) courage
(E) insurrection

6. When Black Elk says that the Wasichus speak with "forked tongues" (line 73), he is referring to their tendency toward

(A) chivalry
(B) gloom
(C) bluntness
(D) accuracy
(E) misrepresentation

GO ON TO THE NEXT PAGE

7. The tone of Black Elk's narrative might be described as

   (A) amused
   (B) soothing
   (C) ominous
   (D) sullen
   (E) reassuring

8. Both the Frank's reaction to Usamah's praying and the Wasichus' reaction to the Indians' dancing might be characterized as

   (A) emotional and fearful
   (B) tolerant and kind
   (C) disgusted and pompous
   (D) pious and devout
   (E) comfortable and gratified

9. The subject of both passages might be summarized as

   (A) freedom of expression
   (B) master and man
   (C) religious intolerance
   (D) after the fall
   (E) warlords and curates

10. What might Usamah's reaction be to hearing of Black Elk's troubles?

    (A) He would not forgive the Indians' rebelliousness.
    (B) He would not tolerate the Wasichus' rudeness.
    (C) He would urge the Indians to go along with the Wasichus.
    (D) He would not understand why the Indians wanted to dance.
    (E) He would try to convert the Wasichus.

STOP

END OF SECTION 4. IF YOU HAVE ANY TIME LEFT, GO OVER YOUR WORK IN THIS SECTION ONLY. DO NOT WORK IN ANY OTHER SECTION OF THE TEST.

SECTION 5

25 Questions • Time—30 Minutes

Directions: Solve the following problems using any available space on the page for scratchwork. On your answer sheet fill in the choice which best corresponds to the correct answer.

Notes: The figures accompanying the problems are drawn as accurately as possible unless otherwise stated in specific problems. Again, unless otherwise stated, all figures lie in the same plane. All numbers used in these problems are real numbers. Calculators are permitted for this test.

Reference Information

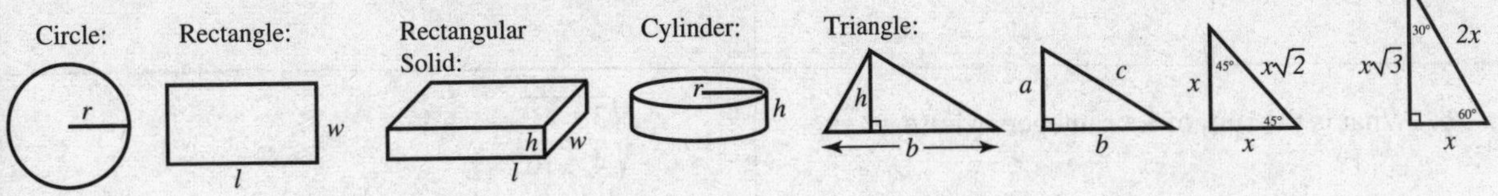

$C = 2\pi r$ $A = lw$ $V = lwh$ $V = \pi r^2 h$ $A = \frac{1}{2}bh$ $a^2 + b^2 = c^2$

$A = \pi r^2$

The number of degrees of arc in a circle is 360.
The measure in degrees of a straight angle is 180.
The sum of the measures in degrees of the angles of a triangle is 180.

1. If $\frac{2}{3} + \frac{3}{4} + \frac{5}{6} + p = 3$, then $p =$

(A) $\frac{4}{3}$
(B) $\frac{3}{4}$
(C) $\frac{2}{3}$
(D) $\frac{1}{2}$
(E) $\frac{1}{3}$

2. In the figure below, $x + y =$

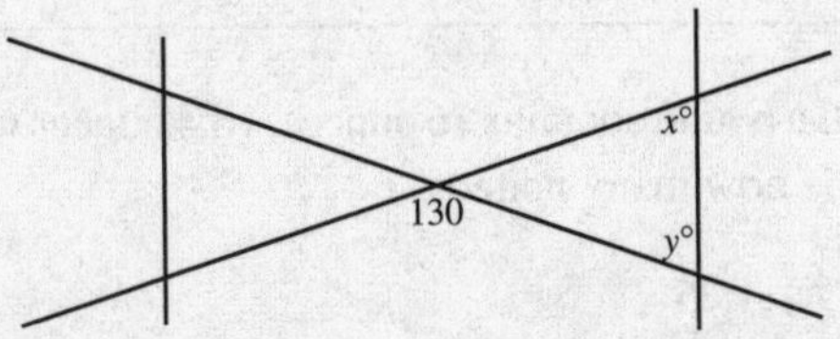

(A) 360
(B) 180
(C) 130
(D) 50
(E) It cannot be determined from the information given.

3. If $P = QR$ and $Q = S + 2$, then which of the following is equal to $\frac{P}{R}$?

(A) $S + 2$
(B) S
(C) $S - 2$
(D) $Q(S + 2)$
(E) SQ

4. If $x = -\frac{1}{2}$, then which of the following is the greatest?

(A) x^5
(B) x^4
(C) x^3
(D) x^2
(E) x

GO ON TO THE NEXT PAGE

5. A man runs 5 miles per hour for one and one-half hours. If a woman runs the same distance in one hour, what is the woman's average speed in miles per hour?

(A) 10

(B) $9\frac{1}{2}$

(C) $7\frac{1}{2}$

(D) 5

(E) $4\frac{1}{2}$

6. What is the sum of four integers whose average is 11?

(A) 36
(B) 38
(C) 40
(D) 42
(E) 44

7. In a basket containing 180 pears, 9 are spoiled. What percent of the pears in the basket are not spoiled?

(A) 95%
(B) 90%
(C) 50%
(D) 25%
(E) 20%

8. A number r is tripled, the new number is decreased by three, and that number is then divided by three. Which of the following reflects the above statements?

(A) $3(r-3)$
(B) $9r$
(C) $r-3$
(D) r
(E) $r-1$

9. If $ABCD$ is a square with a side of 4, then what is the sum of the perimeter of ΔABE and ΔDCF?

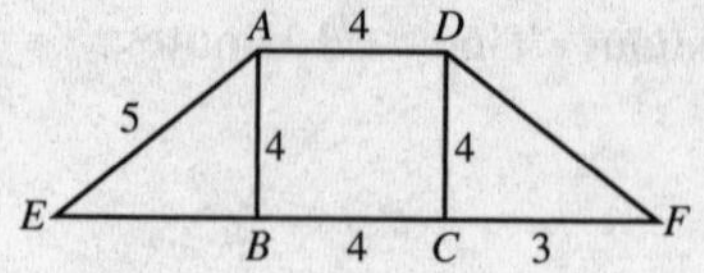

Note: Figure not drawn to scale.

(A) 48
(B) 36
(C) 24
(D) 12
(E) 6

10. $\sqrt{\frac{3}{4}-\frac{3}{16}}=$

(A) $\frac{4}{3}$

(B) $\frac{3}{4}$

(C) $\frac{9}{16}$

(D) $\frac{1}{3}$

(E) $\frac{1}{4}$

11. If $\{w, x, y, z\} = z(w + x + y)$, so that $\{1, 2, 3, 4\} = 4(1 + 2 + 3) = 24$, then all of the following are equal *except*

(A) $\{2, 3, 4, 6\}$
(B) $\{4, 3, 2, 6\}$
(C) $\{3, 5, 1, 6\}$
(D) $\{4, 1, 5, 6\}$
(E) $\{1, 5, 3, 6\}$

12. If a pound contains 16 ounces, 16.4 ounces would be how many pounds?

(A) 1.75
(B) 1.5
(C) 1.25
(D) 1.025
(E) 1.0025

13. If a certain circle has a circumference of x, then which of the following is the radius of the circle?

(A) $\frac{x}{2\pi}$

(B) $\frac{x}{\pi}$

(C) $\frac{2x}{\pi}$

(D) $2\times\pi$

(E) $4\times\pi$

14. If $(x + 1)(x - 2)$ is positive, then

(A) $x < -1$ or $x > 2$
(B) $x > -1$ or $x < 2$
(C) $-1 < x < 2$
(D) $-2 < x < 1$
(E) $x = -1$ or $x = 2$

15. If rectangle $ABCD$ has a length of 12 and a width of 8, what is the ratio of the area of ΔAED to the area of $ABCD$?

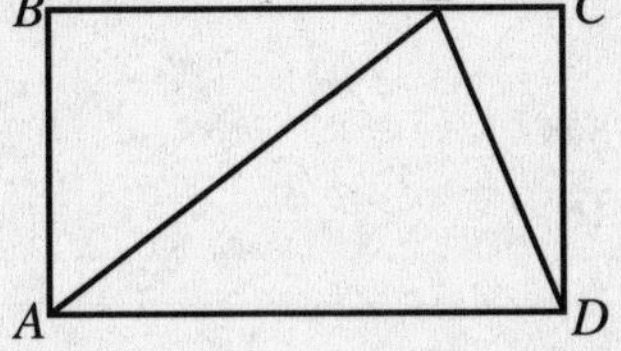

(A) 1 : 6
(B) 1 : 4
(C) 2 : 5
(D) 3 : 7
(E) 1 : 2

16. A "full" number is one that is the sum of all the other numbers besides itself by which it can be divided without leaving a remainder. Which of the following is a "full" number?

I. 6
II. 12
III. 28
IV. 32

(A) I only
(B) I and II only
(C) I and III only
(D) III and IV only
(E) I, III, and IV only

17. ANNUAL SALE OF CASSETTES
ABC SOUND STORES

Year	Number Sold
1985	7,000
1986	9,000
1987	12,000
1988	16,000
1989	20,000
1990	24,000

In the above table, which yearly period had the smallest percent increase in sales?

(A) 1985–86
(B) 1986–87
(C) 1987–88
(D) 1988–89
(E) 1989–90

18. A student scored 70, 75, and 80 on three tests. If the student scored y on the fourth test, what is the average (arithmetic mean) of the four tests?

(A) $\frac{225+y}{4}$

(B) $\frac{225+y}{3}$

(C) $\frac{75+y}{4}$

(D) $\frac{75+y}{2}$

(E) y

GO ON TO THE NEXT PAGE

19. Two snails are three feet apart and directly facing each other. If one snail moves forward continuously at .04 inches per second and the other moves forward continuously at .05 inches per second, how many minutes will it take for the snails to touch?

(A) $3\frac{1}{3}$ minutes

(B) $6\frac{2}{3}$ minutes

(C) 9 minutes

(D) $12\frac{1}{2}$ minutes

(E) 18 minutes

20. A person is hired for a job that pays $500 per month and receives a 10% raise in each following month. In the fourth month, how much will that person earn?

(A) $550
(B) $600.50
(C) $650.50
(D) $665.50
(E) $700

21. John is now four times as old as Anne was six years ago. How old is Anne today if John is 20 years old?

(A) 8
(B) 11
(C) 12
(D) 14
(E) 15

22. If $a^2 - 2ab + b^2 = 36$ and $a^2 - 3ab + b^2 = 22$, what is the value of ab?

(A) 6
(B) 8
(C) 12
(D) 14
(E) It cannot be determined from the information given.

23. In the figure below, four semicircles are drawn on the four sides of a rectangle. What is the total area of the shaded portion?

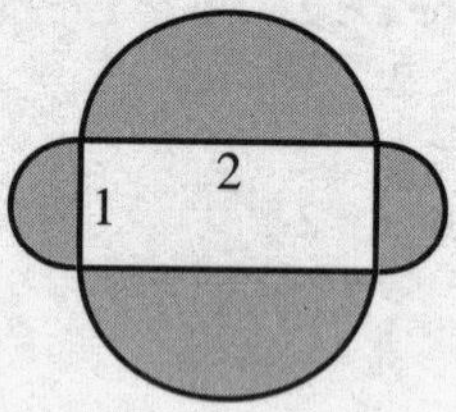

(A) 5π

(B) $\frac{5\pi}{2}$

(C) $\frac{5\pi}{4}$

(D) $\frac{5\pi}{8}$

(E) $\frac{5\pi}{16}$

24. $P = \frac{1}{2} + \frac{1}{3}$ and $Q = P^2$, what is $Q - P$?

(A) 1

(B) $\frac{5}{36}$

(C) 0

(D) $-\frac{5}{36}$

(E) $-\frac{25}{36}$

25. In the figure, the enclosed square has an area of

(A) 9
(B) 18
(C) 24
(D) 27
(E) 36

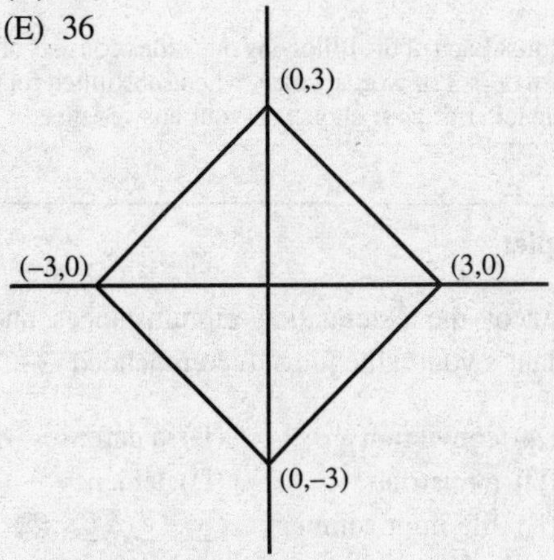

Note: Figure not drawn to scale.

STOP

END OF SECTION 5. IF YOU HAVE ANY TIME LEFT, GO OVER YOUR WORK IN THIS SECTION ONLY. DO NOT WORK IN ANY OTHER SECTION OF THE TEST.

SECTION 6

30 Questions • Time—30 Minutes

Directions: Each of the following questions consists of an incomplete sentence followed by five words or pairs of words. Choose that word or pair of words which, when substituted for the blank space or spaces, *best* completes the meaning of the sentence and mark the letter of your choice on your answer sheet.

Example:

In view of the extenuating circumstances and the defendant's youth, the judge recommended ----.

(A) conviction (B) a defense
(C) a mistrial (D) leniency
(E) life imprisonment Ⓐ Ⓑ Ⓒ ● Ⓔ

1. Because the poet Emily Dickinson led a ---- life, she used her ---- to explore the outside world.

 (A) gregarious..talent
 (B) sociable..books
 (C) fast-paced..telephone
 (D) secluded..imagination
 (E) gracious..friends

2. Spending our money on an expensive restaurant meal will ---- our going to the movies.

 (A) debunk
 (B) evoke
 (C) rescind
 (D) concede
 (E) preclude

3. A ---- student is unlikely to gain admission to a first-rate college.

 (A) contrite
 (B) vicarious
 (C) mediocre
 (D) putative
 (E) mendacious

4. Blue whales grow to ---- size and must eat tons of plankton to ---- their huge appetites.

 (A) prodigious..satiate
 (B) effusive..assuage
 (C) colossal..deplete
 (D) fortuitous..exhort
 (E) obstreperous..vanquish

5. The ---- of the plan ensured its success; the enemy did not ---- such a recklessly bold attempt.

 (A) urbanity..presume
 (B) levity..elude
 (C) audacity..anticipate
 (D) protocol..preclude
 (E) truculence..discern

Directions: Each of the following questions consists of a capitalized pair of words followed by five pairs of words lettered A to E. The capitalized words bear some meaningful relationship to each other. Choose the lettered pair of words whose relationship is most similar to that expressed by the capitalized pair and mark its letter on your answer sheet.

Example:

DAY : SUN : :

(A) sunlight : daylight (B) ray : sun
(C) night : moon (D) heat : cold
(E) moon : star

Ⓐ Ⓑ ● Ⓓ Ⓔ

6. HOUR : TIME : :

(A) hand : clock
(B) digit : electricity
(C) gram : weight
(D) speedometer : car
(E) scale : diet

7. GEM : SETTING : :

(A) diamond : gold
(B) photo : camera
(C) ring : necklace
(D) picture : frame
(E) painting : subject

8. SHIP : ARMADA : :

(A) sail : wind
(B) gun : sword
(C) atom : molecule
(D) chemical : reaction
(E) violin : flute

9. CATERPILLAR : BUTTERFLY : :

(A) tadpole : frog
(B) bird : nest
(C) egg : yolk
(D) puppy : kitten
(E) horse : zebra

10. TREMBLE : FEAR : :

(A) scream : envy
(B) smile : rage
(C) demand : anger
(D) follow : love
(E) weep : grief

11. SPARK : CONFLAGRATION : :

(A) match : light
(B) oxygen : combustion
(C) drizzle : downpour
(D) sugar : sweetness
(E) mountain : hill

12. ROBUST : VIGOR : :

(A) massive : strength
(B) sick : illness
(C) farsighted : glasses
(D) full : appetite
(E) sanguine : hope

13. TRAITOROUS : PERFIDY : :

(A) despicable : country
(B) envious : green
(C) devious : dourness
(D) loyal : steadfastness
(E) smart : average

GO ON TO THE NEXT PAGE

Directions: Each passage below is followed by a set of questions. Read each passage, then answer the accompanying questions, basing your answers on what is stated or implied in the passage and in any introductory material provided. Mark the letter of your choice on your answer sheet.

Questions 14–22 are based on the following passage.

This passage comes from the diary of Mrs. Sarah Kemble Knight, an eighteenth-century teacher and writer. Her journal tells of a trip she took on horseback from her home in Boston to New York City in the year 1704. Here she describes life in colonial New York, comparing and contrasting it to her hometown.

The City of New York is a pleasant, well compacted place, situated on a Commodious River which is a fine harbor for shipping. The Buildings Brick Generally, very stately and high, although not altogether like ours in Boston. The Bricks in some of the Houses are of divers Colors and laid in Checkers, being glazed look very agreeable. The inside of them are neat to admiration, the wooden work, for only the walls are plastered, and the Summers and Joists are planed and kept very white scour'd as so is all the partitions if made of Boards. The fireplaces have no Jambs (as ours have) But the Backs run flush with the walls, and the Hearth is of Tiles and is as far out into the Room at the Ends as before the fire, which is Generally Five foot in the Lower rooms, and the piece over where the mantle tree should be is made as ours with Joiners' work, and as I suppose is fasten'd to iron rods inside. The House where the Vendue was, had Chimney Corners like ours, and they and the hearths were laid with the finest tile that I ever see, and the staircases laid all with white tile which is ever clean, and so are the walls of the Kitchen which had a Brick floor. . . . They are not strict in keeping the Sabbath as in Boston and other places where I had been, But seem to deal with great exactness as far as I see or Deal with. They are sociable to one another and Courteous and Civil to strangers and fare well in their house. The English go very fashionable in their dress. But the Dutch, especially the middling sort, differ from our women, in their habit go loose, wear French muches which are like a Cap and a headband in one, leaving their ears bare, which are set out with Jewels of a large size and many in number. And their fingers hoop't with Rings, some with large stones in them of many Colors as were the pendants in their ears, which You should see very old women wear as well as Young. . . .

Their Diversions in the Winter is Riding Sleighs about three or four Miles out of Town, where they have Houses of entertainment at a place called the Bowery, and some go to friends' Houses who handsomely treat them. Mr. Burroughs carried his spouse and Daughter and myself out to one Madame Dowes, a Gentlewoman that lived at a farmhouse, who gave us a handsome entertainment of five or six Dishes and choice Beer and metheglin, Cider, &c. all which she said was the produce of her farm. I believe we met 50 or 60 sleighs that day—they fly with great swiftness and some are so furious that they'll turn out of the path for none except a Loaden cart. Nor do they spare for any diversion the place affords, and sociable to a degree, their Tables being as free to their Neighbors as to themselves.

14. In her description, Knight includes details about

(A) architecture, dress, and entertainment
(B) hobbies, jobs, and food
(C) animals, people, and plants
(D) the shipping industry and religious practices
(E) English and Dutch customs

15. Knight's use of the word *middling* (line 29) demonstrates her

(A) delight in the ordinary
(B) refusal to become second-rate
(C) moderation in all things
(D) love of the Dutch
(E) awareness of class differences

16. The Dutch women of New York wear all of the following except

(A) earrings
(B) a French-style cap
(C) English-style dresses
(D) rings
(E) colorful jewels

17. When Knight says that Mr. Burroughs "carried" her out (line 41), she means that he

(A) supported her when she became inebriated
(B) displayed her to his friends
(C) communicated her wishes
(D) transported her in a vehicle
(E) shouldered her baggage

18. The word *metheglin* (line 45) refers to a

(A) religion
(B) fair
(C) style
(D) goblet
(E) beverage

19. Compared to Bostonians, Knight notes that New Yorkers

(A) are more fashionable
(B) are less devout
(C) have more money
(D) have larger homes
(E) do not enjoy sleigh riding

20. It seems clear that Knight

(A) has never been out of Boston before
(B) has never been to New York before
(C) thinks Boston's entertainment is superior to New York's
(D) thinks New Yorkers are rude
(E) is homesick for Boston

21. Knight seems least impressed by

(A) the food in New York
(B) her treatment by Mr. Burroughs
(C) Dutch fashions
(D) the brick buildings
(E) New York kitchens

22. The last line of the passage commends New Yorkers for their

(A) thriftiness
(B) manners
(C) hospitality
(D) wit
(E) cooking

Questions 23–30 are based on the following passage.

Stephen Crane (1871–1900) was an American fiction writer who specialized in realistic description. In the following story, originally printed in Harper's Magazine *in 1899, he recounts a harrowing tale of events in a schoolyard.*

"Oh! Oh! Oh! Jimmie Trescott's writing to his girl! Oh! Oh!". . . She managed soon to shy through the door and out upon the playground, yelling, "Oh, Jimmie Trescott's been writing to his girl!"

The unhappy Jimmie was following as closely as he was allowed by his knowledge of the decencies to be preserved under the eye of the teacher.

Jimmie himself was mainly responsible for the scene which ensued on the playground. It is possible that the little girl might have run, shrieking his infamy, without exciting more than a general but unmilitant interest. These barbarians were excited only by the actual appearance of human woe; in that event they cheered and danced. Jimmie made the strategic mistake of pursuing little Rose, and thus exposed his thin skin to the whole school. He had in his cowering mind a vision of a hundred children turning from their play under the maple trees and speeding toward him over the gravel with sudden wild taunts. Upon him drove a yelping demonic mob, to which his words were futile. He saw in this mob boys that he dimly knew, and his deadly enemies, and his retainers, and his most intimate friends. The virulence of his deadly enemy was no greater than the virulence of his intimate friend. From the outskirts the little informer could be heard still screaming the news, like a toy parrot with clock-work inside it. It broke up all sorts of games, not so much because of the mere fact of the letter-writing as because the children knew that some sufferer was at the last point, and like little blood-fanged wolves, they thronged to the scene of his destruction. They galloped about him shrilly chanting insults. He turned from one to another, only to meet with howls. He was baited.

Then, in one instant, he changed all this with a blow. Bang! The most pitiless of the boys near him received a punch, fairly and skillfully, which made him bellow out like a walrus, and then Jimmie laid desperately into the whole world, striking out frenziedly in all directions. Boys who could handily whip him, and knew it, backed away from this onslaught. Here was intention—serious intention. They themselves were not in frenzy and their cooler judgment respected Jimmie's efforts when he ran amuck. They saw that it really was none of their affair. In the meantime the wretched little girl who had caused the bloody riot was away by the fence, weeping because boys were fighting. . . .

Then upon the situation there pealed a brazen bell. It was a bell that these children obeyed, even as nations obey the formal law which is printed in calfskin. It

GO ON TO THE NEXT PAGE

smote them into some sort of inaction; even Jimmie was influenced by its potency, although, as a finale, he kicked out lustily into the legs of an intimate friend who had been one of the foremost in the torture. . . .

The teacher looked carefully down at him. "Come up to the desk. . . ."

He rose amid the awe of the entire schoolroom.

"Who have you been fighting?" she asked.

"I dunno, 'm."

Whereupon the empress blazed out in wrath. "You don't know who you've been fighting?". . . She seemed about to disintegrate to mere flaming fagots of anger. "You don't know who you've been fighting?" she demanded, blazing. "Well, you stay in after school until you find out."

As he returned to his place all the children knew by his vanquished air that sorrow had fallen upon the house of Trescott. When he took his seat he saw gloating upon him the satanic black eyes of the little Goldege girl.

23. Which of the following describes what really happened on the playground?

(A) The little girl started the fight.
(B) The boys who ran over were responsible for the fight.
(C) Jimmie imagined the fight.
(D) The teacher stopped the fight.
(E) Jimmie's reactions started the fight.

24. "The virulence of his deadly enemy was no greater than the virulence of his intimate friend" (lines 23–24) means that

(A) his friends taunted him just as fiercely as his enemies
(B) the little girl became his deadly enemy
(C) the whole school was to blame
(D) the boys didn't like Jimmie
(E) his best friend fought on his side

25. The sentence "He was baited" (line 33) means

(A) he was hooked on a tree
(B) he was goaded into fighting back
(C) he made up his mind
(D) he was ready to run
(E) he held his breath

26. Which of the following is an example of irony?

(A) The little girl keeps yelling.
(B) Decencies are preserved under the eye of the teacher.
(C) Jimmie pursues little Rose.
(D) The little girl weeps when the boys start fighting.
(E) The teacher demands to know who took part in the fight.

27. All of the following participate in the action of the story EXCEPT

(A) Jimmie's girlfriend
(B) Jimmie's intimate friends
(C) Rose
(D) the teacher
(E) Jimmie's deadly enemies

28. The "empress" (line 59) is

(A) Rose
(B) Jimmie's girlfriend
(C) the teacher
(D) the little Goldege girl
(E) Jimmie's mother

29. The word *vanquished* (line 66) most nearly means

(A) envious
(B) defeated
(C) repentant
(D) combative
(E) awesome

30. From the beginning of the story to the end, Rose changes from

(A) teasing to sorry to secretly pleased
(B) shy to combative
(C) cheerful to violent to rueful
(D) cowering to shrieking
(E) excited to wretched to satanic

STOP

END OF SECTION 6. IF YOU HAVE ANY TIME LEFT, GO OVER YOUR WORK IN THIS SECTION ONLY. DO NOT WORK IN ANY OTHER SECTION OF THE TEST.

Practice Examination 6
Answer Key

Section 1: MATH

Part 1

1. D	4. D	7. B	10. C	13. B
2. C	5. D	8. A	11. B	14. A
3. B	6. C	9. C	12. A	15. A

Part 2

16. 22	18. 0	20. $\frac{36}{5} = 7.2$	22. 30	24. 28
17. 85	19. 1	21. 35	23. 90	25. 5

Section 2: VERBAL

1. C	8. B	15. D	22. A	29. B
2. B	9. C	16. D	23. B	30. D
3. B	10. D	17. A	24. E	31. E
4. D	11. A	18. C	25. B	32. A
5. D	12. C	19. C	26. B	33. C
6. E	13. C	20. D	27. A	34. E
7. C	14. D	21. C	28. C	35. A

Section 3: MATH

1. A	3. E	5. A	7. B	9. E
2. B	4. C	6. A	8. E	10. B

Section 4: VERBAL

1. B	3. A	5. E	7. C	9. C
2. A	4. B	6. E	8. A	10. B

Section 5: MATH

1. B	6. E	11. D	16. C	21. B
2. C	7. A	12. D	17. E	22. D
3. A	8. E	13. A	18. A	23. C
4. D	9. C	14. A	19. B	24. D
5. C	10. B	15. E	20. D	25. B

Section 6: VERBAL

1. D	7. D	13. D	19. B	25. B
2. E	8. C	14. A	20. B	26. D
3. C	9. A	15. E	21. C	27. A
4. A	10. E	16. C	22. C	28. C
5. C	11. C	17. D	23. E	29. B
6. C	12. E	18. E	24. A	30. A

Practice Examination 6

Explanatory Answers

Note: A [calculator icon] following a math answer explanation indicates that a calculator could be helpful in solving that particular problem.

Section 1

Part 1

1. **(D)** Each angle of a square is 90°; therefore, the sum of all angles is 360°. A polygon may have any number of sides, and angles, so the sum of all the angles cannot be determined.

2. **(C)** The missing angle measure is 180° – 70° – 55° = 55°. Therefore, the triangle is isosceles, with two equal angles of 55°. In an isosceles triangle, the sides opposite the equal angles are equal. Thus $x = y$.

3. **(B)** The area of the larger triangle is $\frac{1}{2}(9)(7) = 31\frac{1}{2}$. The area of the smaller triangle is $\frac{1}{2}(5)(3) = 7\frac{1}{2}$. The area of the shaded area is the area of the larger triangle minus that of the smaller, $31\frac{1}{2} - 7\frac{1}{2} = 24$. The shaded area has the larger area.

4. **(D)** If $x > 1$, then $\frac{1}{x} < x$. But if $0 < x < 1$, then $\frac{1}{x} > x$. Since the denominator in $\frac{1}{x}$ will be a fraction, it will be 1 times the reciprocal of x. This will be larger than x itself. We cannot tell which is the larger.

5. **(D)** Factoring the equation in Column B, we find $a^2 - 7a + 12 = (a-4)(a-3)$. If $a > 4$, Column A is larger. But if $a \le 4$, Column B is larger. Therefore, we cannot determine which column is larger.

6. **(C)** The circumference of a circle with radius $2r$ is $2\pi(2r) = 4\pi r$. The perimeter of a square with side πr is $4\pi r$, so Column A and Column B are equal.

7. **(B)** In Column A,

$$\sqrt{\frac{1}{3}\times\frac{1}{6}} = \sqrt{\frac{1}{3}\times\frac{1}{3}\times\frac{1}{2}} = \frac{1}{3}\sqrt{\frac{1}{2}}.$$

In Column B,

$$\sqrt{\frac{1}{3}+\frac{1}{6}} = \sqrt{\frac{6}{18}+\frac{3}{18}} = \sqrt{\frac{9}{18}} = \sqrt{\frac{1}{2}}.$$

Column A is $\frac{1}{3}$ the value of Column B.

8. **(A)** Plugging in –2 we get $(-2-1)^2 + (-2) = 9 - 2 = 7$.

Plugging in 2 we get $(2-1)^2 + 2 = 1 + 2 = 3$

9. **(C)** $(0-1)^2 + 0 = 1$

$(1-1)^2 + 1 = 1$

10. **(C)** The easiest way to solve this is to realize that $(a+b) = (b+a)$ and $(c+d) = (d+c)$. You can also use the foil method to multiply out both sides.

11. **(B)** 42% of 165 is $165 \times 0.42 = 69.3$. The number which 80 is 20% of is $N \times 0.20 = 80$, or $N = \frac{80}{0.20} = 400$. Thus, Column B is larger than Column A.

12. **(A)** Each face of the small cube has an area of 1; each small cube thus has a surface area of 6. Each face of the large cube has an area of 4; the large cube thus has a surface area of 24. $\frac{24}{8} = 3$.

13. **(B)** In Column A, a positive number is multiplied by a negative number. In Column B, the negative of M is taken and divided by N, a negative number, thus resulting in a positive number. A positive number is always greater than a negative number.

14. **(A)** $p = \sqrt{8^2 - 4^2}$; hence, $p = \sqrt{48}$. Meanwhile, q is the hypotenuse of a right triangle, so $q = \sqrt{4^2 + 5^2}$. Hence $q = \sqrt{41}$. Therefore, p is larger.

15. **(A)** The value of Column A is –44. The value of Column B is –168. Therefore, Column A is larger.

Part 2

16.

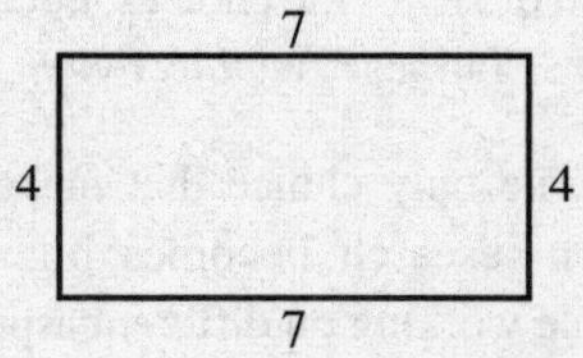

Perimeter $= 4 + 7 + 4 + 7 = 22$

17. The median is the middle score when the data is arrayed in increasing order.
70, 70, 70, 70, 85, 85, 85, 90, 90, 95

85 is the median.

18. $\textcircled{-1} = -1 - 1 = -2$, and $\boxed{1} = 2(1) = 2$

$\textcircled{-1} + \boxed{1} = -2 + 2 = 0$

19. $$\begin{aligned} x + y^2 - z &= (-1) + (-1)^2 - (-1) \\ &= (-1) + (1) - (-1) \\ &= -1 + 1 + 1 \\ &= 1 \end{aligned}$$

20. $$\frac{1}{2} + \frac{1}{3} = \frac{1}{2} \bullet \frac{3}{3} + \frac{1}{3} \bullet \frac{2}{2}$$

$$= \frac{3}{6} + \frac{2}{6} = \frac{5}{6}$$

$$\frac{6}{\frac{1}{2} + \frac{1}{3}} = \frac{6}{\frac{5}{6}} = \frac{6}{1} \bullet \frac{6}{5} = \frac{36}{5}$$

21. Angle AOC is a central angle. Arc $AC = 70°$ as a central angle is equal to its intercepted arc.

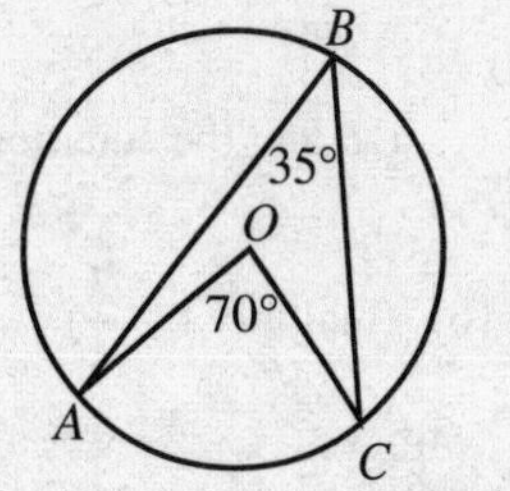

An inscribed angle is equal to $\frac{1}{2}$ the measure of its intercepted arc.

$$m\angle ABC = \frac{1}{2} m\overset{\frown}{AC} = \frac{1}{2}(70°) = 35°$$

22.

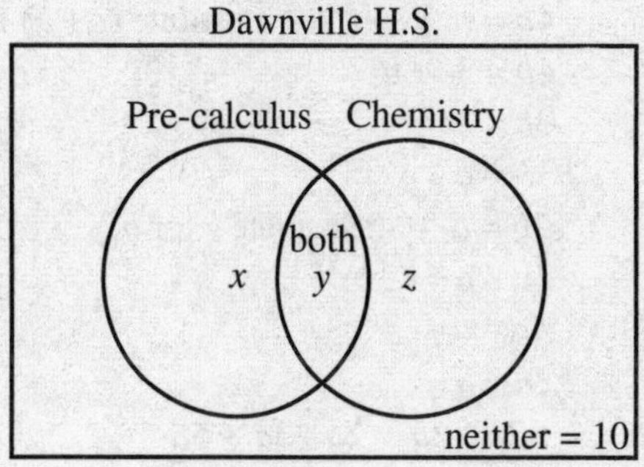

$$\begin{aligned} x + y &= 44 \\ y + z &= 46 \\ x + y + z + \text{neither} &= 70, \\ x + y + z + 10 &= 70 \\ x + y + z &= 60 \end{aligned}$$

but $x + y = 44 \therefore z = 16$

but $y + z = 46 \therefore x = 14$

$$\begin{aligned} \therefore 14 + y + 16 &= 60 \\ y + 30 &= 60 \\ y &= 30 \end{aligned}$$

23. $$\frac{\text{Sum of test scores}}{\text{Number of tests}} = \text{Average}$$

$$\frac{\text{Sum}}{5} = 70 \ \therefore \text{Sum} = 350$$

If two tests are disregarded
the new sum $= 350 - 50 - 30 = 270$
the new number of tests $= 5 - 2 = 3$

The new average

$$= \frac{\text{Sum}}{\text{Number of tests}} = \frac{270}{3} = 90$$

24. $3a + 5b = 10$

$$\begin{array}{l} 3a + 5b = 10 \\ \underline{a - b = 6} \quad \text{(adding the equations)} \\ 4a + 4b = 16 \end{array}$$

$\frac{7}{4}(4a+4b=16)$ (multiply by $\frac{7}{4}$)

$7a+7b=28$

25. $a-b=b-c=c-a$

$a-b=b-c \rightarrow 2b=a+c$

$a-b=c-a \rightarrow 2a=c+b$

$2b=a+c$

$\therefore\ 4b=2a+2c$, but $2a=c+b$

$4b=(c+b)+2c$ (substitute $(c+b)$ for $2a$)

$4b=3c+b$

$3b=3c$

$b=c$

$2b=a+c$ (substitute c for b)

$2c=a+c$

$c=a$

$\therefore\ a=b=c$

$\therefore\ \frac{2a+3b}{c}=\frac{2a+3a}{a}=\frac{5a}{a}=5$

Section 2

1. **(C)** A record collection that includes all kinds of music can be described as *eclectic* (composed of materials from a variety of sources).

2. **(B)** The implication is that the objective is a good one although the plan for achieving it is not. Choice (B), *laudable* (or praiseworthy), is the correct completion of this sentence.

3. **(B)** A statement that is *equivocal* can have more than one interpretation and thus leave doubt about the speaker's intentions.

4. **(D)** One is investigated only if misconduct is suspected. Filing *duplicitous* or deceitful forms would be cause for investigation. It is not likely that one would be investigated for filing true (A), duplicate (B), unnecessary (C), or messy (E) forms.

5. **(D)** The sentence implies that the teacher is being praised. *Commend* is a synonym for praise.

6. **(E)** The first word in each choice is acceptable. Quickly plugging in the choices eliminates the wrong answers.

7. **(C)** Taping every episode implies that the teenagers were *assiduous* (extremely attentive) followers of the soap opera.

8. **(B)** The key word in the sentence is *postponing*. By spinning tales, Scheherazade *temporized* (delayed in order to gain time), thus stalling her planned execution.

9. **(C)** The key word is *fair*. The supervisor could be proud of any of the choices, but the only one that means "fairness" is *objectivity*.

10. **(D)** The only choice that makes sense is (D). When research becomes highly *specialized*, people working on different aspects of the same problem may be unaware of or *unfamiliar with* each other's work.

11. **(A)** The pair of words must be contrasting due to the word *but*. Living in *isolation* is the opposite of living in a *community*.

12. **(C)** One's view is influenced by one's beliefs, or *philosophy*.

13. **(C)** This is the only pair that makes sense.

14. **(D)** The military censors are concerned about maintaining security. If they find passages in a letter that *jeopardize* (endanger) it, they would *expunge* (erase) those passages.

15. **(D)** A *trumpet* is a small brass instrument, while a *tuba* is a large brass instrument. A *piccolo* is a small wind instrument, while a *bassoon* is a large one.

16. **(D)** A *dinghy* is a small boat that operates in the water, and a *glider* is a small flying craft that operates in the *air*.

17. **(A)** A *nail* makes a *puncture*, and a *scalpel* makes an *incision*.

18. **(C)** A *galaxy* is made up of many *stars*, and a *flock* is made up of many *birds*.

19. **(C)** *Silver* is a *metal* and *helium* is a *gas*.

20. **(D)** A *sprinter* has great *speed*, and a *weightlifter* has great *strength*.

21. **(C)** An *interloper* seeks to *meddle* in the affairs of another. An *avenger* seeks to *punish* another.

22. **(A)** *Meteorology* is the study of *weather*, and *ornithology* is the study of *birds*.

23. **(B)** An *innovation* is the brand-new idea that lacks *precedent* (an earlier instance or example). Similarly, an *illusion* by definition lacks *veracity* (truthfulness).

24. **(E)** An *anarchist* is a *lawless* person; a *philistine* is an *uncultured* person.

25. **(B)** *Detrimental* means *harmful*. *Pernicious* means fatal, a greater degree of harm. *Cheerful* means happy. *Exuberant* means uninhibited or high-spirited, denoting a higher degree of joy.

26. **(B)** Each of the choices is a kind of rhetorical element, a form used in speech-making. In this case, the speaker asks what is called a rhetorical question, which is one that doesn't need an answer and is asked only for effect or emphasis. Even if you do not know this term, process of elimination and the fact that the first sentences of the passage are questions should make the answer evident.

27. **(A)** Substituting the choices in place of the italicized word will make your choice clear.

28. **(C)** If you know the word, only one choice is synonymous. If you do not know it, test the choices in context.

29. **(B)** Douglass states (B) in lines 15–16: "There is blasphemy in the thought." He also clearly believes that there is no further point in debating the issue and that arguments over whether or not God ordained slavery are futile.

30. **(D)** Douglass refers to fire, thunder, storm, whirlwind, and earthquake to emphasize the need for drastic—and if necessary, violent—action.

31. **(E)** This kind of interpretation question may be easier to answer if you try restating the phrase in your own words and comparing them to the choices. Here, choices (A), (B), and (D) are relatively meaningless. Choice (C) may be true, but it is not a restatement of the phrase.

32. **(A)** Douglass says that to the American slave, the Fourth of July is a "sham," a "mockery," a "fraud," and a "deception." Nothing in the passage supports choices (B), (C), or (D), and as for (E), Douglass has said that the time for debate is passed.

33. **(C)** The crimes covered up by this thin veil are the crimes of a group worse than savages. Only choice (C) has this connotation.

34. **(E)** A careful reading of the text surrounding this citation shows that in Douglass's view, America compares unfavorably with every other nation, including South America.

35. **(A)** Paragraph 4 contains a furious denunciation of the Fourth of July as hypocritical at a time when some Americans are being held as slaves. Douglass's words most likely shocked and frightened his mostly white Rochester audience.

Section 3

1. **(A)** The number line below shows the approximate location of the five fractions.

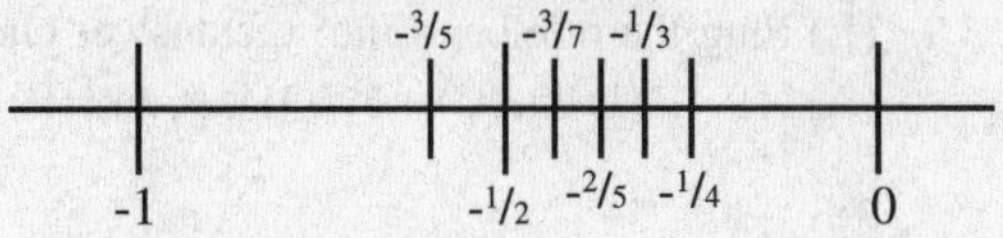

2. **(B)** Be careful in converting the words into an equation.

$$\frac{2}{3}x = 6 + \frac{1}{2}x$$

Subtract $\frac{1}{2}x$ from both sides:

$$\frac{1}{6}x = 6$$

$$x = 36$$

3. **(E)** 10 divided by 2 is equal to 5, which in percent form is 500%.

4. **(C)** The savings on one quart is \$1.39 - \$.59 = .80. The savings on six quarts is $6 \times .80 = \$4.80$.

5. **(A)** Since the square has a side of m, its area is m^2. The unshaded triangle has an area of $\frac{mn}{2}$. The shaded area is equal to the whole square minus the unshaded portion.

6. **(A)** Proposition II is eliminated because it has John 12 inches taller than Henry. Proposition III is eliminated because it does not have Henry at $\frac{3}{4}$ of Mark's height.

7. **(B)** $\dfrac{\frac{2}{3}+\frac{3}{4}+\frac{5}{6}}{3}=$

$$\frac{\frac{8}{12}+\frac{9}{12}+\frac{10}{12}}{3}=\frac{\frac{27}{12}}{3}=\frac{27}{12}\bullet\frac{1}{3}=\frac{27}{36}=\frac{3}{4}$$

8. **(E)** Plug the answer choices into the equation until you find the one that does not allow j to be an integer.

Example: (A) $\frac{3}{4}j=9$

$$j=9\left(\frac{4}{3}\right)$$
$$j=12$$

(E) $\frac{3}{4}j=20$

$$j=20\left(\frac{4}{3}\right)$$
$$j=\frac{80}{3}=26\frac{2}{3}$$

9. **(E)** Plug the number 4 into the answer choices. (A) is 9, (B) is 25, (C) is 3, (D) is 9, and (E) is 12.

10. **(B)** Since a ratio is used, we are free to plug in any numbers that we wish so long as they fit the ratio. Since segment *CD* is the smallest, let's assign a value of 1 to that length. Segment *BC* is twice as long, so it will be 2. Segment *AB* is three times as long as segment *BC*, so it is 6. Segment *AD* has a total length of 9. If we subtract segment *BC*, it has a length of 7.

Section 4

1. **(B)** When Usamah calls new emigrants from Frankish lands "ruder in character" than those who have been around for a while (lines 1–4), he refers not only to a level of civility, but to a level of refinement that can be achieved only by fraternizing with diverse peoples.

2. **(A)** The Frank is violent and emotional in his reaction; he evidently sees this form of prayer as heresy, a gross violation of his own beliefs.

3. **(A)** Usamah, a gentleman himself, cannot understand the behavior of the crude visitor to his land. He says himself that he has "ever been surprised" at his conduct (lines 26–27).

4. **(B)** This line refers to the people's despair rather than to their hunger or illness. Black Elk is saying that to give up their dance would be the last straw.

5. **(E)** The Wasichus would not throw people in jail and mass soldiers near the ridge if they saw the refusal simply as rudeness (A). They are afraid that one refusal will lead to others, and that insurrection is possible.

6. **(E)** The Wasichus have made and broken promises before (lines 49–52), and now Black Elk does not trust them.

7. **(C)** The scenes of wild dancing contrasted with the scenes of soldiers on the move lead to a feeling of tension. Clearly something bad is going to happen.

8. **(A)** Usamah is mystified by the Frank's emotional response to his praying (lines 26–29). Black Elk even says that the Wasichus were "afraid of something" (lines 33–34). Both the reactions seem overly emotional and somewhat fearful—afraid of change, or differences, or possible rebellion.

9. **(C)** In Passage 1, a Frank tries to keep Usamah from praying while facing Mecca. In Passage 2, white men try to keep the Indians from doing their sacred dance.

10. **(B)** Usamah does not fight against the Franks, but neither does he blindly accept their behavior. He accepts their differences even while concluding that his way is better. He would be appalled that the Wasichus were trying to strip a sacred rite from a people they had conquered.

Section 5

1. **(B)** First you must find a common denominator for 3, 4, and 6. The lowest common denominator would be 12.

$$\frac{8}{12}+\frac{9}{12}+\frac{10}{12}+p=3$$
$$\frac{27}{12}+p=3$$
$$p=\frac{36}{12}-\frac{27}{12}$$
$$p=\frac{9}{12}$$
$$p=\frac{3}{4}$$

2. **(C)** The 130-degree angle and the angle next to it must add up to 180 degrees, as they form a straight line. All triangles contain 180 degrees, so
$180 = 50 + x + y$
$130 = x + y$
Note that we can tell the value of $x + y$, but we cannot tell the value of x or y alone.

3. **(A)** Since $Q = S + 2$, we can substitute $S + 2$ in place of Q in the first equation.

Step 1: $P = QR$ is the same as $P = (S + 2)R$

Step 2: Divide both sides by R:
$$\frac{P}{R}=S+2$$

4. **(D)** Answer choices (A), (C), and (E) must be negative, while (B) and (D) are positive. (B) is $\frac{1}{16}$, while (D) is $\frac{1}{4}$.

5. **(C)** $5\times1\frac{1}{2}=7\frac{1}{2}$
If the woman runs $7\frac{1}{2}$ miles in an hour, then that is her average miles per hour.

6. **(E)** If the average of the four numbers is 11, then the sum must be 4×11.

7. **(A)** If 9 pears spoiled, then 171 did not.
$$\frac{171}{180}=\frac{19}{20}=95\%$$

8. **(E)** Follow the instructions one step at a time.

Step 1: $3r$

Step 2: $3r-3$

Step 3: $\frac{3r-3}{3}$

Step 4: The 3's divide out and leave $r-1$.

9. **(C)** Since $ABCD$ is a square, all of the sides must be 4. We know that the triangles are both right triangles since they are adjacent to the square. Therefore, they are both 3, 4, 5 triangles.
$2(3+4+5)=24$

10. **(B)** $\sqrt{\frac{3}{4}-\frac{3}{16}}=\sqrt{\frac{12}{16}-\frac{3}{16}}=\sqrt{\frac{9}{16}}=\frac{3}{4}$

11. **(D)** The easiest way to solve this is to substitute into the formula.

Answer A = $6(2+3+4)=54$
Answer B = $6(4+3+2)=54$
Answer C = $6(3+5+1)=54$
Answer D = $6(4+1+5)=60$
Answer E = $6(1+5+3)=54$

12. **(D)** This is solved by dividing 16.4 by 16.

```
    1.025
16)16.400
   16
   --
     40
     32
     --
      80
      80
      --
```

13. **(A)** Circumference $=2\pi r$
$x=2\pi r$ (substitute x)
$\frac{x}{2\pi}=r$ (divide by 2π)

14. **(A)** The product of the terms can be positive if they are both negative or both positive. This chart shows the combinations.

	$x<-1$	$-1<x<2$	$x>2$
$x+1$	–	+	+
$x-2$	–	–	+
$(x+1)(x-2)$	+	–	+

15. **(E)** Segment AD is the base of the triangle and the length of the rectangle. Segment CD is the height of the triangle and the width of the rectangle. Let's use l and w to represent length and width.

Area $ABCD = l \times w$

Area $\Delta AED = \dfrac{l \times w}{2}$

Since the rectangle is twice as big as the triangle, the ratio is 1 : 2.

16. **(C)** Each of the choices will have to be considered.

I. 6 can be divided by 1, 2, and 3.
$1 + 2 + 3 = 6$
II. 12 can be divided by 1, 2, 3, 4, and 6.
$1 + 2 + 3 + 4 + 6 = 16$
III. 28 can be divided by 1, 2, 4, 7, and 14.
$1 + 2 + 4 + 7 + 14 = 28$
IV. 32 can be divided by 1, 2, 4, 8, and 16.
$1 + 2 + 4 + 8 + 16 = 31$

Only I and III are full numbers.

17. **(E)** The formula for finding percent change is Difference divided by the Original Amount.

(A) $\dfrac{2000}{7000} \cong 28\%$

(B) $\dfrac{3000}{9000} = 33\frac{1}{3}\%$

(C) $\dfrac{4000}{12000} = 33\frac{1}{3}\%$

(D) $\dfrac{4000}{16000} = 25\%$

(E) $\dfrac{4000}{20000} = 20\%$

18. **(A)** To compute an average, add the items to be averaged and then divide that sum by the number of items.

$$\frac{70+75+80+y}{4} = \frac{225+y}{4}$$

19. **(B)** In order to use one measurement, convert 3 feet into 36 inches. Therefore, the two snails have to move a total of 36 inches.

$$.04d + .05d = 36$$
$$.09d = 36$$
$$d = 400$$

It will take 400 seconds, which is equal to $6\frac{2}{3}$ minutes.

20. **(D)** 1st month $= 500$
2nd month $= 500 + .10(500) = 550$
3rd month $= 550 + .10(550) = 605$
4th month $= 605 + .10(605) = 665.50$

21. **(B)** The question translated into algebra would read $J = 4(A-6)$.
$20 = 4A - 24$
$44 = 4A$
$11 = A$

22. **(D)** Set these up as simultaneous equations and solve.

$$a^2 - 2ab + b^2 = 36$$
$$\underline{-(a^2 - 3ab + b^2 = 22)}$$
$$ab = 14$$

23. **(C)** It makes the problem easier if you realize that the facing semicircles form two whole circles. The smaller circle has a diameter of 1 and, therefore, a radius of $\frac{1}{2}$.
Area $= \pi(\frac{1}{2})^2 = \frac{\pi}{4}$
The larger circle has a diameter of 2 and, therefore, a radius of 1. Area $= \pi(1)^2 = \pi$

$$\frac{4\pi}{4} + \frac{\pi}{4} = \frac{5\pi}{4}$$

24. **(D)** $P = \dfrac{1}{2} + \dfrac{1}{3} = \dfrac{3}{6} + \dfrac{2}{6} = \dfrac{5}{6}$

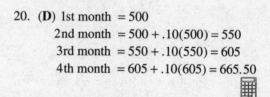

$$Q = P^2 = \left(\frac{5}{6}\right)^2 = \frac{25}{36}$$

$$Q - P = \frac{25}{36} - \frac{5}{6} = \frac{25}{36} - \frac{30}{36} = -\frac{5}{36}$$

25. **(B)** There are several ways to solve this problem. One way would be to divide the square into four triangles each of which would be a 45° - 45° - 90° triangle.
The ratio of the sides of a 45° : 45° : 90° is $1:1:\sqrt{2}$, giving sides of $3:3:3\sqrt{2}$ and an area of $3\sqrt{2}\times3\sqrt{2}=18$.
OR diagonal = 6

$$\text{Area} = \frac{d^2}{2} = \frac{6^2}{2} = 18.$$

Section 6

1. **(D)** A person who leads a *secluded* life has no contact with the outside world and therefore would have to use *imagination* to explore it. None of the other choices makes sense.

2. **(E)** Spending all one's money will *preclude* (make impossible) a trip to the movies.

3. **(C)** One is unlikely to gain admission to a top college with an academic record that is *mediocre* (merely ordinary).

4. **(A)** The blue whale typically grows to *prodigious* (huge) size and must eat tons of plankton to *satiate* (satisfy) its huge appetite.

5. **(C)** A recklessly bold attempt is by definition characterized by *audacity* and was successful because the enemy failed to *anticipate* it.

6. **(C)** An *hour* is a measure of *time*, while a *gram* is a measure of *weight*.

7. **(D)** A *gem* is placed within a *setting* in jewelry, just as a *picture* is placed within a *frame*.

8. **(C)** A *ship* is part of an *armada*, and an *atom* is part of a *molecule*.

9. **(A)** A *caterpillar* changes into a *butterfly*, and a *tadpole* turns into a *frog*.

10. **(E)** To *tremble* is a sign of *fear*, just as to *weep* is a sign of *grief*.

11. **(C)** A *conflagration* is a huge fire, while a *spark* is a very small fire. A *drizzle* is a very light rain, while a *downpour* is very heavy rain.

12. **(E)** *Robust* means full of *vigor*, just as *sanguine* means full of *hope*.

13. **(D)** *Perfidy*, or betrayal of trust, is a characteristic of a *traitorous* person. *Steadfastness*, or constancy, is a characteristic of a *loyal* person.

14. **(A)** Knight talks about the buildings, fashions, and diversions she sees in New York, in that order.

15. **(E)** Knight probably means "middle class"; her point is that this kind of Dutch woman dresses oddly.

16. **(C)** Knight notes that "the English [women] go very fashionable in their dress," but "the Dutch . . . differ from our women, in their habit go loose. . . ." All of the other items are mentioned as forming part of the Dutch women's attire.

17. **(D)** "Mr. Burroughs carried his spouse and Daughter and myself out to one Madame Dowes . . ." (lines 41–42). It is clear from what has gone before that Mr. Burroughs is transporting the women, probably in a sleigh.

18. **(E)** *Metheglin* is a kind of mead, or alcoholic drink. It is part of a list of beverages, so one can infer that it, too, is a beverage.

19. **(B)** Only this point is stated, in lines 22–23.

20. **(B)** Knight's delight and surprise indicate that she has never seen the sights of New York before. She has, however, been out of Boston (A); she mentions "other places where I had been" (lines 23–24). The passage offers no support for choices (C), (D), or (E).

21. **(C)** Lines 28–32 show Knight's condescending attitude toward the Dutch women and their outfits.

22. **(C)** New Yorkers' tables are "as free to their Neighbors as to themselves," a fact that impresses Knight greatly.

23. **(E)** In paragraph 3, it is clearly developed that Jimmie is the reason for the fight. The taunts of his schoolmates put him on the defensive and lead up to the point in paragraph 4 where he takes

matters into his own hands "with a blow." He strikes out at friends and enemies alike.

24. **(A)** *Virulence* means "bitter hostility," and as the playground events developed, Jimmie's friends proved every bit as hostile to him as his enemies—or so it appeared to him.

25. **(B)** In the story, Jimmie is teased mercilessly by the other children until finally their taunts goad him into striking back. They *bait*, or *provoke*, him into starting the fight.

26. **(D)** Irony, in which the result is the opposite of what might be expected, is found in the behavior of the little girl. At the beginning of the passage she is gleefully taunting Jimmie, but once the fight starts, she begins weeping.

27. **(A)** In the opening paragraph, little Rose claims to have seen Jimmie writing to his girlfriend. However, the girlfriend never actually appears in the story.

28. **(C)** The "empress" who demands to know who took part in the fight is clearly the teacher.

29. **(B)** Since "sorrow had fallen upon the house of Trescott" when the teacher reprimanded Jimmie, the boy was clearly defeated.

30. **(A)** Little Rose begins by teasing Jimmie, but she's sorry once the fight starts. Later, however, she gloats, or is secretly pleased, when Jimmie is punished.

Evaluating Practice Examination 6

To determine your Verbal Reasoning Score:

1. Using the Analysis Worksheet, enter the number of correct answers for each verbal reasoning section on the appropriate line in Column A of the Verbal Reasoning grid.
2. Enter the number of incorrect answers for each verbal reasoning section on the appropriate line in Column B of the Verbal Reasoning grid.
3. Total Columns A and B and enter these totals in boxes A and B, respectively.
4. Perform the indicated calculation to find your Raw Score: (value in box A) minus (one-quarter of the value in box B) = Raw Score.
5. Consult the Conversion Chart to find your approximate Scaled Score.

To determine your Mathematical Reasoning Score:

1. Enter the number of correct answers for each mathematical reasoning section on the appropriate line in Column C of the Mathematical Reasoning grid.
2. Enter the number of incorrect answers for each mathematical reasoning section on the appropriate line in Column D, E, or F of the Mathematical Reasoning grid.
3. Total Columns C, D, and E, and enter these totals in boxes C, D, and E, respectively.
4. Perform the indicated calculation to find your Raw Score: (value in box C) minus (one-quarter of the value in box D) minus (one-third of the value in box E) = Raw Score.
5. Consult the Conversion Chart to find your approximate Scaled Score.

   Note: Box F is not used in this calculation.

Analysis Worksheet

VERBAL REASONING

Section	Number of Questions	Column A Number of Correct Answers	Column B Number of Incorrect Answers
2	35		
4	10		
6	30		
	Total	A	B

A − ¼ B = Raw Score → Use Conversion Chart → Scaled Score

MATHEMATICAL REASONING

Section		Number of Questions	Column C Number of Correct Answers	Col. D	Col. E	Col. F
				Number of Incorrect Answers		
3		10				
5		25				
1	Part I	15				
	Part II	10				
		Total	C	D	E	F

C − ¼ D − ⅓ E = Raw Score → Use Conversion Chart → Scaled Score

Conversion Scales for Practice Examination 6

VERBAL REASONING

Raw Score	Scaled Score	Raw Score	Scaled Score
75	800	40	550
70	800	35	520
65	760	30	480
60	710	25	440
55	670	20	410
50	620	15	370
45	590	10	340
		5	290
		0	230

MATHEMATICAL REASONING

Raw Score	Scaled Score	Raw Score	Scaled Score
60	800	25	510
55	760	20	480
50	690	15	440
45	650	10	410
40	610	5	340
35	580	0	200
30	550		

Although you now have some idea of what your scores would look like had they been scaled according to unofficial ETS standards, you will probably want to know how to interpret your Raw Scores in more familiar terms. If so, use the following Self-Evaluation Charts to see what your Raw Scores actually mean.

SELF-EVALUATION CHARTS

VERBAL REASONING: RAW SCORE

Excellent	60 – 75
Good	50 – 60
Average	30 – 50
Fair	20 – 30
Poor	0 – 20

MATHEMATICAL REASONING: RAW SCORE

Excellent	50 – 60
Good	40 – 50
Average	20 – 40
Fair	10 – 20
Poor	0 – 10

P A R T

SIX

Final Practice Examination

CONTENTS

Final Practice Examination

Answer Sheet

If a section has fewer questions than answer ovals, leave the extra ovals blank.

Section 1

1	Ⓐ Ⓑ Ⓒ Ⓓ Ⓔ	11	Ⓐ Ⓑ Ⓒ Ⓓ Ⓔ	21	Ⓐ Ⓑ Ⓒ Ⓓ Ⓔ	31	Ⓐ Ⓑ Ⓒ Ⓓ Ⓔ
2	Ⓐ Ⓑ Ⓒ Ⓓ Ⓔ	12	Ⓐ Ⓑ Ⓒ Ⓓ Ⓔ	22	Ⓐ Ⓑ Ⓒ Ⓓ Ⓔ	32	Ⓐ Ⓑ Ⓒ Ⓓ Ⓔ
3	Ⓐ Ⓑ Ⓒ Ⓓ Ⓔ	13	Ⓐ Ⓑ Ⓒ Ⓓ Ⓔ	23	Ⓐ Ⓑ Ⓒ Ⓓ Ⓔ	33	Ⓐ Ⓑ Ⓒ Ⓓ Ⓔ
4	Ⓐ Ⓑ Ⓒ Ⓓ Ⓔ	14	Ⓐ Ⓑ Ⓒ Ⓓ Ⓔ	24	Ⓐ Ⓑ Ⓒ Ⓓ Ⓔ	34	Ⓐ Ⓑ Ⓒ Ⓓ Ⓔ
5	Ⓐ Ⓑ Ⓒ Ⓓ Ⓔ	15	Ⓐ Ⓑ Ⓒ Ⓓ Ⓔ	25	Ⓐ Ⓑ Ⓒ Ⓓ Ⓔ	35	Ⓐ Ⓑ Ⓒ Ⓓ Ⓔ
6	Ⓐ Ⓑ Ⓒ Ⓓ Ⓔ	16	Ⓐ Ⓑ Ⓒ Ⓓ Ⓔ	26	Ⓐ Ⓑ Ⓒ Ⓓ Ⓔ	36	Ⓐ Ⓑ Ⓒ Ⓓ Ⓔ
7	Ⓐ Ⓑ Ⓒ Ⓓ Ⓔ	17	Ⓐ Ⓑ Ⓒ Ⓓ Ⓔ	27	Ⓐ Ⓑ Ⓒ Ⓓ Ⓔ	37	Ⓐ Ⓑ Ⓒ Ⓓ Ⓔ
8	Ⓐ Ⓑ Ⓒ Ⓓ Ⓔ	18	Ⓐ Ⓑ Ⓒ Ⓓ Ⓔ	28	Ⓐ Ⓑ Ⓒ Ⓓ Ⓔ	38	Ⓐ Ⓑ Ⓒ Ⓓ Ⓔ
9	Ⓐ Ⓑ Ⓒ Ⓓ Ⓔ	19	Ⓐ Ⓑ Ⓒ Ⓓ Ⓔ	29	Ⓐ Ⓑ Ⓒ Ⓓ Ⓔ	39	Ⓐ Ⓑ Ⓒ Ⓓ Ⓔ
10	Ⓐ Ⓑ Ⓒ Ⓓ Ⓔ	20	Ⓐ Ⓑ Ⓒ Ⓓ Ⓔ	30	Ⓐ Ⓑ Ⓒ Ⓓ Ⓔ	40	Ⓐ Ⓑ Ⓒ Ⓓ Ⓔ

Section 2

1	Ⓐ Ⓑ Ⓒ Ⓓ Ⓔ	11	Ⓐ Ⓑ Ⓒ Ⓓ Ⓔ	21	Ⓐ Ⓑ Ⓒ Ⓓ Ⓔ	31	Ⓐ Ⓑ Ⓒ Ⓓ Ⓔ
2	Ⓐ Ⓑ Ⓒ Ⓓ Ⓔ	12	Ⓐ Ⓑ Ⓒ Ⓓ Ⓔ	22	Ⓐ Ⓑ Ⓒ Ⓓ Ⓔ	32	Ⓐ Ⓑ Ⓒ Ⓓ Ⓔ
3	Ⓐ Ⓑ Ⓒ Ⓓ Ⓔ	13	Ⓐ Ⓑ Ⓒ Ⓓ Ⓔ	23	Ⓐ Ⓑ Ⓒ Ⓓ Ⓔ	33	Ⓐ Ⓑ Ⓒ Ⓓ Ⓔ
4	Ⓐ Ⓑ Ⓒ Ⓓ Ⓔ	14	Ⓐ Ⓑ Ⓒ Ⓓ Ⓔ	24	Ⓐ Ⓑ Ⓒ Ⓓ Ⓔ	34	Ⓐ Ⓑ Ⓒ Ⓓ Ⓔ
5	Ⓐ Ⓑ Ⓒ Ⓓ Ⓔ	15	Ⓐ Ⓑ Ⓒ Ⓓ Ⓔ	25	Ⓐ Ⓑ Ⓒ Ⓓ Ⓔ	35	Ⓐ Ⓑ Ⓒ Ⓓ Ⓔ
6	Ⓐ Ⓑ Ⓒ Ⓓ Ⓔ	16	Ⓐ Ⓑ Ⓒ Ⓓ Ⓔ	26	Ⓐ Ⓑ Ⓒ Ⓓ Ⓔ	36	Ⓐ Ⓑ Ⓒ Ⓓ Ⓔ
7	Ⓐ Ⓑ Ⓒ Ⓓ Ⓔ	17	Ⓐ Ⓑ Ⓒ Ⓓ Ⓔ	27	Ⓐ Ⓑ Ⓒ Ⓓ Ⓔ	37	Ⓐ Ⓑ Ⓒ Ⓓ Ⓔ
8	Ⓐ Ⓑ Ⓒ Ⓓ Ⓔ	18	Ⓐ Ⓑ Ⓒ Ⓓ Ⓔ	28	Ⓐ Ⓑ Ⓒ Ⓓ Ⓔ	38	Ⓐ Ⓑ Ⓒ Ⓓ Ⓔ
9	Ⓐ Ⓑ Ⓒ Ⓓ Ⓔ	19	Ⓐ Ⓑ Ⓒ Ⓓ Ⓔ	29	Ⓐ Ⓑ Ⓒ Ⓓ Ⓔ	39	Ⓐ Ⓑ Ⓒ Ⓓ Ⓔ
10	Ⓐ Ⓑ Ⓒ Ⓓ Ⓔ	20	Ⓐ Ⓑ Ⓒ Ⓓ Ⓔ	30	Ⓐ Ⓑ Ⓒ Ⓓ Ⓔ	40	Ⓐ Ⓑ Ⓒ Ⓓ Ⓔ

Section 3

1	Ⓐ Ⓑ Ⓒ Ⓓ Ⓔ	6	Ⓐ Ⓑ Ⓒ Ⓓ Ⓔ	11	Ⓐ Ⓑ Ⓒ Ⓓ Ⓔ	16	Ⓐ Ⓑ Ⓒ Ⓓ Ⓔ
2	Ⓐ Ⓑ Ⓒ Ⓓ Ⓔ	7	Ⓐ Ⓑ Ⓒ Ⓓ Ⓔ	12	Ⓐ Ⓑ Ⓒ Ⓓ Ⓔ	17	Ⓐ Ⓑ Ⓒ Ⓓ Ⓔ
3	Ⓐ Ⓑ Ⓒ Ⓓ Ⓔ	8	Ⓐ Ⓑ Ⓒ Ⓓ Ⓔ	13	Ⓐ Ⓑ Ⓒ Ⓓ Ⓔ	18	Ⓐ Ⓑ Ⓒ Ⓓ Ⓔ
4	Ⓐ Ⓑ Ⓒ Ⓓ Ⓔ	9	Ⓐ Ⓑ Ⓒ Ⓓ Ⓔ	14	Ⓐ Ⓑ Ⓒ Ⓓ Ⓔ	19	Ⓐ Ⓑ Ⓒ Ⓓ Ⓔ
5	Ⓐ Ⓑ Ⓒ Ⓓ Ⓔ	10	Ⓐ Ⓑ Ⓒ Ⓓ Ⓔ	15	Ⓐ Ⓑ Ⓒ Ⓓ Ⓔ	20	Ⓐ Ⓑ Ⓒ Ⓓ Ⓔ

Section 4

1	Ⓐ Ⓑ Ⓒ Ⓓ Ⓔ	6	Ⓐ Ⓑ Ⓒ Ⓓ Ⓔ	11	Ⓐ Ⓑ Ⓒ Ⓓ Ⓔ	16	Ⓐ Ⓑ Ⓒ Ⓓ Ⓔ
2	Ⓐ Ⓑ Ⓒ Ⓓ Ⓔ	7	Ⓐ Ⓑ Ⓒ Ⓓ Ⓔ	12	Ⓐ Ⓑ Ⓒ Ⓓ Ⓔ	17	Ⓐ Ⓑ Ⓒ Ⓓ Ⓔ
3	Ⓐ Ⓑ Ⓒ Ⓓ Ⓔ	8	Ⓐ Ⓑ Ⓒ Ⓓ Ⓔ	13	Ⓐ Ⓑ Ⓒ Ⓓ Ⓔ	18	Ⓐ Ⓑ Ⓒ Ⓓ Ⓔ
4	Ⓐ Ⓑ Ⓒ Ⓓ Ⓔ	9	Ⓐ Ⓑ Ⓒ Ⓓ Ⓔ	14	Ⓐ Ⓑ Ⓒ Ⓓ Ⓔ	19	Ⓐ Ⓑ Ⓒ Ⓓ Ⓔ
5	Ⓐ Ⓑ Ⓒ Ⓓ Ⓔ	10	Ⓐ Ⓑ Ⓒ Ⓓ Ⓔ	15	Ⓐ Ⓑ Ⓒ Ⓓ Ⓔ	20	Ⓐ Ⓑ Ⓒ Ⓓ Ⓔ

Section 5

1	Ⓐ	Ⓑ	Ⓒ	Ⓓ	Ⓔ	6	Ⓐ	Ⓑ	Ⓒ	Ⓓ	Ⓔ	11	Ⓐ	Ⓑ	Ⓒ	Ⓓ	Ⓔ
2	Ⓐ	Ⓑ	Ⓒ	Ⓓ	Ⓔ	7	Ⓐ	Ⓑ	Ⓒ	Ⓓ	Ⓔ	12	Ⓐ	Ⓑ	Ⓒ	Ⓓ	Ⓔ
3	Ⓐ	Ⓑ	Ⓒ	Ⓓ	Ⓔ	8	Ⓐ	Ⓑ	Ⓒ	Ⓓ	Ⓔ	13	Ⓐ	Ⓑ	Ⓒ	Ⓓ	Ⓔ
4	Ⓐ	Ⓑ	Ⓒ	Ⓓ	Ⓔ	9	Ⓐ	Ⓑ	Ⓒ	Ⓓ	Ⓔ	14	Ⓐ	Ⓑ	Ⓒ	Ⓓ	Ⓔ
5	Ⓐ	Ⓑ	Ⓒ	Ⓓ	Ⓔ	10	Ⓐ	Ⓑ	Ⓒ	Ⓓ	Ⓔ	15	Ⓐ	Ⓑ	Ⓒ	Ⓓ	Ⓔ

Note: ONLY the answers entered on the grid are scored.
Handwritten answers at the top of the column are NOT scored.

Grid-in answer boxes 16, 17, 18, 19, 20, 21, 22, 23, 24, 25 (each grid):

	/	/	
.	.	.	.
	0	0	0
1	1	1	1
2	2	2	2
3	3	3	3
4	4	4	4
5	5	5	5
6	6	6	6
7	7	7	7
8	8	8	8
9	9	9	9

Section 6

1	Ⓐ	Ⓑ	Ⓒ	Ⓓ	Ⓔ	11	Ⓐ	Ⓑ	Ⓒ	Ⓓ	Ⓔ	21	Ⓐ	Ⓑ	Ⓒ	Ⓓ	Ⓔ	31	Ⓐ	Ⓑ	Ⓒ	Ⓓ	Ⓔ
2	Ⓐ	Ⓑ	Ⓒ	Ⓓ	Ⓔ	12	Ⓐ	Ⓑ	Ⓒ	Ⓓ	Ⓔ	22	Ⓐ	Ⓑ	Ⓒ	Ⓓ	Ⓔ	32	Ⓐ	Ⓑ	Ⓒ	Ⓓ	Ⓔ
3	Ⓐ	Ⓑ	Ⓒ	Ⓓ	Ⓔ	13	Ⓐ	Ⓑ	Ⓒ	Ⓓ	Ⓔ	23	Ⓐ	Ⓑ	Ⓒ	Ⓓ	Ⓔ	33	Ⓐ	Ⓑ	Ⓒ	Ⓓ	Ⓔ
4	Ⓐ	Ⓑ	Ⓒ	Ⓓ	Ⓔ	14	Ⓐ	Ⓑ	Ⓒ	Ⓓ	Ⓔ	24	Ⓐ	Ⓑ	Ⓒ	Ⓓ	Ⓔ	34	Ⓐ	Ⓑ	Ⓒ	Ⓓ	Ⓔ
5	Ⓐ	Ⓑ	Ⓒ	Ⓓ	Ⓔ	15	Ⓐ	Ⓑ	Ⓒ	Ⓓ	Ⓔ	25	Ⓐ	Ⓑ	Ⓒ	Ⓓ	Ⓔ	35	Ⓐ	Ⓑ	Ⓒ	Ⓓ	Ⓔ
6	Ⓐ	Ⓑ	Ⓒ	Ⓓ	Ⓔ	16	Ⓐ	Ⓑ	Ⓒ	Ⓓ	Ⓔ	26	Ⓐ	Ⓑ	Ⓒ	Ⓓ	Ⓔ	36	Ⓐ	Ⓑ	Ⓒ	Ⓓ	Ⓔ
7	Ⓐ	Ⓑ	Ⓒ	Ⓓ	Ⓔ	17	Ⓐ	Ⓑ	Ⓒ	Ⓓ	Ⓔ	27	Ⓐ	Ⓑ	Ⓒ	Ⓓ	Ⓔ	37	Ⓐ	Ⓑ	Ⓒ	Ⓓ	Ⓔ
8	Ⓐ	Ⓑ	Ⓒ	Ⓓ	Ⓔ	18	Ⓐ	Ⓑ	Ⓒ	Ⓓ	Ⓔ	28	Ⓐ	Ⓑ	Ⓒ	Ⓓ	Ⓔ	38	Ⓐ	Ⓑ	Ⓒ	Ⓓ	Ⓔ
9	Ⓐ	Ⓑ	Ⓒ	Ⓓ	Ⓔ	19	Ⓐ	Ⓑ	Ⓒ	Ⓓ	Ⓔ	29	Ⓐ	Ⓑ	Ⓒ	Ⓓ	Ⓔ	39	Ⓐ	Ⓑ	Ⓒ	Ⓓ	Ⓔ
10	Ⓐ	Ⓑ	Ⓒ	Ⓓ	Ⓔ	20	Ⓐ	Ⓑ	Ⓒ	Ⓓ	Ⓔ	30	Ⓐ	Ⓑ	Ⓒ	Ⓓ	Ⓔ	40	Ⓐ	Ⓑ	Ⓒ	Ⓓ	Ⓔ

Final Practice Examination

SECTION 1

25 Questions • Time—30 Minutes

Directions: Solve the following problems using any available space on the page for scratchwork. On your answer sheet fill in the choice which best corresponds to the correct answer.

Notes: The figures accompanying the problems are drawn as accurately as possible unless otherwise stated in specific problems. Again, unless otherwise stated, all figures lie in the same plane. All numbers used in these problems are real numbers. Calculators are permitted for this test.

Reference Information

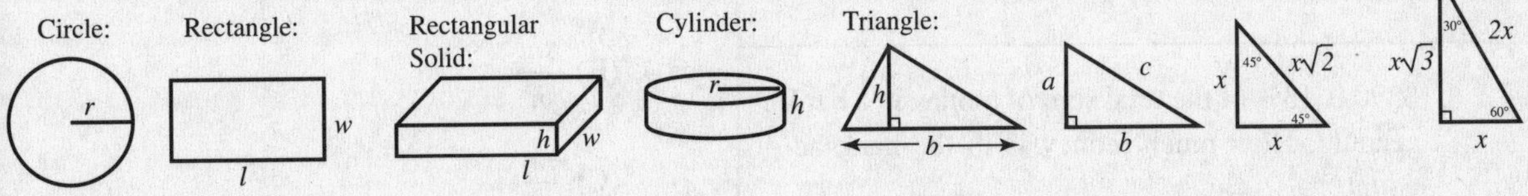

$C = 2\pi r$, $A = \pi r^2$ | $A = lw$ | $V = lwh$ | $V = \pi r^2 h$ | $A = \frac{1}{2}bh$ | $a^2 + b^2 = c^2$

The number of degrees of arc in a circle is 360.
The measure in degrees of a straight angle is 180.
The sum of the measures in degrees of the angles of a triangle is 180.

1. $.2 \times .02 \times .002 =$

(A) .000008
(B) .00008
(C) .0008
(D) .008
(E) .08

2. If $\frac{p}{q} = 6$ and $q = -3$, then $\frac{p+q}{q} =$

(A) –21
(B) –14
(C) –7
(D) 1
(E) 7

3. If s, t, and u are different positive integers and $\frac{s}{t}$ and $\frac{t}{u}$ are also positive integers, which of the following cannot be a positive integer?

(A) $\frac{s}{u}$

(B) $s \cdot t$

(C) $\frac{u}{s}$

(D) $(s + t)u$

(E) $(s - u)t$

GO ON TO THE NEXT PAGE

4. Of the people attending a concert, $\frac{3}{4}$ are seated in the auditorium and the remaining $\frac{1}{4}$ are in the lobby. If $\frac{1}{2}$ of those in the lobby move to seats in the auditorium, then what is the ratio of those seated in the auditorium to those in the lobby?

(A) 16:1
(B) 12:1
(C) 9:1
(D) 7:1
(E) 6:1

5. If the perimeter of the rectangle below is 42, then what is the area of the rectangle?

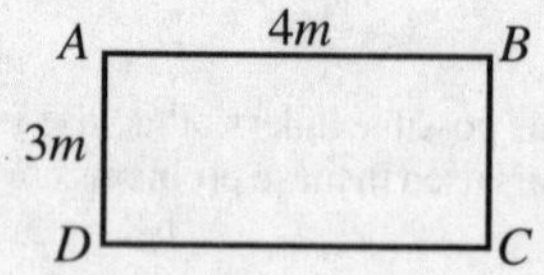

(A) 21
(B) 42
(C) 84
(D) 108
(E) 216

6. $390 is 13% of the total sum of money in a bank account. How much money is in the bank account?

(A) $6,000
(B) $3,000
(C) $1,057
(D) $557
(E) $50.70

7. If $n(q+5)=s$ and $q(n+4)=s$, and n, q, and s are positive integers, then which of the following statements must be true?

I. $n(q+5)=q(n+4)$

II. $\dfrac{n(q+5)}{q(n+4)}=1$

III. $q>n$

(A) I only
(B) II only
(C) III only
(D) I and III only
(E) I, II, and III

8. $\dfrac{\frac{2}{3}(x^2y^3)^4}{\frac{3}{4}(x^4y^3)^2}=$

(A) $\dfrac{8y^6}{9}$

(B) $\dfrac{9y^6}{8}$

(C) $\dfrac{3}{4}xy$

(D) $\dfrac{2y^6}{3}$

(E) $\dfrac{8}{9y^6}$

9. Jane has walked m miles. After a rest she walks n miles. If Jane always walked s steps per mile, then how many steps did Jane take?

(A) $s+m+n$

(B) $\dfrac{sm}{n}$

(C) $\dfrac{m}{sn}$

(D) $(s+m)n$

(E) $s(m+n)$

10. Tim can fold a certain number of brochures in 20 minutes. John can fold the same number in 15 minutes. If Tim and John work together for 3 hours and during that time John folds x brochures, how many brochures will Tim fold?

(A) $\dfrac{4x}{3}$

(B) $\dfrac{5x}{4}$

(C) $\dfrac{3x}{4}$

(D) $\dfrac{2x}{3}$

(E) $\dfrac{x}{2}$

Questions 11 and 12 refer to the table below.

SCORE DISTRIBUTION
MATHEMATICS TEST

Score	No. of students
40–52	5
53–64	11
65–76	7
77–88	32
89–100	40

11. If the lowest passing score is 65, then, to the nearest percent, what percent of the students failed the test?

(A) 5%
(B) 7%
(C) 11%
(D) 17%
(E) 52%

12. If 9 students scored 100, how many scored from 77 to 99?

(A) 72
(B) 63
(C) 51
(D) 40
(E) 31

13. In the figure below, which of the following is x necessarily equal to?

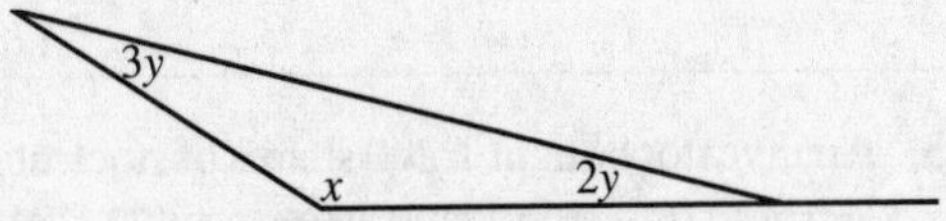

Note: Figure not drawn to scale.

(A) $180 - 5y$
(B) $180 + 5y$
(C) $90 - 5y$
(D) $190 + 5y$
(E) $5y$

14. For which values of x will $x(x + 2)(x - 3)(x + 4)$ be equal to 0?

(A) 0
(B) 2, –3, and 4
(C) 0 and –2
(D) –2, 3, and –4
(E) 0, –2, 3, and –4

For questions 15 and 16 let $a \square b = a^b + b^a$

15. What is the value of $2 \square 3$?

(A) 5
(B) 6
(C) 13
(D) 17
(E) 19

16. If a and b are different positive integers, then which of the following statements must be false?

(A) The smallest value for $a \square b$ is 3.
(B) $a^b \bullet b^a = b^a \bullet a^b$
(C) a^b is never equal to b^a
(D) $a \square b$ can equal 0
(E) $a \square b = b \square a$

17. A pool is filled to $\frac{3}{4}$ of its capacity. $\frac{1}{9}$ of the water in the pool evaporates. If the pool can hold 24,000 gallons when it is full, how many gallons of water will have to be added in order to fill the pool?

(A) 6,000
(B) 8,000
(C) 12,000
(D) 16,000
(E) 18,000

GO ON TO THE NEXT PAGE

18. If $\frac{12m}{7}$ is an integer, m could be any of the following *except*

(A) 63
(B) 49
(C) 21
(D) 15
(E) 7

19. What is side AD + side DC ?

(A) $18\sqrt{2}$
(B) $18\sqrt{2}$
(C) $10\sqrt{2}$
(D) 10
(E) $6\sqrt{2}$

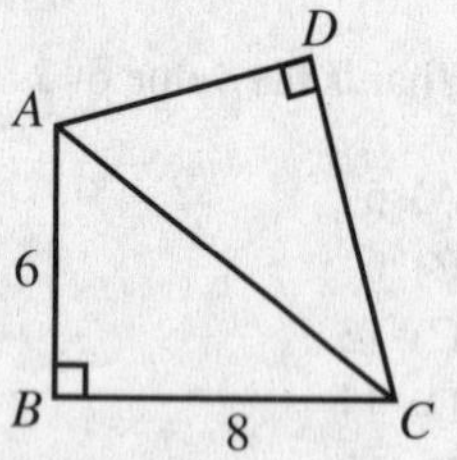

Note: Figure not drawn to scale.

20. Four "*ABCD*" equals three "*EFGH*." Four "*EFGH*" equals five "*IJKL*." How many "*ABCD*" are equal to fifteen "*IJKL*"?

(A) 4
(B) 8
(C) 12
(D) 16
(E) 20

21.

j	k
1	$\frac{2}{3}$
2	$\frac{4}{3}$
3	2
4	$\frac{8}{3}$

According to the above chart, $k =$

(A) $\frac{2}{3}j$
(B) $j - \frac{1}{3}$
(C) $\frac{3}{2}j$
(D) $\frac{j}{2}$
(E) $\frac{j}{3}$

22. In the figure, what is the sum of the six angles divided by the average of the six angles?

(A) 72
(B) 36
(C) 12
(D) 6
(E) It cannot be determined from the information given.

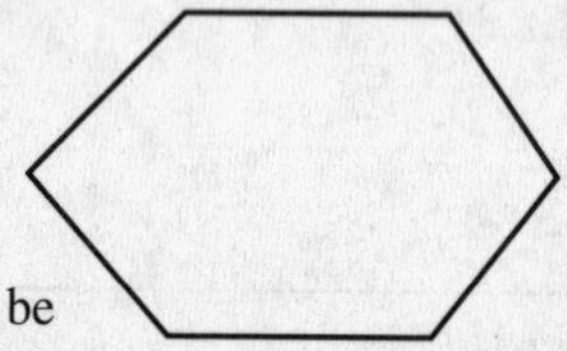

23. An investor bought 1,200 shares of stock at $\$22\frac{5}{8}$ and sold the same 1,200 shares at $\$23\frac{1}{2}$. What is the profit not counting commissions or taxes?

(A) $4,050
(B) $3,050
(C) $2,050
(D) $1,050
(E) $550

24. A certain neon sign flashes every 2 seconds, another sign flashes every 3 seconds, and a third flashes every 5 seconds. If they all start flashing together, how many seconds will pass before they all flash simultaneously again?

(A) 45 seconds
(B) 30 seconds
(C) 20 seconds
(D) 15 seconds
(E) 10 seconds

25. Marianne can read at a rate of 300 words per minute. While taking a speed reading course, Marianne increases her speed by $\frac{1}{3}$. After finishing the course, Marianne's speed drops by 100 words per minute. What percent of her original speed is her current speed?

(A) 200%
(B) 100%
(C) 50%
(D) 20%
(E) 0%

STOP

END OF SECTION 1. IF YOU HAVE ANY TIME LEFT, GO OVER YOUR WORK IN THIS SECTION ONLY. DO NOT WORK IN ANY OTHER SECTION OF THE TEST.

SECTION 2

30 Questions • Time—30 Minutes

Directions: Each of the following questions consists of an incomplete sentence followed by five words or pairs of words. Choose that word or pair of words which, when substituted for the blank space or spaces, *best* completes the meaning of the sentence, and mark the letter of your choice on your answer sheet.

Example:

In view of the extenuating circumstances and the defendant's youth, the judge recommended ----.

(A) conviction (B) a defense
(C) a mistrial (D) leniency
(E) life imprisonment Ⓐ Ⓑ Ⓒ ● Ⓔ

1. Because he had faith in the student's integrity, the teacher offered to ---- with the principal on her behalf.

(A) interpolate
(B) reminisce
(C) intercede
(D) deprecate
(E) repudiate

2. The new contract ---- all previous agreements between the two parties.

(A) subdues
(B) supersedes
(C) precedes
(D) relegates
(E) warrants

3. As volcanic activity ----, the scientist was able to return to the area to ---- her studies.

(A) commenced..augment
(B) intervened..rescind
(C) retreated..revert
(D) encroached..design
(E) abated..resume

4. Some observers believe that an emphasis on ---- has damaged the traditional spirit of societal unity and harmony.

(A) individualism
(B) exercise
(C) tranquillity
(D) syllogisms
(E) fraternity

5. The conspirators met ---- in order to plot a(n) ---- against the oppressive regime.

(A) reclusively..schism
(B) clandestinely..insurrection
(C) vicariously..invocation
(D) imperviously..embargo
(E) insidiously..referendum

Directions: Each of the following questions consists of a capitalized pair of words followed by five pairs of words lettered A to E. The capitalized words bear some meaningful relationship to each other. Choose the lettered pair of words whose relationship is most similar to that expressed by the capitalized pair and mark its letter on your answer sheet.

Example:

DAY : SUN : :

(A) sunlight : daylight
(B) ray : sun
(C) night : moon
(D) heat : cold
(E) moon : star

Ⓐ Ⓑ ● Ⓓ Ⓔ

6. PEAR : FRUIT : :

(A) flower : seed
(B) baseball : sport
(C) building : windows
(D) street : pavement
(E) youth : juvenile

7. DISCIPLINARIAN : OBEDIENCE : :

(A) principal : school
(B) fireman : hose
(C) parent : children
(D) perfectionist : flawlessness
(E) picture : colors

8. DECIBEL : LOUDNESS : :

(A) gram : ounce
(B) meter : yard
(C) length : width
(D) carat : weight
(E) gallon : mile

9. WOOD : CARVE : :

(A) paper : burn
(B) pipe : blow
(C) clay : mold
(D) tree : grow
(E) brick : build

10. GALLERY : ARTWORK : :

(A) museum : children
(B) zoo : animals
(C) theater : exhibits
(D) stadium : field
(E) forest : park

11. FADE : VANISH : :

(A) abate : diminish
(B) meander : wander
(C) chide : reprimand
(D) deplete : replenish
(E) infer : imply

12. BOOK : CHAPTER : :

(A) film : projector
(B) thesis : doctorate
(C) prelude : piano
(D) sculpture : chisel
(E) symphony : movement

13. ROOTS : TREE : :

(A) foundation : building
(B) chimney : smoke
(C) exit : entrance
(D) engine : automobile
(E) sleeve : shirt

GO ON TO THE NEXT PAGE

Directions: Each passage below is followed by a set of questions. Read the passage, then answer the accompanying questions, basing your answers on what is stated or implied in the passage and in any introductory material provided. Mark the letter of your choice on your answer sheet.

Questions 14–22 are based on the following passage.

The Federalist Papers *were written to convince readers to adopt the Constitution in place of the Articles of Confederation, in order to maintain authority with a central, federal government. This particular paper was written in 1788 by John Jay, later to become first Chief Justice of the Supreme Court.*

It is not a new observation that the people of any country (if, like the Americans, intelligent and well-informed) seldom adopt and steadily persevere for many years in an erroneous opinion respecting their interests. That consideration naturally tends to create great respect for the high opinion which the people of America have so long and uniformly entertained of the importance of their continuing firmly united under one federal government, vested with sufficient powers for all general and national purposes.

The more attentively I consider and investigate the reasons which appear to have given birth to this opinion, the more I become convinced that they are cogent and conclusive.

Among the many objects to which a wise and free people find it necessary to direct their attention, that of providing for their *safety* seems to be the first. The *safety* of the people doubtless has relation to a great variety of circumstances and considerations, and consequently affords great latitude to those who wish to define it precisely and comprehensively.

At present I mean only to consider it as it respects security for the preservation of peace and tranquillity, as well as against dangers from *foreign arms and influence*, as from dangers of the *like kind* arising from domestic causes. As the former of these comes first in order, it is proper it should be the first discussed. Let us therefore proceed to examine whether the people are not right in their opinion that a cordial Union, under an efficient national government, affords them the best security that can be devised against *hostilities* from abroad.

The number of wars which have happened or will happen in the world will always be found to be in proportion to the number and weight of the causes, whether *real or pretended,* which *provoke* or *invite* them. If this remark be just, it becomes useful to inquire whether so many *just* causes of war are likely to be given by *United America* as by *disunited* America; for if it should turn out that United America will probably give up the fewest, then it will follow that in this respect the Union tends most to preserve the people in a state of peace with other nations.

The *just* causes of war, for the most part, arise either from violations of treaties or from direct violence. America has already formed treaties with no less than six foreign nations, and all of them, except Prussia, are maritime, and therefore able to annoy and injure us. She has also extensive commerce with Portugal, Spain, and Britain, and, with respect to the two latter, has, in addition, the circumstance of neighborhood to attend to.

It is of high importance to the peace of America that she observe the laws of nations towards all these powers, and to me it appears evident that this will be more perfectly and punctually done by one national government than it could be either by thirteen separate States or by three or four distinct confederacies.

14. Jay opens with the observation that

   (A) Americans are right in wanting a united government
   (B) people often harbor wrong ideas about their welfare
   (C) all Americans are vested with specific powers
   (D) Americans are more intelligent than foreigners
   (E) people in America respect each other's opinions

15. How does Jay narrowly define "safety"?

   (A) Sanctuary in a storm
   (B) Protection from foreign and domestic arms
   (C) Economic security
   (D) Certainty
   (E) Defense against the world's unrest

16. When Jay refers to a "cordial Union" (line 29), he means one that is

(A) friendly to other nations
(B) harmonious
(C) warm
(D) complimentary
(E) spirited

17. Does Jay believe that a war can be just?

(A) No, not if it leads to suffering.
(B) Yes, if it can be proved in court.
(C) Yes, if it is due to broken treaties or invasion.
(D) No, unless it is in defense of the flag.
(E) Yes, if it is caused by disunity.

18. Why does Jay bother to point out that five lands with which America has treaties are maritime (lines 46–48)?

(A) They have the advantage over land-locked America.
(B) America's cannons do not work over water.
(C) The treaties affect ocean commerce.
(D) They can attack America with powerful navies.
(E) The sixth nation is the most powerful of all.

19. What does *punctually* mean in line 56?

(A) seasonably
(B) early
(C) belligerently
(D) timelessly
(E) efficiently

20. From Jay's arguments, you can assume that the Constitution provides for

(A) treaties with maritime nations only
(B) guidelines to help America observe international law
(C) procedures to decide if a war is just
(D) a stronger central government than existed under the Articles of Confederation
(E) thirteen separate states and three distinct confederacies

21. Based on the passage, Jay would most likely support a war to

(A) conquer additional territory for America
(B) expel Native Americans from the thirteen states
(C) defend America against hostilities from Spain
(D) extend the range of American commerce
(E) liberate a colony of Portugal

22. What would you expect Jay to discuss after he finishes talking about foreign hostilities?

(A) Foreign peace initiatives
(B) Hostilities that do not affect America
(C) Effective governments
(D) The role of the militia
(E) Domestic disturbances

Questions 22–30 are based on the following passage.

In between life as a printer and life as a writer, Mark Twain (Samuel Clemens) worked as a pilot aboard a Mississippi steamboat. This piece is from Old Times on the Mississippi *(1875), a collection of reminiscences first published in the* Atlantic Monthly.

At the end of what seemed a tedious while, I had managed to pack my head full of islands, towns, bars, "points," and bends; and a curiously inanimate mass of lumber it was, too. However, inasmuch as I could shut my eyes and reel off a good long string of these names without leaving out more than ten miles of river in every fifty, I began to feel that I could make her skip those little gaps. But of course my complacency could hardly get start enough to lift my nose a trifle into the air, before Mr. Bixby would think of something to fetch it down again. One day he turned on me suddenly with this settler:—

"What is the shape of Walnut Bend?"

He might as well have asked me my grandmother's opinion of protoplasm. I reflected respectfully, and then said I didn't know it had any particular shape. My gunpowdery chief went off with a bang, of course, and then went on loading and firing until he was out of adjectives.

I had learned long ago that he only carried just so many rounds of ammunition, and was sure to subside into a very placable and even remorseful old smoothbore as soon as they were all gone. That word "old" is merely affectionate; he was not more than thirty-four. I waited. By and by he said:—

"My boy, you've got to know the *shape* of the river perfectly. It is all there is left to steer by on a very dark night. Everything else is blotted out and gone. But mind you, it hasn't the same shape in the night that it has in the daytime."

"How on earth am I ever going to learn it, then?"

"How do you follow a hall at home in the dark? Because you know the shape of it. You can't see it."

"Do you mean to say that I've got to know all the million trifling variations of shape in the banks of this interminable river as well as I know the shape of the front hall at home?"

"On my honor, you've got to know them *better* than any man ever did know the shapes of the halls in his own house."

"I wish I was dead!"

"Now I don't want to discourage you, but"—

"Well, pile it on me; I might as well have it now as another time."

"You see, this has got to be learned; there isn't any getting around it. A clear starlight night throws such heavy shadows that, if you didn't know the shape of a shore perfectly, you would claw away from every bunch of timber, because you would take the black shadow of it for a solid cape; and you see you would be getting scared to death every fifteen minutes by the watch. You would be fifty yards from shore all the time when you ought to be within fifty feet of it. You can't see a snag in one of those shadows, but you know exactly where it is, and the shape of the river tells you when you are coming to it. Then there's your pitch-dark night; the river is a very different shape on a pitch-dark night from what it is on a starlight night. All shores seem to be straight lines, then, and mighty dim ones, too; and you'd *run* them for straight lines, only you know better. You boldly drive your boat right into what seems to be a solid straight wall (you knowing very well that in reality there is a curve there), and that wall falls back and makes way for you. Then there's your gray mist. You take a night when there's one of these grisly, drizzly, gray mists, and then there isn't *any* particular shape to a shore. A gray mist would tangle the head of the oldest man that ever lived. Well, then different kinds of *moonlight* change the shape of the river in different ways.

23. In line 12, Twain uses the word *settler* to mean

(A) pioneer
(B) perch on the railing
(C) remark that decides the issue
(D) problem that humbles him
(E) questions about his origins

24. When Twain compares a question to asking his "grandmother's opinion of protoplasm" (lines 14–15), he means that

(A) the question is inane
(B) the speaker is very old
(C) he does not know the answer
(D) his grandmother would be able to respond
(E) the words are meaningless

25 Twain compares his chief to a gun to point out the chief's

(A) accuracy
(B) splendid posture
(C) peppery temper
(D) love of hunting
(E) violent past

26. When Twain writes that Mr. Bixby "carried just so many rounds of ammunition," he means that

(A) Bixby used a pistol to settle arguments
(B) Bixby loaded and fired his gun at random
(C) Bixby was impossible to work for
(D) Bixby's gun was out of bullets
(E) Bixby's hot temper would soon subside

27. Twain's reaction to Mr. Bixby's insistence on the need to know the river at night is

(A) despair
(B) elation
(C) puzzlement
(D) anger
(E) humility

28. The word *cape* (line 50) means

(A) cloak
(B) robe
(C) woodpile
(D) peninsula
(E) waterway

29. Mr. Bixby is shown to be extremely

    (A) knowledgeable
    (B) rude
    (C) condescending
    (D) fearful
    (E) negative

30. According to the passage, which of the following is true?

    (A) On a pitch-dark night, the pilot can't discern the curve of the shoreline.
    (B) A riverboat should always be within 50 feet of the shore.
    (C) On a clear, starlit night the shoreline is easy to see.
    (D) The river's shape gives no hint of underwater snags.
    (E) On a misty night, only old men should pilot riverboats.

STOP

END OF SECTION 2. IF YOU HAVE ANY TIME LEFT, GO OVER YOUR WORK IN THIS SECTION ONLY. DO NOT WORK IN ANY OTHER SECTION OF THE TEST.

SECTION 3

10 Questions • Time—15 Minutes

Directions: Solve the following problems using any available space on the page for scratchwork. On your answer sheet fill in the choice which best corresponds to the correct answer.

Notes: The figures accompanying the problems are drawn as accurately as possible unless otherwise stated in specific problems. Again, unless otherwise stated, all figures lie in the same plane. All numbers used in these problems are real numbers. Calculators are permitted for this test.

Reference Information

Circle: Rectangle: Rectangular Solid: Cylinder: Triangle:

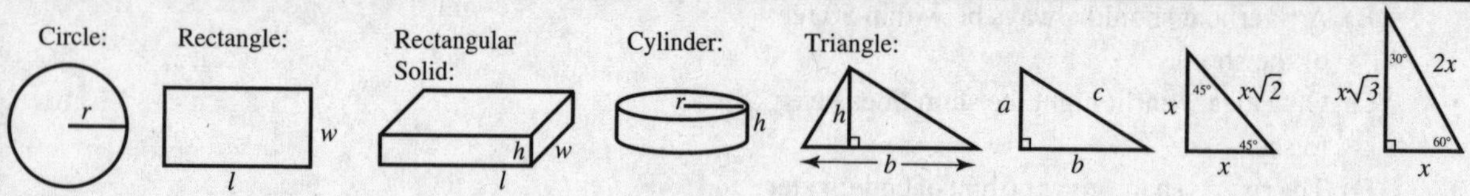

$C = 2\pi r$ $A = lw$ $V = lwh$ $V = \pi r^2 h$ $A = \frac{1}{2}bh$ $a^2 + b^2 = c^2$

$A = \pi r^2$

The number of degrees of arc in a circle is 360.
The measure in degrees of a straight angle is 180.
The sum of the measures in degrees of the angles of a triangle is 180.

1. Which of the following is less than $\frac{1}{2}$?

(A) $\frac{9}{16}$

(B) $\frac{11}{21}$

(C) $\frac{8}{17}$

(D) $\frac{14}{27}$

(E) $\frac{6}{11}$

2. Rectangle R has sides of x and y. Rectangle S has sides of $3x$ and $2y$. What is the area of S minus the area of R?

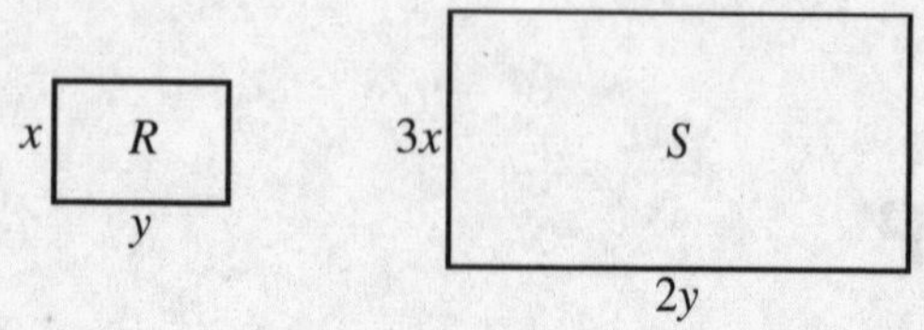

(A) $12xy$
(B) $9xy$
(C) $6xy$
(D) $5xy$
(E) $4xy$

3. If the triangle below is distorted so that angle y is doubled and angle z is tripled, then angle x will become a right angle. Which of the following is a possible value for angle y?

(A) 90
(B) 75
(C) 60
(D) 45
(E) 30

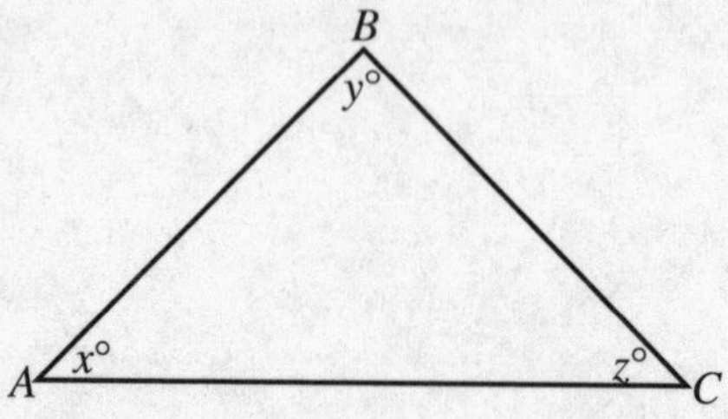

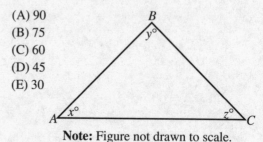

Note: Figure not drawn to scale.

4. If $3x + 3$ is 6 more than $3y + 3$, then $x - y =$

(A) 0
(B) 2
(C) 4
(D) 6
(E) 9

5. Jim's average score for three bowling games was 162. In the second game, Jim scored 10 less than in the first game. In the third game, he scored 13 less than in the second game. What was his score in the first game?

(A) 189
(B) 179
(C) 173
(D) 171
(E) 168

6. $3\times10^3\times2\times10^2=$

(A) 6,000,000
(B) 600,000
(C) 60,000
(D) 6,000
(E) 600

7. A certain machine makes a widget every 2.5 seconds. How many widgets does the machine make in 40 minutes?

(A) 12,600
(B) 9,600
(C) 4,800
(D) 1,200
(E) 960

8. A cassette tape has two sides and each side can record for 45 minutes. A student brings 3 tapes in order to record a three-hour lecture. If the time spent loading and unloading the tapes is negligible, what percent of the total available tape will not be used to record the lecture?

(A) 75%
(B) 50%
(C) $33\frac{1}{3}\%$
(D) 25%
(E) 20%

9. If $\frac{(a+b)}{(c+d)}=5$ and $\frac{(e+f)}{(g+h)}=6$, then what is the value of $\frac{(a+b)}{(g+h)}\bullet\frac{(e+f)}{(c+d)}$?

(A) 0
(B) 1
(C) 11
(D) 30
(E) It cannot be determined from the information given.

10. The fraction $\frac{2}{7}$ is represented by the decimal .285714 repeated. $\frac{2}{7}$ = .285714 285714 285714. . . . What is the 753rd decimal digit?

(A) 2
(B) 8
(C) 5
(D) 7
(E) 1

STOP

END OF SECTION 3. IF YOU HAVE ANY TIME LEFT, GO OVER YOUR WORK IN THIS SECTION ONLY. DO NOT WORK IN ANY OTHER SECTION OF THE TEST.

SECTION 4

10 Questions • Time—15 Minutes

Directions: The two passages given below deal with a related topic. Following the passages are questions about the content of each passage or about the relationship between the two passages. Answer the questions based upon what is stated or implied in the passages and in any introductory material provided. Mark the letter of your choice on your answer sheet.

Questions 1–10 are based on the following passages.

Our nation was little more than fifty years old when the debate began over whether or not we possessed a national literature, a body of work that could be considered truly American. These remarks are by a Boston minister and founder of American Unitarianism, and by one of the first "American" novelists.

Passage 1—William Ellery Channing, from "Remarks on National Literature" (1830)

Do we possess, indeed, what may be called a national literature? Have we produced eminent writers in the various departments of intellectual effort? Are our chief resources of instruction and literary enjoyment furnished from ourselves? We regret that the reply to these questions is so obvious. The few standard works which we have produced, and which promise to live, can hardly, by any courtesy, be denominated a national literature. On this point, if marks and proofs of our real condition were needed, we should find them in the current apologies for our deficiencies. Our writers are accustomed to plead in our excuse, our youth, the necessities of a newly settled country, and the direction of our best talents to practical life. Be the pleas sufficient or not, one thing they prove, and that is, our consciousness of having failed to make important contributions to the interests of the intellect. We have few names to place by the side of the great names in science and literature on the other side of the ocean. We want those lights which make a country conspicuous at a distance. Let it not be said, that European envy denies our just claims. In an age like this, when the literary world forms a great family, and the products of mind are circulated more rapidly than those of machinery, it is a nation's own fault, if its name be not pronounced with honor beyond itself. We have ourselves heard, and delighted to hear, beyond the Alps, our country designated as the land of Franklin. This name had scaled that mighty barrier, and made us known where our institutions and modes of life were hardly better understood than those of the natives of our forests.

We are accustomed to console ourselves for the absence of a commanding literature, by urging our superiority to other nations in our institutions for the diffusion of elementary knowledge through all classes of the community. We have here just cause for boasting, though perhaps less than we imagine. That there are gross deficiencies in our common schools, and that the amount of knowledge which they communicate, when compared with the time spent in its acquisition, is lamentably small, the community begin to feel. There is a crying need for a higher and more quickening kind of instruction than the laboring part of society have yet received, and we rejoice that the cry begins to be heard. But, allowing our elementary institutions to be ever so perfect, we confess that they do not satisfy us. We want something more. A dead level of intellect, even if it should rise above what is common in other nations, would not answer our wishes and hopes for our country. We want great minds to be formed among us, minds which shall be felt afar, and through which we may act on the world. We want the human intellect to do its utmost here. We want this people to obtain a claim on the gratitude of the human race, by adding strength to the foundation, and fullness and splendor to the development of moral and religious truth; by originality of thought, by discoveries of science, and by contributions to the refining pleasures of taste and imagination.

Passage 2—James Fenimore Cooper from "Problems of a Native Literature" (1828)

Solitary and individual works of genius may, indeed, be occasionally brought to light, under the impulses of the high feeling which has conceived them; but, I fear, a good, wholesome, profitable and continued pecuniary support, is the applause that talent most craves. The fact, that an American publisher can get an English work without money, must, for a few years longer, (unless legislative protection shall be extended to their own authors) have a tendency to repress a national literature. No man will pay a writer for an epic, a tragedy, a sonnet, a history, or a romance, when he can get a work of equal merit for nothing. I have conversed with those who are conversant on the subject, and, I confess, I have been astonished at the information they imparted.

A capital American publisher has assured me that there are not a dozen writers in this country, whose works he should feel confidence in publishing at all, while he reprints hundreds of English books without the least hesitation. This preference is by no means so much owing to any difference in merit, as to the fact that, when the price of the original author is to be added to the uniform hazard which accompanies all literary speculations, the risk becomes too great.

1. According to Channing, American writers blame the following for the lack of a national literature:

   (A) the fact that the country is new
   (B) the need to put talents to work elsewhere
   (C) American publishers
   (D) both A and B
   (E) both B and C

2. Channing uses the word *lights* (line 19) to mean

   (A) flickers
   (B) luminaries
   (C) beams
   (D) trivia
   (E) merrymakers

3. Channing uses the example of Benjamin Franklin to show

   (A) how resourceful Americans really are
   (B) that people born in Europe are not necessarily better
   (C) how much more distinguished scientists are than writers
   (D) how the life of the mind lives on after death
   (E) that Americans can become famous overseas

4. Although Americans consider their elementary schools superior because they educate the masses, Channing feels

   (A) that schools should concentrate on educating the elite
   (B) that European schools are better
   (C) their goal should be the formation of great minds
   (D) students are lacking in reading and writing skills
   (E) they should focus on a canon of great literary works

5. In line 62 of Cooper's essay, *pecuniary* means

   (A) unusual
   (B) intellectual
   (C) harmful
   (D) offensive
   (E) monetary

6. Although some people will publish for love, Cooper stresses the need for

   (A) money
   (B) public support
   (C) praise
   (D) confidence
   (E) merit

7. Channing, on the other hand, stresses the need for

   (A) integrity
   (B) international fame
   (C) compensation
   (D) enjoyment
   (E) independence

8. Cooper raises the idea of legislative protection (lines 65–67) to

   (A) imply that no one is able to protect writers
   (B) show how other countries protect writers
   (C) explain why writers are not being protected
   (D) suggest a method of protecting writers
   (E) reject the conventional way of protecting writers

GO ON TO THE NEXT PAGE

9. Unlike Channing, Cooper believes that American writers

(A) are capable right now of great works
(B) need to be better grounded in the classics
(C) are more innovative than European writers
(D) both A and B
(E) both B and C

10. According to Cooper, the main obstacle to a national literature is

(A) the will of the American reading public
(B) a lack of national heroes
(C) the attitude that English literature is better
(D) publishers' unwillingness to take risks
(E) a deluded reliance on tried-and-true texts

STOP

END OF SECTION 4. IF YOU HAVE ANY TIME LEFT, GO OVER YOUR WORK IN THIS SECTION ONLY. DO NOT WORK IN ANY OTHER SECTION OF THE TEST.

SECTION 5

25 Questions • Time—30 Minutes

Directions: Solve the following problems using any available space on the page for scratchwork. On your answer sheet fill in the choice which best corresponds to the correct answer.

Notes: The figures accompanying the problems are drawn as accurately as possible unless otherwise stated in specific problems. Again, unless otherwise stated, all figures lie in the same plane. All numbers used in these problems are real numbers. Calculators are permitted for this test.

Reference Information

Circle: | Rectangle: | Rectangular Solid: | Cylinder: | Triangle:

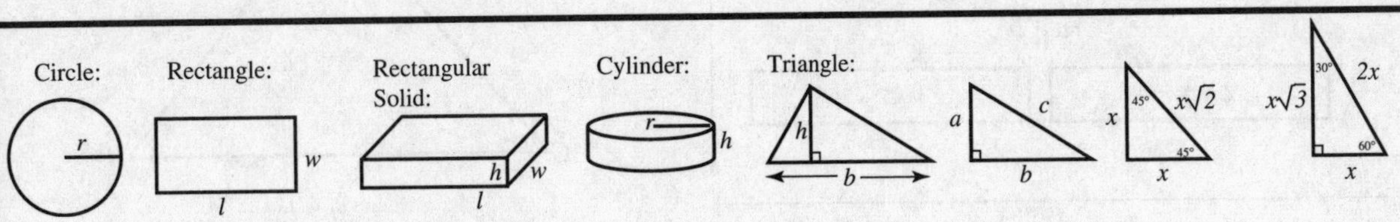

$C = 2\pi r$, $A = \pi r^2$ | $A = lw$ | $V = lwh$ | $V = \pi r^2 h$ | $A = \frac{1}{2}bh$ | $a^2 + b^2 = c^2$

The number of degrees of arc in a circle is 360.
The measure in degrees of a straight angle is 180.
The sum of the measures in degrees of the angles of a triangle is 180.

Part 1: Quantitative Comparison Questions

Directions: For each of the following questions, two quantities are given—one in Column A, the other in Column B. Compare the two quantities and mark your answer sheet as follows:

(A) if the quantity in Column A is greater
(B) if the quantity in Column B is greater
(C) if the quantities are equal
(D) if the relationship cannot be determined from the information given

Notes:

(1) Information concerning one or both of the compared quantities will be centered above the two columns for some items.
(2) Symbols that appear in both columns represent the same thing in Column A as in Column B.
(3) Letters such as *x*, *n*, and *k* are symbols for real numbers.

Examples

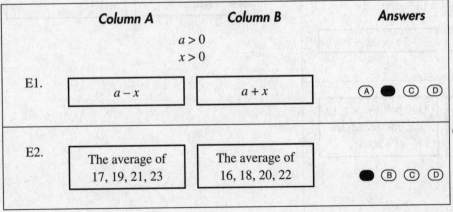

	Column A	Column B	Answers
		$a > 0$ $x > 0$	
E1.	$a - x$	$a + x$	(A) ● (C) (D)
E2.	The average of 17, 19, 21, 23	The average of 16, 18, 20, 22	● (B) (C) (D)

DO NOT MARK CHOICE (E) FOR THESE QUESTIONS. THERE ARE ONLY FOUR ANSWER CHOICES.

GO ON TO THE NEXT PAGE

	Column A	Column B
1.	$(\sqrt{12})(27)(\frac{1}{2})$	$(29)(\sqrt{3})$

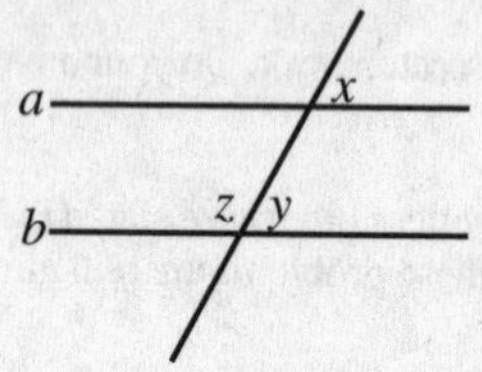

$a \parallel b$

	Column A	Column B
2.	$z+y-x$	z

	Column A	Column B
3.	$(\sqrt{x})^2$	$\frac{1}{x^2}$

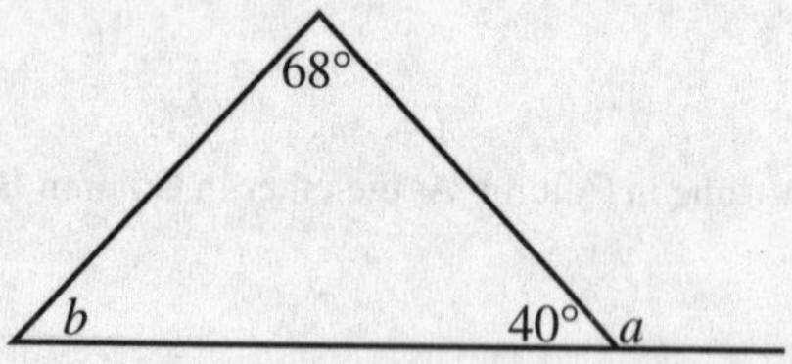

Note: Figure not drawn to scale.

	Column A	Column B
4.	a	b

$x=-3$

	Column A	Column B
5.	$2x^3+6x^2-2$	$5x^2+3x-7$

	Column A	Column B
6.	Twice the sum of the interior angles of a triangle	One-half the sum of the interior angles of a square

	Column A	Column B
7.	y^2-1	y^3+1

Questions 8–9 refer to the figure below.

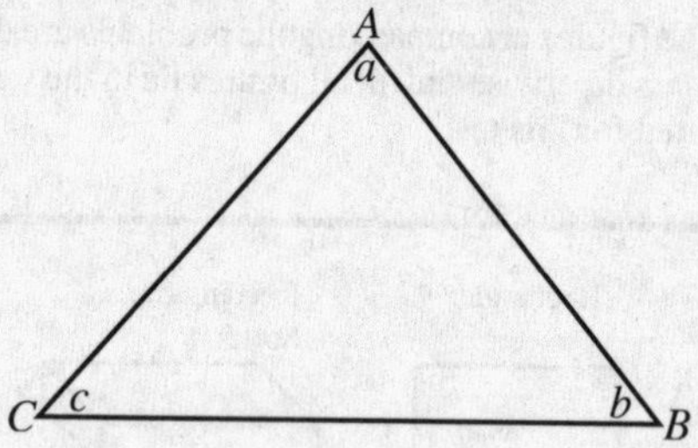

$a>b$

$a>c$

	Column A	Column B
8.	side AC	side AB

	Column A	Column B
9.	side AB	side CB

	Column A	Column B
10.	The area of a triangle with base of 6 and height of 8	The area of a rectangle with sides of 7 and 4

	Column A	Column B
	t, u, and *v* are positive integers	
11.	$\frac{t+u+v}{3}$	The average of *t, u,* and *v*
	$m \neq 2$	
12.	$\frac{m^2-2m}{\frac{1}{2}(m-2)}$	$2m+1$
	$m < n$	
13.	$n-m$	$m-n$

	Column A	Column B
	Note: Both figures are rectangles.	
14.	Area of shaded area	Area of unshaded area
15.	segment *AB*	segment *CD*

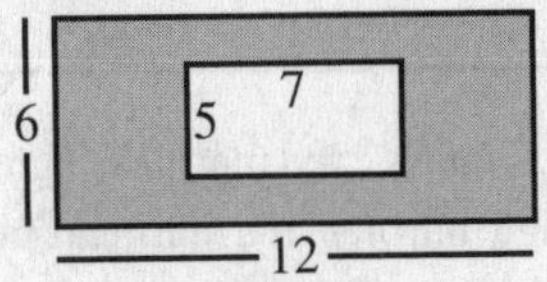

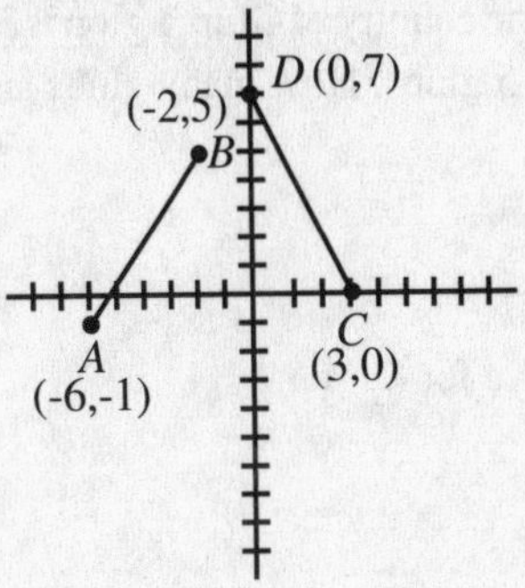

Part 2: Student-Produced Response Questions

Directions: Solve each of these problems. Write the answer in the corresponding grid on the answer sheet and fill in the ovals beneath each answer you write. Here are some examples.

Answer: $\frac{3}{4}$ (= .75; show answer either way)

Answer: 325

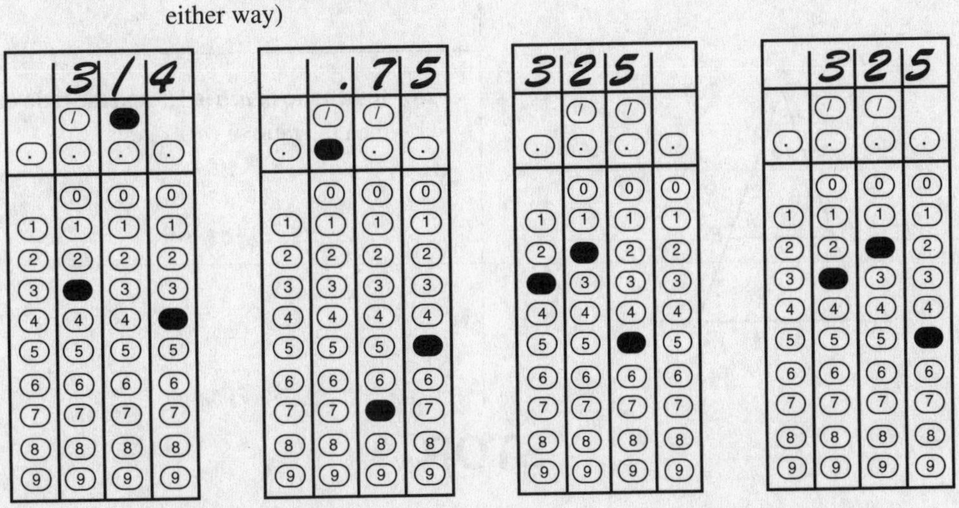

Note: A mixed number such as $3\frac{1}{2}$ must be gridded as 7/2 or as 3.5. If gridded as "3 1/2" it will be read as "thirty-one halves."

Note: Either position is correct.

GO ON TO THE NEXT PAGE

16. What is the value of $(2a^2 - a^3)^2$ when $a = -1$?

17. A jar contains 2 red marbles, 3 green marbles, and 4 orange marbles. If a marble is picked at random, what is the probability that the marble is not orange?

18. In the country of Glup, 1 glop is 3 glips and 4 glips are 5 globs. How many globs are 2 glops?

19. Solve for k: $\frac{k}{3} + \frac{k}{4} = 1$

20. If the area of a square of side x is 5, what is the area of a square of side $3x$?

21. In the diagram below, ΔABC is *similar* to ΔDBF. If $DF = 3, BD = BF = 6$ and $AC = 4$, what is the perimeter of ΔABC?

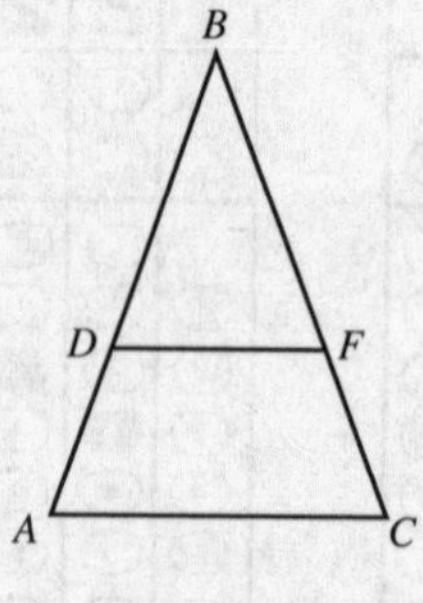

22. In quadrilateral $ABCD$ below, the measure of $\angle A = 120°$, the measure of $\angle B = 82°$, and the measure of $\angle D = 93°$. What is the value of x?

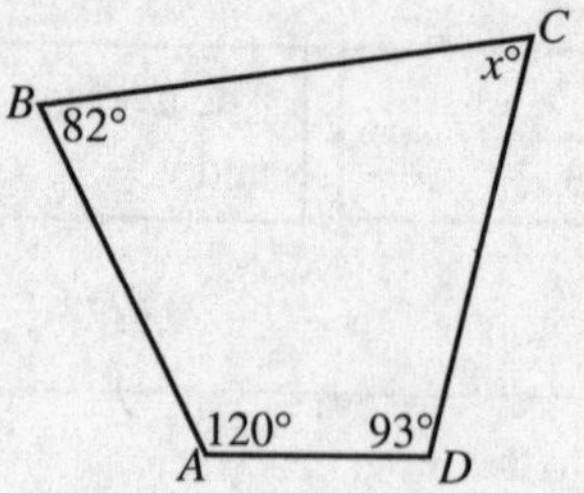

23. If $2x + 2y = 6$ and $3x - 3y = 9$, what is the value of $x^2 - y^2$?

24. If $\frac{4}{5}$ is subtracted from its reciprocal, the result is

25. If the ratio of $a{:}b$ is 1:5 and the ratio of $b{:}c$ is 3:2, then the ratio of $(a + c){:}c$ is

STOP

END OF SECTION 5. IF YOU HAVE ANY TIME LEFT, GO OVER YOUR WORK IN THIS SECTION ONLY. DO NOT WORK IN ANY OTHER SECTION OF THE TEST.

SECTION 6

35 Questions • Time—30 Minutes

Directions: Each of the following questions consists of an incomplete sentence followed by five words or pairs of words. Choose that word or pair of words which, when substituted for the blank space or spaces, *best* completes the meaning of the sentence, and mark the letter of your choice on your answer sheet.

Example:

In view of the extenuating circumstances and the defendant's youth, the judge recommended ----.

(A) conviction
(B) a defense
(C) a mistrial
(D) leniency
(E) life imprisonment
Ⓐ Ⓑ Ⓒ ● Ⓔ

1. The meeting yielded ---- results, yet all participants were convinced that a solution was ----.

(A) negligible..imminent
(B) small..hurried
(C) detrimental..as bad
(D) fleeting..short
(E) guarded..despicable

2. Only 25 years ago a space launching produced widespread interest; it is hard to believe trips into space are now considered ---- events.

(A) demeaning
(B) furtive
(C) comely
(D) commonplace
(E) surly

3. The football team was once ---- by injuries; of the 20 members only 10 were fit to play.

(A) truncated
(B) decimated
(C) invaded
(D) ostracized
(E) reviled

4. Since the city cannot ticket their cars, the diplomats can park anywhere with ----.

(A) penury
(B) impunity
(C) precision
(D) languor
(E) ignominy

5. If you ---- the charges instead of ---- them, people may conclude that you are guilty.

(A) delegate..enumerating
(B) preempt..disclaiming
(C) efface..disavowing
(D) reduce..mitigating
(E) ignore..rebutting

6. On the narrow and ---- mountain road, the truck skidded when it rounded a curve.

(A) pejorative
(B) salutary
(C) propitious
(D) sedulous
(E) tortuous

7. Although her acting was ----, she looked so good on stage that the audience applauded anyway.

(A) dynamic
(B) laudable
(C) implacable
(D) execrable
(E) intrepid

GO ON TO THE NEXT PAGE

8. Because of her unpopular opinions, she was unable to ---- broad support among the voters; however, those who did support her were exceptionally ----.

(A) alienate..many
(B) survey..divided
(C) cut across..quiet
(D) amass..loyal
(E) evoke..languid

9. Philosophical differences ---- the unification of the two parties into one.

(A) delegated
(B) legislated
(C) impeded
(D) enacted
(E) entrusted

10. When a job becomes too ----, workers get ----, their attention wanders, and they start to make careless errors.

(A) diverse..busy
(B) hectic..lazy
(C) tedious..bored
(D) fascinating..interested
(E) rewarding..sloppy

11. His ---- of practical experience and his psychological acuity more than ---- his lack of formal academic training.

(A) claims..compromise
(B) background..repay
(C) breadth..account for
(D) wealth..compensate for
(E) fund..elucidate

12. The merchant ---- a small neighborhood business into a city-wide chain of stores.

(A) appraised
(B) transferred
(C) parlayed
(D) redeemed
(E) instilled

13. It is not always easy to ---- one's mistakes, but it is inevitably more ---- to try to hide them.

(A) cover..suspect
(B) confess..difficult
(C) cancel..attractive
(D) solve..satisfying
(E) anticipate..circumspect

14. A professional journalist will attempt to ---- the facts learned in an interview by independent ----.

(A) endorse..question
(B) query..situation
(C) garnish..sources
(D) verify..investigation
(E) embellish..scrutiny

Directions: Each of the following questions consists of a capitalized pair of words followed by five pairs of words lettered A to E. The capitalized words bear some meaningful relationship to each other. Choose the lettered pair of words whose relationship is most similar to that expressed by the capitalized pair and mark its letter on your answer sheet.

Example:

DAY : SUN : :

(A) sunlight : daylight (B) ray : sun
(C) night : moon (D) heat : cold
(E) moon : star

Ⓐ Ⓑ ● Ⓓ Ⓔ

15. SCRIBBLING : WRITING : :

(A) pen : pencil
(B) sound : vibration
(C) walking : jogging
(D) mumbling : speaking
(E) seeing : vision

16. URGE : INSIST : :

(A) refuse : deny
(B) request : demand
(C) deserve : receive
(D) infer : imply
(E) inspire : revoke

17. SCREAM : FRIGHT : :

(A) moan : loudness
(B) sweat : drops
(C) groan : pain
(D) fly : plane
(E) cry : tears

18. HYPOCRITE : DUPLICITOUS : :

(A) partisan : impartial
(B) traitor : disloyal
(C) soldier : tough
(D) tailor : prosperous
(E) prisoner : repentant

19. SOAR : HOVER : :

(A) trail : hike
(B) sing : harmonize
(C) fall : trip
(D) help : aid
(E) swim : float

20. CARPENTER : CABINET : :

(A) gardener : tree
(B) musician : clarinet
(C) cobbler : boot
(D) banker : deposit
(E) potter : kiln

21. BICEPS : MUSCLE : :

(A) cobra : snake
(B) pump : heart
(C) bat : bird
(D) cup : mug
(E) ball : rubber

22. POVERTY : MONEY : :

(A) elation : joy
(B) despair : remorse
(C) veracity : honesty
(D) erudition : learning
(E) darkness : light

23. ENGAGEMENT : MARRIAGE : :

(A) overture : opera
(B) night : darkness
(C) failure : success
(D) demands : destitution
(E) ballgame : umpire

24. IMPORTANT : PIVOTAL : :

(A) major : minimal
(B) robust : strong
(C) stern : draconian
(D) salient : compulsory
(E) impetuous : perfect

25. EVANESCENT : VANISH : :

(A) effervescent : corrode
(B) iridescent : shine
(C) expressive : admonish
(D) fluorescent : disappear
(E) vacuous : expedite

GO ON TO THE NEXT PAGE

Directions: The reading passage below is followed by a set of questions. Read the passage and answer the accompanying questions, basing your answers on what is stated or implied in the passage. Mark the letter of your choice on your answer sheet.

Questions 26–35 are based on the following passage.

Jane Austen (1775–1817) had an unremarkable life but a keen eye for details even in the most mundane of situations. This excerpt from Mansfield Park *shows how sharply satiric her wit could be.*

Tom Bertram had of late spent so little of his time at home, that he could be only nominally missed; and Lady Bertram was soon astonished to find how very well they did even without his father, how well Edmund could supply his place in carving, talking to the steward, writing to the attorney, settling with the servants, and equally saving her from all possible fatigue or exertion in every particular, but that of directing her letters.

The earliest intelligence of the travellers' safe arrival in Antigua after a favorable voyage, was received; though not before Mrs. Norris had been indulging in very dreadful fears, and trying to make Edmund participate in them whenever she could get him alone; and as she depended on being the first person made acquainted with any fatal catastrophe, she had already arranged the manner of breaking it to all the others, when Sir Thomas's assurances of their both being alive and well, made it necessary to lay by her agitation and affectionate preparatory speeches for a while.

The winter came and passed without their being called for; the accounts continued perfectly good;—and Mrs. Norris in promoting gaieties for her nieces, assisting their toilettes, displaying their accomplishments, and looking for their future husbands, had so much to do as, in addition to all her own household cares, some interference in those of her sister, and Mrs. Grant's wasteful doings to overlook, left her very little occasion to be occupied even in fears for the absent.

The Miss Bertrams were now fully established among the belles of the neighborhood; and as they joined to beauty and brilliant acquirements, a manner naturally easy, and carefully formed to general civility and obligingness, they possessed its favor as well as its admiration. Their vanity was in such good order, that they seemed to be quite free from it, and gave themselves no airs; while the praises attending such behavior, secured, and brought round by their aunt, served to strengthen them in believing they had no faults.

Lady Bertram did not go into public with her daughters. She was too indolent even to accept a mother's gratification in witnessing their success and enjoyment at the expense of any personal trouble, and the charge was made over to her sister, who desired nothing better than a post of such honorable representation, and very thoroughly relished the means it afforded her of mixing in society without having horses to hire.

26. Why does Mrs. Norris have to "lay by" her speeches (line 18)?
    (A) She is forced to defend herself against the others.
    (B) Since no disaster has occurred, she must postpone her grief.
    (C) Her work with her nieces comes first.
    (D) Her audience has left for Antigua.
    (E) The Miss Bertrams are as yet too young to be formally presented.

27. The travellers mentioned in line 9 are
    (A) Lady Bertram and Mrs. Grant
    (B) Sir Thomas Bertram and Tom Bertram
    (C) the two Miss Bertrams
    (D) Edmund and Mrs. Norris
    (E) the steward and the attorney

28. Austen's description of Mrs. Norris's many occupations (paragraph 3) depicts her as a
    (A) drudge
    (B) busybody
    (C) beauty
    (D) prankster
    (E) sinner

29. Austen undercuts her description of the lovely Miss Bertrams by pointing out that they
    (A) believed themselves faultless
    (B) gave themselves no airs
    (C) were frequently praised
    (D) had easy manners
    (E) were beautiful and brilliant

30. In line 42, what does *charge* mean?

(A) fee
(B) attack
(C) duty
(D) accusation
(E) demand

31. The last line of this passage reveals Mrs. Norris as

(A) honorable
(B) clumsy
(C) delightful
(D) cheap
(E) fussy

32. The chief characteristic of Lady Bertram exposed in this excerpt is her

(A) concern for her children
(B) love of country
(C) shyness
(D) incredible vanity
(E) laziness

33. Austen seems to feel that Mrs. Norris is

(A) ludicrous
(B) poignant
(C) charming
(D) forceful
(E) uninteresting

34. Which of the following is an example of Austen's satiric wit?

(A) Tom Bertram had of late spent so little time at home.
(B) Sir Thomas writes that he is alive and well.
(C) Lady Bertram is too indolent to witness her daughters' social success.
(D) The Miss Bertrams were established as belles of the neighborhood.
(E) Edmund carves, talks to the steward, and writes to the attorney.

35. The best description of this excerpt is that it is

(A) coldly unsympathetic
(B) libelous
(C) tongue-in-cheek
(D) tactless and coarse
(E) lovingly tender

STOP

END OF SECTION 6. IF YOU HAVE ANY TIME LEFT, GO OVER YOUR WORK IN THIS SECTION ONLY. DO NOT WORK IN ANY OTHER SECTION OF THE TEST.

Final Practice Examination

Answer Key

Section 1: MATH

1.	A	6.	B	11.	D	16.	D	21.	A
2.	E	7.	E	12.	B	17.	B	22.	D
3.	C	8.	A	13.	A	18.	D	23.	D
4.	D	9.	E	14.	E	19.	C	24.	B
5.	D	10.	C	15.	D	20.	D	25.	B

Section 2: VERBAL

1.	C	7.	D	13.	A	19.	E	25.	C
2.	B	8.	D	14.	A	20.	D	26.	E
3.	E	9.	C	15.	B	21.	C	27.	A
4.	A	10.	B	16.	B	22.	E	28.	D
5.	B	11.	C	17.	C	23.	D	29.	A
6.	B	12.	E	18.	D	24.	C	30.	A

Section 3: MATH

1.	C	3.	E	5.	C	7.	E	9.	D
2.	D	4.	B	6.	B	8.	C	10.	C

Section 4: VERBAL

1.	D	3.	E	5.	E	7.	B	9.	A
2.	B	4.	C	6.	A	8.	D	10.	D

Section 5: MATH

Part 1

1.	B	4.	A	7.	D	10.	B	13.	A
2.	C	5.	B	8.	D	11.	C	14.	A
3.	D	6.	A	9.	B	12.	B	15.	B

Part 2

16.	9	18.	$7.5 = \frac{15}{2}$	20.	45	22.	65	24.	$\frac{9}{20} = .45$
17.	$\frac{5}{9} = .556$	19.	$\frac{12}{7} = 1.71$	21.	20	23.	9	25.	1.3

Section 6: VERBAL

1.	A	8.	D	15.	D	22.	E	29.	A
2.	D	9.	C	16.	B	23.	A	30.	C
3.	B	10.	C	17.	C	24.	C	31.	D
4.	B	11.	D	18.	B	25.	B	32.	E
5.	E	12.	C	19.	E	26.	B	33.	A
6.	E	13.	B	20.	C	27.	B	34.	C
7.	D	14.	D	21.	A	28.	B	35.	C

Final Practice Examination

Explanatory Answers

Note: A [calculator icon] following a math answer explanation indicates that a calculator could be helpful in solving that particular problem.

Section 1

1. **(A)** $2 \times 2 \times 2 = 8$. There are 6 decimal places in the factors; therefore, there must be 5 zeros in front of the 8.

2. **(E)** If $q = -3$, then p must equal -18. Plug these numbers into the problem:

   $$\frac{-18 + (-3)}{-3} = \frac{-21}{-3} = 7$$

3. **(C)** Since $\frac{s}{t}$ is an integer, s must be greater than t. Since $\frac{t}{u}$ is an integer, t must be greater than u. The relationship among the three variables can be written as $s > t > u$. Thus $\frac{u}{s}$ cannot be an integer because the denominator is bigger than the numerator.

4. **(D)** $\frac{1}{2}$ of the $\frac{1}{4}$ go from the lobby into the auditorium. Therefore, multiplying the two fractions, this means that $\frac{1}{8}$ of the total audience returns to the auditorium. The next step would be to add $\frac{1}{8}$ and $\frac{3}{4}$.

   $$\frac{1}{8} + \frac{3}{4} = \frac{1}{8} + \frac{6}{8} = \frac{7}{8}$$

   Since $\frac{7}{8}$ of the people are in the auditorium, the ratio would be 7:1.

5. **(D)**

   $$2(3m + 4m) = 42$$
   $$6m + 8m = 42$$
   $$14m = 42$$
   $$m = 3$$
   $$\text{Area} = 3m \times 4m = 3(3) \times 4(3) = 9 \times 12 = 108$$

6. **(B)** $390 = 13\%$ of the total $= .13x$

   $x = 3{,}000$

   $3{,}000 = \text{total}$

7. **(E)** I. Since both of the expressions equal s, they must equal each other.

   II. Any fraction that has the same value in the numerator and denominator is equal to 1.

   III. $n(q + 5) = q(n + 4)$

   $$nq + 5n = nq + 4q$$
   $$5n = 4q$$

   Therefore, q is greater than n.

8. **(A)**

   $$\frac{\frac{2}{3}(x^2y^3)^4}{\frac{3}{4}(x^4y^3)^2} = \frac{\frac{2}{3}(x^8y^{12})}{\frac{3}{4}(x^8y^6)} = \frac{2}{3} \bullet \frac{4}{3}\frac{x^8y^{12}}{x^8y^6} = \frac{8y^6}{9}$$

9. **(E)** We need to know how many miles Jane walked. We find this by adding m and n. Jane walked s steps in every mile. We would find her total steps by multiplying the steps per mile by the total miles.

10. **(C)** Since Tim works slower than John, choices (A) and (B) must be wrong. A good way to solve this is to act as if Tim folds 1 brochure in 20 minutes, and John folds 1 in 15 minutes. In an hour, John will fold 4 brochures while Tim folds 3. Tim folds $\frac{3}{4}$ as many as John.

11. **(D)** There are 95 students and 16 failed the test. $\frac{16}{95}$ is close to $\frac{16}{100}$. The correct answer must be slightly bigger than 16%, so 17% is correct.

12. **(B)** 72 students scored from 77 to 100. If 9 scored 100, then 72 – 9, or 63, must be the number of students who scored from 77 to 99.

13. **(A)** $180 = x + 3y + 2y$. Subtract $5y$ from both sides. $180 - 5y = x$.

14. **(E)** If x is 0, then the entire statement must equal 0. To find the other values for x, set each factor equal to 0.

$x + 2 = 0 \quad x - 3 = 0 \quad x + 4 = 0$

$x = -2 \quad x = 3 \quad x = -4$

15. **(D)** $2 \,\square\, 3 = 2^3 + 3^2 = 8 + 9 = 17$.

16. **(D)** Since a and b are positive, there is no way that the operation can equal 0.

17. **(B)** If $\frac{1}{9}$ evaporates, then $\frac{8}{9}$ remains. Since the pool is only $\frac{3}{4}$ full, then $\frac{8}{9} \times \frac{3}{4} = \frac{24}{36} = \frac{2}{3}$. Therefore, the pool is $\frac{1}{3}$ empty. To fill the pool, it is necessary to add $\frac{1}{3}$ of 24,000 gallons, or 8,000 gallons.

18. **(D)** The question is made simpler if you realize that $\frac{m}{7}$ has to be an integer, so m must be divisible by 7. 7 does not go evenly into 15.

19. **(C)** You can use the Pythagorean Theorem to solve for side AC.

$6^2 + 8^2 = AC^2$

$36 + 64 = AC^2$

$100 = AC^2$

$10 = AC$

Since side AD equals side DC, ΔADC is a 45°–45°–90° triangle with legs AD and DC and hypotenuse AC. But we know that side AC = 10. Therefore, side AD equals $\frac{1}{2}AC \bullet \sqrt{2} = \frac{1}{2}(10)\sqrt{2} = 5\sqrt{2}$.

$AD + DC = 2(5\sqrt{2}) = 10\sqrt{2}$.

20. **(D)** Two ratios are given, and *"EFGH"* is the common link between them.

4 "*ABCD*" = 3 "*EFGH*"

4 "*EFGH*" = 5 "*IJKL*"

Multiply the top equation by 4 and the second equation by 3 in order to make *"EFGH"* the same.

16 "*ABCD*" = 12 "*EFGH*" = 15 "*IJKL*"

21. **(A)** Plug the values of j into the answer choices in order to see which one consistently gives k as its answer.

22. **(D)** The figure has six sides, so it contains 720 degrees. The average of the six angles, therefore, would be 720 divided by 6, which is equal to 120. Now divide the sum of the angles by the average. 720 divided by 120 equals 6. (When you divide the sum of some numbers by the average of those numbers you *always* obtain the number of numbers.)

23. **(D)** Estimation works well in this problem. We know that the stock went up by almost 1 dollar. Therefore, the profit must be almost 1,200 dollars.

24. **(B)** The question might be phrased, "What is the lowest common denominator for 2, 3, and 5?" $2 \times 3 \times 5 = 30$.

25. **(B)** $300 \times \frac{1}{3} = 100$. Marianne increased her speed by 100 words. When her speed drops by 100 words, she will be back at 300, which is 100% of her original speed.

Section 2

1. **(C)** A teacher who believed in a student's integrity might be expected to *intercede* (intervene with a good word) on her behalf.

2. **(B)** Of the choices, only (B) makes sense; a new contract could *supersede* (replace) all previous agreements.

3. **(E)** The scientist could return to the area only if volcanic activity *abated* (subsided). She could then *resume* her studies.

4. **(A)** The choice must contrast with *unity* and *harmony*.

5. **(B)** Conspirators might meet *reclusively* (in solitude) or *insidiously* (treacherously), but they would be most likely to do so *clandestinely* (in secret). And faced with an oppressive regime, their aim would most likely be to plot an *insurrection* (rebellion).

6. **(B)** A *pear* is a kind of *fruit*, and *baseball* is a kind of *sport*.

7. **(D)** A *disciplinarian* demands *obedience*, and a *perfectionist* demands *flawlessness*.

8. **(D)** A *decibel* is a measure of the *loudness* of sound, just as a *carat* is a measure of the *weight* of a precious stone.

9. **(C)** To *carve wood* is to form it into a desired shape. Likewise, to *mold clay* is to form it into a desired shape.

10. **(B)** A *gallery* is a place for *artwork*, and a *zoo* is a place for *animals*.

11. **(C)** To *fade* is to disappear partially; to *vanish* is to disappear completely. To *chide* is to reprove mildly; to *reprimand* is to reprove severely.

12. **(E)** A *book* normally is comprised of *chapters*, and a *symphony* normally is comprised of *movements*.

13. **(A)** The *roots* support a *tree*, and the *foundation* supports a *building*.

14. **(A)** Paragraph 1 concerns Americans' opinion that they should continue "firmly united" (line 8) and Jay's contention that this opinion could never be considered "erroneous."

15. **(B)** This definition comes at the beginning of paragraph 4.

16. **(B)** Jay is primarily concerned here with the smooth-working efficiency that a harmonious unity can provide.

17. **(C)** Lines 44–45 confirm Jay's opinion that the "just causes of war arise . . . from violations of treaties or from direct violence."

18. **(D)** Jay remarks that the maritime nations are "able to annoy and injure us" (line 48).

19. **(E)** This is the only response that makes sense in context. Jay speaks earlier (line 29–30) of "an efficient national government"; it is one of his key themes.

20. **(D)** According to the introduction, Jay is attempting to convince readers to adopt the Constitution in place of the Articles of Confederation. The reason he offers here is that America needs firm unity under a national government "vested with sufficient powers" for all purposes. Presumably, the Constitution would do a better job of providing such government than would the Articles of Confederation.

21. **(C)** Since Jay believes that wars are just if they are undertaken in response to treaty violations or invasions, he would likely support a war to defend America against hostilities from Spain. None of the other answer choices describes a situation in which Jay would believe that war is justified.

22. **(E)** Paragraph 4 names the two dangers that face the nation and states that Jay will deal with the two in order, beginning with foreign arms.

23. **(D)** The line before refers to Mr. Bixby's ability to "fetch down" Twain's nose when he gets a bit complacent; the *settler* in this case is another question that "settles," or "fetches down," Twain's nose.

24. **(C)** The comparison is comic in intent. Twain knows as much about the shape of Walnut Bend as he does about his grandmother's opinion of protoplasm, which is to say, nothing at all.

25. **(C)** This comparison starts on line 17 with the sobriquet "gunpowdery chief." Twain is describing his chief's tendency to blow up at the slightest provocation.

26. **(E)** There is no mention of a real gun in the selection. Twain is describing his boss's temper, which was quick to explode but subsided just as rapidly.

27. **(A)** Twain's despair is shown in the line "I wish I was dead!" (line 41).

28. **(D)** Mr. Bixby says that Twain might mistake the black shadow of a woodpile for a "solid cape," or peninsula of land.

29. **(A)** The entire passage contrasts Mr. Bixby's knowledge of the river with Twain's ignorance.

30. **(A)** Twain says that on a pitch-dark night, "all shores seem to be straight lines."

Section 3

1. **(C)** If $\frac{9}{18}$ is equal to $\frac{1}{2}$, then $\frac{9}{16}$ must be bigger than $\frac{1}{2}$. If two fractions contain the same numerator, the one with the smaller denominator is larger. If $\frac{8}{16}$ is equal to $\frac{1}{2}$, then $\frac{8}{17}$ must be smaller.

2. **(D)** *R* has an area of *xy* and *S* has an area of 6*xy*.

   $6xy - xy = 5xy$

3. **(E)** Since angle *y* is doubled and angle *x* is a right angle, the answer must be (E). The other answer choices are too big. If you double 45, that would be 90. This is impossible as $90 + 90 = 180$, and you haven't yet added in angle *z*.

4. **(B)**

   $$3x + 3 = 3y + 3 + 6$$
   $$3x + 3 = 3y + 9$$
   $$3x - 3y = 6 \text{ (Subtract } 3y \text{ and 3 from both sides.)}$$
   $$x - y = 2 \text{ (Divide both sides by 3.)}$$

5. **(C)** If the average for the three games was 162, then the total was 3×162 or 486. Let *x* represent the first game.

   $$x + (x - 10) + (x - 10 - 13) = 486$$
   $$3x - 33 = 486$$
   $$3x = 519$$
   $$x = 173$$

6. **(B)** $3 \times 10^3 = 3 \times 1000 = 3000$

   $$2 \times 10^2 = 2 \times 100 = 200$$
   $$200 \times 3000 = 600,000$$

7. **(E)** There are 60 seconds in a minute, $60 \times 40 =$ 2,400. To find the number of widgets made, divide 2,400 by 2.5. This is equal to 960.

8. **(C)** Each cassette has a total of 90 minutes on it; three cassettes contain 270 minutes total. A lecture that is 3 hours long would be 180 minutes. The tape will then have $270 - 180 = 90$ minutes left. $\frac{90}{270} = \frac{1}{3} = 33\frac{1}{3}\%$.

9. **(D)** Since we are given the values of the fractions, we can simply multiply 5 times 6.

10. **(C)** There are 6 numbers in the repeated pattern: $\begin{array}{r}125r3\\ 6\overline{)753}\end{array}$. The pattern repeats 125 complete times and goes 3 digits into the next pattern. The 753rd decimal digit is the same as the 3rd digit. The answer is 5.

Section 4

1. **(D)** The answer begins with the line "Our writers are accustomed to plead in our excuse. . . ." (lines 11–12). It is Cooper, not Channing, who blames publishers (C).

2. **(B)** Channing uses *lights* in a dual sense, but his primary goal is to say that we are lacking those "great names" that allow a country to be noticed abroad.

3. **(E)** Our country is "designated as the land of Franklin" (lines 27–28)—Franklin is known abroad and has made our country known through his fame.

4. **(C)** Lines 36–52 deal with the schools. Channing concentrates on the idea that "we want great minds to be formed among us." As opposed to the idea in (A), Channing remarks that "we have here just cause for boasting" that our schools educate the masses.

5. **(E)** "Monetary" is the only word that works in context here.

6. **(A)** This statement is found in the first sentence of the essay.

7. **(B)** To Channing's mind, the importance of a national literature lies in its ability to highlight America's place in the world. Most of paragraph 1 deals with this opinion.

8. **(D)** This is part of Cooper's point that since American publishers can get English works for free, national literature is suppressed—unless legislative protection is devised to protect American authors.

9. **(A)** The first sentence of Cooper's essay states that "works of genius may, indeed, be occasionally brought to light." Channing, on the other hand, laments that "the few standard works which we have produced . . . can hardly . . . be denominated a national literature" (lines 6–9). Cooper has more faith in American authors' abilities.

10. **(D)** Cooper's whole essay focuses on the fact that American publishers ignore good American writing because they can get English writing for free. If they were more willing and able to take risks, a national literature might thrive.

Section 5

Part 1

1. **(B)** In Column A, $\sqrt{12} = \sqrt{4 \times 3} = \sqrt{4} \times \sqrt{3} = 2\sqrt{3}$; so $(\sqrt{12})(27)(\frac{1}{2}) = (27)(\sqrt{3})$. Column B is $(29)(\sqrt{3})$ and thus is larger than Column A.

2. **(C)** Since x and y are corresponding angles, $x = y$. Therefore, $z + y - x = z$. Column A and Column B are equal.

3. **(D)** $(\sqrt{x})^2 = x$. When x is greater than 1, A is larger than B. But if x is a fraction, A is smaller than B. Plug in 2 for x; then plug in $\frac{1}{2}$.

4. **(A)** Since the sum of all the interior angles of a triangle is 180°, angle $b = 180° - (68° + 40°) = 72°$. Angle a is a supplementary angle to 40°, so $a = 180° - 40° = 140°$. Column A is the larger.

5. **(B)** Substituting -3 for x in Column A gives the value of -2. Substituting in Column B gives the value of 29. Therefore, Column B is larger than Column A.

6. **(A)** Twice the sum of the interior angles of a triangle is $2(180°) = 360°$. One-half the sum of the interior angles of a square is $\frac{1}{2}(360°) = 180°$. Therefore, Column A is greater than Column B $(360° > 180°)$.

7. **(D)** If $y > 0$, $y^3 + 1 > y^2 - 1$. But if $y < 0$, y^3 will be negative and $y^3 + 1 < y^2 - 1$.

8. **(D)** Since we don't know the relationship of angles b and c, we cannot determine anything about the relationship between sides AC and AB.

9. **(B)** Angle a is the largest of the angles. Therefore, side CB is the largest side of the triangle and thus greater than side AB.

10. **(B)** The area of a triangle having a base of 6 and a height of 8 is $\frac{1}{2}(6)(8) = 24$. The area of a rectangle with sides of 7 and 4 is (7)(4) = 28. Therefore, the area of the rectangle—Column B—is larger.

11. **(C)** To figure out the average of three numbers we add them and divide by three. Columns A and B will therefore give the same answer.

12. **(B)** Column A can be simplified: $\frac{m^2 - 2m}{\frac{1}{2}(m-2)} = \frac{m(m-2)}{\frac{1}{2}(m-2)} = \frac{m}{\frac{1}{2}} = 2m$. Column B is $2m + 1$ and is larger than Column A by 1.

13. **(A)** Subtracting the smaller of two numbers from the larger will always be greater than subtracting the larger from the smaller, regardless of what the numbers are.

14. (**A**) The area of the larger square is $6 \times 12 = 72$. The area of the smaller square (the unshaded area) is $5 \times 7 = 35$. The shaded area is $72 - 35 = 37$. Therefore, the shaded area is larger than the unshaded area.

15. (**B**) The length of segment AB is $\sqrt{[-2-(-6)]^2 + [5-(-1)]^2} = \sqrt{(4)^2 + (6)^2} = \sqrt{16+36} = \sqrt{52}$. The length of segment CD is $\sqrt{(0-3)^2 + (7-0)^2} = \sqrt{(-3)^2 + (7)^2} = \sqrt{9+49} = \sqrt{58}$

Segment CD is the larger of the two segments.

Part 2

16. $(2a^2 - a^3)^2$ when $a = -1$

$$(2(-1)^2 - (-1)^3)^2 = (2(1) - (-1))^2$$
$$= (2+1)^2$$
$$= 3^2$$
$$= 9$$

17. Probability of not orange =

$$\frac{\text{Number of ways not to pick an orange}}{\text{Number of ways to pick a marble}} = \frac{2 \text{ red} + 3 \text{ green}}{9 \text{ marbles}} = \frac{5}{9}$$

18. (1 glop = 3 glips)4 multiply by 4

(4 glips = 5 globs)3 multiply by 3

4 glops = 12 glips

12 glips = 15globs

$\therefore$ 4 glops = 15 globs

2 glops = $\frac{15}{2} = 7\frac{1}{2}$ globs = 7.5

19. Multiply by 12: $4k + 3k = 12$

$$7k = 12$$
$$k = \tfrac{12}{7} = 1.71$$

20. If the sides have a ratio 1:3, the areas have a ratio 1:9. Therefore, the area of the large square is 9(5), or 45.

21.

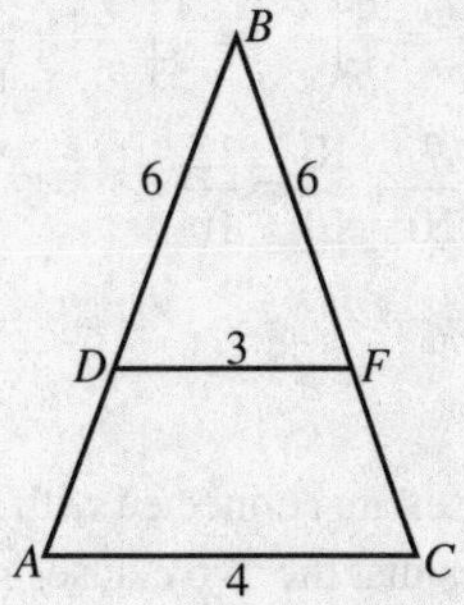

Establish the line ratio between ΔDBF and ΔABC.

$$\frac{\text{side of } \Delta DBF}{\text{corresponding side of } \Delta ABC} = \frac{\text{perimeter of } \Delta DBF}{\text{perimeter of } \Delta ABC}$$

$$\frac{3}{4} = \frac{(3+6+6)}{x}$$
$$\frac{3}{4} = \frac{15}{x}$$
$$3x = 60$$
$$x = 20$$

22. The sum of the measures of the four angles of a quadrilateral is 360°.

$$m\angle A + m\angle B + m\angle C + m\angle D = 360°$$
$$120 + 82 + x + 93 = 360°$$
$$295 + x = 360°$$
$$x = 65°$$

23. $2x + 2y = 6$ $\quad 3x - 3y = 9$

$\therefore x + y = 3$ $\quad \therefore x - y = 3$

$$(x+y)(x-y) = 3(3) = 9$$
$$x^2 - y^2 = 9$$

24. The reciprocal of $\frac{4}{5}$ is $\frac{5}{4}$.

$$\frac{5}{4} - \frac{4}{5} = \frac{25-16}{20} = \frac{9}{20}$$

25. $\frac{a}{b}=\frac{1}{5}, \frac{b}{c}=\frac{3}{2}, \frac{a}{c}=\frac{a}{b}\left(\frac{b}{c}\right)=\frac{1}{5}\left(\frac{3}{2}\right)=\frac{3}{10}$

$\frac{a+c}{c}=\frac{a}{c}+\frac{c}{c}=\frac{3}{10}+\frac{10}{10}=\frac{13}{10}=1.3$

Section 6

1. **(A)** The two clauses are connected with the word *yet*. This indicates that the two clauses represent conflicting ideas. If a negative idea is first presented, a positive one must follow to counteract it.

2. **(D)** The trips into space formerly generated attention; now they are an everyday event.

3. **(B)** A team with so many injured players is said to be *decimated* (in large part destroyed).

4. **(B)** Diplomats who can't be ticketed can park anywhere with *impunity* (freedom from punishment).

5. **(E)** Of the choices, only (E) makes sense. The words "instead of" signal the need for opposing ideas, and only (E) satisfies this condition.

6. **(E)** A *tortuous* road is twisted and winding; therefore, it is likely that a truck could skid while rounding a curve.

7. **(D)** The word *although* indicates that the blank should be filled by a negative word, something not usually applauded. The best choice is *execrable*, meaning "very inferior."

8. **(D)** The candidate was not able to *amass* (gather) support from a majority of the voters; however, those who backed her were *loyal* (devoted).

9. **(C)** Differences would normally *impede*, or block, the unification of two parties.

10. **(C)** Workers' attention is likely to wander if a job is *tedious*; they become *bored*.

11. **(D)** If you lack formal training, you can *compensate* for it with a *wealth* of practical experience.

12. **(C)** A small neighborhood business could likely be *parlayed* (exploited for further gain) into a chain of stores.

13. **(B)** The other choices do not produce a reasonable sentence.

14. **(D)** Journalists routinely *verify* (check) their facts before publishing them. They do so by research and independent *investigation*.

15. **(D)** *Scribbling* is unreadable or messy *writing*. *Mumbling* is inaudible *speaking*.

16. **(B)** *Urge* is a somewhat weaker form of *insist*; the difference is one of degree. Likewise, *request* is a somewhat weaker form of *demand*.

17. **(C)** You *scream* from *fright* and *groan* from *pain*.

18. **(B)** A *hypocrite* is by definition *duplicitous*, and a *traitor* is by definition *disloyal*. The analogy is based on defining characteristics.

19. **(E)** To *soar* is to move through the air, while to *hover* is to remain in one place. To *swim* is to move through water. To *float* is to stay in one place.

20. **(C)** A *carpenter* creates a *cabinet* just as a *cobbler* creates a *boot*.

21. **(A)** A *biceps* is a type of *muscle*: a *cobra* is a type of *snake*.

22. **(E)** *Poverty* is characrerized by a lack of *money*, and *darkness* is characterized by a lack of *light*.

23. **(A)** An *engagement* occurs before a *marriage*, and the *overture* occurs before the *opera*.

24. **(C)** *Pivotal* means extremely *important*, just as *draconian* means extremely *stern*.

25. **(B)** *Evanescent* means "tending to *vanish*"; likewise, *iridescent* means "tending to *shine*."

26. **(B)** Sir Thomas is fine, and all goes well, so Mrs. Norris has no need for her speeches.

27. **(B)** The first paragraph mentions that both Tom Bertram and his father are away from home. The second paragraph says that Sir Thomas has sent assurances that both travellers are alive and well. (You may infer that Sir Thomas is Tom's father and Lady Bertram's husband.)

28. (**B**) Mrs. Norris takes over her nieces' lives and interferes with her sister's household.

29. (**A**) Austen begins with a litany of qualities that the Miss Bertrams are supposed to have, but says that their constantly being praised has made them believe "they had no faults" (line 38).

30. (**C**) Since Lady Bertram is so lazy, she gives the job of going into public with the Miss Bertrams to Mrs. Norris.

31. (**D**) Horses cost money; Mrs. Norris's occupation with her nieces' affairs means she can attend society functions without hiring any.

32. (**E**) Lines 2–8 and 39–46 illustrate Lady Bertram's indolence.

33. (**A**) Mrs. Norris is revealed to be cheap, histrionic, and nosy in this excerpt.

34. (**C**) Satire is defined as holding up a person's follies to ridicule; Austen's depiction of Lady Bertram's laziness is a perfect example.

35. (**C**) Austen's wit is dry, but she reveals the silliness of each character through her careful choice of words.

Evaluating the Final Examination

To determine your Verbal Reasoning Score:

1. Using the Analysis Worksheet, enter the number of correct answers for each verbal reasoning section on the appropriate line in Column A of the Verbal Reasoning grid.

2. Enter the number of incorrect answers for each verbal reasoning section on the appropriate line in Column B of the Verbal Reasoning grid.

3. Total Columns A and B and enter these totals in boxes A and B, respectively.

4. Perform the indicated calculation to find your Raw Score: (value in box A) minus (one-quarter of the value in box B) = Raw Score.

5. Consult the Conversion Chart to find your approximate Scaled Score.

To determine your Mathematical Reasoning Score:

1. Enter the number of correct answers for each mathematical reasoning section on the appropriate line in Column C of the Mathematical Reasoning grid.

2. Enter the number of incorrect answers for each mathematical reasoning section on the appropriate line in Column D, E, or F of the Mathematical Reasoning grid.

3. Total Columns C, D, and E, and enter these totals in boxes C, D, and E, respectively.

4. Perform the indicated calculation to find your Raw Score: (value in box C) minus (one-quarter of the value in box D) minus (one-third of the value in box E) = Raw Score.

5. Consult the Conversion Chart to find your approximate Scaled Score.

   Note: Box F is not used in this calculation.

Analysis Worksheet

VERBAL REASONING

Section	Number of Questions	Column A Number of Correct Answers	Column B Number of Incorrect Answers
2	30		
4	10		
6	35		
	Total	A	B

A − ¼ B = Raw Score → Use Conversion Chart → Scaled Score

MATHEMATICAL REASONING

Section	Number of Questions	Column C Number of Correct Answers	Col. D Number of Incorrect Answers	Col. E Number of Incorrect Answers	Col. F Number of Incorrect Answers
1	25			■	■
3	10			■	■
5 Part 1	15		■		■
Part 2	10		■	■	
	Total	C	D	E	F

C − ¼ D − ⅓ E = Raw Score → Use Conversion Chart → Scaled Score

Conversion Scales For Final Practice Examination

VERBAL REASONING

Raw Score	Scaled Score	Raw Score	Scaled Score
75	800	40	550
70	800	35	520
65	760	30	480
60	710	25	440
55	670	20	410
50	620	15	370
45	590	10	340
		5	290
		0	230

MATHEMATICAL REASONING

Raw Score	Scaled Score	Raw Score	Scaled Score
60	800	25	510
55	760	20	480
50	690	15	440
45	650	10	410
40	610	5	340
35	580	0	200
30	550		

Although you now have some idea of what your scores would look like had they been scaled according to unofficial ETS standards, you will probably want to know how to interpret your Raw Scores in more familiar terms. If so, use the following Self-Evaluation Charts to see what your Raw Scores actually mean.

SELF-EVALUATION CHARTS

VERBAL REASONING: Raw Score

Excellent	60 – 75
Good	50 – 60
Average	30 – 50
Fair	20 – 30
Poor	0 – 20

MATHEMATICAL REASONING: Raw Score

Excellent	50 – 60
Good	40 – 50
Average	20 – 40
Fair	10 – 20
Poor	0 – 10